World Travel Atlas

COLUMBUS
PRESS

Contents

Introduction..iii

■ ˋStatistics

Travel Statistics – World............................iv-v

Travel Statistics – United States...................vi

Travel Statistics – United Kingdom...............vii

Country Statistics.....................................viii

■ General Maps

Key to Map Symbols: The World – Physical..............I

World – Political...2-3

The Arctic and Antarctica..............................4

Europe – Political..5

Scandanavia and the Baltic Lands...................6-7

England and Wales.......................................8-9

Scotland..10

Ireland...11

France..12

Spain and Portugal.....................................13

Italy and the Balkan States..........................14-15

Central Europe..16-17

Eastern Europe, Russia and Central Asia...........18-19

Asia – Political..20

Japan...21

China...22

South-East Asia...23

Southern Asia...24

South-West Asia..25

Northern Africa...26-27

Central and Southern Africa..........................28-29

Africa – Political..30

New Zealand...31

Australia...32-33

Canada...34-35

United States...36-37

Mexico, Central America and the West Indies.....38-39

South America – North................................40-41

South America – South................................42

Index to General Maps.................................43-48

■ Specialist Maps – World and European

Time – World..49

Climate – World...50

Climate – Europe..51

Health – World..52

Driving – World...53

Airports – World..54-55

Airports – Europe.......................................56

International Flight Times – World...................57

Cruise Routes – World.................................58-59

UNESCO Natural Heritage Sites – World...........60-61

UNESCO Cultural Heritage Sites – World..........62-63

UNESCO Cultural Heritage Sites – Europe.........64

■ Specialist Maps – Country

Benelux...65

United Kingdom...66-67

United Kingdom Beaches..............................68

United Kingdom Ferry Routes........................69

United Kingdom Airports..............................70-71

France..72-73

Germany...74-76

Austria and Switzerland...............................77

Italy...78

Italy and Malta..79

Spain...80-81

Portugal..82

Greece and Turkey.....................................83

Mediterranean Beaches...............................84-85

Eastern Europe and the CIS..........................86-87

Africa...88-89

United States...90-91

United States National Parks.........................92-93

Canada...94

Central America and the Caribbean.................95

Far East..96

Index to Specialist Maps..............................97-112

■ Teaching Maps

World...113

Europe..114

United Kingdom...115

Germany...116

France..117

Iberia...118

Iberian Islands..119

Switzerland and Austria...............................120

Italy...121

Greece..122

Central America and the Caribbean.................123

Canada...124

USA...125

North Africa and Israel................................126

Southern Africa...127

Far East..128

Editor: Mike Taylor of the University of Brighton

Specialist Cartography: David Burles

Design Editor: Karen Harkness

Additional Research: Nonke Beyer, Sally McFall, Reid Savage

Circulation Manager: Martin Newman

Circulation Controllers: Jullian Manning, Peter Korniczky

Front Cover Design: Warren Evans

Production: Brian Quinn

Publisher: Stephen Collins

ISBN: 0 946393 48 6

Printed by Eyre & Spottiswoode, Margate.

Colour reproduction and typesetting by Alphabetset, London SW10 and Target Litho, London EC2.

Cartography & index on pp. 1-48 ©1993 Reed International Books Limited.

Cartography on pp. 74-75 ©1994 ICA/EMG.

Other cartography and index ©1995 Columbus Press Limited.

Published by Columbus Press Limited, 28 Charles Square, London N1 6HT, Tel: +44 (0)171 417 0700. Fax: +44 (0)171 417 0710.

The Publishers would like to thank all the tourist offices, airlines and other organisations and individuals who assisted in the preparation of this edition, with particular thanks to Alphabetset, Target Litho, UNESCO, the World Tourism Organisation, the British Tourism Authority and the National Maritime Museum. Whilst every effort is made by the Publishers to ensure the accuracy of the information contained in this edition of the World Travel Atlas, the Publishers accept no responsibility for any loss occasioned to any person acting or refraining from acting as a result of the material contained in this publication or liability for any financial or other agreements which may be entered into with any advertisers, nor with any organisations or individuals listed in the text.

Producing the first edition of the World Travel Atlas was a memorable, if sometimes exhausting, experience. The high point came after publication with the positive reaction of our travel trade clients to the book; while the low point was realising, as we were going to press, how many excellent ideas had reluctantly been put in the 'maybe Edition 2' folder. If every idea and suggestion had been acted upon it's unlikely the first edition would be out even now.

I'm therefore very pleased that many of these ideas have taken shape in the second edition, either as brand new maps or as improvements to existing ones. Look at the Mediterranean Beaches plates, for example, the US National Parks, the Teaching Maps, the Specialist Maps Index . . . These and many other additions and refinements are all, we feel, well worth waiting for.

It's only by continuing to work closely with the travel trade that we can continue to provide high-quality publications to assist you in your business, so please, keep your comments coming. After all, the 'Maybe Edition 3' folder isn't filled up yet . . .

Stephen Collins
Publisher
Columbus Press

ABTA

Have a good look at this work of reference; it is far more than just an atlas. Designed to make decision-taking easier, and the issuing of information more accurate (remember the obligations of the Package Travel Directive!), this is a vital publication.

Like the World Travel Guide, it should be in every ABTA member's office – and indeed in every branch. I congratulate Columbus for creating it: how did we ever manage without it?

Colin Trigger F. Inst. T.T.
President
Association of British Travel Agents

The Travel Training Company

For a long time the need has existed for an atlas which looks at the world through travel and tourism. Columbus Press fulfilled this need admirably with this publication. Indeed, so impressed has The Travel Training Company been that it commends this book to everyone who works or is interested in travel and tourism at any level.

Peter Aley
The Travel Training Company
A Subsidiary of the Association of British Travel Agents

TRAVEL STATISTICS : Worldwide

Figure I **TOURIST ARRIVALS BY REGION (1991)**
Source: World Travel and Tourism Review 1993

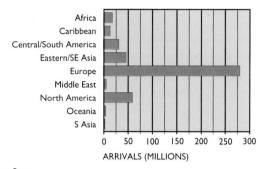

Figure 2 **TOURIST ARRIVALS BY REGION %CHANGE 1986-1991**
Source: World Travel and Tourism Review 1993

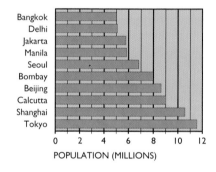

Figures 3a-e
URBAN POPULATIONS

Figure 3a **North & Central America**

Figure 3b **Europe**

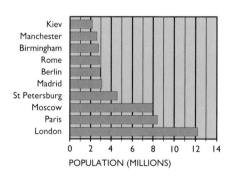

Figure 3c **Asia**

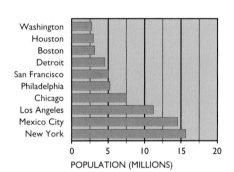

Figure 3d **South America**

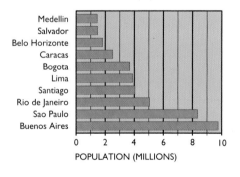

Figure 3e **Africa**

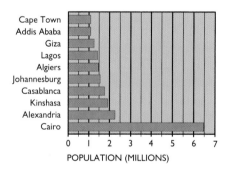

Figure 3f **Oceania**

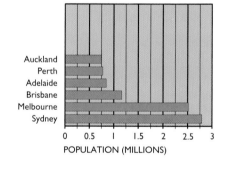

Figure 4
WORLD TOURISM ARRIVALS AND RECEIPTS (1960-1990)
Source: World Travel and Tourism Review 1993

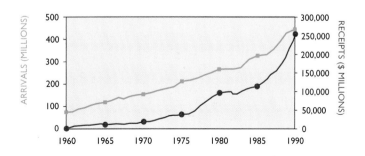

Figure 5
ACTIVITY AT MAJOR AIRPORTS
Source: ICAO Civil Aviation Statistics of the World tables 4.1 and 4.2 1992

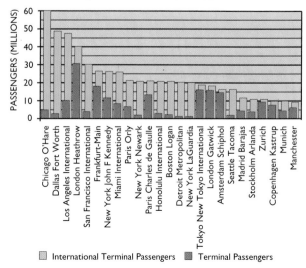

TRAVEL STATISTICS : Worldwide

Figures 6a-e
TOURISM PAYMENTS – RECEIPTS AND EXPENDITURE

Figure 6a **US tourism payments**
Source: World Tourism Organization 1992 statistics

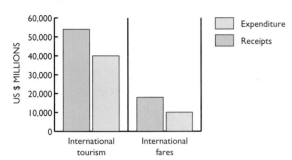

Figure 6b **Canada tourism payments**
Source: World Tourism Organization 1992 statistics

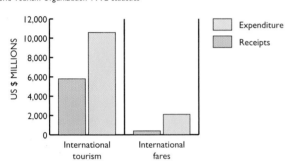

Figure 6c **UK tourism payments**
Source: World Tourism Organization 1992 statistics

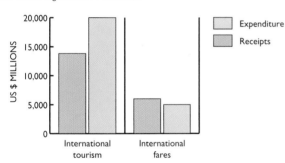

Figure 6d **Germany tourism payments**
Source: World Tourism Organization 1992 statistics

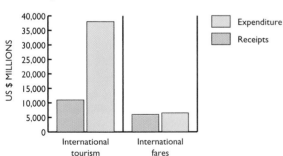

Figure 6e **Japan tourism payments**
Source: World Tourism Organization 1992 statistics

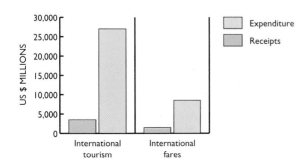

Figures 7a-e
WORLDWIDE DESTINATIONS – WHO GOES WHERE

Figure 7a **US destinations by region**
Source: World Tourism Organization 1992 statistics

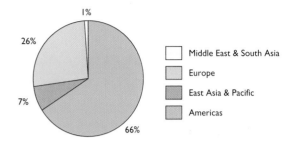

Figure 7b **Canada destinations by region**
Source: World Tourism Organization 1992 statistics

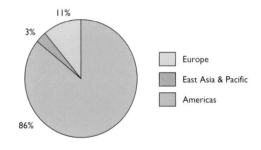

Figure 7c **United Kingdom destinations by region**
Source: World Tourism Organization 1992 statistics

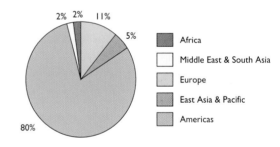

Figure 7d **Germany destinations by region**
Source: World Tourism Organization 1992 statistics

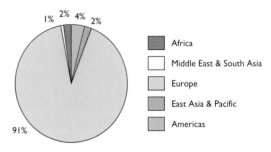

Figure 7e **Japan destinations by region**
Source: World Tourism Organization 1992 statistics

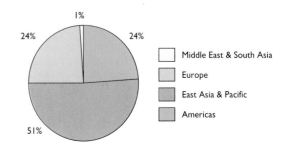

TRAVEL STATISTICS : US

Figure 8
DOMESTIC TRAVEL – EXPENDITURE BY STATE
Source: US Travel Data Center 1991

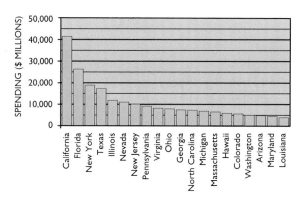

Figure 9
DOMESTIC TRAVEL – EMPLOYMENT BY STATE
Source: US Travel Data Center 1991

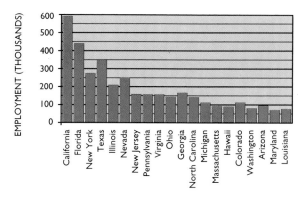

Figure 10
INTERNATIONAL VISITORS TO THE US
Source: US Travel and Tourism Administration 1992

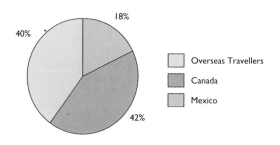

Figure 11
OVERSEAS VISITORS TO THE US
Source: US Travel and Tourism Administration 1992

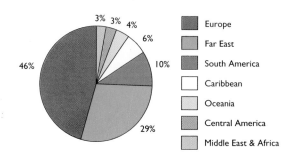

Figure 12a
ARRIVALS BY MODES OF TRANSPORT
Source: World Tourism Organization 1992

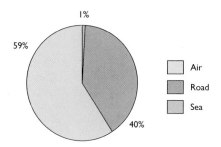

Figure 12b
ARRIVALS BY PURPOSE OF VISIT
Source: World Tourism Organization 1992

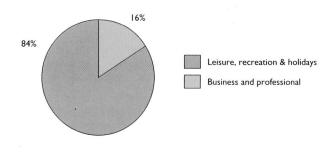

Figure 13
ACTIVITIES PARTICIPATED IN BY OVERSEAS VISITORS
Source: US Travel & Tourism Administration 1992

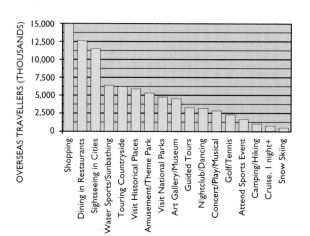

Figure 14
US TOURISM RECEIPTS CONTINUE TO RECORD DRAMATIC GROWTH
Source: World Travel and Tourism Review 1993

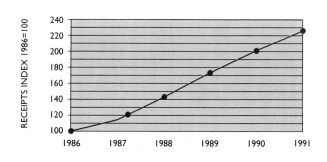

TRAVEL STATISTICS : UK

Figure 15
OVERSEAS VISITS TO THE UK BY AREA OF RESIDENCE
Source: British Tourist Authority 1992

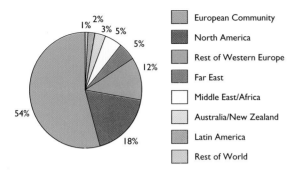

- European Community
- North America
- Rest of Western Europe
- Far East
- Middle East/Africa
- Australia/New Zealand
- Latin America
- Rest of World

Figure 16
OVERSEAS VISITS TO THE UK BY PURPOSE OF VISIT
Source: British Tourist Authority 1992

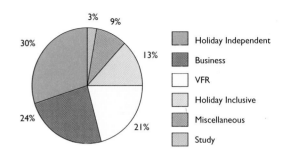

- Holiday Independent
- Business
- VFR
- Holiday Inclusive
- Miscellaneous
- Study

Figure 17
TOP FIVE COUNTRIES OF ORIGIN OF VISITORS TO UK
Source: British Tourist Authority 1991

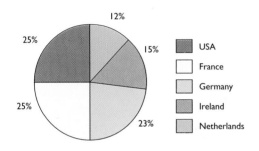

- USA
- France
- Germany
- Ireland
- Netherlands

Figure 18
ENGLAND – TYPES OF LOCATION
Source: British Tourist Authority/English Tourist Board 1994

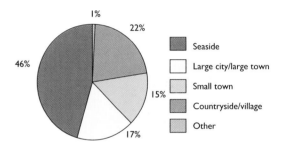

- Seaside
- Large city/large town
- Small town
- Countryside/village
- Other

Figures 19a-d
VISITS TO VARIOUS UK ATTRACTIONS

Figure 19a **Visits to attractions charging admissions**
Source: Statistics supplied to British Tourist Authority/English Tourist Board 1991

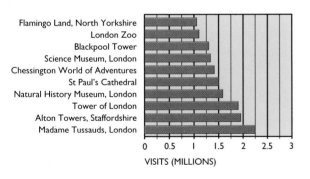

Figure 19b **Visits to historic buildings**
Source: Statistics supplied to British Tourist Authority/English Tourist Board 1991

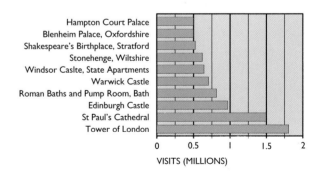

Figure 19c **Visits to gardens**
Source: Statistics supplied to British Tourist Authority/English Tourist Board 1991

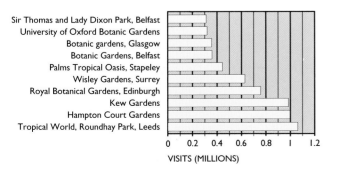

Figure 19d **Visits to museums and galleries**
Source: Statistics supplied to British Tourist Authority/English Tourist Board 1991

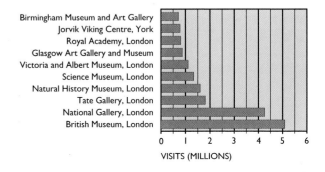

The list below gives information on all the independent states in the world. Many countries have dependencies, overseas possessions, colonies, offshore island groups etc, and with the exception of a few common-sense exceptions (such as Réunion and Hong Kong) these have not been listed. The matter of defining what is and what is not a state is by no means clear-cut, but no political stance has been adopted in the creation of this section. For more information on states and territories worldwide, consult the relevant pages of your *World Travel Guide*.

Some **Country** names have been shortened for reasons of space. **Area** is given in 1,000s of square kilometres, **Population** in 1,000s and **Population Density** as the latter divided by the former. Population figures are based on the most up-to-date information available (usually census returns or official estimates), some being as recent as 1992. In general, refugees are not included. Please see the notes at the foot of the chart regarding **Capitals**, as some countries have more than one, or are in the process of changing over from one to another.

Country	Area	Pop.	Population Density	Capital
Afghanistan	652	18,614	28.5	Kabul
Albania	29	3,300	114.8	Tirana
Algeria	2,382	25,324	10.6	Algiers (el Djezaïr)
American Samoa	0.2	47	240.2	Pago Pago
Andorra	0.47	55	114.5	Andorra la Vella
Angola	1,247	10,020	8.0	Luanda
Anguilla	0.1	9	93.3	The Valley
Antigua & Barbuda	0.4	66	144.7	St John's
Argentina	2,766	32,370	11.7	Buenos Aires
Armenia	30	3,354	112.6	Yerevan
Aruba	0.2	72	373.1	Oranjestad
Australia	7,682	17,292	2.3	Canberra
Austria	84	7,812	93.0	Vienna
Azerbaijan	87	7,174	83.0	Baku
Bahamas	14	254	18.3	Nassau
Bahrain	693	503	725.7	Manama
Bangladesh	148	111,400	754.9	Dhaka
Barbados	0.4	257	597.9	Bridgetown
Belarus	207	10,300	49.6	Minsk
Belgium	31	9,978	328.4	Brussels
Belize	23	191	8.3	Belmopan
Benin	113	4,736	42.1	Porto Novo
Bermuda	0.05	58	1102.5	Hamilton
Bhutan	46	1,375	29.6	Thimphu
Bolivia	1,084	7,612	6.9	La Paz [1]
				Sucre [1]
Bonaire	0.3	11	38.7	Kralendijk
Bosnia-Hercegovina	51	4,365	85.4	Sarajevo
Botswana	582	1,325	2.3	Gaborone
Brazil	8,511	153,322	18.0	Brasília
British Virgin Is.	0.2	17	108.8	Road Town
Brunei	6	256	44.5	Bandar Seri Begawan [2]
Bulgaria	111	8,989	81.0	Sofia
Burkina Faso	274	9,001	32.8	Ouagadougou
Burundi	28	5,620	196.1	Bujumbura
Cambodia	181	8,246	45.5	Phnom Penh
Cameroon	475	11,540	24.3	Yaoundé
Canada	9,971	27,409	2.8	Ottawa
Cape Verde	4	347	86.0	Cidade de Praia
Cayman Is.	0.2	30	114.7	George Town
Cent. African Rep.	623	2,688	4.3	Bangui
Chad	1,284	5,428	4.2	Ndjaména [3]
Chile	757	13,599	18.0	Santiago
China	9,571	1,158,230	121.0	Beijing [4]
Colombia	1,142	32,841	28.8	Santa Fe de Bogotá [5]
Comoro Is.	2	475	255.1	Moroni
Congo	342	1,843	5.4	Brazzaville
Cook Is.	0.2	19	78.0	Avarua
Costa Rica	51	2,994	58.6	San José
Côte d'Ivoire	322	12,600	39.1	Yamoussoukro [6]
				Abidjan [6]
Croatia	57	4,800	84.6	Zagreb
Cuba	111	10,736	96.8	Havana
Curaçao	0.4	144	323.9	Willemstad
Cyprus	9	707	75.1	Nicosia
Czech Rep.	79	10,302	131.0	Prague
Denmark	44	5,162	119.8	Copenhagen
Djibouti	23	520	22.4	Djibouti
Dominica	0.7	71	94.4	Roseau
Dominican Rep.	48	7,749	148.1	Santo Domingo
Ecuador	272	11,078	40.7	Quito
Egypt	998	53,153	53.3	Cairo
El Salvador	21	5,252	249.6	San Salvador
Equatorial Guinea	29	348	12.4	Malabo
Eritrea	124	3,500	21.0	Asmara
Estonia	45	1,566	34.5	Tallinn
Ethiopia	1,235	50,000	40.5	Addis Ababa
Falkland Is.	12	2	0.2	Stanley
Fiji	18	746	40.6	Suva
Finland	338	5,029	14.9	Helsinki
France	544	57,049	104.1	Paris
French Guiana	91	115	0.8	Cayenne
French Polynesia	4	199	47.8	Papeete
Gabon	268	1,206	4.5	Libreville
Gambia, The	11	800	70.8	Banjul
Georgia	70	5,471	78.2	Tbilisi
Germany	357	80,980	227.0	Berlin [7]
				Bonn [7]
Ghana	239	15,509	65.0	Accra
Gibraltar	0.006	28	4319.2	Gibraltar
Greece	132	10,269	77.8	Athens
Greenland	2,176	55	0.03	Nuuk
Grenada	0.03	95	276.7	St George's
Guadeloupe	2	387	217.4	Basse-Terre [8]
				Point-à-Pitre [8]
Guam	0.5	133	242.5	Agaña
Guatemala	108	9,454	86.8	Guatemala City
Guinea Rep.	246	5,718	20.6	Conakry
Guinea-Bissau	36	943	26.1	Bissau
Guyana	215	740	3.4	Georgetown
Haiti	28	6,625	238.7	Port-au-Prince
Honduras	112	4,916	43.9	Tegucigalpa, DC
Hong Kong	1	5,757	5385.0	Victoria
Hungary	93	10,337	111.1	Budapest
Iceland	103	262	2.5	Reykjavík
India	3,287	846,303	257.4	New Delhi
Indonesia	1,904	182,000	93.7	Jakarta
Iran	1,648	57,727	35.0	Tehran
Iraq	438	17,250	39.4	Baghdad
Ireland	70	3,523	50.1	Dublin
Israel	21	5,168	230.9	Jerusalem
Italy	301	57,746	191.7	Rome
Jamaica	11	2,374	216.0	Kingston
Japan	378	123,587	332.0	Tokyo
Jordan	98	4,145	42.4	Amman
Kazakhstan	2,717	16,900	6.2	Almaty
Kenya	580	25,905	44.7	Nairobi
Kiribati	0.1	72	89.2	Baikiri
Korea, DPR (N)	121	22,193	184.1	Pyongyang
Korea, Rep (S)	99	43,663	439.7	Seoul
Kuwait	18	1,350	120.3	Kuwait City
Kyrgyzstan	198	4,421	22.3	Bishkek
Laos	237	4,170	17.6	Vientiane
Latvia	65	2,606	40.4	Riga
Lebanon	10	2,745	262.6	Beirut
Lesotho	30	1,700	56.0	Maseru
Liberia	97	2,520	25.8	Monrovia
Libya	1,775	3,773	2.1	Tripoli
Liechtenstein	0.2	29	183.7	Vaduz
Lithuania	65	3,761	57.6	Vilnius
Luxembourg	3	390	150.7	Luxembourg-Ville
Macau	0.02	356	19,761.0	Macau
Macedonia (FYR)	26	2,034	79.1	Skopje
Madagascar	587	12,660	21.6	Antananarivo
Malawi	118	8,556	72.2	Lilongwe
Malaysia	330	18,178	55.1	Kuala Lumpur
Maldives	0.3	238	799.8	Malé
Mali	1,240	8,461	6.8	Bamako
Malta	0.3	360	1139.0	Valletta
Marshall Is.	0.2	43	240.9	Majuro
Martinique	1	360	326.9	Fort-de-France
Mauritania	1,031	2,036	2.0	Nouakchott
Mauritius	2	1,058	519.0	Port Louis
Mayotte	0.4	94	252.4	Dzaoudzi
Mexico	1,958	85,000	41.5	Mexico City
Micronesia	0.7	100	143.0	Kolonia
Moldova	34	4,394	130.4	Chisinău
Monaco	0.002	30	15,321.0	Monaco-Ville
Mongolia	1,565	2,200	1.4	Ulan Bator
Montserrat	0.1	12	116.7	Plymouth
Morocco	711 [9]	25,208 [9]	35.5	Rabat
Mozambique	799	15,731	19.7	Maputo
Myanmar	677	41,550	61.4	Yangon
Namibia	824	1,427	1.7	Windhoek
Nauru	0.02	9	439.0	Yaren District
Nepal	147	18,462	125.4	Kathmandu
Netherlands	34	15,200	447.0	Amsterdam
New Caledonia	19	164	8.6	Nouméa
New Zealand	271	3,454	12.8	Wellington
Nicaragua	120	4,264	33.3	Managua
Niger	1,267	7,948	6.3	Niamey
Nigeria	924	88,514	95.8	Abuja [10]
Niue	0.3	2	8.6	Alofi
N. Mariana Is.	0.5	31	69.1	Saipan
Norway	324	4,274	13.1	Oslo
Oman	300	1,599	5.3	Muscat
Palau	0.9	15	29.7	Koror
Pakistan	796	115,520	145.1	Islamabad
Panama	75	2,514	33.3	Panama City
Papua New Guinea	463	3,772	8.1	Port Moresby
Paraguay	407	4,397	10.8	Asunción
Peru	1,280	22,453	17.5	Lima
Philippines	300	65,000	202.0	Manila
Poland	313	38,417	123.0	Warsaw
Portugal	92	9,858	106.6	Lisbon
Puerto Rico	9	3,551	396.4	San Juan
Qatar	11	486	42.5	Doha
Réunion	3	598	238.0	Saint-Denis
Romania	237	22,760	96.0	Bucharest
Russian Fed.	17,075	148,485	8.7	Moscow
Rwanda	26	7,148	271.4	Kigali
Saba	0.01	1	85.8	The Bottom
St Eustatius	0.02	2	84.8	Oranjestad
St Kitts & Nevis	0.3	44	168.2	Basseterre
St Lucia	0.6	136	220.7	Castries
St Maarten	0.04	36	888.0	Philipsburg
St Vincent/Gren.	0.3	106	273.6	Kingstown
San Marino	0.06	24	392.0	San Marino
São Tomé	1	116	120.0	São Tomé
Saudi Arabia	2,240	14,870	6.6	Riyadh
Senegal	197	6,881	35.0	Dakar
Seychelles	0.5	68	149.8	Victoria
Sierra Leone	72	4,260	59.4	Freetown
Singapore	0.6	2,818	4499.1	Singapore City
Slovak Rep.	49	5,289	108.0	Bratislava
Slovenia	20	1,966	97.1	Ljubljana
Solomon Is.	28	319	11.6	Honiara
Somalia	638	7,691	12.1	Mogadishu
South Africa	1,221	33,849	27.7	Pretoria [11]
				Cape Town [11]
				Bloemfontein [11]
Spain	505	38,872	77.0	Madrid
Sri Lanka	64	17,240	267.5	Colombo
Sudan	2,506	23,797	9.5	Khartoum
Suriname	163	404	2.5	Paramaribo
Swaziland	17	768	44.2	Mbabane
Sweden	441	8,692	19.3	Stockholm
Switzerland	41	6,834	165.5	Bern
Syria	185	14,894	67.6	Damascus
Taiwan	36	20,557	571.0	Taipei
Tajikistan	143	5,556	38.8	Dushanbe
Tanzania	945	25,635	27.1	Dodama
Thailand	513	56,532	106.3	Bangkok
Togo	57	3,643	64.2	Lomé
Tonga	0.7	94	121.0	Nuku'alofa
Trinidad & Tobago	5	1,253	244.3	Port of Spain
Tunisia	154	8,200	53.3	Tunis
Turkey	779	57,326	73.5	Ankara
Turkmenistan	488	4,254	8.7	Ashgabat
Turks & Caicos Is.	0.5	12	24.7	Cockburn Town
Tuvalu	0.03	10	365.4	Funafuti
Uganda	241	16,582	68.8	Kampala
Ukraine	604	52,057	86.2	Kiev
U.A.E.	78	1,909	24.6	Abu Dhabi
United Kingdom	242	57,649	237.8	London
United States	9,373	255,082	27.2	Washington, DC
US Virgin Is.	0.4	101	286.9	Charlotte Amalie
Uruguay	176	3,112	17.7	Montevideo
Uzbekistan	447	21,207	47.4	Tashkent
Vanuatu	12	147	12.1	Port Vila
Vatican City	0.004	0.8	1709.0	Vatican City
Venezuela	912	20,226	22.2	Caracas
Vietnam	330	66,200	200.4	Hanoi
Western Samoa	3	160	56.5	Apia
Yemen	528	12,500	23.3	Sana'a
Yugoslavia	102	10,407	101.8	Belgrade
Zaïre	2,345	36,672	15.6	Kinshasa
Zambia	753	8,023	10.7	Lusaka
Zimbabwe	391	10,402	26.6	Harare

Notes:

1. La Paz (administrative), Sucre (legislative).
2. Formerly known as Brunei Town.
3. Formerly known as Fort Lamy.
4. Formerly known as Peking.
5. Formerly known as Bogotá.
6. Yamoussoukro (administrative), Abidjan (commercial).
7. Berlin is the capital of Germany, and Bonn is the administrative capital. Berlin will also become an administrative capital by the year 2002.
8. Basse-Terre (administrative), Point-à-Pitre (commercial).
9. The area and population figures for Morocco include the disputed area of Western Sahara.
10. The former capital of Nigeria was Lagos.
11. Pretoria (administrative), Cape Town (legislative), Bloemfontein (judicial). This arrangement is currently under review.

GENERAL REFERENCE

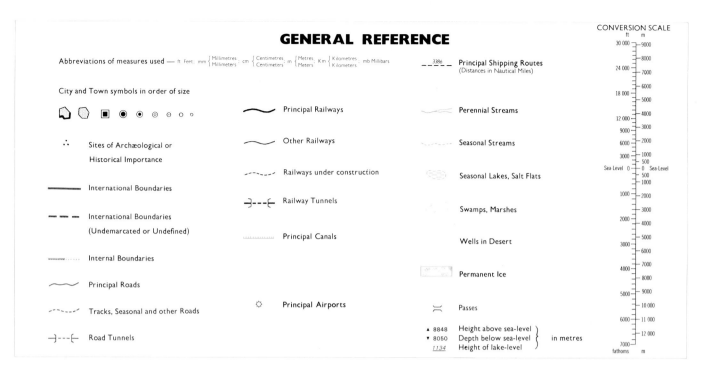

Abbreviations of measures used — ft. Feet; mm {Millimetres Millimeters}: cm {Centimetres Centimeters}; m {Metres Meters} Km {Kilometres Kilometers}; mb Millibars

City and Town symbols in order of size

⬭ ⬡ ▣ ◉ ⦿ ◉ ⊙ ◎ ○ ∘

∴ Sites of Archæological or Historical Importance

─────── International Boundaries

─ ─ ─ ─ International Boundaries (Undemarcated or Undefined)

·─··─··─ Internal Boundaries

⌒ Principal Roads

─ ─ ─ ─ Tracks, Seasonal and other Roads

⊣─ ─ ⊢ Road Tunnels

∿ Principal Railways

∿ Other Railways

─·─·─·─ Railways under construction

⊣─ ─ ⊢ Railway Tunnels

··········· Principal Canals

☼ Principal Airports

─ ─ 3386 Principal Shipping Routes (Distances in Nautical Miles)

∼ Perennial Streams

·─·─·─ Seasonal Streams

Seasonal Lakes, Salt Flats

Swamps, Marshes

Wells in Desert

Permanent Ice

⊃⊂ Passes

▲ 8848 Height above sea-level
▼ 8050 Depth below sea-level   } in metres
1134 Height of lake-level

CONVERSION SCALE

ft	m
30 000	9000
24 000	8000
	7000
18 000	6000
	5000
	4000
12 000	3000
9000	2000
6000	1000
3000	500
Sea-Level 0	0 Sea-Level
	500
	1000
1000	2000
	3000
2000	4000
	5000
3000	6000
	7000
4000	8000
	9000
5000	10 000
	11 000
6000	12 000
7000	
fathoms	m

THE WORLD
Physical
1:150 000 000

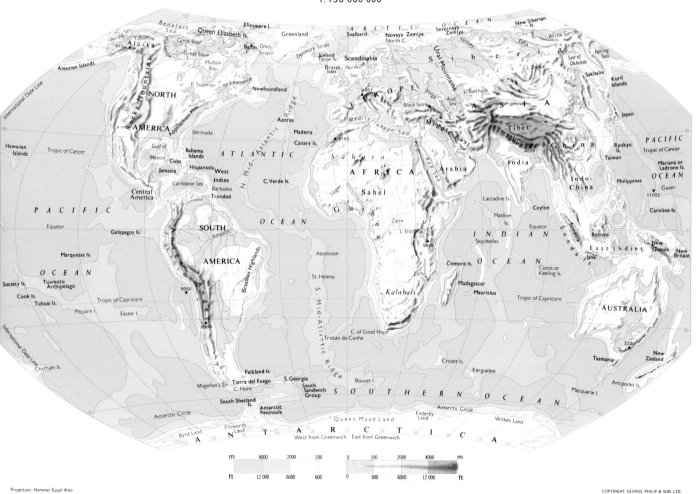

| m | 4000 | 2000 | 200 | 0 | 200 | 2000 | 4000 | m |
| ft | 12 000 | 6000 | 600 | 0 | 600 | 6000 | 12 000 | ft |

Projection: Hammer Equal Area

Projection: *Hammer Equal Area*

For destination information on every country in the world consult the Columbus Press *World Travel Guide* 14th edition. Tel +44 (171) 417 0700.

See also the following specialist world maps: World Time (p. 49); World Climate (p. 50); World Health (p. 52); World Driving (p. 53); World Airports (pp. 54-55); World Flight Times (p. 57); World Cruise Routes (pp. 58-59); UNESCO World Natural Heritage Sites (pp. 60-61); UNESCO World Cultural Heritage Sites (pp. 62-63).

For destination information on every country in the world consult the Columbus Press *World Travel Guide* 14th edition. Tel +44 (171) 417 0700.

See also the following specialist world maps: World Time (p. 49); World Climate (p. 50); World Health (p. 52); World Driving (p. 53); World Airports (pp. 54-55); World Flight Times (p. 57); World Cruise Routes (pp. 58-59); UNESCO World Natural Heritage Sites (pp. 60-61); UNESCO World Cultural Heritage Sites (pp. 62-63).

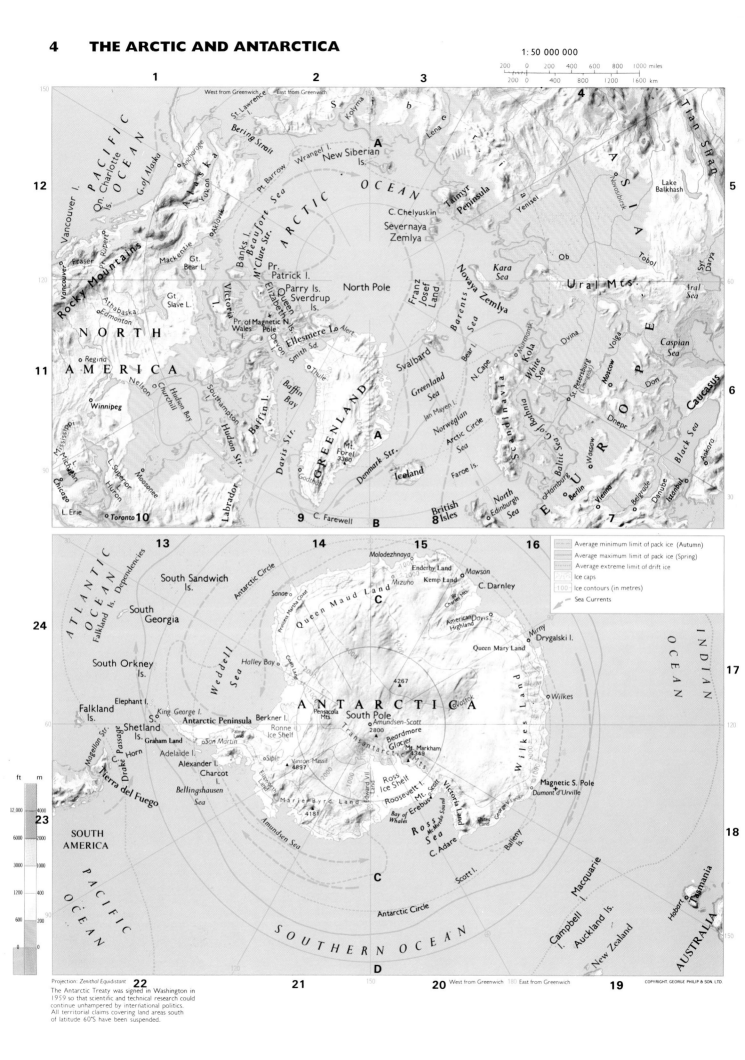

1 : 50 000 000

Legend:
- Average minimum limit of pack ice (Autumn)
- Average maximum limit of pack ice (Spring)
- Average extreme limit of drift ice
- Ice caps
- 100 — Ice contours (in metres)
- Sea Currents

Projection: Zenithal Equidistant

The Antarctic Treaty was signed in Washington in 1959 so that scientific and technical research could continue unhampered by international politics. All territorial claims covering land areas south of latitude 60°S have been suspended.

COPYRIGHT. GEORGE PHILIP & SON. LTD.

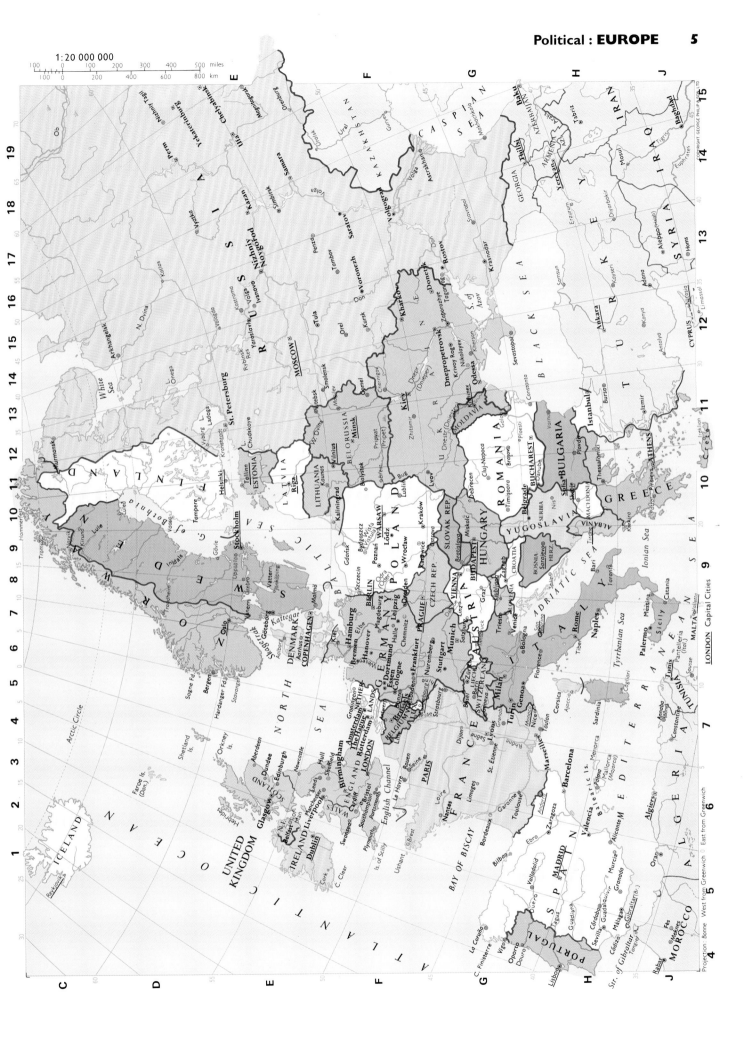

For destination information on every country in the world consult the Columbus Press *World Travel Guide* 14th edition. Tel +44 (171) 417 0700.

See also the following specialist map: Central and Eastern Europe and the CIS (pp. 86-87).

1:5 000 000

For destination information on every country in the world consult the Columbus Press *World Travel Guide* 14th edition. Tel +44 (171) 417 0700.

See also the following specialist map: Central and Eastern Europe and the CIS (pp. 86-87).

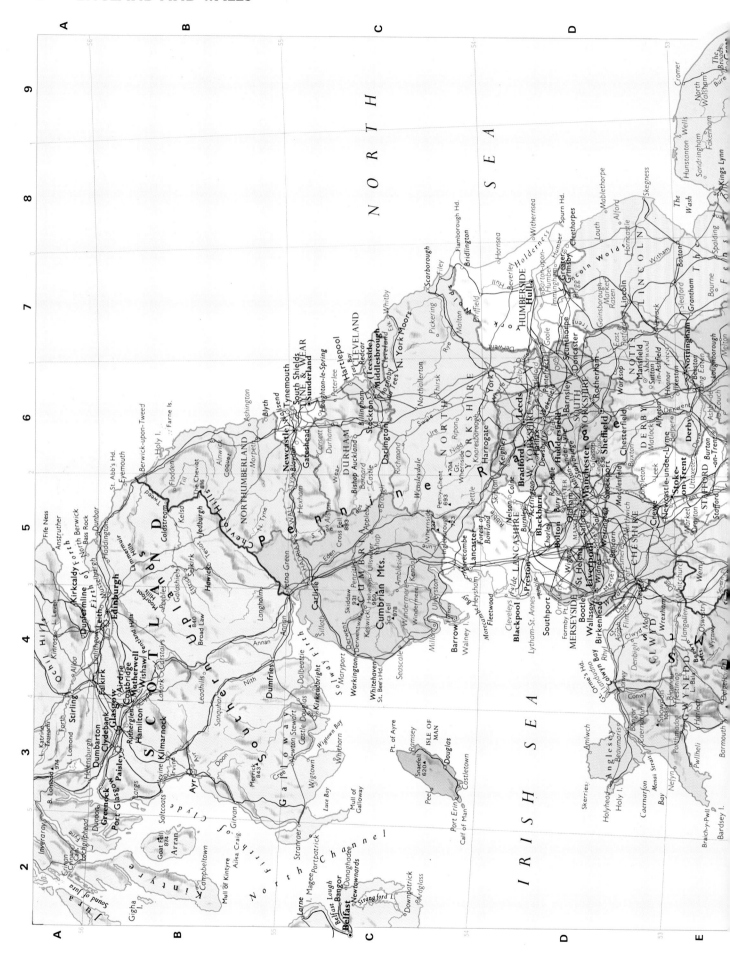

There are currently many proposals being considered which will, over the next few years, significantly alter the administrative map of Great Britain. Changes which now seem likely to come into effect within the next year or so are the abolition of Berkshire in favour of five new 'Unitary' Authorities; the reversion of Hereford and Worcestershire to separate counties; the abolition of the post-1974 counties of Avon, Cleveland and Humberside; the establishment of the Isle of Wight as a separate authority; and the creation of 'Historic County' status for Rutland. In addition, many large municipalities will be removed from County Council control and will govern their own affairs as Unitary Authorities. Any changes will be given wide publicity as they are announced and implemented: they will also be represented in future editions of the *World Travel Atlas*.

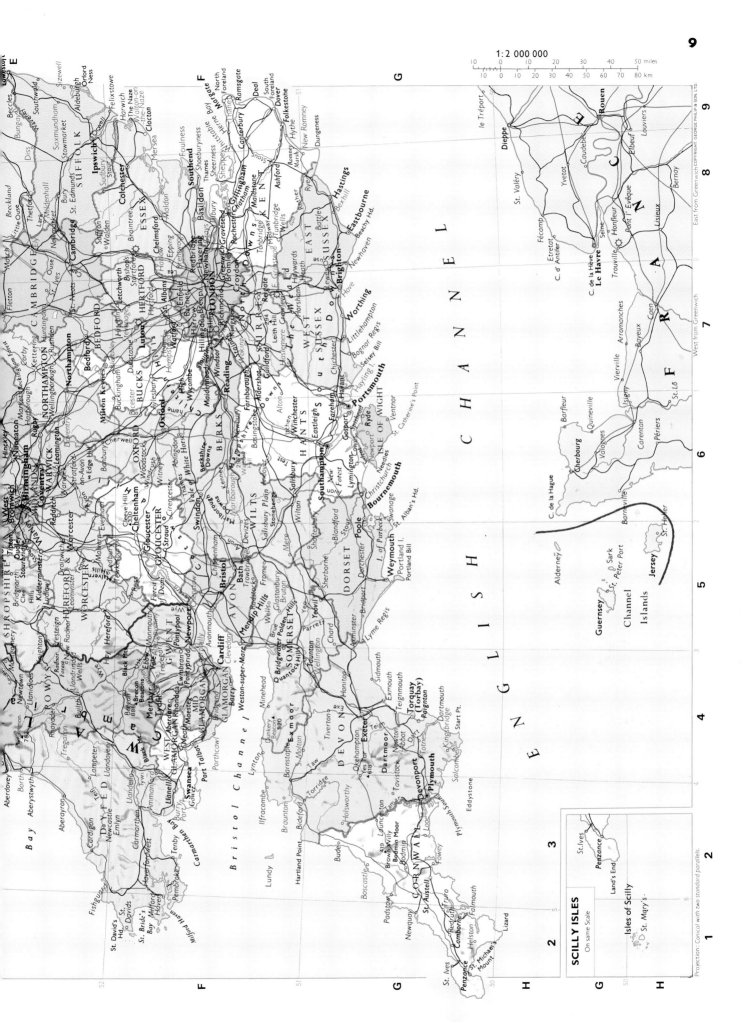

For destination information on every country in the world consult the Columbus Press *World Travel Guide* 14th edition. Tel +44 (171) 417 0700.

See also the following specialist maps: UK Regions (pp. 66-67); UK Beaches (p. 68); UK–Europe Ferries (p. 69); UK Airports and Motorways (pp. 70-71).

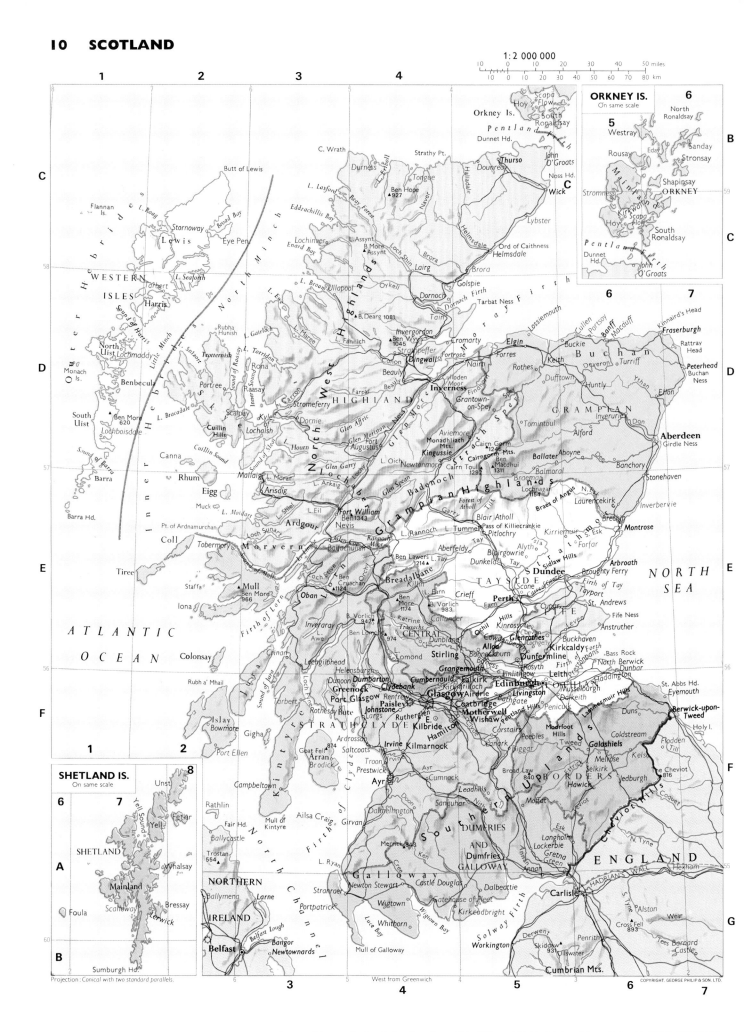

1 : 2 000 000

ORKNEY IS.
On same scale

SHETLAND IS.
On same scale

Projection: Conical with two standard parallels.

COPYRIGHT. GEORGE PHILIP & SON. LTD.

West from Greenwich

For destination information on every country in the world consult the Columbus Press *World Travel Guide* 14th edition. Tel +44 (171) 417 0700.

See also the following specialist maps: UK Regions (pp. 66-67); UK Beaches (p. 68); UK–Europe Ferries (p. 69); UK Airports and Motorways (pp. 70-71).

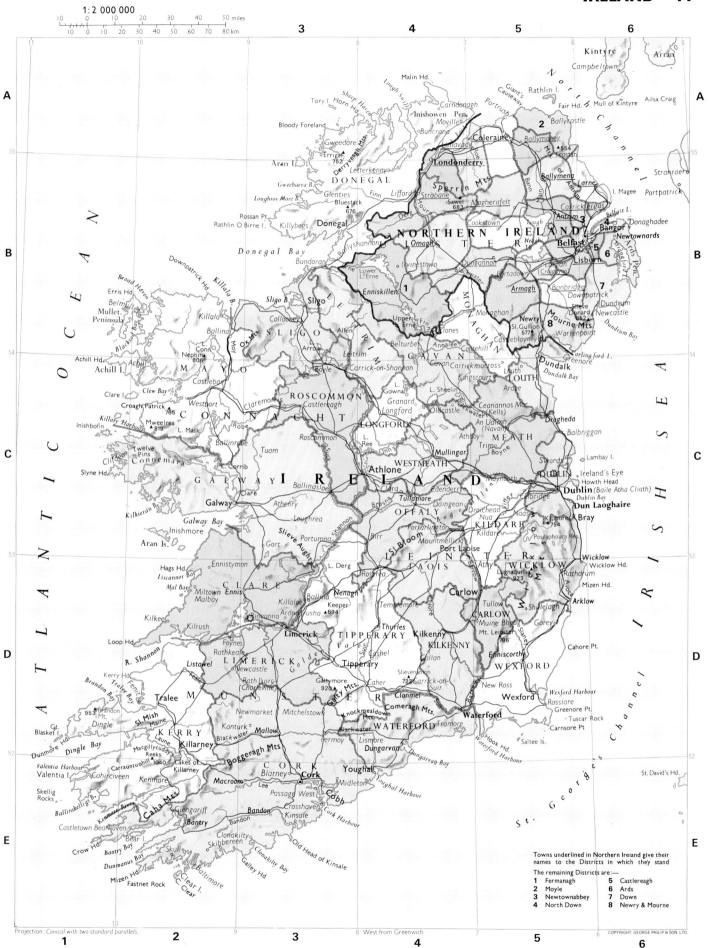

1 : 2 000 000

Projection : Conical with two standard parallels.

Towns underlined in Northern Ireland give their
names to the Districts in which they stand

The remaining Districts are:—

1	Fermanagh	5	Castlereagh
2	Moyle	6	Ards
3	Newtownabbey	7	Down
4	North Down	8	Newry & Mourne

West from Greenwich

COPYRIGHT. GEORGE PHILIP & SON. LTD.

For destination information on every country in the world consult the Columbus Press *World Travel Guide* 14th edition. Tel +44 (171) 417 0700.

See also the following specialist map: UK–Europe Ferries (p. 69);

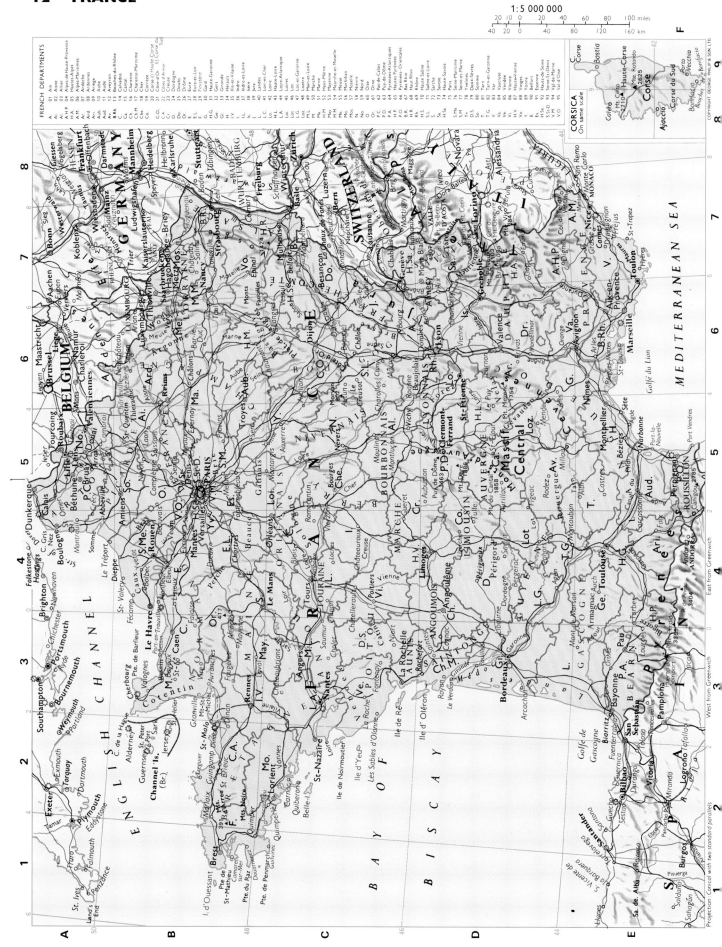

For destination information on every country in the world consult the Columbus Press *World Travel Guide* 14th edition. Tel +44 (171) 417 0700.

See also the following specialist maps: UK–Europe Ferries (p. 69); France Regions (pp. 72–73); Mediterranean Beaches (pp. 84–85).

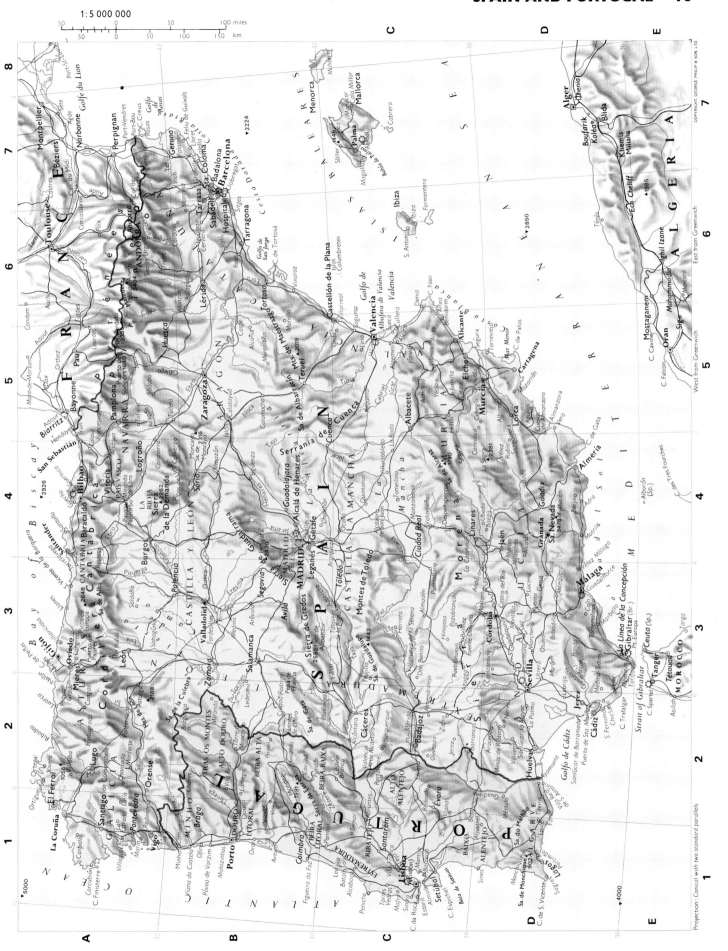

1:5 000 000

For destination information on every country in the world consult the Columbus Press *World Travel Guide* 14th edition. Tel +44 (171) 417 0700.

See also the following specialist maps: UK–Europe Ferries (p. 69); Spain Regions (pp. 80–81); Portugal Regions (p. 82); Mediterranean Beaches (pp. 84–85).

For destination information on every country in the world consult the Columbus Press *World Travel Guide* 14th edition. Tel +44 (171) 417 0700.

See also the following specialist maps: Italy Regions (pp. 78-79); Mediterranean Beaches (pp. 84-85).

1:5 000 000

For destination information on every country in the world consult the Columbus Press *World Travel Guide* 14th edition. Tel +44 (171) 417 0700.

See also the following specialist maps: Greece and Turkey (p. 83); Mediterranean Beaches (pp. 84-85).

For destination information on every country in the world consult the *World Travel Guide* Travel Guide 14th edition. Tel +44 (171) 417 0700.

See also the following specialist maps: Benelux (p. 65); UK–Europe Ferries (p. 69); France Regions (pp. 72-73); Germany (pp. 74-75); Germany Regions (p. 76); Austria and Switzerland (p. 77); Italy Regions (pp. 78-79); Mediterranean Beaches (pp. 84-85); Central and Eastern Europe and the CIS (pp. 86-87).

1:5 000 000

For destination information on every country in the world consult the Columbus Press *World Travel Guide* 14th edition. Tel +44 (171) 417 0700.

See also the following specialist maps: Benelux (p. 65); UK–Europe Ferries (p. 69); France Regions (pp. 72-73); Germany (pp. 74-75); Germany Regions (p. 76); Austria and Switzerland (p. 77); Italy Regions (pp. 78-79); Mediterranean Beaches (pp. 84-85); Central and Eastern Europe and the CIS (pp. 86-87).

Projection: Conical Orthomorphic with two standard parallels

East from Greenwich

For destination information on every country in the world consult the Columbus Press *World Travel Guide* 14th edition. Tel +44 (171) 417 0700.

See also the following specialist map: Central and Eastern Europe and the CIS (pp. 86-87).

For destination information on every country in the world consult the Columbus Press *World Travel Guide* 14th edition. Tel +44 (171) 417 0700.

See also the following specialist map: Central and Eastern Europe and the CIS (pp. 86-87).

For destination information on every country in the world consult the Columbus Press *World Travel Guide* 14th edition. Tel +44 (171) 417 0700.

See also the following specialist maps: Central and Eastern Europe and the CIS (pp. 86-87); Thailand, Malaysia and Singapore (p. 96).

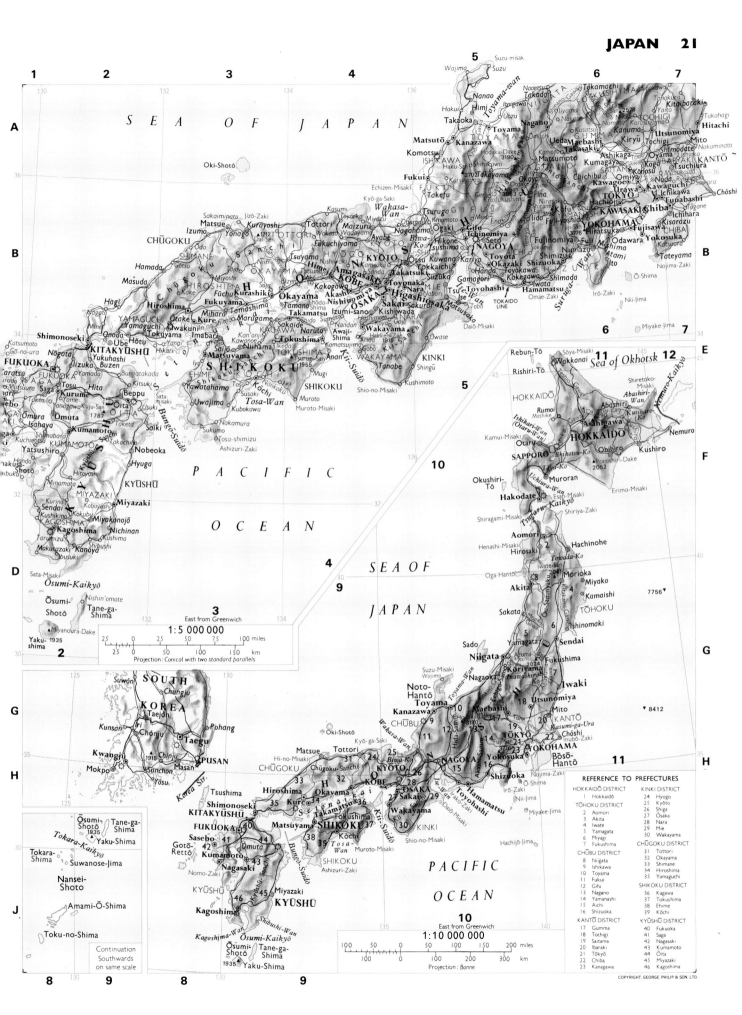

SEA OF JAPAN

A

Oki-Shotō

CHŪGOKU

B

Hamada
Masuda
Hagi

Shimonoseki
FUKUOKA
KITAKYŪSHŪ

SHIKOKU

C

D

Ōsumi-Kaikyō
Ōsumi-Shotō
Tane-ga-Shima

Yaku-shima 1935
Miyanoura-Dake

3
East from Greenwich
1:5 000 000

25   0   25   50   75   100 miles
25   0   50   100   150   km
Projection: Conical with two standard parallels

SOUTH KOREA

Suwŏn
Chŏngju
Taejŏn
Pohang
Kunsan
Chŏnju
Kwangju
Chinju 1915
PUSAN
Mokpo
Yŏsu
Masan
Sunchŏn

Korea Str.

Tsushima

CHŪGOKU

Hiroshima
Okayama
Shimonoseki
KITAKYŪSHŪ
FUKUOKA
Sasebo
Gotō-Rettō
Kumamoto
Nagasaki
KYŪSHŪ

Matsue
Tottori
Kyōto
KŌBE
ŌSAKA
Sakai
Wakayama
KINKI

Oki-Shotō

REBUN-TŌ
Sōya-Misaki
Wakkanai
Sea of Okhotsk

Rishiri-Tō

HOKKAIDŌ

SAPPORO
Otaru
Okushiri-Tō
Hakodate
Muroran

Aomori
Hirosaki
Hachinohe
Towada-Ko

Akita
Morioka
Miyako
Kamaishi
TŌHOKU
Sakata
Yamagata
Sendai
Niigata
Fukushima
Iwaki
Utsunomiya
Mito
KANTŌ
TOKYO
YOKOHAMA
Yokosuka
NAGOYA
Shizuoka
Hamamatsu
Toyohashi

PACIFIC

OCEAN

Ōsumi-Shotō 1935
Tane-ga-Shima
Tokara-Kaikyō
Yaku-Shima
Tokara-Shima
Suwanose-Jima
Nansei-Shotō
Amami-Ō-Shima
Toku-no-Shima

Continuation
Southwards
on same scale

PACIFIC
OCEAN

10
East from Greenwich
1:10 000 000

100   50   0   50   100   150   200 miles
100   0   100   200   300   km
Projection: Bonne

REFERENCE TO PREFECTURES	
HOKKAIDŌ DISTRICT	KINKI DISTRICT
1 Hokkaidō	24 Hyogo
TŌHOKU DISTRICT	25 Kyōto
2 Aomori	26 Shiga
3 Akita	27 Ōsaka
4 Iwate	28 Nara
5 Yamagata	29 Mie
6 Miyagi	30 Wakayama
7 Fukushima	CHŪGOKU DISTRICT
CHŪBU DISTRICT	31 Tottori
8 Niigata	32 Okayama
9 Ishikawa	33 Shimane
10 Toyama	34 Hiroshima
11 Fukui	35 Yamaguchi
12 Gifu	SHIKOKU DISTRICT
13 Nagano	36 Kagawa
14 Yamanashi	37 Tokushima
15 Aichi	38 Ehime
16 Shizuoka	39 Kōchi
KANTŌ DISTRICT	KYŪSHŪ DISTRICT
17 Gumma	40 Fukuoka
18 Tochigi	41 Saga
19 Saitama	42 Nagasaki
20 Ibaraki	43 Kumamoto
21 Tōkyō	44 Ōita
22 Chiba	45 Miyazaki
23 Kanagawa	46 Kagoshima

1:20 000 000

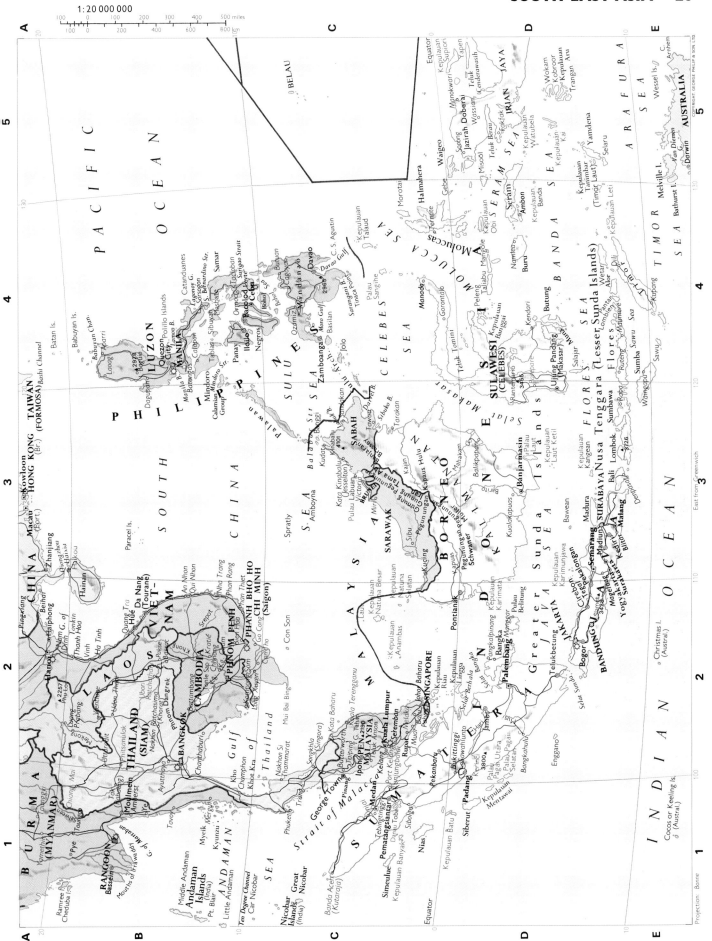

1 : 20 000 000

PACIFIC OCEAN

CHINA

BURMA (MYANMAR)

THAILAND (SIAM)

LAOS

VIET-NAM

CAMBODIA

BANGKOK

RANGOON

PHNOM PENH

PHANH BHO HO CHI MINH (Saigon)

HONG KONG (Br.)

TAIWAN (FORMOSA)

Macau (Port.)

Hainan

PHILIPPINES

LUZON

MANILA

Davao

SOUTH CHINA SEA

SULU SEA

CELEBES SEA

MALAYSIA

Kuala Lumpur

SINGAPORE

SABAH

SARAWAK

BRUNEI

BORNEO

KALIMANTAN

SUMATERA

Medan

Padang

Palembang

JAKARTA

BANDUNG

SURABAYA

SEMARANG

INDONESIA

JAVA

Greater Sunda Islands

Lesser Sunda Islands

Nusa Tenggara

SULAWESI (CELEBES)

Ujung Pandang (Makasar)

MOLUCCAS

Ambon

BANDA SEA

SERAM SEA

IRIAN JAYA

FLORES SEA

TIMOR SEA

ARAFURA SEA

AUSTRALIA

Darwin

INDIAN OCEAN

ANDAMAN SEA

Andaman Islands (India)

Nicobar Islands (India)

Cocos or Keeling Is. (Austral.)

Christmas I. (Austral.)

Equator

East from Greenwich

Projection: Bonne

COPYRIGHT GEORGE PHILIP & SON LTD

For destination information on every country in the world consult the Columbus Press *World Travel Guide* 14th edition. Tel +44 (171) 417 0700.

See also the following specialist map: Thailand, Malaysia and Singapore (p. 96).

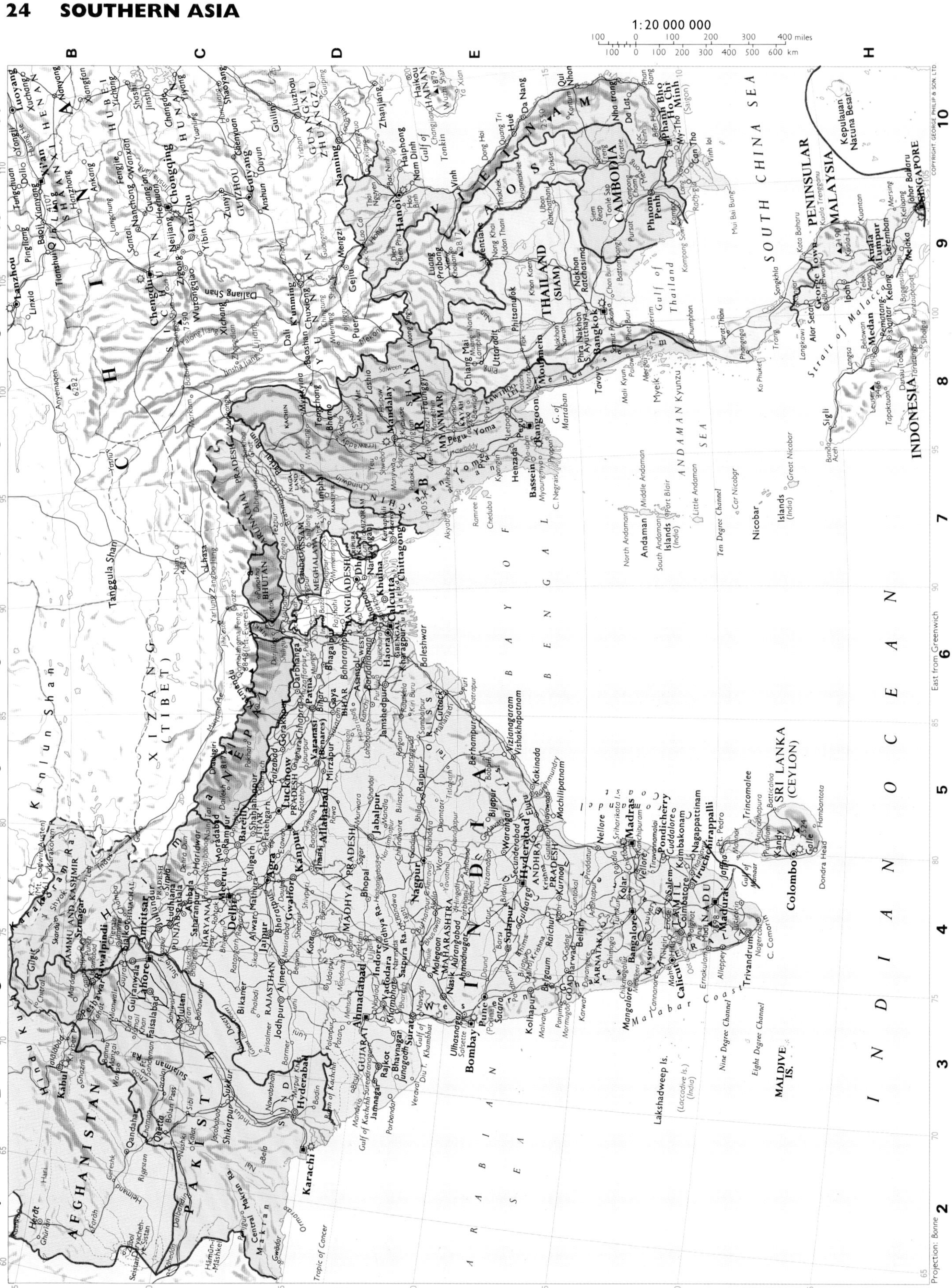

1:20 000 000

C H I N A

AFGHANISTAN

PAKISTAN

I N D I A

NEPAL

BHUTAN

BANGLADESH

XIZANG (TIBET)

MYANMAR (BURMA)

VIETNAM

LAOS

THAILAND (SIAM)

CAMBODIA

PENINSULAR MALAYSIA

INDONESIA

SRI LANKA (CEYLON)

SOUTH CHINA SEA

ANDAMAN SEA

BAY OF BENGAL

ARABIAN SEA

INDIAN OCEAN

Gulf of Thailand

Strait of Malacca

MALDIVE IS.

Lakshadweep Is. (Laccadive Is.) (India)

Andaman Islands (India)

Nicobar Islands (India)

Tropic of Cancer

East from Greenwich

Projection: Bonne

For destination information on every country in the world consult the Columbus Press *World Travel Guide* 14th edition. Tel +44 (171) 417 0700.

See also the following specialist map: Thailand, Malaysia and Singapore (p. 96).

© GEORGE PHILIP & SON LTD.

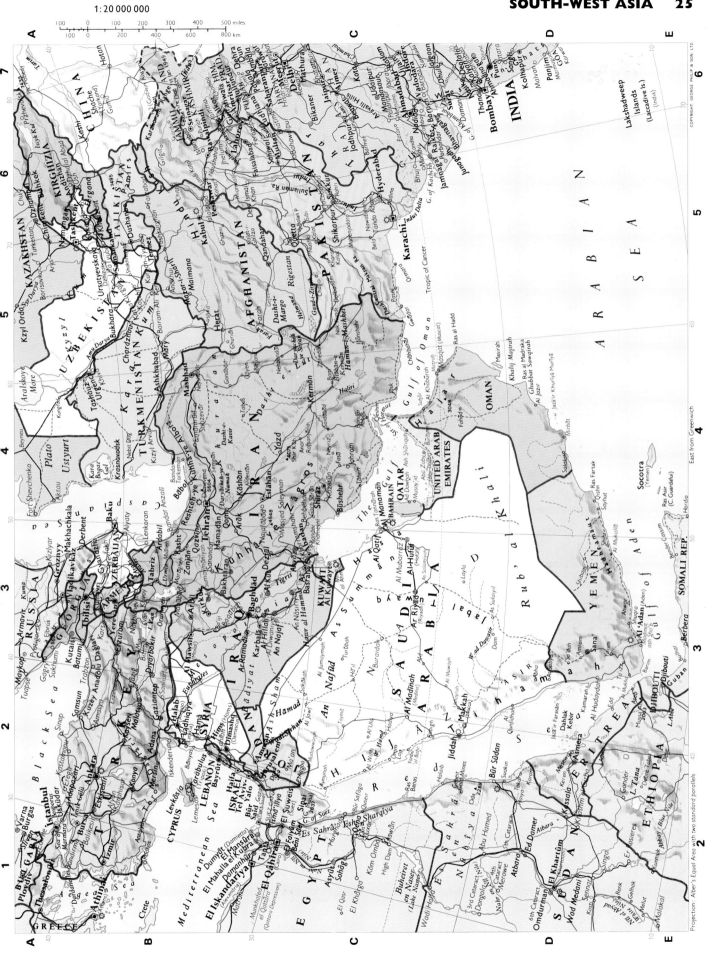

For destination information on every country in the world consult the Columbus Press *World Travel Guide* 14th edition. Tel +44 (171) 417 0700.

See also the following specialist maps: Mediterranean Beaches (pp. 84-85); Central and Eastern Europe and the CIS (pp. 86-87); Thailand, Malaysia and Singapore (p. 96).

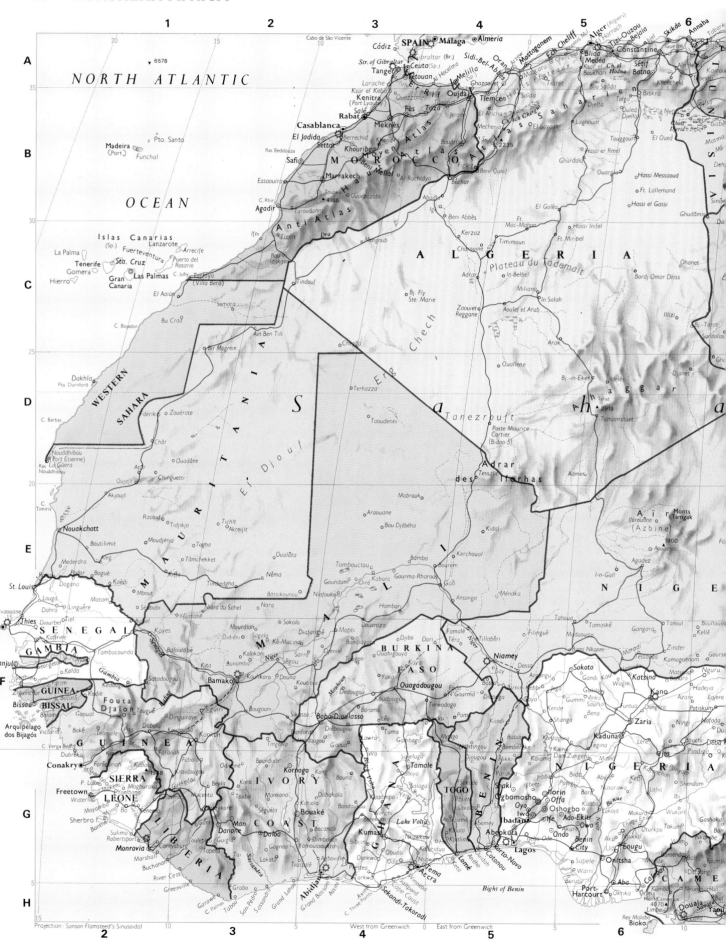

For destination information on every country in the world consult the Columbus Press *World Travel Guide* 14th edition. Tel +44 (171) 417 0700.

See also the following specialist maps: Mediterranean Beaches (pp. 84-85); Africa (pp. 88-89).

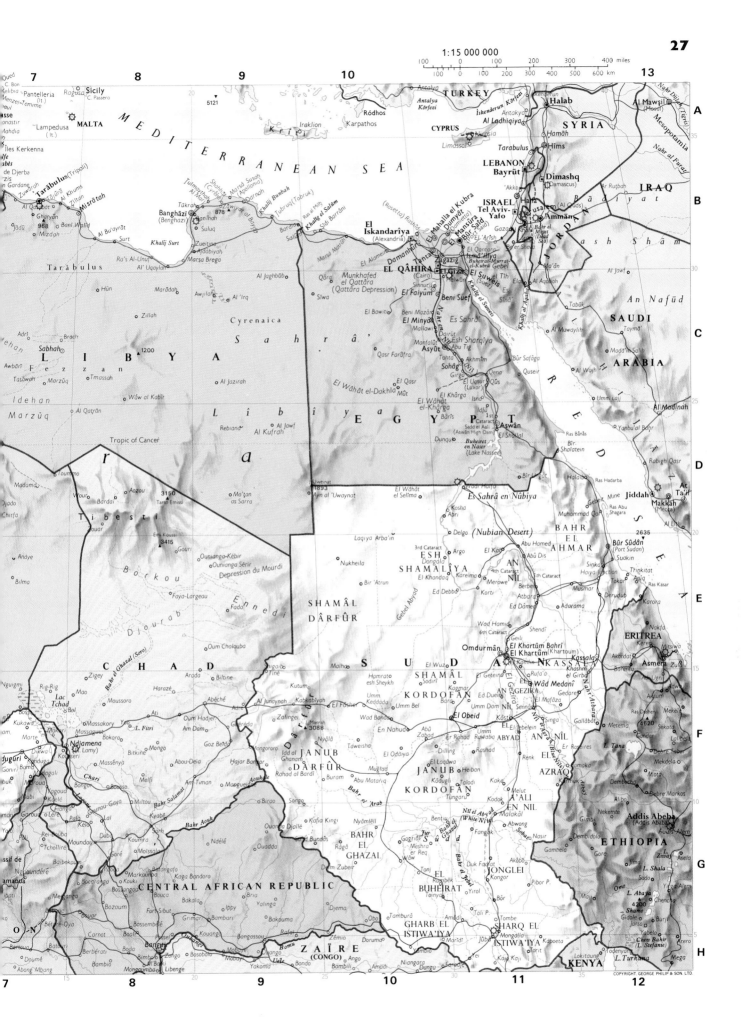

1:15 000 000

100   0   100   200   300   400 miles
100   0   100   200   300   400   500   600 km

7   **8**   **9**   **10**   **13**

MEDITERRANEAN SEA

Sicily

MALTA

TURKEY

CYPRUS

SYRIA

Halab

Al Mawşil (Mosul)

LEBANON
Bayrût

Dimashq
(Damascus)

IRAQ

ISRAEL
Tel Aviv-
Yafo

Ammân

JORDAN

El Iskandariya
(Alexandria)

EL QÂHIRA
(Cairo)

SAUDI

ARABIA

Munkhafed
el Qattâra
(Qattâra Depression)

LIBYA

Cyrenaica

Sahrâ'

EGYPT

Tropic of Cancer

Tibesti

Aswân

Buheiret
en Naser
(Lake Nasser)

Jiddah
(Mecca)
Makkah

Es Sahrâ en Nûbiya

(Nubian Desert)

BAHR
EL
AHMAR

Bûr Sûdân
(Port Sudan)

CHAD

ESH
SHAMALÎYA

AN
NÎL

ERITREA

Asmera

SHAMÂL
DÂRFÛR

JANUB
DÂRFÛR

SUDAN

SHAMÂL

KORDOFAN

El Obeid

AN
NÎL

NÎL

GEZIRA

EL
AZRAQ

Kassala

ETHIOPIA

Addis Abeba
(Addis Ababa)

CENTRAL AFRICAN REPUBLIC

JANUB
KORDOFAN

BAHR
EL
GHAZAL

EL
BUHEIRAT

JONGLEI

A'ALI
EN NIL

White Nile

GHARB EL
ISTIWA'IYA

SHARQ EL
ISTIWA'IYA

ZAÏRE
(CONGO)

KENYA

L. Turkana

COPYRIGHT. GEORGE PHILIP & SON. LTD.

7   **8**   **9**   **10**   **11**   **12**

For destination information on every country in the world consult the Columbus Press *World Travel Guide* 14th edition. Tel +44 (171) 417 0700.

See also the following specialist maps: Mediterranean Beaches (pp. 84-85); Africa (pp. 88-89).

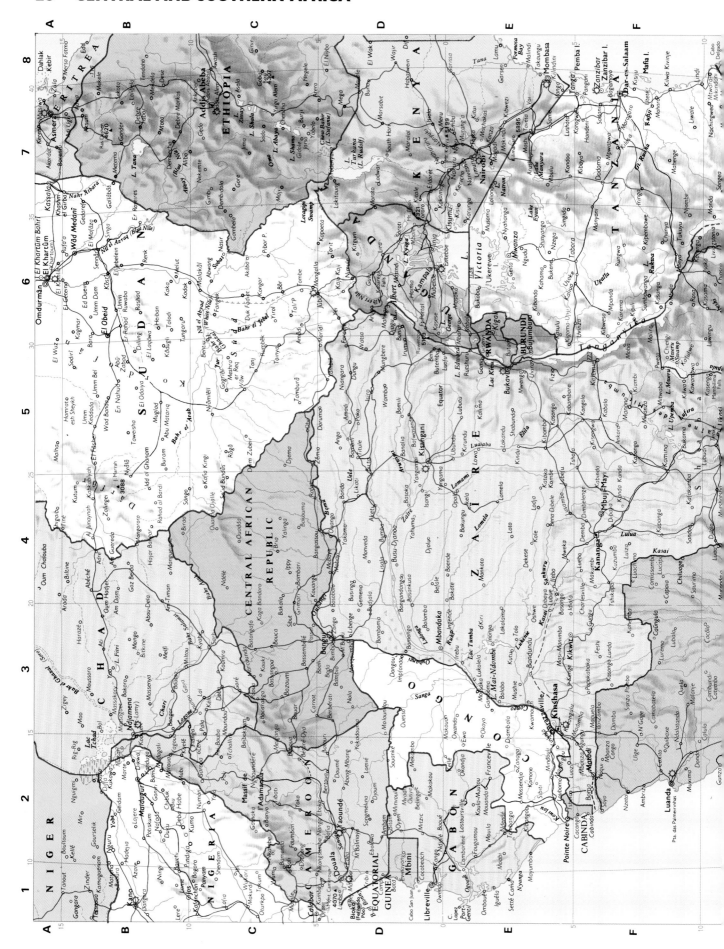

For destination information on every country in the world consult the Columbus Press *World Travel Guide* 14th edition. Tel +44 (171) 417 0700.

See also the following specialist map: Africa (pp. 88-89).

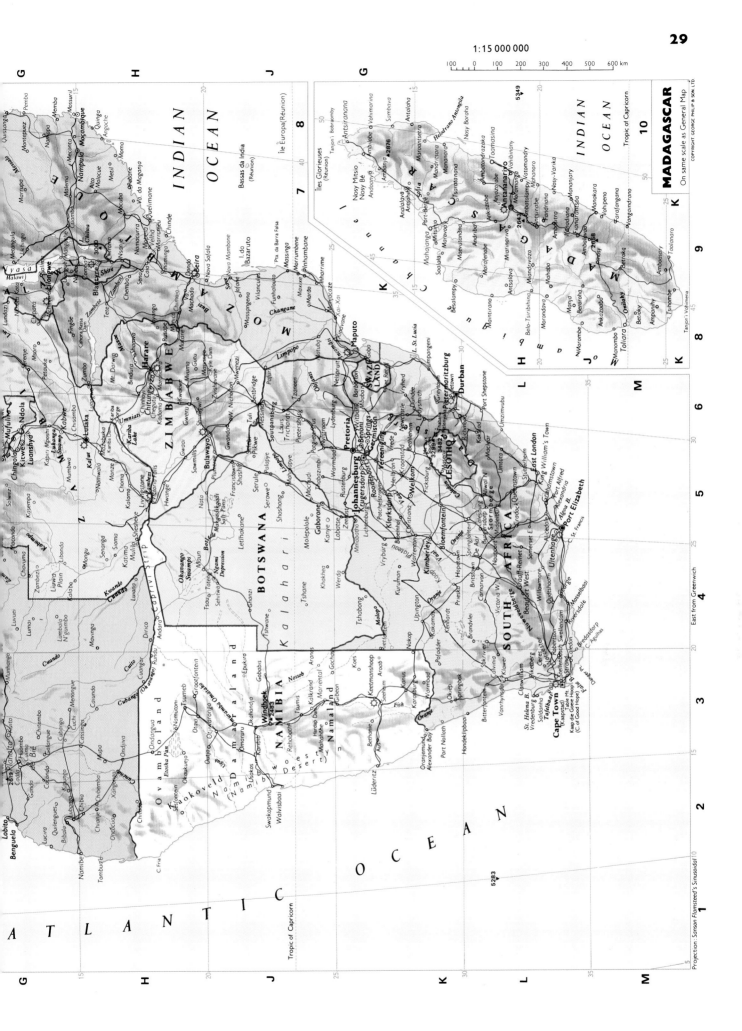

1:15 000 000

100 0 100 200 300 400 500 600 km

MADAGASCAR

On same scale as General Map

COPYRIGHT GEORGE PHILIP & SON LTD.

Projection: Sanson Flamsteed's Sinusoidal

For destination information on every country in the world consult the Columbus Press *World Travel Guide* 14th edition. Tel +44 (171) 417 0700.

See also the following specialist map: Africa (pp. 88-89).

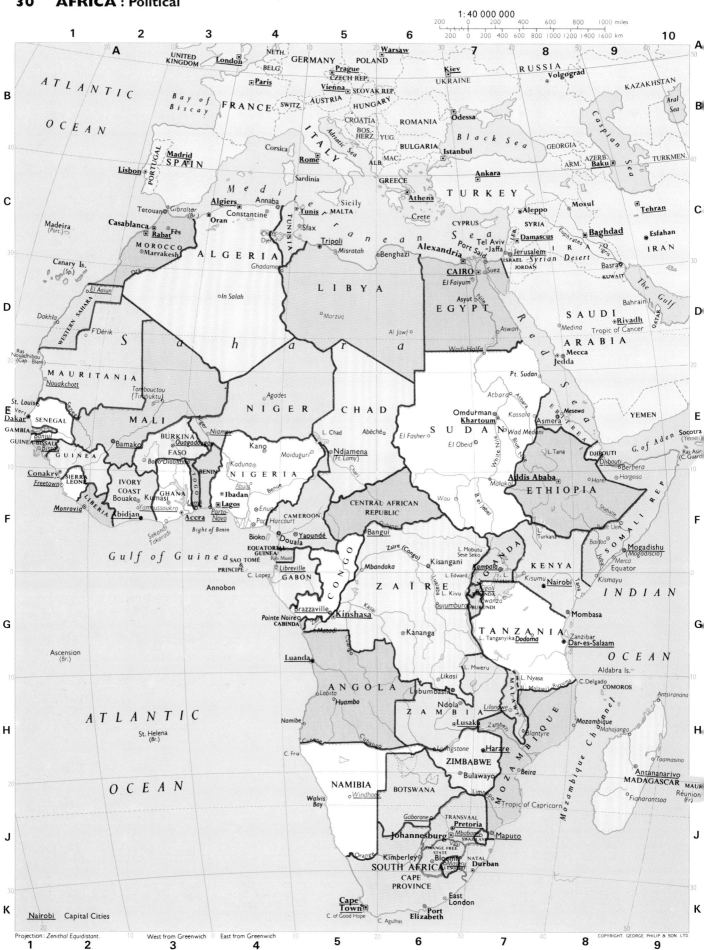

1 : 40 000 000

200   0   200   400   600   800   1000 miles

200   0   200   400   600   800 1000 1200 1400 1600 km

Projection: Zenithal Equidistant.

West from Greenwich | East from Greenwich

Nairobi   Capital Cities

COPYRIGHT GEORGE PHILIP & SON LTD

For destination information on every country in the world consult the Columbus Press *World Travel Guide* 14th edition. Tel +44 (171) 417 0700.

See also the following specialist map: Africa (pp. 88-89).

1:6 000 000
20 0 20 40 60 80 100 miles
20 0 40 80 120 160 km

KIRIBATI

TUVALU
(Ellice Is.)

Tokelau Is. (N.Z.)

WESTERN
SAMOA

Wallis &
Futuna
(Fr.)

Rotuma

Vanua Levu
FIJI
Viti
Levu

Lau or
Eastern
Group

Savaii
Upolu

Tutuila
AMER.
SAMOA
(U.S.)

TONGA
(Friendly
Is.)

Niue
(N.Z.)

Pukapuka

Nassau

Suwarrow

Northern Group
Cook Is. (N.Z.)

Palmerston
Atoll

Rakahanga

Mahiki

Tongareva
(Penrhyn) I.

Îles de la
Société

Aitutaki
Lower Group
Rarotonga

Mitiaro
Atiu Mauke

Mangaia

FRENCH
POLYNESIA

VAN-
UATU

Tropic of Capricorn

PACIFIC OCEAN

Macauley
Raoul (Sunday) I.

Kermadec Is.
(N.Z.)
Curtis

Three Kings Is.
Auckland
NORTH I.

Cook Strait
NEW
ZEALAND
SOUTH I.
Wellington
Christchurch
Dunedin

Chatham I.
Chatham Is.
Pitt I.

Bounty Is.

Tasman
Sea

Stewart I.
Snares

Antipodes Is.

Auckland Is.
Macquarie I.
(Austr.)

Campbell I.

SOUTHERN
OCEAN

NEW ZEALAND &
S.W. PACIFIC
1:60 000 000
200 0 200 400 600 800 miles
200 0 400 800 1200 km

NORTH ISLAND

Three Kings Is.
North C.
C. Reinga
C. Maria
van Diemen
Houhora
Rangaunu Bay
Doubtless Bay
Mangonui Bay
Whangaroa Bay
Ahipara Bay
Kaitaia
Tauroa Pt.
Opua
B. of Islands
C. Brett
Rawene
Hikurangi
Whangarei
Hokianga Harb.
Whangarei Harb.
Bream Hd.
Donnelly's Crossing
Bream Bay
Dargaville
Waipu
Lit. Barrier I.
Gt. Barrier I.
Kaipara Harb.
C. Rodney
C.Colville
Warkworth
Cuvier I.
Helensville
Hauraki
Gulf
Coromandel
Takapuna
Devonport
Whitianga
AUCKLAND
Onehunga
Manukau
Thames
Waiuku
Pukekohe
Mayor I.
Waikato
Mercer
Paeroa
Waihi
Tauranga Harb.
Huntly
Morrinsville
Te Aroha
Bay of Plenty
Raglan
Tauranga
White I.
C. Runaway
Kawhia
Hamilton
Te Puke
Whakatane
Cambridge
Opotiki
East C.
Te Awamutu
Putaruru
Rotorua
Kawerau
Raukumara Ra.
Otorohanga
Hikurangi
Te Kuiti
Kinleith
Murupara
Waipiro
Mokau
Makai
Taupo
Motu
North Taranaki
Bight
Wairoa
Ongarue
Waikaremoana
Tolaga Bay
Waitara
Taumarunui
Ormond
New Plymouth
Turangi
Gisborne
Inglewood
Mt. Egmont
Poverty Bay
Stratford
Raetihi
Nuhaka
Opunake
Eltham
Ohakune
Waiouru
Wairoa
Waikokopu
Kapuni
Mahia
Peninsula
Hawera
Taihape
Bay Hawke Bay
View
South Taranaki
Bight
Mangaweka
Napier
Waverley
Ruahine Ra.
C. Kidnappers
Patea
Hunterville
Hastings
Wanganui
Marton
Bulls
Feilding
Waipawa
Sanson
Waipukurau
Palmerston N.
Foxton
Woodville
Dannevirke
Shannon
Pohiatua
Levin
Eketahuna
Otaki
C. Turnagain
Paraparaumu
Tararua Ra.
Up. Hutt
Masterton
Carterton
Featherston
Greytown
Petone
Martinborough
Lr. Hutt
Eastbourne
WELLINGTON

PACIFIC
OCEAN

SOUTH ISLAND

C. Farewell
Golden
Bay
Collingwood
D'Urville I.
Takaka
Tasman
Bay
Tasman
Mts.
Motueka
Karamea
Bight
Pelorus Sd.
Kapiti I.
Seddonville
Richmond
Havelock
Granity
Nelson
Picton
Wakefield
Blenheim
Westport
Lyell Ra.
Murchison
Rotoroa
Renwick
Seddon
Reefton
Inangahua
Junction
Mt. Traverse
Tapuaenuku
Ward
Blackball
Spenser
Mts.
Runanga
Hanmer
Clarence
Greymouth
Stillwater
Amuri P.
Kaikoura
Kumara
L. Brunner
Jacksons
Springs
Hokitika
Waiau
Ross
Arthur's
Pass
Waikari
Culverden
Waiau
Waipara
Amberley
Colleridge
Oxford
Abut Hd.
Okarito
Rangiora
Pegasus Bay
Kaiapoi
New Brighton
Springfield
Whitecliffs
Riccarton
Christchurch
Methven
Lyttelton
Mt. Cook
3753
Rakaia
Lincoln
Stavely
Southbridge
L. Ellesmere
Banks Peninsula
SOUTHERN ALPS
Fairlie
Akaroa
Jackson B.
Okuru
Mt. Cook
Haast
Little River
Geraldine
Mt.
Aspiring
3027
L. Coleridge
Temuka
Pukaki
Timaru
Mt.
Earnslaw
2819
L. Ohau
Hawea
St.
Andrews
Milford Sd.
Wanaka
Kurow
Waimate
Bligh Sd.
George Sd.
Omarama
Tokarahi
Ngapara
Queenstown
Arrowtown
Cromwell
Oamaru
Secretary I.
Kakanui
Mts.
Maheno
Doubtful
Sd.
Wakatipu
Clyde
Naseby
Hampden
Dunback
Te Anau
Kingston
Alexandra
Waikouaiti
Breaksea
Roxburgh
Dunedin
Resolution
I.
Manapouri
Mossburn
Port Chalmers
Dusky
Sd.
Lumsden
Edievale
Mosgiel
Otago Harbour
Lawrence
Kelso
Fairfield
St. Kilda
C. Saunders
Chalky
Inlet
Ohai
Nightcaps
Clinton
Milton
Preservation
Inlet
Winton
Gore
Balclutha
Te Waewae B.
Orepuki
Hedgehope
Mataura
Kaitangata
Riverton
Wyndham
Nugget Pt.
Invercargill
Bluff
Owaka
Ruapuke I.
Tokanui
Waikawa
Foveaux Str.
Halfmoon Bay
Stewart I.
S.W. Cape
Port Pegasus

TASMAN
SEA

Westland Bight

Canterbury Plain

SAMOA ISLANDS
1:12 000 000
WESTERN
SAMOA
AMERICAN
SAMOA
Savai'i
Apia
Upolu
Pago Pago
Manua Is.
Tutuila
Rose I.

FIJI AND TONGA
ISLANDS
1:12 000 000
50 0 50 100 150 miles
50 0 50 100 150 200 250 km

Wallis & Futuna (Fr.)
Futuna
WESTERN SAMOA
Niuafo'ou
(Tonga)
Thikombia
L'ambasa
Vanua Levu
Yasawa Group
Taveuni
FIJI
Koro
Vanua Balavu
Lautoka
Levuka
Lau or Eastern Group
TONGA
(Friendly Is.)
Nandi
Viti Levu
Ovalau
Ngau
Lakemba
Vava'u
Suva
Koro Sea
Moala
Vatoa
Tofua I.
Kandavu
Tongatapu
Nuku'alofa

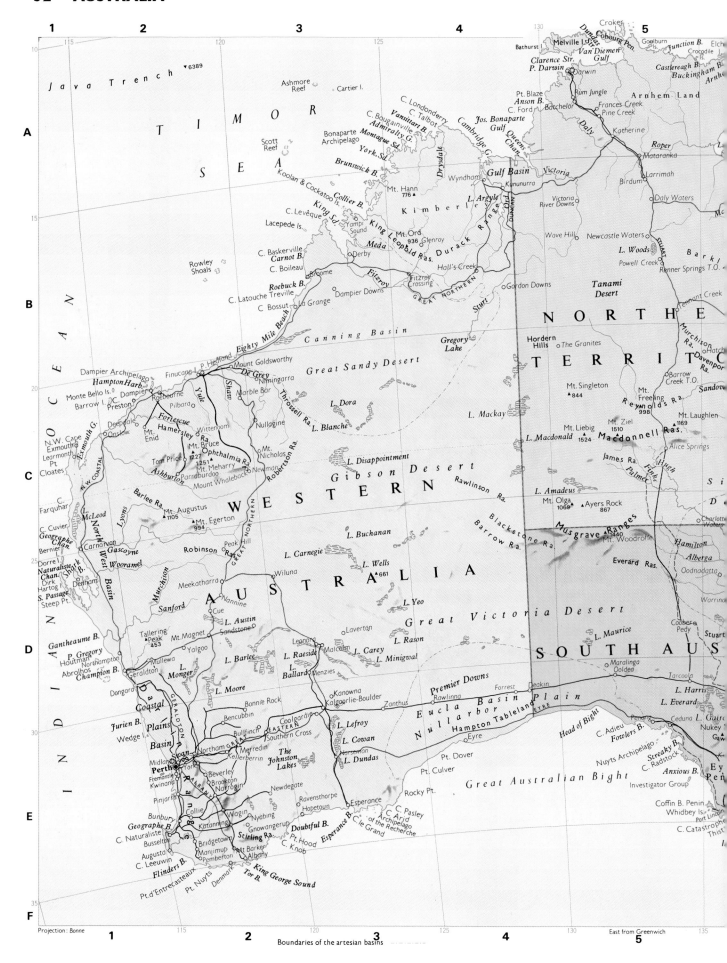

Projection: Bonne

Boundaries of the artesian basins

East from Greenwich

1:12 000 000

100   0   100   200 miles
100 0 100 200 300 400 km

AUSTRALASIA
PHYSICAL
1:80 000 000

200 0 200 400 600 800 1000 miles
200 0 400 600 1200 1600 km

	ft	m
	12000	4000
	6000	2000
	600	200
	0	0
	200	600
	2000	6000
	4000	12000
	ft	m

Gulf of Carpentaria

Cape York Peninsula

QUEENSLAND

Great Dividing Range

Great Barrier Reef

CORAL SEA ISLANDS TERRITORY

PACIFIC OCEAN

NEW SOUTH WALES

VICTORIA

SOUTH AUSTRALIA

NEW ZEALAND

TASMANIA

Tasman Sea

Bass Strait

MELBOURNE

TASMANIA

Hobart

on same scale

COPYRIGHT. GEORGE PHILIP & SON LTD

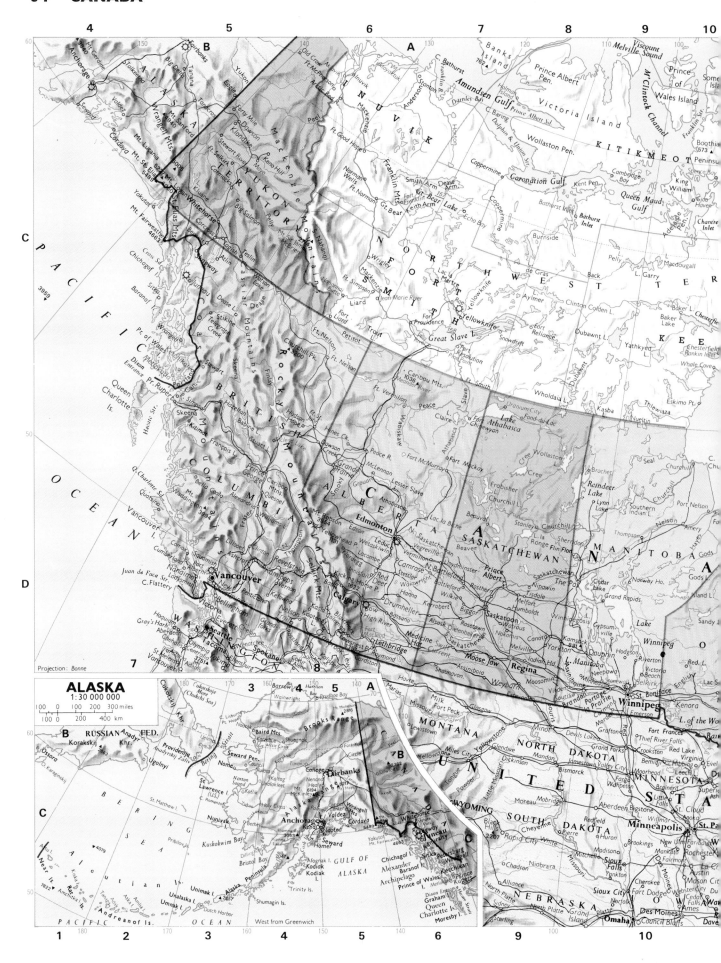

ALASKA
1:30 000 000

Projection: Bonne

For destination information on every country in the world consult the Columbus Press *World Travel Guide* 14th edition. Tel +44 (171) 417 0700.

See also the following specialist map: Canada Regions (p. 94).

1:15 000 000

West from Greenwich

COPYRIGHT. GEORGE PHILIP & SON. LTD

For destination information on every country in the world consult the Columbus Press *World Travel Guide* 14th edition. Tel +44 (171) 417 0700.

See also the following specialist map: Canada Regions (p. 94).

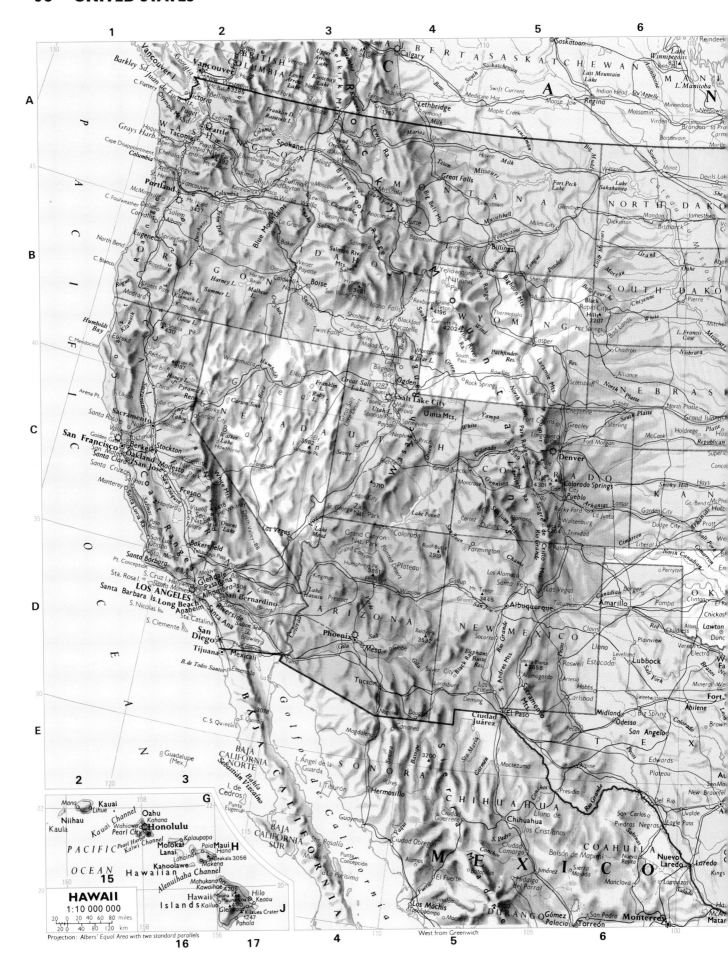

For destination information on every country in the world consult the Columbus Press *World Travel Guide* 14th edition. Tel +44 (171) 417 0700.

See also the following specialist maps: USA Regions (pp. 90-91); USA National Parks (pp. 92-93).

For destination information on every country in the world consult the Columbus Press *World Travel Guide* 14th edition. Tel +44 (171) 417 0700.

See also the following specialist maps: USA Regions (pp. 90-91); USA National Parks (pp. 92-93).

For destination information on every country in the world consult the Columbus Press *World Travel Guide* 14th edition. Tel +44 (171) 417 0700.

See also the following specialist maps: USA Regions (pp. 90–91); USA National Parks (pp. 92–93); Central America, Mexico and the Caribbean (p. 95).

1:15 000 000

COPYRIGHT. GEORGE PHILIP & SON. LTD.

For destination information on every country in the world consult the Columbus Press *World Travel Guide* 14th edition. Tel +44 (171) 417 0700.

See also the following specialist maps: USA Regions (pp. 90-91); USA National Parks (pp. 92-93); Central America, Mexico and the Caribbean (p. 95).

For destination information on every country in the world consult the Columbus Press *World Travel Guide* 14th edition. Tel +44 (171) 417 0700.

See also the following specialist map: Central America, Mexico and the Caribbean (p. 95).

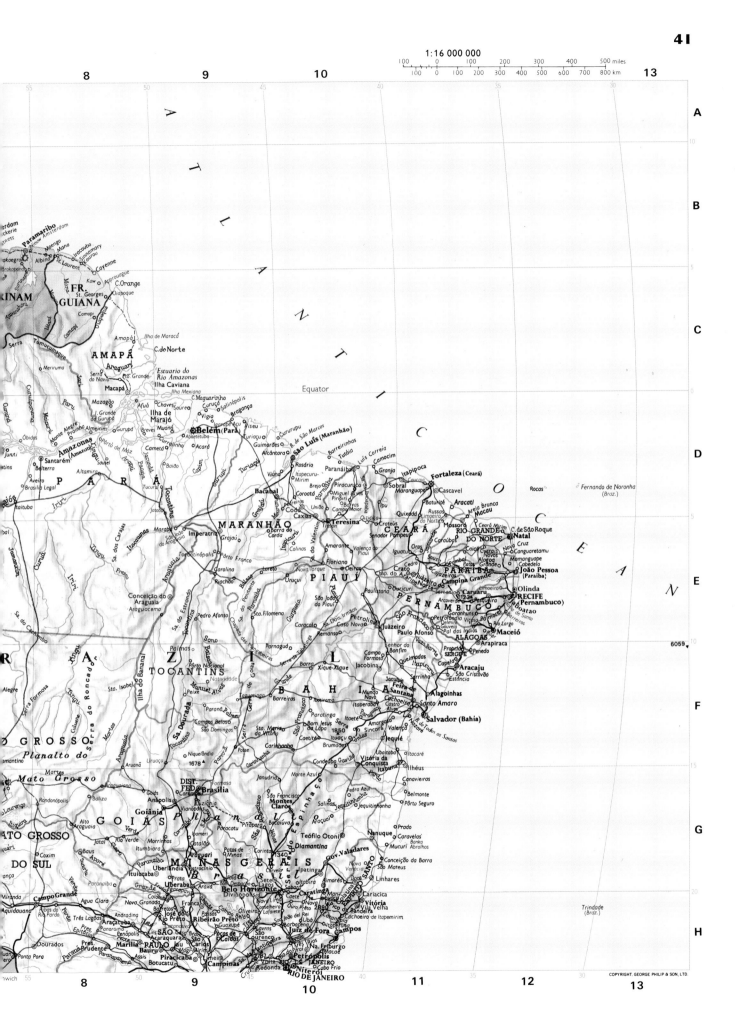

1:16 000 000

1:16 000 000

For destination information on every country in the world consult the Columbus Press *World Travel Guide* 14th edition. Tel +44 (171) 417 0700.

INDEX

he index contains the names of all the principal places and features shown on e maps. Each name is followed by an additional entry in italics giving the ountry or region within which it is located.

hysical features composed of a proper name (Erie) and a description (Lake) e positioned alphabetically by the proper name. The description is positioned ter the proper name and is usually abbreviated.

he number in bold type which follows each name in the index refers to the umber of the map page where that feature or place will be found. This is usually the largest scale at which the place or feature appears. The letter and figure which are in bold type immediately after the page number give the grid square on the map page, within which the feature is situated. The letter represents the latitude and the figure the longitude.

In some cases the feature itself may fall within the specified square, while the name is outside. This is usually the case only with features which are larger than a grid square. Rivers are indexed to their mouths or confluences, and carry the symbol ≈ after their names. A solid square ■ follows the name of a country while, an open square □ refers to a first order administrative area.

Abbreviations used in the index:

Afghan - *Afghanistan*
Arch. - *Archipelago*
Amer. - *America*
Atl. - *Atlantic*
B. - *Bay*
Bulg. - *Bulgaria*
C. - *Cape*
Cent. - *Central*
Chan. - *Channel*
Den. - *Denmark*
Dom. Rep. - *Dominican Republic*
Eq. - *Equatorial*
Fin. - *Finland*
G. - *Gulf*
Ger. - *Germany*
I(s). - *Island(s), Isle(s)*
Ind. - *Indian*
Ire. - *Ireland*
L. - *Lake, Loch, Lough*
Mong. - *Mongolia*
Mt(s). - *Mount(s), Mountains(s)*
N. - *North*
N.Z. - *New Zealand*
Neth. - *Netherlands*
Norw. - *Norway*
Pac. - *Pakistan*
Pen. - *Peninsula*
Port. - *Portugal*
Rep. - *Republic*
Rom. - *Romania*
S. - *South*
S. Arabia - *Saudi Arabia*
Str. - *Strait*
Swed. - *Sweden*
Switz. - *Switzerland*
U.A.E. - *United Arab Emirates*
U.K. - *United Kingdom*
U.S.A. - *United States of America*
W. - *West*
Yug. - *Yugoslavia*

achen, *Ger.* 16 C3
a, *Nigeria* 26 G6
adan, *Iran* 25 B3
ashiri, *Japan* 21 F11
beville, *France* 12 A4
eokuta, *Nigeria* 26 G5
erdare, *U.K.* 9 F4
erdeen, *U.K.* 10 D6
erystwyth, *U.K.* 9 E3
idjan, *Ivory Coast* 26 G4
ilene, *U.S.A.* 36 D7
ruzzi, □ *Italy* 14 C5
u Dhabi, *U.A.E.* 25 C4
capulco, *Mexico* 38 D5
ccra, *Ghana* 26 G4
hill I., *Ire.* 11 C1
concagua, *Argentina* 42 C3
cre, □ *Brazil* 40 E4
damaoua, Massif de l', *Cameroon* 28 C2
dana, *Turkey* 25 B2
ddis Abeba, *Ethiopia* 28 C7
delaide, *Australia* 33 E6
den, Gulf of, *Asia* 25 D3
driatic Sea, *Italy* 14 C6
gean Sea, *Greece* 15 E11
fghanistan, ■ *Asia* 25 B5
rica 30
gadir, *Morocco* 26 B3
gra, *India* 24 C4
guascalientes, *Mexico* 38 C4
haggar, *Algeria* 26 D6
hmadabad, *India* 24 D3
hvāz, *Iran* 25 B3
rdrie, *U.K.* 10 F5
accio, *France* 14 D3
kershus, *Norw.* 7 F11
kita, *Japan* 21 G11
kron, *U.S.A.* 37 B10
kureyri, *Iceland* 6 D4
'Adan, *Yemen* 25 D3
Basrah, *Iraq* 25 B3
Hillah, *Iraq* 25 B3
Hufūf, *S. Arabia* 25 C3
Kut, *Iraq* 25 B3
Kuwayt, *Kuwait* 25 C3
Madinah, *S. Arabia* 25 C2
Manamāh, *S. Arabia* 25 C4
l Mawsil, *Iraq* 25 B3
l Qatif, *S. Arabia* 25 C3
labama, □ *U.S.A.* 37 D9
agôas, □ *Brazil* 41 E11
agoinhas, *Brazil* 41 F11
and, *Fin.* 7 F16
laska, □ *U.S.A.* 34 B4
lba Iulia, *Rom.* 17 E11
lbacete, *Spain* 13 C5
lbania, ■ *Europe* 15 D9
lbany, *U.S.A.* 37 B12
lberta, □ *Canada* 34 C8
lborg, *Den.* 7 H10
lbuquerque, *U.S.A.* 36 C5
ldabra Is., *Africa* 30 F8
lderney, *Channel Is.* 12 B2
ldershot, *U.K.* 9 F7
leppo = Halab, *Syria* 25 B2
lessándria, *Italy* 14 B3
lesund, *Norw.* 6 E9
leutian Is., *U.S.A.* 34 C2
lexandria = El Iskandarîya, *Egypt* 27 B10
lfreton, *U.K.* 8 D6
lgarve, □ *Port.* 13 D1
Alger, *Algeria* 26 A5
Algeria, ■ *Africa* 26 C5
Algiers = Alger, *Algeria* 26 A5
Alicante, *Spain* 13 C5
Alice Springs, *Australia* 32 C5
Alkmaar, *Neth.* 16 B2
Allahabad, *India* 24 C5
Allentown, *U.S.A.* 37 B11
Alloa, *U.K.* 10 E5
Alma Ata, *Kazakhstan* 18 E8
Almeria, *Spain* 13 D4
Alps, *Europe* 12 D7
Alsace, □ *France* 12 B7
Altona, *Ger.* 16 B4
Älvsborg, □ *Swed.* 7 G12
Amagasaki, *Japan* 21 B4
Amapá, □ *Brazil* 41 C8
Amarillo, *U.S.A.* 36 C6
Amazonas, ≈ *S. Amer.* 41 D8
Amazonas, □ *Brazil* 40 D5
Amiens, *France* 12 B5
Ammān, *Jordan* 25 B2
Amritsar, *India* 24 B3
Amsterdam, *Neth.* 16 B2
Amundsen Gulf, *Canada* 34 A7
An Najaf, *Iraq* 25 B3
Anaheim, *U.S.A.* 36 D3
Anápolis, *Brazil* 41 G9
Anchorage, *Alaska* 34 B5
Ancohuma, *Bolivia* 40 G5
Ancona, *Italy* 14 C5
Andalucía, □ *Spain* 13 D3
Andaman Is., *India* 24 F7
Andes, Cord. de los, *S. Amer.* 40 G4
Andhra Pradesh, □ *India* 24 E4
Andorra, ■ *Europe* 13 A6
Andria, *Italy* 14 D7
Andros, *Greece* 15 F11
Andros I., *W. Indies* 39 C9
Angers, *France* 12 C3
Anglesey, *U.K.* 8 D3
Angola, ■ *Africa* 29 G3
Angoulême, *France* 12 D4
Angoumois, □ *France* 12 D3
Anguilla, *W. Indies* 38 J19
Anjou, □ *France* 12 C3
Ankara, *Turkey* 25 B2
Annaba, *Algeria* 26 A6
Anshan, *China* 22 B7
Antananarivo, *Madagascar* 29 H9
Antarctica 4 24C
Anticosti, Î. d', *Canada* 35 D13
Antigua & Barbuda, ■ *W. Indies* 38 K20
Antofagasta, *Chile* 42 A2
Antrim, *U.K.* 11 B5
Antwerpen, *Belgium* 16 C2
Aomori, *Japan* 21 F11
Apeldoorn, *Neth.* 16 B2
Appalachian Mts., *U.S.A.* 37 C10
Appennini, *Italy* 14 C5
Ar Ramadi, *Iraq* 25 B3
Ar Riyād, *S. Arabia* 25 C3
Arabian Sea, *Asia* 25 D5
Aracajú, *Brazil* 41 F11
Arad, *Rom.* 17 E10
Aragon, □ *Spain* 13 B5
Arāk, *Iran* 25 B3
Aral Sea = Aralskoye More, *Asia* 18 E6
Aralskoye More, *Asia* 18 E6
Arbil, *Iraq* 25 B3
Arbroath, *U.K.* 10 E6
Arctic Ocean, 4 12A
Ardabil, *Iran* 25 B3
Ardennes, *Belgium* 16 C2
Ardgour, *U.K.* 10 E3
Arenal, *Spain* 13 C7
Arequipa, *Peru* 40 G4
Argentina, ■ *S. Amer.* 42 E3
Århus, *Den.* 7 H11
Arizona, □ *U.S.A.* 36 D4
Arkansas, ≈ *U.S.A.* 37 C7
Arkansas, □ *U.S.A.* 37 D8
Arkhangelsk, *Russia* 18 C5
Arklow, *Ire.* 11 D5
Armagh, *U.K.* 11 B5
Armenia, ■ *Asia* 18 E5
Armenia, *Colombia* 40 C3
Arnhem, *Neth.* 16 C2
Arnhem Land, *Australia* 32 A5
Arran, *U.K.* 10 F3
Artois, □ *France* 12 A5
Aru Is., *Indonesia* 23 D5
Arunachal Pradesh, □ *India* 24 C7
Asahikawa, *Japan* 21 F11
Ascension, *Atl. Ocean* 30 F2
Ascoli Piceno, *Italy* 14 C5
Ashkhabad, *Turkmenistan* 18 F6
Asmera, *Ethiopia* 28 A7
Assam □ *India* 24 C7
Astrakhan, *Russia* 18 E5
Asturias, □ *Spain* 13 A2
Asunción, *Paraguay* 42 B5
Aswân, *Egypt* 27 D11
Asyût, *Egypt* 27 C11
Athabasca, L., *Canada* 34 C9
Athens = Athínai, *Greece* 15 F10
Athínai, *Greece* 15 F10
Athlone, *Ire.* 11 C4
Atlanta, *U.S.A.* 37 D10
Atlantic Ocean 2 C7
Auckland, *N.Z.* 31 G5
Augsburg, *Ger.* 16 D5
Augusta, *U.S.A.* 37 D10
Aust-Agder, □ *Norw.* 7 G9
Austin, *U.S.A.* 36 D7
Australia, ■ *Australasia* 32
Australian Alps, *Australia* 33 F8
Australian Capital Territory, □ *Australia* 33 F8
Austria, ■ *Europe* 16 E6
Auvergne, □ *France* 12 D5
Avellaneda, *Argentina* 42 C5
Aviemore, *U.K.* 10 D5
Avignon, *France* 12 D6
Avila, *Spain* 13 B3
Avon, □ *U.K.* 9 F5
Ayers Rock, *Australia* 32 D5
Ayr, *U.K.* 10 F4
Azerbaijan, ■ *Asia* 18 E5
Azores, *Atl. Ocean* 2 C8
Azovskoye More, *Ukraine* 18 E4

B

Bābol, *Iran* 25 B4
Bacău, *Rom.* 17 E13
Bacabal, *Brazil* 41 D10
Badajoz, *Spain* 13 C2
Badalona, *Spain* 13 B7
Baden-Württemberg, □ *Ger.* 16 D4
Badenoch, *U.K.* 10 E4
Baffin Bay, *N. Amer.* 35 A13
Baffin I., *Canada* 35 B12
Baghdād, *Iraq* 25 B3
Bahamas, ■ *W. Indies* 39 C9
Bahia, □ *Brazil* 41 F10
Bahía Blanca, *Argentina* 42 D4
Bahrain, ■ *Asia* 25 C4
Baidoa, *Somalia* 30 F8
Baja California, □ *Mexico* 38 B2
Bakersfield, *U.S.A.* 36 C3
Bakhtaran, *Iran* 25 B3
Baku, *Azerbaijan* 18 E5
Balboa, *Panama* 38 H14
Baleares, Is., *Spain* 13 C6
Bali, *Indonesia* 23 D3
Balkhash, Ozero, *Kazakhstan* 18 E8
Ballarat, *Australia* 33 F7
Ballater, *U.K.* 10 D5
Ballymena, □ *U.K.* 11 B5
Ballymoney, □ *U.K.* 11 A5
Balmoral, *U.K.* 10 D5
Baltic Sea, *Europe* 7 H15
Baltimore, *U.S.A.* 37 C11
Bamako, *Mali* 26 F3
Bamberg, *Ger.* 16 D5
Banbridge, *U.K.* 11 B5
Bandon, *Ire.* 11 E3
Bandung, *Indonesia* 23 D2
Banff, *U.K.* 10 D6
Bangalore, *India* 24 F4
Banghāzi, *Libya* 27 B8
Bangkok, *Thailand* 23 B2
Bangladesh, ■ *Asia* 24 D6
Bangor, *U.K.* 11 B6
Bangui, *Cent. Afr. Rep.* 28 D3
Banjarmasin, *Indonesia* 23 D3
Banks I., *Canada* 34 A7
Bantry, *Ire.* 11 E2
Baotou, *China* 22 B5
Baranof I., *Alaska* 34 C6
Barbados, ■ *W. Indies* 38 P22
Barbuda, *W. Indies* 38 K20
Barcelona, *Spain* 13 B7
Bardsey I., *U.K.* 8 E3
Bareilly, *India* 24 C4
Barents Sea, *Arctic* 18 B4
Bari, *Italy* 14 D7
Barkly Tableland, *Australia* 32 B6
Barletta, *Italy* 14 D7
Barnsley, *U.K.* 8 D6
Barquisimeto, *Venezuela* 40 A5
Barra, *U.K.* 10 E1
Barrancabermeja, *Colombia* 40 B4
Barranquilla, *Colombia* 40 A4
Barrow-in-Furness, *U.K.* 8 C4
Barry, *U.K.* 9 F4
Basel, *Switz.* 16 E3
Basildon, *U.K.* 9 F8
Basilicata, □ *Italy* 14 D6
Basingstoke, *U.K.* 9 F6
Bass Strait, *Australia* 33 F8
Basse Terre, *Guadeloupe* 38 L20
Bath, *U.K.* 9 F5
Baton Rouge, *U.S.A.* 37 D8
Bauru, *Brazil* 41 H9
Bayern, □ *Ger.* 16 D5
Baykal, Ozero, *Russia* 19 D11
Bayonne, *France* 12 E3
Bayrūt, *Lebanon* 25 B2
Beaujolais, *France* 12 C6
Beaumont, *U.S.A.* 37 D8
Bedford, *U.K.* 9 E7
Bedfordshire, □ *U.K.* 9 E7
Beijing, *China* 22 C6
Beira, *Mozambique* 29 H7
Belcher Is., *Canada* 35 C12
Belém, *Brazil* 41 D9
Belet Uen, *Somalia* 30 F8
Belfast, *U.K.* 11 B6
Belgium, ■ *Europe* 16 C2
Belgrade = Beograd, *Yug.* 15 B9
Belize, ■ *Cent. Amer.* 38 D7
Belmopan, *Belize* 38 D7
Belo Horizonte, *Brazil* 41 G10
Belorussia, ■ *Europe* 18 D3
Beloye More, *Russia* 18 C4
Ben Nevis, *U.K.* 10 E4
Benares = Varanasi, *India* 24 C5
Benbecula, *U.K.* 10 D1
Bengal, B. of, *Ind. Ocean* 24 E6
Bengbu, *China* 22 C6
Benguela, *Angola* 29 G2
Beni Suef, *Egypt* 27 C11
Benidorm, *Spain* 13 C5
Benin, ■ *Africa* 26 G5
Benin, Bight of, *Africa* 26 H5
Benin City, *Nigeria* 26 G6
Benoni, *S. Africa* 29 K5
Benue, ≈ *Africa* 26 G6
Benxi, *China* 22 B7
Beograd, *Yug.* 15 B9
Bergamo, *Italy* 14 B3
Bergen, *Norw.* 7 F8
Bering Sea, *Arctic* 19 D17
Berkeley, *U.S.A.* 36 C2
Berkshire, □ *U.K.* 9 F6
Berlin, *Ger.* 16 B6
Bermuda, □ *Atl. Ocean* 39 A12
Bern, *Switz.* 16 E3
Berwick-upon-Tweed, *U.K.* 8 B6
Besançon, *France* 12 C7
Béziers, *France* 12 E5
Bhopal, *India* 24 D4
Bhutan, ■ *Asia* 24 C7
Białystok, *Poland* 17 B11
Biarritz, *France* 12 E3
Biel, *Switz.* 16 E3
Bielefeld, *Ger.* 16 B4
Bielsko-Biała, *Poland* 17 D9
Bihar, □ *India* 24 D6
Bijagos, Arquipélago dos, *Guinea-Bissau* 26 F1
Bilbao, *Spain* 13 A4
Billings, *U.S.A.* 36 A5
Bioko, *Eq. Guinea* 28 D1
Birkenhead, *U.K.* 8 D4
Birmingham, *U.K.* 9 E6
Birmingham, *U.S.A.* 37 D9
Biscay, B. of, *Europe* 12 D1
Bishkek, *Kirghizia* 18 E8
Bișhop Auckland, *U.K.* 8 C6
Bitola, *Macedonia* 15 D9
Biwa-Ko, *Japan* 21 B5
Black Sea, *Europe* 18 E4
Blackburn, *U.K.* 8 D5
Blackpool, *U.K.* 8 D4
Blanc, Mt., *France* 12 D7
Blantyre, *Malawi* 29 H7
Blaydon, *U.K.* 8 C6
Blekinge, □ *Swed.* 7 H13
Bloemfontein, *S. Africa* 29 K5
Blue Nile = Nîl el Azraq, ≈ *Africa* 27 E11
Blyth, *U.K.* 8 B6
Bobo-Dioulasso, *Burkina Faso* 26 F4
Bochum, *Ger.* 16 C3
Boden, *Swed.* 6 D16
Bodmin Moor, *U.K.* 9 G3
Boggeragh Mts., *Ire.* 11 D3
Bogotá, *Colombia* 40 C4
Böhmerwald, *Ger.* 16 D6
Bolivia, ■ *S. Amer.* 40 G5

Index

Bologna, *Italy* 14 B4
Bolton, *U.K.* 8 D5
Bombay, *India* 24 E3
Bonn, *Ger.* 16 C3
Boothia, Gulf of, *Canada* ...35 A11
Bootle, *U.K.* 8 D4
Borås, *Swed.* 7 H12
Bordeaux, *France* 12 D3
Borders, □ *U.K.* 10 F5
Borlänge, *Swed.* 7 F13
Borneo, □ *Indonesia* 23 C3
Bornholm, *Den.* 7 J13
Bosnia-Herzegovina, ■ *Europe* ...14 B7
Bosporus, *Turkey* 25 A1
Boston, *U.S.A.* 37 B12
Boston, *U.K.* 8 E7
Bothnia, G. of, *Scandinavia* ...6 E16
Botoşani, *Rom.* 17 E13
Botswana, ■ *Africa* 29 J4
Bouaké, *Ivory Coast* 26 G3
Boulogne, *France* 12 A4
Bourbonnais, □ *France* 12 C5
Bourges, *France* 12 C5
Bournemouth, *U.K.* 9 G6
Bowland, Forest of, *U.K.* ...8 D5
Boyne, ≈ *Ire.* 11 C5
Brăila, *Rom.* 17 F13
Bradford, *U.K.* 8 D6
Braga, *Port.* 13 B1
Brahmaputra, ≈ *India* 24 C7
Brandenburg, *Ger.* 16 B6
Brantford, *Canada* 35 D11
Brasília, *Brazil* 41 G9
Braşov, *Rom.* 17 F12
Bratislava, *Slovak Rep.* ...16 D8
Bratsk, *Russia* 19 D11
Braunschweig, *Ger.* 16 B5
Bray, *Ire.* 11 C5
Brazil, ■ *S. Amer.* 41 F8
Brazzaville, *Congo* 28 E3
Breadalbane, *U.K.* 10 E4
Brecon Beacons, *U.K.* 9 F4
Breda, *Neth.* 16 C2
Bremen, *Ger.* 16 B4
Bremerhaven, *Ger.* 16 B4
Brentwood, *U.K.* 9 F8
Bréscia, *Italy* 14 B4
Bressay, *U.K.* 10 A7
Brest, *France* 12 B1
Bretagne, □ *France* 12 B2
Bridgeport, *U.S.A.* 37 B12
Bridgetown, *Barbados* 38 P22
Bridgwater, *U.K.* 9 F4
Bridlington, *U.K.* 8 C7
Brighton, *U.K.* 9 G7
Bríndisi, *Italy* 15 D7
Brisbane, *Australia* 33 D9
Bristol, *U.K.* 9 F5
Bristol Channel, *U.K.* 9 F3
British Columbia, □ *Canada* ...34 C7
Brno, *Czech Rep.* 16 D8
Broads, The, *U.K.* 8 E9
Brooks Range, *Alaska* 34 B5
Brugge, *Belgium* 16 C1
Brunei, ■ *Asia* 23 C3
Brussel, *Belgium* 16 C2
Bruxelles = Brussel, *Belgium* ...16 C2
Bucaramanga, *Colombia* ...40 B4
Buchan, *U.K.* 10 D6
Bucharest = Bucureşti, *Rom.* ...17 F13
Buckinghamshire, □ *U.K.* ...9 F7
Bucureşti, *Rom.* 17 F13
Budapest, *Hungary* 17 E9
Buenaventura, *Colombia* ...40 C3
Buenos Aires, *Argentina* ...42 C5
Buffalo, *U.S.A.* 37 B11
Buga, *Colombia* 40 C3
Bujumbura, *Burundi* 28 E5
Bukavu, *Zaïre* 28 E5
Bulawayo, *Zimbabwe* 29 J5
Bulgaria, ■ *Europe* 15 C11
Bûr Saîd, *Egypt* 27 B11
Bûr Sûdân, *Sudan* 27 E12
Burgas, *Bulg.* 15 C12
Burgenland, □ *Austria* 16 E8
Burgos, *Spain* 13 A4
Burkina Faso, ■ *Africa* 26 F4
Burma, ■ *Asia* 24 D8
Bursa, *Turkey* 25 A1
Burton-on-Trent, *U.K.* 8 E6
Buru, *Indonesia* 23 D4
Burundi, ■ *Africa* 28 E5
Buskerud, □ *Norw.* 7 F10
Bute, *U.K.* 10 F3
Bydgoszcz, *Poland* 17 B8
Bylot I., *Canada* 35 A12
Bytom, *Poland* 17 C9

C

Cabimas, *Venezuela* 40 A4
Cabinda, □ *Angola* 28 F2
Cáceres, *Spain* 13 C2
Cádiz, *Spain* 13 D2
Caen, *France* 12 B3
Caernarfon B., *U.K.* 8 D3
Cágliari, *Italy* 14 E3
Caha Mts., *Ire.* 11 E2
Cairngorm Mts., *U.K.* 10 D5

Cairo = El Qâhira, *Egypt* ...27 B11
Calabar, *Nigeria* 26 G6
Calabria, □ *Italy* 14 E7
Calais, *France* 12 A4
Calcutta, *India* 24 D6
Calgary, *Canada* 34 C8
Cali, *Colombia* 40 C3
Calicut, *India* 24 F4
California, □ *U.S.A.* 36 C2
Callao, *Peru* 40 F3
Caltanissetta, *Italy* 14 F5
Camagüey, *Cuba* 39 C9
Cambodia, ■ *Asia* 23 B2
Camborne, *U.K.* 9 G2
Cambrian Mts., *U.K.* 9 E4
Cambridge, *U.K.* 9 E8
Cambridgeshire, □ *U.K.* 9 E8
Camden, *U.S.A.* 37 C12
Cameroon, ■ *Africa* 28 C2
Cameroon, Mt., *Cameroon* ...28 D1
Campania, □ *Italy* 14 D6
Campbeltown, *U.K.* 10 F3
Campeche, G. de, *Mexico* ...38 D6
Campina Grande, *Brazil* 41 E11
Campinas, *Brazil* 41 H9
Campo Grande, *Brazil* 41 H8
Campos, *Brazil* 41 H10
Canada, ■ *N. Amer.* 34 C10
Canarias, Is., *Atl. Ocean* ...26 C1
Canaveral, C., *U.S.A.* 37 E10
Canberra, *Australia* 33 F8
Cannes, *France* 12 E7
Canouan, *W. Indies* 38 Q20
Cantabria, □ *Spain* 13 A3
Canterbury, *U.K.* 9 F9
Canton = Guangzhou, *China* ...22 D6
Cape Province, □ *S. Africa* ...29 L4
Cape Town, *S. Africa* 29 L3
Cape York Pen., *Australia* ...33 A7
Caprivi Strip, *Namibia* 29 H4
Caracas, *Venezuela* 40 A5
Caratinga, *Brazil* 41 G10
Cardiff, *U.K.* 9 F4
Cardigan B., *U.K.* 9 E3
Carlisle, *U.K.* 8 C5
Carlow, *Ire.* 11 D5
Carmarthen B., *U.K.* 9 F3
Carnegie, L., *Australia* 32 D3
Caroline Is., *Pac. Ocean* ...3 D17
Carpathians, *Europe* 17 E12
Carpentaria, Gulf of, *Australia* ...33 A6
Carrara, *Italy* 14 B4
Carrickfergus, *U.K.* 11 B6
Cartagena, *Spain* 13 D5
Cartagena, *Colombia* 40 A3
Cartago, *Colombia* 40 C3
Caruaru, *Brazil* 41 E11
Carúpano, *Venezuela* 40 A6
Casablanca, *Morocco* 26 B3
Caspian Sea, *Asia* 18 E6
Castellón de la Plana, *Spain* ...13 C5
Castilla - La Mancha, □ *Spain* ...13 C3
Castilla y Leon, □ *Spain* 13 B3
Castries, *St. Lucia* 38 N21
Cataluña, □ *Spain* 13 B6
Catánia, *Italy* 14 F6
Catanzaro, *Italy* 14 E7
Cavan, □ *Ire.* 11 B4
Caviana, I., *Brazil* 41 C9
Ceara, □ *Brazil* 41 E11
Cebu, *Philippines* 23 B4
Cedar L., *Canada* 34 C10
Celebes Sea, *Asia* 23 C4
Celebes = Sulawesi, *Indonesia* ...23 D4
Central, □ *U.K.* 10 E4
Central African Rep., ■ *Africa* ...28 C4
Central America, *N. Amer.* ...38 E7
Ceram, *Indonesia* 23 D4
Cerignola, *Italy* 14 D6
Ceylon = Sri Lanka, ■ *Asia* ...24 G5
Chad, ■ *Africa* 27 E8
Champagne, □ *France* 12 B6
Chang, ≈ *China* 22 C6
Changchun, *China* 22 B7
Changsha, *China* 22 D6
Changzhou, *China* 22 C7
Channel Is., *U.K.* 12 B2
Charleston, *U.S.A.* 37 D10
Charlotte, *U.S.A.* 37 C10
Charlottenburg, *Ger.* 16 B6
Charlottetown, *Canada* 35 D13
Chatham, *U.K.* 9 F8
Chattanooga, *U.S.A.* 37 C9
Cheju Do, *S. Korea* 22 C7
Chelmsford, *U.K.* 9 F8
Cheltenham, *U.K.* 9 F5
Chelyabinsk, *Russia* 18 D7
Chemnitz, *Ger.* 16 C6
Chengdu, *China* 22 C5
Cherbourg, *France* 12 B3
Cheremkhovo, *Russia* 19 D11
Chesapeake B., *U.S.A.* 37 C11
Cheshire, □ *U.K.* 8 D5
Chester, *U.K.* 8 D5
Chesterfield, *U.K.* 8 D6
Cheviot Hills, *U.K.* 8 B5
Chiba, *Japan* 21 B7
Chicago, *U.S.A.* 37 B9
Chichagof I., *Alaska* 34 C6

Chiclayo, *Peru* 40 E3
Chihuahua, *Mexico* 38 B3
Chile, ■ *S. Amer.* 42 D2
Chiloe I. de, *Chile* 42 E2
Chiltern Hills, *U.K.* 9 F7
Chimborazo, *Ecuador* 40 D3
China, ■ *Asia* 22 C4
Chingola, *Zambia* 29 G5
Chişinau = Kishinev, *Moldavia* ...18 E3
Chita, *Russia* 19 D12
Chittagong, *Bangladesh* ...24 D7
Chongqing, *China* 22 D5
Chonos, Arch. de los, *Chile* ...42 E2
Chorzów, *Poland* 17 C9
Christchurch, *N.Z.* 31 K4
Christmas I., *Australia* 23 E2
Chukotskoye More, *Russia* ...19 C19
Chungking = Chongqing, *China* ...22 D5
Ciénaga, *Colombia* 40 A4
Cienfuegos, *Cuba* 39 C8
Cincinnati, *U.S.A.* 37 C10
Ciudad Bolivar, *Venezuela* ...40 B6
Ciudad Guayana, *Venezuela* ...40 B6
Ciudad Juárez, *Mexico* 38 A3
Ciudad Real, *Spain* 13 C4
Clacton, *U.K.* 9 F9
Clare, □ *Ire.* 11 D2
Cleethorpes, *U.K.* 8 D7
Clermont-Ferrand, *France* ...12 D5
Cleveland, *U.S.A.* 37 B10
Cleveland, □ *U.K.* 8 C6
Clonmel, *Ire.* 11 D4
Cluj-Napoca, *Rom.* 17 E11
Clwyd, □ *U.K.* 8 D4
Clyde, ≈ *U.K.* 10 F5
Clyde, Firth of, *U.K.* 10 F3
Clydebank, *U.K.* 10 F4
Coalville, *U.K.* 8 E6
Coast Ranges, *U.S.A.* 36 C2
Coatbridge, *U.K.* 10 F4
Coats I., *Canada* 35 B11
Cobh, *Ire.* 11 E3
Cochabamba, *Bolivia* 40 G5
Cocos or Keeling Is., *Australia* ...23 E1
Coimbra, *Port.* 13 B1
Colchester, *U.K.* 9 F8
Coleraine, □ *U.K.* 11 A5
Coll, *U.K.* 10 E2
Cologne = Köln, *Ger.* 16 C3
Colombia, ■ *S. Amer.* 40 C4
Colombo, *Sri Lanka* 24 G5
Colón, *Panama* 38 H14
Colonsay, *U.K.* 10 E2
Colorado, □ *U.S.A.* 36 C5
Colorado, ≈ *U.S.A.* 36 D4
Colorado Springs, *U.S.A.* ...36 C5
Columbia, ≈ *U.S.A.* 36 A2
Columbia, □ *U.S.A.* 37 D10
Columbus, Georgia, *U.S.A.* ...37 D10
Columbus, Ohio, *U.S.A.* 37 C10
Colwyn Bay, *U.K.* 8 D4
Comeragh Mts., *Ire.* 11 D4
Como, *Italy* 14 B4
Comoros, ■ *Africa* 30 G8
Conakry, *Guinea* 26 G2
Concepcion, *Chile* 42 D2
Congo, ■ *Africa* 28 E3
Congo = Zaïre, ≈ *Africa* 28 E3
Connacht, □ *Ire.* 11 C2
Connecticut, □ *U.S.A.* 37 B12
Connemara, *Ire.* 11 C2
Constanţa, *Rom.* 17 F14
Constantine, *Algeria* 26 A6
Cookstown, □ *U.K.* 11 B5
Cooper Creek, ≈ *Australia* ...33 D6
Córdoba, *Spain* 13 D3
Córdoba, *Argentina* 42 C4
Corfu = Kérkira, *Greece* 15 E8
Cork, *Ire.* 11 E3
Cornwall, □ *U.K.* 9 G3
Coronation Gulf, *Canada* ...34 B8
Corpus Christi, *U.S.A.* 36 E7
Corse, *France* 14 C3
Corsica = Corse, *France* 14 C3
Corumba, *Brazil* 40 G7
Cosenza, *Italy* 14 E7
Costa Blanca, *Spain* 13 C5
Costa Brava, *Spain* 13 B7
Costa del Sol, *Spain* 13 D3
Costa Dorada, *Spain* 13 B7
Costa Rica, ■ *Cent. Amer.* ...39 F8
Cote d'Ivoire = Ivory Coast,
■ *Africa* 26 G3
Cotonou, *Benin* 26 G5
Cotopaxi, *Ecuador* 40 D3
Cotswold Hills, *U.K.* 9 F6
Cottbus, *Ger.* 16 C7
Coventry, *U.K.* 9 E6
Craiova, *Rom.* 17 F11
Crawley, *U.K.* 9 F7
Cremona, *Italy* 14 B4
Crete = Kriti, *Greece* 15 G11
Crewe, *U.K.* 8 D5
Croatia, ■ *Europe* 14 B6
Cromarty, *U.K.* 10 D4
Cuba, ■ *W. Indies* 39 C8
Cúcuta, *Colombia* 40 B4
Cuenca, *Ecuador* 40 D3

Cuenca, *Spain* 13 B4
Cuiaba, *Brazil* 41 G7
Cumaná, *Venezuela* 40 A6
Cumbernauld, *U.K.* 10 F4
Cumbria, □ *U.K.* 8 C5
Cumbrian Mts., *U.K.* 8 C4
Curaçao, *Neth. Ant.* 40 A5
Curitiba, *Brazil* 42 B7
Cuzco, *Peru* 40 F4
Cwmbran, *U.K.* 9 F4
Cyclades = Kikládhes, *Greece* ...15 F11
Cyprus, ■ *Asia* 25 B2
Czech Rep., ■ *Europe* 16 D7
Czestochowa, *Poland* 17 C9

D

Dakar, *Senegal* 26 F1
Dalian, *China* 22 C7
Dallas, *U.S.A.* 37 D7
Damaraland, *Namibia* 29 J3
Damascus = Dimashq, *Syria* ...25 B2
Dandong, *China* 22 B7
Danube = Dunarea, ≈ *Europe* ...17 F14
Dar-es-Salaam, *Tanzania* ...28 F7
Dardanelles, *Turkey* 25 A1
Darién, G. del, *S. Amer.* 40 B3
Darling, ≈ *Australia* 33 E7
Darlington, *U.K.* 8 C6
Darmstadt, *Ger.* 16 D4
Dartmoor, *U.K.* 9 G4
Dartmouth, *Canada* 35 D13
Darwin, *Australia* 32 A5
Datong, *China* 22 B6
Dauphine, □ *France* 12 D6
Davao, *Philippines* 23 C4
Davis Str., *N. Amer.* 35 B14
Dayton, *U.S.A.* 37 C10
Dead Sea, *Asia* 25 B2
Deal, *U.K.* 9 F9
Dean, Forest of, *U.K.* 9 F5
Debrecen, *Hungary* 17 E10
Delaware, □ *U.S.A.* 37 C11
Delhi, *India* 24 C4
Denmark, ■ *Europe* 7 J10
Denver, *U.S.A.* 36 C6
Derby, *U.K.* 8 E6
Derbyshire, □ *U.K.* 8 D6
Derryveagh Mts., *Ire.* 11 A4
Des Moines, *U.S.A.* 37 B8
Dessau, *Ger.* 16 C6
Detroit, *U.S.A.* 37 B10
Devon, □ *U.S.A.* 9 G4
Devon I., *Canada* 35 A11
Dezful, *Iran* 25 B3
Dhaka, *Bangladesh* 24 D7
Dhodhekanisos, *Greece* ...15 F12
Dieppe, *France* 12 B4
Dijon, *France* 12 C6
Dimashq, *Syria* 25 B2
Dingle B., *Ire.* 11 D1
Dingwall, *U.K.* 10 D4
Disappointment, L., *Australia* ...32 C3
Diyarbakir, *Turkey* 25 B3
Djibouti, ■ *Africa* 30 D8
Dnepropetrovsk, *Ukraine* ...18 E4
Dnestr, ≈ *Ukraine* 18 E4
Dolomiti, *Italy* 14 A4
Dominica, ■ *W. Indies* 38 M20
Dominican Rep., ■ *W. Indies* ...39 D10
Don, ≈ *Russia* 18 E5
Doncaster, *U.K.* 8 D6
Donegal, □ *Ire.* 11 B3
Donetsk, *Ukraine* 18 E4
Dordrecht, *Neth.* 16 C2
Dornoch, *U.K.* 10 D4
Dorset, □ *U.K.* 9 G5
Dortmund, *Ger.* 16 C3
Douala, *Cameroon* 28 D1
Douglas, *U.K.* 8 C3
Dounreay, *U.K.* 10 C5
Douro, ≈ *Port.* 13 B1
Dover, *U.K.* 9 F9
Down, □ *U.K.* 11 B6
Drakensberg, *S. Africa* 29 K5
Drammen, *Norw.* 7 G11
Dresden, *Ger.* 16 C6
Drogheda, *Ire.* 11 C5
Dublin, *Ire.* 11 C5
Dubrovnik, *Croatia* 15 C8
Dudley, *U.K.* 9 E5
Duisburg, *Ger.* 16 C3
Duluth, *U.S.A.* 37 A8
Dumbarton, *U.K.* 10 F4
Dumfries, *U.K.* 10 F5
Dumfries and Galloway, □ *U.K.* ...10 F5
Dumyât, *Egypt* 27 B11
Dunarea, ≈ *Europe* 17 F14
Dundalk, *Ire.* 11 B5
Dundee, *U.K.* 10 E6
Dunedin, *N.Z.* 31 L3
Dunfermline, *U.K.* 10 E5
Dungannon, □ *U.K.* 11 B5
Dungarvan, *Ire.* 11 D4
Dunkerque, *France* 12 A5
Durango, *Mexico* 38 C4
Durban, *S. Africa* 29 K6
Durham, *U.K.* 8 C6
Dushanbe, *Tajikistan* 18 F7

Düsseldorf, *Ger.* 16 C3
Dyfed, □ *U.K.* 9 F3

E

East China Sea, *Asia* 22 C7
East Kilbride, *U.K.* 10 F4
East London, *S. Africa* 29 L5
East Siberian Sea, *Arctic* ...19 B17
East Sussex, □ *U.K.* 9 G8
Eastbourne, *U.K.* 9 G8
Easter Is., *Pac. Ocean* 2 F16
Ebbw Vale, *U.K.* 9 F4
Ebro, ≈ *Spain* 13 B5
Ech Cheliff, *Algeria* 26 A5
Ecuador, ■ *S. Amer.* 40 D3
Eday, *U.K.* 10 B6
Edinburgh, *U.K.* 10 F5
Edmonton, *Canada* 34 C8
Edward, L., *Africa* 28 E5
Egypt, ■ *Africa* 27 D11
Eifel, *Ger.* 16 C3
Eigg, *U.K.* 10 E2
Eighty Mile Beach, *Australia* ...32 B3
Eindhoven, *Neth.* 16 C2
El Faiyûm, *Egypt* 27 C11
El Ferrol, *Spain* 13 A1
El Gîza, *Egypt* 27 C11
El Iskandarîya, *Egypt* 27 B11
El Khartûm, *Sudan* 27 E11
El Mahalla el Kubra, *Egypt* ...27 B11
El Mansûra, *Egypt* 27 B11
El Minyâ, *Egypt* 27 C11
El Obeid, *Sudan* 27 F11
El Paso, *U.S.A.* 36 D5
El Qâhira, *Egypt* 27 B11
El Salvador, ■ *Cent. Amer.* ...38 E7
El Suweis, *Egypt* 27 C11
Elba, *Italy* 14 C4
Elbe, ≈ *Ger.* 16 B5
Elblag, *Poland* 17 A9
Elburz Mts., *Iran* 25 B4
Elche, *Spain* 13 C5
Eleuthera I., *W. Indies* 39 C9
Elgin, *U.K.* 10 D5
Ellesmere Port, *U.K.* 8 D5
Emilia Romagna, □ *Italy* ...14 B4
England, □ *U.K.* 8 D6
English Channel, *Europe* ...9 G5
Ennis, *Ire.* 11 D2
Enniscorthy, *Ire.* 11 D5
Enschede, *Neth.* 16 B3
Enugu, *Nigeria* 26 G6
Equatorial Guinea, ■ *Africa* ...28 D1
Erawadi Myit, ≈ *Burma* 24 D8
Erfurt, *Ger.* 16 C5
Erie, L., *N. Amer.* 35 D11
Eritrea, ■ *Africa* 27 F12
Erzurum, *Turkey* 25 B3
Esbjerg, *Den.* 7 J10
Esfahán, *Iran* 25 B4
Eskilstuna, *Swed.* 7 G13
Eskisehir, *Turkey* 25 B2
Espirito Santo, □ *Brazil* 41 G10
Essen, *Ger.* 16 C3
Essex, □ *U.K.* 9 F8
Estonia, ■ *Europe* 18 D3
Ethiopia, ■ *Africa* 30 D7
Etna, Mt., *Italy* 14 F6
Euphrates, ≈ *Asia* 25 B3
Evansville, *U.S.A.* 37 C9
Everest, Mt., *Nepal* 24 C6
Everglades, *U.S.A.* 37 E10
Évora, *Port.* 13 C2
Évvoia, *Greece* 15 E11
Exeter, *U.K.* 9 G4
Exmoor, *U.K.* 9 F4
Extremadura, □ *Spain* 13 C2
Eyre, L., *Australia* 33 D6
Eyre Peninsula, *Australia* ...32 E5

F

Fairbanks, *Alaska* 34 B5
Falkirk, *U.K.* 10 F5
Falkland Is, *Atl. Ocean* 42 G5
Fareham, *U.K.* 9 G6
Farnborough, *U.K.* 9 F7
Faroe Is., *Atl. Ocean* 5 C4
Feira de Santana, *Brazil* ...41 F11
Fens, The, *U.K.* 8 E7
Fermanagh, □ *U.K.* 11 B4
Ferrara, *Italy* 14 B4
Fès, *Morocco* 26 B3
Fetlar, *U.K.* 10 A8
Fife, □ *U.K.* 10 E5
Fiji, ■ *Pac. Ocean* 31 C16
Finland, ■ *Europe* 6 C10
Finnmark, □ *Norw.* 6 B10
Firenze, *Italy* 14 C4
Flandre, *Belgium* 16 C1
Fleetwood, *U.K.* 8 D4
Flensburg, *Ger.* 16 A4
Flinders I., *Australia* 33 F8
Flint, *U.S.A.* 37 B10
Florence = Firenze, *Italy* ...14 C4
Flores, *Indonesia* 23 D4
Florida, □ *U.S.A.* 37 E10
Fóggia, *Italy* 14 D6

Folkestone, *U.K.* 9 F9
Fort de France, *Martinique* 38 N20
Fort Smith, *U.S.A.* 37 C8
Fort Wayne, *U.S.A.* 37 B9
Fort William, *U.K.* 10 E3
Fort Worth, *U.S.A.* 36 D7
Fortaleza, *Brazil* 41 D11
Forth, Firth of, *U.K.* 10 E6
Foula, *U.K.* 10 A6
Foxe Channel, *Canada* 35 B11
France, ■ *Europe* 12 C4
Franche-Comte, □ *France* 12 C6
Frankfurt am Main, *Ger.* 16 C4
Frankfurt an der Oder, *Ger.* 16 B7
Fränkische Alb, *Ger.* 16 D5
Fraser I., *Australia* 33 D9
Fraserburgh, *U.K.* 10 D6
Frederikshavn, *Den.* 7 H11
Frederikstad, *Norw.* 7 G11
Freetown, *Sierra Leone* 26 G2
Freiburg, *Ger.* 16 D3
French Guiana, ■ *S. Amer.* 41 C8
Fresno, *U.S.A.* 36 C3
Friuli Venezia Giulia, □ *Italy* 14 A5
Frome, L., *Australia* 33 E6
Frunze = Bishkek, *Kirghizia* 18 E8
Fuji-San, *Japan* 21 B6
Fukuoka, *Japan* 21 C2
Fukushima, *Japan* 21 G11
Funabashi, *Japan* 21 B7
Furneaux Group, *Australia* 33 G8
Fürth, *Ger.* 16 D5
Fushun, *China* 22 B7
Fuzhou, *China* 22 D6
Fyn, *Den.* 7 J11

G

Gabon, ■ *Africa* 28 E2
Gaborone, *Botswana* 29 J5
Gairdner, L., *Australia* 32 E6
Galaţi, *Rom.* 17 F14
Galapagos Is., *Pac. Ocean* 2 E5
Galashiels, *U.K.* 10 F6
Galicia, □ *Spain* 13 A1
Gällivare, *Swed.* 6 C16
Galloway, *U.K.* 10 G4
Galveston, *U.S.A.* 37 E8
Galway, *Ire.* 11 C2
Gambia, ■ *Africa* 26 F1
Gamboa, *Panama* 38 H14
Ganga = Ind./Bangla. 24 C4
Ganges = Ganga, ≈ *Ind./Bangla.* 24 C4
Gaoxiong, *Taiwan* 22 D7
Garda, L. di, *Italy* 14 B4
Gascogne, □ *France* 12 E3
Gaspé, Pén de, *Canada* 35 D13
Gateshead, *U.K.* 8 C6
Gatun, *Panama* 38 H14
Gävle, *Swed.* 7 F14
Gavleborg, □ *Swed.* 7 F14
Gaza, *Israel* 25 B2
Gaziantep, *Turkey* 25 B2
Gdansk, *Poland* 17 A9
Gdynia, *Poland* 17 A9
Geelong, *Australia* 33 F7
Gelsenkirchen, *Ger.* 16 C3
Genève, *Switz.* 16 E3
Génova, *Italy* 14 B3
Gent, *Belgium* 16 C1
George Town, *Malaysia* 23 C2
Georgetown, *Guyana* 40 B7
Georgia, ■ *Asia* 18 E5
Georgia, □ *U.S.A.* 37 D10
Gera, *Ger.* 16 C6
Germany, ■ *Europe* 16 C5
Germiston, *S. Africa* 29 K5
Gerona, *Spain* 13 B7
Ghana, ■ *Africa* 26 G4
Giant's Causeway, *U.K.* 11 A5
Gibraltar, ■ *Europe* 13 D3
Gibson Desert, *Australia* 32 C3
Gifu, *Japan* 21 B5
Gigha, *U.K.* 10 F3
Gijón, *Spain* 13 A3
Gillingham, *U.K.* 9 F8
Gisborne, *N.Z.* 31 H7
Gjøvik, *Norw.* 7 F11
Glasgow, *U.K.* 10 F4
Glendale, *U.S.A.* 36 D3
Glenrothes, *U.K.* 10 E5
Gliwice, *Poland* 17 C9
Głogów, *Poland* 16 C8
Gloucester, *U.K.* 9 F5
Gloucestershire, □ *U.K.* 9 F5
Goa, □ *India* 24 E3
Goiânia, *Brazil* 41 G9
Goias, □ *Brazil* 41 F9
Good Hope, C. of, *S. Africa* 29 L3
Gorkiy = Nizhniy Novgorod, *Russia* .18 D5
Görlitz, *Ger.* 16 C7
Gosport, *U.K.* 9 G6
Göteborg, *Swed.* 7 H11
Gotland, *Swed.* 7 H15
Götaland, *Swed.* 7 G12
Gozo, *Malta* 14 F6
Grampian, □ *U.K.* 10 D6
Grampian Highlands, *U.K.* 10 E4

Gran Canaria, *Canary Is.* 26 C1
Granada, *Spain* 13 D4
Grand Bahama I., *W. Indies* 39 B9
Grand Canyon, *U.S.A.* 36 C4
Grand Cayman, *W. Indies* 39 D8
Grand Rapids, *U.S.A.* 37 B9
Grangemouth, *U.K.* 10 E5
Grantham, *U.K.* 8 E7
Gravesend, *U.K.* 9 F8
Graz, *Austria* 16 E7
Great Abaco I., *W. Indies* 39 B9
Great Australian Bight, *Australia* ...32 E4
Great Barrier Reef, *Australia* 33 B8
Great Bear L., *Canada* 34 B7
Great Divide, *Australia* 33 C8
Great Falls, *U.S.A.* 36 A4
Great Inagua I., *W. Indies* 39 C10
Great Salt Lake, *U.S.A.* 36 B4
Great Sandy Desert, *Australia* 32 C3
Great Slave L., *Canada* 34 B8
Great Victoria Desert, *Australia* ...32 D4
Great Wall, The, *China* 22 C5
Great Yarmouth, *U.K.* 8 E9
Greater Antilles, *W. Indies* 39 D9
Greater Manchester, □ *U.K.* 8 D5
Greece, ■ *Europe* 15 E9
Green Bay, *U.S.A.* 37 B9
Greenland, ■ *N. Amer.* 4 A9
Greenock, *U.K.* 10 F4
Greensboro, *U.S.A.* 37 C11
Grenada, ■ *W. Indies* 38 Q20
Grenoble, *France* 12 D6
Gretna Green, *U.K.* 10 F5
Grey Range, *Australia* 33 D7
Grimsby, *U.K.* 8 D7
Groningen, *Neth.* 16 B3
Groot Karoo, *S. Africa* 29 L4
Groote Eylandt, *Australia* 33 A6
Gross Glockner, *Austria* 16 E6
Grudziadz, *Poland* 17 B9
Guadalajara, *Mexico* 38 C4
Guadalajara, *Spain* 13 B4
Guadarrama, Sierra de, *Spain* 13 B4
Guadeloupe, ■ *W. Indies* 38 L20
Guadiana, ≈ *Port.* 13 D2
Guadix, *Spain* 13 D4
Guangzhou, *China* 22 D6
Guantanamo, *Cuba* 39 C9
Guatemala, ■ *Cent. Amer.* 38 D6
Guatemala City, *Guatemala* 38 E6
Guayaquil, *Ecuador* 40 D2
Guelph, *Canada* 35 D11
Guernsey, *Channel Is.* 12 B2
Guildford, *U.K.* 9 F7
Guinea, ■ *Africa* 26 F2
Guinea-Bissau, ■ *Africa* 26 F1
Guiyang, *China* 22 D5
Gujarat, □ *India* 24 D3
Gulf, The, *Asia* 25 C4
Guyana, ■ *S. Amer.* 40 B7
Guyenne, □ *France* 12 D4
Gwalior, *India* 24 C4
Gwent, □ *U.K.* 9 F4
Gwynedd, □ *U.K.* 8 E4
Győr, *Hungary* 17 E8

H

Haarlem, *Neth.* 16 B2
Hachinohe, *Japan* 21 F11
Hadrian's Wall, *U.K.* 8 C5
Hagen, *Ger.* 16 C3
Haifa, *Israel* 25 B2
Hainan Dao, *China* 22 E6
Hakodate, *Japan* 21 F11
Halab, *Syria* 25 B2
Halberstadt, *Ger.* 16 C5
Halifax, *Canada* 35 D13
Halifax, *U.K.* 8 D6
Halland, □ *Swed.* 7 H12
Halle, *Ger.* 16 C5
Halmstad, *Swed.* 7 H12
Hamã, *Syria* 25 B2
Hamadãn, *Iran* 25 B3
Hamamatsu, *Japan* 21 B5
Hamar, *Norw.* 7 F11
Hamburg, *Ger.* 16 B5
Hame, □ *Fin.* 7 F17
Hameln, *Ger.* 16 B4
Hamilton, *N.Z.* 31 G5
Hamilton, *U.K.* 10 F4
Hamilton, *Canada* 35 D11
Hamm, *Ger.* 16 C3
Hammerfest, *Norw.* 6 A17
Hammond, *U.S.A.* 37 B9
Hampshire, □ *U.K.* 9 F6
Hangzhou, *China* 22 C6
Hannover, *Ger.* 16 B4
Hanoi, *Vietnam* 23 A2
Harare, *Zimbabwe* 29 H6
Harbin, *China* 22 B7
Hargeisa, *Somalia* 30 F8
Harlow, *U.K.* 9 F8
Härnösand, *Swed.* 6 E15
Harrogate, *U.K.* 8 D6
Hartlepool, *U.K.* 8 C6
Haryana, □ *India* 24 C4
Hastings, *N.Z.* 31 H6

Hastings, *U.K.* 9 G8
Haugesund, *Norw.* 7 G8
Haut Atlas, *Morocco* 26 B4
Havana = La Habana, *Cuba* 39 C8
Havant, *U.K.* 9 G7
Hawaii, *Pac. Ocean* 2 C2
Hawaii, □ *U.S.A.* 36 H16
Hawick, *U.K.* 10 F6
Hedmark, □ *Norw.* 7 F11
Hefei, *China* 22 C6
Heidelberg, *Ger.* 16 D4
Heilbronn, *Ger.* 16 D4
Helmsdale, *U.K.* 10 C5
Helsingborg, *Swed.* 7 H12
Helsingor, *Den.* 7 H12
Helsinki, *Fin.* 7 F18
Hemel Hempstead, *U.K.* 9 F7
Hengyang, *China* 22 D6
Herat, *Afghan.* 25 B5
Hereford, *U.K.* 9 E5
Hereford & Worcester, □ *U.K.* ...9 E5
Herford, *Ger.* 16 B4
Hermosillo, *Mexico* 38 B2
Hertfordshire, □ *U.K.* 9 F7
Hessen, □ *Ger.* 16 C4
Higashiōsaka, *Japan* 21 B4
High Wycombe, *U.K.* 9 F7
Highland, □ *U.K.* 8 D4
Hildesheim, *Ger.* 16 B4
Hilversum, *Neth.* 16 B2
Himachal Pradesh, □ *India* 24 B4
Himalaya, *Asia* 24 C5
Himeji, *Japan* 21 B4
Hims, *Syria* 25 B2
Hindu Kush, *Afghan.* 25 B5
Hirosaki, *Japan* 21 F11
Hiroshima, *Japan* 21 B3
Hobart, *Australia* 33 G8
Hohhot, *China* 22 B6
Hokkaido, *Japan* 21 F11
Holderness, *U.K.* 8 D7
Holguin, *Cuba* 39 C9
Hollywood, *U.S.A.* 36 D3
Honduras, ■ *Cent. Amer.* 38 E7
Honefoss, *Norw.* 7 F11
Hong Kong, ■ *Asia* 22 D6
Honolulu, *Hawaii* 36 H16
Honshu, *Japan* 21 B4
Hordaland, □ *Norw.* 7 F9
Hormuz, Str. of, *Asia* 25 C4
Horn, C. = Hornos, C. de, *Chile* ..42 H3
Hornos, C. de, *Chile* 42 H3
Horsens, *Den.* 7 J10
Hospitalet, *Spain* 13 B7
Houghton-le-Spring, *U.K.* 8 C6
Houston, *U.S.A.* 37 E7
Howrah, *India* 24 D6
Hoy, *U.K.* 10 C5
Hradec Kralove, *Czech Rep.* 16 C7
Huainan, *China* 22 C6
Huang, ≈ *China* 22 C6
Huascarán, *Peru* 40 E3
Huddersfield, *U.K.* 8 D6
Hudson Bay, *Canada* 35 B11
Hudson Str., *Canada* 35 B12
Huelva, *Spain* 13 D2
Huesca, *Spain* 13 A5
Hull, *U.K.* 8 D7
Humber, ≈ *U.K.* 8 D7
Humberside, □ *U.K.* 8 D7
Hungary, ■ *Europe* 17 E9
Hunsrück, *Ger.* 16 D3
Huron, L., *N. Amer.* 37 B10
Hyderabad, *India* 24 E4
Hyderabad, *Pak.* 24 C2

I

Iaşi, *Rom.* 17 E13
Ibadan, *Nigeria* 26 G5
Ibagué, *Colombia* 40 C3
Ibiza, *Spain* 13 C6
Iceland, ■ *Europe* 6 D4
Ichinomiya, *Japan* 21 B5
Idaho, □ *U.S.A.* 36 B3
Ikaria, *Greece* 15 F12
Île-de-France, □ *France* 12 B5
Illinois, □ *U.S.A.* 37 B9
Ilorin, *Nigeria* 26 G5
Imphal, *India* 24 D7
Inch'on, *S. Korea* 22 C7
India, ■ *Asia* 24 E4
Indian Ocean, ...24 H3
Indiana, □ *U.S.A.* 37 C9
Indianapolis, *U.S.A.* 37 C9
Indonesia, ■ *Asia* 23 D3
Indore, *India* 24 D4
Indus, ≈ *Pakistan* 24 C2
Ingolstadt, *Ger.* 16 D5
Inishowen Pen., *Ire.* 11 A4
Inner Hebrides, *U.K.* 10 E2
Innsbruck, *Austria* 16 E5
Inveraray, *U.K.* 10 E3
Invercargill, *N.Z.* 31 M2
Invergordon, *U.K.* 10 D4
Inverness, *U.K.* 10 D4
Iona, *U.K.* 10 E2
Ionian Sea, *Europe* 15 E8
Iónioi Nisoi, □ *Greece* 15 E9

Iowa, □ *U.S.A.* 37 B8
Ípiros, □ *Greece* 15 E9
Ipswich, *U.K.* 9 E9
Iquique, *Chile* 40 H4
Iquitos, *Peru* 40 D4
Iráklion, *Greece* 15 G11
Iran, ■ *Asia* 25 B4
Iraq, ■ *Asia* 25 B3
Ireland, ■ *Europe* 11 C4
Irian Jaya, □ *Indonesia* 23 D5
Irish Sea, *Europe* 8 D2
Irkutsk, *Russia* 19 D11
Irrawady = Erawadi Myit, ≈ *Burma* ..24 E8
Irvine, *U.K.* 10 F4
Islay, *U.K.* 10 F2
Israel, ■ *Asia* 25 B2
Istanbul, *Turkey* 25 A1
Italy, ■ *Europe* 14 C4
Ivory Coast, ■ *Africa* 26 G3
Iwaki, *Japan* 21 G11
Iwo, *Nigeria* 26 G5
Izmir, *Turkey* 25 B1

J

Jabalpur, *India* 24 D5
Jackson, *U.S.A.* 37 D8
Jacksonville, *U.S.A.* 37 D10
Jaén, *Spain* 13 D4
Jaipur, *India* 24 C4
Jakarta, *Indonesia* 23 D2
Jamaica, ■ *W. Indies* 39 D9
James Bay, *Canada* 35 C11
Jammu & Kashmir, □ *India* 24 B3
Jämtland, □ *Norw.* 6 E13
Japan, ■ *Asia* 21 G10
Japan, Sea of, *Asia* 21 A3
Java, *Indonesia* 23 D2
Jena, *Ger.* 16 C5
Jerez, *Spain* 13 D2
Jersey, *Channel Is.* 12 B2
Jersey City, *U.S.A.* 37 B12
Jerusalem, *Israel* 25 B2
Jiddah, *S. Arabia* 25 C2
Jilin, *China* 22 B7
Jilong, *Taiwan* 22 D7
Jinan, *China* 22 C6
Jinzhou, *China* 22 B7
João Pessoa, *Brazil* 41 E12
Johannesburg, *S. Africa* 29 K5
John O'Groats, *U.K.* 10 C5
Johnstone, *U.K.* 10 F4
Jönköping, □ *Swed.* 7 H12
Jordan, ■ *Asia* 25 B2
Juàzeiro do Norte, *Brazil* 41 E11
Juiz de Fora, *Brazil* 41 H10
Jundiaí, *Brazil* 42 A7
Jura, *Europe* 12 C6
Jura, *U.K.* 10 F3

K

Kabul, *Afghan.* 25 B5
Kaduna, *Nigeria* 26 F6
Kagoshima, *Japan* 21 D2
Kaiserslautern, *Ger.* 16 D3
Kalahari, *Africa* 29 J4
Kaliningrad, *Russia* 18 D3
Kalisz, *Poland* 17 C9
Kalmar, □ *Swed.* 7 H14
Kamaishi, *Japan* 21 G11
Kampala, *Uganda* 28 D6
Kampuchea = Cambodia, ■ *Asia* ...23 B2
Kananga, *Zaïre* 28 F4
Kanazawa, *Japan* 21 A5
Kandahar, *Afghan.* 25 B5
Kangaroo I., *Australia* 33 F6
Kano, *Nigeria* 26 F6
Kanpur, *India* 24 C5
Kansas, □ *U.S.A.* 36 C7
Kansas City, *U.S.A.* 37 C8
Kaokoveld, *Namibia* 29 H2
Kaolack, *Senegal* 26 F1
Kara Sea, *Arctic* 18 B7
Karachi, *Pak.* 24 D2
Karaganda, *Kazakhstan* 18 E8
Karbalã, *Iraq* 25 B3
Kariba L., *Africa* 29 H5
Karlskrona, *Swed.* 7 H13
Karlsruhe, *Ger.* 16 D4
Karlstad, *Swed.* 7 G12
Kärnten, □ *Austria* 16 E6
Kárpathos, *Greece* 15 G12
Kãshãn, *Iran* 25 B4
Kassel, *Ger.* 16 C4
Katmandu, *Nepal* 24 C6
Katowice, *Poland* 17 C9
Katsina, *Nigeria* 26 F6
Kattegat, *Scandinavia* 7 H11
Kawaguchi, *Japan* 21 B6
Kawasaki, *Japan* 21 B6
Kayseri, *Turkey* 25 B2
Kazakhstan, ■ *Asia* 18 E7
Kazan, *Russia* 18 D5
Kecskemét, *Hungary* 17 E9
Kefallinia, *Greece* 15 E9
Keflavik, *Iceland* 6 D2
Keighley, *U.K.* 8 D6
Kemãn, *Iran* 25 B4

Kemi, *Fin.* 6 D18
Kenitra, *Morocco* 26 B3
Kent, □ *U.K.* 9 F8
Kentucky, □ *U.S.A.* 37 C9
Kenya, ■ *Africa* 28 D7
Kenya, Mt., *Kenya* 28 E7
Kerala, □ *India* 24 F4
Kérkira, *Greece* 15 E8
Kerry, □ *Ire.* 11 D2
Keski - Suomen, □ *Fin.* 6 E18
Key West, *U.S.A.* 37 F10
Khabarovsk, *Russia* 19 E14
Kharkov, *Ukraine* 18 E4
Khartoum = El Khartûm, *Sudan* ...27 E11
Khios, *Greece* 15 E11
Khulna, *Bangladesh* 24 D6
Kidderminster, *U.K.* 9 E5
Kiel, *Ger.* 16 A5
Kielce, *Poland* 17 C10
Kikládhes, *Greece* 15 F11
Kikwit, *Zaïre* 28 E3
Kildare, □ *Ire.* 11 C5
Kilimanjaro, *Tanzania* 28 E7
Kilkenny, *Ire.* 11 D4
Killarney, *Ire.* 11 D2
Kilmarnock, *U.K.* 10 F4
Kimberley, *Australia* 32 B4
Kimberley, *S. Africa* 29 K4
King I., *Australia* 33 F7
King William I., *Canada* 34 B10
Kings Lynn, *U.K.* 8 E8
Kingston, *Jamaica* 38 J17
Kingston, *U.K.* 9 F7
Kingussie, *U.K.* 10 D4
Kinshasa, *Zaïre* 28 E3
Kintyre, *U.K.* 10 F3
Kirghizia, ■ *Asia* 18 E8
Kiribati, ■ *Pac. Ocean* 3 D18
Kirkūk, *Iraq* 25 B3
Kirkcaldy, *U.K.* 10 E5
Kirkwall, *U.K.* 10 C6
Kiruna, *Swed.* 6 C15
Kisangani, *Zaïre* 28 D5
Kishinev, *Moldavia* 18 E3
Kitakyūshū, *Japan* 21 C2
Kitchener, *Canada* 35 D11
Kíthira, *Greece* 15 F10
Kitwe, *Zambia* 29 G5
Kiva, L., *Africa* 28 E5
Kiyev, *Ukraine* 18 D4
Klagenfurt, *Austria* 16 E7
Knockmealdown Mts., *Ire.* 11 D4
Knossos, *Greece* 15 G11
Knoxville, *U.S.A.* 37 C10
Kobe, *Japan* 21 B4
København, *Den.* 7 J12
Koblenz, *Ger.* 16 C3
Kōchi, *Japan* 21 C3
Kodiak I., *Alaska* 34 C4
Kolding, *Den.* 7 J10
Köln, *Ger.* 16 C3
Komsomolsk, *Russia* 19 D14
Kongsvinger, *Norw.* 7 F12
Konya, *Turkey* 25 B2
Kopervik, *Norw.* 7 G8
Kopparberg, □ *Swed.* 7 F12
Kōriyama, *Japan* 21 G11
Kos, *Greece* 15 F12
Košice, *Slovak Rep.* 17 D10
Koskiusko, Mt., *Australia* 33 F8
Kosovo, □ *Yug.* 15 C9
Kowloon, *Hong Kong* 22 D6
Kraków, *Poland* 17 C9
Krasnodar, *Russia* 18 E4
Krasnoyarsk, *Russia* 19 D10
Krefeld, *Ger.* 16 C3
Kristiansand, *Norw.* 7 G10
Kristianstad, □ *Swed.* 7 J13
Kristiansund, *Norw.* 6 E9
Kriti, *Greece* 15 G11
Krivoy Rog, *Ukraine* 18 E4
Kronoberg, □ *Swed.* 7 H13
Kuala Lumpur, *Malaysia* 23 C2
Kumamoto, *Japan* 21 C2
Kumasi, *Ghana* 26 G4
Kuopio, □ *Fin.* 6 E19
Kurashiki, *Japan* 21 B3
Kure, *Japan* 21 B3
Kurilskiye Ostrova, *Russia* 19 E16
Kushiro, *Japan* 21 F11
Kuwait, ■ *Asia* 25 C3
Kuybyshev = Samara, *Russia* ...18 D6
Kwangju, *S. Korea* 22 C7
Kyūshu, *Japan* 21 C2
Kyle of Lochalsh, *U.K.* 10 D3
Kyoga, L., *Uganda* 28 D6
Kyōto, *Japan* 21 B4
Kyyiv = Kiev, *Ukraine* 18 D4

L

La Boca, *Panama* 38 H14
La Chorrera, *Panama* 38 H14
La Coruña, *Spain* 13 A1
La Habana, *Cuba* 39 C8
La Paz, *Bolivia* 40 G5
La Plata, *Argentina* 42 D5
La Rioja, □ *Spain* 13 A4
La Rochelle, *France* 12 C3

Index

La Spézia, Italy — 14 B3
Labrador, Coast of, Canada — 35 C13
Ladozhskoye, Ozero, Russia — 18 C4
Lagos, Port. — 13 D1
Lagos, Nigeria — 26 G5
Lahore, Pak. — 24 B3
Lahti, Fin. — 7 F18
Lakshadweep Is., India — 24 F3
Lancashire, □ U.K. — 8 D5
Lancaster, U.K. — 8 C5
Lancaster Sd., Canada — 35 A11
Landskrona, Swed. — 7 J12
Languedoc, □ France — 12 E5
Lansing, U.S.A. — 37 B10
Lanzhou, China — 22 C5
Laois, □ Ire. — 11 D4
Laos, ■ Asia — 23 B2
Lapi, □ Fin. — 6 C19
Lappland, Fin. — 6 B18
Laptev Sea, Arctic — 19 B13
Laredo, U.S.A. — 36 E7
Lárisa, Greece — 15 E10
Larne, U.K. — 11 B6
Las Palmas, Canary Is. — 26 C1
Las Vegas, U.S.A. — 36 C3
Latvia, ■ Europe — 18 D3
Lauchhammer, Ger. — 16 C6
Launceston, Australia — 33 G8
Lausanne, Switz. — 16 E3
Lawton, U.S.A. — 36 D7
Le Havre, France — 12 B4
Le Mans, France — 12 B4
Le Moule, Guadeloupe — 38 L20
Leamington, U.K. — 9 E6
Lebanon, ■ Asia — 25 B2
Lecce, Italy — 15 D8
Leeds, U.K. — 8 D6
Leeuwarden, Neth. — 16 B2
Leeward Is., W. Indies — 39 D12
Legnica, Poland — 16 C8
Leicester, U.K. — 9 E6
Leicestershire, □ U.K. — 9 E6
Leiden, Neth. — 16 B2
Leinster, Ire. — 11 C4
Leipzig, Ger. — 16 C6
Leith, U.K. — 10 F5
Leitrim, □ Ire. — 11 B3
Lena, ≈ Russia — 19 B13
Leningrad = St. Peterburg, Russia — 18 D4
León, Mexico — 38 C4
León, Spain — 13 A3
Lérida, Spain — 13 B6
Lesotho, ■ Africa — 29 K5
Lesser Antilles, W. Indies — 39 E12
Lésvos, Greece — 15 E11
Letchworth, U.K. — 9 F7
Lethbridge, Canada — 34 D8
Leuven, Belgium — 16 C2
Levkás, Greece — 15 E9
Levkòsia, Cyprus — 25 B2
Lewis, U.K. — 10 C2
Lhasa, China — 22 D4
Lianyungang, China — 22 C6
Liberec, Czech. Rep. — 16 C7
Liberia, ■ Africa — 26 G3
Lîbîya, Sahrâ', Africa — 27 C9
Libreville, Gabon — 28 D1
Libya, ■ Africa — 27 C8
Liechtenstein, ■ Europe — 16 E4
Liège, Belgium — 16 C2
Liffey, ≈ Ire. — 11 C5
Liguria, □ Italy — 14 B3
Ligurian Sea, Italy — 14 C3
Likasi, Zaïre — 28 G5
Lille, France — 12 A5
Lillehammer, Norw. — 7 F11
Lilongwe, Malawi — 29 G6
Lima, Peru — 40 F3
Limavady, U.K. — 11 A5
Limerick, Ire. — 11 D3
Límnos, Greece — 15 E11
Limoges, France — 12 C4
Limousin, □ France — 12 D4
Limpopo, ≈ Africa — 29 K6
Linares, Spain — 13 C4
Lincoln, U.S.A. — 37 B7
Lincoln, U.K. — 8 D7
Lincolnshire, □ U.K. — 8 D7
Linköping, Swed. — 7 G13
Linz, Austria — 16 D7
Lisboa, Port. — 13 C1
Lisburn, U.K. — 11 B5
Listowel, Ire. — 11 D2
Lithuania, ■ Europe — 18 D3
Little Minch, U.K. — 10 D2
Little Rock, U.S.A. — 37 D8
Liverpool, U.K. — 8 D5
Livingston, U.K. — 10 F5
Livingstone, Zambia — 29 H5
Livorno, Italy — 14 C4
Lizard, U.K. — 9 H2
Ljubljana, Slovenia — 14 A6
Llanelli, U.K. — 9 F3
Lloret, Spain — 13 B7
Lobito, Angola — 29 G2
Locarno, L. di, Italy — 14 A3
Lochaber, U.K. — 10 E4
Lockerbie, U.K. — 10 F5
Łódź, Poland — 17 C9

Lofoten, Norw. — 6 B12
Logroño, Spain — 13 A4
Loire, ≈ France — 12 C2
Lolland, Den. — 7 J11
Lombardia, □ Italy — 14 B3
Lombok, Indonesia — 23 D3
Lomé, Togo — 26 G5
Lomond, L., U.K. — 10 E4
Lomza, Poland — 17 B10
London, U.K. — 9 F7
London, Canada — 35 D11
Londonderry, U.K. — 11 B4
Londrina, Brazil — 42 A6
Long Beach, U.S.A. — 36 D3
Long Island, U.S.A. — 37 B12
Longford, □ Ire. — 11 C4
Lorca, Spain — 13 D5
Lorne, U.K. — 10 E4
Lorraine, □ France — 12 B7
Los Angeles, U.S.A. — 36 D3
Lothian, □ U.K. — 10 F5
Loughborough, U.K. — 8 E6
Louisiana, □ U.S.A. — 37 D8
Louisville, U.S.A. — 37 C9
Lourdes, France — 12 E3
Louth, □ Ire. — 11 C5
Lower Hutt, N.Z. — 31 J5
Lowestoft, U.K. — 8 E9
Luanda, Angola — 28 F2
Luanshya, Zambia — 29 G5
Lubbock, U.S.A. — 36 D6
Lübeck, Ger. — 16 B5
Lublin, Poland — 17 C11
Lubumbashi, Zaïre — 29 G5
Lucca, Italy — 14 C4
Lucknow, India — 24 C5
Ludwigshafen, Ger. — 16 D4
Lugo, Spain — 13 A2
Luleå, Swed. — 6 D17
Lüneburger Heide, Ger. — 16 B5
Luoyang, China — 22 C6
Lurgan, U.K. — 11 B5
Lusaka, Zambia — 29 H5
Luton, U.K. — 9 F7
Luxembourg, ■ Europe — 16 D3
Luzern, Switz. — 16 E4
Luzhou, China — 22 D5
Luzon, Philippines — 23 B4
Lvov, Ukraine — 18 E3
Lyckele, Swed. — 6 D15
Lymington, U.K. — 9 G6
Lyon, France — 12 D6

M
M'Clintock Chan., Canada — 34 B9
Macapá, Brazil — 41 C8
Macau, ■ Asia — 22 D6
Macclesfield, U.K. — 8 D5
Macdonnell Ranges, Australia — 32 C5
Macedonia, ■ Europe — 15 D9
Maceió, Brazil — 41 E11
Mackenzie, ≈ Canada — 34 B6
Mackenzie Mts., Canada — 34 B6
Macroom, Ire. — 11 E3
Madagascar, ■ Africa — 29 J9
Madeira, Atl. Ocean — 26 B1
Madeira, ≈ S. Amer. — 40 E6
Madhya Pradesh, □ India — 24 D4
Madison, U.S.A. — 37 B9
Madras, India — 24 F5
Madre, L., Mexico — 38 B5
Madrid, □ Spain — 13 B4
Madrid, Spain — 13 B4
Madurai, India — 24 G4
Maebashi, Japan — 21 A6
Mafia I., Tanzania — 28 F7
Magadan, Russia — 19 D16
Magalluf, Spain — 13 C7
Magdeburg, Ger. — 16 B5
Magherafelt, □ U.K. — 11 B5
Maharashtra, □ India — 24 D4
Mahon, Spain — 13 C8
Mai-Ndombe, L., Zaïre — 28 E3
Maidenhead, U.K. — 9 F7
Maidstone, U.K. — 9 F8
Maiduguri, Nigeria — 26 F7
Maimana, Afghan. — 25 B5
Maine, □ France — 12 B3
Maine, □ U.S.A. — 37 A13
Mainz, Ger. — 16 D4
Makasar = Ujung Pandang,
 Indonesia — 23 D3
Makedhona, □ Greece — 15 D10
Makgadikgadi Salt Pans, Botswana — 29 J5
Makkah, S. Arabia — 25 C3
Malaga, Spain — 13 D3
Malatya, Turkey — 25 B2
Malawi, ■ Africa — 29 G6
Malaysia, ■ Asia — 23 C2
Maldives, ■ Ind. Ocean — 24 G3
Mali, ■ Africa — 26 E4
Mallorca, Spain — 13 C7
Mallow, Ire. — 11 D3
Malmö, Swed. — 7 J12
Malmöhus, □ Swed. — 7 J12
Malta, ■ Europe — 14 G6
Malvern Hills, U.K. — 9 E5
Man, I. of, U.K. — 8 C3

Managua, Nicaragua — 38 E7
Manaus, Brazil — 40 D6
Manchester, U.K. — 8 D5
Mandalay, Burma — 24 D8
Manila, Philippines — 23 B4
Manitoba, □ Canada — 34 C10
Manitoba, L., Canada — 34 C10
Manizales, Colombia — 40 B3
Mannheim, Ger. — 16 D4
Mansel I., Canada — 35 B11
Mansfield, U.K. — 8 D6
Mantova, Italy — 14 B4
Maputo, Mozambique — 29 K6
Mar del Plata, Argentina — 42 D5
Maracaibo, Venezuela — 40 A4
Maracay, Venezuela — 40 A5
Marajó, I. de, Brazil — 41 D9
Maranhão, □ Brazil — 41 E9
Marbella, Spain — 13 D3
Marche, □ France — 12 C4
Marche, □ Italy — 14 C5
Margate, U.K. — 9 F9
Mariana Is., Pac. Ocean — 3 D17
Maribor, Slovenia — 14 A6
Marie-Galante, W. Indies — 38 M20
Marília, Brazil — 41 H8
Maringá, Brazil — 42 A6
Marmara, Sea of, Turkey — 25 A1
Marquesas Is., Pac. Ocean — 2 E3
Marrakech, Morocco — 26 B3
Marseille, France — 12 E6
Marshall Is., Pac. Ocean — 3 D18
Martha's Vineyard, U.S.A. — 37 B12
Martinique, □ W. Indies — 38 N21
Maryland, □ U.S.A. — 37 C11
Mashhad, Iran — 25 B4
Masqat, Oman — 25 C4
Massachusetts, □ U.S.A. — 37 B12
Massif Central, France — 12 D5
Matadi, Zaïre — 28 F2
Matamoros, Mexico — 38 B5
Mato Grosso, □ Brazil — 41 F7
Mato Grosso do Sul, □ Brazil — 41 G7
Matsuyama, Japan — 21 C3
Matterhorn, Switz. — 16 E3
Maturín, Venezuela — 40 B6
Mauritania, ■ Africa — 26 E2
Mauritius, ■ Ind. Ocean — 30 H9
Mayo, □ Ire. — 11 C2
Mazar-i-Sharif, Afghan. — 25 B5
Mbandaka, Zaïre — 28 D3
Meath, □ Ire. — 11 C5
Mecca = Makkah, S. Arabia — 25 C2
Mechelen, Belgium — 16 C2
Medan, Indonesia — 23 C1
Medellin, Colombia — 40 B3
Medicine Hat, Canada — 34 D8
Medina = Al Madinah, S. Arabia — 25 C2
Mediterranean Sea, — 5 H7
Meerut, India — 24 C4
Mekong, ≈ Asia — 23 B2
Melbourne, Australia — 33 F8
Melrose, U.K. — 10 F6
Melville Is., Australia — 32 A5
Memphis, U.S.A. — 37 C9
Menai Strait, U.K. — 8 D3
Mendip Hills, U.K. — 9 F5
Mendoza, Argentina — 42 C3
Menorca, Spain — 13 B7
Mentawai Is., Indonesia — 23 D1
Merca, Somalia — 30 F8
Mérida, Mexico — 38 C7
Mersey, ≈ U.K. — 8 D5
Merseyside, □ U.K. — 8 D5
Merthyr Tydfil, U.K. — 9 F4
Messina, Italy — 14 E6
Metz, France — 12 B7
Mexicali, Mexico — 38 A1
Mexico, ■ Cent. Amer. — 38 B3
Mexico City, Mexico — 38 D5
Mexico, G. de, Cent. Amer. — 38 B6
Miami, U.S.A. — 37 E10
Michigan, □ U.S.A. — 37 A9
Michigan, L., U.S.A. — 37 B9
Micronesia, ■ Pac. Ocean — 3 D17
Mid Glamorgan, □ U.K. — 9 F4
Middlesbrough, U.K. — 8 C6
Midland, U.S.A. — 36 D6
Mikkeli, □ Fin. — 6 E19
Milano, Italy — 14 B3
Milton Keynes, U.K. — 9 E7
Milwaukee, U.S.A. — 37 B9
Minas Gerais, □ Brazil — 41 G9
Mindanao, Philippines — 23 C4
Minneapolis, U.S.A. — 37 B8
Minnesota, □ U.S.A. — 37 A8
Minsk, Belorussia — 18 D3
Miskolc, Hungary — 17 D10
Misrātah, Libya — 27 B8
Mississippi, □ U.S.A. — 37 D9
Mississippi, ≈ U.S.A. — 37 E9
Missouri, □ U.S.A. — 37 C8
Missouri, ≈ U.S.A. — 37 C8
Miyako, Japan — 21 G11
Mobile, U.S.A. — 37 D9
Mobutu, L., Africa — 28 D6
Moçambique, Mozambique — 29 H8
Módena, Italy — 14 B4

Mogadishu, Somalia — 30 E8
Moldavia, ■ Europe — 18 E3
Molise, □ Italy — 14 D6
Mölndal, Swed. — 7 H12
Moluccas, Indonesia — 23 C4
Mombasa, Kenya — 28 E7
Mona, Canal de la, W. Indies — 39 D11
Monaco, ■ Europe — 12 E7
Monaghan, □ Ire. — 11 B5
Mönchengladbach, Ger. — 16 C3
Moncton, Canada — 35 D13
Mongolia, ■ Asia — 22 B5
Monrovia, Liberia — 26 G2
Mont St. - Michel, France — 12 B3
Montana, □ U.S.A. — 36 A4
Monte Carlo, Monaco — 12 E7
Montes Claros, Brazil — 41 G10
Montevideo, Uruguay — 42 C5
Montgomery, U.S.A. — 37 D9
Montpellier, France — 12 E5
Montréal, Canada — 35 D12
Montrose, U.K. — 10 E6
Montserrat, W. Indies — 38 L19
Moray Firth, U.K. — 10 D5
More og Romsdal, □ Norw. — 6 E9
Morecambe B., U.K. — 8 C4
Morelia, Mexico — 38 D4
Morena, Sierra, Spain — 13 C3
Morioka, Japan — 21 G11
Morocco, ■ Africa — 26 B3
Morvern, U.K. — 10 E3
Moscow = Moskva, Russia — 18 D4
Mosel, ≈ Europe — 16 C3
Moskva, Russia — 18 D4
Mostaganem, Algeria — 26 A5
Motala, Swed. — 7 G13
Motherwell, U.K. — 10 F5
Moulamyaing, Burma — 24 E8
Mourne Mts., U.K. — 11 B5
Mozambique, ■ Africa — 29 J6
Mozambique Chan., Africa — 29 H8
Muck, U.K. — 10 E3
Mufulira, Zambia — 29 G5
Mülheim, Ger. — 16 C3
Mulhouse, France — 12 C7
Mull, U.K. — 10 E3
Mullet Pen., Ire. — 11 B1
Mullingar, Ire. — 11 C4
Multan, Pak. — 24 B3
München, Ger. — 16 D5
Munich = München, Ger. — 16 D5
Munster, Ire. — 11 D3
Münster, Ger. — 16 C3
Murcia, □ Spain — 13 D5
Murcia, Spain — 13 C5
Murmansk, Russia — 18 C4
Murray River, ≈ Australia — 33 F6
Murray River Basin, Australia — 33 F7
Musgrave Ranges, Australia — 32 D5
Mustique, W. Indies — 38 Q20
Mwanza, Tanzania — 28 E6
Myanmar = Burma, ■ Asia — 24 D8
Mysore, India — 24 F4

N
Nagano, Japan — 21 A6
Nagaoka, Japan — 21 G10
Nagasaki, Japan — 21 C1
Nagoya, Japan — 21 B5
Nagpur, India — 24 D4
Nairobi, Kenya — 28 E7
Nakhodka, Russia — 19 E14
Namaland, Namibia — 29 J3
Namibia, ■ Africa — 29 J3
Namibwoestyn, Namibia — 29 J2
Namsos, Norw. — 6 D11
Nanchang, China — 22 D6
Nancy, France — 12 B7
Nanjing, China — 22 C6
Nanning, China — 22 D5
Nansei-Shoto, Japan — 21 J8
Nantes, France — 12 C3
Napier, N.Z. — 31 H6
Napoli, Italy — 14 D6
Narbonne, France — 12 E5
Narvik, Norw. — 6 B14
Naser, Buheiret en, Egypt — 27 D11
Nashville, U.S.A. — 37 C9
Nassau, Bahamas — 39 B9
Natal, □ S. Africa — 29 K6
Natal, Brazil — 41 E11
Nauru, ■ Pac. Ocean — 3 E18
Navarra, □ Spain — 13 A5
Náxos, Greece — 15 F11
Ndjamena, Chad — 27 F8
Ndola, Zambia — 29 G5
Nebraska, □ U.S.A. — 36 B6
Negro, ≈ Brazil — 40 D6
Neiva, Colombia — 40 C3
Nemuro, Japan — 21 F12
Nemuro-Kaikyô, Japan — 21 F12
Nenagh, Ire. — 11 D3
Nepal, ■ Asia — 24 C5
Ness, L., U.K. — 10 D4

Netherlands, ■ Europe — 16 B2
Nevada, □ U.S.A. — 36 C3
Nevers, France — 12 C5
New Bedford, U.S.A. — 37 B12
New Britain, Pac. Ocean — 3 E17
New Brunswick, □ Canada — 35 D13
New Caledonia, Pac. Ocean — 3 F18
New Forest, U.K. — 9 G6
New Hampshire, □ U.S.A. — 37 B12
New Haven, U.S.A. — 37 B12
New Jersey, □ U.S.A. — 37 C12
New Mexico, □ U.S.A. — 36 D5
New Orleans, U.S.A. — 37 D8
New Plymouth, N.Z. — 31 H5
New Providence I., W. Indies — 39 B9
New South Wales, □ Australia — 33 E8
New York, U.S.A. — 37 B12
New York, □ U.S.A. — 37 B11
New Zealand, ■ Pac. Ocean — 31 J5
Newark, U.S.A. — 37 B12
Newbury, U.K. — 9 F6
Newcastle, Australia — 33 E9
Newcastle, U.K. — 8 C5
Newcastle-under-Lyme, U.K. — 8 D5
Newfoundland, □ Canada — 35 C14
Newport, U.K. — 9 F5
Newport News, U.S.A. — 37 C11
Newquay, U.K. — 9 G2
Newry, U.K. — 11 B5
Newtownabbey, □ U.K. — 11 B6
Newtownards, U.K. — 11 B6
Niagara Falls, N. Amer. — 35 D12
Niamey, Niger — 26 F5
Nicaragua, ■ Cent. Amer. — 38 E7
Nice, France — 12 E7
Nicobar Is., India — 24 H9
Niederösterreich, □ Austria — 16 D7
Niedersachsen, □ Ger. — 16 B4
Niger, ■ Africa — 26 E6
Niger, ≈ Africa — 26 G6
Nigeria, ■ Africa — 26 G6
Niigata, Japan — 21 G10
Nijmegen, Neth. — 16 C3
Nîl el Abyad, ≈ Africa — 27 E11
Nîl el Azraq, ≈ Africa — 27 E11
Nîl, Nahr en, ≈ Africa — 27 C11
Nile = Nîl, Nahr en, ≈ Africa — 27 C11
Nîmes, France — 12 E6
Ningbo, China — 22 D7
Nishinomiya, Japan — 21 B4
Niteroi, Brazil — 41 H10
Nizhniy Novgorod, Russia — 18 D5
Nord-Trondelag, □ Norw. — 6 D11
Nordland, □ Norw. — 6 C13
Nordrhein - Westfalen, □ Ger. — 16 C3
Norfolk, U.S.A. — 37 C11
Norfolk, □ U.K. — 8 E8
Normandie, □ France — 12 B3
Norrbotten, □ Norw. — 6 C15
Norrköping, Swed. — 7 G14
North Carolina, □ U.S.A. — 37 C11
North Channel, Europe — 8 C2
North Dakota, □ U.S.A. — 36 A6
North Downs, U.K. — 9 F7
North Island, N.Z. — 31 H5
North Korea, ■ Asia — 22 B9
North Minch, U.K. — 10 C3
North Ronaldsay, U.K. — 10 C8
North Sea, Europe — 8 D1
North Uist, U.K. — 10 D1
North West Highlands, U.K. — 10 D3
North West Territories, □ Canada — 34 B8
North Yorkshire, □ U.K. — 8 C6
North Yorkshire Moors, U.K. — 8 C7
Northampton, U.K. — 9 E7
Northamptonshire, □ U.K. — 9 E7
Northern Ireland, □ U.K. — 11 B4
Northern Territory, □ Australia — 32 B5
Northumberland, □ U.K. — 8 B5
Norway, ■ Europe — 6 E11
Norwegian Sea, Atl. Ocean — 6 D9
Norwich, U.K. — 8 E9
Nottingham, U.K. — 8 D6
Nottinghamshire, □ U.K. — 8 D6
Nouakchott, Mauritania — 26 E1
Nova Scotia, □ Canada — 35 D13
Novaya Zemlya, Russia — 18 B6
Novi Sad, Yug. — 15 B8
Novokuznetsk, Russia — 18 D9
Novosibirsk, Russia — 18 D9
Novosibirskiye Ostrova, Russia — 19 B15
Núbîya, Es Sahrâ en, Sudan — 27 D11
Nullarbor Plain, Australia — 32 E4
Nuneaton, U.K. — 9 E6
Nunivak I., Alaska — 34 B3
Nürnberg, Ger. — 16 D5
Nyasa, L., Africa — 29 G6
Nykøbing, Den. — 7 J12

O
Oakland, U.S.A. — 36 C2
Ob, ≈ Russia — 18 C7
Oban, U.K. — 10 E3
Oberhausen, Ger. — 16 C3
Oberösterreich, □ Austria — 16 D6
Obihiro, Japan — 21 F12
Odense, Den. — 7 J11
Oder, ≈ Europe — 16 B7

Index

Odessa, *Ukraine* ...18 E4
Odessa, *U.S.A.* ...36 D6
Offaly, □ *Ire.* ...11 C4
Offenbach, *Ger.* ...16 C4
Ogbomosho, *Nigeria* ...26 G5
Ogden, *U.S.A.* ...36 B4
Ohio, ≈ *U.S.A.* ...37 C9
Ohio, □ *U.S.A.* ...37 B10
Okavango Swamps, *Botswana* ...29 H4
Okayama, *Japan* ...21 B3
Okazaki, *Japan* ...21 B5
Okhotsk, *Russia* ...19 D15
Okhotsk Sea of, *Arctic* ...19 D15
Oki-Shotō, *Japan* ...21 A3
Oklahoma, □ *U.S.A.* ...37 C7
Oklahoma City, *U.S.A.* ...37 C7
Okushiri-Tō, *Japan* ...21 F10
Öland, *Swed.* ...7 H14
Oldenburg, *Ger.* ...16 B4
Oldham, *U.K.* ...8 D5
Olimbos, *Greece* ...15 D10
Olomouc, *Czech Rep.* ...16 D8
Olympia, *Greece* ...15 F9
Omagh, *U.K.* ...11 B4
Omaha, *U.S.A.* ...37 B7
Oman, ■ *Asia* ...25 C4
Oman, Gulf of, *Asia* ...25 C4
Omdurmân, *Sudan* ...27 E11
Omsk, *Russia* ...18 D8
Omuta, *Japan* ...21 C2
Onezhskoye, Ozero, *Russia* ...18 C4
Onitsha, *Nigeria* ...26 G6
Ontario, □ *Canada* ...35 C11
Ontario, L., *N. Amer.* ...35 D12
Opava, *Czech Rep.* ...17 D8
Oppland, □ *Norw.* ...7 F10
Oradea, *Rom.* ...17 E10
Oran, *Algeria* ...26 A4
Orange, ≈ *S. Africa* ...29 K3
Oranje-Vrystaat, □ *S. Africa* ...29 K5
Örebro, □ *Swed.* ...7 G13
Oregon, □ *U.S.A.* ...36 B2
Orense, *Spain* ...13 A2
Orinoco, ~ *S. Amer.* ...40 B6
Orissa, □ *India* ...24 D5
Orkney, □ *U.K.* ...10 B5
Orlando, *U.S.A.* ...37 E10
Orleanais, □ *France* ...12 C4
Orleans, *France* ...12 C4
Orumiyeh, *Iran* ...25 B3
Oruro, *Bolivia* ...40 G5
Osaka, *Japan* ...21 B4
Oshawa, *Canada* ...35 D12
Oshogbo, *Nigeria* ...26 G5
Osijek, *Croatia* ...15 B8
Oskarshamn, *Swed.* ...7 H14
Oslo, *Norw.* ...7 G11
Osnabrück, *Ger.* ...16 B4
Östersund, *Swed.* ...6 E13
Ostfriesische Inseln, *Ger.* ...16 B3
Ostrava, *Czech Rep.* ...17 D9
Ostrov Vrangelya, *Russia* ...19 B18
Osumi-Kaikyō, *Japan* ...21 D2
Osumi-Shotō, *Japan* ...21 D2
Otaru, *Japan* ...21 F11
Otranto, Str. of, *Italy* ...15 D8
Ottawa, *Canada* ...35 D12
Ötztal, *Austria* ...16 E5
Ouagadougou, *Burkina Faso* ...26 F4
Oujda, *Morocco* ...26 B4
Oulu, *Fin.* ...6 D18
Outer Hebrides, *U.K.* ...10 D1
Oviedo, *Spain* ...13 A3
Owambo, *Namibia* ...29 H3
Ox Mts., *Ire.* ...11 B3
Oxford, *U.K.* ...9 F6
Oxfordshire, □ *U.K.* ...9 F6

P
Pacaraima, Sierra, *S. Amer.* ...40 C6
Pacific Ocean, ...2 D3
Padang, *Indonesia* ...23 D2
Padova, *Italy* ...14 B4
Paisley, *U.K.* ...10 F4
Pakistan, ■ *Asia* ...24 C4
Palawan, *Philippines* ...23 B3
Palembang, *Indonesia* ...23 D2
Palencia, *Spain* ...13 A3
Palermo, *Italy* ...14 E5
Palma, *Spain* ...13 C7
Palmerston North, *N.Z.* ...31 J5
Palmira, *Colombia* ...40 C3
Pamplona, *Spain* ...13 A5
Panama, ■ *Cent. Amer.* ...39 F8
Panama Canal, *Panama* ...38 H14
Panama City, *Panama* ...39 H14
Panama, G. de, *Panama* ...39 F9
Papua New Guinea, ■ *Pac. Ocean* ...3 E17
Pará, □ *Brazil* ...41 D8
Paraguay, ■ *S. Amer.* ...42 A5
Paraiba, □ *Brazil* ...41 E11
Paramaribo, *Surinam* ...41 B7
Paraná, □ *Brazil* ...42 A6
Paraná, *Argentina* ...42 C4
Parecis, Serra dos, *Brazil* ...40 F6
Paris, *France* ...12 B5
Parma, *Italy* ...14 B4

Pasadena, *U.S.A.* ...36 D3
Pasto, *Colombia* ...40 C3
Patna, *India* ...24 C6
Patos L. dos, *Brazil* ...42 C6
Patrai, *Greece* ...15 E9
Pavia, *Italy* ...14 B3
Pecs, *Hungary* ...17 E9
Peking = Beijing, *China* ...22 C6
Pelopónnisos, □ *Greece* ...15 F10
Pelotas, *Brazil* ...42 C6
Pemba I., *Tanzania* ...28 F7
Pennine Range, *U.K.* ...8 C5
Pennsylvania, □ *U.S.A.* ...37 B11
Pentland Firth, *U.K.* ...10 C5
Penzance, *U.K.* ...9 G2
Peoria, *U.S.A.* ...37 B9
Pereira, *Colombia* ...40 C3
Perm, *Russia* ...18 D6
Pernambuco, □ *Brazil* ...41 E11
Perpignan, *France* ...12 E5
Perth, *Australia* ...32 E2
Perth, *U.K.* ...10 E5
Peru, ■ *S. Amer.* ...40 E3
Perúgia, *Italy* ...14 C5
Pésaro, *Italy* ...14 C5
Pescara, *Italy* ...14 C6
Peshawar, *Pak.* ...24 B3
Peterboro', *Canada* ...35 D12
Peterborough, *U.K.* ...8 E7
Peterhead, *U.K.* ...10 D7
Petropavlovsk-Kamchatskiy, *Russia* 19 D16
Petrópolis, *Brazil* ...41 H10
Pforzheim, *Ger.* ...16 D4
Phanh Bho Ho Chi Minh, *Vietnam* ...23 B2
Philadelphia, *U.S.A.* ...37 B12
Philippi, *Greece* ...15 D11
Philippines, ■ *Asia* ...23 B4
Phnom Penh, *Cambodia* ...23 B2
Phoenix, *U.S.A.* ...36 D4
Phoenix Is., *Pac. Ocean* ...2 E1
Piacenza, *Italy* ...14 B3
Piauí, □ *Brazil* ...41 E10
Picardie, □ *France* ...12 A5
Piemonte, □ *Italy* ...14 B2
Pietermaritzburg, *S. Africa* ...29 K6
Pindos Oros, *Greece* ...15 E9
Piotrków Trybunalsk, *Poland* ...17 C9
Piracicaba, *Brazil* ...41 H9
Piraievs, *Greece* ...15 F10
Pisa, *Italy* ...14 C4
Pistóia, *Italy* ...14 C4
Piteå, *Swed.* ...6 D16
Pittsburgh, *U.S.A.* ...37 B11
Plauen, *Ger.* ...16 C6
Pleven, *Bulg.* ...15 C11
Ploieşti, *Rom.* ...17 F13
Plovdiv, *Bulg.* ...15 C11
Plymouth, *U.K.* ...9 G3
Plzeň, *Czech Rep.* ...16 D6
Po, ≈ *Italy* ...14 B5
Podgorica, *Yug.* ...15 C8
Pointe Noire, *Congo* ...28 E2
Pointe-à Pitre, *Guadeloupe* ...38 L20
Poitou, □ *France* ...12 C3
Poland, ■ *Europe* ...17 C9
Ponce, *Puerto Rico* ...39 D11
Pondicherry, *India* ...24 F4
Ponta Grossa, *Brazil* ...42 B6
Pontefract, *U.K.* ...8 D6
Pontevedra, *Spain* ...13 A1
Pontiac, *U.S.A.* ...37 B10
Pontypool, *U.K.* ...9 F4
Pontypridd, *U.K.* ...9 F4
Poole, *U.K.* ...9 G6
Poona = Pune, *India* ...24 E3
Poopó, L., *Bolivia* ...40 G5
Popocatepetl, *Mexico* ...38 D5
Pori, *Fin.* ...7 F16
Port au Prince, *Haiti* ...39 D10
Port Elizabeth, *S. Africa* ...29 L5
Port Glasgow, *U.K.* ...10 F4
Port Harcourt, *Nigeria* ...26 H6
Port Laoise, *Ire.* ...11 C4
Port of Spain, *Trinidad* ...38 S20
Port Said = Bûr Saïd, *Egypt* ...27 B11
Port Talbot, *U.K.* ...9 F4
Portland, *U.S.A.* ...36 A2
Porto, *Port.* ...13 B1
Pôrto Alegre, *Brazil* ...42 C6
Portree, *U.K.* ...10 D2
Portsmouth, *U.K.* ...9 G6
Portsmouth, *U.S.A.* ...37 C11
Portugal, ■ *Europe* ...13 C1
Potosí, *Bolivia* ...40 G5
Potsdam, *Ger.* ...16 B6
Powys, □ *U.K.* ...9 E4
Poznań, *Poland* ...16 B8
Prague = Praha, *Czech Rep.* ...16 C7
Praha, *Czech Rep.* ...16 C7
Prato, *Italy* ...14 C4
Preston, *U.K.* ...8 D5
Pretoria, *S. Africa* ...29 K5
Prince Albert, *Canada* ...34 C9
Prince Charles I., *Canada* ...35 B12
Prince Edward I., □ *Canada* ...35 D13
Prince of Wales I., *Alaska* ...34 C6
Prince of Wales I., *Canada* ...34 A10
Provence, □ *France* ...12 E6
Providence, *U.S.A.* ...37 B12

Puebla, *Mexico* ...38 D5
Pueblo, *U.S.A.* ...36 C6
Puerto Rico, ■ *W. Indies* ...39 D11
Puglia, □ *Italy* ...14 D7
Pula, *Croatia* ...14 B5
Pune, *India* ...24 E3
Punjab, □ *India* ...24 B4
Purbeck, I. of, *U.K.* ...9 G5
Pusan, *S. Korea* ...22 C7
Pyongyang, *N. Korea* ...22 C7
Pyrenées, *France* ...12 E4

Q
Qatar, ■ *Asia* ...25 C4
Qingdao, *China* ...22 C7
Qiqihar, *China* ...22 B7
Quantock Hills, *U.K.* ...9 F4
Quebec, □ *Canada* ...35 C13
Quebec, *Canada* ...35 D12
Queen Charlotte Is., *Canada* ...34 C6
Queen Maud Gulf, *Canada* ...34 B9
Queensland, □ *Australia* ...33 C7
Quezon City, *Philippines* ...23 B4
Quito, *Ecuador*, ...40 D3

R
Rabat, *Morocco* ...26 B3
Radom, *Poland* ...17 C10
Ragusa, *Italy* ...14 F6
Rajasthan, □ *India* ...24 C3
Ramsgate, *U.K.* ...9 F9
Randers, *Den.* ...7 H11
Rangoon, *Burma* ...23 B8
Rasht, *Iran* ...25 B3
Rathlin I., *U.K.* ...11 A5
Rauma, *Fin.* ...7 F16
Ravenna, *Italy* ...14 B5
Rawalpindi, *Pak.* ...24 B3
Reading, *U.K.* ...9 F7
Rebun-Tō, *Japan* ...21 E11
Recife, *Brazil* ...41 E12
Red River, ≈ *U.S.A.* ...37 D8
Red Sea, *Asia* ...25 C2
Redditch, *U.K.* ...9 E6
Regensburg, *Ger.* ...16 D6
Réggio di Calábria, *Italy* ...14 E6
Réggio nell'Emília, *Italy* ...14 B4
Regina, *Canada* ...34 C9
Reichenbach, *Ger.* ...16 C6
Reigate, *U.K.* ...9 F7
Reims, *France* ...12 B6
Reina Adelaida, Arch., *Chile* ...42 G2
Reindeer L., *Canada* ...34 C9
Remscheid, *Ger.* ...16 C3
Rennes, *France* ...12 B3
Reno, *U.S.A.* ...36 C3
Réunion, □ *Ind. Ocean* ...30 H9
Reykjavik, *Iceland* ...6 C3
Rhein, ≈ *Europe* ...16 C3
Rheinland Pfalz, □ *Ger.* ...16 C3
Rhine = Rhein, ≈ *Europe* ...16 C3
Rhode Island, □ *U.S.A.* ...37 B12
Rhodes = Ródhos, *Greece* ...15 F13
Rhodopi Planina, *Bulg.* ...15 D11
Rhön, *Ger.* ...16 C5
Rhondda, *U.K.* ...9 F4
Rhône, ≈ *France* ...12 D6
Rhum, *U.K.* ...10 E2
Ribeirão Prêto, *Brazil* ...41 H9
Richmond, *U.K.* ...8 C6
Richmond, *U.S.A.* ...37 C11
Riga, *Latvia* ...18 D3
Rijeka, *Croatia* ...14 B6
Rimini, *Italy* ...14 B5
Rio Branco, *Brazil* ...40 E5
Rio de Janeiro, *Brazil* ...41 H10
Rio Gallegos, *Argentina* ...42 G3
Rio Grande, *Brazil* ...42 C6
Rio Grande do Norte, □ *Brazil* ...41 E11
Rio Grande do Sul, □ *Brazil* ...42 C5
Rishiri-Tō, *Japan* ...21 E11
Riyadh = Ar Riyâd, *S. Arabia* ...25 C3
Rochefort, *France* ...12 D3
Rochester, *U.K.* ...9 F8
Rochester, *U.S.A.* ...37 B11
Rocky Mts., *N. Amer.* ...36 A4
Ródhos, *Greece* ...15 F13
Rogaland, □ *Norw.* ...7 G9
Roma, *Italy* ...14 D5
Romania, ■ *Europe* ...17 F12
Rondônia, □ *Brazil* ...40 F6
Roodepoort-Maraisburg, *S. Africa* ...29 K5
Roraima, □ *Brazil* ...40 C6
Roscommon, □ *Ire.* ...11 C3
Roseau, *Dominica* ...38 M20
Roskilde, *Den.* ...7 J12
Rostock, *Ger.* ...16 A6
Rostov, *Russia* ...18 E4
Rotherham, *U.K.* ...8 D6
Rotterdam, *Neth.* ...16 C2
Roubaix, *Belgium* ...16 C1
Rouen, *France* ...12 B4
Rousay, *U.K.* ...10 B5
Ruse, *Bulg.* ...15 C12
Russia, ■ *Europe/Asia* ...18 D7
Rwanda, ■ *Africa* ...28 E5

Ryde, *U.K.* ...9 G6

S
's-Gravenhage, *Neth.* ...16 B2
's-Hertogenbosch, *Neth.* ...16 C2
Saarbrucken, *Ger.* ...16 D3
Saarland, □ *Ger.* ...16 D3
Sabadell, *Spain* ...13 B6
Sabah, □ *Malaysia* ...23 C3
Sacramento, *U.S.A.* ...36 C2
Sado, *Japan* ...21 G10
Safi, *Morocco* ...26 B3
Saginaw, *U.S.A.* ...37 B10
Sahara, *Africa* ...26 D4
Saigon = Phanh Bho Ho Chi Minh, *Vietnam* ...23 B2
Saint John, *Canada* ...35 D13
Saintonge, □ *France* ...12 D3
Sakai, *Japan* ...21 B4
Sakata, *Japan* ...21 G10
Sakhalin, *Russia* ...19 D15
Salamanca, *Spain* ...13 B3
Salerno, *Italy* ...14 D6
Salford, *U.K.* ...8 D5
Salisbury, *U.K.* ...9 F6
Salt Lake City, *U.S.A.* ...36 B4
Salta, *Argentina* ...42 A3
Saltillo, *Mexico* ...38 B4
Salvador, *Brazil* ...41 F11
Salzburg, *Austria* ...16 E6
Salzgitter, *Ger.* ...16 B5
Samara, *Russia* ...18 D6
Samarkand, *Uzbekistan* ...18 F7
Samoa Is., *Pac. Ocean* ...31 A12
Sámos, *Greece* ...15 F12
Samothráki, *Greece* ...15 D11
San Angelo, *U.S.A.* ...36 D6
San Antonio, *U.S.A.* ...36 E7
San Cristóbal, *Venezuela* ...40 B4
San Diego, *U.S.A.* ...36 D3
San Fernando, *Trinidad* ...38 S20
San Francisco, *U.S.A.* ...36 C2
San Francisco de Macoris, *Dom. Rep.* ...39 D10
San Jose, *U.S.A.* ...36 C2
San Juan, *Argentina* ...42 C3
San Juan, *Puerto Rico* ...39 D11
San Luis Potosi, *Mexico* ...38 C4
San Marino, ■ *Europe* ...14 C5
San Miguel de Tucuman, *Argentina* 42 B3
San Salvador, *El Salvador* ...38 E7
San Sebastian, *Spain* ...13 A4
San'a, *Yemen* ...25 D3
Sancti Spiritus, *Cuba* ...39 C9
Sanday, *U.K.* ...10 B6
Santa Ana, *U.S.A.* ...36 D3
Santa Barbara, *U.S.A.* ...36 D3
Santa Catarina, □ *Brazil* ...42 B7
Santa Clara, *Cuba* ...39 C9
Santa Clara, *U.S.A.* ...36 C2
Santa Cruz, *Bolivia* ...40 G6
Santa Cruz, *Canary Is.* ...26 C1
Santa Fe, *Argentina* ...42 C4
Santa Marta, *Colombia* ...40 A4
Santander, *Spain* ...13 A4
Santarém, *Port.* ...13 C1
Santarem, *Brazil* ...41 D8
Santiago, *Chile* ...42 C2
Santiago, *Dom. Rep.* ...39 D10
Santiago, *Spain* ...13 A1
Santiago de Cuba, *Cuba* ...39 C9
Santo Domingo, *Dom. Rep.* ...39 D11
Santos, *Brazil* ...42 A7
São Francisco, ≈ *Brazil* ...41 F11
São Luís, *Brazil* ...41 D10
São Paulo, □ *Brazil* ...41 H9
São Paulo, *Brazil* ...42 A7
São Tomé & Principe, ■ *Africa* ...30 E4
Sapporo, *Japan* ...21 F11
Sarajevo, *Bosnia* ...15 C8
Saratov, *Russia* ...18 D5
Sarawak, □ *Malaysia* ...23 C3
Sardegna, □ *Italy* ...14 D3
Sardinia = Sardegna, □ *Italy* ...14 D3
Sark, *Channel Is.* ...12 B2
Sasebo, *Japan* ...21 C1
Saskatchewan, □ *Canada* ...34 C9
Saskatoon, *Canada* ...34 C9
Satu Mare, *Rom.* ...17 E11
Saudi Arabia, ■ *Asia* ...25 C3
Sault Ste. Marie, *Canada* ...35 D11
Savannah, *U.S.A.* ...37 D10
Savoie, □ *France* ...12 D7
Savona, *Italy* ...14 B3
Scapa Flow, *U.K.* ...10 C5
Scarborough, *U.K.* ...8 C7
Schleswig - Holstein, □ *Ger.* ...16 A4
Schwäbische Alb, *Ger.* ...16 D4
Schwarzwald, *Ger.* ...16 D4
Schwerin, *Ger.* ...16 B5
Scilly, Is. of, *U.K.* ...9 H2
Scotland, □ *U.K.* ...10 E4
Scunthorpe, *U.K.* ...8 D7
Seattle, *U.S.A.* ...36 A2
Segovia, *Spain* ...13 B3
Seine, ≈ *France* ...12 B4
Sekondi - Takoradi, *Ghana* ...26 H4
Selkirk, *U.K.* ...10 F6

Semarang, *Indonesia* ...23 D3
Sendai, *Japan* ...21 G11
Senegal, ■ *Africa* ...26 F2
Serbia, □ *Yug.* ...15 C9
Setonaikai, *Japan* ...21 C3
Setúbal, *Port.* ...13 C1
Sevastopol, *Ukraine* ...18 E4
Severn, ≈ *U.K.* ...9 F5
Severnaya Zemlya, *Russia* ...19 B10
Sevilla, *Spain* ...13 D3
Seychelles, ■ *Ind. Ocean* ...3 E12
Sfax, *Tunisia* ...27 B7
Shache, *China* ...22 C2
Shanghai, *China* ...22 C7
Shannon, ≈ *Ire.* ...11 D2
Shantou, *China* ...22 D6
Shapinsay, *U.K.* ...10 B6
Sheffield, *U.K.* ...8 D6
Shenyang, *China* ...22 B7
Sherwood Forest, *U.K.* ...8 D6
Shetland, □ *U.K.* ...10 A7
Shikoku, *Japan* ...21 C3
Shimonoseki, *Japan* ...21 C2
Shiraz, *Iran* ...25 C4
Shizuoka, *Japan* ...21 B6
Sholapur, *India* ...24 E4
Shreveport, *U.S.A.* ...37 D8
Shrewsbury, *U.K.* ...8 E5
Shropshire, □ *U.K.* ...9 E5
Siam = Thailand, ■ *Asia* ...23 B2
Sibiu, *Rom.* ...17 F12
Sichuan, □ *China* ...22 D5
Sicilia, □ *Italy* ...14 F5
Siena, *Italy* ...14 C4
Sierra Leone, ■ *Africa* ...26 G2
Sierra Nevada, *U.S.A.* ...36 C3
Silver City, *Panama* ...38 H14
Simpson Desert, *Australia* ...32 C6
Singapore, ■ *Asia* ...23 C2
Sioux City, *U.S.A.* ...37 B7
Sioux Falls, *U.S.A.* ...37 B7
Siracusa, *Italy* ...14 F6
Sitges, *Spain* ...13 B6
Sjælland, *Den.* ...7 J11
Skagerrak, *Europe* ...7 H10
Skien, *Norw.* ...7 G10
Skikda, *Algeria* ...26 A6
Skopje, *Macedonia* ...15 C9
Skye, I. of, *U.K.* ...10 D2
Slieve Aughty, *Ire.* ...11 C3
Slieve Bloom, *Ire.* ...11 C4
Slieve Mish, *Ire.* ...11 D2
Sligo, *Ire.* ...11 B3
Slough, *U.K.* ...9 F7
Slovak Rep., ■ *Europe* ...17 D9
Slovenia, ■ *Europe* ...14 B6
Snake, ≈ *U.S.A.* ...36 A3
Snowdon, *U.K.* ...8 D3
Society Is., *Pac. Ocean* ...2 E2
Socotra, *Yemen* ...25 D4
Söderhamn, *Swed.* ...7 F14
Sofiya, *Bulg.* ...15 C10
Sogn og Fjordane, □ *Norw.* ...7 F9
Solimoes, ≈ *Brazil* ...40 D5
Solomon Is., ■ *Pac. Ocean* ...3 E17
Solway Firth, *U.K.* ...8 C4
Somali Rep., ■ *Africa* ...30 E8
Somerset, □ *U.K.* ...9 F4
Somerset I., *Canada* ...34 A10
Sør-Trondelag, □ *Norw.* ...6 E12
Soria, *Spain* ...13 B4
Sorocaba, *Brazil* ...42 A7
Sosnowiec, *Poland* ...17 C9
Söul, *S. Korea* ...22 C7
Sousse, *Tunisia* ...27 A7
South Africa, ■ *Africa* ...29 L3
South Australia, □ *Australia* ...32 D5
South Bend, *U.S.A.* ...37 B9
South Carolina, □ *U.S.A.* ...37 D10
South China Sea, *Asia* ...23 B3
South Dakota, □ *U.S.A.* ...36 B6
South Downs, *U.K.* ...9 G7
South Georgia, *Atl. Ocean* ...42 G9
South Glamorgan, □ *U.K.* ...9 F4
South Island, *N.Z.* ...31 K7
South Korea, ■ *Asia* ...22 C7
South Ronaldsay, *U.K.* ...10 C6
South Shields, *U.K.* ...8 C6
South Uist, *U.K.* ...10 D1
South Yorkshire, □ *U.K.* ...8 D6
Southampton, *U.K.* ...9 G6
Southampton I., *Canada* ...35 B11
Southend, *U.K.* ...9 F8
Southern Alps, *N.Z.* ...31 K3
Southern Ocean, ...3 G12
Southern Uplands, *U.K.* ...10 F5
Southport, *U.K.* ...8 D4
Soutpansberge, *S. Africa* ...29 J5
Spain, ■ *Europe* ...13 B4
Spandau, *Ger.* ...16 B6
Spanish Town, *Jamaica* ...38 K17
Spencer Gulf, *Australia* ...33 E6
Sperrin Mts., *U.K.* ...11 B4
Spessart, *Ger.* ...16 D4
Split, *Croatia* ...14 C7
Spokane, *U.S.A.* ...36 A3
Sporádhes Voríai, *Greece* ...15 E11
Springfield, *U.S.A.* ...37 B12
Springs, *S. Africa* ...29 K5

Index

Sri Lanka, ■ Asia — 24 G5
Srinagar, India — 24 B3
St. Albans, U.K. — 9 F7
St. Andrews, U.K. — 10 E6
St. Austell, U.K. — 9 G3
St. Boniface, Canada — 34 D10
St. Christopher-Nevis = St. Kitts - Nevis, ■ W. Indies — 38 K19
St. Croix, W. Indies — 39 D12
St. - Étienne, France — 12 D6
St. Gallen, Switz. — 16 E4
St. George's, Grenada — 38 Q20
St. George's Channel, Europe — 11 E5
St. Helena, Atl. Ocean — 30 G3
St. Helens, U.K. — 8 D5
St. John's, Antigua — 38 K20
St. John's, Canada — 35 D14
St. Kitts - Nevis, ■ W. Indies — 38 K19
St. Lawrence, ≈ Canada — 35 D14
St. Louis, U.S.A. — 37 C8
St. Lucia, ■ W. Indies — 38 P21
St. Maarten, □ W. Indies — 38 J18
St. Malo, France — 12 B2
St. Martin, □ W. Indies — 38 J18
St. Michael's Mt., U.K. — 9 H4
St. Nazaire, France — 12 C2
St. Paul, U.S.A. — 37 B8
St. Peterburg, Russia — 18 D4
St. Petersburg, U.S.A. — 37 E10
St. Pierre et Miquelon, □ N. Amer. — 35 D14
St. Thomas, W. Indies — 39 D12
St. - Denis, France — 12 B5
St. - Tropez, France — 12 E7
St. Vincent & the Grenadines, ■ W. Indies — 38 P20
Stafford, U.K. — 8 E5
Staffordshire, □ U.K. — 8 E5
Staines, U.K. — 9 F7
Stalingrad = Volgograd, Russia — 18 E5
Stanley, Falkland Is. — 42 G5
Stara Planina, Bulg. — 15 C11
Stavanger, Norw. — 7 G8
Steiermark, □ Austria — 16 E7
Sterea Ellas, □ Greece — 15 E9
Stewart I., N.Z. — 31 M1
Stirling, U.K. — 10 E5
Stockholm, Swed. — 7 G15
Stockport, U.K. — 8 D5
Stockton, U.K. — 8 C6
Stockton, U.S.A. — 36 C2
Stoke-on-Trent, U.K. — 8 D5
Stonehenge, U.K. — 9 F6
Stourbridge, U.K. — 8 E5
Strabane, U.K. — 11 B4
Stralsund, Ger. — 16 A6
Strasbourg, France — 12 B7
Stratford-on-Avon, U.K. — 9 E6
Strath Spey, U.K. — 10 D5
Strathclyde, □ U.K. — 10 F3
Stromeferry, U.K. — 10 D3
Stronsay, U.K. — 10 B6
Stuttgart, Ger. — 16 D4
Subotica, Yug. — 15 A8
Sucre, Bolivia — 40 G5
Sudan, ■ Africa — 27 E10
Sudbury, Canada — 35 D11
Suez Canal, Egypt — 25 B2
Suez = El Suweis, Egypt — 27 C11
Suffolk, □ U.K. — 9 E8
Sulawesi, Indonesia — 23 D4
Sumatera, Indonesia — 23 D2
Sumba, Indonesia — 23 D3
Sumbawa, Indonesia — 23 D3
Sunderland, U.K. — 8 C6
Sundsvall, Swed. — 6 E14
Superior, L., N. Amer. — 37 A9
Surabaja, Indonesia — 23 D3
Surat, India — 24 D3
Surinam, ■ S. Amer. — 41 C7
Surrey, □ U.K. — 9 F7
Sutton-in-Ashfield, U.K. — 8 D6
Suva, Fiji — 31 D8
Suzhou, China — 22 C7
Svendborg, Den. — 7 J11
Sverdlovsk = Yekaterinburg, Russia — 18 D7
Swansea, U.K. — 9 F4
Swaziland, ■ Africa — 29 K6
Sweden, ■ Europe — 7 F13
Swindon, U.K. — 9 F6
Switzerland, ■ Europe — 16 E4
Sydney, Australia — 33 E9
Syracuse, U.S.A. — 37 B11
Syria, ■ Asia — 25 B2
Syrian Desert, Asia — 25 B2
Szczecin, Poland — 16 B9
Szeged, Hungary — 17 E10

T
Tabrīz, Iran — 25 B3
Tacoma, U.S.A. — 36 A2
Taegu, S. Korea — 22 C7
Tahiti, Pac. Ocean — 2 E2
Taibei, Taiwan — 22 D7
Tainan, Taiwan — 22 D7
Taiwan, ■ Asia — 22 D7
Taiyuan, China — 22 C6
Taizhong, Taiwan — 22 D7
Tajikistan, ■ Asia — 18 F7

Takamatsu, Japan — 21 B4
Talcahuano, Chile — 42 D2
Tallinn, Estonia — 18 D3
Tamil Nadu, □ India — 24 F4
Tampa, U.S.A. — 37 E10
Tampere, Fin. — 7 F17
Tampico, Mexico — 38 C5
Tamworth, U.K. — 9 E6
Tane-ga-Shima, Japan — 21 D2
Tanga, Tanzania — 28 F7
Tanganyika, L., Africa — 28 F5
Tangshan, China — 22 C6
Tanimbar Is., Indonesia — 23 D5
Tanta, Egypt — 27 B11
Tanzania, ■ Africa — 28 F7
Tarābulus, Lebanon — 25 B2
Tarābulus, Libya — 27 B7
Taranto, Italy — 14 D7
Tarragona, Spain — 13 B6
Tarrasa, Spain — 13 B6
Tashkent, Uzbekistan — 18 E7
Tasman Sea, Pac. Ocean — 31 J2
Tasmania, Australia — 33 G8
Tauern, Austria — 16 E6
Taunton, U.K. — 9 F4
Taunus, Ger. — 16 C4
Tay, ≈ U.K. — 10 E5
Tayside, □ U.K. — 10 E5
Tbilisi, Georgia — 18 E5
Tchad, L., Chad — 27 F7
Teeside, U.K. — 8 C6
Tegucigalpa, Honduras — 38 E7
Tehrān, Iran — 25 B4
Tehuantepec, Istme de, Mexico — 38 D5
Tejo, ≈ Port. — 13 C1
Tel Aviv - Yafo, Israel — 25 B2
Telemark, □ Norw. — 7 G10
Telford, U.K. — 8 E5
Tennessee, □ U.S.A. — 37 C9
Tennessee, ≈ U.S.A. — 37 C9
Teresina, Brazil — 41 E10
Terni, Italy — 14 C5
Teruel, Spain — 13 B5
Tetouan, Morocco — 26 A3
Teutoburger Wald, Ger. — 16 B4
Tevere, ≈ Italy — 14 C5
Texas, □ U.S.A. — 36 D6
Thailand, ■ Asia — 23 B2
Thames, ≈ U.K. — 9 F8
Thásos, Greece — 15 D11
The Hague = 's-Gravenhage, Neth. — 16 B2
Thessalia, □ Greece — 15 E10
Thessaloniki, Greece — 15 D10
Thies, Senegal — 26 F1
Thráki, □ Greece — 15 D11
Thunder Bay, Canada — 35 D11
Thüringer Wald, Ger. — 16 C5
Thurles, Ire. — 11 D4
Thurso, U.K. — 10 C5
Tianjin, China — 22 C6
Tiber = Tevere, ≈ Italy — 14 C5
Tibesti, Chad — 27 D8
Tibet = Xizang, □ China — 22 C3
Tientsin = Tianjin, China — 22 C6
Tierra del Fuego, S. Amer. — 42 G3
Tigris, ≈ Iraq — 25 B3
Tijuana, Mexico — 38 A1
Tilburg, Neth. — 16 C2
Timaru, N.Z. — 31 L3
Timişoara, Rom. — 17 F10
Timor, Indonesia — 23 D4
Tinos, Greece — 15 F11
Tipperary, □ Ire. — 11 D4
Tipperary, Ire. — 11 D3
Tipton, U.K. — 9 E5
Tirana, Alb. — 15 D8
Tirol, □ Austria — 16 E5
Tiree, U.K. — 10 E3
Tiruchchirappalli, India — 24 F4
Titicaca, L., S. Amer. — 40 G5
Titograd = Podgorica, Yug. — 15 C8
Tizi-Ouzou, Algeria — 26 A5
Tobago, W. Indies — 39 E12
Tokelau Is., Pac. Ocean — 2 E1
Togo, ■ Africa — 26 G5
Tōkyō, Japan — 21 B6
Toledo, Spain — 13 C3
Toledo, U.S.A. — 37 B10
Toluca, Mexico — 38 D5
Tomsk, Russia — 18 D9
Tonga, ■ Pac. Ocean — 31 D11
Toowoomba, Australia — 33 D9
Topeka, U.S.A. — 37 C7
Torbay, U.K. — 9 G4
Torino, Italy — 14 B2
Toronto, Canada — 35 D12
Torquay, U.K. — 9 G4
Torremolinos, Spain — 13 D3
Torrens, L., Australia — 33 E6
Tortosa, Spain — 13 B6
Torún, Poland — 17 B9
Toscana, □ Italy — 14 C4
Toulon, France — 12 E6
Toulouse, France — 12 E4
Touraine, □ France — 12 C4
Tourcoing, Belgium — 16 C1

Tours, France — 12 C4
Townsville, Australia — 33 B8
Toyama, Japan — 21 A5
Toyohashi, Japan — 21 B5
Toyonaka, Japan — 21 B4
Tralee, Ire. — 11 D2
Transilvania, Rom. — 17 E12
Transvaal, □ S. Africa — 29 K5
Trápani, Italy — 14 E5
Trelleborg, Swed. — 7 J12
Trentino Alto-Adige, □ Italy — 14 A4
Treviso, Italy — 14 B5
Trier, Ger. — 16 D3
Trieste, Italy — 14 B5
Trincomalee, Sri Lanka — 24 G5
Trinidad & Tobago, ■ W. Indies — 39 E12
Tripoli = Tarābulus, Libya — 27 B7
Tristan da Cunha, Atl. Ocean — 2 F9
Trois-Rivières, Canada — 35 D12
Trollhättan, Swed. — 7 G12
Troms, □ Norw. — 6 B15
Tromso, Norw. — 6 B15
Trondheim, Norw. — 6 E11
Trossachs, U.K. — 10 E4
Trujillo, Peru — 40 E3
Tsugaru-Kaikyō, Japan — 21 F11
Tsushima, Japan — 21 H8
Tuamotu Arch., Pac. Ocean — 2 E2
Tubuai Is., Pac. Ocean — 2 F2
Tucson, U.S.A. — 36 D4
Tula, Russia — 18 D4
Tullamore, Ire. — 11 C4
Tulsa, U.S.A. — 37 C7
Tulua, Colombia — 40 C3
Tunis, Tunisia — 26 A6
Tunisia, ■ Africa — 26 A6
Turin = Torino, Italy — 14 B2
Turkana, L., Kenya — 28 D7
Turkey, ■ Asia — 25 B2
Turkmenistan, ■ Asia — 18 F6
Turku, Fin. — 7 F17
Turnu-Severin, Rom. — 17 F11
Turun ja Pori, □ Fin. — 7 F17
Tuvalu, ■ Pac. Ocean — 3 E18
Tver, Russia — 18 D4
Tyler, U.S.A. — 37 D7
Tyne & Wear, □ U.K. — 8 C6
Tynemouth, U.K. — 8 C6
Tyrrhenian Sea, Italy — 14 E5

U
Uberaba, Brazil — 41 G9
Uddevalla, Swed. — 7 G11
Udine, Italy — 14 A5
Ufa, Russia — 18 D6
Uganda, ■ Africa — 28 D6
Ujpest, Hungary — 17 E9
Ujung Pandang, Indonesia — 23 D3
Ukraine, ■ Europe — 18 E4
Ulaanbaatar, Mong. — 22 B5
Ulan Ude, Russia — 19 D11
Ullapool, U.K. — 10 D3
Ulm, Ger. — 16 D4
Ulster, □ Ire. — 11 B4
Umbria, □ Italy — 14 C5
Ungava Pen., Canada — 35 C12
United Arab Emirates, ■ Asia — 25 C4
United Kingdom, ■ Europe — 4 E5
United States of America, ■ N. Amer. — 36 C6
Unst, U.K. — 10 A8
Uppsala, Swed. — 7 G14
Urmia, L., Iran — 25 B3
Uruguay, ■ S. Amer. — 42 C5
Uruguay, ≈ S. Amer. — 42 C5
Urumqi, China — 22 B3
Usti nad Labem, Czech Rep. — 16 C7
Utah, □ U.S.A. — 36 C4
Utrecht, Neth. — 16 B2
Utsunomiya, Japan — 21 A6
Uttar Pradesh, □ India — 24 C5
Uudenmaa, □ Fin. — 7 F18
Uzbekistan, ■ Asia — 18 E7

V
Vaal, ≈ S. Africa — 29 K4
Vaasa, □ Fin. — 6 E17
Vadso, Norw. — 6 A20
Valence, France — 12 D6
Valencia, □ Spain — 13 C5
Valencia, Spain — 13 C5
Valencia, Venezuela — 40 A5
Valladolid, Spain — 13 B3
Valle d'Aosta, □ Italy — 14 B2
Valletta, Malta — 14 G6
Valparaíso, Chile — 42 C2
Vancouver, Canada — 34 D7
Vancouver I., Canada — 34 D7
Vanuatu, ■ Pac. Ocean — 3 E18
Varanasi, India — 24 C5
Värmland, □ Swed. — 7 G12
Varna, Bulg. — 15 C12
Västerbotten, □ Norw. — 6 D14
Västerås, Swed. — 7 G14
Vasternorrland, □ Norw. — 6 E14
Västervik, Swed. — 7 H14
Västmanland, □ Swed. — 7 G14

Vatnajökull, Iceland — 6 D5
Veneto, □ Italy — 14 B4
Venézia, Italy — 14 B5
Venezuela, ■ S. Amer. — 40 B5
Veracruz, Mexico — 38 D5
Vereeniging, S. Africa — 29 K5
Vermont, □ U.S.A. — 37 B12
Verona, Italy — 14 B4
Versailles, France — 12 B5
Vest-Agder, □ Norw. — 7 G9
Vesterålen, Norw. — 6 B13
Vestfjorden, Norw. — 6 B13
Vesuvio, Italy — 14 D6
Viborg, Den. — 7 H10
Vichy, France — 12 C5
Victoria, Australia — 33 F7
Victoria, Canada — 34 D7
Victoria Falls, Zimbabwe — 29 H5
Victoria I., Canada — 34 A8
Victoria, L., Africa — 28 E6
Vienna = Wien, Austria — 16 D8
Vientos, Paso de los, W. Indies — 39 C10
Vietnam, ■ Asia — 23 B2
Vigo, Spain — 13 A1
Vilnius, Lithuania — 18 D3
Viña del Mar, Chile — 42 C2
Virgin Is., W. Indies — 39 D12
Virginia, □ U.S.A. — 37 C11
Visby, Swed. — 7 H15
Vitória, Brazil — 41 H10
Vitoria, Spain — 13 A4
Vladivostok, Russia — 19 E14
Vojvodina, □ Yug. — 15 B8
Volga, ≈ Russia — 18 E5
Volgograd, Russia — 18 E5
Vólos, Greece — 15 E10
Volta, L., Ghana — 26 G4
Vorarlberg, □ Austria — 16 E4
Voronezh, Russia — 18 D4
Vyatka, Russia — 18 D5

W
Waco, U.S.A. — 37 D7
Wād Medanī, Sudan — 27 F11
Wakayama, Japan — 21 B4
Wakefield, U.K. — 8 D6
Wakkanai, Japan — 21 E11
Wałbrzych, Poland — 16 C8
Wales, □ U.K. — 9 E4
Wallasey, U.K. — 8 B6
Wallsend, U.K. — 8 C6
Walney I., U.K. — 8 C4
Walsall, U.K. — 9 E6
Walvisbaai, S. Africa — 29 J2
Wanganui, N.Z. — 31 H5
Warley, U.K. — 9 E6
Warrington, U.K. — 8 D5
Warszawa, Poland — 17 B10
Warwick, U.K. — 9 E6
Warwickshire, □ U.K. — 9 E6
Wash, The, U.K. — 8 E8
Washington, □ U.S.A. — 36 A2
Washington D.C., U.S.A. — 37 C11
Waterbury, U.S.A. — 37 B12
Waterford, Ire. — 11 D4
Watford, U.K. — 9 F7
Weald, The, U.K. — 9 F7
Welkom, S. Africa — 29 K5
Wellesley Is., Australia — 33 B6
Wellington, N.Z. — 31 J5
Wellington I., Chile — 42 F2
Wenzhou, China — 22 D7
West Bromwich, U.K. — 9 E6
West Glamorgan, □ U.K. — 9 F4
West Indies — 39 D10
West Midlands, □ U.K. — 9 E6
West Sussex, □ U.K. — 9 F7
West Virginia, □ U.S.A. — 37 C10
West Yorkshire, □ U.K. — 8 D6
Western Australia, □ Oceania — 32 C3
Western Is., □ U.K. — 10 D1
Western Sahara, ■ Africa — 26 C2
Western Samoa, ■ Pac. Ocean — 2 E1
Westerwald, Ger. — 16 C3
Westmeath, □ Ire. — 11 C4
Weston-super-Mare, U.K. — 9 F6
Westray, U.K. — 10 B5
Wexford, Ire. — 11 D5
Weymouth, U.K. — 9 G5
Whalsay, U.K. — 10 A8
White Nile = Nīl el Abyad, ≈ Africa — 27 E11
White Sea = Beloye More, Russia — 18 C4
Whitehaven, U.K. — 8 C4
Whitehorse, Canada — 34 B6
Wichita, U.S.A. — 37 C7
Wichita Falls, U.S.A. — 37 D7
Wick, U.K. — 10 C5
Wicklow, Ire. — 11 D5
Wien, Austria — 16 D8
Wiesbaden, Ger. — 16 C4
Wigan, U.K. — 8 D5
Wight, I. of, □ U.K. — 9 G6
Wilhelmshaven, Ger. — 16 B4
Wilmington, U.S.A. — 37 C11
Wiltshire, □ U.K. — 9 F6
Winchester, U.K. — 9 F6
Windermere, L., U.K. — 8 C5
Windhoek, Namibia — 29 J3

Windsor, U.K. — 9 F7
Windsor, Canada — 35 D11
Windward Is., W. Indies — 39 E12
Winnipeg, Canada — 34 D10
Winnipeg, L., Canada — 34 C10
Winston Salem, U.S.A. — 37 C10
Winterthur, Switz. — 16 E4
Wirral, The, U.K. — 8 D4
Wisconsin, □ U.S.A. — 37 B9
Wishaw, U.K. — 10 F5
Włocławek, Poland — 17 B9
Woking, U.K. — 9 F7
Wollongong, Australia — 33 E9
Wolverhampton, U.K. — 9 E5
Worcester, U.K. — 9 E5
Worcester, U.S.A. — 37 B12
Workington, U.K. — 8 C4
Worksop, U.K. — 8 D6
Worms, Ger. — 16 D4
Worthing, U.K. — 9 G7
Wrexham, U.K. — 8 D5
Wrocław, Poland — 16 C8
Wuhan, China — 22 C6
Wuhu, China — 22 C6
Wuppertal, Ger. — 16 C3
Würzburg, Ger. — 16 D4
Wyoming, □ U.S.A. — 36 B5

X
Xi'an, China — 22 C5
Xiaguan, China — 22 D5
Xingu, ≈ Brazil — 41 D8
Xinjiang Uygur, □ China — 22 B3
Xizang, □ China — 22 C3
Xuzhou, China — 22 C6

Y
Yakushima, Japan — 21 D2
Yakutsk, Russia — 19 C13
Yamagata, Japan — 21 G11
Yaoundé, Cameroon — 28 D2
Yaroslavl, Russia — 18 D4
Yazd, Iran — 25 B4
Yell, U.K. — 10 A8
Yellow Sea, Asia — 22 C7
Yellowknife, Canada — 34 B8
Yellowstone National Park, U.S.A. — 36 B4
Yemen, ■ Asia — 25 D3
Yenisey, ≈ Russia — 18 C9
Yeovil, U.K. — 9 G5
Yerevan, Armenia — 18 E5
Yining, China — 22 B3
Yokohama, Japan — 21 B6
Yokosuka, Japan — 21 B6
York, U.K. — 8 D6
Youghal, Ire. — 11 E4
Ystad, Swed. — 7 J12
Yucatan, □ Mexico — 38 D7
Yugoslavia, ■ Europe — 15 B9
Yukon, ≈ N. Amer. — 34 B6
Yukon Territory, □ Canada — 34 B6

Z
Zabrze, Poland — 17 C9
Zagazig, Egypt — 27 B11
Zagreb, Croatia — 14 B6
Zagros Mts., Iran — 25 B3
Zaire, ≈ Africa — 28 E4
Zaïre, ■ Africa — 28 E4
Zákinthos, Greece — 15 F9
Zambezi, ≈ Africa — 29 H6
Zambia, ■ Africa — 29 G5
Zamora, Spain — 13 B3
Zanzibar, Tanzania — 28 F7
Zaporozhye, Ukraine — 18 E4
Zaragoza, Spain — 13 B5
Zaria, Nigeria — 26 F6
Zemlya Frantsa Iosifa, Russia — 18 B6
Zhanghua, Taiwan — 22 D7
Zhangjiakou, China — 22 B6
Zhengzhou, China — 22 C6
Zhenjiang, China — 22 C6
Zibo, China — 22 C6
Zigong, China — 22 D5
Zimbabwe, ■ Africa — 29 H5
Zürich, Switz. — 16 E4
Zwickau, Ger. — 16 C6

TIME

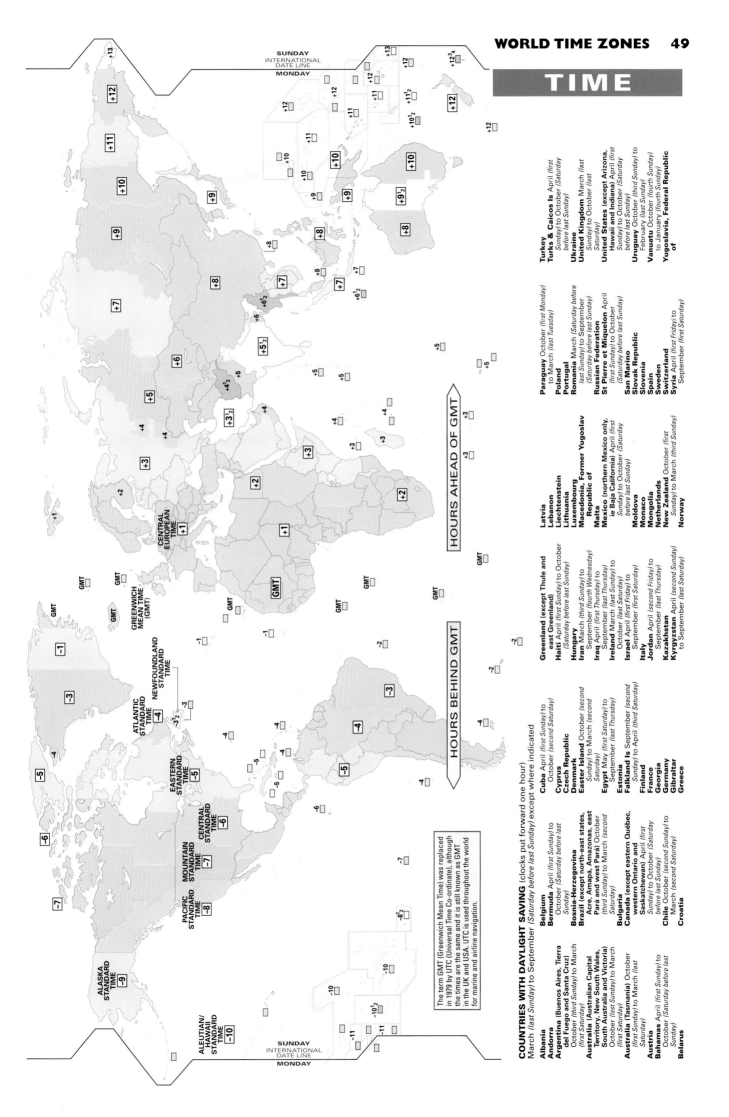

HOURS AHEAD OF GMT

HOURS BEHIND GMT

GREENWICH MEAN TIME (GMT)

CENTRAL EUROPEAN TIME

NEWFOUNDLAND STANDARD TIME

ATLANTIC STANDARD TIME

EASTERN STANDARD TIME

CENTRAL STANDARD TIME

MOUNTAIN STANDARD TIME

PACIFIC STANDARD TIME

ALASKA STANDARD TIME

ALEUTIAN/ HAWAII STANDARD TIME

SUNDAY INTERNATIONAL DATE LINE MONDAY

The term GMT (Greenwich Mean Time) was replaced in 1979 by UTC (Universal Time Co-ordinate), although the times are the same and it is still known as GMT in the UK and USA. UTC is used throughout the world for marine and airline navigation.

COUNTRIES WITH DAYLIGHT SAVING (clocks put forward one hour)
March (last Sunday) to September (Saturday before last Sunday) except where indicated

Albania
Andorra
Argentina (Buenos Aires, Tierra del Fuego and Santa Cruz) October (third Sunday) to March (first Saturday)
Australia (Australian Capital Territory, New South Wales, South Australia and Victoria) October (last Sunday) to March (first Saturday)
Australia (Tasmania) October (first Sunday) to March (last Saturday)
Austria
Bahamas April (first Sunday) to October (Saturday before last Sunday)
Belarus

Belgium
Bermuda April (first Sunday) to October (Saturday before last Sunday)
Bosnia-Herzegovina
Brazil (except north-east states, Acre, Amapá, Amazonas, east Pará and west Pará) October (third Sunday) to March (second Saturday)
Bulgaria
Canada (except eastern Quebec, western Ontario and Saskatchewan) April (first Sunday) to October (Saturday before last Sunday)
Chile October (second Sunday) to March (second Saturday)
Croatia

Cuba April (first Sunday) to October (second Saturday)
Cyprus
Czech Republic
Denmark
Easter Island October (second Sunday) to March (second Saturday)
Egypt May (first Saturday) to September (last Thursday)
Estonia
Falkland Is September (second Sunday) to April (third Saturday)
Finland
France
Georgia
Germany
Gibraltar
Greece

Greenland (except Thule and east Greenland)
Haiti April (first Sunday) to October (Saturday before last Sunday)
Hungary
Iran March (third Sunday) to September (fourth Wednesday)
Iraq April (first Thursday) to September (last Thursday)
Ireland March (last Sunday) to September (last Sunday)
Israel April (first Friday) to September (first Saturday)
Italy
Jordan April (second Friday) to September (last Thursday)
Kazakhstan
Kyrgyzstan April (second Sunday) to September (last Saturday)

Latvia
Lebanon
Liechtenstein
Lithuania
Luxembourg
Macedonia, Former Yugoslav Republic of
Malta
Mexico (northern Mexico only, ie Baja California) April (first Sunday) to October (Saturday before last Sunday)
Moldova
Monaco
Mongolia
Netherlands
New Zealand October (first Sunday) to March (third Sunday)
Norway

Paraguay October (first Monday) to March (last Tuesday)
Poland
Portugal
Romania March (Saturday before last Sunday) to September (Saturday before last Sunday)
Russian Federation
St Pierre et Miquelon April (first Sunday) to October (Saturday before last Sunday)
San Marino
Slovak Republic
Slovenia
Spain
Sweden
Switzerland
Syria April (first Friday) to September (first Saturday)

Turkey
Turks & Caicos Is April (first Sunday) to October (Saturday before last Sunday)
Ukraine
United Kingdom March (last Sunday) to October (last Saturday)
United States (except Arizona, Hawaii and Indiana) April (first Sunday) to October (Saturday before last Sunday)
Uruguay October (third Sunday) to February (first Sunday)
Vanuatu October (fourth Sunday) to January (fourth Sunday)
Yugoslavia, Federal Republic of

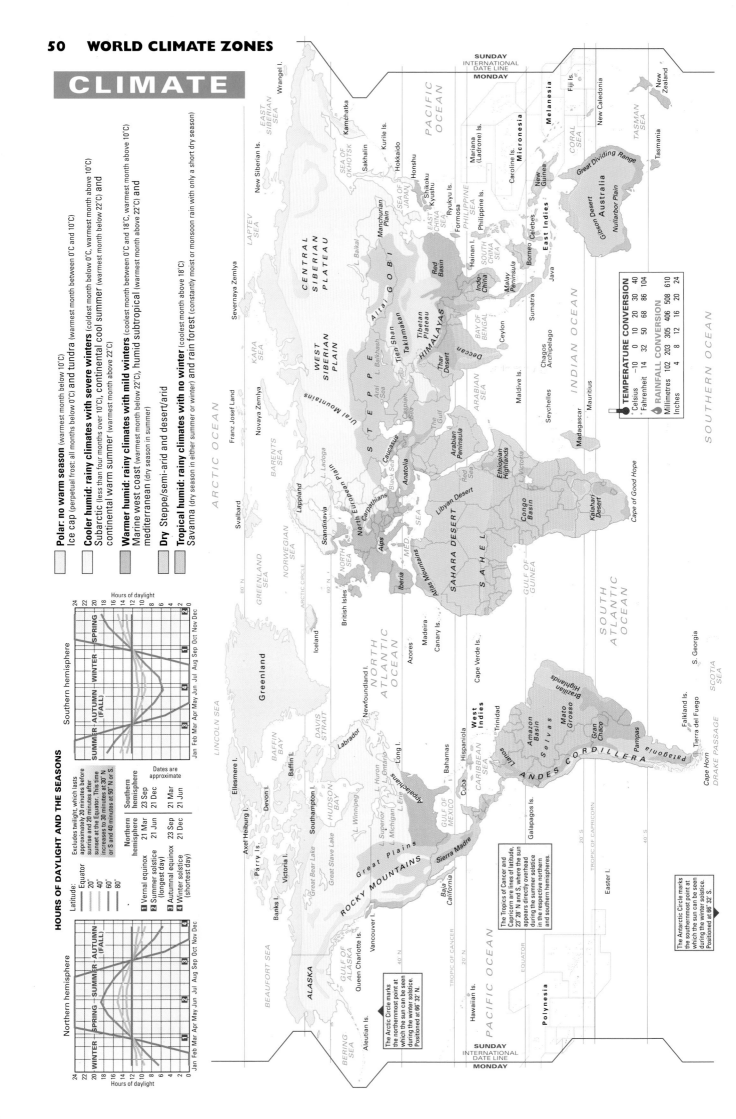

CLIMATE

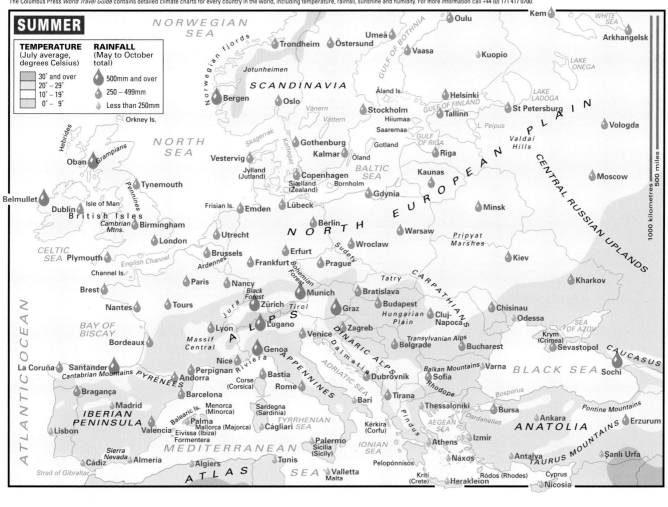

The Columbus Press *World Travel Guide* contains detailed climate charts for every country in the world, including temperature, rainfall, sunshine and humidity. For more information call +44 (0) 171 417 0700.

HEALTH

MALARIA

The main antimalarial drugs

CHL Chloroquine. Usually well tolerated. The few people who may experience uncomfortable side-effects, such as gastrointestinal disturbance, may tolerate it better by taking the drug with meals and in divided twice-weekly doses.

C+P Chloroquine + proguanil. Often causes gastrointestinal upsets (see above).

MEF Mefloquine. Usually well tolerated. Mild side-effects such as dizziness or gastrointestinal effects may occur for a while during early prophylaxis, but spontaneously resolve. If these side-effects are unacceptable, C+P or DOX can be used instead. Neurological and psychiatric disorders may rarely occur.

DOX Doxycycline. Side-effects are common. Tablets should always be taken with plenty of fluid, and never taken just prior to lying down.

All antimalarial drugs to be taken at weekly intervals should be started one week before departure, and those to be taken daily should be started one day before departure. All drugs should be continued for four weeks after the last possible exposure to infection.

In many countries of the Americas and south-east Asia (for example, China, Indonesia, Malaysia, Mexico, Myanmar and Philippines), malaria is largely confined to rural areas not visited by most travellers. Any travel to these areas is most often during day-time when there is minimal risk of exposure. Chemoprophylaxis is recommended only for those travellers who will be exposed outdoors during the evening or night-time in rural areas. Although chemoprophylaxis is not recommended in areas with very limited risk, travellers should be advised to use insect repellents and other personal protection measures.

Travellers are reminded that protection from biting mosquitoes is the first line of defence against malaria, and no antimalarial prophylactic regimen gives complete protection

Malaria zones:

A Risk generally low and seasonal, no risk in many areas (for example urban areas). *Plasmodium falciparum* absent or sensitive to chloroquine.

Recommended prophylaxis:
Chloroquine, or in case of very low risk), no prophylaxis, with chloroquine as a stand-by when prompt medical attention unavailable.

B Low risk in most areas. Chloroquine alone will protect against *P. vivax.* Chloroquine with proguanil will give some protection against *P. falciparum* and may alleviate the disease if it occurs despite prophylaxis.

Recommended prophylaxis:
Chloroquine + proguanil *or* chloroquine alone (if proguanil unavailable) *or* (in the case of very low risk), no prophylaxis.

Recommended stand-by (to be used under medical guidance or when prompt medical attention unavailable): Quinine *or* sulfadoxine-pyrimethamine *or* sulfalene-pyrimethamine *or* mefloquine *or* halofantrine.

C In Africa, risk high except in some high-altitude areas. In Asia and America, risk low in most areas except in the Amazon basin (colonisation and mining areas), where the risk is high. Resistance to sulfadoxine-pyrimethamine is common in Asia, but variable in America. It is effective in most of Africa.

Recommended prophylaxis:
Chloroquine + proguanil (except for south-east Asia) *or* doxycycline *or* mefloquine *or* (in the case of very low risk), no prophylaxis.

Recommended stand-by (to be used under medical guidance or when prompt medical attention unavailable): As zone B.

This page is based on information supplied by the World Health Organisation (WHO). In all cases, travellers should seek up-to-date medical advice before departure regarding recent developments and further health requirements.

YELLOW FEVER

SUDAN

The yellow fever endemic zones cover areas of Africa and South America. Countries named in red type are either fully within a zone or have part of their area affected by it. Countries only partially within the yellow fever zones are:

Africa: southern parts of Mali, Niger, Chad, Sudan; east and north-east part of Somalia; far west of Zambia; and all of Zaire except the far south are regarded as endemic zones.

South America: all of Colombia except the south-west coast; eastern parts of Ecuador, Peru, Bolivia; and all of Brazil except the eastern coastal states are regarded as endemic zones.

EGYPT

Countries are named in **black type** on the map require an *international certificate of vaccination against yellow fever* from travellers arriving from a yellow fever endemic zone.

All countries where yellow fever is endemic (marked in red type: see left) also require the certificate if travelling from an endemic area, with the exception of Colombia, Panama, Venezuela and Zambia, where no certificate is required.

CHAD

Countries marked with a box require a yellow fever vaccination certificate from *all* travellers, whether they are arriving from an infected area or not. Due to the risks involved, pregnant women and children under one year of age (or in some cases six to nine months of age) usually do not require a yellow fever certificate. However, those travelling with children should seek advice before entering the country by contacting the relevant embassies or telephoning the Travellers Healthline on 0891 224100 (in UK only).

Countries marked with an asterisk (*) may require yellow fever certificates from those arriving from non-infected countries if they are staying for more than two weeks. Travellers should seek advice as above before entering the country by contacting the relevant embassies or telephoning the Travellers Healthline on 0891 224100 (in UK only).

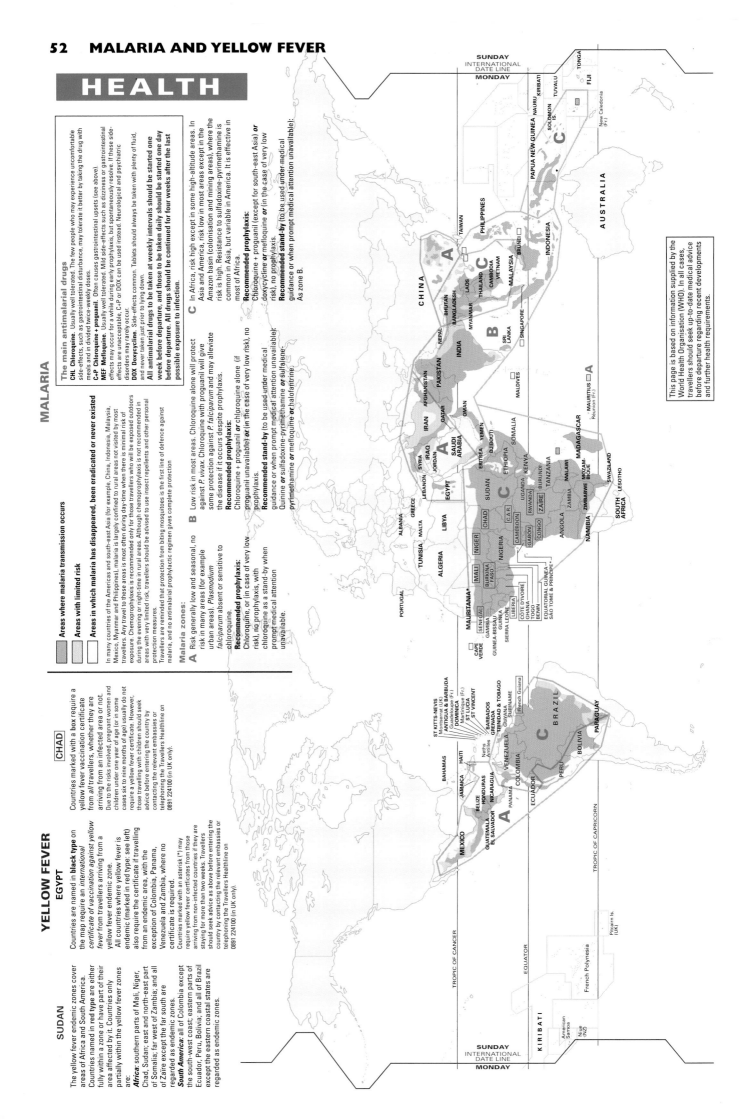

Areas where malaria transmission occurs

Areas with limited risk

Areas in which malaria has disappeared, been eradicated or never existed

DRIVING

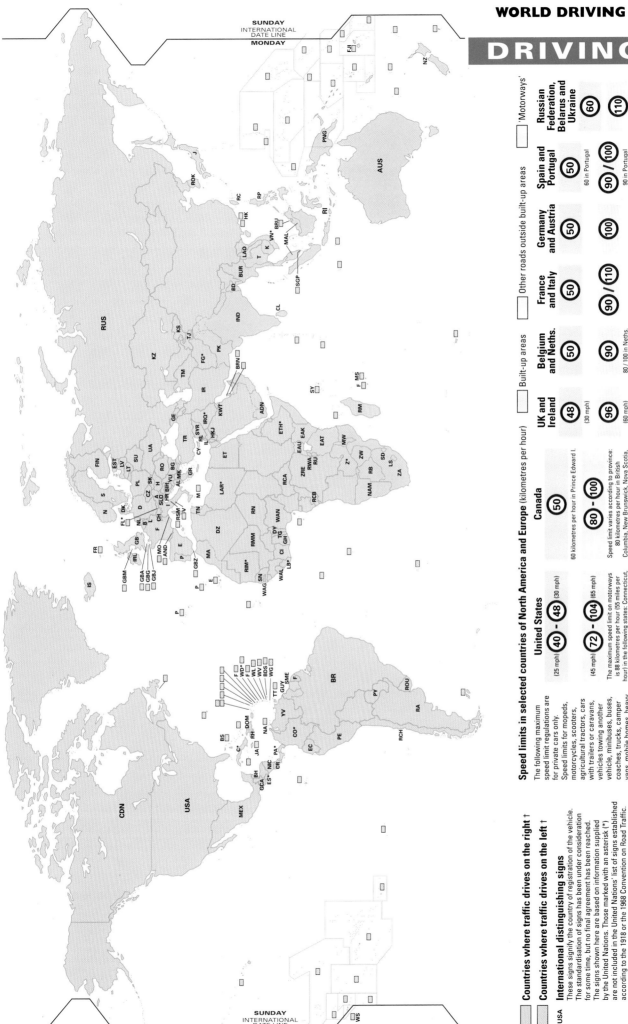

Countries where traffic drives on the right †

Countries where traffic drives on the left †

International distinguishing signs
These signs signify the country of registration of the vehicle. The standardisation of signs has been under consideration for some time, but no final agreement has been reached. The signs shown here are based on information supplied by the United Nations. Those marked with an asterisk (*) are not included in the United Nations' list of signs established according to the 1918 or the 1968 Convention on Road Traffic.

† Information supplied by the RAC.

Speed limits in selected countries of North America and Europe (kilometres per hour)

United States
(25 mph) 40 – 48 (30 mph)

(45 mph) 72 – 104 (65 mph)

The maximum speed limit on motorways is 88 kilometres per hour (55 miles per hour) in the following states: Connecticut, Delaware, District of Columbia, Hawaii, Maryland, Massachusetts, Nevada, New Jersey, New York, Pennsylvania, Rhode Island and South Carolina.

The following maximum speed limit regulations are for private cars only.
Speed limits for mopeds, motorcycles, scooters, agricultural tractors, cars with trailers or caravans, vehicles towing another vehicle, minibuses, buses, coaches, trucks, camper vans, mobile homes, heavy goods vehicles and recently qualified drivers often vary from those shown.

Canada
50

60 kilometres per hour in Prince Edward I.

80 – 100

Speed limit varies according to province: 80 kilometres per hour in British Columbia, New Brunswick, Nova Scotia, Ontario and Saskatchewan; 90 kph in Manitoba, Newfoundland, NW Territories, Prince Edward Island and Yukon; 100 kph in Alberta and between 60-100 kph in Québec, depending on the road.

	Built-up areas	Other roads outside built-up areas	'Motorways'
UK and Ireland	48 (30 mph)	96 (60 mph)	112 (70 mph)
Belgium and Neths.	50	90 80 / 100 in Neths.	120
France and Italy	50	90 / 110	130
Germany and Austria	50	100	130 Germany: recommended only
Spain and Portugal	50 60 in Portugal	90 / 100 90 in Portugal	120
Russian Federation, Belarus and Ukraine	60	110	110

AIRPORTS

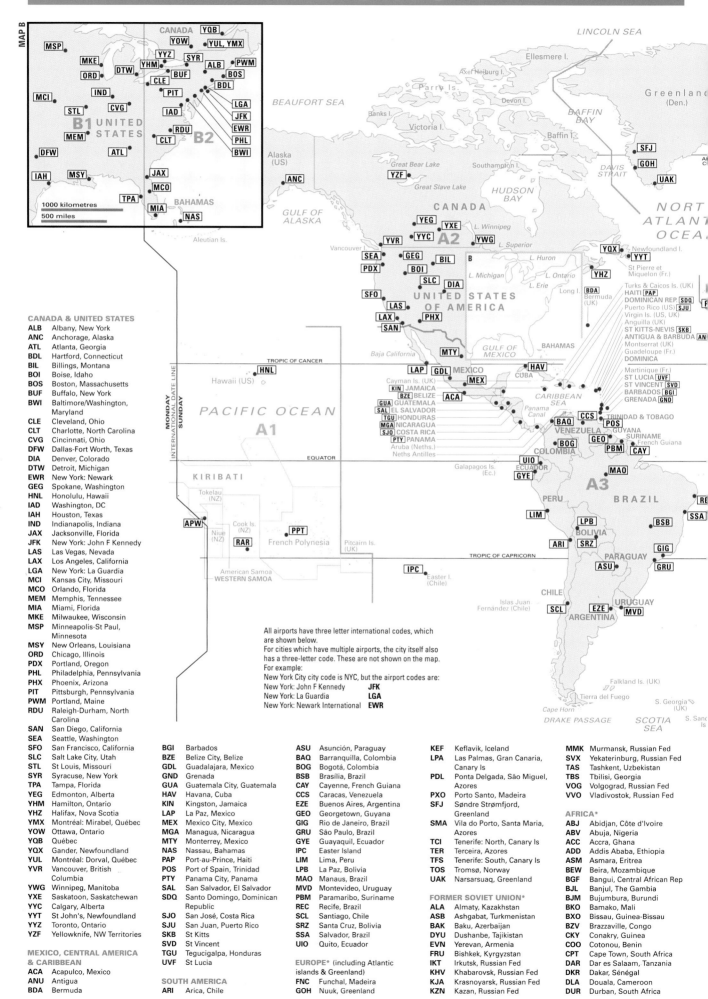

All airports have three letter international codes, which are shown below.
For cities which have multiple airports, the city itself also has a three-letter code. These are not shown on the map.
For example:
New York City city code is NYC, but the airport codes are:

New York: John F Kennedy	JFK
New York: La Guardia	LGA
New York: Newark International	EWR

CANADA & UNITED STATES
ALB Albany, New York
ANC Anchorage, Alaska
ATL Atlanta, Georgia
BDL Hartford, Connecticut
BIL Billings, Montana
BOI Boise, Idaho
BOS Boston, Massachusetts
BUF Buffalo, New York
BWI Baltimore/Washington, Maryland
CLE Cleveland, Ohio
CLT Charlotte, North Carolina
CVG Cincinnati, Ohio
DFW Dallas-Fort Worth, Texas
DIA Denver, Colorado
DTW Detroit, Michigan
EWR New York: Newark
GEG Spokane, Washington
HNL Honolulu, Hawaii
IAD Washington, DC
IAH Houston, Texas
IND Indianapolis, Indiana
JAX Jacksonville, Florida
JFK New York: John F Kennedy
LAS Las Vegas, Nevada
LAX Los Angeles, California
LGA New York: La Guardia
MCI Kansas City, Missouri
MCO Orlando, Florida
MEM Memphis, Tennessee
MIA Miami, Florida
MKE Milwaukee, Wisconsin
MSP Minneapolis-St Paul, Minnesota
MSY New Orleans, Louisiana
ORD Chicago, Illinois
PDX Portland, Oregon
PHL Philadelphia, Pennsylvania
PHX Phoenix, Arizona
PIT Pittsburgh, Pennsylvania
PWM Portland, Maine
RDU Raleigh-Durham, North Carolina
SAN San Diego, California
SEA Seattle, Washington
SFO San Francisco, California
SLC Salt Lake City, Utah
STL St Louis, Missouri
SYR Syracuse, New York
TPA Tampa, Florida
YEG Edmonton, Alberta
YHM Hamilton, Ontario
YHZ Halifax, Nova Scotia
YMX Montréal: Mirabel, Québec
YOW Ottawa, Ontario
YQB Québec
YQX Gander, Newfoundland
YUL Montréal: Dorval, Québec
YVR Vancouver, British Columbia
YWG Winnipeg, Manitoba
YXE Saskatoon, Saskatchewan
YYC Calgary, Alberta
YYT St John's, Newfoundland
YYZ Toronto, Ontario
YZF Yellowknife, NW Territories

MEXICO, CENTRAL AMERICA & CARIBBEAN
ACA Acapulco, Mexico
ANU Antigua
BDA Bermuda

BGI Barbados
BZE Belize City, Belize
GDL Guadalajara, Mexico
GND Grenada
GUA Guatemala City, Guatemala
HAV Havana, Cuba
KIN Kingston, Jamaica
LAP La Paz, Mexico
MEX Mexico City, Mexico
MGA Managua, Nicaragua
MTY Monterrey, Mexico
NAS Nassau, Bahamas
PAP Port-au-Prince, Haiti
POS Port of Spain, Trinidad
PTY Panama City, Panama
SAL San Salvador, El Salvador
SDQ Santo Domingo, Dominican Republic
SJO San José, Costa Rica
SJU San Juan, Puerto Rico
SKB St Kitts
SVD St Vincent
TGU Tegucigalpa, Honduras
UVF St Lucia

SOUTH AMERICA
ARI Arica, Chile

ASU Asunción, Paraguay
BAQ Barranquilla, Colombia
BOG Bogotá, Colombia
BSB Brasília, Brazil
CAY Cayenne, French Guiana
CCS Caracas, Venezuela
EZE Buenos Aires, Argentina
GEO Georgetown, Guyana
GIG Rio de Janeiro, Brazil
GRU São Paulo, Brazil
GYE Guayaquil, Ecuador
IPC Easter Island
LIM Lima, Peru
LPB La Paz, Bolivia
MAO Manaus, Brazil
MVD Montevideo, Uruguay
PBM Paramaribo, Suriname
REC Recife, Brazil
SCL Santiago, Chile
SRZ Santa Cruz, Bolivia
SSA Salvador, Brazil
UIO Quito, Ecuador

EUROPE* (including Atlantic islands & Greenland)
FNC Funchal, Madeira
GOH Nuuk, Greenland

KEF Keflavik, Iceland
LPA Las Palmas, Gran Canaria, Canary Is
PDL Ponta Delgada, São Miguel, Azores
PXO Porto Santo, Madeira
SFJ Søndre Strømfjord, Greenland
SMA Vila do Porto, Santa Maria, Azores
TCI Tenerife: North, Canary Is
TER Terceira, Azores
TFS Tenerife: South, Canary Is
TOS Tromsø, Norway
UAK Narsarsuaq, Greenland

FORMER SOVIET UNION*
ALA Almaty, Kazakhstan
ASB Ashgabat, Turkmenistan
BAK Baku, Azerbaijan
DYU Dushanbe, Tajikistan
EVN Yerevan, Armenia
FRU Bishkek, Kyrgyzstan
IKT Irkutsk, Russian Fed
KHV Khabarovsk, Russian Fed
KJA Krasnoyarsk, Russian Fed
KZN Kazan, Russian Fed

MMK Murmansk, Russian Fed
SVX Yekaterinburg, Russian Fed
TAS Tashkent, Uzbekistan
TBS Tbilisi, Georgia
VOG Volgograd, Russian Fed
VVO Vladivostok, Russian Fed

AFRICA*
ABJ Abidjan, Côte d'Ivoire
ABV Abuja, Nigeria
ACC Accra, Ghana
ADD Addis Ababa, Ethiopia
ASM Asmara, Eritrea
BEW Beira, Mozambique
BGF Bangui, Central African Rep
BJL Banjul, The Gambia
BJM Bujumbura, Burundi
BKO Bamako, Mali
BXO Bissau, Guinea-Bissau
BZV Brazzaville, Congo
CKY Conakry, Guinea
COO Cotonou, Benin
CPT Cape Town, South Africa
DAR Dar es Salaam, Tanzania
DKR Dakar, Sénégal
DLA Douala, Cameroon
DUR Durban, South Africa

AIRPORTS

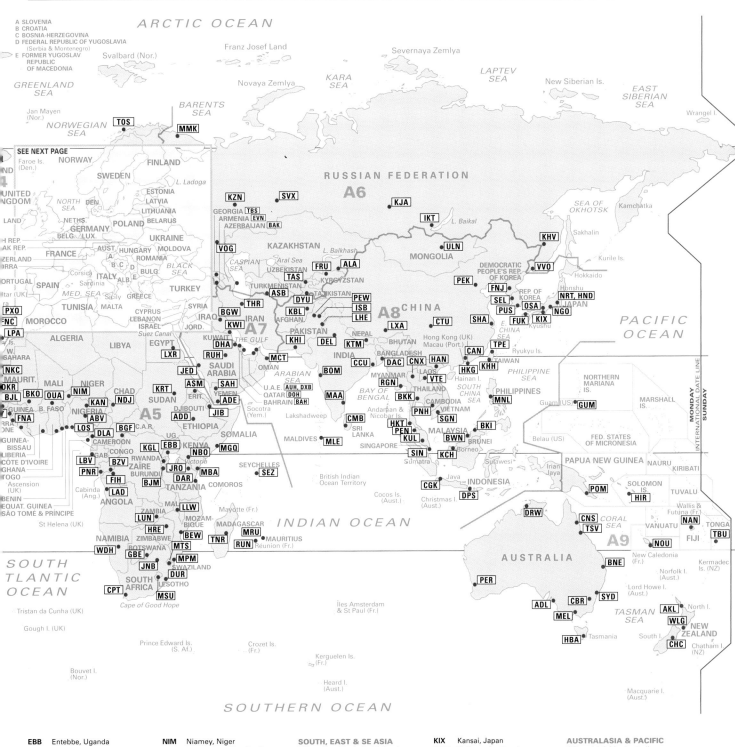

A SLOVENIA
B CROATIA
C BOSNIA-HERZEGOVINA
D FEDERAL REPUBLIC OF YUGOSLAVIA
(Serbia & Montenegro)
E FORMER YUGOSLAV REPUBLIC OF MACEDONIA

EBB	Entebbe, Uganda	**NIM**	Niamey, Niger	**SOUTH, EAST & SE ASIA**		**KIX**	Kansai, Japan	**AUSTRALASIA & PACIFIC**
FIH	Kinshasa, Zaïre	**NKC**	Nouakchott, Mauritania	**BKI**	Kota Kinabalu, Malaysia	**KTM**	Kathmandu, Nepal	**ADL**	Adelaide, Australia

EBB Entebbe, Uganda
FIH Kinshasa, Zaïre
FNA Freetown, Sierra Leone
GBE Gaborone, Botswana
HRE Harare, Zimbabwe
JIB Djibouti
JNB Johannesburg, South Africa
JRO Kilimanjaro, Tanzania
KAN Kano, Nigeria
KGL Kigali, Rwanda
KRT Khartoum, Sudan
LAD Luanda, Angola
LBV Libreville, Gabon
LFW Lomé, Togo
LLW Lilongwe, Malawi
LOS Lagos, Nigeria
LUN Lusaka, Zambia
LXR Luxor, Egypt
MBA Mombasa, Kenya
MGQ Mogadishu, Somalia
MPM Maputo, Mozambique
MRU Mauritius
MSU Maseru, Lesotho
MTS Manzini, Swaziland
NBO Nairobi, Kenya
NDB Nouadhibou, Mauritania
NDJ Ndjamena, Chad

NIM Niamey, Niger
NKC Nouakchott, Mauritania
OUA Ouagadougou, Burkina Faso
PNR Pointe-Noire, Congo
ROB Monrovia, Liberia
RUN Réunion
SEZ Mahé, Seychelles
SID Sal, Cape Verde
SSG Malabo, Equatorial Guinea
TNR Antananarivo, Madagascar
WDH Windhoek, Namibia

MIDDLE EAST*
ADE Aden, Yemen
AUH Abu Dhabi, UAE
BAH Bahrain
BGW Baghdad, Iraq
DHA Dhahran, Saudi Arabia
DOH Doha, Qatar
DXB Dubai, UAE
JED Jeddah, Saudi Arabia
KWI Kuwait
MCT Muscat, Oman
RUH Riyadh, Saudi Arabia
SAH Sana'a, Yemen
THR Tehran, Iran

SOUTH, EAST & SE ASIA
BKI Kota Kinabalu, Malaysia
BKK Bangkok, Thailand
BOM Bombay, India
BWN Bandar Seri Begawan, Brunei
CAN Guangzhou (Canton), China
CCU Calcutta, India
CGK Jakarta, Indonesia
CMB Colombo, Sri Lanka
CNX Chieng Mai, Thailand
CTU Chengdu, China
DAC Dhaka, Bangladesh
DEL Delhi, India
DPS Denpasar, Bali, Indonesia
FNJ Pyongyang, Dem People's Rep of Korea
FUK Fukuoka, Japan
HAN Hanoi, Vietnam
HKG Hong Kong
HKT Phuket, Thailand
HND Tokyo: Haneda, Japan
ISB Islamabad, Pakistan
KBL Kabul, Afghanistan
KCH Kuching, Malaysia
KHH Kaohsiung, Taiwan
KHI Karachi, Pakistan

KIX Kansai, Japan
KTM Kathmandu, Nepal
KUL Kuala Lumpur, Malaysia
LHE Lahore, Pakistan
LXA Lhasa, China
MAA Madras, India
MLE Malé, Maldives
MNL Manila, Philippines
NGO Nagoya, Japan
NRT Tokyo: Narita, Japan
OSA Osaka, Japan
PEK Beijing (Peking), China
PEN Pinang (Penang), Malaysia
PEW Peshawar, Pakistan
PNH Phnom Penh, Cambodia
PUS Pusan, Republic of Korea
RGN Yangon (Rangoon), Myanmar
SEL Seoul, Republic of Korea
SGN Ho Chi Minh City, Vietnam
SHA Shanghai, China
SIN Singapore
TPE Taipei, Taiwan
ULN Ulan Bator, Mongolia
VTE Vientiane, Laos

AUSTRALASIA & PACIFIC
ADL Adelaide, Australia
AKL Auckland, New Zealand
APW Apia, Western Samoa
BNE Brisbane, Australia
CBR Canberra, Australia
CHC Christchurch, New Zealand
CNS Cairns, Australia
DRW Darwin, Australia
GUM Guam
HBA Hobart, Tasmania, Australia
HIR Honiara, Solomon Is
MEL Melbourne, Australia
NAN Nadi, Fiji
NOU Nouméa, New Caledonia
PER Perth, Australia
POM Port Moresby, Papua New Guinea
PPT Papeete, Tahiti, Fr Polynesia
RAR Rarotonga, Cook Is
SYD Sydney, Australia
TBU Tongatapu, Tonga
TSV Townsville, Australia
WLG Wellington, New Zealand

* See next page for other airports in these areas

AIRPORTS

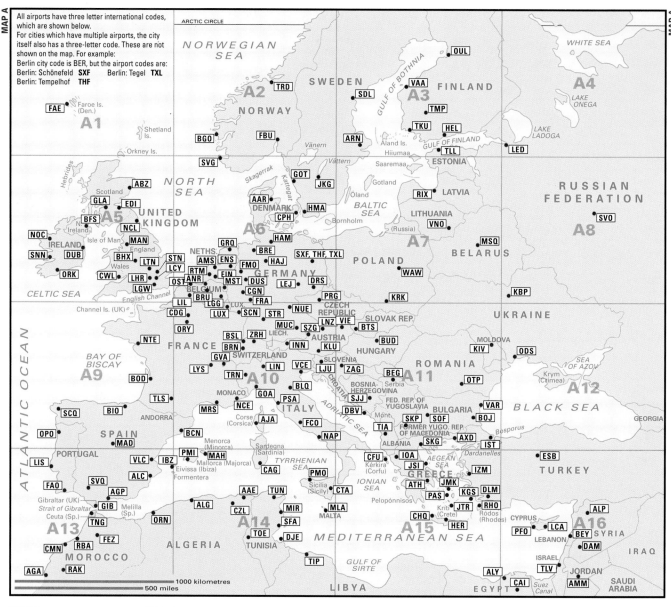

All airports have three letter international codes, which are shown below.
For cities which have multiple airports, the city itself also has a three-letter code. These are not shown on the map. For example:
Berlin city code is BER, but the airport codes are:
Berlin: Schönefeld **SXF**   Berlin: Tegel **TXL**
Berlin: Tempelhof **THF**

EUROPE

AAR	Århus, Denmark
ABZ	Aberdeen, Scotland
AGP	Málaga, Spain
AJA	Ajaccio, France
ALC	Alicante, Spain
AMS	Amsterdam, Netherlands
ANR	Antwerpen (Antwerp), Belgium
ARN	Stockholm, Sweden
ATH	Athína (Athens), Greece
AXD	Alexandroúpoli, Greece
BCN	Barcelona, Spain
BEG	Belgrade, Federal Republic of Yugoslavia
BFS	Belfast, N Ireland
BGO	Bergen, Norway
BHX	Birmingham, England
BIO	Bilbao, Spain
BLQ	Bologna, Italy
BOD	Bordeaux, France
BOJ	Burgas, Bulgaria
BRE	Bremen, Germany
BRN	Bern (Berne), Switzerland
BRU	Bruxelles (Brussel/Brussels), Belgium
BSL	Basel (Basle), Switzerland
BTS	Bratislava, Slovak Republic
BUD	Budapest, Hungary
CAG	Cágliari, Italy
CDG	Paris: Charles de Gaulle, France
CFU	Kérkira (Corfu), Greece
CGN	Köln (Cologne) / Bonn, Germany
CHQ	Haniá (Canea), Greece
CPH	København (Copenhagen), Denmark
CTA	Catánia, Italy
CWL	Cardiff, Wales

DBV	Dubrovnik, Croatia
DLM	Dalaman, Turkey
DRS	Dresden, Germany
DUB	Dublin, Ireland
DUS	Düsseldorf, Germany
EDI	Edinburgh, Scotland
EIN	Eindhoven, Netherlands
ENS	Enschede, Netherlands
ESB	Ankara, Turkey
FAE	Vágar, Faroe Is
FAO	Faro, Portugal
FBU	Oslo, Norway
FCO	Roma (Rome), Italy
FMO	Münster/Osnabrück, Germany
FRA	Frankfurt am Main, Germany
GIB	Gibraltar
GLA	Glasgow, Scotland
GOA	Génova (Genoa), Italy
GOT	Göteborg (Gothenburg), Sweden
GRQ	Groningen, Netherlands
GVA	Genève (Geneva), Switzerland
HAJ	Hannover, Germany
HAM	Hamburg, Germany
HEL	Helsinki, Finland
HER	Iráklio (Herakleion), Greece
HMA	Malmö, Sweden
IBZ	Eivissa (Ibiza), Spain
INN	Innsbruck, Austria
IOA	Ioanina, Greece
IST	Istanbul, Turkey
IZM	Izmir, Turkey
JKG	Jönköping, Sweden
JMK	Míkonos, Greece
JSI	Skiathos, Greece
JTR	Thíra, Greece
KGS	Kós (Cos), Greece

KLU	Klagenfurt, Austria
KRK	Kraków (Cracow), Poland
LCA	Larnaca, Cyprus
LCY	London: City, England
LEJ	Leipzig/Halle, Germany
LGG	Liège, Belgium
LGW	London: Gatwick, England
LHR	London: Heathrow, England
LIL	Lille, France
LIN	Milano (Milan), Italy
LIS	Lisboa (Lisbon), Portugal
LJU	Ljubljana, Slovenia
LNZ	Linz, Austria
LTN	London: Luton, England
LUX	Luxembourg
LYS	Lyon, France
MAD	Madrid, Spain
MAH	Maó (Mahón), Spain
MAN	Manchester, England
MLA	Malta
MRS	Marseille, France
MST	Maastricht, Netherlands
MUC	München (Munich), Germany
NAP	Nápoli (Naples), Italy
NCE	Nice, France
NCL	Newcastle, England
NOC	Knock, Ireland
NTE	Nantes, France
NUE	Nürnberg (Nuremberg), Germany
OPO	Porto (Oporto), Portugal
ORK	Cork, Ireland
ORY	Paris: Orly, France
OST	Oostende (Ostend), Belgium
OTP	Bucharest, Romania
OUL	Oulu, Finland
PAS	Páros, Greece
PFO	Paphos, Cyprus
PMI	Palma de Mallorca, Spain

PMO	Palermo, Italy
PRG	Prague, Czech Republic
PSA	Pisa, Italy
RHO	Ródos (Rhodes), Greece
RTM	Rotterdam, Netherlands
SCN	Saarbrücken, Germany
SCQ	Santiago de Compostela, Spain
SDL	Sundsvall, Sweden
SJJ	Sarajevo, Bosnia-Herzegovina
SKG	Thessaloníki (Salonika), Greece
SKP	Skopje, Former Yugoslav Republic of Macedonia
SNN	Shannon, Ireland
SOF	Sofia, Bulgaria
STN	London: Stansted, England
STR	Stuttgart, Germany
SVG	Stavanger, Norway
SVQ	Sevilla (Seville), Spain
SXF	Berlin: Schönefeld, Germany
SZG	Salzburg, Austria
THF	Berlin: Tempelhof, Germany
TIA	Tirana, Albania
TKU	Turku, Finland
TLS	Toulouse, France
TMP	Tampere, Finland
TRD	Trondheim, Norway
TRN	Torino (Turin), Italy
TXL	Berlin: Tegel, Germany
VAA	Vaasa, Finland
VAR	Varna, Bulgaria
VCE	Venézia (Venice), Italy
VIE	Wien (Vienna), Austria
VLC	Valencia, Spain
WAW	Warsaw, Poland
ZAG	Zagreb, Croatia

ZRH	Zürich, Switzerland

FORMER SOVIET UNION

KBP	Kiev, Ukraine
KIV	Chisinau, Moldova
LED	St Petersburg, Russian Federation
MSQ	Minsk, Belarus
ODS	Odessa, Ukraine
RIX	Riga, Latvia
SVO	Moscow, Russian Fed
TLL	Tallinn, Estonia
VNO	Vilnius, Lithuania

MIDDLE EAST

ALP	Halab (Aleppo), Syria
AMM	Amman, Jordan
BEY	Beirut, Lebanon
DAM	Damascus, Syria
TLV	Tel Aviv-Yafo, Israel

AFRICA

AAE	Annaba, Algeria
AGA	Agadir, Morocco
ALG	Algiers, Algeria
ALY	Alexandria, Egypt
CAI	Cairo, Egypt
CMN	Casablanca, Morocco
CZL	Constantine, Algeria
DJE	Jerba, Tunisia
FEZ	Fès, Morocco
MIR	Monastir, Tunisia
ORN	Oran, Algeria
RAK	Marrakech, Morocco
RBA	Rabat, Morocco
SFA	Sfax, Tunisia
TIP	Tripoli, Libya
TNG	Tanger (Tangiers), Morocco
TOE	Tozeur, Tunisia
TUN	Tunis, Tunisia

FLIGHT TIMES

Average flight times from London, New York and Singapore to other major destinations. Hours do not include stopover time, when necessary, from one destination to another.

Less than 2 hours

2 hours – 4 hours 59 mins

5 hours – 8 hours 59 mins

9 hours – 14 hours 59 mins

15 hours – 24 hours 59 mins

25 hours and over

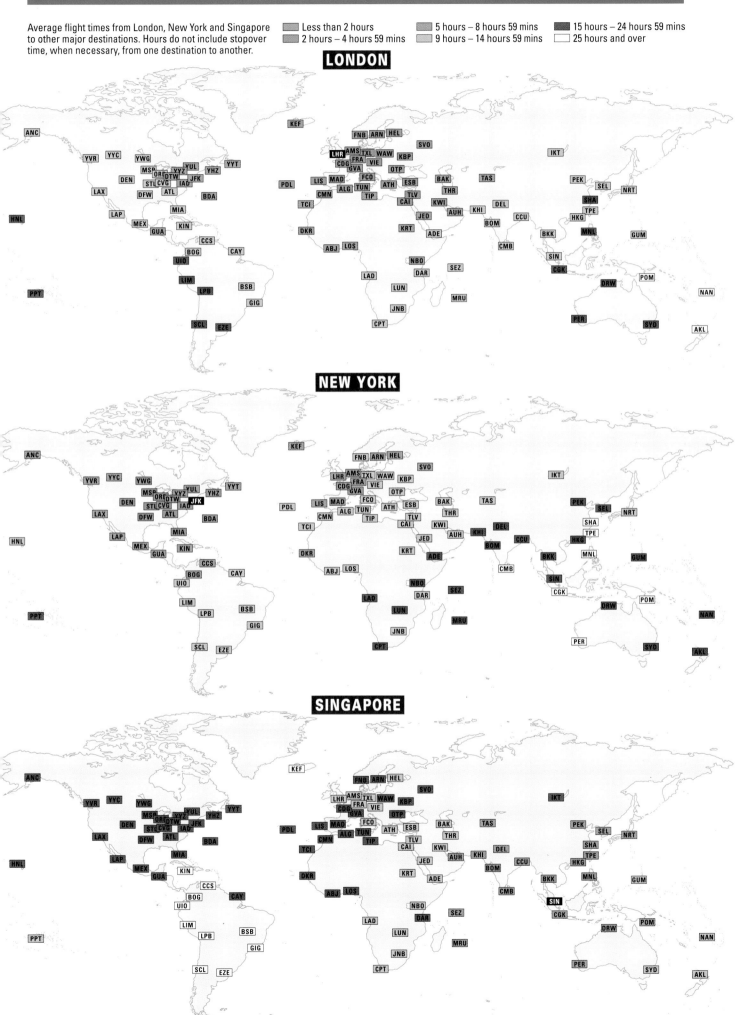

CRUISE ROUTES

Cruising is one of the fastest-growing holiday choices in the world and, as new ships are built and new lines created, there is a continuing search for new ports of call. This map includes ports that are now beginning to be visited for the first time along with those which have featured in cruise brochures for decades.

The map highlights the main cruising areas and also includes ports outside these areas that appear only on the schedules of world cruises.

Some of the places marked are accessable only by tender or, in some cases (notably Antarctica) by zodiac or other powered inflatable boat from the ship which will be anchored offshore.

The 'Round-the-World' cruise routes shown on the map are examples used by some passenger shipping companies. There are considerable variations, but cruise programmes offering 'Round-the-World' trips will call at most of the ports marked. Route variations might be caused due to size of ship, port-berthing facilities, weather conditions at particular times of year or marketing considerations.

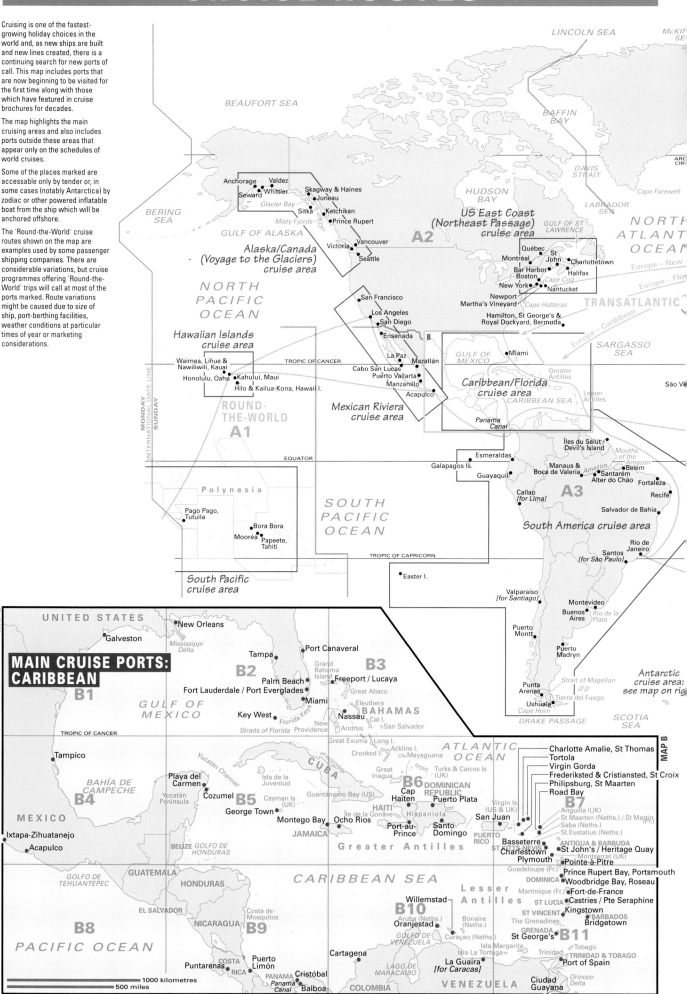

MAIN CRUISE PORTS: CARIBBEAN

CRUISE ROUTES

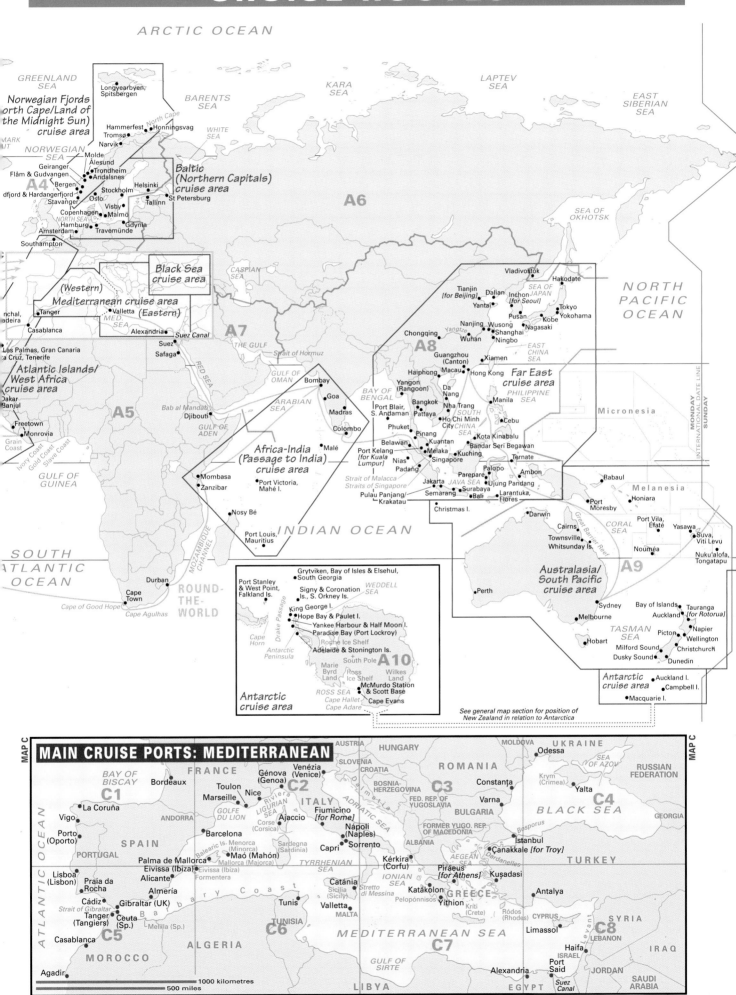

NATURAL HERITAGE

All properties which belong to the *UNESCO World Heritage List* are considered to be of world importance either because of their natural features or their significant man-made contribution to world culture. Sites for consideration of heritage status are submitted by the appropriate government ministry. UNESCO then considers each proposal under strict criteria and designates sites where appropriate.

Some countries are not signatories to the convention, and so the UNESCO list is not fully comprehensive worldwide.

There are two main categories of property: natural and cultural.

Cultural sites.
(i) *Monuments:* including sculptures, memorial stones, obelisks, cave paintings and inscriptions;
(ii) *Groups of buildings:* these can be separated or connected but are usually set in a unique landscape;
(iii) *Sites of anthropological or archaeological importance.*

For further information, contact:

The World Heritage Centre,
UNESCO,
7 place de Fontenoy,
75352 Paris 07-SP,
France.

Tel: +33 1 45 68 10 00.

The World Heritage Committee met in 1994 for its 18th session and added 22 cultural sites to the list. A further three already established have had extensions to their sites recognised.
These are shown below and on the following pages in red.

CANADA & UNITED STATES

1 Kluane National Park, Wrangell-St Elias Parks and Tatshenshini-Alsek Provincial Wilderness Park, Alaska/Yukon
2 Nahanni National Park, NW Territories
3 Wood Buffalo National Park, NW Territories/ Alberta
4 Canadian Rocky Mountains Parks, British Columbia/Alberta
5 Dinosaur Provincial Park, Alberta
6 Gros Morne National Park, Newfoundland
7 Hawaii Volcanoes National Park, Hawaii
8 Olympic National Park, Washington
9 Redwood National Park, California
10 Yosemite National Park, California
11 Grand Canyon National Park, Arizona
12 Yellowstone National Park, Wyoming
13 Mammoth Cave National Park, Kentucky
14 Great Smoky Mountains National Park, Tennessee/North Carolina
15 Everglades National Park, Florida

MEXICO & CENTRAL AMERICA

1 Sian Ka'an Biosphere Reserve, Mexico
2 Tikal National Park, Guatemala
3 Río Platano Biosphere Reserve, Honduras
4 Talamanca Range and La Amistad International Park, Costa Rica/Panama
5 Darien National Park, Panama

SOUTH AMERICA

1 Galapagos Islands National Park
2 Los Katios National Park, Colombia
3 Canaima National Park, Venezuela
4 Sangay National Park, Ecuador
5 Río Abiseo National Park, Peru
6 Huascarán National Park, Peru
7 Manu National Park, Peru
8 Machu Picchu Historic Sanctuary, Peru
9 Serra de Capivara National Park, Brazil
10 Iguaçu National Park, Brazil
11 Iguazu National Park, Argentina
12 Los Glaciares National Park, Argentina

EUROPE (including Atlantic islands)

1 St Kilda, Scotland
2 Giant's Causeway and its coast, N Ireland
3 Mont-St-Michel and its bay, France
4 Paris: banks of the Seine, France
5 Girolata and Porto Gulfs and Scandola Reserve, Corsica, France
6 Doñana National Park, Spain
7 Garajonay National Park, Gomera, Canary Is
8 Skocjan Caves, Slovenia
9 Plitvice Lakes National Park, Croatia
10 Durmitor National Park, Fed Rep of Yugoslavia
11 Kotor and its gulf, Fed Rep of Yugoslavia
12 Ohrid Lake and its region, Former Yugoslav Republic of Macedonia
13 Meteora, Greece
14 Olympia: archaeological site, Greece
15 Mount Athos, Greece
16 Pirin National Park, Bulgaria
17 Srebarna Nature Reserve, Bulgaria
18 Danube Delta, Romania
19 Bialowieza National Park, Poland
20 Hierapolis-Pamukkale, Turkey
21 Göreme National Park and Cappadocia rock sites, Turkey

AFRICA

1 Ichkeul National Park, Tunisia
2 Tassili n'Ajjer, Algeria
3 Bandiagara Cliff: Land of the Dogon, Mali
4 Banc d'Arguin National Park, Mauritania
5 Djoudj National Bird Sanctuary, Sénégal
6 Niokolo-Koba National Park, Sénégal
7 Mount Nimba Strict Nature Reserve, Guinea/ Côte d'Ivoire
8 Comoë National Park, Côte d'Ivoire

NATURAL HERITAGE

A SLOVENIA
B CROATIA
C BOSNIA-HERZEGOVINA
D FEDERAL REPUBLIC OF YUGOSLAVIA
(Serbia & Montenegro)
E FORMER YUGOSLAV
REPUBLIC
OF MACEDONIA

9 Tai National Park, Côte d'Ivoire
10 Aïr-Ténéré Strict Nature Reserve, Niger
11 Simen National Park, Ethiopia
12 Parc national du Manovo-Gounda St Floris, Central African Republic
13 Dja Faunal Reserve, Cameroon
14 Salonga National Park, Zaïre
15 Garamba National Park, Zaïre
16 Virunga National Park, Zaïre
17 Kahuzi-Biega National Park, Zaïre
18 Ruwenzori Mountains National Park, Uganda
19 Bwindi Impenetrable National Park, Uganda
20 Serengeti National Park, Tanzania
21 Ngorongoro Conservation Area, Tanzania
22 Kilimanjaro National Park, Tanzania
23 Selous Game Reserve, Tanzania
24 Lake Malawi National Park, Malawi
25 Victoria Falls and Mosi-oa-Tunya, Zambia/ Zimbabwe
26 Mana Pools National Park and Safi & Chewore safari areas, Zimbabwe
27 Mozambique Island
28 Tsingy Bemaraha Strict Nature Reserve,

Madagascar
29 Aldabra Atoll, Seychelles
30 Vallée de Mai Nature Reserve, Seychelles

MIDDLE EAST
1 Arabian Oryx Sanctuary, Oman

SOUTH, EAST & SE ASIA
1 Sagarmatha National Park, Nepal
2 Chitwan National Park, Nepal
3 Nanda Devi National Park, India
4 Keoladeo National Park, India
5 Manas Wildlife Sanctuary, India
6 Kaziranga National Park, India
7 Sundarbans National Park, India
8 Dambulla Golden Rock Temple, Sri Lanka
9 Sinharaja Forest Reserve, Sri Lanka
10 Taishan, China
11 Huangshan, China
12 Ha Long Bay, Vietnam
13 Sukhothai and its region: historic towns, Thailand
14 Thung Yai-Huai Kha Khaeng Wildlife

Sanctuary, Thailand
15 Ujung Kulon National Park and Krakatau Nature Reserve, Indonesia
16 Komodo National Park, Indonesia

AUSTRALASIA & PACIFIC
1 Shark Bay, Australia
2 Kakadu National Park, Australia
3 Queensland wet tropics, Australia
4 Australian east coast temperate and sub-tropical rainforest parks and central eastern rainforest, Nautralia
5 Great Barrier Reef, Australia
6 Uluru National Park, Australia
7 Fossil mammal sites, Australia
8 Willandra lakes region, Australia
9 Tasmanian wilderness, Australia
10 Lord Howe Island group, Australia
11 Tongariro National Park, New Zealand
12 Westland and Mt Cook National Parks, New Zealand
13 Fjordland National Park, New Zealand
14 Henderson Island, to UK

CULTURAL HERITAGE

All properties which belong to the *UNESCO World Heritage List* are considered to be of world importance either because of their natural features or their significant man-made contribution to world culture. Sites for consideration of heritage status are submitted by the appropriate government ministry. UNESCO then considers each proposal under strict criteria and designates sites where appropriate.

Some countries are not signatories to the convention, and so the UNESCO list is not fully comprehensive worldwide.

There are two main categories of property: natural and cultural.

Cultural sites.
(i) *Monuments:* including sculptures, memorial stones, obelisks, cave paintings and inscriptions;
(ii) *Groups of buildings:* these can be separated or connected but are usually set in a unique landscape;
(iii) *Sites of anthropological or archaeological importance.*

For further information, contact:

The World Heritage Centre, UNESCO, 7 place de Fontenoy, 75352 Paris 07-SP, France.

Tel: +33 1 45 68 10 00.

The World Heritage Committee met in 1994 for its 18th session and added 22 cultural sites to the list. A further three already established have had extensions to their sites recognised. These are shown below and on the following pages in red.

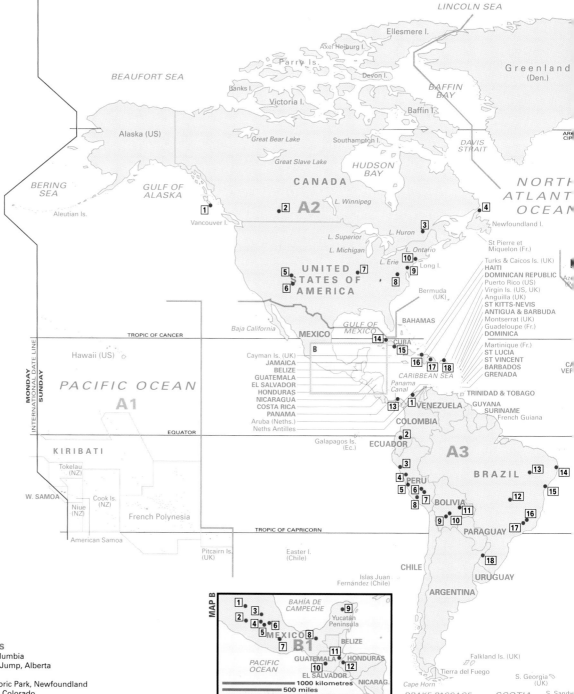

CANADA & UNITED STATES
1 Anthony Island, British Columbia
2 Head-Smashed-In Buffalo Jump, Alberta
3 Québec: historic area
4 L'Anse aux Meadows Historic Park, Newfoundland
5 Mesa Verde National Park, Colorado
6 Chaco Culture National Historical Park, New Mexico
7 Cahokia Mounds State Historic Site, Illinois
8 Charlottesville: Monticello and University of Virginia, Virginia
9 Philadelphia: Independence Hall, Pennsylvania
10 Statue of Liberty, New Jersey

MEXICO, CENTRAL AMERICA & CARIBBEAN
1 Guanajuato: historic town and adjacent mines, Mexico
2 Morelia: historic centre, Mexico
3 Teotihuacan: pre-Hispanic city, Mexico
4 Mexico City: historic centre and Xochimilco, Mexico
5 Popocatepetl: monasteries, Mexico
6 Puebla: historic centre, Mexico
7 Oaxaca: historic centre and Monte Alban: archaeological site, Mexico
8 Palenque: pre-Hispanic city and national park, Mexico
9 Chichén-Itzá: pre-Hispanic city, Mexico
10 Antigua, Guatemala
11 Quirigua: archaeological park & ruins, Guatemala
12 Copán: Maya site, Honduras
13 Portobelo and San Lorenzo: fortifications, Panama
14 Havana: old town and its fortifications, Cuba
15 Trinidad and Valley de los Ingenios, Cuba

16 Citadel, Sans-Souci and Ramiers Historic Park, Haiti
17 Santo Domingo: colonial city, Dominican Rep
18 La Fortaleza and San Juan: historic site, Puerto Rico

SOUTH AMERICA
1 Cartagena: port, fortress and monuments, Colombia
2 Quito: old city, Ecuador
3 Chan Chan: archaeological area, Peru
4 Chavin: archaeological site, Peru
5 Lima: historic centre, Peru
6 Machu Picchu Historic Sanctuary, Peru
7 Cuzco: old city, Peru
8 Nazca: geoglyphs, Peru
9 Potosí: mining town, Bolivia
10 Sucre: historic city, Bolivia
11 Chiquitos Jesuit missions, Bolivia
12 Brasília, Brazil
13 Serra de Capivara National Park, Brazil
14 Olinda: historic centre, Brazil
15 Salvador de Bahia: historic centre, Brazil
16 Ouro Preto: historic town, Brazil
17 Congonhas: Sanctuary of Bom Jesus, Brazil
18 Sao Miguel das Missoes: Jesuit mission ruins,

Brazil and Guarani Jesuit missions of San Ignacio Mini, Santa Ana, Nuestra Señora de Loreto & Santa Maria Mayor, Argentina

EUROPE* (including Atlantic islands)
1 Angra do Heroismo: central area, Azores
2 Alta: rock drawings, Norway

FORMER SOVIET UNION*
1 Kutaisi: Bagrati Cathedral and Gelati Monastery, Georgia
2 Itchan Kala, Uzbekistan

AFRICA*
1 Thebes: ancient city and its necropolis, Egypt
2 Abu Simbel to Philae: Nubian monuments, Egypt
3 Aksum: archaeological site, Ethiopia
4 Fasil Ghebbi & Gondar monuments, Ethiopia
5 Lalibela: rock-hewn churches, Ethiopia
6 Awash Lower Valley, Ethiopia
7 Tiya: carved steles, Ethiopia
8 Omo Lower Valley, Ethiopia
9 Tadrart Acacus: rock-art sites, Libya
10 Tassili n'Ajjer, Algeria
11 Timbuktu, Mali
12 Djenné: old towns, Mali

CULTURAL HERITAGE

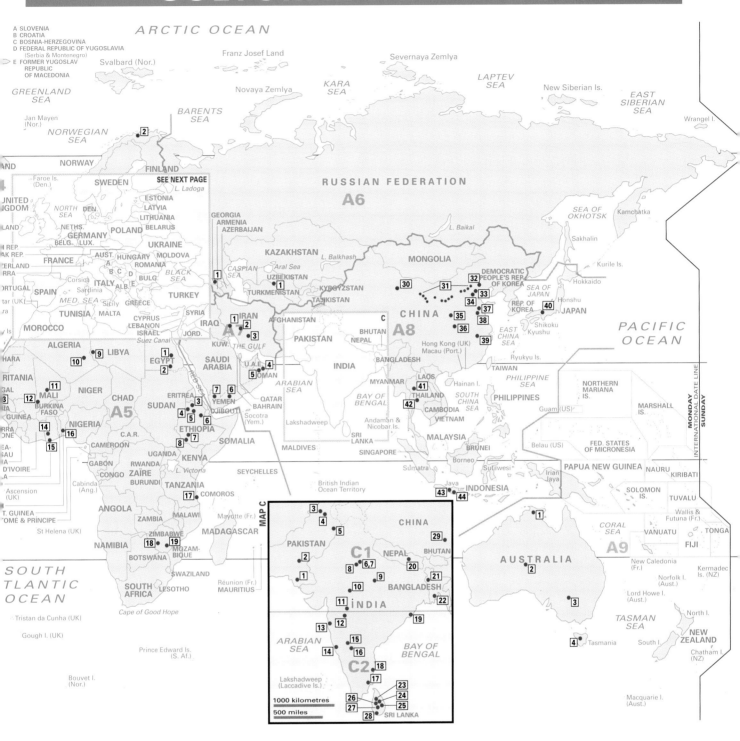

13 Gorée Island, Sénégal
14 Ashante traditional buildings, Ghana
15 Accra and Volta areas: forts & castles, Ghana
16 Abomey: royal palaces, Benin
17 Kilwa Kisiwani and Songo Mnara: ruins, Tanzania
18 Khami Ruins National Monument, Zimbabwe
19 Great Zimbabwe National Monument, Zimbabwe

MIDDLE EAST*
1 Tchogha Zambil, Iran
2 Esfahan (Isfahan): Meidam Emam, Iran
3 Persepolis: ancient city, Iran
4 Bat, Al-Khutm and Al-Ayn: archaeolgical sites, Oman
5 Bahla: fort, Oman
6 Shibam: old walled city, Yemen
7 Sana'a: old city, Yemen

SOUTH, EAST & SE ASIA
1 Thatta: historical monuments, Pakistan
2 Mohendojaro: archaeological site, Pakistan
3 Takht-i-Bakhi: Buddhist ruins & Sahr-i-Bahlol: remains of city, Pakistan
4 Taxila: archaeological site, Pakistan
5 Lahore: fort and Shalimar Gardens, Pakistan
6 Agra Fort, India

7 Taj Mahal, Agra, India
8 Fatehpur Sikri: Mongol city, India
9 Khajuraho: group of monuments, India
10 Sanchi: Buddhist monuments, India
11 Ajanta Caves, India
12 Ellora Caves, India
13 Elephanta Caves, India
14 Goa: churches and convents, India
15 Pattadakal: group of monuments, India
16 Hampi: group of monuments, India
17 Thanjavur: Brihadisvara Temple, India
18 Mahabalipuram: group of monuments, India
19 Konarak: Sun Temple, India
20 Kathmandu Valley, Nepal
21 Paharpur: ruins of the Buddhist Vihara, Bangladesh
22 Bagerhat: historic mosque city, Bangladesh
23 Anuradhapura: sacred city, Sri Lanka
24 Sigiriya: ancient city, Sri Lanka
25 Polonnaruwa: ancient city, Sri Lanka
26 Dambulla Golden Rock Temple, Sri Lanka
27 Kandy: sacred city, Sri Lanka
28 Galle: old town and its fortifications, Sri Lanka
29 Lhasa: Potala Palace, Tibet, China
30 Mogao Caves, Dunhuang, China
31 Great Wall, China

32 Chengde: mountain resort and outlying temples, China
33 Beijing (Peking): Imperial Palace of the Ming and Qing Dynasties, China
34 Zhoukoudian: Peking Man site, China
35 Xi'an area: Mausoleum of the first Qin Emperor, China
36 Wudang Mountains: ancient building complex, China
37 Taishan, China
38 Qufu: temple and cemetery of Confucius and Kong family mansion, China
39 Huangshan, China
40 Kyoto: historic monuments of ancient city, Japan
41 Sukhothai & its region: historic towns, Thailand
42 Ayutthaya & its region: historic towns, Thailand
43 Borobudur: temple compound, Indonesia
44 Prambanan: temple compound, Indonesia

AUSTRALASIA & PACIFIC
1 Kakadu National Park, Australia
2 Uluru National Park, Australia
3 Willandra Lakes Region, Australia
4 Tasmanian Wilderness, Australia

* See next page for other sites in these areas

CULTURAL HERITAGE

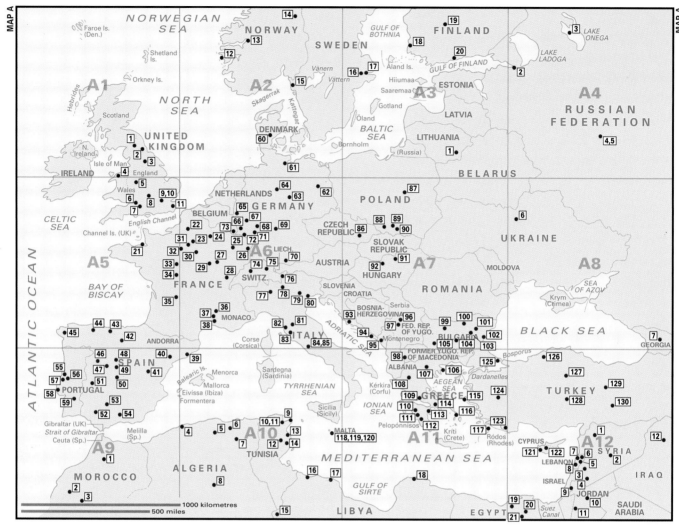

The World Heritage Committee met in 1994 for its 18th session and added 22 cultural sites to the list. A further three already established have had extensions to their sites recognised. These are shown below and on the previous pages in red.

EUROPE

1 Hadrian's Wall, England
2 Durham: castle and cathedral, England
3 Studley Royal Park and ruins of Fountains Abbey, England
4 Gwynedd: castles and town walls of King Edward, Wales
5 Ironbridge Gorge, England
6 Bath, England
7 Stonehenge, Avebury & associated megalithic sites, England
8 Blenheim Palace, England
9 London: Tower of London, England
10 London: Westminster Palace and Abbey and St Margaret's Church, England
11 Canterbury: cathedral, St Augustine's Abbey and St Martin's Church, England
12 Bergen: Bryggen area, Norway
13 Urnes: stave church, Norway
14 Røros: mining town, Norway
15 Tanum: rock carvings, Sweden
16 Drottningholm Palace, Sweden
17 Stockholm: Skogskyrkogarden, Sweden
18 Rauma: old town, Finland
19 Petäjävesi: old church, Finland
20 Helsinki: Suomenlinna Fortress, Finland
21 Mont-St-Michel and its bay, France
22 Amiens: cathedral, France
23 Paris: banks of the Seine, France
24 Reims: Notre-Dame Cathedral, former Abbey of St-Remi and Tau Palace, France
25 Nancy: Place Stanislas, Place de la Carrière and Place d'Alliance, France
26 Strasbourg: Grand Île, France
27 Fontenay: Cistercian abbey, France
28 Arc-et-Senans: royal salt works, France
29 Vézelay: basilica and hill, France
30 Fontainebleau: palace and park, France
31 Versailles: palace and park, France
32 Chartres: cathedral, France
33 Chambord: château and estate, France
34 St-Savin-sur-Gartempe: church, France
35 Vézère Valley: decorated grottoes, France
36 Orange: Roman theatre and its surroundings and triumphal arch, France
37 Pont du Gard: Roman aqueduct, France
38 Arles: Roman and Romanesque monuments, France
39 Barcelona: Parque & Palacio Güell and Casa Milá, Spain
40 Poblet: monastery, Spain
41 Teruel: Mujedar architecture, Spain
42 Burgos: cathedral, Spain
43 Altamira Cave, Spain
44 Asturias: churches of the Asturias Kingdom, Spain

45 Santiago de Compostela: old town, Spain
46 Salamanca: old city, Spain
47 Ávila: old town with its extra-muros churches, Spain
48 Segovia: old town and aqueduct, Spain
49 El Escorial: monastery, Spain
50 Toledo: historic city, Spain
51 Cáceres: old town, Spain
52 Sevilla (Seville): cathedral, alcazar and Archivo de Indias, Spain
53 Córdoba: mosque and historic centre, Spain
54 Granada: Alhambra, Generalife and Albaicin quarter, Spain
55 Batalha: monastery, Portugal
56 Tomar: Convent of Christ, Portugal
57 Alcobaça monastery, Portugal
58 Lisboa (Lisbon): Monastery of the Hieronymites and Tower of Belém , Portugal
59 Évora: historic centre, Portugal
60 Jelling: mounds, runic stones and church, Denmark
61 Lübeck: Hanseatic city, Germany
62 Berlin & Potsdam: palaces and parks, Germany
63 Quedlinburg: Collegiate church, castle and old town, Germany
64 Hildesheim: St Mary's Cathedral and St Michael's Church, Germany
65 Aachen: cathedral, Germany
66 Trier: Roman monuments, cathedral and Liebfrauen Church, Germany
67 Brühl: Augustusburg and Falkenlust Castles, Germany
68 Lorsch: abbey and Altenmünster, Germany
69 Würzburg: Residence with the Court Gardens and Residence Square, Germany
70 Wies: pilgrimage church, Germany
71 Speyer: cathedral, Germany
72 Volklingen: ironworks, Germany
73 Luxembourg-Ville: old quarters and fortifications
74 Bern (Berne): old city, Switzerland
75 St Gallen: convent, Switzerland
76 Müstair: Benedictine Convent of St John, Switzerland
77 Milano (Milan): Church and Dominican Convent of Santa Maria delle Grazie with "The Last Supper" by L. da Vinci, Italy
78 Val Camónica: rock drawings, Italy
79 Vicenza, Italy
80 Venézia (Venice) and its lagoon, Italy
81 Firenze (Florence): historic centre, Italy
82 Pisa: Piazza del Duomo, Italy
83 San Gimignano: historic centre, Italy
84 Roma (Rome): historic centre, including extraterritorial properties of the Holy See and San Paolo fuori le Mura, Italy
85 Vatican City
86 Zelená Hora: St John of Nepomuk, Czech Republic
87 Warsaw: historic centre, Poland
88 Auschwitz: concentration camp, Poland
89 Kraków (Cracow): historic centre, Poland
90 Wieliczka: salt mine, Poland
91 Hollokö: traditional village, Hungary
92 Budapest: banks of Danube and Buda Castle area, Hungary
93 Split: historic centre with Diocletian Palace, Croatia

94 Dubrovnik: old city, Croatia
95 Kotor and its gulf, Federal Republic of Yugoslavia
96 Studenica: monastery, Federal Republic of Yugoslavia
97 Stari Ras and Sopocani, Federal Republic of Yugoslavia
98 Ohrid Lake and its region, Former Yugoslav Republic of Macedonia
99 Boyana: church, Bulgaria
100 Svechtari: Thracian tomb, Bulgaria
101 Madara Rider, Bulgaria
102 Nessebar: ancient city, Bulgaria
103 Ivanovo: rock-hewn churches, Bulgaria
104 Kazanlák: Thracian tomb, Bulgaria
105 Rila: monastery, Bulgaria
106 Mount Áthos, Greece
107 Thessaloniki (Salonika): Palaeochristian and Byzantine monuments, Greece
108 Metéora, Greece
109 Delphi: archaeological site, Greece
110 Olympia: archaeological site, Greece
111 Bassáe: Temple of Apollo Epicurius, Greece
112 Mistras, Greece
113 Epidaurus: archaeological site, Greece
114 Athina (Athens): Acropolis, Greece
115 Hios (Chios): Daphni, Hossios, Luckas and Néa Moni monasteries, Greece
116 Dilos, Greece
117 Ródos (Rhodes): mediaeval city, Greece
118 Hal Saflieni Hypogeum, Malta
119 Valletta: old city, Malta
120 Ggantija: temples, Malta
121 Paphos: archaeological site, Cyprus
122 Troödos region: painted churches, Cyprus
123 Xanthos-Letoon, Turkey
124 Hierapolis-Pamukkale, Turkey
125 Istanbul: historic areas, Turkey
126 Safranbolu, Turkey
127 Hattusha: Hittite city, Turkey
128 Göreme National Park and Cappadocia rock sites, Turkey
129 Divrigi: Great Mosque and hospital, Turkey
130 Nemrut Dag: archaeological site, Turkey

FORMER SOVIET UNION

1 Vilnius: old city, Lithuania
2 St Petersburg: historic centre and related monuments, Russian Federation
3 Khizi Pogost, Russian Federation
4 Moscow: Kremlin and Red Square, Russian Federation
5 Moscow: Church of the Ascension at Kolomenskoye, Russian Federation
6 Kiev: St Sophia Cathedral, related monastic buildings and Lavra of Kiev-Pechersk, Ukraine
7 Kutaisi: Bagrati Cathedral and Gelati Monastery, Georgia

AFRICA

1 Fès: medina, Morocco

BENELUX

BELGIAN COAST

Knokke-Heist
Zeebrugge
Blankenberge
Wenduine
De Haan
Bredene-aan-Zee
Oostende (Ostend)
Westende-Bad
Lombardsijde-Bad
Nieuwpoort-aan-Zee
Oostduinkerke-Bad
Koksijde-Bad
de Sint-Idesbald
Panne Veurne
Middelkirke-Bad
Gistel
Loppem
Torhout
Diksmuide
Tielt
Brugge (Bruges)
Kanaal van Gent naar Oostende
NETHS.
MAP C
C1
C2
WEST VLAANDEREN
FR.

20 kilometres
10 miles

MAP B

SCHIERMONNIKOOG
AMELAND
TERSCHELLING
Eemshaven
Uithuizen
Emden
Delfzijl
B4 GRONINGEN
Dokkum
Marssum
Leeuwarden
Groningen
EELDE
Hoogezand
VLIELAND
B3 Harlingen
Bolsward
FRIESLAND
Assen
TEXEL
Sneek
Heerenveen
DRENTHE
Den Helder
Stavoren
WIERINGER-MEER
IJSSELMEER
NOORDOOST POLDER
Havelte
Emmen
Hoogeveen
Coevorden
Broek op Langedijk
Enkhuizen
Emmeloord
Giethoorn
Meppel
Wanneperveen
Alkmaar
Hoorn
MARKER-WAARD
Kampen
Zwolle
Ommen
Nordhorn
Edam
Volendam
Lelystad
FLEVOLAND
OVERIJSSEL
NOORD-HOLLAND
Zaandam
MARKEN
Almelo
TWENTE
Noordzee Kanaal
AMSTERDAM
Almere
Harderwijk
Deventer
Hengelo
B8
B5
B6
B7
Haarlem
SCHIPHOL
Muiden
Naarden
Hilversum
Apeldoorn
Enschede
Zandvoort
Amstelveen
Soestdijk
GELDERLAND
Zutphen
Keukenhof
Lisse
Aalsmeer
Baarn
Amersfoort
Noordwijk aan Zee
Katwijk aan Zee
Wassenaar
Leiden
Utrecht
NATIONAAL PARK DE HOGE VELUWE
1944
Scheveningen
Boskoop
Madurodam
UTRECHT
Oosterbeek, 1944
Arnhem
Winterswijk
Den Haag ('s-Gravenhage, The Hague)
Delft
Gouda
Oudewater
Lek
Hoek van Holland (Hook of Holland)
Ter Heijde
ZESTIENHOVEN
Rotterdam
NETHERLANDS
Bocholt
Europoort
Schiedam
Kinderdijk
Gorinchem
1944
Nijmegen
Dorsten
VOORNE
Zwijndrecht
Waal
GOEREE
Dordrecht
Grave, 1944
Xanten
Bottrop
PUTTEN
Kaatsheuvel
Gelsenkirchen
HOEKSE WAARD
's-Hertogenbosch
Overloon
B12
Oberhausen
Essen
SCHOUWEN
OVERFLAKKEE
Sprookjespark De Efteling
NOORD-BRABANT
DUIVELAND
Breda
Moers
Krefeld
Roosendaal
Tilburg
Helmond
Duisburg
NOORD BEVELAND
THOLEN
B10
B11
Hilvarenbeek
Veere
Middelburg
ZUID BEVELAND
Bergen op Zoom
Eindhoven
Venlo
Düsseldorf
Neuss
Vlissingen (Flushing)
WALCHEREN
WELSCHAP
Turnhout
Roermond
Solingen
Breskens
Mönchengladbach
Zeebrugge
IJzendijke
Terneuzen
Bree
Oostende (Ostend)
Brugge (Bruges)
OOST VLAANDEREN
Antwerpen (Antwerp)
DEURNE
Köln (Cologne)
Nieuwpoort
Biervliet
Herentals
LIMBURG
Veurne
WEST VLAANDEREN
Lier
Geelen
Heerlen
Dunkerque
Gent (Gand, Ghent)
Laarne
Mechelen
Genk
Valkenburg
Düren
BONN
FLANDERS
Passendale, 1917
Aalst
BELGIUM
Leuven
Hasselt
Maastricht
BEEK
Aachen (Aix-la-Chapelle)
Poperinge
1914 & 1915
Zonnebeke, 1915 & 1917
Oudenaarde
Tienen
BRABANT
St-Omer
Ieper (Ypres)
Kortrijk
BRUXELLES (BRUSSEL, BRUSSELS)
ZAVENTEM
BIERSET
Liège
GERMANY
Tourcoing
B14
Rixensart
B15
B16
B13
Lille
Roubaix
Ath
Attre
Waterloo, 1815
Nivelles
Húy
Verviers
Spa
Béthune
Tournai
Beloeil
GOSSELIES
Namur
Modave
Château de Reinhardstein
Amblève
Lens
Douai
Le Rœulx
Mons
Charleroi
Profondeville
MEUSE VALLEY
Sankt Vith
St-Pol-sur-Ternoise
Valenciennes
Annevoie
Godinne
Spontin
Hotton
Gerolstein
Arras
Maubeuge
Yvoir 1944
Dinant
Marche-en-Famenne
Doullens
Cambrai
Rochefort
La Roche-en-Ardenne
Clervaux
ARDENNES
Albert
FRANCE
Oise
Hirson
Bohan
Han-sur-Lesse
1944
Wiltz
Vianden
Bitburg
Amiens
B17
Rochehaut
LUXEMBOURG B19
Bastogne
Esch-sur-Sûre
Bourscheid
Echternach
Royle
St-Quentin
Vervins
Rocroi
Rochehaut
Bouillon
Neufchâteau
Diekirch
Beaufort
Larochette
Mosel
B18
Charleville-Mézières
Sedan
Arlon
Mersch
LUXEMBOURG
Trier
Florenville
Steinsel
FINDEL
province capital
battlefield (with date)
Chauny
Laon
Noyon
Rethel
Stenay
Longuyon
Abbaye-d'Orval
Virton
Semois
Meuse
Esch-sur-Alzette
LUXEMBOURG-VILLE
Remich
Mondorf-les-Bains
Land tints: below sea level, 0-200m, over 200m

100 kilometres
50 miles

NORTH SEA
B9
HAINAUT
Sambre
Escaut
Scheldo
Armentières
Lille
Ourthe
Sûre
NAMUR

2 Marrakech: medina, Morocco
3 Aït Benhaddou: fortified village, Morocco
4 Tipasa: archaeological site, Algeria
5 Beni Hammad: Al Qal'a, Algeria
6 Djemila: Roman ruins, Algeria
7 Timgad: Roman ruins, Algeria
8 M'Zab Valley, Algeria
9 Kerkuane: Punic town and its necropolis, Tunisia
10 Tunis: medina, Tunisia
11 Carthage: archaeological site, Tunisia
12 Kairouan, Tunisia
13 Sousse: medina, Tunisia
14 El Jem: amphitheatre, Tunisia
15 Ghadamès: old town, Libya

16 Sabratha: archaeological site, Libya
17 Leptis Magna: archaeological site, Libya
18 Cyrene: archaeological site, Libya
19 Abu Mena: Christian ruins, Egypt
20 Cairo: Islamic city, Egypt
21 Memphis: Pyramid fields from Giza to Dahshur and its necropolis, Egypt

MIDDLE EAST
1 Halab: ancient city of Aleppo, Syria
2 Tadmur: archaeological site of Palmyra, Syria
3 Damascus: ancient city, Syria
4 Bosra: ancient city, Syria
5 Anjar: archaeological site, Lebanon

6 Baalbek, Lebanon
7 Byblos, Lebanon
8 Soûr: archaeological site of Tyre, Lebanon
9 Jerusalem: old city and its walls, Jordan
10 Qasr Amra, Jordan
11 Petra, Jordan
12 Hatra, Jordan

UNITED KINGDOM

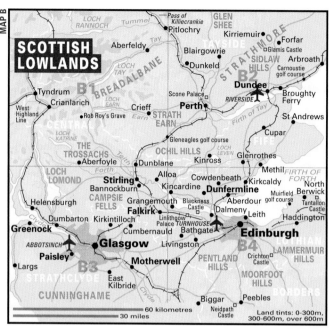

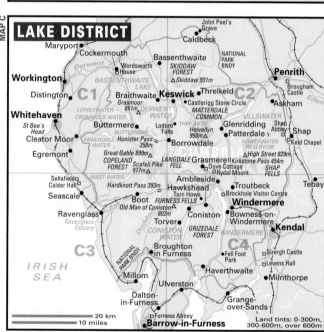

UK HERITAGE

Since 1895 *The National Trust* has worked for the preservation of places of historic interest or natural beauty in England, Wales and Northern Ireland. Under the National Trust Act of 1907 it is empowered to declare its land and buildings inalienable, which means they cannot be sold or mortgaged. The Trust, which is a charity, is the largest private landowner and conservation society in Britain. Many National Trust properties are under the guardianship of English Heritage and Cadw: Welsh Historic Monuments.

For further information, contact:

The National Trust,
36 Queen Anne's Gate,
London SW1H 9AS.

Tel. +44 (0) 171 222 9251.

The National Trust for Scotland was founded in 1931 with similar aims to The National Trust. It presently has more than 100 properties in its care.

For further information, contact:

The National Trust for Scotland,
5 Charlotte Square,
Edinburgh EH2 4DU.

Tel. +44 (0) 131 243 9501.

English Heritage was founded in 1984 to protect some of England's most important historic buildings and archaeological sites.

For further information, contact:

English Heritage,
429 Oxford Street,
London W1R 2HD.

Tel. +44 (0) 171 973 3396.

Historic Scotland maintains over 300 monuments and properties on behalf of the Secretary of State for Scotland.

For further information, contact:

Friends of Historic Scotland,
Room 214,
20 Brandon Street,
Edinburgh EH3 5RA.

Tel. +44 (0) 131 244 3099.

Cadw: Welsh Historic Monuments, founded in 1984, looks after 131 monuments from prehistoric sites to medieval fortresses to early industrial monuments, all of which are in the care of the Secretary of State for Wales.

For further information, contact:

Cadw: Welsh Historic Monuments,
Brunel House,
2 Fitzalan Road,
Cardiff CF2 1UY.

Tel. +44 (0) 1222 465511.

◼ The National Trust
☐ The National Trust for Scotland
◼ English Heritage
☐ Historic Scotland
☐ Cadw: Welsh Historic Monuments

This map shows a selection of the major buildings, monuments and gardens open to the public, all of which are open for at least six months of the year. Most properties shown charge admission.

Ten of the most beautiful expanses of country in England and Wales have been given the status of *National Park* by Parliament in recognition of their scenic importance and use for open-air recreation.

For further information, contact:

The Countryside Commission,
John Dower House,
Crescent Place,
Cheltenham,
Gloucestershire GL50 3RA.

Tel. +44 (0) 1242 521381.

Scotland
☐ 1 Skara Brae stone age house
☐ 2 Maes Howe tomb
☐ 3 Urquhart Castle
☐ 4 Fort George
☐ 5 Dallas Dhu Distillery
☐ 6 Elgin Cathedral
☐ 7 Huntly Castle
☐ 8 Arbroath Abbey
☐ 9 Huntingtower Castle
☐ 10 St Andrews Cathedral and Castle
☐ 11 Dunfermline Palace and Abbey
☐ 12 Castle Campbell
☐ 13 Stirling Castle
☐ 14 Dumbarton Castle
☐ 15 Arduaine Garden
☐ 16 Rothesay Castle
☐ 17 Brodick Castle, Garden and Country Park
☐ 18 Culzean Castle and Country Park
☐ 19 Bothwell Castle, Uddingston
☐ 20 Linlithgow Palace
☐ 21 Edinburgh Castle
☐ 22 Craigmillar Castle
☐ 23 Dirleton Castle and Garden
☐ 24 Melrose Abbey
☐ 25 Dryburgh Abbey
☐ 26 Jedburgh Abbey
☐ 27 Caerlaverock Castle
☐ 28 New Abbey Corn Mill
☐ 29 Threave Garden and estate

Northumbria
◼ 30 Berwick-upon-Tweed Castle
◼ 31 Lindisfarne Castle
◼ 32 Cragside House, Garden and grounds
◼ 33 Hadrian's Wall, Housesteads Museum and Fort
◼ 34 Cherryburn, Mickley
◼ 35 Gibside Chapel and grounds
◼ 36 Souter Lighthouse
◼ 37 Washington Old Hall
◼ 38 Hylton Castle
◼ 39 Guisborough Priory
◼ 40 Egglestone Abbey
◼ 41 Barnard Castle
◼ 42 Bowes Castle

Cumbria
◼ 43 Acorn Bank Garden
◼ 44 Beatrix Potter's Lake District multi-media show
◼ 45 Wordsworth House
◼ 46 Hawkshead Courthouse
◼ 47 Stagshaw Garden

Yorkshire & Humberside
☐ 48 Rievaulx Abbey
◼ 49 Rievaulx Terrace and Temples
◼ 50 York: Treasurer's House
◼ 51 Skipsea Castle
◼ 52 Maister House
◼ 53 Thornton Abbey

North West
◼ 54 Warton Old Rectory
◼ 55 Salley Abbey
◼ 56 Whalley Abbey Gatehouse
◼ 57 Speke Hall
◼ 58 Chester Roman Ampitheatre
◼ 59 Tatton Park
◼ 60 Quarry Bank Mill and Styal Country Park

East Midlands
◼ 61 Peveril Castle
◼ 62 Winster Market House
◼ 63 Sutton Scarsdale Hall
◼ 64 Bolsover Castle
◼ 65 Mattersey Priory
◼ 66 Clumber Park
◼ 67 Rufford Abbey
◼ 68 Lincoln: Bishop's Palace
◼ 69 Tattershall Castle
◼ 70 Bolingbroke Castle
◼ 71 Ashby de la Zouch Castle
◼ 72 Kirby Muxloe Castle
◼ 73 Leicester: Jewry Hall
◼ 74 Lyddington Bede House
◼ 75 Lyveden New Bield
◼ 76 Geddington: Eleanor Cross

Heart of England
◼ 77 Croxden Abbey
◼ 78 Shugborough Estate
◼ 79 Letocetum baths and museum
◼ 80 Old Oswestry Hill Fort
◼ 81 Lilleshall Abbey
◼ 82 Acton Burnell Castle
◼ 83 Clun Castle
◼ 84 Bantock House Museum
◼ 85 Kenilworth Castle
◼ 86 Charlecote Park
◼ 87 Kinwarton Dovecote
◼ 88 Fleece Inn
◼ 89 Hawford Dovecote
◼ 90 Berrington Hall
◼ 91 Longtown Castle
◼ 92 Kempley: St Mary's Church
◼ 93 Deerhurst: Odda's Chapel
◼ 94 Hailes Abbey
◼ 95 Hidcote Manor Garden

East Anglia
◼ 96 Creake Abbey
◼ 97 Horsey Windpump
◼ 98 Great Yarmouth: 4 South Quay
◼ 99 King's Lynn: St George's Guildhall
◼ 100 Oxburgh Hall
◼ 101 Leiston Abbey

◼ 102 Framlingham Castle
◼ 103 Lavenham Guildhall
◼ 104 Bury St Edmunds: Theatre Royal
◼ 105 Moulton Packhorse Bridge
◼ 106 Isleham Priory Church
◼ 107 Ramsey Abbey Gatehouse
◼ 108 Anglesey Abbey and garden
◼ 109 Colchester: St Botolph's Priory
◼ 110 Hadleigh Castle
◼ 111 Waltham Abbey Gatehouse and Bridge
◼ 112 St Alban's Roman Wall
◼ 113 Berkhamsted Castle

London
◼ 114 Kenwood: The Iveagh Bequest
◼ 115 Chiswick House
◼ 116 Southwark: George Inn
◼ 117 Westminster: Jewel Tower

South East
◼ 118 Claremont Garden
◼ 119 Farnham Castle Keep
◼ 120 Waverley Abbey
◼ 121 Ightham Mote
◼ 122 Old Soar Manor
◼ 123 Deal Castle
◼ 124 Walmer Castle and Gardens
◼ 125 Dover Castle
◼ 126 Smallhythe Place
◼ 127 Bodiam Castle
◼ 128 Battle Abbey and site of Battle of Hastings
◼ 129 Pevensey Castle
◼ 130 Alfriston Clergy House
◼ 131 Bateman's
◼ 132 Standen House
◼ 133 Wakehurst Palace Garden
◼ 134 Nymans Garden
◼ 135 Petworth House
◼ 136 Uppark

Central Southern England
◼ 137 Pitstone Windmill
◼ 138 Long Crendon Courthouse
◼ 139 Hughenden Manor
◼ 140 Cliveden
◼ 141 Deddington Castle
◼ 142 Great Coxwell Barn
◼ 143 Uffington Castle
◼ 144 Donnington Castle
◼ 145 The Vyne
◼ 146 Northington: The Grange
◼ 147 Winchester City Mill
◼ 148 Wolvesley: Old Bishop's Palace
◼ 149 Netley Abbey
◼ 150 Titchfield Abbey
◼ 151 Bembridge Windmill
◼ 152 Osborne House
◼ 153 Carisbrook Castle
◼ 154 Yarmouth Castle
◼ 155 The Needles Old Battery
◼ 156 Christchurch Castle and Norman House
◼ 157 Knowlton Church and Earthworks

West Country
◼ 158 Abbotsbury Abbey
◼ 159 Thomas Hardy's Cottage
◼ 160 Avebury
◼ 161 Lacock Abbey and Fox Talbot Museum
◼ 162 The Courts garden
◼ 163 Stourhead Garden
◼ 164* Salisbury: Mompesson House
◼ 165 Horton Court
◼ 166 Bath Assembly Rooms
◼ 167 Clevedon Court
◼ 168 King John's Hunting Lodge
◼ 169 Montacute House
◼ 170 Stoke-sub-Hamdon Priory
◼ 171 Dunster Castle
◼ 172 Dunster Watermill
◼ 173 Watersmeet House
◼ 174 Knightshayes Court
◼ 175 Loughwood Meeting House
◼ 176 A la Ronde house
◼ 177 Killerton house and garden
◼ 178 Castle Drogo
◼ 179 Buckland Abbey
◼ 180 Saltram
◼ 181 Wembury: The Old Mill
◼ 182 Overbecks Museum and garden
◼ 183 Cotehele house and mill
◼ 184 Tintagel Old Post Office
◼ 185 Lanhydrock House and garden
◼ 186 Pendennis Castle
◼ 187 Halliggye Fogou tunnel
◼ 188 St Michael's Mount

Wales
◼ 189 Erddig House
◼ 190 Chirk Castle
☐ 191 Conwy Castle
◼ 192 Bodnant Garden
☐ 193 Beaumaris Castle
◼ 194 Plas Newydd house
◼ 195 Penrhyn Castle
◼ 196 Segontium Fort
☐ 197 Caernarfon Castle
☐ 198 Plas-yn-Rhiw house and garden
◼ 199 Ty Mawr Wybrnant
◼ 200 Powis Castle
☐ 201 Skenfrith Castle
☐ 202 Raglan Castle
☐ 203 Tintern Abbey
☐ 204 Chepstow Castle
☐ 205 Caerphilly Castle
☐ 206 Carreg Cennen Castle
☐ 207 Dinefwr Park
☐ 208 Colby Woodland Garden

Northern Ireland
◼ 209 Rowallane Garden

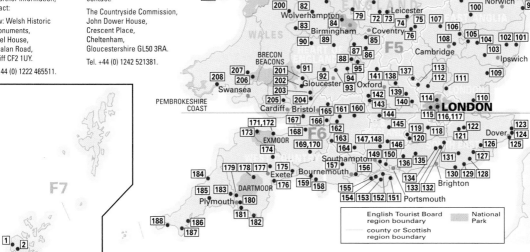

English Tourist Board region boundary		National Park
county or Scottish region boundary		

UK BEACHES

The *European Blue Flag Campaign* is an environmental awareness raising activity of the Foundation for Environmental Education in Europe (Feee).

To qualify for a Blue Flag, a beach has to fulfill a number of strict criteria regarding water quality (compliance with the EU Bathing Water Directive), environment, education and information, beach area management and safety. The Blue Flag is awarded annually and is valid for one year.

On 16th May 1994 the Campaign jury awarded Blue Flags to 17 beaches in the UK.

For further information, contact:

Tidy Britain Group,
Lion House,
26 Muspole Street,
Norwich NR3 1DJ.

Tel. +44 (0) 1603 762888.

The *Seaside Award* is awarded annually by the Tidy Britain Group to resort and rural beaches in the UK and the Channel Islands.

Resort beaches: busy beaches in or close to towns are assessed on 29 criteria including general cleanliness, water quality, safety provisions, beach facilities and provision for the disabled.

Rural beaches: situated in more remote locations, are assessed on 13 key points but are not expected to maintain the same standard of supervision or facilities as resort beaches.

If the water quality of an award beach complies with the EU Bathing Water Directive, it qualifies for the *Premier Seaside Award*.

165 beaches qualified for the *Seaside Award* for 1994, with 65 achieving the Premier standard.

Legend

- ● European Blue Flag
- ● Premier Seaside Award (resort)
- ● Premier Seaside Award (rural)
- ○ Seaside Award (resort)
- ○ Seaside Award (rural)

Scotland
- 1 Troon South
- 2 Nairn Central
- 3 Sandend
- 4 Inverboyndie
- 5 Fraserburgh
- 6 Cruden Bay
- 7 Balmedie
- 8 St Andrews West
- 9 Kingsbarns
- 10 Elie
- 11 Aberdour: Silver Sands
- 12 Gullane Bents

Northumbria
- 13 Bamburgh
- 14 Beadnell Bay
- 15 Low Newton
- 16 Warkworth
- 17 Amble Links
- 18 Tynemouth: Cullercoats
- 19 Tynemouth: Longsands South

Yorkshire & Humberside
- 20 Runswick Bay
- 21 Sandsend
- 22 Whitby: West Cliff
- 23 Robin Hood's Bay
- 24 Scarborough: North Bay
- 25 Scarborough: South Bay
- 26 Filey
- 27 Flamborough: South Landing
- 28 Bridlington: North
- 29 Bridlington: South

East Anglia
- 30 Snettisham
- 31 Hunstanton
- 32 Wells-next-the-Sea
- 33 Mundesley
- 34 Lowestoft South
- 35 Kessingland
- 36 Southwold
- 37 Dunwich
- 38 Aldeburgh
- 39 Shoeburyness East
- 40 Southend: Three Shells
- 41 Southend: Leigh Bell Wharf

South East
- 42 Sheerness: Beach Street
- 43 Sheerness: Minster Leas
- 44 Birchington: Minnis Bay
- 45 Margate
- 46 Broadstairs: Viking Bay
- 47 Dymchurch
- 48 Romney Sands near Littlestone & Greatstone
- 49 Camber
- 50 Winchelsea
- 51 Bexhill
- 52 Pevensey Bay
- 53 Eastbourne (pier to Wishtower)
- 54 Birling Gap
- 55 Littlehampton
- 56 Bognor Regis
- 57 West Wittering

Central Southern England
- 58 Hayling Island West
- 59 Hill Head (near Fareham)
- 60 Lepe Country Park
- 61 Christchurch: Friars Cliff
- 62 Christchurch: Highcliffe Castle
- 63 Bournemouth: Fisherman's Walk
- 64 Bournemouth: Durley
- 65 Poole: Sandbanks

Isle of Wight
- 66 Colwell Bay
- 67 Gurnard
- 68 Cowes
- 69 East Cowes
- 70 Ryde West
- 71 Ryde East
- 72 Springvale
- 73 St Helens Duver
- 74 Yaverland
- 75 Sandown
- 76 Shanklin

West Country
- 77 Weymouth Central
- 78 Dawlish Warren
- 79 Dawlish: Coryton Cove
- 80 Teignmouth: Main Beach
- 81 Shaldon: Ness Cove
- 82 Torbay: Maidencombe
- 83 Torbay: Watcombe
- 84 Torbay: Oddicombe
- 85 Torbay: Redgate
- 86 Torbay: Meadfoot
- 87 Torbay: Corbyn Head
- 88 Torbay: Paignton
- 89 Torbay: Goodrington's Sands
- 90 Torbay: Broadsands
- 91 Torbay: Elberry Cove
- 92 Torbay: Churston Cove
- 93 Dartmouth: Strete Gate
- 94 Blackpool Sands
- 95 Torcross
- 96 Inner Hope: Hope Cove
- 97 Outer Hope: Mouthwell
- 98 Thurlestone: South Milton Sands
- 99 Bantham
- 100 Bigbury-on-Sea: Challaborough
- 101 Crinnis
- 102 Sennen Cove
- 103 Porthmeor
- 104 St Merryn: Treyarnon
- 105 St Merryn: Constantine Bay
- 106 St Merryn: Harlyn Bay
- 107 Polzeath
- 108 Bude: Widemouth Sand
- 109 Bude: Crooklets
- 110 Bude: Sandymouth
- 111 Woolacombe

Wales
- 112 Southerndown
- 113 Oxwych Bay
- 114 Cefn Sidan Pembrey Country Park
- 115 Saundersfoot: Amroth
- 116 Saundersfoot: Wiseman's Bridge
- 117 Saundersfoot: Coppet Hall
- 118 Tenby North
- 119 Tenby South
- 120 Lydstep Bay
- 121 Skrinkle
- 122 Manorbier
- 123 Freshwater East
- 124 Barafundle
- 125 Broadhaven South
- 126 West Angle Bay
- 127 Dale
- 128 Milford Haven: Marloes
- 129 Haverfordwest: Broad Haven
- 130 Nolton Haven
- 131 Newgale
- 132 St David's: Caerfai
- 133 St David's: Whitesands
- 134 Abereiddy
- 135 Pwllgwaelod
- 136 Fishguard: Cym-yr-Eglwys
- 137 Aberporth: Traeth y Dyffryn
- 138 St Dogmaels: Poppit
- 139 Mwnt
- 140 Tresaith
- 141 Penbryn
- 142 Cwmtydu
- 143 Llangrannog
- 144 New Quay: Traethgwyn
- 145 New Quay: Traeth Harbwr
- 146 New Quay: Traeth cei Bach
- 147 Aberaeron: Traeth y De
- 148 Gilfach yr Halen
- 149 Aberystwyth: Traeth y Gogledd
- 150 Borth
- 151 Llandanwg
- 152 Dinas Dinlle (near Caernarfon)

Anglesey
- 153 Llanddwyn
- 154 Rhosneigr: Traeth Crigyll
- 155 Rhoscolyn: Borth Wen
- 156 Trearddur Bay
- 157 Holyhead: Porth Dafarch
- 158 Benllech
- 159 Llanddona

Northern Ireland
- 160 Benone
- 161 Portrush: West Bay Strand
- 162 Cranfield Bay

Channel Islands
Guernsey
- 163 Vazon Bay, Cobo
- 164 Port Soif
- 165 Pembroke / L'Ancresse

Thurso

WESTERN ISLES

A1

HIGHLAND

Inverness

GRAMPIAN

Aberdeen

SCOTLAND

A2

TAYSIDE
Dundee
Perth

Oban

FIFE

CENTRAL

Glasgow

Edinburgh

LOTHIAN

STRATHCLYDE

Ayr

BORDERS

A3

DUMFRIES AND GALLOWAY

NORTHUMBERLAND

Newcastle upon Tyne   TYNE & WEAR

Carlisle

CUMBRIA

DURHAM
Middlesbrough   CLEVELAND

NORTH YORKSHIRE

Leeds   York   HUMBERSIDE

Kingston upon Hull

LANCASHIRE

W YORKS

MERSEYSIDE
GTR MANCHESTER   S YORKS
Liverpool   Manchester
Sheffield

A4

CHESHIRE

CLWYD
Stoke-on-Trent

DERBYSHIRE

NOTTINGHAMSHIRE
Derby   Nottingham

LINCOLNSHIRE

GWYNEDD

STAFFORDSHIRE

SHROPSHIRE

NORFOLK

Norwich

Wolverhampton   LEICESTERSHIRE
W MIDLANDS   Leicester
Birmingham

A5

WARWICKSHIRE

POWYS   HEREFORD AND WORCESTER

NORTHAMPTONSHIRE

CAMBRIDGESHIRE

Coventry

DYFED

EAST ANGLIA

SUFFOLK

Cambridge

Ipswich

BEDFORDSHIRE

Gloucester

OXFORDSHIRE

GLOUCESTERSHIRE   Oxford

BUCKINGHAMSHIRE   HERTFORDSHIRE

ESSEX

Swansea   W GLAMORGAN
MID GLAMORGAN   Cardiff

S GLAMORGAN

Bristol

LONDON

GTR LONDON

AVON   Bath   WILTSHIRE   BERKSHIRE   KENT

Dover

A6

SOMERSET

HAMPSHIRE   SURREY

Southampton   W SUSSEX   E SUSSEX
Portsmouth   Brighton

DEVON

DORSET

Exeter

Bournemouth

CORNWALL   Plymouth

ISLES OF SCILLY

ISLE OF WIGHT

IRELAND

NORTHERN IRELAND

Londonderry
LONDONDERRY

ANTRIM

TYRONE

FERMANAGH   Belfast

ARMAGH   DOWN

ISLE OF MAN

SHETLAND

A7

ORKNEY

Thurso

GUERNSEY

JERSEY   FRANCE

CHANNEL ISLANDS

A8

English Tourist Board region boundary
county or Scottish region boundary

UK FERRIES

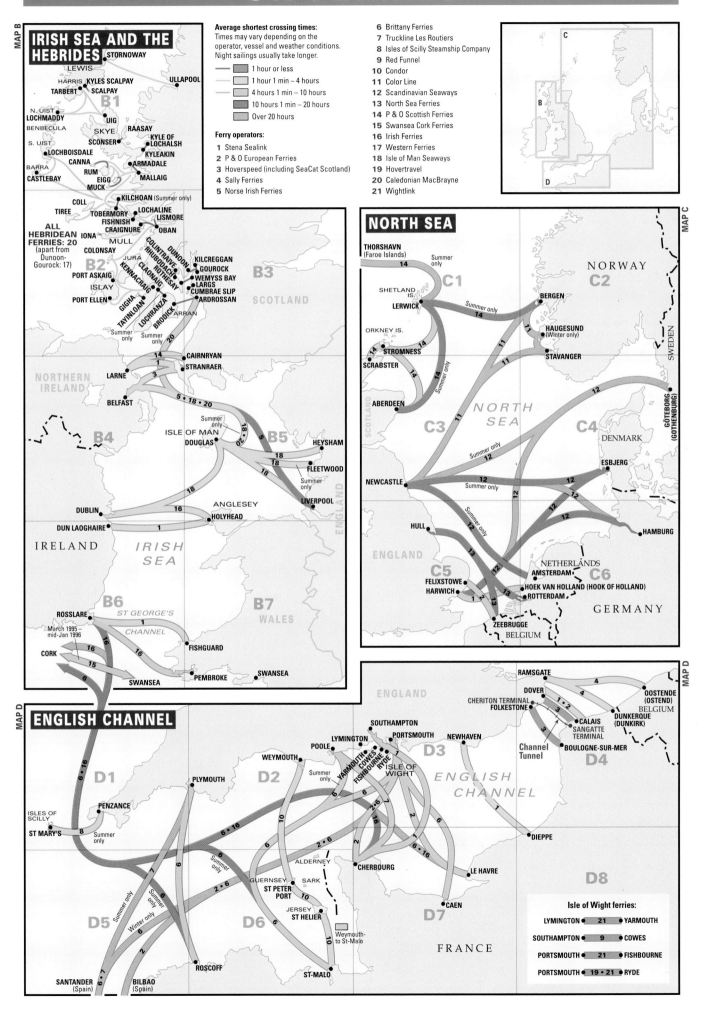

IRISH SEA AND THE HEBRIDES

Average shortest crossing times:
Times may vary depending on the operator, vessel and weather conditions. Night sailings usually take longer.

- 1 hour or less
- 1 hour 1 min – 4 hours
- 4 hours 1 min – 10 hours
- 10 hours 1 min – 20 hours
- Over 20 hours

Ferry operators:
1 Stena Sealink
2 P & O European Ferries
3 Hoverspeed (including SeaCat Scotland)
4 Sally Ferries
5 Norse Irish Ferries
6 Brittany Ferries
7 Truckline Les Routiers
8 Isles of Scilly Steamship Company
9 Red Funnel
10 Condor
11 Color Line
12 Scandinavian Seaways
13 North Sea Ferries
14 P & O Scottish Ferries
15 Swansea Cork Ferries
16 Irish Ferries
17 Western Ferries
18 Isle of Man Seaways
19 Hovertravel
20 Caledonian MacBrayne
21 Wightlink

NORTH SEA

ENGLISH CHANNEL

Isle of Wight ferries:

LYMINGTON ●—21—● YARMOUTH		
SOUTHAMPTON ●—9—● COWES		
PORTSMOUTH ●—21—● FISHBOURNE		
PORTSMOUTH ●—19 · 21—● RYDE		

UK AIRPORTS

This map lists international destinations available on *scheduled* passenger flights from UK airports. Domestic routes within the UK (England, Wales, Scotland and Northern Ireland) have not been included, but flights to the Isle of Man and the Channel Islands are shown.

Routes listed are those licensed for operation during 1995 and do not reflect periods of operation or frequency. In addition, commercial or other considerations may result in services being suspended or withdrawn at short notice. Please check with the appropriate airport and/or airline to confirm all details of service.

For London airports, see opposite page.

All airports have three letter international codes, which are shown here. For cities which have multiple airports, the city itself also has a three letter code. These are not listed here. For example:
London city code is LON, but the airport codes are:

London: Biggin Hill	**BQH**
London: City	**LCY**
London: Gatwick	**LGW**
London: Heathrow	**LHR**
London: Luton	**LTN**
London: Stansted	**STN**

ABZ Aberdeen
Flights to five destinations

Denmark: Esbjerg	EBJ
Germany: Frankfurt-a-Main	FRA
Netherlands: Amsterdam	AMS
Norway: Bergen	BGO
Norway: Stavanger	SVG

EDI Edinburgh
Flights to eight destinations

Belgium: Brussels	BRU
Channel Islands: Jersey	JER
France: Paris	CDG
Germany: Düsseldorf	DUS
Germany: Munich	MUC
Ireland: Dublin	DUB
Netherlands: Amsterdam	AMS
Switzerland: Zürich	ZRH

GLA Glasgow
Flights to 17 destinations

Canada: Toronto	YYZ
Channel Islands: Jersey	JER
Denmark: Copenhagen	CPH
France: Paris	CDG
Germany: Düsseldorf	DUS
Germany: Frankfurt-a-Main	FRA
Germany: Hannover	HAJ
Iceland: Reykjavik	KEF
Ireland: Donegal	CFN
Ireland: Dublin	DUB
Ireland: Londonderry	LDY
Isle of Man	IOM
Malta	MLA
Netherlands: Amsterdam	AMS
USA: New York	JFK/LGA
USA: Washington	IAD

PIK Prestwick
Flights to one destination

Ireland: Dublin	DUB

NCL Newcastle
Flights to 11 destinations

Belgium: Brussels	BRU
Channel Islands: Guernsey	GCI
Channel Islands: Jersey	JER
France: Paris	CDG
Germany: Düsseldorf	DUS
Germany: Frankfurt-a-Main	FRA
Ireland: Dublin	DUB
Netherlands: Amsterdam	AMS
Norway: Bergen	BGO
Norway: Oslo	FBU
Norway: Stavanger	SVG

MME Teesside
Flights to two destinations

Channel Islands: Jersey	JER
Netherlands: Amsterdam	AMS

HUY Humberside
Flights to two destinations

Belgium: Brussels	BRU
Netherlands: Amsterdam	AMS

MAN Manchester
Flights to 64 destinations

Australia: Melbourne	MEL
Australia: Sydney	SYD
Austria: Vienna	VIE
Belgium: Brussels	BRU
Canada: Toronto	YYZ
Channel Islands: Guernsey	GCI
Channel Islands: Jersey	JER
Cyprus: Larnaca	LCA
Cyprus: Paphos	PFO
Czech Republic: Prague	PRG
Denmark: Copenhagen	CPH
Denmark: Billund	BLL
Egypt: Cairo	CAI
Finland: Helsinki	HEL
France: Bordeaux	BOD
France: Lille	LIL
France: Lyon	LYS
France: Nantes	NTE
France: Nice	NCE
France: Paris	CDG
Germany: Düsseldorf	DUS
Germany: Frankfurt-a-Main	FRA
Germany: Hamburg	HAM
Germany: Hannover	HAJ
Germany: Munich	MUC
Germany: Stuttgart	STR
Gibraltar	GIB
Greece: Athens	ATH
Hong Kong	HKG
Ireland: Cork	ORK
Ireland: Dublin	DUB
Ireland: Kerry	KIR
Ireland: Knock	NOC
Ireland: Londonderry	LDY
Ireland: Shannon	SNN
Ireland: Waterford	WAT
Isle of Man	IOM
Israel: Tel Aviv-Yafo	TLV
Italy: Milan	LIN
Italy: Rome	FCO
Malta	MLA
Netherlands: Amsterdam	AMS
Netherlands: Maastricht	MST
Netherlands: Rotterdam	RTM
Norway: Oslo	FBU
Oman: Muscat	MCT
Pakistan: Islamabad	ISB
Romania: Bucharest	OTP
Russian Fed: Moscow	SVO
Singapore	SIN
Spain: Barcelona	BCN
Spain: Madrid	MAD
Sweden: Stockholm	ARN
Switzerland: Geneva	GVA
Switzerland: Zürich	ZRH
Turkey: Istanbul	IST
UAE: Abu Dhabi	AUH
UAE: Dubai	DBX
USA: Atlanta	ATL
USA: Boston	BOS
USA: Chicago	CHI
USA: Dallas	DFW
USA: New York	JFK
Uzbekistan: Tashkent	TAS

LBA Leeds / Bradford
Flights to five destinations

Belgium: Brussels	BRU
France: Paris	CDG
Ireland: Dublin	DUB
Isle of Man	IOM
Netherlands: Amsterdam	AMS

BLK Blackpool
Flights to one destination

Isle of Man	IOM

LPL Liverpool
Flights to three destinations

Channel Islands: Jersey	JER
Ireland: Dublin	DUB
Isle of Man	IOM

EMA East Midlands
Flights to seven destinations

Belgium: Brussels	BRU
Channel Islands: Guernsey	GCI
Channel Islands: Jersey	JER
France: Paris	CDG
Germany: Düsseldorf	DUS
Ireland: Dublin	DUB
Netherlands: Amsterdam	AMS

BHX Birmingham
Flights to 27 destinations

Belgium: Brussels	BRU
Channel Islands: Guernsey	GCI
Channel Islands: Jersey	JER
Cyprus: Larnaca	LCA
Cyprus: Paphos	PFO
Denmark: Copenhagen	CPH
Denmark: Billund	BLL
France: Lyon	LYS
France: Paris	CDG
Germany: Düsseldorf	DUS
Germany: Frankfurt-a-Main	FRA
Germany: Hamburg	HAM
Germany: Hannover	HAJ
Germany: Munich	MUC
Germany: Stuttgart	STR
Ireland: Cork	ORK
Ireland: Dublin	DUB
Isle of Man	IOM
Italy: Milan	LIN
Netherlands: Amsterdam	AMS
Netherlands: Eindhoven	EIN
Netherlands: Rotterdam	RTM
Spain: Barcelona	BCN
Spain: Málaga	AGP
Switzerland: Basel	BSL
Switzerland: Zürich	ZRH
USA: New York	JFK

BHX Coventry
Flights to two destinations

Channel Islands: Jersey	JER
Ireland: Waterford	WAT

NWI Norwich
Flights to two destinations

Netherlands: Amsterdam	AMS
Spain: Alicante	ALC

CBG Cambridge
Flights to one destination

Netherlands: Amsterdam	AMS

GLO Gloucester
Flights to one destination

Ireland: Dublin	DUB

BRS Bristol
Flights to eight destinations

Belgium: Brussels	BRU
Channel Islands: Guernsey	GCI
Channel Islands: Jersey	JER
France: Paris	CDG
Germany: Frankfurt-a-Main	FRA
Ireland: Cork	ORK
Ireland: Dublin	DUB
Netherlands: Amsterdam	AMS

SOU Southampton
Flights to ten destinations

Belgium: Brussels	BRU
Channel Islands: Alderney	ACI
Channel Islands: Guernsey	GCI
Channel Islands: Jersey	JER
France: Caen	CFR
France: Cherbourg	CER
France: Paris	CDG
Ireland: Dublin	DUB
Isle of Man	IOM
Netherlands: Amsterdam	AMS

BOH Bournemouth
Flights to four destinations

Belgium: Brussels	BRU
France: Paris	CDG
Ireland: Dublin	DUB
Netherlands: Amsterdam	AMS

EXT Exeter
Flights to eight destinations

Belgium: Brussels	BRU
Channel Islands: Guernsey	GCI
Channel Islands: Jersey	JER
France: Paris	CDG
Ireland: Cork	ORK
Ireland: Dublin	DUB
Isle of Man	IOM
Netherlands: Amsterdam	AMS

PLH Plymouth
Flights to three destinations

Channel Islands: Guernsey	GCI
Channel Islands: Jersey	JER
Ireland: Cork	ORK

CWL Cardiff
Flights to six destinations

Belgium: Brussels	BRU
Channel Islands: Guernsey	GCI
Channel Islands: Jersey	JER
France: Paris	CDG
Ireland: Dublin	DUB
Netherlands: Amsterdam	AMS

BFS Belfast International
Flights to one destination

Netherlands: Amsterdam	AMS

BHD Belfast City
Flights to two destinations

Channel Islands: Guernsey	GCI
Isle of Man	IOM

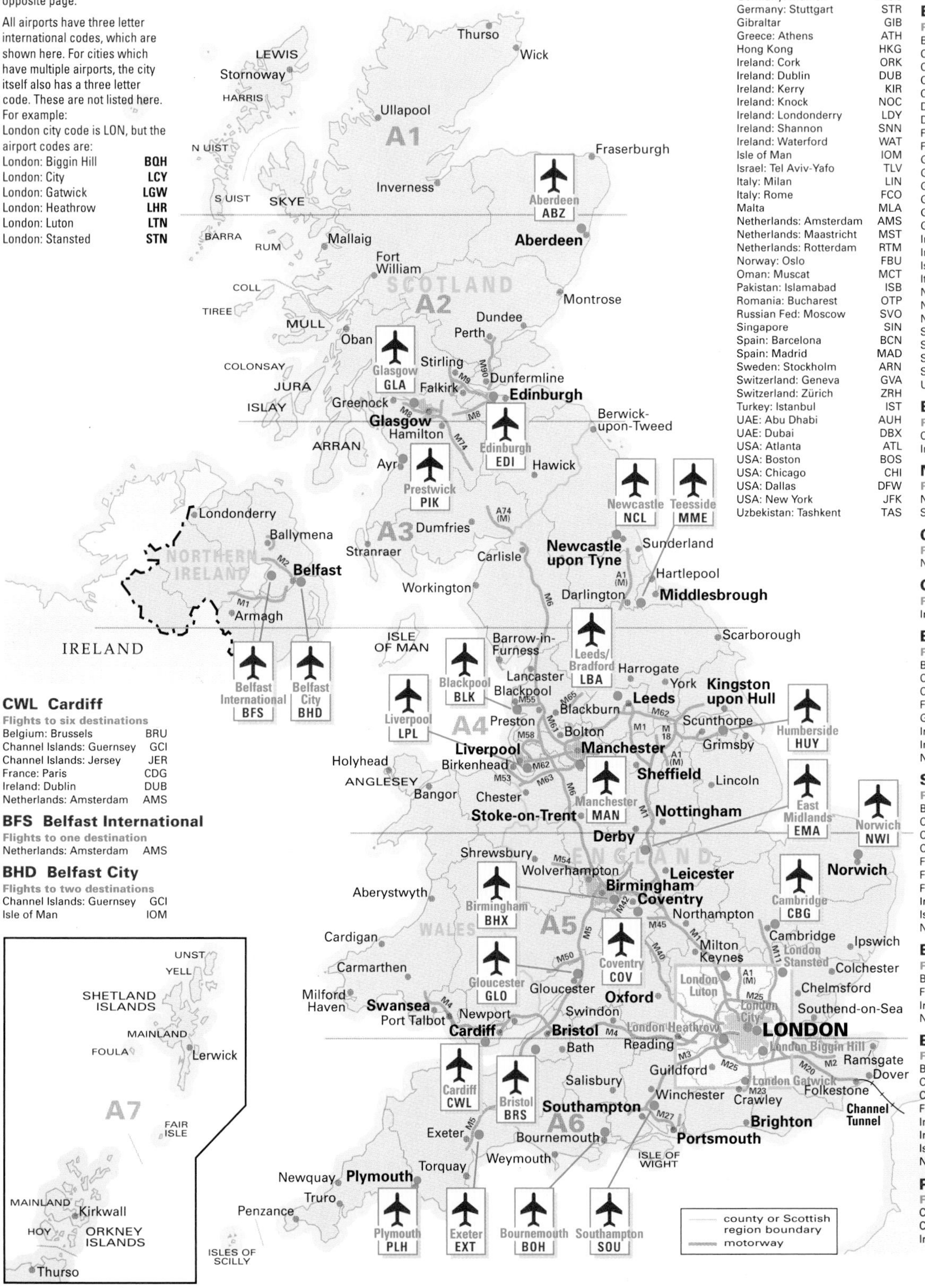
Thurso
Wick
LEWIS
Stornoway
HARRIS
Ullapool
A1
N UIST
Fraserburgh
Inverness
Aberdeen
ABZ
S UIST
SKYE
BARRA
RUM
Mallaig
Aberdeen
Fort William
SCOTLAND
COLL
A2
Montrose
TIREE
Dundee
MULL
Perth
Oban
Glasgow
GLA
COLONSAY
Stirling
JURA
Dunfermline
Falkirk
Edinburgh
ISLAY
Greenock
Glasgow
Hamilton
Berwick-upon-Tweed
ARRAN
Edinburgh
EDI
Ayr
Prestwick
PIK
Hawick
Newcastle
NCL
Teesside
MME
Londonderry
Ballymena
Dumfries
A3
NORTHERN IRELAND
Belfast
Stranraer
Carlisle
Newcastle upon Tyne
Sunderland
Hartlepool
Workington
Darlington
Middlesbrough
Armagh
IRELAND
ISLE OF MAN
Barrow-in-Furness
Leeds/Bradford
LBA
Scarborough
Belfast International
BFS
Belfast City
BHD
Blackpool
BLK
Lancaster
Harrogate
York
Kingston upon Hull
Blackpool
Leeds
Liverpool
LPL
A4
Preston
Blackburn
Scunthorpe
Humberside
HUY
Bolton
Grimsby
Liverpool
Manchester
Holyhead
Birkenhead
Sheffield
ANGLESEY
Lincoln
Bangor
Chester
Manchester
MAN
East Midlands
EMA
Norwich
NWI
Stoke-on-Trent
Nottingham
Derby
Shrewsbury
ENGLAND
Wolverhampton
Leicester
Norwich
Birmingham
Coventry
Aberystwyth
Birmingham
BHX
Cambridge
CBG
Northampton
WALES
A5
Cardigan
Coventry
COV
Cambridge
Ipswich
Milton Keynes
London Stansted
Carmarthen
Colchester
Gloucester
GLO
Gloucester
London Luton
Chelmsford
Milford Haven
Oxford
Swansea
London City
Southend-on-Sea
Port Talbot
Newport
Swindon
London Heathrow
LONDON
Cardiff
Bristol
Bath
Reading
London Biggin Hill
Ramsgate
Guildford
London Gatwick
Dover
Cardiff
CWL
Bristol
BRS
Salisbury
Folkestone
Winchester
Crawley
Southampton
Channel Tunnel
A6
Brighton
Exeter
Bournemouth
Portsmouth
ISLE OF WIGHT
Weymouth
Torquay
Newquay
Plymouth
Truro
Penzance
ISLES OF SCILLY
Plymouth
PLH
Exeter
EXT
Bournemouth
BOH
Southampton
SOU
county or Scottish region boundary
motorway
UNST
YELL
SHETLAND ISLANDS
MAINLAND
FOULA
Lerwick
A7
FAIR ISLE
MAINLAND
Kirkwall
HOY
ORKNEY ISLANDS
Thurso

LONDON AIRPORTS

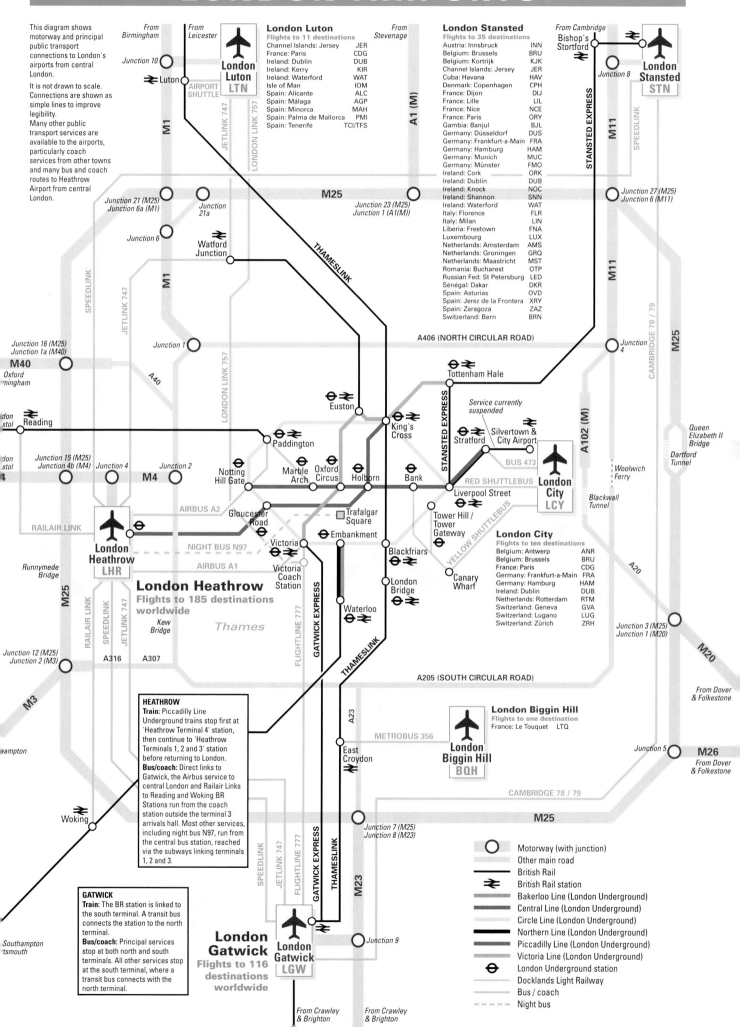

This diagram shows motorway and principal public transport connections to London's airports from central London.

It is not drawn to scale. Connections are shown as simple lines to improve legibility.

Many other public transport services are available to the airports, particularly coach services from other towns and many bus and coach routes to Heathrow Airport from central London.

London Luton
Flights to 11 destinations

Channel Islands: Jersey	JER
France: Paris	CDG
Ireland: Dublin	DUB
Ireland: Kerry	KIR
Ireland: Waterford	WAT
Isle of Man	IOM
Spain: Alicante	ALC
Spain: Málaga	AGP
Spain: Minorca	MAH
Spain: Palma de Mallorca	PMI
Spain: Tenerife	TCI/TFS

London Stansted
Flights to 35 destinations

Austria: Innsbruck	INN
Belgium: Brussels	BRU
Belgium: Kortrijk	KJK
Channel Islands: Jersey	JER
Cuba: Havana	HAV
Denmark: Copenhagen	CPH
France: Dijon	DIJ
France: Lille	LIL
France: Nice	NCE
France: Paris	ORY
Gambia: Banjul	BJL
Germany: Düsseldorf	DUS
Germany: Frankfurt-a-Main	FRA
Germany: Hamburg	HAM
Germany: Munich	MUC
Germany: Münster	FMO
Ireland: Cork	ORK
Ireland: Dublin	DUB
Ireland: Knock	NOC
Ireland: Shannon	SNN
Ireland: Waterford	WAT
Italy: Florence	FLR
Italy: Milan	LIN
Liberia: Freetown	FNA
Luxembourg	LUX
Netherlands: Amsterdam	AMS
Netherlands: Groningen	GRQ
Netherlands: Maastricht	MST
Romania: Bucharest	OTP
Russian Fed: St Petersburg	LED
Sénégal: Dakar	DKR
Spain: Asturias	OVD
Spain: Jerez de la Frontera	XRY
Spain: Zaragoza	ZAZ
Switzerland: Bern	BRN

London Heathrow
Flights to 185 destinations worldwide

London City
Flights to ten destinations

Belgium: Antwerp	ANR
Belgium: Brussels	BRU
France: Paris	CDG
Germany: Frankfurt-a-Main	FRA
Germany: Hamburg	HAM
Ireland: Dublin	DUB
Netherlands: Rotterdam	RTM
Switzerland: Geneva	GVA
Switzerland: Lugano	LUG
Switzerland: Zürich	ZRH

London Biggin Hill
Flights to one destination
France: Le Touquet   LTQ

London Gatwick
Flights to 116 destinations worldwide

HEATHROW
Train: Piccadilly Line Underground trains stop first at 'Heathrow Terminal 4' station, then continue to 'Heathrow Terminals 1, 2 and 3' station before returning to London.
Bus/coach: Direct links to Gatwick, the Airbus service to central London and Railair Links to Reading and Woking BR Stations run from the coach station outside the terminal 3 arrivals hall. Most other services, including night bus N97, run from the central bus station, reached via the subways linking terminals 1, 2 and 3.

GATWICK
Train: The BR station is linked to the south terminal. A transit bus connects the station to the north terminal.
Bus/coach: Principal services stop at both north and south terminals. All other services stop at the south terminal, where a transit bus connects with the north terminal.

○	Motorway (with junction)
	Other main road
	British Rail
⇌	British Rail station
	Bakerloo Line (London Underground)
	Central Line (London Underground)
	Circle Line (London Underground)
	Northern Line (London Underground)
	Piccadilly Line (London Underground)
	Victoria Line (London Underground)
⊖	London Underground station
	Docklands Light Railway
	Bus / coach
	Night bus

Service currently suspended

BUS 473
RED SHUTTLEBUS
YELLOW SHUTTLEBUS
METROBUS 356

FRANCE

For names of départements,
see facing page →

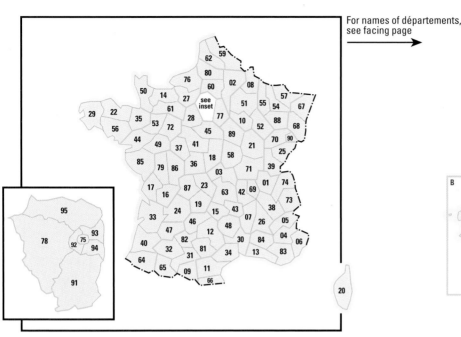

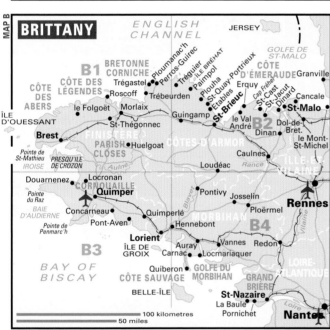

BRITTANY

ENGLISH CHANNEL

JERSEY

GOLFE DE ST-MALO

B1 BRETONNE CORNICHE
Ploumanac'h, Perros-Guirec, Tréguier, ÎLE BRÉHAT
Paimpol, Plouha, St-Quay-Portrieux
CÔTE D'ÉMERAUDE
Granville

CÔTE DES LÉGENDES
Trégastel, Roscoff, Trébeurden
Erquy, St-Cast, Cap Fréhel, St-Jacut, Dinard
Étables, **St-Brieuc**, Cancale

CÔTE DES ABERS
le Folgoët, Morlaix, Guingamp, le Val André, Dol-de-Bret., **St-Malo**

ÎLE D'OUESSANT
St-Thégonnec, Dinan, le Mont-St-Michel

FINISTÈRE PARISH CLOSES
Huelgoat, CÔTES-D'ARMOR, Caulnes, ILLE-ET-VILAINE **B2**

Brest

Pointe de St-Mathieu, IROISE, PRESQU'ÎLE DE CROZON, Aulne
Loudéac, Rance

Douarnenez, Locronan, CORNOUAILLE, Blavet, Pontivy, Josselin
Rennes

Pointe du Raz, **Quimper**

BAIE D'AUDIERNE, Concarneau, Quimperlé, Hennebont, MORBIHAN, Ploërmel **B4**

Pointe de Penmarc'h, Pont-Aven

B3 ÎLE DE GROIX, **Lorient**, Auray, Vannes, Redon, LOIRE-ATLANTIQUE
Carnac, Locmariaquer

BAY OF BISCAY
Quiberon, GOLFE DU MORBIHAN
CÔTE SAUVAGE, GRAND BRIÈRE

BELLE-ÎLE
St-Nazaire
La Baule, Pornichet, Loire, **Nantes**

100 kilometres
50 miles

LOIRE

Mayenne, la Ferté-Bernard, Nogent-le-Rotrou, EURE-ET-LOIR

MAYENNE, MAINE, Bonneval

Vitré
Rennes
Laval, Sablé-sur-Sarthe, **Le Mans**, St-Calais, Châteaudun
ILLE-ET-VILAINE **C1** SARTHE
Beaugency, **Orléans** LOIRET

Châteaubriant, le Plessis-Bourré, la Flèche, Vendôme, Talcy, **C2** LOIR-ET-CHER

LOIRE-ATLANTIQUE, le Lude, Roche-Racan, Chambord, Beauregard, Villesavin, Cheverny, Troussay, Moulin

Angers ANJOU, Montgeoffroy, Langeais, Vouvray, Baudry, **Tours**, Amboise, Chaumont, Chenonceaux, Chémery

Ancenis, Serrant, Brissac, Boumois, Azay-le-Rideau, Villandry, Nitray, Saché, Montpoupon, Valençay

Nantes MAINE-ET-LOIRE, Chemillé, Fontevraud, Saumur, Ussé, Chinon, TOURAINE, Loches, Romorantin-Lanthenay

Cholet, Thouars, Loudun, Descartes, Châtillon-sur-Indre, le Grand-Pressigny, Azay-le-Ferron, **Châteauroux** INDRE

VENDÉE, Bressuire, Châtellerault, Boussay, le Bouchet, Argenton-sur-Creuse

la Roche-sur-Yon, Parthenay, DEUX-SÈVRES, Vienne, **C4**, Chauvigny

C3 Fontenay-le-Comte, **Poitiers**

ÎLE DE RÉ, Luçon, Niort, POITOU, VIENNE, Lussac-les-Châteaux, la Souterraine, HAUTE-VIENNE

□ château
La Rochelle, Bellac, CREUSE

100 kilometres
50 miles

PYRÉNÉES (WEST)

Biarritz, **Bayonne**, Sauveterre, Orthez, GERS, Miélan

Hendaye, St-Jean-de-Luz, Cambo-les-Bains, Ascain, Pau, HAUTES-PYRÉNÉES, HAUTE-GARONNE

San Sebastián, PAYS BASQUE, PYRÉNÉES-ATLANTIQUES, Tarbes, Lannemezan **D1**

CÔTE BASQUE, Mauléon, Oloron-Ste-Marie, Lourdes, BIGORRE, Argelès-Gazost, Saint-Gaudens

St-Jean-Pied-de-Port, Larrau, Col du Tourmalet 2114m, la Mongie, Valcabrère

Roncesvalles, Behérobie, Sainte-Engrâce, Cauterets, Luz, Barèges, St-Lary Soulan **D2**

SPAIN, **Pamplona**, Gavarnie, Luchon Superbagnères, PYRÉNÉES OCCIDENTALES

Pico de Aneto 3404m

PARC NATIONAL DES PYRÉNÉES OCCIDENTALES

100 kilometres
50 miles
Land tints: 0-1000m, 1000-2000m, over 2000m

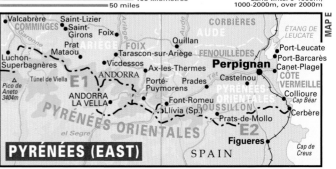

PYRÉNÉES (EAST)

Valcabrère, Saint-Lizier, Saint-Girons, Foix, CORBIÈRES, COMMINGES, AUDE, ÉTANG DE LEUCATE

Prat Mataou, ARIÈGE, FOIX, Quillan, FENOUILLÈDES, Port-Leucate

Luchon-Superbagnères, Vicdessos, Tarascon-sur-Ariège, Port-Barcarès, Canet-Plage, Ax-les-Thermes, Prades, **Perpignan**

ANDORRA, Porté-Puymorens, Castelnou, CÔTE VERMEILLE, Collioure, Cap Béar

Pico de Aneto 3404m, **ANDORRA LA VELLA**, Font-Romeu, PYRÉNÉES-ORIENTALES, ROUSSILLON

el Segre, Llívia (Sp.), Prats-de-Mollo, Cerbère **E2**

PYRÉNÉES ORIENTALES
Figueres, Cap de Creus

PYRÉNÉES (EAST)
SPAIN

FRANCE

01 Ain	33 Gironde	65 Hautes-Pyrénées
02 Aisne	34 Hérault	66 Pyrénées-Orientales
03 Allier	35 Ille-et-Vilaine	67 Bas-Rhin
04 Alpes-de-Haute-Provence	36 Indre	68 Haut-Rhin
05 Hautes-Alpes	37 Indre-et-Loire	69 Rhône
06 Alpes-Maritimes	38 Isère	70 Haute-Saône
07 Ardèche	39 Jura	71 Saône-et-Loire
08 Ardennes	40 Landes	72 Sarthe
09 Ariège	41 Loir-et-Cher	73 Savoie
10 Aube	42 Loire	74 Haute-Savoie
11 Aude	43 Haute-Loire	75 Paris
12 Aveyron	44 Loire-Atlantique	76 Seine-Maritime
13 Bouches-du-Rhône	45 Loiret	77 Seine-et-Marne
14 Calvados	46 Lot	78 Yvelines
15 Cantal	47 Lot-et-Garonne	79 Deux-Sèvres
16 Charente	48 Lozère	80 Somme
17 Charente-Maritime	49 Maine-et-Loire	81 Tarn
18 Cher	50 Manche	82 Tarn-et-Garonne
19 Corrèze	51 Marne	83 Var
20 Corse	52 Haute-Marne	84 Vaucluse
21 Côte-d'Or	53 Mayenne	85 Vendée
22 Côtes-d'Armor	54 Meurthe-et-Moselle	86 Vienne
23 Creuse	55 Meuse	87 Haute-Vienne
24 Dordogne	56 Morbihan	88 Vosges
25 Doubs	57 Moselle	89 Yonne
26 Drôme	58 Nièvre	90 Territoire de Belfort
27 Eure	59 Nord	91 Essonne
28 Eure-et-Loir	60 Oise	92 Hauts-de-Seine
29 Finistère	61 Orne	93 Seine-Saint-Denis
30 Gard	62 Pas-de-Calais	94 Val-de-Marne
31 Haute-Garonne	63 Puy-de-Dôme	95 Val-d'Oise
32 Gers	64 Pyrénées-Atlantiques	

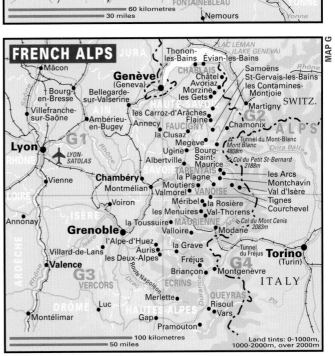

GERMANY

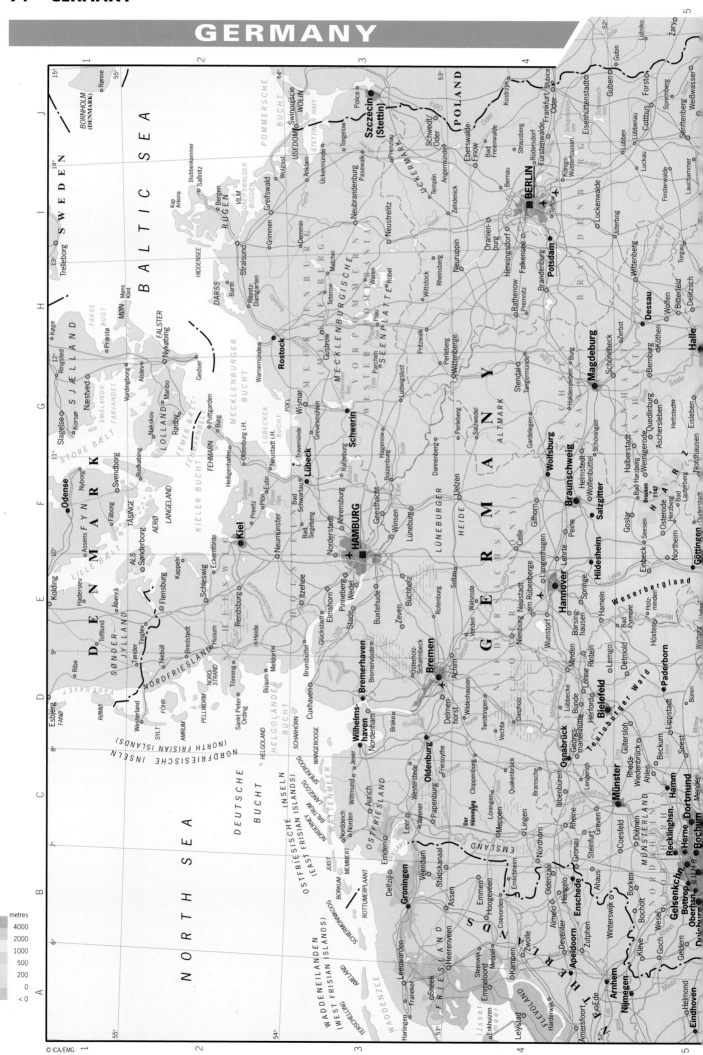

metres
4000
2000
1000
500
200
0
< 0

© ICA/EMG

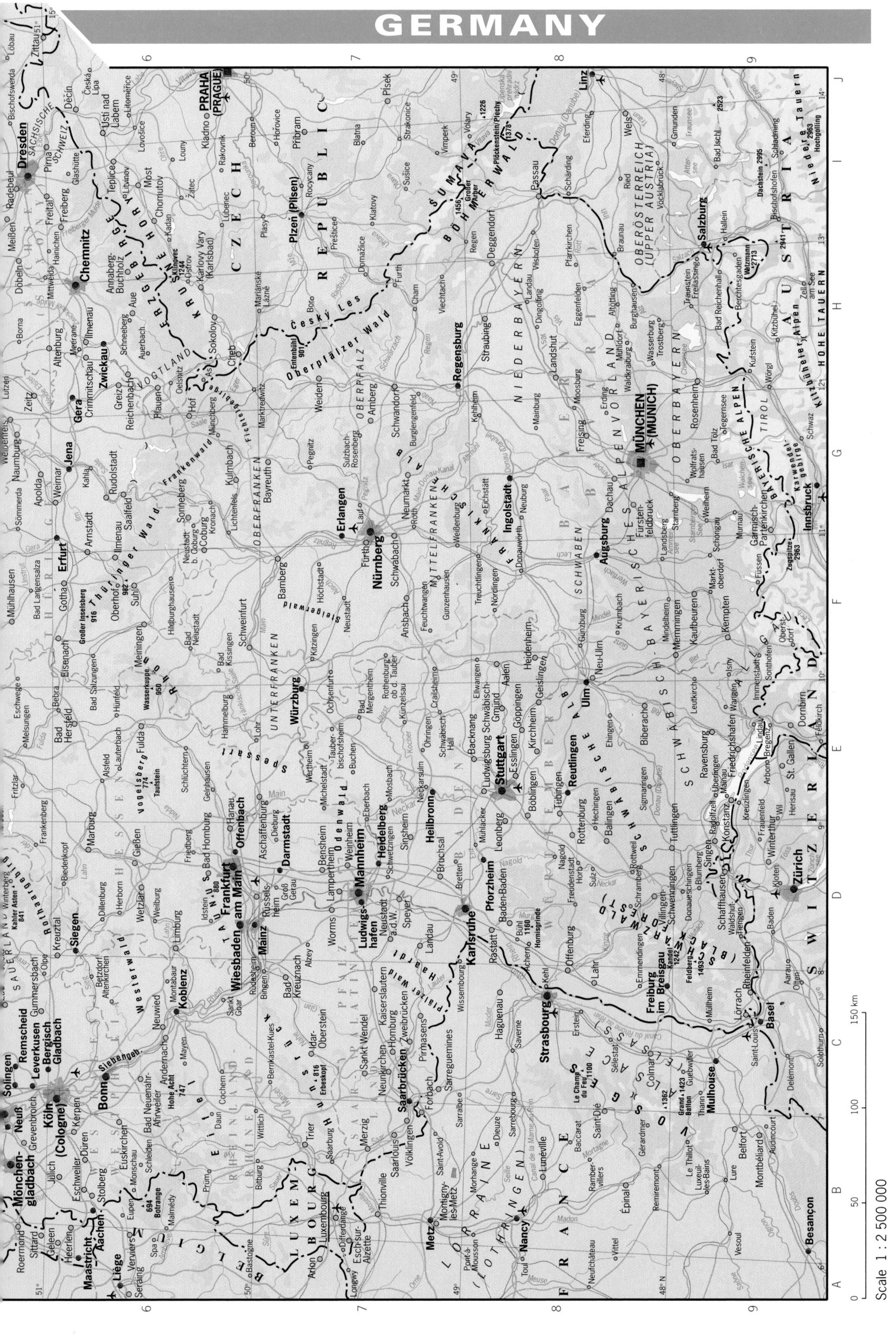

GERMANY

Scale 1 : 2 500 000

0 50 100 150 km

Major places and features labelled on the map include:

PRAHA (PRAGUE), Dresden, Chemnitz, Zwickau, Gera, Jena, Erfurt, Plzeň (Pilsen), CZECH REPUBLIC, Linz, Salzburg, AUSTRIA, OBERÖSTERREICH (UPPER AUSTRIA), Passau, Regensburg, NIEDERBAYERN, MÜNCHEN (MUNICH), OBERBAYERN, Innsbruck, TIROL, Erlangen, Nürnberg, Fürth, OBERFRANKEN, Bayreuth, MITTELFRANKEN, Ingolstadt, Augsburg, SCHWABEN, Ulm, Neu-Ulm, BAYERN, BAYERISCHE ALPEN, Frankfurt am Main, Offenbach, Darmstadt, Mannheim, Ludwigshafen, Heidelberg, Heilbronn, Stuttgart, Esslingen, Reutlingen, Pforzheim, Karlsruhe, Baden-Baden, SCHWÄBISCHE ALB, HESSEN, Wiesbaden, Mainz, Würzburg, UNTERFRANKEN, Spessart, Odenwald, Koblenz, Bonn, Köln (Cologne), Leverkusen, Bergisch Gladbach, Remscheid, Solingen, Mönchengladbach, Neuß, Aachen, Maastricht, Liège, Siegen, SAUERLAND, WESTERWALD, Strasbourg, ELSASS, Freiburg im Breisgau, SCHWARZWALD (BLACK FOREST), Basel, Zürich, SWITZERLAND, St. Gallen, Konstanz, Friedrichshafen, Ravensburg, Memmingen, Kempten, Garmisch-Partenkirchen, Zugspitze 2963, Saarbrücken, Trier, LUXEMBOURG, Luxembourg, Metz, Nancy, FRANCE, LORRAINE, BELGIE / BELGIQUE, SACHSEN, ERZGEBIRGE, VOGTLAND, THÜRINGEN, THÜRINGER WALD, BÖHMERWALD, ŠUMAVA, ČESKÝ LES, OBERPFÄLZER WALD, FRANKENWALD, Dachstein 2995, Wetterstein, HOHE TAUERN, Hochgölling 2863

GERMANY

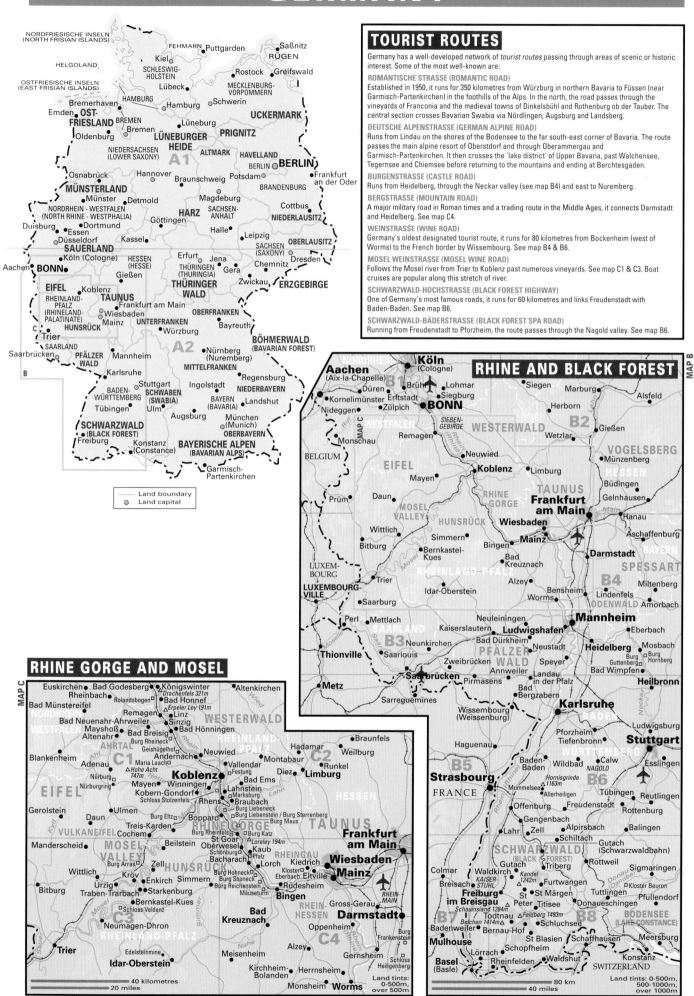

TOURIST ROUTES

Germany has a well-developed network of *tourist routes* passing through areas of scenic or historic interest. Some of the most well-known are:

ROMANTISCHE STRASSE (ROMANTIC ROAD)
Established in 1950, it runs for 350 kilometres from Würzburg in northern Bavaria to Füssen (near Garmisch-Partenkirchen) in the foothills of the Alps. In the north, the road passes through the vineyards of Franconia and the medieval towns of Dinkelsbühl and Rothenburg ob der Tauber. The central section crosses Bavarian Swabia via Nördlingen, Augsburg and Landsberg.

DEUTSCHE ALPENSTRASSE (GERMAN ALPINE ROAD)
Runs from Lindau on the shores of the Bodensee to the far south-east corner of Bavaria. The route passes the main alpine resort of Oberstdorf and through Oberammergau and Garmisch-Partenkirchen. It then crosses the 'lake district' of Upper Bavaria, past Walchensee, Tegernsee and Chiemsee before returning to the mountains and ending at Berchtesgaden.

BURGENSTRASSE (CASTLE ROAD)
Runs from Heidelberg, through the Neckar valley (see map B4) and east to Nuremberg.

BERGSTRASSE (MOUNTAIN ROAD)
A major military road in Roman times and a trading route in the Middle Ages, it connects Darmstadt and Heidelberg. See map C4.

WEINSTRASSE (WINE ROAD)
Germany's oldest designated tourist route, it runs for 80 kilometres from Bockenheim (west of Worms) to the French border by Wissembourg. See map B4 & B6.

MOSEL WEINSTRASSE (MOSEL WINE ROAD)
Follows the Mosel river from Trier to Koblenz past numerous vineyards. See map C1 & C3. Boat cruises are popular along this stretch of river.

SCHWARZWALD-HOCHSTRASSE (BLACK FOREST HIGHWAY)
One of Germany's most famous roads, it runs for 60 kilometres and links Freudenstadt with Baden-Baden. See map B6.

SCHWARZWALD-BÄDERSTRASSE (BLACK FOREST SPA ROAD)
Running from Freudenstadt to Pforzheim, the route passes through the Nagold valley. See map B6.

RHINE AND BLACK FOREST

RHINE GORGE AND MOSEL

SWITZERLAND AND AUSTRIA

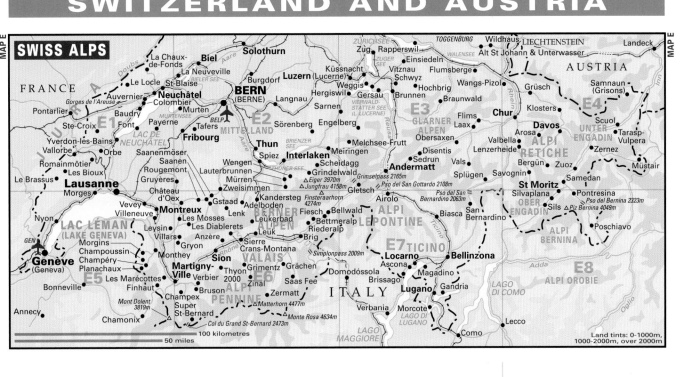

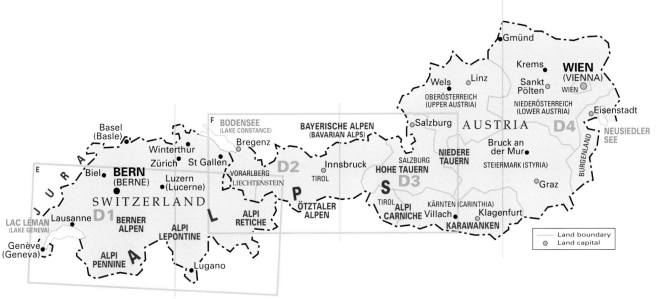

ITALY

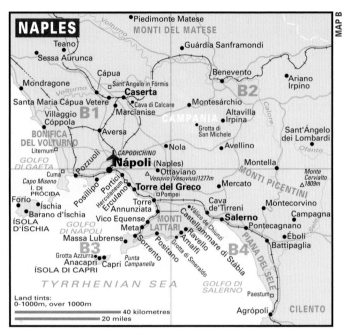

ITALY AND MALTA

SPAIN

CANARY IS

TENERIFE (B1)
LOS RODEOS
La Laguna
Puerto de la Cruz
Santa Cruz
Garachico
La Orotava
Candelaria
Güímar
Los Gigantes
△ Pico de Teide 3715m
Playa Paraiso
Playa de las Americas
Los Cristianos
El Medano
REINA SOFIA
El Abrigo
Las Galletas
COSTA DEL SILENCIO
40 kilometres
20 miles

GRAN CANARIA (B2)
San Nicolás de Tolentino
Arucas
Las Palmas
Tejeda
Bandama 574m
Telde
△ Pico de las Nieves 1949m
La Playa de Mogan
Ingenio
Puerto Rico
Arguineguin
San Agustín
Playa del Inglés
Maspalomas
40 kilometres
20 miles

LANZAROTE (B3)
MONTAÑA CLARA
GRACIOSA
Orzola
Arrieta
LA ISLETA
Teguise
Oasis de Nazaret
La Veguita
Costa Teguise
Islote de Hilario
Montaña Blanca
Tías
Arrecife
Atalaya de Femés 608m △
Los Pocillos
Puerto del Carmen
Playa Blanca
40 kilometres
20 miles

ALEGRANZA
GRACIOSA

LA PALMA (B4)
Santa Cruz
TENERIFE
Puerto de la Cruz
Santa Cruz
GOMERA
San Sebastián
Valverde
HIERRO
200 kilometres
100 miles

LANZAROTE (B5)
Arrecife
Corralejo
Betancuria
Puerto del Rosario
FUERTEVENTURA
Las Palmas
Gran Tarajal
Jandía Playa
GRAN CANARIA

(B6)
ATLANTIC OCEAN
MOROCCO
Tarfaya
W. SAHARA

For location see general map section

Land tints: 0-500m, 500-1000m, over 1000m

COSTA VERDE
La Coruña
Gijón
Oviedo
Santiago de Compostela
PRINCIPADO DE ASTURIA
Lugo
GALICIA
CAN
León
Vigo
Orense
CA Y
Valladol
PORTUGAL
Salamanca
EXTREMADURA
Badajoz
Mérida
A
D
Córdoba
Huelva
Sevilla (Seville)
ANDALUCÍA
Má
COSTA DE LA LUZ
Cádiz
Gib (U

COSTA BRAVA
Llívia (Sp.)
FRANCE
Sant Pere de Rodes
ANDORRA
Puigcerdà
La Jonquera
Portbou
Llançà
La Seu d'Urgell
Empúries
Cadaqués
Figueres
Roses
Cap de Creus
Olot
EMPORDA
Berga
Sant Pere Pescador
L'Escala
COSTA DE LA MORT
L'Estartit
Vic
Girona
Begur
Palafrugell
Palamós
COSTA DE LEVANT
Platja d'Aro
Sant Feliu d.G.
Manresa
Blanes
Tossa de Mar
Monestir de Montserrat
Granollers
Calella
Lloret de Mar
Malgrat de Mar
Igualada
Terrassa
Sabadell
Arenys de Mar
Reial Monestir de Poblet
Martorell
Mataró
COSTA BRAVA
Montblanc
Vilafranca del Penèdes
Badalona
Monestir de Santes Creus
Valls
El Vendrell
Barcelona
DEL PRAT
Comaruga
Calafell
Castelldefels
Reus
Sitges
MEDITERRANEAN SEA
Torredembarra
Vilanova i la Geltrú
Tarragona
COSTA DORADA
la Pineda
Salou / Port Aventura
Cambrils de Mar
CATALUNYA
Llobregat
Ter
100 kilometres
50 miles
Land tints: 0-500m, 500-1000m, over 1000m

COSTA DEL SOL
Aracena
Constantina
Córdoba
Huéscar
Almodóvar del Rio
Torredonjimeno
Jaen
Vélez Rubio
Palma del Rio
Baena
La Antilla
Montilla
Baza
El Rompido
Carmona
Ecija
Alcala la Real
Huercal-Overa
Huelva
Estepa
Guadix
Punta Umbria
Mazagón
Loja
Mojácar
Isla Cristina
COTO DE DOÑANA
Granada
SIERRA NEVADA
Carboneras
Torre de la Higuera
LAS MARISMAS
Pico de Veleta 3392m △
Mulhacén 3482m △
Nijar
Antequera
Capileira
Sanlúcar de Barrameda
Algodonales
Vélez-Málaga
El Ejido
Almería
El Cabo de Gata
Chipiona
SERRANÍA DE RONDA
Salobreña
Motril
Adra
Aguadulce
GOLFO DE ALMERÍA
COSTA DE LA LUZ
Rota
Jerez de la Frontera
Málaga
Nerja
Almuñécar
San José
Calahonda
Cabo de Gata
BAHÍA DE CÁDIZ
El Puerto de Santa María
Ronda
El Palo
Torrox
Almerimar
Cádiz
San Pedro Alcántara
Torremolinos
Torre del Mar
COSTA TROPICAL
Almería
Roquetas de Mar
COSTA DE ALMERÍA
Chiclana de la Frontera
Casares
Marbella
Benalmádena Costa
GOLFO DE CÁDIZ
Estepona
Fuengirola
Mijas Costa
Puerto Banús
COSTA DEL SOL
Conil de la Frontera
Barbate de Franco
San Roque
MEDITERRANEAN SEA
Cabo de Trafalgar
Algeciras
La Línea
Gibraltar (UK)
Punta de Europa
Tarifa
Punta Marroqui o de Tarifa
ANDALUCÍA
MURCIA
Guadalquivir
Genil
Playa de Castilla
SERRANÍA DE RONDA
100 km
50 miles
Land tints: 0-500m, 500-1000m, over 1000m

SPAIN

Map legend:
— autonomous community boundary
◉ autonomous community capital

PYRÉNÉES

San Sebastián
Pamplona
COMUNIDAD FORAL DE NAVARRA
Logroño
LA RIOJA
BASQUE COUNTRY
PAIS VASCO
Zaragoza (Saragossa)
ARAGÓN
A1
Girona
CATALUNYA (CATALONIA)
COSTA BRAVA
Barcelona
COSTA DORADA
Tortosa
Guadalajara
MADRID
Aranjuez
Castellón de la Plana
Vinaròs (Vinaroz)
COSTA DEL AZAHAR
COMUNIDAD DE VALENCIANA
ILLA-LA MANCHA
Valencia
Albacete
ISLAS BALEARES (BALEARIC IS.)
MENORCA (MINORCA)
G
H
Palma de Mallorca
MALLORCA (MAJORCA)
F
EIVISSA (IBIZA)
E
Ciudad Real
Linares
Alicante
Murcia
REGIÓN DE MURCIA
COSTA BLANCA
D
ANDALUCÍA
Cartagena
Granada
COSTA CÁLIDA
Almería
COSTA DE ALMERÍA
SOL

NOT SHOWN ON MAIN MAP:
CANARIAS (CANARY IS.)
◉ Las Palmas de Gran Canaria / Santa Cruz de Tenerife

MINORCA

MEDITERRANEAN SEA

MAP H

Cap de Cavalleria
H1
Cala Morell
Cala Tirant
Fornells
H2
Es Delfins
Cala Forcat
Cala Blanes
Ciutadella
S'Albufeira
Son Parc
Arena d'en Castell
Port d'Addaia
Cala Santandria
Naveta d'Es Tudóns
Es Mercadal
El Torro △350m
Cap de Favàritx
Cala Blanca
Ferreries
ILLA D'EN COLOM
Cala Santa Galdana
Es Migjorn Redones
Gran Sant Cristóbal
Es Grau
Shangri-La
Tamarinda
Cap d'Artrutx
Cala En Bosc
Sant Tomàs
Alaior
Maó (Mahón)
Cala Llonga
Platja de Son Bou
Sant Jaume Mediterrani
Son Bou de Baix
Sant Climent
Villa Carlos
H3
Cala En Porter
Cales Coves
Es Canutells
H4
Sant Lluis
S'Algar
Binissafúller
Binibequer Vell
Cala Torret
Punta Prima
Biniancolla

20 kilometres
10 miles

MAJORCA

MAP G

Cap de Formentor
Cala de Sant Vicenç
Formentor
Port de Pollença
MEDITERRANEAN SEA
Pollença
Cap d'es Pinar
Sa Calobra
Alcúdia
Sa Mesquida de Baix
Monestir de Lluc
Port de Alcúdia
BADIA DE ALCUDIA
Puig Major 1445m
Platja de Muro
Cala Ratjada
Port de Sóller
Can Picafort
Capdepera
Son Moll
G1
Sóller
Muro
Coves d'Artà
Deià
Orient
Inca
Santa Margalida
Arta
G2
Banyalbufar
Valldemossa
Sant Llorenç des Cardassar
Cala Bona
Mirador de Ses Ànimas
Sinéu
ES PLA
Cala Millor
Estellencs
Manacor
Sa Coma
S'Illot
Sant Telm
Palma de Mallorca
Porto Cristo
Calvià Castell de Bendinat
SON SANT JOAN
Santuari de Nostra Senyora de Cura
Cala Estany
Coves del Drac
Andratx
5 2 6
Cales de Mallorca
Peguera
9 8 1
Santa Ponça
10
Platges de Mallorca
Llucmajor
Santuari de Sant Salvador
Felanitx
Cala Antena
Cala Murada
Port de Andratx
3
Cala Marçal
Porto Colom
11
Campos
Cala d'Or
Bahia Grande
BADIA DE PALMA
La Rapita
Cala Llonga
Porto Petro
Cala Pi
Santanyí
Cala Mondragó
Colònia de Sant Jordi
Platja dels Dols
Cala Figuera
G3
G4
Cala Santanyi

BADIA DE PALMA:
1 Cala Blava   6 El Molinar
2 Cala Major   7 Illetes
3 Cala Vinyes   8 Magalluf
4 Can Pastilla 9 Palma Nova
5 Costa d'en Blanes 10 Portals Nous
                11 S'Arenal

ILLA CONILLERA
ILLA DE CABRERA

40 kilometres
20 miles
Land tints: 0-500m, 500-1000m, over 1000m

COSTA BLANCA

MAP E

Denia
Jávea
Alcoy
Guadaleste
Benissa
Teulada
Cabo de la Nao
VALENCIA
Calpe
Moraira
Yecla
Villena
Alfaz del Pi
Altea
Peñón de Ifach
Finestrat
Benidorm
E1
Elda
Villajoyosa
E2
Jumilla
Novelda
COSTA BLANCA
ALTET
Campello
Cieza
Elx (Elche)
Alicante
Crevillente
Los Arenales del Sol
Orihuela
Santa Pola
ISLOTE DE LA CANTERA
Segura
Guardamar del Segura
MEDITERRANEAN SEA
Murcia
Torrevieja
Pilar de la Horadada
Campoamor
COSTA CÁLIDA
MURCIA
Santiago de la Ribera
San Pedro del Pinatar
E3
San Javier
E4
Los Alcázares
MAR MENOR
Mazarrón
La Unión
La Manga del Mar Menor
Cabo de Palos
Puerto de Mazarrón
Cartagena

Land tints:
0-500m,
500-1000m,
over 1000m

100 kilometres
50 miles

IBIZA

MAP F

Portinatx
Port de Sant Miquel
Sant Joan de Labritja
Sant Miquel de Balansat
Cala de Sant Vicenç
Sant Carles de Peralta
ILLA DE TAGOMAGO
F1
Cala Gracio
EIVISSA (IBIZA)
F2
SA CONILLERA
Sant Antoni de Portmany
Cala Llenya
ILLES BLEDES
Es Canyar
Cala Bassa
Port d'es Torrent
Sant Rafael
S'Argamassa
Santa Eulària del Riu
Cala Tarida
Sant Josep de sa Talaia
Fantasylandia
Cala Llonga
Cala Vadella
Platja Talamanca
△ Sa Talaiassa de Sant Josep 475m
Eivissa (Ibiza)
Cubells
Ses Figueretes
ILLA ES VEDRA
Platja d'En Bossa
La Canal
Punta de ses Portes
ILLA DES PENJAT
MEDITERRANEAN SEA
ILLA ESPARDELL
F3
ILLA ESPALMADOR
F4
Es Savina
ESTANY PUDENT
Es Pujols
Cala Sahona
FORMENTERA
Sant Fransesc de Formentera
Platja de Migjorn
El Pilar

20 km
10 miles

PORTUGAL

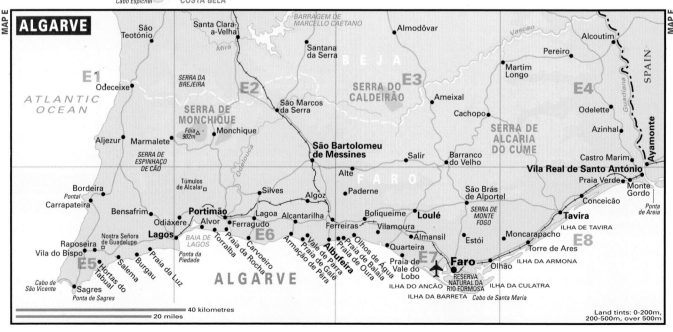

GREECE AND TURKEY

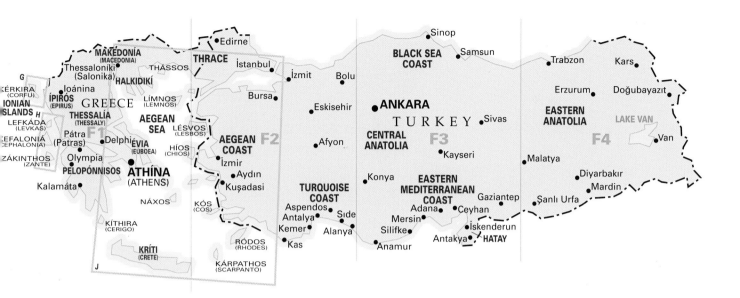

MEDITERRANEAN BEACHES

The *European Blue Flag Campaign* is an environmental awareness raising activity of the Foundation for Environmental Education in Europe (Feee). This map shows Blue Flag beaches in the Mediterranean. For UK beaches, see page 68.

To qualify for a Blue Flag, a beach has to fulfill a number of strict criteria regarding water quality (compliance with the EU Bathing Water Directive), environment, education and information, beach area management and safety. The Blue Flag is awarded annually and is valid for one year. On 16th May 1994 the Campaign jury awarded Blue Flags to 1,454 beaches and 337 marinas in 15 countries across Europe.

The member countries are Belgium, Denmark, Estonia, Finland, France, Germany, Greece, Ireland, Italy, Netherlands, Portugal, Spain, Sweden, Turkey and United Kingdom. In addition, Bulgaria and Cyprus are associated members. The list below gives further details on member countries shown on this map:

FRANCE
Blue Flags awarded to 302 beaches and 54 marinas (including one marina in Guadeloupe).
Certain criteria are examined at municipal level and not only for the territory of the beaches. Moreover, a municipality can only fly the Blue Flag if a minimum of 50% of its beaches fulfill the criteria for water quality. The municipalities for which all beaches fulfilled the criteria are marked with an asterisk (*).
For further information, contact:
F.E.E.E.F.,
127 rue de Flandre,
75019 Paris.

GREECE
Blue Flags awarded to 287 beaches and four marinas.
For further information, contact:
Hellenic Society for the Protection of Nature,
24 Nikis Street,
GR-105 57 Athens.

ITALY
Blue Flags awarded to 221 beaches and 43 marinas.
For further information, contact:
Associazione Bandiere Blu d'Europa,
c/o ISMES,
Via dei Crociferi 44,
00187 Roma.

SPAIN
Blue Flags awarded to 306 beaches and 60 marinas (including 15 beaches and six marinas in the Canary Islands).
For further information, contact:
Asociación de Educación Ambiental (A.D.E.A.C.),
Avenida America 33, 5A,
28002 Madrid.

TURKEY
Blue Flags awarded to 12 beaches and nine marinas as part of a pilot project.
For further information, contact:
Türkiye Cevre Egitim Vakfi,
Cumhuriyet Cad. no. 187/3,
Elmadag-Istanbul.

Other countries:
(B = beaches, M = marinas)
Belgium: 7 natural inland waters
Denmark: 139 B, 84 M
Estonia: 2 M (pilot project)
Finland: 29 M
Germany: 47 M
Ireland: 55 B
Netherlands: 12 B, 3 M
Portugal: 95 B (incl. 1 B in Azores & 4 B in Madeira)
Sweden: 1 M (pilot project)
UK: 17 B

FRANCE

Also see map E, page 72 and map F, page 73

Languedoc-Roussillon
Pyrénées-Orientales département
1 **Cerbère***: Centre Village, Peyrefite, Piscine Eau de Mer
2 **Banyuls-sur-Mer***: Centrale, Centre Héliomarin, Plage des Elmes, Troc Pinell
3 **Port-Vendres***: Anse de Paulilles, Plage de l'Oli, Plage d'en Baux
4 **Collioure***: Plage des Pêcheurs, Plage du Faubourg, Plage Saint Vincent, Plage Saint Vincent Nord
5 **Argèles-sur-Mer**: Plage de la Sardane, Plage de l'emissaire en mer, Plage du Mas Larrieu, Plage du Racou
6 **Saint-Cyprien***: Plage au Sud Port, Plage du Cala à Gogo, Plage du Jimmy's, Plage face station Total, Plage Poste de secours no. 3
7 **Canet-en-Roussillon**: Plage Centrale, Plage de la Marenda, Plage du Lido, Plage du Mar Estang, Plage du Roussillon, Plage du Sardinal (Niveau GCU), Plage du Sardinal (Poste de secours)
8 **Sainte-Marie-la-Mer***: Plage Centrale, Plage du 1er Epi, Plage du 2ème Epi, Plage du 3ème Epi, Plage du 4ème Epi, Plage du camping municipal
9 **Toreilles***: Plage Centre, Plage Nord, Plage Sud
10 **Le Barcarès***: Plage de la Coudalère, Plage du Lydia, Plage du Village
Aude département
11 **Port-la-Nouvelle***: Côte Vermeille, Plage Nord, Plage Sud
12 **Gruissan**: Étang de Mateille, Étang des Ayguades, Grazel, Les Ayguades, Les Chalets
13 **Narbonne***: 1er Poste de secours, 2ème Poste de secours, 3ème Poste de secours, Créneau de Nature
14 **Fleury-d'Aude***: Les Cabanes-de-Fleur, Pissevaches, Saint Pierre-la-Mer
Hérault département
15 **Valras**: Allée de Gaulle, Bel Horizon, Poste de secours central
16 **Sérignan***: Sérignan Plage, Sérignan Plage Nature
17 **Portiragnes***: La Redoute-Le Blockaus, La Redoute-Le Bosquet
18 **Vias***: La Grande Cosse, Farinette
19 **Agde**: La Tamarissière, Le Mole, Plage Naturiste, Richelieu, Roche Notre-Dame, Saint Vincent
20 **Sète***: Crique de l'Anau, La Corniche-Lazaret, Le Lido, Les Quilles
21 **Villeneuve-les-Maguelonne**: Maguelonne
22 **Mauguio-Carnon***: Carnon Est-L'Eglise, Carnon Est-Les Dunes, Carnon Ouest
23 **La Grande-Motte**: Le Couchant
Provence-Alpes-Côte d'Azur
Bouches-du-Rhône département
24 **Saintes-Maries-de-la-Mer**: Brise de Mer
25 **Fos-sur-Mer***: Caravaou, Grande Plage
26 **Martigues***: Carro, Grand Vallat, Les Laurons, Sainte-Croix, Verdon
27 **Sausset-les-Pins***: Baumettes, Corniche, Roches Plates
28 **Marseille**: Anse des Phocéens, Bains des Dames, Bains Militaires, Bonneveine, Corbières, David, En Vau, Grand Roucas, La Lave, Morgiou, Port Pin, Petit Roucas, Pointe Rouge, Prophete, Saint-Estève, Samena, Vieille Chapelle
29 **La Ciotat***: Casino, Clos des Plages, Figuerolles, Liouquet, Mugel, Saint-Jean
Var département
30 **Saint-Cyr-sur-Mer***: La Madrague de Saint-Cyr, Les Lecques Ouest, Les Lecques Saint-Come, Port d'Alon
31 **Bandol***: Anse de Renecros, Casino, Île de Bandor Plage, Île de Bandor Soukana, L'Anglaise
32 **Sanary-sur-Mer***: Baie de Cousse, La Gorguette, Plage Dorée Centre, Port Issol
33 **Le Pradet***: Bonnettes, La Garonne, Monaco, Oursinières, Pin de Galles
34 **Carqueiranne**: Coupereau, Peno
35 **Hyères***: Badine Giens, Baie de la Palud, Baie de Niels Giens, Ceinturon Est, Ceinturon Ouest, Île de Porquerelles Grande Plage, Île de Porquerelles Plage d'Argent, Île de Port-Cros sud-Anse de Janets, La Capte, L'Almanarre Centre, L'Almanarre Nord, La Madrague, L'Hyppodrome, Port-Pothuau les Salins
36 **La Londe-les-Maures***: L'Argentière, L'Ayguade, Les Bormettes
37 **Le Lavandou***: Aiguebelle, Batailler, Cap Nègre, Cavalière, Jean Blanc, La Fossette, La Vieille, Pramousquier, Saint-Clair
38 **Cavalaire-sur-Mer***: Bonporteau, Cavalaire Centre, Cavalaire Est, Cavalaire Ouest
39 **La Croix-Valmer***: Gigaro, Héracles, La Douane, Vergeron
40 **Ramatuelle**: Bonne Terrasse, L'Escalet, Pampelonne Chavarel, Pampelonne Neptune, Pampelonne Grand Vallat
41 **Cogolin***: Cogolin
42 **Grimaud***: Beauvallon, Grimaud Nord, Les Cigales, Les Rives de Beauvaillon, Port Grimaud
43 **Sainte-Maxime***: Garonnette Val d'Esquières, L'Eléphant, La Nartelle, Sainte-Maxime-Ville, Tardieu
44 **Fréjus**: Corailleurs, La Fougasse, Pébrier, Petit Boucharel, Port de Saint-Aygulf
Alpes-Maritimes département
45 **Antibes**: Bonne Auberge, Cap d'Antibes, Fontonne Est, Fontonne Ouest, Fort Carré, Hôtel Belles Rives, Juan-les-Pins Arc-en-Ciel, Juan-les-Pins Armorial, Juan-les-Pins Le Bretagne, Juan-les-Pins Le Provence, La Garoupe, La Godille, La Gravette, La Salis, Limité Commune, Limité de Commune, Neptune, Port Gallice, Rayon, Sablettes, Siesta, Voile Blanche
46 **Nice**: Bambou, Beau Rivage, Carras, Castel, Coco Beach, Florida, Forum, Gallion, La Paiolle, Lido, Miami, Militaire, Mini Tunnel Magnan, Neptune, Opéra, Paillon Epi, Palais de la Mer, Poincaré, Régence, Voilier
47 **Cap-d'Ail***: Mala, Marquet, Pissarelles
Corse (Corsica)
48 **Saint-Florent***: Hameau Foce, HLM, Roya Est, Roya Ouest

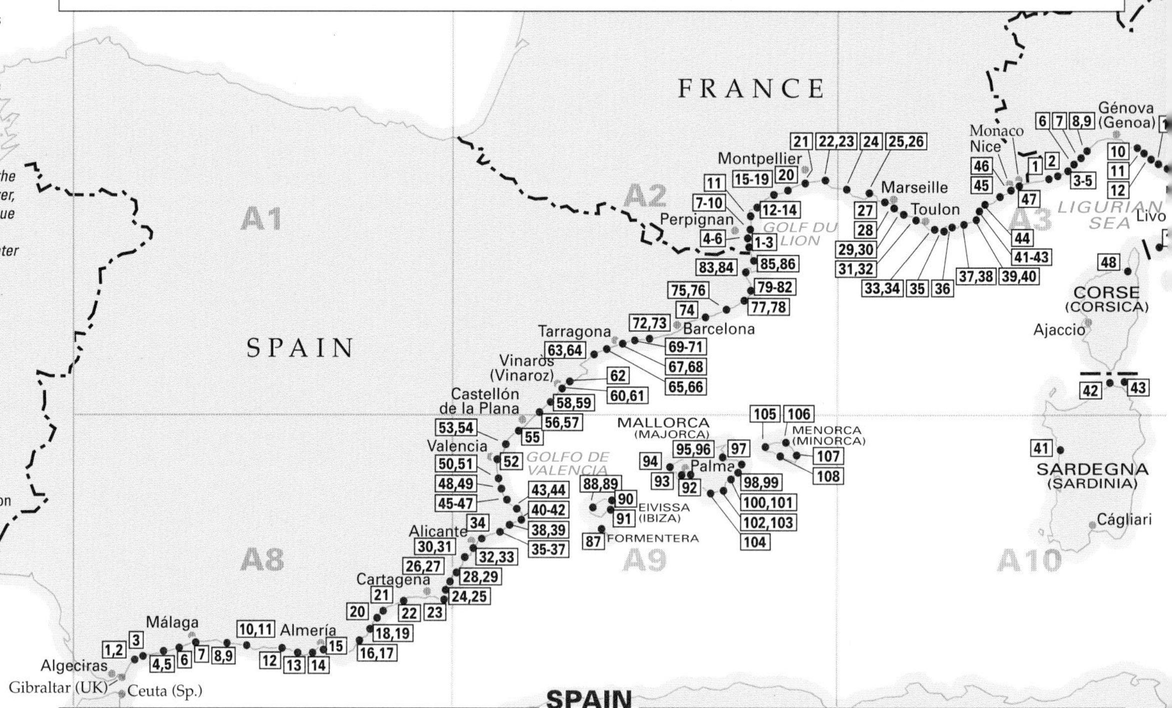

SPAIN

Also see maps C and D, page 80 and maps E, F, G and H, page 81

Andalucía
Málaga province
1 **Casares**: Ancha
2 **Estepona**: La Rada
3 **Marbella**: Guadalmina-San Pedro, Ciudad Sindical
4 **Fuengirola**: Gaviotas-Boliches, Torreblanca
5 **Benalmádena**: Carvajal-La Perla, Malapesquera
6 **Torremolinos**: Bajondillo
7 **Málaga**: Malagueta Paseo Marítimo, El Palo-Dedo
8 **Torrox**: Ferrara
9 **Nerjá**: Burriana
Granada province
10 **Almuñécar**: La Herradura, San Cristóbal, Altillo
11 **Salobreña**: El Peñón
Almeria province
12 **Adra**: Poniente-Sirena Loca
13 **El Ejido**: Balerma, Poniente-Almerimar
14 **Roquetas**: Cerrillos-Playa Serena, Roquetas, Aguadulce
15 **Almería**: Las Conchas-San Miguel, Retamar, Cabo de Gata
16 **Níjar**: San José, Agua Amarga
17 **Carboneras**: El Ancón
18 **Mojácar**: Venta del Bancal, Rumina
19 **Vera**: Bolaga, Puerto Rey-El Playazo
20 **Pulpí**: Terreros
Murcia
21 **Águilas**: Las Delicias
22 **Mazarrón**: Bolnuevo, Bahía
23 **Cartagena**: Azohía, Mar de Cristal
24 **Los Alcázares**: Manzanares, El Espejo, Los Narejos
25 **San Javier**: Veneciola, Colón
26 **San Pedro del Pinatar**: La Llana
Valencia
Alicante province
27 **Pilar de la Horadada**: Las Villas-Higuericas, Jesuitas-Cala Rincón
28 **Orihuela**: Cabo Roig, La Zenia, Flamenca
29 **Torrevieja**: El Cura
30 **Guardamar del Segura**: La Roqueta, Aparcamiento
31 **Santa Pola**: Llevant, Varador
32 **Elx (Elche)**: El Altet
33 **Alicante**: Saladar, El Postiguet, San Juan
34 **Campello**: Muchavista, Carrer la Mar
35 **Villajoyosa**: La Caleta, Bon Nou, Parais, Ciutat
36 **Finestrat**: La Cala
37 **Benidorm**: Poniente, Mal Pas, Levante
38 **Alfaz del Pi**: Racó de L'Albir
39 **Altea**: Cap Blanc Sur, La Roda
40 **Calpe**: Arenal, La Fossa
41 **Benissa**: Cala Fustera
42 **Teulada**: Les Playetes
43 **Jávea**: La Granadella, Cala Blanca, El Arenal
44 **Denia**: Las Rutas, Marineta Cassiana, Las Marinas, Les Deveses
Valencia province
45 **Oliva**: Aigua Blanca, Terranova
46 **Piles**: Piles
47 **Gandia**: Nord
48 **Xeraco**: Xeraco
49 **Tabernes de Valldigna**: Tabernes
50 **Cullera**: Sant Antoni, L'Illa, El Faro, El Dosser
51 **Sueca**: Mareny de Vilxes
52 **Valencia**: El Recatí, La Devesa
53 **Sagunto**: Port de Sagunto
54 **Canet d'En Berenguer**: Racó de la Mar
Castellón province
55 **Moncófar**: Moncófar
56 **Benicácim**: Torre de San Vicente,Voramar-Almadrava
57 **Oropesa**: La Conxa
58 **Torreblanca**: Torrenostra, Nord
59 **Alcalá de Chivert**: El Moro, La Romana, El Cargador
60 **Peñíscola**: Nord
61 **Vinaròs (Vinaroz)**: Vinaròs, Triador
Catalunya (Catalonia)
Tarragona province
62 **Alcanar**: Les Cases
63 **L'Ametlla de Mar**: Calafató
64 **Vandellós i l'Hospitalet de l'infant**: L'Almadrava, L'Arenal
65 **Mont Roig del Camp**: L'Estany Gelat
66 **Cambrils de Mar**: Prat d'en Fores, Vilafortuny-Esquirol
67 **Tarragona**: L'Arrabassada, La Savinosa, La Mora, Tamarit
68 **Torredembarra**: Torredembarra
69 **El Vendrell**: Francás, Coma-ruga, St Salvador
70 **Calafell**: Calafell
71 **Cunit**: Cunit
Barcelona province
72 **Vilanova i la Geltrú**: Platja Ribes Roges
73 **Sitges**: La Barra-Riera Chica, La Ribera, Sant Sebastiá, Aiguadolç
74 **Calella**: Calella
Girona province
75 **Blanes**: Sabanell
76 **Lloret de Mar**: Santa Cristina, Sa Boadella, Fenals, Lloret
77 **Tossa de Mar**: Platja de Tossa
78 **Sant Feliu de Guixols**: Sant Feliu, Sant Pol
79 **Castell-Platja d'Aro**: Sa Conca, Platja d'Aro
80 **Calonge/Palamós**: Torretes
Calonge: Torre Valentina, Sant Antoni
81 **Palamós**: Platja Gran
82 **Palafrugell**: Canadell, Llafranc, Tamariu
83 **L'Escala**: Moll Grec
84 **Roses**: Roses, l'Almadrava
85 **Llancà**: Platja del Port, Grifeu
86 **Portbou**: Portbou
Islas Baleares (Balearic Islands)
Formentera
87 Arenals, Illetes, Llevant, Sa Roqueta
Eivissa (Ibiza)
88 **Sant Josep de sa Talaia**: Salines, Cala Vadella, Cala Conta, Cala Bassa
89 **Sant Antoni de Portmany**: Cala Gració
90 **Sant Joan de Labritja**: S'Illot, Port de San Miquel, Benirrás, Cala Portinatx, S'Arenal Gros, Cala Sant Vinceng
91 **Sant Eulária del Riu**: Cala Llenya, Santa Eulária, Cala Llonga
Mallorca (Majorca)
92 **Palma de Mallorca**: Platja de Palma
93 **Calviá**: Palma Nova, Magalluf, Santa Ponça, Peguera Tora, Peguera Romana
94 **Andratx**: Sant Telm
95 **Muro**: Platja de Muro
96 **Santa Margalida**: Can Picafort
97 **Capdepera**: Cala Mesquida, Cala Agulla, Son Moll, Font de sa Cala
98 **Son Servera**: Es Ribell, Port Vell, Cala Millor, Port Roig
99 **Sant Llorenç des Cardassar**: Cala Millor, Sa Coma
100 **Sant Llorenç/Manacor**: S'Illot-Cala Moreia, Cala Antena, Cala Anguila
101 **Manacor**: Cala Murada, Cala Mandia, Estany d'En Mas
102 **Felanitx**: Cala Marçal, Cala Ferrera
103 **Santanyí**: Cala Esmeralda, Cala Gran, Cala d'Or, Cala Mondragó, Cala Santanyí, Cala Llombards
104 **Ses Salines**: Des Dols
Menorca (Minorca)
105 **Ciutadella**: Son Xoriguer, Cala En Bosc, Cala de Santandria, Cala Blanes
106 **Es Mercadal**: Cala Tirant, Son Saura, Arenal d'en Castell
107 **Maó (Mahón)**: Es Grau
108 **Ferreries**: Cala Santa Galdana

MEDITERRANEAN BEACHES

GREECE

Also see maps G, H and J, page 83

Iónioi Nissoi (Ionian Islands) region

Kérkira (Corfu)
1 **Pélekas:** Glifáda, Kontogialos
2 **Gianades:** Ermónes
3 **Magoulades:** Arilas
4 **Thinalio:** Ágios Spyridonas
5 **Pagoi:** Ágios Georgios
6 **Peroulades:** Canal d'Amour
7 **Spartilas:** Mparmpati (Barbati)
8 **Káto Korakiana:** Dassia, Ípsos
9 **Kérkira (Corfu):** Alykes Potamou, Gouvia, Kanoni, Kommeno, Kontokali
10 **Lefkími:** Alykes, Kávos, Mpouka (Buka)
Kefaloniá (Cephalonia)
11 **Argostóli:** Makrys Gialos, Platys Gialos
12 **Skála:** Kaminia (Skála)
Zákinthos (Zante)
13 **K. Gerakari:** Ampoula *1*
14 **Plános:** Tsilivi
15 **Zákinthos:** Zákinthos
16 **Tragaki:** Ampoula *2*
17 **Kalamáki:** Kalamáki

Ípirós region

Thesprotia
18 **Igoumenítsa:** Drepano, Makrygiali
Préveza
19 **Kanali:** Kastrosykia
20 **Mitikas:** Monolithi
21 **Préveza:** Kyani Akti

Sterea Elláda region, southwest

Fokída
22 **Itéa:** Maiami, Trokantero
Viotia
23 **Antikira:** Ágios Isidoros

Pelopónnisos region, north

Kórinthia (Corinth), north
24 **Loutráki:** Loutráki
25 **Vraháti:** Vraháti
26 **Nérantza (Kokoni):** Nérantza (Kokoni)

Ditiki Elláda region, south

Ahaïa
27 **Lakópetra:** Lakópetra
28 **Araxos (Metóhi):** Kalógria
Ilia
29 **Kástro:** Kástro
30 **Amaliáda:** Kourouta, Palouki
31 **Zaháro:** Zaháro

Pelopónnisos region, south

Messinia
32 **Kiparissia:** Ai Lagoudis
33 **Methóni:** Methóni *1*, *2*
34 **Kalamáta:** Anatol. kalamata *1*, *2* (Vérga), *3* (Vérga)
35 **Vérga:** Argilia
36 **Mikra Mandínia:** Mikra Mandínia
Lakonia
37 **Githio:** Githio (Selinitsa)
38 **Neápoli:** Neápoli *1*, *2*
Arkadia
39 **Parálio Ástros:** Ástros
Argolida
40 **Kivéri:** Kivéri
41 **Árgos:** Naftikos Omilos
42 **Nafplio:** Arvanitia EOT, Karathonas
43 **Toló:** Toló
44 **Asíni:** Glyfos Melisinou, Kastraki
45 **Drépano:** Plaka, Vivari
46 **Kiláda:** Lepitsa
47 **Portohéli:** Kósta, Ntrasiza, Portohéli *1*, *2*
48 **Ermióni:** Bisti, Dardeza, Kouverta
49 **Thermisía:** Thermisía
50 **Paleá Epidavros:** Nisi, Paleá Epidavros *1*, *2*
Kórinthia (Corinth), south
51 **Ágios Theódori:** Ágios Theódori

Sterea Elláda region, northeast

Évia (Euboea)
52 **Erétria:** Erétria *1*, *2*, *3*, Erétria EOT, Malakonta *1*, *2*
53 **Halkída:** Halkída *1*, *2*, Liani Ammos, Souvala
Fthiótida
54 **Atalánti:** Skála
55 **Kaména Voúrla:** Kaména Voúrla EOT
56 **Karavómilos:** Karavómilos
57 **Ráhes:** Ráhes

Thessalía (Thessaly) region

Magnissia
58 **Vólos:** Anavros, Vólos EOT
59 **Kalá Nerá:** Kalá Nerá
60 **Neohóri (Afetes):** Afysos-Ampovos
61 **Mileai:** Boufa
62 **Mouréssi:** Ntamouchari, Papa Nero
63 **Ágios Dimítrios:** Ágios Ioannis
Skíathos
64 **Skíathos:** Achladia, Kanapitsa, Koukounariés, Mandraki, Megali Ammos, Platanias-Agia Paraskevi, Sklithri, Troullos, Vromolimnos
Skópelos
65 **Skópelos:** Agnontas, Limnonari, Milia, Panormos, Stafylos, Velanio
Lárissa
66 **Skíti:** Ágiokampos
67 **Melívia:** Velika

Kentriki Makedonía region

Pieria
68 **Platamónas:** Platamónas *1*, *2*
69 **Pandeleimónas:** Pandeleimónas
70 **Skotína:** Skotina *1* / EOT, Skotina *2*
71 **Leptokariá:** Leptokariá *1*, *2*
72 **Litohórou:** Litohórou *1*, *2*-Plaka
73 **Peristasi:** Katerínoskala
74 **Paralia:** Paralía
75 **Korinós:** Korinós
76 **Magrigialos:** Archaia Pydna, Magrígialos
Thessaloníki (Salonika), west
77 **Néi Epivates:** Néi Epivates
78 **Ágia Triás:** Ágia Triás EOT
79 **Epanomí:** Epanomí EOT
Halkidiki
80 **Kassándra:** Saní *1*, *3*
81 **Kalándra:** Poseidi *1* / EOT, Poseidi *2*
82 **Foúrka:** Foúrka
83 **Pefkohóri:** Pefkohóri
84 **Haniótis:** Haniótis *1*, *2*
85 **Polihrono:** Polihrono
86 **Kriopigí:** Kassándra, Kriopigí *1*, *2*, *3* (Pigadakia)
87 **Áfitos:** Áfitos
88 **Néa Fókea:** Saní *2*
89 **Polígiros:** Gerakiní
90 **Ormília:** Psakoudia
91 **Metamórfossi:** Metamórfossi *1*
92 **Ágios Nikólaos:** Metamórfossi *2*
93 **Nikítas:** Elia, Nikitas
94 **Néos Marmarás:** Marmarás, Pórto Carras *1*, *2*
95 **Sikía:** Kalamitsi
96 **Sárti:** Sárti *1*, *2*
97 **Pirgadíkia:** Pirgadikia
98 **Ouranópoli:** Ouranópoli *1*, *2*, *3* (Kampoudi)
99 **Olimbiáda:** Olimbiáda
Thessaloníki (Salonika), east
100 **Kato Stavrós:** Stavrós Platania
101 **Vrassná:** Vrassná
102 **Asproválta:** Asproválta *1*, *2* / EOT

Anatolikí Makedonía Kai Thráki region

Kavála
103 **Kariani:** Kariani
104 **Kavála:** Batis, Kalamitsi, Tosca
Thássos
105 **Prinos:** Prinos Dasylio
106 **Panagiá:** Panagiá
107 **Thássos:** Makryammos
Xánthi
108 **Mángana:** Mángana
109 **Mirodato:** Mirodato
110 **Mándra:** Paralia Mándras
111 **Néa Kessáni:** Porto Lágos
Rodópi
112 **Fanári:** Fanári EOT, Fanári KAOA
113 **Méssi:** Akti Méssis, Arogí
114 **Ímeros:** Ímeros
115 **Marónia:** Platanitis
Évros
116 **Alexandroúpoli:** Plaz Dimou

Vório Aigaío (N Aegean) region

Lésvos (Lesbos)
117 **Eressós:** Scala Eresou
118 **Messótopos:** Tavari
119 **Kerámi:** Scala Kallonis
120 **Polihnitos:** Nyfida
121 **Vrissa:** Vatera
122 **Pirgi Thermis:** Kanoni Thermis
123 **Mitlíni:** Tsamakia
124 **Paleókipos:** Evreiaki
125 **Plomári:** Ágios Isidoros
Hios (Chios)
126 **Omiroupoli:** Ormos Lo
127 **Kardámila:** Paralia Nagou
128 **Neohóri:** Agia Foteini
129 **Thimiana:** Karfas, Megas Limnionas
Sámos
130 **Vourliotes:** Tsampou (Tsabou)

Notio Aigaío (S Aegean) region

Kikládes (Cyclades)
Tínos
131 **Tínos:** Kionia
Míkonos
132 **Míkonos:** Platí Gialó
133 **Ano Meria:** Kalafati
134 **Míkonos-(A. Meria):** Elia
Náxos
135 **Náxos:** Ágios Georgios, Vintzi
Síros
136 **Ano Síros:** Kini
Mílos
137 **Adámanta:** Papikinou
Dodekánissos (Dodecanese)
Kós (Cos)
138 **Kós:** Kritika *1*, *2*, *3*
Ródos (Rhodes)
139 **Ialisos:** Ixiá, Ixiá *A*, *B*, Triánda
140 **Ródos (Rhodes):** Psaropoula Kanari, Reni *1*, *2*
141 **Koskinoú:** Faliráki *1*, *2*, *3*, *4*
142 **Koskinoú/Kalithiés:** Faliráki *5*
143 **Koskinoú:** Faliráki-Kastraki, Kavourakia
144 **Kalithiés:** Faliráki *A*-Kalithion, Faliráki *B*-Kalithion, Kathara Falirákiou
145 **Afántou:** Afántou *1*, *2*, Katholiki, Kolímbia
146 **Arhángelos:** Tholos, Tsampika
147 **Líndos:** Vlícha
148 **Lárdos:** Glístra, Lothiarika

Kríti (Crete) region

Haniá (Canea)
149 **Paleohóra:** Pacheia Ammos
150 **Kolimvári:** Kolimvári
151 **Máleme:** Máleme
152 **Plataniás:** Plataniás
153 **N. Kidonia:** Ág. Apostoli EOT *1*, Ág. Apostoli EOT *2*, Kalamaki, Stalos
154 **Haniá (Canea):** Haniá EOT Chrysi Akti
155 **Plakas:** Almyrida
156 **Kalíves:** Kalíves
Réthimno
157 **Réthimno:** Réthimno *1*, *2*-Koutsolidi, *3*, *4*
158 **Adéle:** Adélianos Kampos
159 **Pigi:** Pigianos Kampos
Iráklio (Herakleion)
160 **Achlada:** Ágia Pelagia
161 **Rodiá:** Linoperámata
162 **Gazi:** Ammoudara
163 **Elia:** Amnissos
164 **Gouves:** Gouves *1*, *2*
165 **Mália:** Ágios Dimitrios, Potamos
Lassíthi
166 **Vrahási:** Mpoufou (Boufou)
167 **Eloúnda:** Eloúnda, Poros *1*, *2*, Schisma
168 **Ágios Nikólaos:** Ágios Nikólaos *1*, *2*, *3*, *5*, *6*, Almíros, Amoudi-Ágios Nikólaos *4*, Ammos-Plaz EOT
169 **Kritsa:** Ammoudara-Ágios Nikólaos
170 **Kaló Horió:** Kaló Horió
171 **Sitía:** Sitía
172 **Palékastro:** Kouremenos, Vai
173 **Péfki:** Makrigialos
174 **Ágios Ioánnis:** Koutsounari
175 **Ierápetra:** Ierápetra *1*, *2*
176 **Mírtos:** Mírtos

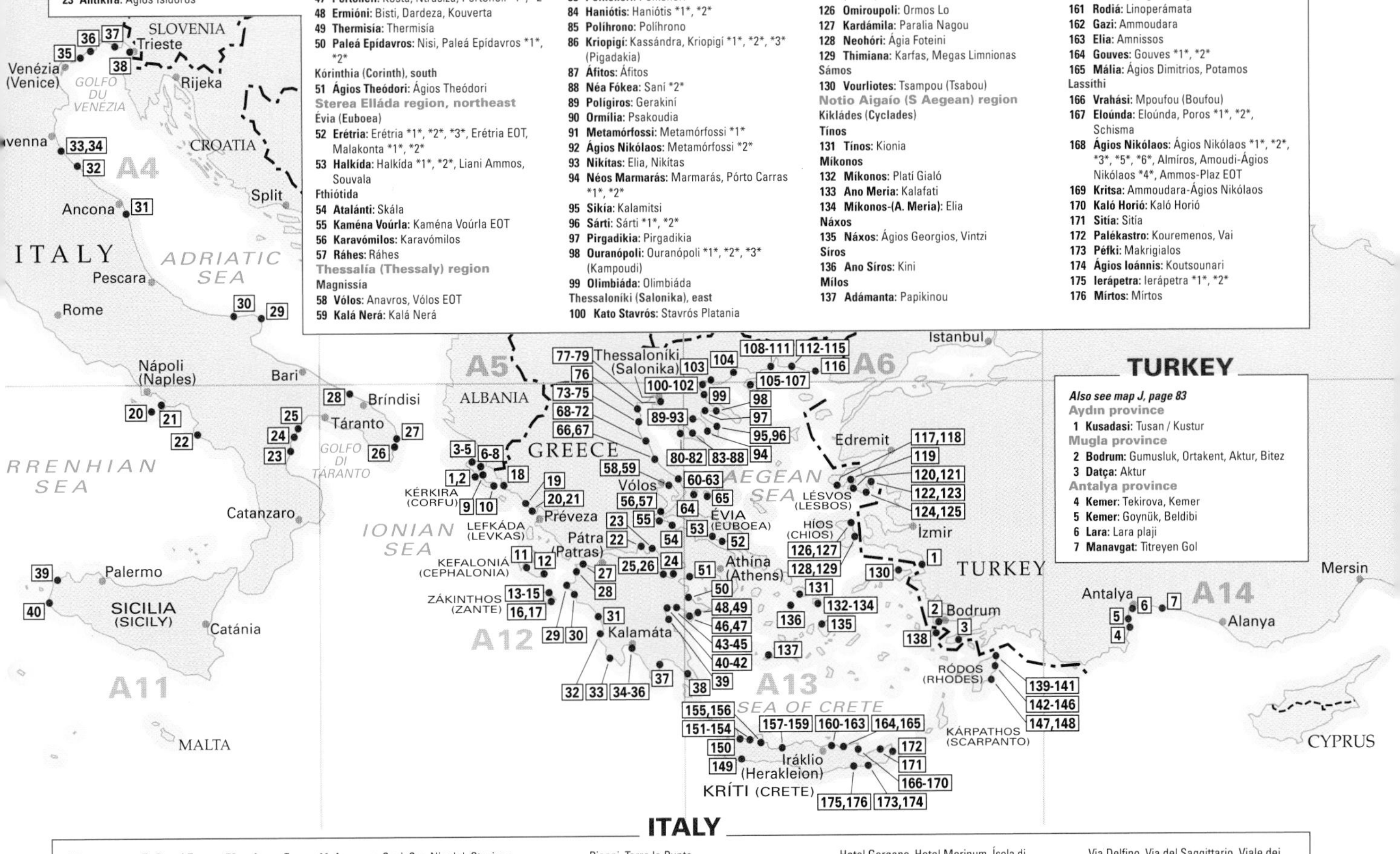

TURKEY

Also see map J, page 83

Aydın province

1 **Kusadasi:** Tusan / Kustur

Mugla province

2 **Bodrum:** Gumusluk, Ortakent, Aktur, Bitez
3 **Datça:** Aktur

Antalya province

4 **Kemer:** Tekirova, Kemer
5 **Kemer:** Goynük, Beldibi
6 **Lara:** Lara plaji
7 **Manavgat:** Titreyen Gol

ITALY

Also see maps B, D and E, page 78 and map F, page 79

Liguria

Imperia province
1 **Ospedaletti:** Bagni Ambrosiana, Capo Néro, Hotel Madison, Pubblico Macello, Rio Carrubo, Rio Crosio, Rio Pellotta, Rio Porrine, Villa Sada
2 **Tággia:** Bagni Annunziata, Colonia Ruffini
3 **Diano Marina:** Acquario, Hotel Jasmine, Hotel Majestic, Mortole, San Pietro, San Sebastiano, Varcavello
4 **San Bartolomeo al Mare:** Bagni Lido, Hotel Majola, Via Palmaria
5 **Cervo:** Capo Mimosa, Foce Steria, Miramare, Molo Centrale, Porteghetto
Savona province
6 **Laiguéglia:** Bagni Diana, Bagni Molo, Bagni Ondina, Colonia Braidese
7 **Finale Ligure:** Arco di Margherita, Arene Candide, Bagni San Donato, Colonia Cremasca, Colonia Lancia
8 **Noli:** Bagni Anita, Bagni Ondina, Bagni Vittoria
9 **Spotorno:** Molo Sant'Antonio, Molo Sirio, Rio Crovetto
Génova (Genoa) province
10 **Rapallo:** Bagni Bristol, Bagni Lido, Bagni Porticciolo, San Michele
11 **Lavagna:** Cavi, San Nicolo', Stazione
12 **Monéglia:** Bisagno, La Secca, Molo Bernero, Posato, San Lorenzo
La Spézia province
13 **Déiva Marina:** Centro, Ovest
14 **Framura:** Arena, Camping Framura, Porto Pidocchio, Spiaggia Confine, Torsei
15 **Bonassola:** Est, Ovest
'Cinque Terre':
16 **Monterosso:** Centro Golfo, Fegina, Lo Scoglio, Valle
17 **Vernazza:** Guvano, La Nave, Scalo Corniglia, Stazione Corniglia

Toscana (Tuscany)

Lucca province
18 **Forte dei Marmi:** Bagno Bonaccia, Bagno Graziella
Livorno (Leghorn) province
19 **Ísola di Capráia:** Centro, Fiumarella, Il Porto, Le Grotte

Campania

Nápoli (Naples) province
20 **Anacapri:** Grotta Azzurra, Punta Arciera, Punta Campitiello, Punta Carena
21 **Vico Equense:** Bagni di Scraio, Cuccurullo, Stabilimento Bikini
Salerno province
22 **Póllica:** Punta Caléo, Spiaggia Acciaroli Est, Spiaggia Acciaroli Ovest, Spiaggia Pioppi, Torre la Punta

Calabria

Cosenza province
23 **Roseto Capo Spúlico:** Baja Bella, Cardona, Castello, Gabbiano Azzurro, La Grilla, La Jonica, Rosetano, Scoglio della Galera

Basilicata

Matera province
24 **Scanzano Iónico:** Bufalória Nord, Bufalória Sud, Foce Agri, Foce Cavone, Lido Bufalória, Lido tre Madonna, Scanzano Nord, Scanzano Sud, Terzo Cavone
25 **Lido di Metaponto Bernalda:** Basento, Bradano, Centro, Nord, Sud

Puglia

Lecce province
26 **Andrano:** La Botte
27 **Castro Marina:** Grotta Romanelli, Grotta Zinzulusa, La Sorgente
Brindisi province
28 **Ostuni:** Cala di Fronte, Camping Pilone, Casa Rossa, Costa Merlata, Diana Marina, Dogana, Fontanelle, Lamaforca, Lido Morelli, Monticelli, Platja Residence, Rosa Marina, San Leonardo, Santa Libera, Villaggio Valtur
Fóggia province
29 **Vieste:** Baia San Felice, Camping Calacampi, Camping Girarrosto, Hollidey, Hotel Gergano, Hotel Merinum, Ísola di Chianco, Marina Piccola Nord, Marina Piccola Sud, Pugnochiuso, San Lorenzo, Scialmarino, Spiaggia San Lorenzo, Villagio Gattarella
30 **Chieuti:** Fantine, Saccione

Marche

Ancona province
31 **Sirolo:** Bagni Penne, Campanile, Camping, Camping Nord, Due Sorelle, Rocce Nere, Villa Bianchelli
Pesaro e Urbino province
32 **Gabicce Mare:** Hotel Majestic, Hotel Venus, Mississippi Nord, Mississippi Sud, Tavollo

Emília-Romagna

Forli province
33 **San Máuro Pascoli:** Vena
34 **Cesenático:** Canale Tagliata Nord, Canale Tagliata Sud, Porto Canale Nord, Porto Canale Sud, Scaricatore, Valverde Nord, Valverde Sud, Villamarina

Veneto

Venézia (Venice) province
35 **Jésolo:** Albergo Bagni, Albergo Danmark, Aurora, Casa Bianca, Centro Spiaggia, Fiume Piave, Fiume Piave Nord, Fiume Sile, Navigatori, Piazza Milano, Villaggio Marzotto
36 **San Michele al Tagliamento:** Capalonga, Via Delfino, Via del Saggittario, Viale dei Lauri, Via Veneto

Friuli-Venézia Giulia

Gorizia province
37 **Grado:** Camping Belvedere, Camping Europa, Costa Azzurra, Punta di Barbacale, Rotta Primero Camping Tenuta, Spiaggia Principale, Terrazza Mare
Trieste province
38 **Trieste:** Aurisina Filtri, Bagni Ausonia e Lanterna, Bagno Sticco, Barcola California Inn, Barcola ex CEDAS, Barcola Topolini, EAPT, Excelsior, Grignano, Santa Croce Porto

Sicilia (Sicily)

Trápani province
39 **Érice:** Bonagia, Hotel Tirreno
40 **Marsala:** Circolo Canottieri, Idroscalo, Lido Marinella, Lido Mediterraneo, Lido Signorino, San Teodore, Spiaggia Spagnolo

Sardegna (Sardinia)

Nuoro province
41 **Bosa:** Lido Chelo, Lido Lotti
Sassari province
42 **Santa Teresa Gallura:** Albergo Esit, Fiume Liscia, Porto Pozzo, Valle dell'Erica
43 **Ísola la Maddalena:** Abbatoggia, Cala Garibaldi, Punta Cannone, Puntanella, Punta San Giorgio, Spalmatore, Tegge

CENTRAL EUROPE AND...

ORIENT EXPRESS

The original Orient Express service started on 4th October 1883 and ran from Paris to Romania. This service linked up to London in 1889. The Paris-Milan-Venice route began in 1906 with the opening of the Simplon Tunnel and the route was later extended to Belgrade, Sofia, Athens and then Constantinople (present-day Istanbul).

Reduction of service due to competition from air travel started in the 1950s and the service was discontinued in 1977. The present service, which began in May 1982, runs from London to Venice via Paris, Basel, Zürich, Innsbruck and Verona with another route from Düsseldorf via Köln, Frankfurt am Main and Basel.

For further information on this and the Eastern Oriental Express and British Pullman, contact:
Venice-Simplon-Orient-Express Ltd.,
Sea Containers House,
20 Upper Ground,
London SE1 9PF.   Tel. +44 (0) 171 928 6000.

Distance from Paris

	Kilometres	Miles
Paris	0	0
Lausanne	508	316
Milan	820	510
Venice	1069	664
Treiste	1226	762
Zagreb	1551	964
Belgrade	1984	1233
Sofia	2401	1492
Istanbul	3035	1886

--- former boundary of Soviet Union

The commonly accepted division between Europe and Asia is formed by the Ural Mountains, Caspian Sea, Caucasus Mountains, Black Sea and the Bosporus.

Trans-Siberian Railway

CENTRAL EUROPE

THE VOLGA

600 kilometres
300 miles

THE DANUBE

300 kilometres
150 miles

400 km
200 miles

...THE FORMER SOVIET UNION

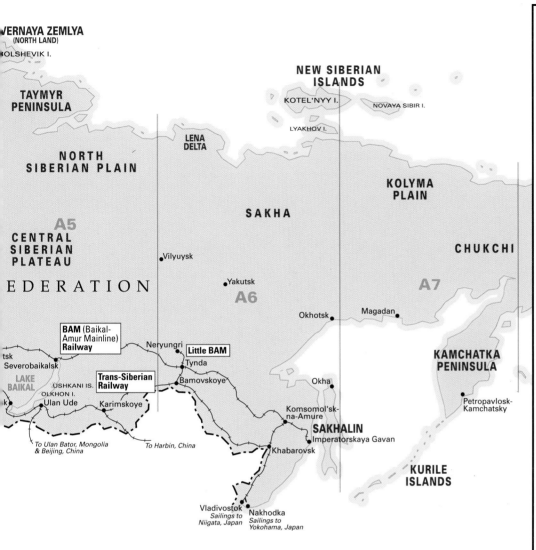

SEVERNAYA ZEMLYA
(NORTH LAND)
BOLSHEVIK I.

TAYMYR
PENINSULA

NORTH
SIBERIAN PLAIN

LENA DELTA

NEW SIBERIAN
ISLANDS

KOTEL'NYY I.

NOVAYA SIBIR I.

LYAKHOV I.

CENTRAL
SIBERIAN
PLATEAU

A5

SAKHA

Vilyuysk

Yakutsk

A6

KOLYMA
PLAIN

CHUKCHI

A7

EDERATION

BAM (Baikal-
Amur Mainline)
Railway

Neryungri

Little BAM

Tynda

Bamovskoye

Okhotsk

Magadan

KAMCHATKA
PENINSULA

Petropavlosk-
Kamchatsky

tsk
Severobaikalsk

LAKE
BAIKAL

USHKANI IS.
OLKHON I.

k

Ulan Ude

Karimskoye

Trans-Siberian
Railway

Okha

Komsomol'sk-
na-Amure

SAKHALIN

Imperatorskaya Gavan

KURILE
ISLANDS

To Ulan Bator, Mongolia
& Beijing, China

To Harbin, China

Khabarovsk

Vladivostok
Sailings to
Niigata, Japan

Nakhodka
Sailings to
Yokohama, Japan

TRANS-SIBERIAN RAILWAY

	Distance from Moscow	
	Kilometres	Miles
Moscow	0	0
Alexandrov	112	70
Yaroslavl'	282	175
Danilov	357	222
Buy	450	280
Kotelnich	870	541
Kirov	957	595
Perm	1437	893
Yekaterinburg	1818	1130
Tyumen	2144	1332
Ishim	2433	1512
Omsk	2716	1688
Tatarsk	2585	1606
Novosibirsk	3343	2077
Yurga	3498	2174
Tayga	3571	2219
Achinsk	3920	2436
Krasnoyarsk	4104	2550
Uyar	4235	2632
Kansk	4351	2704
Tayshet	4522	2810
Irkutsk	5191	3226
Slyudyanka	5317	3304
Ulan Ude	5647	3509
Ulan Bator	6304	3917
Beijing	7865	4887
Khilok	5940	3691
Chita	6204	3855
Karimskoye	6300	3915
Harbin	7610	4729
Bamovskoye	7281	4524
Skovorodino	7313	4544
Belogorsk	7873	4892
Izvestkovyy	8242	5121
Khabarovsk	8531	5301
Bikin	8764	5446
Spassk Dalny	9057	5628
Ussuriysk	9185	5707
Nakhodka	9446	5869
Ugolnaya	9264	5756
Vladivostok	9297	5777

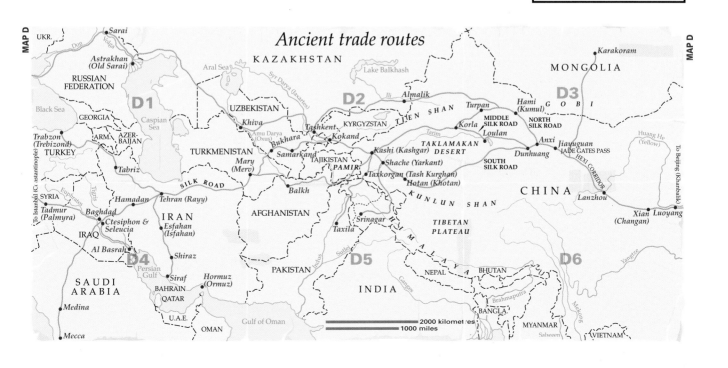

Ancient trade routes

MAP D

UKR.

Sarai

Astrakhan
(Old Sarai)

Don

Volga

KAZAKHSTAN

Aral Sea

Lake Balkhash

MONGOLIA

Karakoram

RUSSIAN
FEDERATION

Black Sea

GEORGIA

Caspian
Sea

D1

UZBEKISTAN

Syr Darya (Jaxartes)

Khiva

Ili

Almalik

D2

Lake Balkhash

TIEN SHAN

Turpan

Hami
(Kumul)

GOBI

D3

Trabzon
(Trebizond)

TURKEY

ARM.
AZER-
BAIJAN

Tabriz

Amu Darya
(Oxus)

Bukhara

TURKMENISTAN

Tashkent

KYRGYZSTAN

Kokand

Samarkand

TAJIKISTAN

PAMIR

Kashi (Kashgar)

Korla

Tarim

TAKLAMAKAN
DESERT

Loulan

MIDDLE
SILK ROAD

NORTH
SILK ROAD

Anxi

Dunhuang

Jiayuguan
JADE GATES PASS

HEXI CORRIDOR

Huang He
(Yellow)

To Beijing (Khanbalik)

To Istanbul (Constantinople)

SYRIA

Tadmur
(Palmyra)

Baghdad

Ctesiphon &
Seleucia

IRAQ

Hamadan

Tehran (Rayy)

IRAN

Esfahan
(Isfahan)

Mary
(Merv)

SILK ROAD

Balkh

AFGHANISTAN

Shache (Yarkant)

Taxkorgan (Tash Kurghan)

Hotan (Khotan)

SOUTH
SILK ROAD

KUNLUN SHAN

CHINA

Lanzhou

Xian
(Changan)

Luoyang

Al Basrah

SAUDI
ARABIA

D4

Shiraz

Siraf

Hormuz
(Ormuz)

BAHRAIN
QATAR

Srinagar

Taxila

PAKISTAN

Sutlej

Indus

D5

NEPAL

TIBETAN
PLATEAU

HIMALAYA

BHUTAN

Brahmaputra

D6

Mecca

Medina

U.A.E.

OMAN

Gulf of Oman

Persian Gulf

INDIA

Ganges

BANGLA.

MYANMAR

Yangtze

Mekong

Salween

VIETNAM

2000 kilometres
1000 miles

MAP D

AFRICA

French is widely spoken throughout the country, except in the north where Spanish is more predominant. French is used for most official and business transactions.

French is used for most business transactions. English is spoken in major cities and resorts.

English is normally understood in hotels, restaurants and shops.

English and French are widely spoken throughout the country.

English is widely spoken throughout the country.

Arabic and Tigrinya are the official languages. English and Italian are the most common foreign languages.

Ahmaric is the official language, with English as the second official language. Italian and French are still widely spoken.

Arabic and Somali are the official languages. Some English and Italian is also spoken.

10 English is the official language, Kiswahili is the national language.

11 French and Kinyarwanda are the official languages. Kisiwahili is used for trade and commerce.

12 English and Swahili are the official languages.

13 Chichewa is widely spoken and is regarded as the national language by Malawi's largest ethnic group, the Chewa.

14 The official languages are English and the Shona and Ndebele dialects.

15 The official languages are English and Afrikaans.

16 The official languages are English and Siswati.

17 The official languages are English and Sesotho.

18 The majority speak Comoran, a blend of Arabic and Swahili.

19 The official language is Creole, but English and French are widely spoken.

20 The official languages are French and Malagasy. Very little English is spoken.

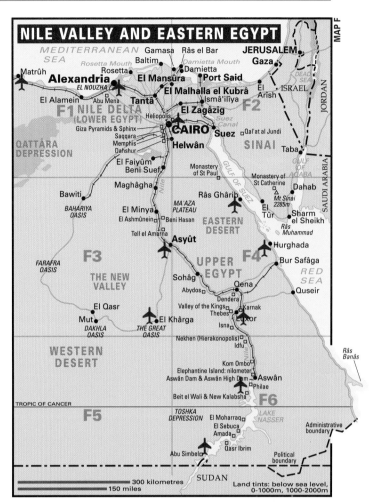

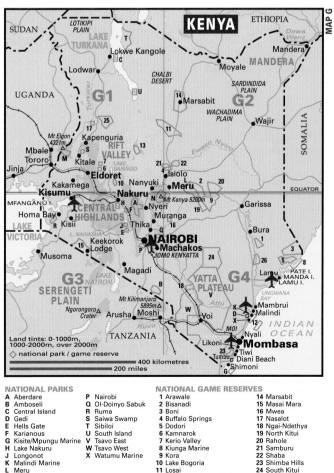

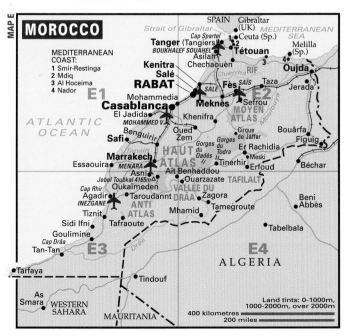

NATIONAL PARKS

A Aberdare
B Amboseli
C Central Island
D Gedi
E Hells Gate
F Karianous
G Kisite/Mpungu Marine
H Lake Nakuru
J Longonot
K Malindi Marine
L Meru
M Mount Elgon
N Mount Kenya
P Nairobi
Q Ol-Doinyo Sabuk
R Ruma
S Saiwa Swamp
T Sibiloi
U South Island
V Tsavo East
W Tsavo West
X Watumu Marine

NATIONAL GAME RESERVES

1 Arawale
2 Bisanadi
3 Boni
4 Buffalo Springs
5 Dodori
6 Kamnarok
7 Kerio Valley
8 Kiunga Marine
9 Kora
10 Lake Bogoria
11 Losai
12 Malindi/Waitamu Marine
13 Maralal (National Sanctuary)
14 Marsabit
15 Masai Mara
16 Mwea
17 Nasalot
18 Ngai-Ndethya
19 North Kitui
20 Rahole
21 Samburu
22 Shaba
23 Shimba Hills
24 South Kitui
25 South Turkana
26 Tana River Primate

UNITED STATES

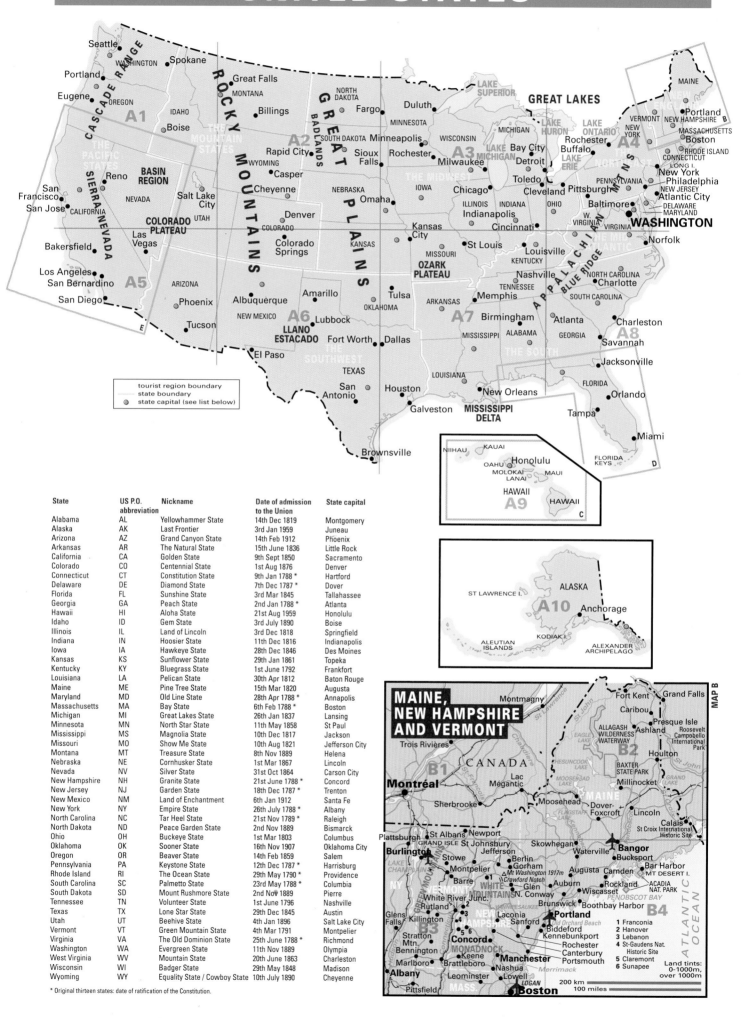

tourist region boundary
state boundary
○ state capital (see list below)

State	US P.O. abbreviation	Nickname	Date of admission to the Union	State capital
Alabama	AL	Yellowhammer State	14th Dec 1819	Montgomery
Alaska	AK	Last Frontier	3rd Jan 1959	Juneau
Arizona	AZ	Grand Canyon State	14th Feb 1912	Phoenix
Arkansas	AR	The Natural State	15th June 1836	Little Rock
California	CA	Golden State	9th Sept 1850	Sacramento
Colorado	CO	Centennial State	1st Aug 1876	Denver
Connecticut	CT	Constitution State	9th Jan 1788 *	Hartford
Delaware	DE	Diamond State	7th Dec 1787 *	Dover
Florida	FL	Sunshine State	3rd Mar 1845	Tallahassee
Georgia	GA	Peach State	2nd Jan 1788 *	Atlanta
Hawaii	HI	Aloha State	21st Aug 1959	Honolulu
Idaho	ID	Gem State	3rd July 1890	Boise
Illinois	IL	Land of Lincoln	3rd Dec 1818	Springfield
Indiana	IN	Hoosier State	11th Dec 1816	Indianapolis
Iowa	IA	Hawkeye State	28th Dec 1846	Des Moines
Kansas	KS	Sunflower State	29th Jan 1861	Topeka
Kentucky	KY	Bluegrass State	1st June 1792	Frankfort
Louisiana	LA	Pelican State	30th Apr 1812	Baton Rouge
Maine	ME	Pine Tree State	15th Mar 1820	Augusta
Maryland	MD	Old Line State	28th Apr 1788 *	Annapolis
Massachusetts	MA	Bay State	6th Feb 1788 *	Boston
Michigan	MI	Great Lakes State	26th Jan 1837	Lansing
Minnesota	MN	North Star State	11th May 1858	St Paul
Mississippi	MS	Magnolia State	10th Dec 1817	Jackson
Missouri	MO	Show Me State	10th Aug 1821	Jefferson City
Montana	MT	Treasure State	8th Nov 1889	Helena
Nebraska	NE	Cornhusker State	1st Mar 1867	Lincoln
Nevada	NV	Silver State	31st Oct 1864	Carson City
New Hampshire	NH	Granite State	21st June 1788 *	Concord
New Jersey	NJ	Garden State	18th Dec 1787 *	Trenton
New Mexico	NM	Land of Enchantment	6th Jan 1912	Santa Fe
New York	NY	Empire State	26th July 1788 *	Albany
North Carolina	NC	Tar Heel State	21st Nov 1789 *	Raleigh
North Dakota	ND	Peace Garden State	2nd Nov 1889	Bismarck
Ohio	OH	Buckeye State	1st Mar 1803	Columbus
Oklahoma	OK	Sooner State	16th Nov 1907	Oklahoma City
Oregon	OR	Beaver State	14th Feb 1859	Salem
Pennsylvania	PA	Keystone State	12th Dec 1787 *	Harrisburg
Rhode Island	RI	The Ocean State	29th May 1790 *	Providence
South Carolina	SC	Palmetto State	23rd May 1788 *	Columbia
South Dakota	SD	Mount Rushmore State	2nd Nov 1889	Pierre
Tennessee	TN	Volunteer State	1st June 1796	Nashville
Texas	TX	Lone Star State	29th Dec 1845	Austin
Utah	UT	Beehive State	4th Jan 1896	Salt Lake City
Vermont	VT	Green Mountain State	4th Mar 1791	Montpelier
Virginia	VA	The Old Dominion State	25th June 1788 *	Richmond
Washington	WA	Evergreen State	11th Nov 1889	Olympia
West Virginia	WV	Mountain State	20th June 1863	Charleston
Wisconsin	WI	Badger State	29th May 1848	Madison
Wyoming	WY	Equality State / Cowboy State	10th July 1890	Cheyenne

* Original thirteen states: date of ratification of the Constitution.

MAINE, NEW HAMPSHIRE AND VERMONT

1 Franconia
2 Hanover
3 Lebanon
4 St-Gaudens Nat. Historic Site
5 Claremont
6 Sunapee

Land tints:
0-1000m,
over 1000m

200 km
100 miles

UNITED STATES

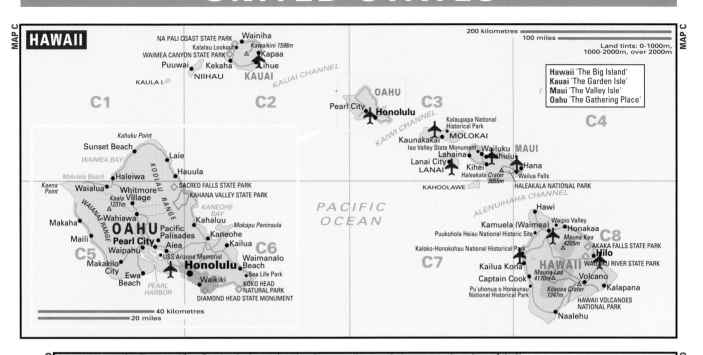

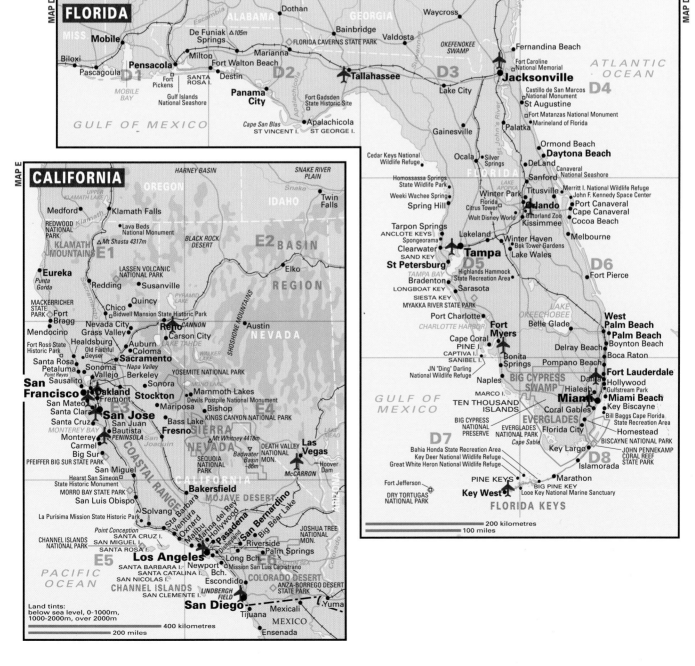

UNITED STATES PARKS

The National Park Service Act was signed in 1916 by President Woodrow Wilson "to conserve the scenery and the natural and historic objects and the wild life therein". Thirty-six national parks were brought under a single federal agency by this law. The National Park Service is now responsible for over 360 sites set aside to preserve the natural, historical and cultural heritage of the United States.

For further information, contact:

National Park Service
1849-C Street Northwest
Washington DC
20240

Tel. +1 202 208 4747

This map also lists a selection of the more well-known theme parks, from Disneyland in California to Sea World in Florida.

● National Park
　National Preserve
○ National Memorial
● National Monument
○ National Recreation Area
　National Seashore
　National Lakeshore
● National Battlefield
　National Battlefield Park
　National Battlefield Site
　National Military Park
○ National Historic Site
　National Historical Park

The Pacific States
Alaska
1 Cape Krusenstern National Monument
2 Noatak National Preserve
3 Gates of the Arctic National Park and Preserve
4 Kobuk Valley National Park
5 Bering Land Bridge National Preserve
6 Yukon-Charley Rivers National Preserve
7 Denali National Park and Preserve
8 Lake Clark National Park and Preserve
9 Katmai National Park and Preserve
10 Aniachak National Monument and Preserve
11 Kenai Fjords National Park
12 Wrangell-St Elias National Park and Preserve
13 Glacier Bay National Park and Preserve
14 Sitka National Historical Park
15 Klondike Gold Rush National Historical Park
Hawaii
16 USS Arizona Memorial
17 Kalaupapa National Historical Park
18 Haleakala National Park
19 Puukohola Heiau National Historic Site
20 Kaloko-Honokohau National Historical Park
21 Pu'uhonua o Honaunau National Historical Park
22 Hawaii Volcanoes National Park
Washington
23 San Juan Island National Historical Park
24 Olympic National Park
25 Ebey's Landing National Historical Reserve
26 North Cascades National Park
27 Ross Lake National Recreation Area
28 Lake Chelan National Recreation Area
29 Coulee Dam National Recreation Area
30 Whitman Mission National Historic Site
31 Mount Ranier National Park
32 Fort Vancouver National Historic Site
Oregon
33 Fort Clatsop National Memorial
34 McLoughlin House National Historic Site
35 John Day Fossil Beds National Monument
36 Crater Lake National Park
37 Oregon Caves National Monument
California
38 Redwood National Park
39 Lava Beds National Monument
40 Whiskeytown-Shasta-Trinity National Recreation Area
41 Lassen Volcanic National Park
42 Point Reyes National Seashore
43 Muir Woods National Monument
44 Fort Point National Historic Site
45 Golden Gate National Recreation Area
46 San Francisco Maritime National Historical Park
47 Port Chicago Naval Magazine National Memorial
48 John Muir National Historic Site
49 Eugene O'Neill National Historic Site
50 Pinnacles National Monument
51 Yosemite National Park
52 Devils Postpile National Monument
53 Sequoia and Kings Canyon National Parks
54 Manzanar National Historic Site
55 Death Valley National Monument
56 Channel Islands National Park
57 Santa Monica Mountains National Recreation Area
58 Cabrillo National Monument
59 Joshua Tree National Monument
Nevada
60 Lake Mead National Recreation Area
61 Great Basin National Park
The Mountain States
Idaho
62 Nez Perce National Historical Park
63 Hagerman Fossil Beds National Monument
64 City of Rocks National Reserve

65 Craters of the Moon National Monument
Montana
66 Glacier National Park
67 Grant-Kohrs Ranch National Historic Site
68 Big Hole National Battlefield
69 Bighorn Canyon National Recreation Area
70 Little Bighorn Battlefield National Monument
Wyoming
71 Devils Tower National Monument
72 Fort Laramie National Historic Site
73 Yellowstone National Park
74 John D. Rockefeller Jr. Memorial Parkway
75 Grand Teton National Park
76 Fossil Butte National Monument
Utah
77 Golden Spike National Monument
78 Timpanogos Cave National Monument
79 Zion National Park
80 Cedar Breaks National Monument
81 Bryce Canyon National Park
82 Capitol Reef National Park
83 Rainbow Bridge National Monument
84 Natural Bridges National Monument
85 Canyonlands National Park
86 Arches National Park
Colorado
87 Dinosaur National Monument
88 Rocky Mountain National Park
89 Colorado National Monument
90 Black Canyon of the Gunnison National Monument
91 Curecanti National Recreation Area
92 Florissant Fossil Beds National Monument
93 Hovenweep National Monument
94 Yucca House National Monument
95 Mesa Verde National Monument
96 Great Sand Dunes National Monument
97 Bent's Old Fort National Historic Site
The Southwest
Arizona
98 Pipe Spring National Monument
99 Grand Canyon National Park
100 Glen Canyon National Recreation Area (also in Utah)
101 Navajo National Monument
102 Canyon de Chelly National Monument
103 Hubbell Trading Post National Historic Site

104 Wupatki National Monument
105 Sunset Crater National Monument
106 Walnut Canyon National Monument
107 Tuzigoot National Monument
108 Montezuma Castle National Monument
109 Petrified Forest National Park
110 Tonto National Monument
111 Hohokam Pima National Monument
112 Casa Grande National Monument
113 Organ Pipe Cactus National Monument
114 Tumacacori National Monument
115 Coronado National Memorial
116 Saguaro National Monument
117 Fort Bowie National Historic Site
118 Chiricahua National Monument
New Mexico
119 Gila Cliff Dwellings National Monument
120 White Sands National Monument
121 Carlsbad Caverns National Park
122 Salinas Pueblo Missions National Monument
123 Aztec Ruins National Monument
124 Chaco Culture National Historical Park
125 Zuni-Cibola National Historical Park
126 El Morro National Monument
127 El Malpais National Monument
128 Petroglyph National Monument
129 Bandelier National Monument
130 Pecos National Historical Park
131 Fort Union National Monument
132 Capulin Volcano National Monument
Texas
133 Lake Meredith National Recreation Area
134 Alibates Flint Quarries National Monument
135 Guadalupe Mountains National Park
136 Chamizal National Memorial
137 Fort Davis National Historic Site
138 Big Bend National Park
139 Amistad National Recreation Area
140 Lyndon B. Johnson National Historical Park
141 San Antonio Missions National Historical Park
142 Padre Island National Seashore
143 Palo Alto Battlefield National Historic Site
144 Big Thicket National Preserve
Oklahoma
145 Chickasaw National Recreation Area

The Midwest
North Dakota
146 International Peace Garden
147 Fort Union Trading Post National Historic Site
148 Theodore Roosevelt National Park (North and South Units)
149 Knife River Indian Villages National Historic Site
South Dakota
150 Jewel Cave National Monument
151 Mount Rushmore National Memorial
152 Wind Cave National Park
153 Badlands National Park
Minnesota
154 Pipestone National Monument
155 Voyageurs National Park
156 Grand Portage National Monument
Wisconsin
157 Apostle Islands National Lakeshore
158 Ice Age Scientific Reserve
Michigan
159 Isle Royale National Park
160 Keweenaw National Historical Park
161 Pictured Rocks National Lakeshore
162 Father Marquette National Memorial and Museum
163 Sleeping Bear Dunes National Lakeshore
Nebraska
164 Agate Fossil Beds National Monument
165 Scotts Bluff National Monument
166 Chimney Rock National Historic Site
167 Homestead National Monument of America
Iowa
168 Effigy Mounds National Monument
169 Herbert Hoover National Historic Site
Kansas
170 Fort Larned National Historic Site
171 Brown v. Board of Education National Historic Site
172 Fort Scott National Historic Site
Missouri
173 Harry S. Truman National Historic Site
174 George Washington Carver National Monument
175 Wilson's Creek National Battlefield
176 Ulysses S. Grant National Historic Site
177 Jefferson National Expansion Memorial
Illinois
178 Lincoln Home National Historic Site

UNITED STATES PARKS

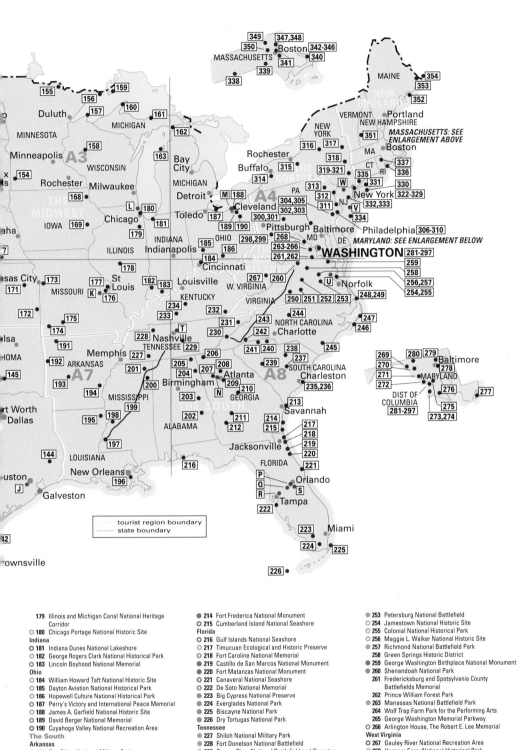

291 Rock Creek Park
O 292 Sewall-Belmont House National Historic Site
O 293 Theodore Roosevelt Island
O 294 Thomas Jefferson Memorial
O 295 Vietnam Veterans Memorial
O 296 Washington Monument
297 The White House

The Northeast
Pennsylvania
O 298 Friendship Hill National Historic Site
● 299 Fort Necessity National Battlefield
O 300 Johnstown Flood National Memorial
O 301 Allegheny Portage Railroad National Historic Site
O 302 Eisenhower National Historic Site
O 303 Gettysburg National Military Park
O 304 Hopewell Furnace National Historic Site
O 305 Valley Forge National Historical Park
● 306 Benjamin Franklin National Memorial
O 307 Edgar Allen Poe National Historic Site
O 308 Gloria Dei (Old Swedes') Church National Historic Site
O 309 Independence National Historical Park
O 310 Thaddeus Kosciuszko National Memorial
311 Delaware and Lehigh Navigation Canal National Heritage Corridor
O 312 Delaware Water Gap National Recreation Area
O 313 Steamtown National Historic Site
New York
O 314 Theodore Roosevelt Inaugural National Historic Site
O 315 Women's Rights National Historical Park
● 316 Fort Stanwix National Monument
O 317 Saratoga National Historical Park
O 318 Martin Van Buren National Historic Site
O 319 Eleanor Roosevelt National Historic Site
O 320 Vanderbilt Mansion National Historic Site
O 321 Home of Franklin Delano Roosevelt National Historic Site
● 322 Castle Clinton National Monument
O 323 Federal Hall National Memorial
● 324 Gateway National Recreation Area
O 325 General Grant National Memorial
O 326 Hamilton Grange National Memorial
O 327 Saint Paul's Church National Historic Site
● 328 Statue of Liberty National Monument
O 329 Theodore Roosevelt Birthplace National Historic Site
O 330 Fire Island National Seashore
O 331 Sagamore Hill National Historic Site
New Jersey
O 332 Edison National Historical Site
O 333 Morristown National Historical Park
334 Pinelands National Reserve
New England
Connecticut
O 335 Weir Farm National Historic Site
Rhode Island
O 336 Touro Synagogue National Historic Site
O 337 Roger Williams National Memorial
Massachusetts
● 338 Springfield Armory National Historic Site
339 Blackstone River Valley National Heritage Corridor
O 340 Cape Cod National Seashore
O 341 Adams National Historic Site
O 342 Boston African American National Historical Site
O 343 Boston National Historical Park
O 344 Frederick Law Olmsted National Historic Site
O 345 John F. Kennedy National Historic Site
O 346 Longfellow National Historic Site
O 347 Saugus Iron Works National Historic Site
O 348 Salem Maritime National Historic Site
O 349 Lowell National Historical Park
O 350 Minute Man National Historical Park
New Hampshire
O 351 Saint-Gaudens National Historic Site
Maine
● 352 Acadia National Park
O 353 Saint Croix Island International Historic Site
Canada
New Brunswick
354 Roosevelt Campobello International Park

(Not shown on map):
Puerto Rico
O 355 San Juan National Historic Site
US Virgin Islands
● 356 Buck Island Reef National Monument
O 357 Christiansted National Historic Site
O 358 Salt River Bay National Historical Park and Ecological Preserve
● 359 Virgin Islands National Park
American Samoa
● 360 The National Park of American Samoa
Northern Mariana Islands
361 American Memorial Park
O 362 War in the Pacific National Historical Park

THEME PARKS

A Great America, Santa Clara, California
B Six Flags Magic Mountain, Valencia, California
C Knott's Berry Farm, Buena Park, California
D Universal Studios, Hollywood, California
E Disneyland, Anaheim, California
F Sea World, San Diego, California
G Six Flags Over Texas, Arlington, Texas
H Sea World of Texas, San Antonio, Texas
J AstroWorld, Houston, Texas
K Six Flags Over Mid-America, Eureka, Missouri
L Six Flags Great America, Gurnee, Illinois
M Sea World of Ohio, Aurora, Ohio
N Six Flags Over Georgia, Atlanta, Georgia
P Universal Studios, Orlando, Florida
Q Walt Disney World Resort Complex (including the Magic Kingdom theme park, EPCOT Center, Disney/MGM Studios theme park, Fort Wilderness recreation area), Lake Buena Vista, Florida
R Busch Gardens, Tampa, Florida
S Sea World, Orlando, Florida
T Opryland USA, Nashville, Tennessee
U Busch Gardens, Williamsburg, Virginia
V Six Flags Great Adventure, Jackson, New Jersey
W Great Gorge Resort Action Park, McAfee, New Jersey

179 Illinois and Michigan Canal National Heritage Corridor
O 180 Chicago Portage National Historic Site
Indiana
O 181 Indiana Dunes National Lakeshore
● 182 George Rogers Clark National Historical Park
● 183 Lincoln Boyhood National Memorial
Ohio
O 184 William Howard Taft National Historic Site
● 185 Dayton Aviation National Historical Park
● 186 Hopewell Culture National Historical Park
● 187 Perry's Victory and International Peace Memorial
● 188 James A. Garfield National Historic Site
● 189 David Berger National Memorial
O 190 Cuyahoga Valley National Recreation Area
The South
Arkansas
● 191 Pea Ridge National Military Park
● 192 Fort Smith National Historic Site
● 193 Hot Springs National Park
● 194 Arkansas National Memorial
Louisiana
O 195 Poverty Point National Monument
O 196 Jean Lafitte National Historical Park
Mississippi
O 197 Natchez National Historical Park
● 198 Vicksburg National Military Park
199 Natchez Trace Parkway (also in Alabama and Tennessee)
● 200 Tupelo National Battlefield
● 201 Brices Cross Roads National Battlefield Site
Alabama
● 202 Tuskegee Institute National Historic Site
● 203 Horseshoe Bend National Military Park
● 204 Little River Canyon National Preserve
● 205 Russell Cave National Monument
Georgia
● 206 Chickamauga and Chattanooga National Military Park
● 207 Kennesaw Mountain National Battlefield Park
● 208 Chattahoochee River National Recreation Area
● 209 Martin Luther King Jr. National Historic Site
● 210 Ocmulgee National Monument
● 211 Andersonville National Historic Site
● 212 Jimmy Carter National Historic Site
● 213 Fort Pulaski National Monument

● 214 Fort Frederica National Monument
● 215 Cumberland Island National Seashore
Florida
● 216 Gulf Islands National Seashore
● 217 Timucuan Ecological and Historic Preserve
● 218 Fort Caroline National Memorial
● 219 Castillo de San Marcos National Monument
● 220 Fort Matanzas National Monument
● 221 Canaveral National Seashore
● 222 De Soto National Memorial
● 223 Big Cypress National Preserve
● 224 Everglades National Park
● 225 Biscayne National Park
● 226 Dry Tortugas National Park
Tennessee
● 227 Shiloh National Military Park
● 228 Fort Donelson National Battlefield
● 229 Stones River National Battlefield and Cemetery
● 230 Great Smoky Mountains National Park
● 231 Andrew Johnson National Historic Site
Kentucky
O 232 Cumberland Gap National Historical Park
O 233 Mammoth Cave National Park
O 234 Abraham Lincoln Birthplace National Historic Site
South Carolina
O 235 Fort Sumter National Monument
O 236 Charles Pinckney National Historic Site
O 237 Congaree Swamp National Monument
238 Historic Camden
O 239 Ninety Six National Historic Site
O 240 Kings Mountain National Military Park
O 241 Cowpens National Battlefield
North Carolina
● 242 Carl Sandburg Home National Historic Site
243 Blue Ridge Parkway (also in Virginia)
● 244 Guilford Courthouse National Military Park
● 245 Moores Creek National Battlefield
O 246 Cape Lookout National Seashore
O 247 Cape Hatteras National Seashore
O 248 Fort Raleigh National Historic Site
O 249 Wright Brothers National Memorial
The Mid Atlantic
Virginia
● 250 Booker T. Washington National Monument
● 251 Red Hill Patrick Henry National Memorial
O 252 Appomattox Court House National Historical Park

O 253 Petersburg National Battlefield
O 254 Jamestown National Historic Site
O 255 Colonial National Historical Park
O 256 Maggie L. Walker National Historic Site
O 257 Richmond National Battlefield Park
O 258 Green Springs Historic District
O 259 George Washington Birthplace National Monument
O 260 Shenandoah National Park
O 261 Fredericksburg and Spotsylvania County Battlefields Memorial
O 262 Prince William Forest Park
O 263 Manassas National Battlefield Park
O 264 Wolf Trap Farm Park for the Performing Arts
O 265 George Washington Memorial Parkway
O 266 Arlington House, The Robert E. Lee Memorial
West Virginia
O 267 Gauley River National Recreation Area
O 268 Harpers Ferry National Historical Park
Maryland
O 269 Antietam National Battlefield
O 270 Monocacy National Batlefield
O 271 Chesapeake and Ohio Canal National Historical Park
O 272 Clara Barton National Historic Site
273 Fort Washington Park
274 Piscataway Park
275 Greenbelt Park
O 276 Thomas Stone National Historic Site
O 277 Assateague Island National Seashore
O 278 Fort McHenry National Monument and Historic Shrine
O 279 Hampton National Historic Site
280 Catoctin Mountain Park
District of Columbia
281 Constitution Gardens
O 282 Ford's Theatre National Historic Site
283 Frederick Douglass Memorial Home
O 284 John F. Kennedy Center for the Performing Arts
O 285 Lincoln Memorial
O 286 Lyndon Baines Johnson Memorial Grove on the Potomac
O 287 Mary McLeod Bethune Council House National Historic Site
288 National Capital Region
289 National Mall
O 290 Pennsylvania Avenue National Historic Site

---

tourist region boundary
state boundary

CANADA

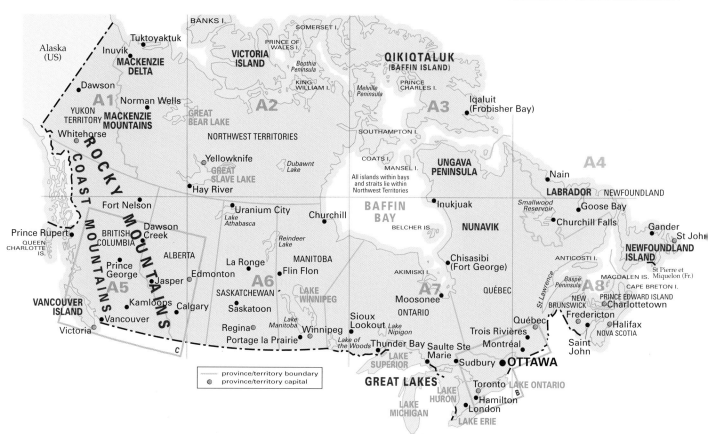

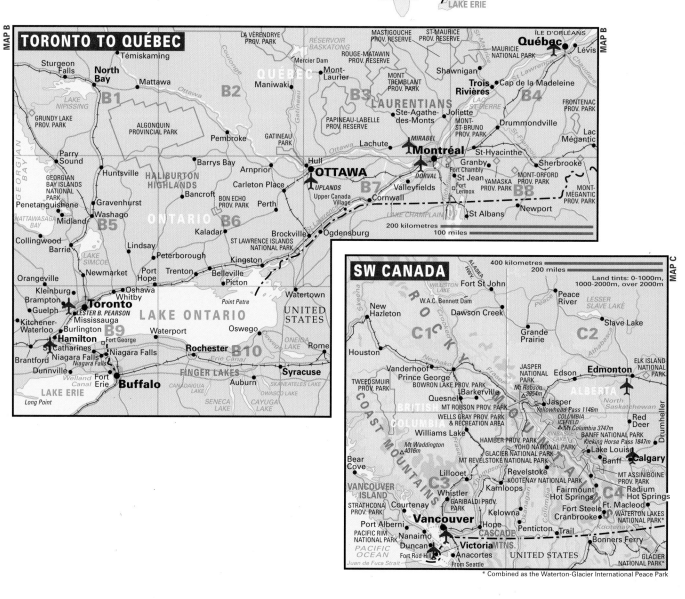

CARIBBEAN

Great Exuma
Long I.
BAHAMAS
Archipelago de Camagüey
Mayaguana
Crooked I.
Acklins I.
Turks & Caicos Is. (UK)
Isla de la Juventud
CUBA
Great Inagua
D2
D3
HAITI
DOMINICAN REPUBLIC
Cayman Is. (UK)
D1
British Virgin Is. (UK)
Puerto Rico (US)
Swan Is. (Hon.)
JAMAICA
Bajo Nuevo (Col.)
US Virgin Is. (US)
de Bahia s., Hon.)
DURAS
Cayos Miskito (Nic.)
CARIBBEAN SEA
ST KITTS-NEVIS
Montserrat (UK)
Aves (Bird I., Ven.)
ARAGUA
Isla de Providencia (Col.)
Isla de San Andrés (Col.)
Cayos de Albuquerque (Col.)
D5
D6
Curaçao (Neths.) **18**
Bonaire (Neths.) **18**
Aruba (Neths.)
Islas Las Aves (Ven.)
Isla Blanquilla (Ven.)
COSTA RICA
PANAMA
Islas Los Roques (Ven.)
Isla La Tortuga (Ven.)
Isla Margarita (Ven.)
D7
TRINIDAD & TOBAGO
COLOMBIA
VENEZUELA
GUYANA

Anguilla (UK)
St Maarten (Neths.) **9**
St Martin (Fr.) **10**
St Barthélemy (Fr.) **10**
Saba (Neths.) **9**
St Eustatius (Neths.) **11**
ANTIGUA & BARBUDA **12**
Guadeloupe (Fr.) **10**
DOMINICA **13**
Martinique (Fr.) **14**
ST LUCIA **15**
BARBADOS **16**
ST VINCENT & THE GRENADINES
GRENADA **17**

OFFICIAL LANGUAGES
(Numbers in top right corner of countries refer to the notes below)

English | French | Spanish
Dutch | Other

1 English is widely spoken by the West Indian settlers in the north and on the Bay Islands.
2 English-speaking communities are found on the Caribbean coast.
3 English is widely spoken.
4 Some English is spoken.
5 English, French, German and Portuguese are spoken by sections of the community.
6 Some English and French are spoken.
7 The official languages are French and Creole. English is widely spoken in tourist areas.
8 Spanish and Creole are widely spoken.
9 English is the most popularly-spoken language.
10 The islanders speak Creole. *Patois* and English are also widely spoken.
11 Papiamento (a combination of Dutch, English, Portuguese, Spanish and African and Indian languages), English, French and Spanish may also be spoken.
12 English *patois* is widely spoken.
13 Creole French is the national language and is spoken by most of the population, Cocoy, a variant of English, is spoken in some areas.
14 The main local dialect is Creole.
15 Local French *patois* is also spoken.
16 Local Bajan dialect is also spoken.
17 French, Spanish, Hindi and Chinese are also spoken.
18 English and Spanish are also spoken. The islanders speak Papiamento (see note on St Eustatius).

MEXICO

MAP E
CENTRAL MEXICO

TROPIC OF CANCER
Matehuala
Ciudad Victoria
Zacatecas
Ciudad Mante
SIERRA MADRE OCCIDENTAL
San Luis Potosí
Ciudad Madero
Tampico
Río Verde
San Blas
Tepic
Aguascalientes
E1
Lago de Moreno
León
Guanajuato
San Miguel de Allende
SIERRA MADRE ORIENTAL
E2
LAGUNA DE TAMIAHUA
Tuxpan
Puerto Vallarta
Guadalajara
MIGUEL HIDALGO
Irapuato
Salamanca
Querétaro
Tula
Pachuca
El Tajín
Poza Rica
El Pital
Yelapa
LAGO DE CHAPALA
Sahuayo
Cuitzeo
Nevado de Toluca 4577m
Toluca
Toluca
Teotihuacán
Tulancingo
Xalapa (Jalapa)
CARIBBEAN SEA
Barra de Navidad
Pátzcuaro
Morelia
Ixtapan del Oro
Huexotla
Tlaxco
MEXICO CITY
Veracruz
Manzanillo
Colima
Uruapan
Valle de Bravo
Puebla
Córdoba
Tres Zapotes
Ciudad Altamirano
Cuernavaca
BENITO JUAREZ
Cholula
Cerro de las Mesas
Cacahuamilpa
Santiago
Lázaro Cárdenas
Los Monos
Taxco
Iguala
Izúcar de Matamoros
Tuxtla
Ixtapa-Zihuatanejo
SIERRA MADRE DEL SUR
Popocatepetl 5452m
Teposcolula
Huajuápan de León
E3
Balsas
Chilpancingo
E4
Oaxaca
Monte Albán
Mitla
PACIFIC OCEAN
Acapulco
GENERAL JUAN N. ALVAREZ
Salina Cruz
Lagunas de Chacahua
Puerto Escondido
Puerto Ángel

400 kilometres
200 miles
Land tints: 0-1000m, 1000-2000m, over 2000m

Important Maya sites
Sites which are UNESCO World Heritage sites are shown below in red.

MEXICO
1 Comalcalco
2 Pajón
3 Izapa
4 Lagartero
5 Chinkultic
6 Toniná
7 Bonampak
8 Yaxchilán
9 La Mar
10 El Cayo
11 Palenque
12 Edzna
13 Tabasqueño
14 Hochob
15 Dzibilnocac
16 Nohcacab
17 Tahcob (Tahcok)
18 Santa Rosa Xtampak
19 Xkichmook
20 Chacmultún
21 Labná
22 Sayil
23 Kabáh
24 Xcalumkin
25 Uxmal
26 Oxkintok
27 Mayapán
28 Dzibilchaltún
29 Aké
30 Ikil

31 Chichén Itza
32 Xlacah
33 Culuba
34 Ek Balam
35 Ecab (Gran Cairo)
36 El Meco
37 El Rey
38 Xcaret (Pole)
39 Cobá
40 Aguada Grande
41 San Gervasio
42 Xelha
43 Tulum
44 Muyil (Chunyaxche)
45 Ichpaatun
46 Kohunlich
47 Ramonal
48 Rio Bec
49 Tortuga
50 Xpuhil
51 Becan
52 Chicanná
53 Hermiguero
54 Calakmul

BELIZE
55 Santa Rita
56 Cerros
57 Sarteneja
58 Shipstern
59 Aventura

60 Nohmul
61 Cuello
62 El Pozito
63 Altun Ha
64 Lamanai
65 Chan Chich (Kaxil Uínic)
66 Baking Pot
67 Buenavista del Cayo
68 Xunantunich
69 Caracol
70 Nim li punit
71 Lubaantun

GUATEMALA
72 Rio Azul
73 Kinal
74 Xultún
75 Uaxactún
76 El Mirador
77 Piedras Negras
78 San Diego
79 Motul de San José
80 Tikal
81 Nakum
82 Naranjo
83 Yaxhá
84 Topoxte
85 Ixkun
86 Seibal
87 Altar de Sacrificios
88 Dos Pilas

89 Aguateca
90 Machaquilá
91 Zaculeu
92 Abaj Takalik
93 Rio Jesus
94 Utatlán
95 Iximché
96 El Baúl
97 Kaminaljuyu
98 Mixco Viejo
99 Cahyup
100 Chuitinamit
101 Quiriguá

HONDURAS
102 Copán
103 Nispero
104 Salitron

EL SALVADOR
105 Cihuatan
106 Tazumal
107 Cara Sucia

THE MAYAN CIVILIZATION

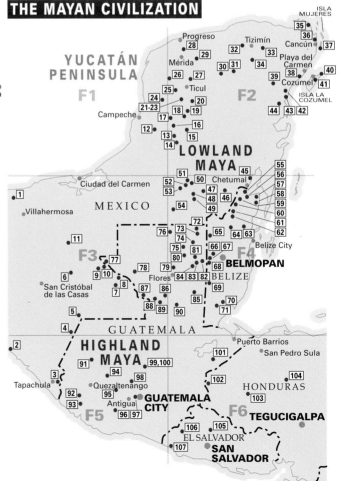

ISLA MUJERES
Progreso **28**
Tizimín
35
Cancún
36
37
YUCATÁN PENINSULA
Mérida
32
33
Playa del Carmen
F1
26 **27**
29
30 **31** **34**
38
Cozumel
39
40
24 **25**
Ticul
F2
41
ISLA LA COZUMEL
Campeche
21-23
18 **19**
20
17
44 **43** **42**
16
12
13 **15**
14
LOWLAND MAYA
Ciudad del Carmen
51
45
55
56
52 **50**
Chetumal
57
53
47
58
1
MEXICO
54
48 **46**
59
Villahermosa
49
60
61
73
72
62
11
76
74
65
64 **63**
Belize City
F3
75
81
66 **67**
F4
77
80
68
BELMOPAN
78
79
6
9 **10**
82
7
Flores
84 **83**
BELIZE
69
San Cristóbal de las Casas
87
86
85
70
88 **89**
71
5
90
4
GUATEMALA
2
HIGHLAND MAYA
99,100
Puerto Barrios
101
San Pedro Sula
91
94
98
101
3
102
104
Tapachula
95
Quezaltenango
HONDURAS
92
GUATEMALA CITY
103
93
Antigua
F5
96 **97**
F6
TEGUCIGALPA
106 **105**
EL SALVADOR
107
SAN SALVADOR

THAILAND, MALAYSIA AND SINGAPORE

ENERAL NOTES

This index refers to the 'specialist maps' from pages 49-96. This map section contains a variety of map styles, most of them falling into three categories:

■ Locator maps. Usually appearing in a buff colour with a blue band accentuating the coastline, often with administrative boundaries in orange or grey. Administrative areas are shown in capital letters in condensed black type, while areas of tourist interest and physical regions are shown in red or blue type (eg France, map A pp 72-73).

■ General tourist maps. These maps are in black frames and show towns, resorts and places of interest as well as roads, railways, high land and rivers (eg Lake District, map C p 66).

■ Special subject maps. These maps highlight a particular item and show the locations of these (eg UK beaches on p 68).

This index only refers to maps which contain a reference grid (A1, A2, etc). The page number is shown first, followed by its location on the page. Many entries have been shortened for clarity, with descriptive abbreviation used – please see the appropriate map for the full name. Abbreviations are usually omitted for physical names where the name itself indicates its identity, eg island, cape or lake, either in English or in another language but easily recognisable, eg Ile, Cap or Lac (in French).

The following criteria have been applied to the maps:

■ On general tourist maps, all locations, regions and complete or nearly complete administrative areas are indexed.

■ On locator maps, locations and areas not marked on any larger-scale general tourist maps are listed.

■ On special subject maps, all locations are indexed including general place names and administrative areas if they do not appear at a larger scale or on a locator map elsewhere.

Where a place is shown on two or more of the general tourist maps, the index only refers to the most relevant map. Usually this is also the largest scale that the place can be found (eg Nice appears in the France section, map F p 73 and also in the Italy section, map F p 79. The index refers only to the map in the France section).

All special subject locations (eg cruise ports and ferry terminals, airports, UNESCO World Heritage sites, etc) which take the same name as resorts, towns, cities or islands also shown in this map section are given separate entries in the index.

Where a place is listed on a special subject map and also appears on a general tourist map or locator map, the index refers to the tourist map or the locator map, as it is drawn to a larger scale and so the location is more accurately shown, and is also shown in relation to other features (eg Redwood National Park is listed on the US national parks special subject map, pp 92-93, and also

marked on the California tourist map, p 91; the index refers to the California map). UNESCO cultural sites, however, are all indexed to the cultural heritage maps where a full description of the site is given. Some of these locations may appear elsewhere in the atlas with a separate, normal entry in the index. UNESCO combined cultural and natural sites are indexed to the cultural site.

For places which have alternative (English and local) spellings, there is a separate entry for each.

ABBREVIATIONS

Adm	Administrative area within a country
AmS	American Samoa
Apt	Airport
Bat	Battlefield (Belgium and Netherlands)
Bch	Beach
Bosnia-Herz.	Bosnia-Herzegovina
B Res	Biosphere Reserve
Brit.	British
CAR	Central African Republic
Cadw	Cadw: Welsh Historic Monuments
Ch	Château (France and Belgium)
Co Bat Mem	County Battlefields Memorial (USA)
Con Area	Conservation Area
Cru	Cruise port
EH	English Heritage
Est	Estuary
Fed.	Federation
Ferry	Ferry terminal
F Pk	Forest Park
F Res	Forest Reserve
Gf	Golf course
G Res	Game Reserve
His Pk	Historic Park
His Sanc	Historic Sanctuary
His Sc	Historic Scotland
Int His	International Historic Site
Int Pc Pk	International Peace Park
Int Pk	International Park
I	Island
Is	Islands
Korea, DPR	Democratic People's Republic of Korea
Korea, Rep.	Republic of Korea
Lag	Lagoon
Mac, FYR	Former Yugoslav Republic of Macedonia
Mt	Mount (as part of name)
Mtn	Mountain/volcano (peak)
Mtns	Major mountain range (for ranges of hills or less important mountain ranges, Reg is used)

N Bat	National Battlefield/National Battlefield Park/National Battlefield Site (USA)
N Bd Sanc	National Bird Sanctuary
N Her Cor	National Heritage Corridor (USA)
N His	National Historic Site/National Historical Park (USA)
N His Res	National Historical Reserve (USA)
N Lake	National Lakeshore (USA)
N Mar	National Marine Sanctuary (USA)
N Mem	National Memorial (USA)
N Mil	National Military Park (USA)
N Mon	National Monument
N Pk	National Park
N Pres	National Preserve (USA)
N Rec	National Recreation Area (USA)
N Res	National Reserve (USA)
N Sea	National Seashore (USA)
NT	National Trust (UK)
Ntr Res	Nature Reserve/Strict Nature Reserve
NT Sc	National Trust for Scotland
N W R	National Wildlife Refuge (USA)
Pen	Peninsula
P Pk	Provincial Park (Canada)
P Res	Provincial Reserve (Canada)
P Wd Pk	Provincial Wilderness Park (Canada)
Rail	Railway
Reg	Physical region/tourist area/area of high land (except major mountain ranges)
Rep.	Republic
Riv	River
S His	State Historic Site / State Historic Park (USA)
S His Mon	State Historic Monument (USA)
S Mon	State Monument (USA)
S Pk	State Park (USA)
S Rec	State Recreation Area (USA)
St	Saint, Sankt, Sant, Sint
Sta	Santa (for US entries, Santa is written in full)
Ste	Sainte
Str	Strait
S W Pk	State Wildlife Park (USA)
Terr.	Territory
UAE	United Arab Emirates
UK	United Kingdom
UN C	UNESCO Heritage site (cultural)
UN CN	UNESCO Heritage site (combined cutural and natural)
UN N	UNESCO Heritage site (natural)
USA	United States of America
Wfall	Waterfall
W Sanc	Wildlife Sanctuary
Yugo, FR	Federal Republic of Yugoslavia

a la Ronde house NT UK 67 F6
aachen UN C Germany 64 A6
aachen Germany 76 B1
alsmeer Netherlands 75 F8
alst Belgium 65 B14
aare Riv Switzerland 77 E2
arau Switzerland 75 D9
baj Takalik Guatemala 95 F5
bano Italy ....
bbatoggia, Isola la Maddalena Bch Sardinia 84 A3
bbotsbury Abbey EH UK 67 F6
bbotsinch Apt UK 66 B3
benrå Denmark 74 E1
beraeron UK 68 A5
beraeron: Traeth y De Bch UK 68 A5
berdare N Pk Kenya 89 G3
berdeen Apt UK 70 A1
berdeen Ferry UK 69 C3
berdeen UK 70 A2
berdeen South Africa 88 C3
berdour UK 66 B4
berdour UK 68 A2
bereiddy Bch UK 68 A5
berfeldy UK 66 B1
berfoyle UK 66 B1
bergavenny UK 66 D3
berporth UK 68 A5
berystwyth UK 70 A5
bidjan Apt Côte d'Ivoire 55 A5
bomey UN C Benin 63 A5
bony Nigeria ....
braham Lincoln Birthplace N His USA 93 A8
bruzzo Adm Italy 78 A2
bu Dhabi Apt UAE 55 A7
bu Mena UN C Egypt 64 A12
bu Mena Egypt 89 F1
bu Simbel Egypt 89 F6
bu Simbel Apt Egypt 89 F6
bu Simbel to Philae UN C Egypt 63 A5
buja Apt Nigeria 55 A5
bydos Egypt 89 F4
cadia N Pk USA 90 B4
capulco Apt Mexico 94 E4
capulco Cru Mexico 58 B4
capulco Mexico 95 E4
ccra Apt Ghana 55 A5
ccra and Volta areas UN C Ghana 63 A5
chern Germany 75 D8
chim Germany 74 E3
chlada Crete 85 A13
chladia, Skiathos Bch Greece 85 A13
ci Trezza Sicily 78 E4
cireale Sicily 78 E4
cklins I. Bahamas 58 B6
cores Is Spain ....82 B
corn Bank Garden NT UK 67 F3
cquario, Diano Marina Bch Italy 84 A3
cquarosa Italy 79 F12
cquasparta Italy 78 C1
cqui Italy 79 F6
cton Burnell Castle EH UK 67 F5
dámanta Greece 85 A13
dámas Greece 83 J7
dams N His USA 93 A4
dana Turkey 83 F3
ddis Ababa Apt Ethiopia 55 A5
ddo Elephant N Pk South Africa 88 C3
delaide Apt Australia 55 A9
delaide I. Cru Antarctica 59 A10
delboden Switzerland 77 E6
déle Crete 85 A13
délianos Kampos, Adéle Bch Crete 85 A13
den Apt Yemen 55 A7
den, Gulf of 59 A5
denau Germany 76 C1
dige Riv Italy 79 F7
dnan Menderes Apt Turkey 83 J3
dour Riv France 72 D2
dra Spain 80 D8
driana, Villa Italy 78 C1
driatic Coast Reg Croatia 86 B2
gegean Coast Reg Turkey 83 F2
gean Sea Greece ....83 J
gerø I Denmark 74 F2

Afántou Greece 85 A13
Ajaccio Apt France 56 A10
Ajaccio Cru France 59 C2
Afyssos Greece 85 C2
Ajaccio Corsica 73 A2
Afetes Greece 85 A12
Afganistan ....
Afitos Greece 85 A13
Afíssos Greece 85 A13
Africa-India Cruise Area 59 A5/8
Afsluitdijk Netherlands 65 B3
Afyon Turkey 83 F2
Afysos-Ampovos, Neohóri Bch Greece 85 A12
Agadir Apt Morocco 89 E3
Agadir Cru Morocco 59 C5
Agadir Morocco 89 E3
Agate Fossil Beds N Mon USA 92 A2
Agathoníssi I Greece 83 J8
Agde France 84 A2
Agia Foteiní, Neohóri Bch Greece 85 A13
Agia Galíni Crete 83 J10
Agia Marína Greece 83 J4
Agia Pelagía Greece 83 J7
Agia Pelagía, Achlada Bch Crete 85 A13
Agia Triás Greece 85 A12
Agia Triás Bch Greece 85 A12
Agiokampos, Skíti Bch Greece 85 A12
Agios Apostóli, N. Kidonia Bch Greece 85 A13
Agios Dimítrios Greece 83 J4
Agios Dimítrios, Mália Bch Crete 85 A13
Agios Efstratios I Greece 83 J4
Agios Geórgios, Náxos Bch Greece 85 A13
Agios Geórgios, Pagoí Bch Greece 85 A12
Ágios Ioánnis Crete ....
Agia Pelagía Greece 83 J7
Agios Ioánnis, Ágios Dimítrios Bch Greece 85 A12
Agios Isídoros, Antikíra Bch Greece 85 A12
Agios Isídoros, Plomári Bch Greece 85 A13
Ágios Kirikos Greece 83 J8
Agios Nikítas Greece 83 H1
Agios Nikólaos Crete 83 J11
Agios Nikólaos Greece 85 A13
Agios Nikólaos "1* – *3* Bch Crete 85 A13
Agios Nikólaos "5* – *6* Bch Crete 85 A13
Agios Spyridonas, Thinalío Bch Greece 85 A12
Ágios Theódori Greece 85 A13
Agios Theódori Crete 85 A13
Agios Theódoros Greece 85 A13
Agnontas, Skópelos Bch Greece 85 A13
Agostóli Greece 83 H2
Agra Fort UN C India 63 C1
Agriá Greece 83 J4
Agrigento Sicily 78 E3
Agro Romano Reg Italy 78 C1
Agua Amarga, Níjar Bch Spain 81 G2
Agua de Pena Madeira 82 C2
Aguada Grande Mexico 95 F2
Aguadulce Spain 80 D8
Aguadulce, Roquetas Bch Spain 84 A8
Aguas de Moura Portugal 82 D2
Aguascalientes Mexico 95 E1
Aguateca Guatemala 95 F3
Aguilas Spain 84 A8
Agulhas, Cape South Africa 88 C6
Ahaus Germany 74 B4
Ahlen Germany 74 C5
Ahr Riv Germany 76 C1
Ahrensburg Germany 74 F3
Ahrtal Germany ....
Ai Lagoudís, Kiparissía Bch Greece 85 A12
Aiéa Hawaiian Is. 91 C5
Aierbach Germany 75 H6
Aigua Blanca, Oliva Bch Spain 84 A2
Aiguadolç, Sitges Bch Spain 84 A2
Aiguebelle, Le Lavandou Bch France 84 A2
Ain Adm France 72 G1
Air Hitam Malaysia 96 B1
Air Hitam Dam Malaysia 96 B1
Aïr-Ténéré Ntr Res, UN N Niger 61 A5
Airolo Switzerland 77 E7
Aisawan Tippaya Asna Thailand 96 C1
Aisch Riv Germany 75 F7
Aisne Adm France ....
Aisne Riv France 72 H1
Aït Benhaddou UN C Morocco 89 E3
Aït Benhaddou Morocco 89 E3
Aix-en-Provence France 72 F3
Aix-la-Chapelle Germany 76 B1

Ajaccio Apt France 56 A10
Ajaccio Cru France 59 C2
Ajaccio Corsica 73 A2
Ajanta Caves UN C India 63 C1
Ajim Tunisia 89 D6
Akaka Falls S Pk Hawaiian Is. 91 C8
Aké Mexico 95 F2
Akhisar Turkey 83 J6
Akhtubinsk Russian Fed. 86 C1
Akimiski I. Canada 94 A7
Akrotíri Greece 83 J8
Aksum UN C Ethiopia 63 A5
Akti Pen Greece 83 J1
Akti Méssis, Méssi Bch Greece 85 A6
Aktion Greece 83 H1
Aktur, Bodrum Bch Turkey 85 A13
Aktur, Datça Bch Turkey 85 A13
Al Basrah Iraq 87 D4
Al Hoceima Morocco 89 E2
Al-Ayn UN C Oman 63 A7
Al-Khutm UN C Oman 63 A7
Alabama Adm USA 90 A7
Alaior Menorca 81 H4
Åland Is. 56 A3
Alanya Turkey 83 F2
Alasehir Turkey 83 J6
Alaska Adm USA 90 A10
Alaska Highway Canada 94 C1
Alaska, Gulf of 58 A2
Alaska/Canada Cruise Area 58 A2
Alàssio Italy 79 F9
Alba Italy 79 F5
Albacete Spain 81 A2
Albania 86 B2
Albano Laziale Italy 78 C3
Albano, Lago Italy 78 C3
Albany Apt USA 54 B2
Albany USA 90 B3
Albena Bulgaria 86 B2
Albenga Italy 79 F9
Albergo Baigi, Jésolo Bch Italy 85 A4
Albergo Danmark, Jésolo Bch Italy 85 A4
Albergo Esit, Sta Teresa Gallura Bch Sardinia 84 A3
Albert France 65 B17
Alberta Adm Canada 94 A5
Albertville France 72 G2
Albufeira Portugal 82 E6
Albuquerque Apt USA 90 A6
Albuquerque, Cayos de Is 95 D5
Alcalà de Chivert Spain 81 A2
Alcalà la Real Spain 80 D3
Alcalar, Túmulos de Portugal 82 E6
Alcanar Spain 84 A2
Alcantarilha Portugal 82 E6
Alcaria do Cume, Serra de Reg Portugal 82 E4
Alcobaça UN C Portugal 64 A9
Alcochete Portugal 82 D2
Alcoutim Portugal 82 E4
Alcoy Spain 81 E1
Alcúdia Mallorca 81 G2
Alcúdia, Badia de Bay Mallorca 81 G2
Aldabra Atoll UN N Seychelles 61 A5
Aldeburgh UK 68 A5
Alderney I Channel Is. 69 B6
Aleganza I Canary Is. 80 B2
Alenhuihaha Channel Hawaiian Is. 91 C8
Alenquer Portugal 82 D2
Alentejo Adm Portugal 82 A3
Aleppo Apt Syria 56 A16
Aleppo UN C Syria 64 A12
Alessándra Italy 79 F6
Ålesund Cru Norway 59 A4
Aletschgletscher Switzerland 77 E6
Aleutian Is. USA 90 A10
Alexander Archipelago Is USA 90 A10
Alexandria Apt Egypt 89 F1
Alexandria Cru Egypt 59 C8
Alexandria South Africa 88 C8
Alexandria Egypt 89 F1
Alexandroúpoli Greece 83 J2
Alexandroúpoli Apt Greece 83 F2
Alfa del Pi Spain 81 E2
Alfeizerão Portugal ....
Alfriston Clergy House NT UK 67 F6
Algarve Reg ....82 E
Algarve Adm Portugal 82 A3
Algeciras Spain 80 D6

Algeria 88 A1
Alghero Sardinia 78 D1
Algiers Apt Algeria 56 A14
Algoa Bay South Africa 88 C8
Algodonales Spain 80 D6
Algonquin P Pk Canada 94 B1
Algoz Portugal 82 E6
Alhama de Aragón Spain ....
Alibates Flint Quarries N Mon USA 92 A6
Alibey I Turkey 83 J5
Alicante Apt Spain 81 E1
Alicante Cru Spain 59 C5
Alicante Spain 81 E1
Alicudi, Isola Sicily 78 E2
Alikés Greece 83 H3
Alimnia I Greece 83 J9
Alimos Greece 83 J7
Aljezur Portugal 82 E1
Almalmar Netherlands 65 B7
Allagash Wilderness Waterway USA 90 B2
Allée de Gaulle, Valras Bch France 84 A2
Alleghe Italy 85 A4
Allegheny Portage Railroad N His USA 93 A4
Aller Riv Germany 74 E4
Allerheiligen Wfall Germany 76 B6
Allgäu Reg Germany 75 F9
Alloa UK 66 B3
Almada Portugal 82 D1
Almalik Kazakhstan 87 D2
Almalik Kazakhstan 87 D2
Almansil Portugal 82 E7
Almaty Apt Kazakhstan 55 A6
Almaty Kazakhstan 86 A3
Almelo Netherlands 65 B8
Almere Netherlands 65 B7
Almería Cru Spain 59 C5
Almería Spain 80 D8
Almería, Golfo de Spain 80 D8
Almerimar Spain 80 D8
Almirós, Agios Nikólaos Bch Crete 85 A13
Almodóvar Portugal 82 E3
Almodóvar del Rio Spain 80 D2
Almuñecar Spain 80 D7
Amoudi-Ágios Nikólaos *4*, Ág. N's Bch Crete 85 A13
Almyrida, Plakas Bch Crete 85 A13
Alónissos I Greece 83 J4
Alpbach Austria 77 F3
Alpe de Suisi Italy 79 F3
Alpe-d'Huez, l' France 72 G3
Alpes-de-Haute-Provence Adm France 72 F1
Alpes-Maritimes Adm France 72 F2
Alpi Bernina Mtns Italy 77 E8
Alpi Carniche Mtns Italy 79 F4
Alpi Cozi Mtns France/Italy 79 F5
Alpi Graie Mtns France/Italy 79 F5
Alpi Marittime Mtns France/Italy 79 F5
Alpi Leopontine Mtns Italy/Switzerland 77 E7
Alpi Pennine Mtns Italy/Switzerland 77 E6
Alpi Retiche Mtns Switzerland/Italy 77 E4
Alpi Venosti Mtns Italy 79 F3
Alpirsbach Germany 76 B6
Alps Mtns ....77 D
Als I Denmark 74 E2
Alsace Adm France 73 A1
Alsfeld Germany 75 E6
Alsenz Germany ....
Alslev Denmark 74 G2
Alta UN C Norway 63 A4
Altai Mtns Russian Fed. 86 A4
Altamira Cave UN C Spain 64 A5
Altar de Sacrificios Guatemala 95 F3
Altavilla Irpina Italy 78 B2
Alte Portugal 82 E7
Altea Spain 81 E2
Altenahr Germany 76 C1
Altenburg Germany 75 H6
Altenkirchen Germany 76 C2
Alter do Chão Cru Brazil ....
Altet Apt Spain 81 E1
Altillo, Almuñécar Bch Spain 84 A8
Altinkum Turkey 83 J8
Altmark Reg Germany 74 A1
Altmühl Riv Germany 75 G8
Altötting Germany 75 G8

Alur Setar Malaysia 96 A2
Alvor Portugal 82 E6
Alykes Potamou, Kérkira Bch Greece 85 A12
Alykes, Lefkími Bch Greece 85 A12
Alz Riv Germany 75 H8
Alzey Germany 76 C4
Amada Egypt 89 F6
Amadora Portugal 82 D1
Amalfi Italy 78 B4
Amaliáda Greece 85 A12
Aman, Pulau I Malaysia 96 B4
Amarillo USA 90 A6
Amazon Riv Brazil 58 A3
Amazon, Mouths of the Reg Brazil 58 A3
Amberg Germany 75 G7
Ambérieu-en-Bugey France 72 G1
Amble Links Bch UK ....
Ambleside UK 66 C4
Amblève Belgium 65 B16
Amboise France 72 C2
Ambon Cru Indonesia 59 A8
Amboseli N Pk Kenya 89 G3
Ameixal Portugal 82 E3
Ameland I Netherlands 65 B3
Amélia Italy 78 C1
American Memorial Park Northern Mariana Is. 93
American Samoa Is 54 A1
Amersfoort Netherlands 65 B7
Amiens UN C France 64 A6
Amiens France 65 B17
Amistad N Rec USA 92 A6
Amman Apt Jordan 56 A16
Ammersee Lake Germany 75 G8
Ammos-Plaz, Ágios Nikólaos Bch Crete 85 A13
Ammoudara, Gazi Bch Crete 85 A13
Ammoudara-Agios Nikólaos, Kritsa Bch Crete 85 A13
Amnissos, Elia Bch Crete 85 A13
Amoliani I Greece 83 J1
Amorbach Germany 76 B4
Amorgós I Greece 83 J8
Amper Riv Germany 75 G8
Ampoula *1*, K. Gerakari Bch Greece 85 A12
Ampoula *2*, Tragaki Bch Greece 85 A12
Amroth, Saundersfoot Bch UK 74 D2
Amrum I Germany 74 D2
Amsterdam Apt Netherlands 65 B7
Amsterdam Cru Netherlands 59 A4
Amsterdam Netherlands 65 B7
Amsterdam Ferry Netherlands 69 C6
Amsterdam, Île 65 A5
Amu Darya Riv Turkmenistan/Uzbekistan 87 D2
Amvrakikós Kólpos Gulf Greece 83 H1
Anacapri Italy 78 B3
Anacortes USA 90 B2
Anáfi I Greece 83 J8
Anafonítria Greece 83 H3
Anagni Italy 78 C4
Anamur Turkey 83 F3
Anatol. kalamata, Kalamáta Bch Greece 85 A12
Anatolia, Central Reg Turkey 83 F3
Anatolia, Eastern Reg Turkey 83 F3
Anavros, Vólos Bch Greece 85 A12
Anca, Casares Bch Spain 84 A8
Anchorage Apt USA 54 A2
Anchorage Cru USA 58 A2
Anchorage USA 90 A10
Anclote Keys Is USA 91 C5
Ancona Italy 78 A1
Ancona Cru Italy 79 F12
Andalo Italy 79 F3
Andalsnes Cru Norway 59 A4
Andalucía Adm Spain 80 A2
Andalsnes Norway 55 A8
Andelys, les France 72 H1
Andermatt Switzerland 77 E7
Andernach Germany 76 C1
Andersonville N His USA 93 A8
Andikíthira I Greece 83 J10
Andíparos I Greece 83 J8
Andorra 72 E1

Index

Andorra la Vella Andorra ... 72 E1
Andrano Italy ... 85 A12
Andratx Mallorca ... 81 G1
Andrew Johnson N His USA ... 93 A8
Andros I Bahamas ... 58 B3
Andros I Greece ... 83 J7
Andros Greece ... 83 J7
Aneto, Pico de Mtn Spain ... 72 D2
Angermünde Germany ... 74 J3
Angers France ... 72 C1
Anglesey I UK ... 70 A4
Anglesey Abbey and garden NT UK ... 67 F5
Angola ... 88 A3
Angra do Heroismo UN C Azores ... 62 A4
Angra do Heroismo Azores ... 82 B2
Anguilla ... 95 D3
Aniachak N Mon, N Pres USA ... 92 A9
Anjar UN C Lebanon ... 64 A12
Anjou Reg France ... 72 C1
Ankara Apt Turkey ... 56 A16
Ankara Turkey ... 83 F3
Anklam Germany ... 74 I3
Annaba Apt Algeria ... 56 A14
Annaba Algeria ... 89 D1
Annaberg-Buchholz Germany ... 75 I6
Annapolis USA ... 90 A4
Annecy France ... 72 G1
Annevoie Belgium ... 65 B15
Annonay France ... 72 G3
Annweiler Germany ... 76 B6
Ano Meria Greece ... 85 A13
Ano Siros Greece ... 85 A13
Ansbach Germany ... 75 F7
Anse de Paulilles, Port-Vendres Bch France ... 84 A2
Anse de Renecros, Bandol Bch France ... 84 A3
Anse des Phocéens, Marseille Bch France ... 84 A3
Antakya Turkey ... 83 F3
Antalya Cru Turkey ... 59 C8
Antalya Turkey ... 83 F2
Antananarivo Apt Madagascar ... 55 A5
Antarctic Cruise Area ... 59 A10
Antarctic Peninsula Antarctica ... 59 A10
Antequera Spain ... 80 D3
Anthony Island UN C Canada ... 62 A2
Anti Atlas Reg Morocco ... 89 E3
Antibes France ... 72 F4
Antibes, Cap d' France ... 72 F4
Antibes, Cap d' Bch France ... 84 A3
Anticosti I. Canada ... 94 A8
Antietam N Bat USA ... 93 A4
Antigua Apt ... 54 A3
Antigua UN C Guatemala ... 62 B1
Antigua Guatemala ... 95 F5
Antigua and Barbuda ... 95 D3
Antikira Greece ... 85 A12
Antrim Adm UK ... 68 A3
Antwerp Apt Belgium ... 65 B10
Antwerp Belgium ... 65 B10
Antwerpen Apt Belgium ... 65 B10
Antwerpen Belgium ... 65 B10
Antwerpen Adm Belgium ... 65 B11
Anuradhapura UN C Sri Lanka ... 63 C2
Anxi China ... 87 D3
Anza-Borrego Desert S Pk USA ... 91 E6
Anzère Switzerland ... 77 E6
Ánzio Italy ... 78 A1
Aosta Italy ... 78 A1
Aosta Italy ... 79 F1
Apalachicola USA ... 91 D2
Apalachicola Riv USA ... 91 D2
Aparcamiento, Guardamar del Segura Bch Spain ... 84 A9
Apeldoorn Netherlands ... 65 B8
Apia Apt Western Samoa ... 54 A1
Apolda Germany ... 75 G5
Apollo Beach Greece ... 83 J7
Apopka, Lake USA ... 91 D5
Apostle Is. N Lake USA ... 93 A3
Appalachian Mountains USA ... 90 A8
Appennino Mtns Italy ... 78 A1
Appomattox Court House N His USA ... 93 A8
Aprilia Apt Italy ... 79 F2
Aprilia Italy ... 78 C3
Apt France ... 72 F1
Aqaba, Gulf of Egypt/Saudi Arabia ... 89 F2
Aquileia Italy ... 79 F4
Aquitaine Adm France ... 72 A2
Arabba Italy ... 79 F3
Arabian Oryx Sanctuary UN N Oman ... 61 A7
Arabian Sea ... 59 A8
Aracena Spain ... 80 D1
Aragón Adm Spain ... 81 A1
Aral Sea Kazakhstan/Uzbekistan ... 86 A3
Aranjuez Spain ... 80 C3
Arawale G Res Kenya ... 89 G4
Araxos Greece ... 85 A12
Árbatax Sardinia ... 78 D4
Arbon Switzerland ... 75 E9
Arbroath UK ... 66 B2
Arbroath Abbey His Sc UK ... 67 F2
Arc Riv France ... 72 G4
Arc-et-Senans UN C France ... 64 A6
Archaia Pydna, Magrigialos Bch Greece ... 85 A12
Arches N Pk USA ... 92 A6
Arco di Margherita, Finale Ligure Bch Italy ... 84 A3
Arcs, les France ... 72 G2
Arctic Ocean ... 59
Ardèche Reg France ... 72 G3
Ardennes Reg Belgium ... 65 B19
Ardrossan Ferry UK ... 69 B3
Arduaine Garden NT Sc UK ... 67 F2
Areia, Ponta de Cape Portugal ... 82 E8
Areiro, Pico de Mtn Madeira ... 82 C2
Arena d'en Castell Menorca ... 81 H2
Arena, Framura Bch Italy ... 84 A3
Arenal d'en Castell, Es Mercadal Bch Menorca ... 84 A9
Arenal, Calpe Bch Spain ... 84 A9
Arenals Bch Formentera ... 84 A9
Arene Candide, Finale Ligure Bch Italy ... 84 A3
Arenys de Mar Spain ... 80 C4
Areuse, Gorges de l' Switzerland ... 77 E1
Arezzo Italy ... 79 F11
Argássi Greece ... 83 H3
Argelès-Gazost France ... 72 D2
Argelès-sur-Mer France ... 84 A2
Argentina ... 54 A3
Argenton-sur-Creuse France ... 72 C3
Argilia, Vérga Bch Greece ... 85 A12
Argos Greece ... 83 J7
Arguineguin Canary Is. ... 80 B2
Arhángelos Greece ... 85 A13
Århus Apt Denmark ... 56 A6
Ariano Irpino Italy ... 78 A1
Arica Apt Chile ... 54 A3
Ariège Adm France ... 72 E1
Ariège Riv France ... 72 E1
Arilas, Magoulades Bch Greece ... 85 A12
Arizona Adm USA ... 90 A5
Arkansas Adm USA ... 93 A7
Arkansas N Mem USA ... 93 A7
Arkhangel'sk Russian Fed. ... 86 A2
Arki I Greece ... 83 J8
Arkona, Kap Germany ... 74 I2
Arkoúdi I Greece ... 83 H1
Arles UN C France ... 64 A6
Arlington House, Robert E. Lee Mem. N Mem USA 93 A4

Arlon Belgium ... 65 B20
Armação de Pera Portugal ... 82 E6
Armadale Ferry UK ... 69 B1
Armagh Apt UK ... 68 A3
Armagh UK ... 70 A3
Armenia ... 86 A2
Armentières France ... 65 B13
Armier Bay Malta ... 79 G1
Armona, Ilha da I Portugal ... 82 E8
Arnel, Ponta de Cape Azores ... 82 B2
Arnhem Netherlands ... 65 B9
Arno Riv Italy ... 79 F11
Arnprior Canada ... 94 B6
Arnsberg Germany ... 74 D5
Arnstadt Germany ... 75 G6
Arogi, Méssi Bch Greece ... 85 A6
Arona Italy ... 79 F2
Arosa Switzerland ... 77 E4
Arpajon France ... 72 H3
Arrábida, Serra da Reg Portugal ... 82 D2
Arran I UK ... 70 A3
Arras France ... 65 B13
Arras, Burg Germany ... 76 C3
Arrecife Canary Is. ... 80 B3
Arrieta Canary Is. ... 80 B3
Arta Mallorca ... 81 G2
Artà, Coves d' Mallorca ... 81 G2
Artrutx, Cap d' Menorca ... 81 H3
Aruba I ... 95 D6
Arucas Canary Is. ... 80 B2
Arusha Tanzania ... 89 G3
Arvanitia, Náfplio Bch Greece ... 85 A12
As Czech Rep. ... 75 H6
As Smara Western Sahara ... 89 E3
Ascain France ... 72 D1
Ascension I ... 55 A5
Aschaffenburg Germany ... 76 B4
Aschersleben Germany ... 74 G5
Ascoli Italy ... 79 F12
Ascona Switzerland ... 77 E7
Ashante traditional buildings UN C Ghana ... 63 A5
Ashby de la Zouch Castle EH UK ... 67 F5
Ashdown Forest UK ... 66 E3
Ashford UK ... 66 E4
Ashgabat Apt Turkmenistan ... 55 A6
Ashgabat Turkmenistan ... 86 A3
Ashland USA ... 90 B2
Asia, Central ... 87
Asilah Morocco ... 89 E2
Asinara, Golfo del' Sardinia ... 78 D1
Asinara, Ìsola Sardinia ... 78 D1
Asini Greece ... 85 A12
Askham UK ... 66 C2
Asmara Apt Eritrea ... 55 A5
Asni Morocco ... 89 E3
Ásola Italy ... 79 F7
Aspendos Turkey ... 83 F2
Asprókavos, Akr. Cape Greece ... 83 G1
Asproválta Greece ... 85 A13
Asproválta Bch Greece ... 85 A13
Assateague Island N Sea USA ... 93 A4
Assen Netherlands ... 65 B4
Assens Denmark ... 74 E1
Assiniboine, Mt P Pk Canada ... 94 C4
Assisi Italy ... 79 F12
Assos Greece ... 83 H2
Astérix, Parc France ... 72 H2
Asti Italy ... 79 F5
Astipálea I Greece ... 83 J8
Astrakhan Russian Fed. ... 86 A2
Ástros, Parálio Ástros Bch Greece ... 85 A12
AstroWorld USA ... 93 A7
Astura, Torre Italy ... 78 C3
Asturias UN C Spain ... 64 A5
Asturias, Principado de Adm Spain ... 80 A1
Asunción Apt Paraguay ... 54 A3
Aswân Apt Egypt ... 89 F6
Aswân Egypt ... 89 F6
Aswân Dam Egypt ... 89 F6
Aswân High Dam Egypt ... 89 F6
Asyût Egypt ... 89 F3
Asyût Egypt ... 89 F6
Atalánti Greece ... 85 A12
Atalaya de Femés Mtn Canary Is. ... 80 B3
Atatürk Apt Turkey ... 83 J3
Aterno Riv Italy ... 78 C2
Ath Belgium ... 65 B14
Athabasca Riv Canada ... 94 C2
Athabasca, Lake Canada ... 94 A6
Athens Apt Greece ... 83 J7
Athens UN C Greece ... 64 A11
Athens Greece ... 83 J4
Athi Riv Kenya ... 89 G4
Athína Apt Greece ... 83 J7
Athína UN C Greece ... 64 A11
Athína Greece ... 83 J4
Athos UN CN Greece ... 64 A11
Athos Mtn Greece ... 83 J1
Atlanta Apt USA ... 54 B1
Atlanta USA ... 90 A8
Atlantic City USA ... 90 A4
Atlantic Islands Cruise Area ... 59 A5
Atlantic Ocean ... 58-59
Atlas Mountains Algeria/Morocco ... 88 A1
Átokos I Greece ... 83 H2
Attersee Lake Austria ... 77 F4
Attre Belgium ... 65 B14
Atyrau Kazakhstan ... 86 A2
Au Austria ... 77 F1
Aubagne France ... 72 F1
Auburn, California USA ... 91 E3
Auburn, Maine USA ... 90 B4
Auckland Apt New Zealand ... 55 A9
Auckland Cru New Zealand ... 59 A9
Auckland I. Cru ... 59 A9
Aude Adm France ... 72 E2
Aude Riv France ... 72 E2
Audierne, Baie d' Bay France ... 72 B3
Audincourt France ... 75 B9
Aue Germany ... 75 H6
Auffach Austria ... 77 F2
Augsburg Germany ... 75 F8
Augusta Sicily ... 78 E4
Augusta USA ... 90 B4
Aulne Riv France ... 72 B1
Auray France ... 72 B2
Aurich Germany ... 74 C3
Aurisina Filtri, Trieste Bch Italy ... 85 A4
Auron France ... 72 G3
Aurora, Jésolo Bch Italy ... 85 A4
Aurunci, Monti Reg Italy ... 78 C4
Auschwitz UN C Poland ... 64 A7
Auschwitz Poland ... 86 B1
Ausoni, Monti Reg Italy ... 78 C4
Austin, Texas USA ... 90 A6
Austin, Texas USA ... 90 A6
Australasia Cruise Area ... 59 A9
Australia ... 55 A9
Australian Cent E. rainforest UN N Australia ... 61 A9
Australian E.coast rainforest UN N Australia ... 61 A9
Austria ... 77
Austrian Alps Mtns Austria ... 77 F
Auvergne Adm France ... 72 A2
Auvernier Switzerland ... 77 E1

Avebury UN C UK ... 64 A5
Avebury NT UK ... 67 F6
Aveiro Portugal ... 82 A1
Avellino Italy ... 78 B2
Aventura Belize ... 95 F4
Aversa Italy ... 78 B1
Aves I ... 95 D3
Avezzano Italy ... 78 C2
Avignon France ... 73 A2
Ávila UN C Spain ... 64 A9
Avola Sicily ... 78 E4
Avon Riv UK ... 66 D2
Avon Adm UK ... 68 A6
Avoriaz France ... 72 G2
Awash Lower Valley UN C Ethiopia ... 63 A5
Axamer Lizum Austria ... 77 F6
Ax-les-Thermes France ... 72 E1
Axel Heiburg I. Canada ... 54 A2
Axios Riv Greece ... 83 J1
Ayamonte Spain ... 82 E4
Aydin Turkey ... 83 J9
Aydin Turkey ... 83 J9
Ayer Chawan, Pulau I Singapore ... 96 C5
Ayer Merbau, Pulau I Singapore ... 96 C5
Ayr UK ... 70 A3
Ayutthaya UN C Thailand ... 63 A8
Ayutthaya Thailand ... 96 D1
Azay-le-Ferron Ch France ... 72 C4
Azay-le-Rideau Ch France ... 72 C2
Azerbaijan ... 86 A2
Azinhal Portugal ... 82 E4
Azohia, Cartagena Bch Spain ... 84 A8
Azores to Spain ... 82 B
Azov, Sea of Russian Fed./Ukraine ... 86 A2
Aztec Ruins N Mon USA ... 92 A6
Azure Window Malta ... 79 G1
Azzurra, Grotta Italy ... 78 B3

Baalbek UN C Lebanon ... 64 A12
Baarn Netherlands ... 65 B7
Bab al Mandab Str ... 59 A5
Baccarat France ... 75 B8
Bacharach Germany ... 76 C4
Backnang Germany ... 75 E8
Bad Aussee Austria ... 77 F4
Bad Bergzabern Germany ... 76 B6
Bad Breisig Germany ... 76 C1
Bad Dürkheim Germany ... 76 B5
Bad Ems Germany ... 76 C2
Bad Freienwalde Germany ... 74 J4
Bad Godesberg Germany ... 76 C1
Bad Goisern Austria ... 77 F4
Bad Harzburg Germany ... 74 F5
Bad Hersfeld Germany ... 75 E6
Bad Hofgastein Austria ... 77 F3
Bad Homburg Germany ... 75 D6
Bad Honnef Germany ... 76 C1
Bad Hönningen Germany ... 76 C1
Bad Ischl Austria ... 77 F4
Bad Kissingen Germany ... 75 E6
Bad Kreuznach Germany ... 76 C4
Bad Langensalza Germany ... 75 F5
Bad Lauterberg Germany ... 74 F5
Bad Mergentheim Germany ... 75 F7
Bad Münstereifel Germany ... 76 C1
Bad Neuenahr-Ahrweiler Germany ... 76 C1
Bad Neustadt Germany ... 75 F6
Bad Pyrmont Germany ... 74 E5
Bad Reichenhall Germany ... 75 H9
Bad Salzungen Germany ... 75 F5
Bad Schwartau Germany ... 74 F3
Bad Segeberg Germany ... 74 F3
Bad Tölz Germany ... 75 G9
Bad Wimpfen Germany ... 76 B4
Badajoz Spain ... 80 A2
Badalona Spain ... 80 C4
Baden Switzerland ... 75 D9
Baden-Baden Germany ... 76 B6
Baden-Württemberg Adm Germany ... 76 B2
Badenweiler Germany ... 76 B7
Badgastein Austria ... 77 F8
Badia di Palma Bay Mallorca ... 81 G3
Badine Giens, Hyères Bch France ... 84 A3
Badlands USA ... 90 A2
Badlands N Pk USA ... 92 A2
Badwater Basin USA ... 91 E4
Baena Spain ... 80 D3
Baffin Bay ... 58 A2
Baffin I. Canada ... 94 A3
Bagerhat UN C Bangladesh ... 63 C1
Baghdad Apt Iraq ... 55 A6
Baghdad Iraq ... 87 D4
Bagington Apt UK ... 66 D2
Bagni Ambrosiana, Ospedaletti Bch Italy ... 84 A3
Bagni Anita, Noli Bch Italy ... 84 A3
Bagni Annunziata, Tággia Bch Italy ... 84 A3
Bagni Ausonia e Lanterna, Trieste Bch Italy ... 85 A4
Bagni Bristol, Rapallo Bch Italy ... 84 A3
Bagni di Scraio, Vico Equense Bch Italy ... 85 A11
Bagni Diana, Laiguéglia Bch Italy ... 84 A3
Bagni Lido, Rapallo Bch Italy ... 84 A3
Bagni Lido, San Bartolomeo al Mare Bch Italy ... 84 A3
Bagni Molo, Laiguéglia Bch Italy ... 84 A3
Bagni Ondina, Laiguéglia Bch Italy ... 84 A3
Bagni Ondina, Noli Bch Italy ... 84 A3
Bagni Penne, Sirolo Bch Italy ... 85 A4
Bagni Porticciolo, Rapallo Bch Italy ... 84 A3
Bagni San Donato, Finale Ligure Bch Italy ... 84 A3
Bagni Vittoria, Noli Bch Italy ... 84 A3
Bagno Bonaccia, Forte dei Marmi Bch Italy ... 84 A3
Bagno Graziella, Forte dei Marmi Bch Italy ... 84 A3
Bagno Sticco, Trieste Bch Italy ... 85 A4
Bahariya Oasis Egypt ... 89 F3
Bahia Grande Mallorca ... 81 G3
Bahia Honda S Rec USA ... 91 D8
Bahia, Islas de Honduras ... 95 D1
Bahia, Mazarrón Bch Spain ... 84 A8
Bahla UN C Oman ... 63 A7
Bahr el Ghazal Reg Sudan ... 88 A2
Bahrain ... 55 A7
Bahrain Apt ... 55 A7
Baia de Zarco Reg Madeira ... 82 C2
Baia San Felice, Vieste Bch Italy ... 85 A4
Bäia Sardinia ... 78 D2
Baie de Cousse, Sanary-sur-Mer Bch France ... 84 A3
Baie de la Palud, Hyères Bch France ... 84 A3
Baie de Niels Giens, Hyères Bch France ... 84 A3
Baikal, Lake Russian Fed. ... 59 A7
Baikonur Cosmodrome Kazakhstan ... 86 A3
Bainbridge USA ... 91 D2
Bains des Dames, Marseille Bch France ... 84 A3
Bains Militaires, Marseille Bch France ... 84 A3
Baja Bella, Roseto Capo Spúlico Bch Italy ... 85 A11
Baja California Reg ... 54 A3
Bajo Nuevo I ... 95 D1
Bajondillo, Torremolinos Bch Spain ... 84 A8
Baking Pot Belize ... 95 F4
Baku Apt Azerbaijan ... 55 A6
Baku Azerbaijan ... 86 A2
Balaton, Lake Hungary ... 86 B2
Balboa Cru Panama ... 58 B9
Baleares, Islas Spain ... 81 A2
Balearic Is. Spain ... 81 A2
Balerma, El Ejido Bch Spain ... 84 A8

Bali Cru Indonesia ... 59 A8
Balik Pulau F Res Malaysia ... 96 B3
Balikesir Turkey ... 83 J3
Balingen Germany ... 76 B6
Balkh Afghanistan ... 87 D5
Balkhash, Lake Kazakhstan ... 86 A3
Ballina Italy ... 78 B1
Ballymena UK ... 70 A3
Balmedie Bch UK ... 68 A2
Balsas Riv Mexico ... 95 E4
Balta Is. Romania ... 86 C2
Baltic Coast Reg Poland ... 86 B1
Baltic Cruise Area ... 59 A4
Baltic Republics Reg ... 86 A1
Baltic Sea ... 56 A7
Baltim Egypt ... 89 F1
Baltimore USA ... 90 A4
Baltimore/Washington Apt USA ... 74 C3
Baltrum I Germany ... 74 C3
BAM Railway Russian Fed. ... 87 A6
Bamako Apt Mali ... 55 A5
Bamberg Germany ... 75 F7
Bambou, Nice Bch France ... 84 A3
Bamburgh Bch UK ... 68 A3
Bamovskoye Russian Fed. ... 87 A6
Ban Klaeng Thailand ... 96 D4
Ban Laem Thailand ... 96 D3
Ban Pae Thailand ... 96 D3
Ban Pong Thailand ... 96 D1
Ban Tah Thailand ... 96 D3
Banās, Ras Egypt ... 89 F6
Banbury UK ... 66 D2
Banc d'Arguin N Pk, UN N Mauritania ... 61 A5
Bancroft Canada ... 94 B6
Bandama Mtn Canary Is. ... 80 B2
Bandar Seri Begawan Apt Brunei ... 55 A8
Bandar Seri Begawan Cru Brunei ... 59 A8
Bandelier N Mon USA ... 92 A6
Bandiagara Cliff UN N Mali ... 61 A5
Bandirma Turkey ... 83 J3
Band el Wali Egypt ... 89 F?
Bandol France ... 72 F3
Banff N Pk Canada ... 94 C4
Banff Canada ... 94 C4
Banff UK ... 66 B2
Bang Pa-In Thailand ... 96 D1
Bang Saen Thailand ... 96 D1
Bangkok Apt Thailand ... 55 A8
Bangkok Cru Thailand ... 59 A8
Bangkok Thailand ... 96 D1
Bangkok, Bight of Thailand ... 96 D1
Bangladesh ... 55 A8
Bangor UK ... 66 C1
Bangor USA ... 90 B4
Bangui Apt Central African Rep. ... 55 A5
Banjul Apt The Gambia ... 55 A5
Banjul Cru The Gambia ... 59 A5
Bankberg Reg South Africa ... 88 C4
Banks I. Canada ... 94 A2
Bannockburn UK ... 66 B2
Bantham Bch UK ... 68 A6
Bantock House Museum NT UK ... 67 F5
Banyalbufar Mallorca ... 81 G1
Banyuls-sur-Mer France ... 84 A2
Bar Harbor USA ... 58 A2
Bar Harbor USA ... 90 B4
Barafundle Bch UK ... 68 A5
Barano d'Ischia Italy ... 78 B3
Barbados Apt ... 54 A3
Barbados ... 95 D7
Barbary Coast ... 59 C5-6
Barbate de Franco Spain ... 80 D5
Barbati, Spartilas Bch Greece ... 85 A12
Barbate Apt Spain ... 80 C3
Barcelona Cru Spain ... 59 C2
Barcelona UN C Spain ... 64 A10
Barcelona Spain ... 80 C3
Barcelonette France ... 72 F2
Barcola California Inn, Trieste Bch Italy ... 85 A4
Barcola ex CEDAS, Trieste Bch Italy ... 85 A4
Barcola Topolini, Trieste Bch Italy ... 85 A4
Bardonècchia Italy ... 79 F5
Bardsea Bch UK ... 66 C3
Bareges France ... 72 D2
Barentin France ... 72 C1
Barents Sea ... 59 A6
Bari Italy ... 78 A1
Baringo, Lake Kenya ... 89 G1
Barkerville Canada ... 94 C3
Barnard Castle EH UK ... 67 F3
Baronia Reg Sardinia ... 78 D2
Barra I UK ... 70 A2
Barra de Navidad Mexico ... 95 E3
Barranco do Velho Portugal ... 82 E3
Barranquilla Apt Colombia ... 54 A3
Barre USA ... 90 B3
Barreiro Portugal ... 82 D2
Barreta, Ilha da I Portugal ... 82 E7
Barrie Canada ... 94 B6
Barrow-in-Furness UK ... 66 C3
Barrys Bay Canada ... 94 B6
Barsinghausen Germany ... 74 E4
Barth Germany ... 74 H2
Barúmini Sardinia ... 78 D4
Basel Apt Switzerland ... 56 A10
Basel Switzerland ... 77 D1
Basento, Lido di Metaponto Bernalda Bch Italy ... 85 A11
Basildon UK ... 66 E2
Basilicata Adm Italy ... 79 A2
Basin Region Canada ... 91 E2
Baskatong, Réservoir Canada ... 94 B3
Basle Apt Switzerland ... 56 A10
Basle Switzerland ... 77 D1
Basque Country Reg Spain ... 81 A1
Bass Lake USA ... 91 E3
Bassae UN C Greece ... 64 A11
Basse-Normandie Adm France ... 72 A1
Bassenthwaite UK ... 66 C1
Bassenthwaite Lake UK ... 66 C1
Basseterre Cru St Kitts ... 58 B7
Bastia Corsica ... 73 A2
Bastogne Belgium ... 65 B19
Bat UN C Oman ... 63 A7
Batailler, Le Lavandou Bch France ... 84 A3
Batalha UN C Portugal ... 64 A9
Bateman's NT UK ... 67 F6
Bath UN C UK ... 64 A5
Bath UK ... 66 D2
Bath Assembly Rooms NT UK ... 67 F6
Bathgate UK ... 66 B2
Batis, Kavála Bch Greece ... 85 A6
Baton Rouge USA ... 78 B4
Battaglia Italy ... 79 F8
Battle UK ... 66 E3
Battle Abbey and site of Battle of Hastings NT UK ... 67 F6
Batton, Grand Mtn France ... 72 C2
Baudry Ch France ... 72 C2
Baumettes, Sausset-les-Pins Bch France ... 84 A3
Bautzen Germany ... 75 J5
Bavaria Adm Germany ... 76 A2
Bavarian Alps Mtns Germany ... 75 G9
Bavarian Forest Reg Germany ... 76 A2
Bawiti Egypt ... 89 F3
Baxter S Pk USA ... 90 B2
Bay City USA ... 90 B2
Bay Is. Honduras ... 95 D1
Bay of Islands Cru New Zealand ... 59 A9
Bay of Isles Cru S Georgia ... 59 A10

Bayan Lepas Malaysia ... 96 B3
Bayan Lepas Apt Malaysia ... 96 B3
Bayerische Alpen Mtns Germany ... 76 A1
Bayern Adm Germany ... 76 A1
Bayonne France ... 72 C2
Bayreuth Germany ... 75 G7
Baza Spain ... 80 D3
Bazias Romania ... 86 C1
Beach Street, Sheerness Bch UK ... 68 A5
Beachy Head Cape UK ... 66 E3
Beadnell Bay Bch UK ... 68 A3
Bear Cove Canada ... 94 C2
Béar, Cap France ... 72 E2
Bearn Reg France ... 72 D2
Beatrix Potter's Lake District NT UK ... 67 F3
Beau Rivage, Nice Bch France ... 84 A3
Beaufort Luxembourg ... 65 B20
Beaufort Sea ... 58 A1
Beaufort West South Africa ... 88 C3
Beaugency France ... 72 C2
Beaulieu-sur-Mer France ... 72 F2
Beaumaris Castle Cadw UK ... 67 F5
Beauregard Ch France ... 72 C2
Beauvais France ... 72 H1
Beauvallon, Grimaud Bch France ... 84 A3
Bebra Germany ... 75 E6
Becan Mexico ... 95 F5
Béchar Algeria ... 89 E2
Beckum Germany ... 74 D5
Bedfordshire Adm UK ... 68 A5
Beek Apt Netherlands ... 65 B11
Begur Spain ... 80 C4
Beherobie France ... 72 C1
Beijing Apt China ... 55 A8
Beijing: Imperial Palace UN C China ... 63 A7
Beilstein Germany ... 76 C3
Beira Apt Mozambique ... 55 A5
Beirut Apt Lebanon ... 56 A16
Beirut Lebanon ... 87 D4
Beit el Wali Egypt ... 89 F6
Beja Portugal ... 82 A2
Beja Alban Portugal ... 82 E3
Béja Tunisia ... 89 D1
Bel Horizon, Valras Bch France ... 84 A2
Belarus ... 86 A1
Belau Is ... 55 A9
Belawan Cru Indonesia ... 59 A8
Belchen Mtn Germany ... 76 B7
Belcher Is. Canada ... 94 A4
Beldibi, Kemer Bch Turkey ... 85 A1
Belém Cru Brazil ... 58 A4
Belém Portugal ... 82 C2
Belfast Ferry UK ... 69 B2
Belfast UK ... 70 A3
Belfast: City Apt UK ... 70 A4
Belfast: International Apt UK ... 70 A4
Belfort France ... 75 B9
Belfry, The Gf UK ... 66 D2
Belgrade Apt Yugo, FR. ... 56 A?
Belgrade Yugo, FR. ... 86 B1
Bélice Riv Sicily ... 78 E4
Belize ... 58 B8
Belize City Apt Belize ... 54 A3
Belize City Belize ... 95 F4
Bellac France ... 72 C3
Bellágio Italy ... 79 F?
Belle Glade USA ... 91 D7
Belle-Ile France ... 72 B2
Bellegarde-sur-Valserine France ... 72 G1
Belleville Canada ... 94 B6
Bellinzona Switzerland ... 77 E7
Bellville South Africa ... 88 C3
Bellwald Switzerland ... 77 E7
Belmopan Belize ... 95 F4
Belœil Belgium ... 65 B14
Belp Apt Switzerland ... 77 E1
Bembridge Windmill NT UK ... 67 F6
Benalmádena Costa Spain ... 80 C3
Benavente Portugal ... 82 D2
Bendinat, Castell de Mallorca ... 81 G3
Benevento Italy ... 78 B2
Benguérir Morocco ... 89 E2
Beni Abbès Algeria ... 89 E2
Beni Hammad UN C Algeria ... 64 A12
Beni Hasan Egypt ... 89 F3
Beni Suef Egypt ... 89 F2
Benicàsim Spain ... 84 A5
Benidorm Spain ... 81 E2
Benin ... 88 A2
Benirràs, St Joan de Labritja Bch Ibiza ... 84 A9
Benissa Spain ... 81 E2
Benito Juarez Apt Mexico ... 95 E5
Benitses Greece ... 83 G2
Benjamin Franklin N Mem USA ... 93 A4
Benllech Bch UK ... 68 A4
Bennington USA ... 90 B3
Benone UK ... 68 A2
Bensafrim Portugal ... 82 E2
Bent's Old Fort N His USA ... 92 A6
Beograd Apt Yugo. FR. ... 56 A?
Berchtesgaden Germany ... 75 H9
Berga Spain ... 80 C4
Bérgamo Italy ... 79 F7
Bergen Cru Norway ... 56 A?
Bergen UN C Norway ... 64 A4
Bergen Ferry Norway ... 69 C2
Bergen op Zoom Netherlands ... 65 B10
Bergerac France ... 72 A2
Bergisch Gladbach Germany ... 74 D6
Bergün Switzerland ... 77 E7
Bering Land Bridge N Pres USA ... 92 A8
Bering Sea ... 58 A1
Berkhamsted Castle EH UK ... 67 F6
Berkshire Adm UK ... 68 A6
Berlin UN C Germany ... 64 A1
Berlin Germany ... 74 I4
Berlin USA ... 90 B3
Berlin: Schönefeld Apt Germany ... 74 I4
Berlin: Tegel Apt Germany ... 74 I4
Berlin: Tempelhof Apt Germany ... 74 I4
Bermuda ... 54 A2
Bermuda Apt ... 54 A2
Bern Apt Switzerland ... 77 E1
Bern UN C Switzerland ... 64 A4
Bern Switzerland ... 77 E1
Bernau Germany ... 74 I4
Bernau-Hof Germany ... 77 D?
Bernburg Germany ... 74 G5
Berne Apt Switzerland ... 77 E1
Berne UN C Switzerland ... 64 A4
Berne Switzerland ... 77 E1
Berner Alpen Mtns Switzerland ... 77 E6
Bernina, Passo del Switzerland ... 77 E7
Bernina, Piz Mtn Switzerland ... 77 E7
Bernkastel-Kues Germany ... 76 C3
Beroun Czech Rep. ... 75 J?
Berounka Riv Czech Rep. ... 75 J?
Berrington Hall NT UK ... 67 F5
Berry Reg France ... 72 C?

ierwick-upon-Tweed UK 70 A3
ierwick-upon-Tweed Castle EH UK ...67 F3
lesançon France 73 A1
ietancuria Canary Is. 80 B5
iéthune France 65 B13
ietong, Pulau l Malaysia 96 B3
ettmeralp Switzerland 77 E6
etzdorf Germany 75 C6
euren, Kloster Germany 76 B8
exhill UK 68 A6
exhill-on-Sea UK 66 E4
ihutan 55 A8
ialowieza N Pk, UN N Poland 61 A4
iiarritz France 72 D1
iiasca Switzerland 77 E7
iiberach Germany 75 E8
iibione Italy 79 F8
iiddeford UK 90 B3
iiedenkopf Germany 75 D6
iiel Switzerland 77 E2
iielefeld Germany 74 D4
iieler See Lake Switzerland 77 E2
iiella Italy 79 F5
iierset Apt Belgium 65 B15
iiervliet Netherlands 65 B10
iig Bear Lake USA 91 E6
iig Bend N Pk USA 92 A6
iig Cypress N Pres USA 91 D8
iig Cypress Swamp USA 91 D7
iig Hole N Bat USA 92 A1
iig Pine Key l USA 91 D7
iig Sur USA 91 E3
iiggin Hill Apt UK 70 A6
iighorn Canyon N Rec USA 92 A2
iigorre Reg France 72 D2
iilbao Apt Spain 56 A9
iilbao Ferry Spain 69 D5
iilbao Spain 81 A1
iill Baggs Cape Florida S Rec USA 91 D7
iillings Apt USA 54 A2
iillings USA 90 A2
iiloxi USA 91 D1
iingen Germany 76 C4
iinancolla Menorca 81 H4
iinibequer Vell Menorca 81 H4
iinssafüller Menorca 81 H4
iira International Racing Circuit Thailand 96 C4
iirchington UK 68 A6
iird I. 95 D3
iirhet el Bibane Lag Tunisia 89 D6
iirkenhead UK 70 A4
iirling Gap Bch UK 68 A6
iirmingham Apt UK 66 D2
iirmingham UK 66 D3
iirmingham USA 90 A7
iirzebbuga Malta 79 G4
iisagno, Monéglia Bch Italy 84 A3
iisanadi G Res Kenya 89 G2
iiscay, Bay of 59 C1
iiscayne N Pk USA 91 D8
iischofshofen Austria 75 H9
iischofswerda Germany 75 J5
iishkek Apt Kyrgyzstan 55 A6
iishkek Kyrgyzstan 86 A3
iishop USA 91 E4
iishop's Stortford UK 66 E1
iismarck USA 90 A2
iissau Apt Guinea-Bissau 55 A5
iisti, Ermióni Bch Greece 85 A13
iitburg Germany 76 C3
iiterbo, Bodrum Bch Turkey 85 A13
iitterfeld Germany 74 H5
iizerte Tunisia 89 D2
ilack Canyon of the Gunnison N Mon USA ..92 A6
ilack Country Reg UK 66 C2
ilack Forest Germany 76 B8
ilack Mountains UK 66 D3
ilack Rock Desert USA 91 E2
ilack Sea 86 A1
ilack Sea Coast Reg Turkey 83 F3
ilack Sea Coast Bulgaria/Romania 86 B2
ilack Sea Cruise Area ....59 C
ilackburn UK 70 A4
ilackness Castle His Sc UK 66 B4
ilackpool Apt UK 70 A4
ilackpool UK 70 A4
ilackpool Sands Bch UK 68 A6
ilackstone River Valley N Her Cor USA .93 A4
ilairgowrie UK 66 B2
ilanc, Cap Tunisia 89 D2
ilanc, Mont Mtn France/Italy 72 G2
ilanes Spain 80 C4
ilankenberge Belgium 65 B14
ilankenheim Germany 76 C1
ilanquilla, Isla Venezuela 95 D7
ilatna Czech Rep. 75 I7
ilavet Riv France 72 B4
iled Slovenia 86 B2
iledes, Illes Is Ibiza 81 F1
ilenheim Palace UN C UK 64 A5
ilenheim Palace UK 64 D4
iloemfontein South Africa 88 B2
ilois France 72 C2
ilue Grotto Malta 79 G1
ilue Lagoon Malta 79 G1
ilue Ridge USA 93 A8
ilue Ridge Parkway USA 93 A8
ilue Train Rail South Africa 88 B2
ilumberg Germany 75 D9
ioaventura Madeira 82 C1
iöblingen Germany 75 E8
ióbr Poland 74 K5
ioca de Valeria Cru Brazil 58 A3
ioca Raton USA 91 D6
iocholt Germany 74 B5
iochum Germany 74 C5
iode Riv Germany 74 G5
iodensee Lake Austria/Germany/Switzerland ..77 F1
iodiam Castle NT UK 67 F6
iodnant Garden NT UK 67 F4
iodrum Turkey 83 J9
iognor Regis UK 66 E3
iognor Regis Bch UK 68 A6
iogoria, Lake G Res Kenya 89 G1
iogotá Apt Colombia 54 A3
iohan Belgium 65 B19
iohemia Reg Czech Rep. 86 B1
iöhmerwald Reg Germany 76 A2
ioise Apt USA 54 A2
ioise USA 90 A1
ioizenburg Germany 74 F3
iok Tower Gardens USA 91 D5
iolaga, Vera Bch Spain 84 A8
iolingbroke Castle EH UK 67 F4
ioliqueime Portugal 82 E5
iolivia 54 A3
iolnuevo, Mazarrón Bch Spain 84 A8
iologna Apt Italy 79 F7
iologna Italy 79 F7
iolsena Italy 78 C1

Bolsena, Lago di Italy 78 C1
Bolshevik I. Russian Fed. 87 A5
Bolsover Castle EH UK 67 F4
Bolsward Netherlands 65 B3
Bolton UK 70 A4
Bolu Turkey 83 F2
Bolzano Italy 79 F3
Bombay Apt India 55 A8
Bombay Cru India 59 A8
Bon Echo P Pk Canada 94 B6
Bon Nou, Villajoyosa Bch Spain 84 A9
Bon, Cap Tunisia 89 D2
Bonagia, Érice Bch Sicily 85 A11
Bonaire I. 95 D6
Bonampak Mexico 95 F3
Bonassola Italy 84 A3
Boni G Res Kenya 89 G4
Bonifacio, Strait of Corsica/Sardinia ..78 D2
Bonifica del Volturno Reg Italy 78 B1
Bonita Springs USA 91 D7
Bonn Germany 76 B1
Bonne Auberge, Antibes Bch France ..84 A3
Bonne Terrasse, Ramatuelle Bch France ..84 A3
Bonners Ferry USA 94 C4
Bonnettes, Le Pradet Bch France 84 A3
Bonneval France 72 C2
Bonneveine, Marseille Bch France 84 A3
Bonneville France 77 E5
Bonporteau, Cavalaire-sur-Mer Bch France ..84 A3
Bontebok N Pk South Africa 88 C6
Booker T. Washington N Mon USA 93 A8
Boot UK 66 C3
Boothbay Harbor USA 90 B4
Boothia Peninsula Canada 94 A2
Boppard Germany 76 C2
Bor Czech Rep. 75 H7
Bora Bora Cru French Polynesia 58 A1
Bordeaux Apt France 56 A9
Bordeaux Cru France 59 C1
Bordeaux France 72 A2
Bordeira Portugal 82 E5
Borders Adm UK 68 A3
Bordighera Italy 79 F9
Boréon, le France 72 F2
Borgo Panigale Apt Italy 79 F7
Borj Bourguiba Tunisia 89 D6
Borken Germany 74 B3
Børmio Italy 79 F3
Borna Germany 75 H5
Bornem Germany 65 B14
Borkum I Germany 74 B3
Bornholm I Denmark 56 A6
Borobodur UN C Indonesia 63 A8
Borovets Bulgaria 86 B2
Borrowdale UK 66 C4
Borth UK 68 A5
Borth Wen, Rhoscolyn Bch UK 68 A4
Bosa Sardinia 78 D1
Boscobel House EH UK 66 D1
Boskoop Netherlands 65 B7
Bosnia-Herzegovina 86 B2
Bosphorus Str Turkey 83 J3
Bosra UN C Syria 64 A12
Boston Apt USA 90 B3
Boston Cru USA 58 A2
Boston USA 90 B3
Boston N His USA 93 A4
Boston African American N His USA ...93 A4
Bosworth Field UK 66 D2
Bothnia, Gulf of 56 A3
Bothwell Castle His Sc UK 67 F2
Botrange Mtn Belgium 75 B6
Botswana 88 A4
Bottrop Germany 74 B5
Bou Grara, Golfe de Tunisia 89 D6
Bouârfa Morocco 89 D2
Bouches-du-Rhône Adm France 72 F3
Bouchet, le Ch France 72 C4
Boufa, Mileai Bch Greece 85 A12
Boufou, Vrahási Bch Crete 85 A11
Bouillon Belgium 65 B19
Boukhalef Souahel Apt Morocco 89 C2
Boulogne-sur-Mer Ferry France 69 D4
Boulogne-sur-Mer France 72 A1
Boumois Ch France 72 C1
Bourg-en-Bresse France 72 G1
Bourg-St-Maurice France 72 G2
Bourges France 72 A1
Bourgogne Adm France 73 A1
Bournemouth Apt UK 70 A6
Bournemouth UK 70 A6
Bournescheid Luxembourg 65 B20
Bourton-on-the-Water UK 66 D4
Boussay Ch France 72 C4
Bouvet I. 55 A5
Bowes Castle EH UK 67 F3
Bowness-on-Windermere UK 66 C4
Bowron Lake P Pk Canada 94 C1
Boynton Beach USA 91 D6
Bozcaada I Turkey 83 J2
Bozeman USA 90 A1
Bracciano I. 78 C1
Bracciano, Lago di Italy 78 C1
Bradano, Lido di Metaponto Bernalda Bch Italy ..85 A11
Bradenton USA 91 D5
Braga Portugal 82 A1
Bragança Portugal 82 A1
Brahmaputra Riv Bangladesh/China/India ..87 D6
Braila Romania 86 C2
Braithwaite UK 66 C1
Brampton Canada 94 B9
Bramsche Germany 74 C4
Brand Austria 77 F5
Brandenburg Germany 74 H4
Brandenburg Adm Germany 76 A1
Brands Hatch UK 66 E1
Brani, Pulau l Singapore 96 C4
Brantford Canada 94 B9
Braodway UK 66 D4
Brasília Apt Brazil 54 A3
Brasília UN C Brazil 62 A3
Bratislava Apt Slovak Rep. 56 A11
Bratislava Slovak Rep. 86 B2
Bratsk Russian Fed. 87 A5
Brattleboro USA 90 B3
Braubach Germany 76 C2
Braunau Austria 75 H8
Braunfels Germany 76 C2
Braunschweig Germany 74 F4
Braunwald Switzerland 77 E3
Brazil 54 A3
Brazzaville Apt Congo 55 A5
Breadalbane Reg UK 66 B1
Brecon Beacons N Pk UK 66 C3
Bredasdorp South Africa 88 C6
Bredene-aan-Zee Belgium 65 C1
Bredstedt Germany 74 D1
Bree Belgium 65 B11
Breede Riv South Africa 88 C6
Bregenz Austria 77 F1
Bréhat, Île France 72 B2
Breisach Germany 76 B7

Brejeira, Serra da Reg Portugal 82 E2
Bremen Apt Germany 74 D3
Bremen Germany 74 D3
Bremen Adm Germany 76 A1
Bremerhaven Germany 74 D3
Bremervörde Germany 74 E3
Brenner Pass Austria/Italy 77 F7
Brenta Reg Italy 79 F3
Bréscia Italy 79 F6
Breskens Netherlands 65 B10
Bressanone Italy 79 F3
Bressuire France 72 C3
Brest France 72 B1
Brest Belarus 86 A1
Bretagne Adm France ....72 B
Bretonne Corniche Reg France 72 B1
Bretten Germany 75 D7
Breuil-Cervinia Italy 79 F1
Briançon France 72 G4
Brices Cross Roads N Bat USA 93 A7
Bridgetown Cru Barbados 58 B11
Bridgnorth UK 66 D1
Bridlington UK 68 A4
Bridlington North Bch UK 68 A4
Bridlington South Bch UK 68 A4
Brie Reg France 72 H4
Brienzer See Lake Switzerland 77 E2
Brig Switzerland 77 E6
Brighton UK 66 E3
Brignoles France 72 F3
Brindisi Italy 79 A2
Brise de Mer, Stes-Maries-de-la-Mer Bch France ..84 A3
Brissac Ch France 72 C1
Brissago Switzerland 77 E7
Bristol Apt UK 70 A6
Bristol UK 70 A5
British Columbia Adm Canada 94 A5
British Indian Ocean Terr. Is. 55 A8
British Virgin Is. 95 D3
Brittany France ....72 B
Brno Czech Rep. 86 B1
Broad Haven, Haverfordwest Bch UK ..68 A5
Broadhaven South Bch UK 68 A5
Broadsands, Torbay Bch UK 68 A6
Broadstairs UK 66 E2
Brocken Mtn Germany 74 F5
Brockhole Visitor Centre UK 66 C4
Brockville Canada 94 B7
Brodick Ferry UK 69 B2
Brodick Castle, Garden/Country Park NT Sc UK ..67 F3
Broek op Langedijk Netherlands 65 B7
Brougham Castle EH UK 66 C2
Broughton in Furness UK 66 C3
Broughty Ferry UK 66 B2
Brown v. Board of Education N His USA ..93 A7
Brownsville USA 90 A6
Bruchsal Germany 75 D7
Bruck an der Mur Austria 77 D4
Bruges France 65 C2
Brugge Belgium 65 C2
Brühl UN C Germany 64 A6
Brühl Germany 76 B1
Brunei 55 A8
Brunico Italy 79 F3
Brunnen Switzerland 77 E3
Brunsbüttel Germany 74 E3
Brunswick USA 90 B4
Bruson Switzerland 77 E6
Brussel Apt Belgium 65 B14
Brussel Belgium 65 B14
Brussels Apt Belgium 65 B14
Brussels Belgium 65 B14
Bruxelles Apt Belgium 65 B14
Bruxelles Belgium 65 B14
Bryce Canyon N Pk USA 92 A5
Bucharest Apt Romania 56 A11
Bucharest Romania 86 B2
Buchen Germany 75 E7
Buck I. Reef N Mon US Virgin Is. 93
Buckinghamshire Adm UK 68 A5
Buckland Abbey NT UK 67 F6
Bucksport USA 90 B4
Budapest Apt Hungary 56 A11
Budapest UN C Hungary 64 A7
Budapest Hungary 86 B2
Bude UK 68 A6
Büdingen Germany 76 B2
Buenavista del Cayo Belize 95 F4
Buenos Aires Apt Argentina 54 A3
Buenos Aires Argentina 58 A3
Bufalória Nord, Scanzano Iónico Bch Italy ..85 A11
Bufalória Sud, Scanzano Iónico Bch Italy ..85 A11
Buffalo Apt USA 90 A4
Buffalo USA 90 A4
Buffalo Springs G Res Kenya 89 G2
Buffels Bay South Africa 88 C7
Bugibba Malta 79 G2
Bühl Germany 75 D8
Bujumbura Apt Burundi 55 A5
Buka, Lefkimi Bch Greece 85 A12
Bukhara Uzbekistan 86 A3
Bukit Bendara Hill Malaysia 96 B1
Bukit Ferringhi Malaysia 96 B3
Bukit Gemuruh F Res Malaysia 96 B3
Bukit Genting F Res Malaysia 96 B3
Bukit Juru F Res Malaysia 96 B4
Bukit Kerajaan F Res Malaysia 96 B3
Bukit Pulau Malaysia 96 B3
Bukit Relau F Res Malaysia 96 B4
Bukit Tengah Malaysia 96 B4
Bukit Timah N Res Singapore 96 C1
Bukit Western Mtn Malaysia 96 B1
Bukovina Reg Romania/Ukraine 86 B2
Bukum, Pulau l Singapore 96 C1
Bulgaria 86 B2
Bulla Regia Tunisia 89 D1
Bulawayo Zimbabwe 88 A4
Bur Safâga Egypt 89 F4
Bura Kenya 89 G4
Büren Germany 74 D5
Burg Germany 74 G2
Burg Germany 74 G4
Burgas Apt Bulgaria 56 A11
Burgas Bulgaria 86 B2
Burgau Portugal 82 E5
Burgdorf Switzerland 77 E2
Burgenland Adm Austria 77 D4
Burghausen Germany 75 H8
Burglengenfeld Germany 75 H7
Burgos UN C Spain 64 A6
Burgos Spain 81 A1
Burgundy Adm France 73 A1
Burkina Faso 88 A2
Burlington USA 90 B3
Burlington USA 90 B3
Burlington Canada 94 B9
Burriana, Nerja Bch Spain 84 A8
Bursa Turkey 83 J3
Bürserberg Austria 77 F5
Burundi 55 A5
Bury St Edmunds: Theatre Royal NT UK ..67 F5
Busch Gardens, Tampa USA 93 A8
Busch Gardens, Williamsburg USA 93 A8

Busing, Pulau l Singapore 96 C3
Bussana Italy 79 F9
Büsum Germany 74 D2
Buthrotum Albania 83 G1
Buttermere Lake UK 66 C4
Buttermere UK 66 C1
Butterworth Malaysia 96 B2
Buxtehude Germany 74 E3
Büyük Menderes Riv Turkey 83 J9
Bwindi Impenetrable N Pk, UN N Uganda ..61 A5
Byblos UN C Lebanon 64 A12

Cabinda Angola 88 A3
Cabo de Gata, Almería Bch Spain 84 A8
Cabo Roig, Orihuela Bch Spain 84 A9
Cabo San Lucas Cru Mexico 58 A3
Cabrera, Illa de l Mallorca 81 G4
Cabrillo N Mon USA 92 A5
Cacahuamilpa Mexico 95 E4
Cáceres UN C Spain 64 A9
Cachopo Portugal 82 E3
Cadaqués Spain 80 C2
Cadenábbia Italy 79 F2
Cádiz Cru Spain 59 C5
Cádiz Apt Spain 56 A9
Cádiz Spain 80 D5
Cádiz, Bahía de Bay Spain 80 D5
Cádiz, Golfo de Spain 80 D5
Caen Ferry France 69 D7
Caen France 72 A1
Caerfai, St David's Bch UK 68 A5
Caerlaverock Castle His Sc UK 67 F3
Caernarfon UK 68 A4
Caernarfon Castle NT UK 67 F4
Caerphilly Castle Cadw UK 67 F5
Cágliari Apt Italy 78 D4
Cágliari Sardinia 78 D4
Cágliari, Golfo di Sardinia 78 D4
Cagnes-sur-Mer France 72 F4
Cahokia Mounds S His, UN C USA 62 A2
Cahuyp Guatemala 95 F5
Cairngorms Reg UK 66 A1
Cairnryan Ferry UK 69 B4
Cairns Apt Australia 55 A9
Cairns Australia 59 A9
Cairns Cru Australia 89 F2
Cairo UN C Egypt 64 A12
Cairo Egypt 89 F1
Cala Agulla, Capdepera Bch Mallorca ..84 A9
Cala Antena Mallorca 81 G4
Cala Antena, St Llorenç/Manacor Bch Mallorca ..84 A9
Cala Bassa Ibiza 81 F1
Cala Bassa, St Josep de sa Talaia Bch Ibiza ..84 A9
Cala Blanca Mallorca 81 H1
Cala Blanca, Jávea Bch Spain 84 A9
Cala Blanes Menorca 81 H1
Cala Blanes, Ciutadella Bch Menorca ..84 A9
Cala Blava Mallorca 81 G3
Cala Bona Mallorca 81 G2
Cala Conta, St Josep de sa Talaia Bch Ibiza ..84 A9
Cala d'Or Mallorca 81 G4
Cala d'Or, Santanyí Bch Mallorca 84 A9
Cala de Santandría Menorca 81 H1
Cala de Santandría, Ciutadella Bch Menorca ..84 A9
Cala de St Vicenç Ibiza 81 F2
Cala de St Vicenç Mallorca 81 G2
Cala di Fronte, Ostuni Bch Italy 85 A12
Cala En Bosc Menorca 81 H3
Cala En Bosc, Ciutadella Bch Menorca ..84 A9
Cala En Porter Menorca 81 H4
Cala Esmeralda, Santanyí Bch Mallorca ..84 A9
Cala Estany Mallorca 81 G4
Cala Ferrera, Felanitx Bch Mallorca ...84 A9
Cala Figuera Mallorca 81 G4
Cala Figuera, Santanyí Bch Mallorca ..84 A9
Cala Forcat Menorca 81 H1
Cala Fustera, Benissa Bch Spain 84 A9
Cala Gració Ibiza 81 F1
Cala Gració, St Antoni de Portmany Bch Ibiza ..84 A9
Cala Gran, Santanyí Bch Mallorca 84 A9
Cala Liberotto Sardinia 78 D2
Cala Llenya Ibiza 81 F2
Cala Llenya, St Eulària del Riu Bch Ibiza ..84 A9
Cala Llombards, Santanyí Bch Mallorca ..84 A9
Cala Llonga Ibiza 81 F2
Cala Llonga Menorca 81 H4
Cala Llonga, St Eulària del Riu Bch Ibiza ..84 A9
Cala Major Mallorca 81 G3
Cala Mandia, Manacor Bch Mallorca ..84 A9
Cala Marçal Mallorca 81 G4
Cala Marçal, Felanitx Bch Mallorca ...84 A9
Cala Mesquida, Capdepera Bch Mallorca ..84 A9
Cala Millor Mallorca 81 G2
Cala Millor, St Llorenç des Cardassar Bch Mallorca ..84 A9
Cala Mondragó Mallorca 81 G4
Cala Mondragó, Santanyí Bch Mallorca ..84 A9
Cala Morell Menorca 81 H1
Cala Murada Mallorca 81 G4
Cala Murada, Manacor Bch Mallorca ..84 A9
Cala Pi Mallorca 81 G3
Cala Portinatx, St Joan de Labritja Bch Ibiza ..84 A9
Cala Ratjada Mallorca 81 G2
Cala Sahona Formentera 81 F3
Cala Santa Galdana, Ferreries Bch Menorca ..84 A9
Cala Santanyí, Santanyí Bch Mallorca ..84 A9
Cala St Vicenç, St Joan de Labritja Bch Ibiza ..84 A9
Cala Sta Galdana Menorca 81 H3
Cala Tarida Ibiza 81 F1
Cala Tirant Menorca 81 H2
Cala Tirant, Es Mercadal Bch Menorca ..84 A9
Cala Torret Menorca 81 H4
Cala Vadella Ibiza 81 F1
Cala Vadella, St Josep de sa Talaia Bch Ibiza ..84 A9
Cala Vinyes Mallorca 81 G3
Calabria Adm Italy 79 A2
Calafató, L'Ametlla de Mar Bch Spain ..84 A2
Calafell Spain 80 C3
Calafell Bch Spain 84 A2
Calahonda Spain 80 D7
Calais Ferry France 69 D4
Calais France 72 A1
Calakmul Mexico 95 F4
Calcarre, Cava di Italy 79 A2
Calcutta Apt India 55 A8
Caldbeck UK 66 C1
Caldeirão, Serra do Reg Portugal 82 E3
Calder Hall UK 66 C3
Caledon South Africa 88 C6
Calella Spain 80 C4
Calella Bch Spain 84 A2
Cales Coves Menorca 81 H4
Cales de Mallorca Mallorca 81 G4
Caletta, la Sardinia 78 D2
Calgary Apt Canada 54 A2
Calgary Canada 94 C4
Calheta Azores 82 B2
Calheta Madeira 82 C1
California Adm USA ....91 E
Calitzdorf South Africa 88 C6
Callao Cru Peru 58 A3
Calonge Spain 80 C4

Calore Riv Italy 78 B2
Calpe Spain 81 E2
Caltanissetta Sicily 78 E4
Calvià Sicily 81 G1
Calvinia South Africa 88 C2
Calw Germany 76 B6
Camagüey, Archipelago de Is. 95 D1
Câmara de Lobos Madeira 82 C1
Camber Bch UK 68 A6
Cambo-les-Bains France 72 D1
Cambodia 55 A8
Cambrai France 65 B17
Cambrian Mountains UK 66 C2
Cambridge Apt UK 70 A5
Cambridge UK 70 A5
Cambridgeshire Adm UK 68 A5
Cambrils de Mar Spain 80 C3
Camden USA 90 B4
Camden USA 93 A8
Cameron Highlands Malaysia 88 A2
Cameroon 88 A2
Campania Italy 78 B3
Campanella, Punta Cape Italy 79 A2
Campania, Sirolo Bch Italy 85 A4
Campbell I. Cru 55 A9
Campeche Mexico 95 F1
Campeche, Bahía de Gulf Mexico 58 B4
Campello Spain 81 E2
Camping Belvedere, Grado Bch Italy ..85 A4
Camping Calacampi, Vieste Bch Italy ..85 A4
Camping Europa, Grado Bch Italy 85 A4
Camping Framura Bch Italy 85 A4
Camping Girarrosto, Vieste Bch Italy ..85 A4
Camping Nord, Sirolo Bch Italy 85 A4
Camping Pilone, Ostuni Bch Italy 85 A12
Camping, Sirolo Bch Italy 85 A4
Campo Tures Italy 79 F3
Campoamor Spain 81 E3
Campobasso Italy 79 A2
Campos Mallorca 81 G4
Campotosto, Lago di Italy 78 C2
Campsie Fells UK 66 B3
Can Pastilla Mallorca 81 G3
Can Picafort Mallorca 81 G3
Can Picafort, Santa Margalida Bch Mallorca ..84 A9
Canada 94
Canadaigua Lake USA 94 B10
Canadell, Palafrugell Bch Spain 84 A2
Canadian Rocky Mountains parks UN N Canada ..94 C
Canaima N Pk, N N Venezuela 60 A3
Çanakkale Cru Turkey 59 C3
Çanakkale Turkey 83 J2
Çanakkale Bogazi Str Turkey 83 J2
Canal d'Amour, Peroulades Bch Greece ..85 A12
Canale Tagliata Nord, Cesenático Bch Italy ..85 A4
Canale Tagliata Sud, Cesenático Bch Italy ..85 A4
Canarias Is Spain ....80 B
Canary Is. Spain ....80 B
Canaveral N Sea USA 91 D4
Canazei Italy 79 F3
Canberra Apt Australia 55 A9
Cancale France 72 B2
Cancún Mexico 95 F2
Candelaria Canary Is. 80 B1
Candé Apt Greece 83 J10
Canea Crete 83 J10
Canea 83 J10
Canet d'En Berenguer Spain 84 A9
Canet-en-Roussillon France 84 A2
Canet-Plage France 84 A2
Cango Caves South Africa 88 C7
Caniçal Madeira 82 C2
Caniço Madeira 82 C2
Canna Ferry UK 69 B1
Cannes France 72 F4
Cannock Chase Reg UK 91 E3
Cannon Apt USA 91 E3
Cantabria Adm Spain 80 A1
Cantera, Islote de la I Spain 81 E1
Canterbury UN C UK 64 A5
Canterbury UK 66 E4
Canterbury Canada 90 B3
Canton Apt China 55 A8
Canton Cru China 59 A8
Canvey I. UK 66 E2
Canyon de Chelly N Mon USA 92 A6
Canyonlands N Pk USA 92 A6
Caorle Italy 79 F8
Cap Blanc Sur, Altea Bch Spain 84 A9
Cap d'Antibes Bch France 84 A3
Cap de La Madeleine Canada 94 B4
Cap Haïtien Cru Haiti 58 B6
Cap Nègre, Le Lavandou Bch France ..84 A3
Capalonga, San Michele al Tagliamento Bch Italy ..85 A4
Capdepera Mallorca 81 G2
Cape Adare Antarctica 59 A10
Cape Breton I. Canada 94 A8
Cape Canaveral USA 91 D6
Cape Cod USA 58 A2
Cape Cod N Sea USA 93 A4
Cape Evans Cru Antarctica 59 A10
Cape Hallet Antarctica 59 A10
Cape Hatteras USA 58 A2
Cape Hatteras N Sea USA 93 A4
Cape Krusenstern N Mon USA 92 A9
Cape Lookout N Sea USA 93 A8
Cape of Good Hope South Africa 88 C5
Cape of Good Hope N Pk Ntr Res South Africa ..88 C5
Cape Peninsula South Africa 88 C5
Cape Sounio Greece 83 J7
Cape Town Apt South Africa 88 C5
Cape Town Cru South Africa 59 A5
Cape Town South Africa 88 C5
Cape Verde 88 A2
Capileira Spain 80 D3
Capitol Reef N Pk USA 92 A5
Capo Boi Sardinia 78 D4
Capo Mimosa, Cervo Bch Italy 84 A3
Capo Néro, Ospedaletti Bch Italy 84 A3
Capodichino Apt Italy 78 B1
Capodimonte Italy 78 C1
Cappadócia UN C Turkey 64 A12
Capráia, Ísola di Italy 79 F10
Capraia, Ísola Sardinia 79 F10
Capri Cru Italy 59 C2
Capri Italy 78 B3
Capri, Ísola di Italy 79 A2
Captain Cook Hawaiian Is. 91 C8
Captiva I. USA 91 D5
Câpua Italy 78 B1
Capulin Volcano N Mon USA 92 A6
Cara Sucia El Salvador 95 F6
Caracas Apt Venezuela 54 A3
Caracol Belize 95 F4
Caravaca, Fos-sur-Mer Bch France 84 A3
Carbonara, Capo Sardinia 78 D4
Carbonara Spain 80 D4
Carcavelos Portugal 82 D1
Cardiff Apt UK 70 A6
Cardiff UK 70 A5
Cardigan UK 70 A5
Cardona, Roseto Capo Spúlico Bch Italy ..85 A11
Carezza Italy 79 F3
Caribbean Sea ....95 D

Index

Caribbean/Florida Cruise Area................58 B
Caribou USA................90 B2
Carinthia Adm Austria................77 D3
Carisbrook Castle EH UK................67 F6
Carl Sandburg Home N His USA................93 A8
Carleton Place Canada................94 B6
Carlisle UK................70 A3
Carlsbad Caverns N Pk USA................92 A6
Carmel USA................91 E3
Carmona Spain................80 D2
Carnac France................72 B4
Carnarvon South Africa................88 C3
Carnon Est-L'Église, Mauguio-Carnon France................84 A2
Carnon Est-Les Dunes, Mauguio-Carnon Bch France................84 A2
Carnon Ouest, Mauguio-Carnon Bch France................84 A2
Carnoustie Gf UK................66 B2
Carpathians Mtns Romania/Ukraine................86 B2
Carqueiranne France................84 A3
Carrapateira Portugal................82 E5
Carrara Italy................79 F10
Carras, Nice Bch France................84 A3
Carreg Cennen Castle Cadw UK................67 F5
Carrer la Mar, Campello Bch Spain................84 A9
Carro, Martigues Bch France................84 A3
Carroz d'Arâches, les France................72 G2
Carson City USA................91 E3
Cartagena Cru Colombia................58 B10
Cartagena UN C Colombia................62 A3
Cartagena Spain................81 E3
Carthage UN C Tunisia................64 A10
Carthage N Mem USA................93 A8
Carthage Apt Tunisia................89 D2
Carvajal-La Perla, Benalmádena Bch Spain................84 A8
Carvoeiro Portugal................82 E6
Casa Bianca, Jésolo Bch Italy................85 A4
Casa Grande N Mon USA................92 A5
Casa Rossa, Ostuni Bch Italy................85 A12
Casablanca Apt Morocco................89 E1
Casablanca Cru Morocco................59 C5
Casablanca Morocco................89 E1
Casale Italy................79 F6
Casamari, Abbazia di Italy................78 C4
Casares Spain................80 D6
Cascade Range Mtns USA................90 A1
Cascais Portugal................82 D1
Caselle Apt Italy................79 F5
Caserta Italy................78 B1
Casino, Bandol Bch France................84 A3
Casino, La Ciotat Bch France................84 A3
Casper USA................90 A2
Caspian Sea................86 A2
Castel Gandolfo Italy................78 C3
Castel, Nice Bch France................84 A3
Castell Spain................84 A2
Castellammare di Stábia Italy................78 B3
Castellammare, Golfo di Sicily................78 E1
Castellane France................72 F2
Castelldefels Spain................80 C3
Castelli Romani Reg Italy................78 C3
Castello, Roseto Capo Spúlico Bch Italy................85 A11
Castellón de la Plana Spain................81 E3
Castelnou France................72 E2
Castelo Branco Portugal................82 A2
Castelo, PÓnto do Cape Madeira................82 C2
Castiglioncello Italy................79 F11
Castiglione del Lago Italy................79 F11
Castiglione della Pescáia Italy................79 F11
Castilla y Leon Adm Spain................80 A1
Castilla, Playa de Bch Spain................80 D1
Castilla-La Mancha Adm Spain................81 A2
Castillo de San Marcos N Mon USA................91 D4
Castle Campbell His Sc UK................67 F2
Castle Clinton N Mon USA................93 A4
Castle Drogo NT UK................67 F6
Castlebay Ferry UK................69 B1
Castlerigg Stone Circle NT UK................66 C2
Castries Cru St Lucia................58 B11
Castro Marim Portugal................82 E4
Castro Marina Italy................85 A12
Cat I. Bahamas................58 B3
Catalonia Adm Spain................81 A1
Catalunya Adm Spain................81 A1
Catánia Apt Italy................78 E4
Catánia Cru Sicily................59 C6
Catánia Sicily................78 E4
Catánia, Golfo di Sicily................78 E4
Catoctin USA................93 A4
Cattólica Italy................79 F12
Caucasus Mtns Azerbaijan/Georgia/Russian Fed................86 A2
Caulnes France................72 B2
Cauterets France................72 D2
Cava de'Tirreni Italy................78 B4
Cavalaire Centre, Cavalaire-sur-Mer Bch France................84 A3
Cavalaire Est, Cavalaire-sur-Mer Bch France................84 A3
Cavalaire Ouest, Cavalaire-sur-Mer Bch France................84 A3
Cavalaire-sur-Mer France................73 F3
Cavalière, Le Lavandou Bch France................84 A3
Cavalleria, Cap de Menorca................81 H2
Cavi, Lavagna Bch Italy................85 A4
Cayenne Apt French Guiana................58 B8
Cayman Is.................95 D1
Cayuga Lake USA................94 B10
Cebu Cru Philippines................59 A8
Ceccano Italy................78 C1
Cedar Breaks N Mon USA................92 A5
Cedar Keys N W R USA................91 D3
Cefalú Sicily................78 E2
Cefn Sidan Pembrey Country Park Bch UK................68 A5
Ceinturon Est, Hyères Bch France................84 A3
Ceinturon Ouest, Hyères Bch France................84 A3
Celano Italy................78 C2
Celle Italy................74 F4
Celtic Sea................56 A5
Cento Italy................79 F7
Central Adm UK................66 B1
Central African Rep................61 A5
Central African Republic................88 A2
Central Highlands Reg Kenya................89 G3
Central I. N Pk Kenya................89 G1
Central Plains Reg Kenya................96 A1
Central Siberian Plateau Russian Fed................87 A5
Central Southern England Reg UK................66 B8
Centrale, Banyuls-sur-Mer France................84 A2
Centre Apt Portugal................82 A1
Centre Héliomarin, Banyuls-sur-Mer Bch France................84 A2
Centro Apt Portugal................82 A2
Centro Golfo, Monterosso Bch Italy................84 A3
Centro Spiaggia, Jésolo Bch Italy................85 A4
Centro, Déiva Marina Bch Italy................84 A3
Centro, Ísola di Capráia Bch Italy................84 A3
Centro, Lido di Metaponto Bernalda Bch Italy................85 A11
Cephalonia I Greece................83 H2
Cephalonia Apt Greece................83 H2
Cerbère France................72 E2
Ceres South Africa................88 C5
Cergy-Pontoise France................72 H1
Cerigo I Greece................83 J7
Cerigo Apt Greece................83 J10
Cernóbbio Italy................79 F2
Cerrillos-Playa Serena, Roquetas Bch Spain................84 A8
Cerro de las Mesas Mexico................95 E4
Cerros Belize................95 F4
Cervéteri Italy................78 C1

Cérvia Italy................79 F8
Cervialto, Monte Mtn Italy................78 B4
Cervo Italy................79 F9
Cesenático Italy................79 F8
Ceska Lipa Czech Rep................75 J6
Ceske Budejovice Czech Rep................86 B1
Cesky Krumlov Czech Rep................86 B1
Cesky Les Reg Czech Rep................75 H7
Çesme Turkey................83 J5
Ceuta Cru Spain................59 C5
Ceuta Spain................89 E2
Ceuta................89 E2
Ceyhan Turkey................83 F3
Cha-Am Thailand................96 D3
Chaâlis, Abbaye de France................72 H2
Challaborough, Bigbury-on-Sea Bch UK................68 A6
Châlons-sur-Marne France................73 A1
Chablais Reg France................72 G2
Chacahua, Lagunas de Mexico................95 E4
Chachoengsao Thailand................96 D2
Chacmultún Mexico................95 F2
Chaco Culture N His, UN C USA................62 A2
Chad................88 A2
Chalbi Desert Kenya................89 G1
Challans France................72 C3
Chambery France................72 G1
Chambi, Jebel Mtn Tunisia................89 D3
Chambly France................72 H1
Chambly, Fort Canada................94 B7
Chambord Ch, UN C France................64 C2
Chambord France................72 C2
Chamizal N Mem USA................92 A6
Chamois Italy................79 F1
Chamonix France................72 G2
Champ de Feu, le Mtn France................75 C8
Champagne-Ardenne Adm France................73 A1
Champéry Switzerland................77 E5
Champex Switzerland................77 E6
Champigny-sur-Marne France................72 H4
Champlain, Lake USA................90 B3
Champoussin Switzerland................77 E5
Chan Chan UN C Peru................62 A3
Chan Chich Belize................95 F4
Changan China................87 D6
Changi Apt Singapore................96 C2
Channel Is.................68 A8
Channel Is. Reg USA................91 E5
Channel Is. N Pk USA................91 E5
Channel Tunnel................66 E4
Chantilly France................72 H2
Chantilly, Forêt de France................72 H2
Chao Phraya Riv Thailand................96 D1
Chapala, Lago de Mexico................95 E1
Charlecote Park NT UK................67 F5
Charleroi Belgium................65 B14
Charleroi Apt Belgium................65 B14
Charles de Gaulle Apt France................72 H2
Charles Pinckney N His USA................93 A8
Charleston, South Carolina USA................90 A8
Charleston, West Virginia USA................90 A8
Charlestown Cru Nevis................58 B7
Charleville-Mézières France................65 B19
Charlotte Apt USA................54 B2
Charlotte USA................90 A8
Charlotte Amalie Cru US Virgin Is.................58 B7
Charlotte Harbor USA................91 D5
Charlottesville USA................62 A2
Charlottetown Cru Canada................58 A2
Charlottetown Canada................94 A8
Charnwood Forest UK................66 D2
Chartres UN C France................64 A6
Chartres France................72 H3
Chartwell NT UK................66 E3
Château d'Oex Switzerland................77 E6
Château-Thierry France................72 H2
Châteaubriant France................72 C1
Châteauroux France................72 C4
Châtel France................72 G2
Châtellerault France................72 C4
Chatham UK................66 E2
Chatham I.................55 A4
Châtillon-sur-Indre France................72 C4
Chattahoochee River N Rec USA................93 A8
Chaudière Riv Canada................94 B4
Chaumont France................72 C2
Chauny France................72 H2
Chauvigny France................72 C4
Chavin UN C Peru................62 A3
Chbika Tunisia................89 D3
Cheb Czech Rep................75 H6
Cheboksary Russian Fed................86 C1
Cheboksary Reservoir Russian Fed................86 C1
Chechaouen Morocco................89 E2
Chedworth Roman Villa NT UK................66 D4
Chelmsford UK................66 E2
Chelsea UK................66 E1
Cheltenham UK................66 D4
Chémery Ch France................72 C2
Chemillé France................72 C3
Chemnitz Germany................75 H6
Chengde UN C China................63 A8
Chengdu Apt China................55 A8
Chenini Tunisia................89 D6
Chenonceaux Ch France................72 C2
Chepstow UK................66 D3
Chepstow Castle Cadw UK................67 F5
Cher Riv France................72 C2
Cherating Malaysia................96 A2
Cherbourg Ferry France................69 D2
Cherbourg France................72 A1
Chergui, Ile Tunisia................89 D4
Cheriton Channel Tunnel Terminal UK................69 D4
Cherryburn, Mickley NT UK................67 F3
Chesapeake and Ohio Canal N His USA................93 A4
Cheshire Adm UK................68 A4
Chessington World of Adventures UK................66 E1
Chester UK................70 A4
Chester Roman Ampitheatre EH UK................67 F4
Chester: St Botolph's Priory EH UK................67 F5
Chetumal Mexico................95 F4
Cheverny Ch France................72 C2
Cheviot Hills UK................66 A1
Chewore safari area UN N Zimbabwe................61 A5
Cheyenne USA................90 A3
Chia Sardinia................78 D4
Chiang Rai Thailand................96 A1
Chianti Reg Italy................79 F11
Chiávari Italy................79 F6
Chicago Apt USA................54 B1
Chicago USA................90 A3
Chicago Portage N His USA................93 A3
Chicanná Mexico................95 F4
Chichén Itza Mexico................95 F2
Chichén Itzá UN C Mexico................62 B1
Chichester UK................66 E3
Chickamauga and Chattanooga N Mil USA................93 A8
Chicksan N Rec USA................93 A7
Chiclana de la Frontera Spain................80 D5
Chico USA................91 E1
Chiemsee Lake Germany................75 H9
Chieng-Mai Apt Thailand................55 A8
Chieng-Mai Thailand................96 A1
Chiesa Italy................79 F2
Chieuti Italy................85 A4
Chile................54 A3
Chilia Riv Romania/Ukraine................86 C2

Chilpancingo Mexico................95 E4
Chiltern Hills UK................66 E1
Chimkent Kazakhstan................86 A3
Chimney Rock N His USA................92 A2
China................55 A8
Chinese and Japanese Garden Singapore................96 C1
Chinkultic Mexico................95 F3
Chinon Ch France................72 C4
Chióggia Italy................79 F8
Chios UN C Greece................64 A11
Chios I Greece................83 J5
Chios Apt Greece................83 J5
Chipiona Spain................80 D5
Chiquitos Jesuit missions UN C Bolivia................62 A3
Chiricahua N Mon USA................92 A6
Chirk Castle NT UK................67 F4
Chisasibi Canada................94 A7
Chisinau Apt Moldova................56 A1
Chisinau Moldova................86 A1
Chiswick House EH UK................67 F5
Chitwan N Pk, UN N Nepal................61 A8
Chiunzi, Válico de Italy................78 B4
Chivasso Italy................79 F5
Cholet France................72 C3
Cholula Mexico................95 E2
Chomutov Czech Rep................75 I6
Chon Buri Thailand................96 D4
Chongqing Cru China................59 A8
Christchurch Apt New Zealand................55 A9
Christchurch New Zealand................59 A9
Christchurch UK................66 A6
Christchurch Castle and Norman House EH UK................67 F6
Christiansted Cru US Virgin Is.................58 B7
Christiansted N His US Virgin Is.................93
Christmas I.................55 A8
Christmas I. Cru................59 A8
Chuitinamit Guatemala................95 F5
Chukchi Reg Russian Fed................87 B7
Chunyaxche Mexico................95 F2
Chur Switzerland................77 E4
Churchill Canada................94 A6
Churchill Falls Canada................94 A4
Churston Cove, Torbay Bch UK................68 A6
Ciampino Apt Italy................78 C3
Cieza Spain................81 E1
Cihuatan El Salvador................95 F5
Cilento Reg Italy................78 B4
Cimini, Monti Reg Italy................78 C1
Cincinnati Apt USA................54 B1
Cincinnati USA................90 A3
Cinque Terre Italy................79 F10
Circolo Canottieri, Marsala Bch Sicily................85 A11
Cirencester UK................66 D4
Cirque de Jáffar Morocco................89 E2
Cirque de l'Anau, Sète Bch France................84 A1
Cistóbal Cru Panama................58 B9
Citadel UN C Haiti................62 A3
Città del Castello Italy................79 F12
Cittadella Italy................79 F7
City of London UK................66 E1
City of Rocks N Res USA................92 A1
Ciudad Altamirano Mexico................95 E3
Ciudad del Carmen Mexico................95 F3
Ciudad Guayana Cru Venezuela................58 B11
Ciudad Madero Mexico................95 E2
Ciudad Mante Mexico................95 E2
Ciudad Real Spain................81 A2
Ciudad Sindical, Marbella Bch Spain................84 A8
Ciudad Victoria Mexico................95 E2
Ciutadella Menorca................81 H1
Ciutat, Villajoyosa Bch Spain................84 A9
Civita Castellana Italy................78 C1
Civitanova Italy................79 F12
Civitavécchia Italy................78 C1
Clacton-on-Sea UK................66 E2
Clanwilliam South Africa................88 C1
Claonaig Ferry UK................69 B2
Clara Barton N His USA................93 A4
Claremont USA................90 B3
Claremont Garden NT UK................67 F6
Clavière Italy................79 F5
Clearwater USA................91 D5
Cleator Moor UK................66 C1
Clermont France................72 H2
Clermont-Ferrand France................72 A2
Clervaux Luxembourg................65 B20
Clevedon Court NT UK................67 F6
Cleveland Apt USA................54 B2
Cleveland Adm UK................68 A3
Cleveland USA................90 A4
Cliveden NT UK................67 F5
Clos des Plages, La Ciotat Bch France................84 A3
Clumber Park NT UK................66 D2
Clun Castle EH UK................67 F5
Clun Forest UK................66 D1
Clusaz, la France................72 G2
Clwyd Adm UK................68 A4
Clyde Riv UK................66 B3
Clyde UK................66 B3
Coast Mountains Canada................94 A5
Coastal Range Mtns USA................91 E3
Coats I. Canada................94 A3
Cobá Mexico................95 F2
Cobo Channel Is.................68 A8
Coburg Germany................75 F6
Cochem Germany................76 C1
Cockermouth UK................66 C1
Coco Beach, Nice Bch France................84 A3
Cocoa Beach USA................91 D6
Cocos Is.................55 A8
Coesfeld Germany................74 C5
Coevorden Netherlands................65 B8
Cognac France................72 A2
Cogolin France................72 F2
Cogolin Bch France................84 A3
Coimbra Portugal................82 A2
Colares Portugal................82 D1
Colby Woodland Garden NT UK................67 F5
Colchester UK................66 E2
Colchester: St Botolph's Priory EH UK................67 F5
Colfosco Italy................79 F3
Colima Mexico................95 E3
Colintraive Ferry UK................69 B2
Coll Ferry UK................69 B2
Coll I UK................70 A2
Colline del Po Italy................79 F5
Collingwood Canada................94 B5
Collioure France................72 E2
Collioure Bch France................84 A2
Colmar France................72 D1
Cologne Germany................76 B1
Cologne/Bonn Apt Germany................76 B1
Coloma USA................91 E3
Colombia................54 A3
Colombier Switzerland................77 E1
Colombo Apt Sri Lanka................55 A8
Colombo Cru Sri Lanka................59 A8
Colón, San Javier Bch Spain................84 A8
Colonia Braidese, Laiguéglia Bch Italy................84 A3
Colonia Cremasca, Finale Ligure Bch Italy................84 A3
Colònia de St Jordi Mallorca................81 G4
Colonia Lancia, Finale Ligure Bch Italy................84 A3
Colonia Ruffini, Tággia Bch Italy................84 A3
Colonial National Historical Park UN C USA................93 A8
Colonsay Ferry UK................69 B2
Colonsay I UK................70 A2
Colorado Adm USA................90 A2

Colorado Riv USA................91 E6
Colorado N Mon USA................92 A6
Colorado Plateau USA................90 A1
Colorado Springs USA................90 A2
Columbia USA................90 A8
Columbia Riv Canada/USA................94 C4
Columbia Icefield Canada................94 C4
Columbia, Mt Canada................94 C4
Columbine, Cape South Africa................88 C1
Columbus USA................90 A4
Coma-ruga, El Vendrell Bch Spain................84 A2
Comalcalco Mexico................95 F3
Comaruga Spain................80 C3
Comino I Malta................79 G1
Cominotto I Malta................79 G1
Commenges Reg France................72 E1
Como, Lago di Italy................79 F2
Como Italy................79 F2
Comoé N Pk, UN N Côte d'Ivoire................61 A5
Comoros................88 A3
Compiègne France................72 H2
Compiègne, Forêt de France................72 H2
Cracow Apt Poland................64 A1
Cracow Poland................86 B1
Cradock South Africa................88 B3
Cragside House, Garden and grounds NT UK................67 F3
Craigmillar Castle His Sc UK................67 F1
Craignure Ferry UK................69 B2
Crailsheim Germany................75 F1
Cranbrooke Canada................94 C4
Cranfield Bay Bch UK................68 A6
Crans-Montana Switzerland................77 E6
Crater Lake N Pk USA................91 A1
Craters of the Moon N Mon USA................92 A1
Crawford Notch Pass USA................90 B3
Crawley UK................66 E1
Creake Abbey EH UK................67 F4
Creil France................72 H2
Crema Italy................79 F6
Cremona Italy................79 F7
Créneau de Nature, Narbonne Bch France................84 A1
Crépy-en-Valois France................72 H2
Crete I Greece................83 J10
Crete, Sea of Greece................83 J11
Creus, Cap de Spain................80 C2
Creuse Adm France................72 C4
Creuse Riv France................72 C4
Crevillente Spain................81 E1
Crianlarich UK................66 B1
Crichton Castle His Sc UK................66 B1
Crieff UK................66 B2
Crimea Reg................86 A2
Crimmitschau Germany................75 H6
Crinnis UK................68 A6
Crique de l'Anau, Sète Bch France................84 A1
Cristofo Colombo Apt Italy................79 F6
Croatia................86 B2
Croatia................86 B2
Crocodile Farm Singapore................96 C2
Crocodile Farm Thailand................96 D1
Crocodile Paradise Singapore................96 C1
Crooked Riv Canada................94 A5
Crooked I. Bahamas................58 B4
Crooklets, Bude Bch UK................68 A6
Croxden Abbey EH UK................67 F4
Croydon UK................66 E1
Cruden Bay Bch UK................66 B1
Crummock Water Lake UK................66 C1
Ctesiphon Iraq................55 D1
Cuba................95 D1
Cubells Ibiza................81 F3
Cuccurullo, Vico Equense Bch Italy................85 A11
Cuello Belize................95 F4
Cuernavaca Mexico................95 E4
Cuitzeo Mexico................95 E1
Culatra, Ilha da I Portugal................82 E4
Culebra Is................84 A9
Cullera Spain................81 E1
Cullercoats, Tynemouth Bch UK................68 A3
Culloden Moor UK................66 B1
Culross His Sc UK................67 F2
Culuba Mexico................95 F2
Culzean Castle and Country Park NT Sc UK................67 F2
Cuma Italy................78 B4
Cumberland Gap N His USA................93 A8
Cumberland Island N Sea USA................93 A8
Cumbernauld UK................66 B3
Cumbrae Slip Ferry UK................69 B2
Cumbria UK................66 C1
Cumbria Reg UK................68 A3
Cúneo Italy................79 F5
Cunninghame Reg UK................66 B3
Cupar UK................66 B2
Curaçao I................95 D6
Curecanti N Rec USA................92 A6
Curral das Freiras Madeira................82 C1
Cuxhaven Germany................74 C3
Cuyahoga Valley N Rec USA................93 A3
Cuzco UN C Peru................62 A3
Cwmtydu Bch UK................68 A5
Cyclades Is Greece................83 J8
Cym-yr-Eglwys, Fishguard Bch UK................68 A5
Cyprus................56 A10
Cyrene UN C Libya................64 A11
Czech Republic................86 B1
Czestochowa Poland................86 B1

Da Nang Cru Vietnam................59 A8
Dachau Germany................75 G8
Dachstein Reg Austria................77 F4
Dadès, Gorges du Morocco................89 E2
Dafnoúdi, Akr. Cape Greece................83 H2
Dagomys Russian Fed................86 A2
Dahab Egypt................89 F4
Dahme Riv Germany................74 I4
Dakar Apt Sénégal................55 A5
Dakar Sénégal................55 A5
Dakhla Oasis Egypt................89 F3
Dalaas Austria................77 F4
Dalaman Apt Turkey................83 J5
Dalaman Turkey................83 J5
Dale Bch UK................68 A5
Dalian Cru China................59 A8
Dallas Apt USA................54 B2
Dallas USA................90 A7
Dallas Dhu Distillery His Sc UK................67 F1
Dallas-Fort Worth Apt USA................54 B1
Dalmeny UK................66 B2
Dalton-in-Furness UK................66 C3
Daluis, Gorges de France................72 F2
Damascus UN C Syria................64 A11
Damascus Apt Syria................56 A10
Dambulla Golden Rock Temple UN CN Sri Lanka................63 D2
Damietta Egypt................89 F2
Damietta Mouth Riv Egypt................89 F2
Damüls Austria................77 F4
Danbury UK................66 E2
Danger Point Cape South Africa................88 C5
Dania USA................91 D7
Dannenberg Germany................74 C4
Danube Riv Austria................77 F4
Danube, Lower Riv Bulgaria/Romania................86 B2
Danube Delta UN N Romania................61 A4
Danube Delta Romania................86 B2
Danube, Middle Riv Croatia/Hungary/Yugo. FR................86 B2
Dar es Salaam Apt Tanzania................55 A7

ardanelles Str Turkey 83 J2
ardeza, Ermióni Greece 85 A13
arfur Reg Chad/Sudan 88 A2
arien N Pk, UN N Panama 60 A3
arlington UK 70 A3
armstadt Germany 76 C4
arss I Germany 74 H2
artmoor N Pk UK 67 F6
artmouth UK 68 A6
arwin Apt Australia 55 A9
arwin Cru Australia 59 A9
assen I. South Africa 88 C5
assía Greece 83 G1
assía, Káto Korakiana Bch Greece 85 A12
atça Turkey 83 J9
aun Germany 76 C1
auphiné Reg France 73 A2
avid Berger N Mem USA 93 A4
avid, Marseille Bch France 84 A3
avis Strait 58 A2
avos Switzerland 77 E4
awa Wenz Riv Ethiopia 89 G2
awlish UK 68 A6
awlish Warren Bch UK 68 A6
awson Canada 94 A1
awson Creek Canada 94 C1
ayton Aviation N His USA 93 A4
aytona Beach USA 91 D4
e Aar South Africa 88 B2
e Funiak Springs USA 91 D2
e Haan Belgium 65 C2
e Hoop Ntr Res South Africa 88 C6
e Land USA 91 D4
e Panne Belgium 65 C1
e Rust South Africa 88 C7
e Soto N Mem USA 93 A8
ead Sea Israel/Jordan 89 F2
eal UK 66 E4
eal Castle EH UK 67 F6
ean, Forest of UK 66 D3
earborn USA 91 E4
eath Valley N Mon USA 91 E4
ebrecen Hungary 86 B2
ecin Czech Rep. 75 J6
eddington Castle EH UK 67 F5
eerhurst: Odda's Chapel EH UK 67 F5
eggendorf Germany 75 H8
eia Mallorca 81 G1
eiva Marina Italy 84 A3
el Prat Apt Spain 80 D2
elaware Adm USA 90 A4
elaware & Lehigh Nav'n Canal N Her Cor USA 93 A4
elaware Water Gap N Rec USA 93 A4
elft Netherlands 65 B6
elfzijl Netherlands 65 B4
elhi Apt India 55 A8
elimara Point Malta 79 G4
elitzsch Germany 74 H5
ella Tolfa, Monti Reg Italy 78 C1
elmenhorst Germany 74 D3
elphi UN C Greece 64 A11
elphi Greece 83 F1
elray Beach USA 91 D6
els Dolc, Ses Salines Bch Mallorca 84 A9
emmin Germany 74 I3
en Haag Netherlands 65 B6
en Helder Netherlands 65 B3
enali N Pres USA 54 A2
endera Egypt 89 F4
enia Spain 81 E2
enizli Turkey 83 J9
enmark 56 A6
enmark Strait 59 A4
enpasar Apt Indonesia 55 A8
enver Apt USA 54 A2
enver USA 90 A2
erby UK 70 A4
erbyshire Adm UK 68 A4
erwent Riv UK 66 C1
erwent Water Lake UK 66 C2
es Moines USA 90 A3
esaru Bulgaria 96 A2
escartes France 72 C4
esenzano Italy 79 F7
espotikó I Greece 83 J7
essau Germany 74 H5
essau Germany 91 D2
estin USA 91 D2
etmold Germany 74 D5
etroit Apt USA 54 B1
etroit USA 90 A3
eurne Apt Belgium 65 B10
eutsche Bucht Bay 74 C2
eux-Alpes, les France 72 G3
eux-Sèvres Adm France 72 C3
eventer Netherlands 65 B8
evil's I. Cru French Guiana 59 A11
evils Postpile N Mon USA 91 E4
evils Tower N Mon USA 92 A2
evon Adm UK 68 A6
evon I. Canada 54 A2
ahran Apt Saudi Arabia 55 A7
aka Apt Bangladesh 55 A8
ía I Greece 83 J11
amond Head S Mon Hawaiian Is. 91 C6
ana Marina, Ostuni Bch Italy 85 A12
ani Beach Kenya 89 G4
ano Marina Italy 79 F9
dyma Turkey 83 J8
eburg Germany 75 D7
ekirch Luxembourg 65 B20
emel Riv Germany 74 D5
epholz Germany 74 D4
eppe Ferry France 69 D8
eppe France 72 A1
euze France 75 B8
ez Germany 76 C2
ferdange Luxembourg 75 A7
gne France 72 F1
on France 73 A1
ksmuide Belgium 65 C1
lenburg Germany 75 D6
os UN C Greece 64 A11
os I Greece 83 J8
an France 72 B2
est Belgium 65 B19
nard France 72 B2
naric Alps Mtns Bosnia-Herz./Croatia 86 B2
nas Diníle Bch UK 68 A4
nefur Park N Pk UK 67 F5
ngli Cliffs Malta 79 G4
ngolfing Germany 75 H8
nosaur P Pk, UN N Canada 60 A2
nosaur N Mon USA 92 A2
neton Castle and Garden His Sc UK 67 F2
sentis Switzerland 77 E3
sneyland USA 91 E6
sneyland Paris France 72 H4
stington UK 66 C1
rigi UN C Turkey 64 A12
varbakir Turkey 83 F3
a Faunal Res, UN N Cameroon 61 A5
mitsáe UN C Algeria 64 A10
enné UN C Mali 63 A5
bouti Apt 88 A2
bouti Cru 59 A5

Djibouti 88 A2
Djoudj N Bd Sanc, UN N Sénégal 61 A5
Dobaccio Italy 79 F3
Döbeln Germany 75 I5
Dodecanese Is Greece 83 J8
Dodori G Res Kenya 89 G4
Dogana, Ostuni Bch Italy 85 A12
Dogubayazit Turkey 83 F3
Doha Apt Qatar 55 A7
Dokkum Netherlands 65 B3
Dokós I Greece 83 J7
Dol-de-Bretagne France 72 B2
Dolent, Mont Mtn France/Italy/Switzerland 77 E5
Dollart Bay Germany 74 C3
Dolomites Mtns Italy 78 A1
Dolomiti Mtns Italy 79 F3
Dolphin Coast Reg South Africa 88 B2
Domazlice Czech Rep. 75 H7
Dominica 95 D3
Dominican Rep. 95 D2
Domodóssola Italy 79 F2
Don Muang Apt Thailand 96 D2
Doñana I N Pk, UN N Spain 61 A4
Doñana, Coto de Reg Spain 80 D1
Donau Riv Germany 76 B8
Donaueschingen Germany 76 B8
Donauwörth Germany 75 F8
Donets Basin Reg Russian Fed./Ukraine 86 A2
Donnington Castle EH UK 67 F6
Donoússa I Greece 83 J8
Dora Baltea Riv Italy 79 F5
Dordogne Reg France 72 A2
Dordrecht Netherlands 65 B11
Doring Riv South Africa 88 C7
Dornbirn Austria 77 F1
Dorset Adm UK 68 A6
Dorsten Germany 65 B12
Dortmund Germany 74 C5
Dortmund-Ems-Kanal Germany 74 C4
Dos Pilas Guatemala 95 F3
Dothan USA 91 D2
Douai France 65 B13
Douala Apt Cameroon 55 A5
Douarnenez France 72 B3
Doubs Riv France 77 E1
Dougga Tunisia 89 D1
Douglas Ferry UK 69 B5
Doukáto, Akr. Cape Greece 83 H1
Doullens France 65 B17
Dourdan France 72 H3
Douz Tunisia 89 D5
Dove Cottage UK 66 C2
Dover UK 66 E4
Dover Ferry UK 69 D4
Dover USA 90 A4
Dover Castle EH UK 67 F6
Dover, Strait of 66 E4
Dover-Foxcroft USA 90 B2
Down Adm UK 68 A3
Dráa Riv Algeria/Morocco 89 E3
Dráa, Cap Morocco 89 E3
Drac, Coves del Mallorca 81 G2
Drac Riv France 72 G2
Drachenfels Hill Germany 76 C1
Draguignan France 72 F4
Drake Passage Str 59 A10
Dráma Greece 83 J1
Drau Riv Austria 77 F8
Drenthe Adm Netherlands 65 B4
Drépano Greece 85 A12
Drepano, Igoumenitsa Bch Greece 85 A12
Dresden Apt Germany 55 A6
Dresden Germany 75 I5
Dreux France 72 H3
Drôme Adm France 72 F1
Drôme Riv France 72 G3
Drottningholm Palace UN C Sweden 64 A3
Drumheller Canada 94 C4
Drummondville Canada 94 B4
Druzba Bulgaria 86 B2
Dry Tortugas N Pk USA 91 D7
Dryburgh Abbey His Sc UK 67 F3
Dubai Apt UAE 55 A7
Dubawnt Lake Canada 94 A2
Dublin Apt Ireland 56 A5
Dublin Ferry Ireland 69 B4
Dubrovnik Apt Croatia 56 A11
Dubrovnik UN C Croatia 64 A7
Dubrovnik Croatia 86 B2
Duddon Riv UK 66 C3
Duderstadt Germany 74 F5
Due Sorelle, Sirolo Bch Italy 85 A4
Duino Italy 79 F4
Duisburg Germany 74 B5
Duiveland I Netherlands 65 B10
Dülmen Germany 74 C5
Duluth USA 90 A3
Dumbarton UK 66 B3
Dumbarton Castle His Sc UK 67 F2
Dumfries UK 70 A3
Dumfries and Galloway Adm UK 66 B2
Dun Laoghaire Ferry Ireland 69 B6
Dunblane UK 66 B1
Duncan Canada 94 C3
Dundee Apt UK 66 B2
Dundee UK 66 B2
Dundee UK 66 B2
Dunedin Cru New Zealand 59 A9
Dunfermline UK 66 B4
Dunfermline Palace and Abbey His Sc UK 66 B4
Dungeness Cape UK 66 E4
Dunhuang UN C China 63 A8
Dunhuang China 87 D3
Dunkeld UK 66 B1
Dunkerque France 65 B13
Dunkerque Ferry France 69 D4
Dunkirk Ferry France 69 D4
Dunnville Canada 94 B9
Dunoon UK 69 B3
Dunster Castle NT UK 67 F6
Dunster Watermill NT UK 67 F6
Dunwich Bch UK 68 A5
Durance Riv France 72 F1
Durban Apt South Africa 55 A5
Durban Cru South Africa 59 A5
Durban South Africa 88 B2
Düren Germany 74 A1
Durham UN C UK 64 A1
Durham Adm UK 68 A4
Durley, Bournemouth Bch UK 68 A6
Durmitor N Pk, UN N Yugo, FR 61 A4
Dushanbe Apt Tajikistan 55 A6
Dushanbe Tajikistan 58 B9
Dusky Sound Cru New Zealand 59 A9
Düsseldorf Apt Germany 55 B5
Düsseldorf Germany 75 B5
Dyfed Adm UK 68 A5
Dymchurch UK 66 E4
Dymchurch Bch UK 68 A6
Dzhambul Kazakhstan 86 A3
Dzibilchaltún Mexico 95 F2
Dzibilnocac Mexico 95 F2

Eagle Lake USA 90 B2

EAPT, Trieste Bch Italy 85 A4
Earn Riv UK 66 B1
Earn, Loch UK 66 B1
East Anglia Reg UK 68 A5
East China Sea 59 A8
East Coast Park Singapore 96 C4
East Frisian Is. Germany 74 C3
East Kilbride UK 66 B3
East London South Africa 88 B2
East Midlands UK 68 A4
East Midlands Apt UK 70 A5
East Siberian Sea 59 A6
Eastbourne UK 66 E3
Eastbourne Bch UK 68 A6
Easter I. 54 A3
Easter I. Cru 58 A3
Easter Island Apt. 54 A3
Eastern Cape Adm South Africa 88 B2
Eastern Desert Egypt 89 F4
Eastern Mediterranean Coast Reg Turkey 83 F3
Eastern Transvaal Adm South Africa 88 B1
Eberbach Germany 76 B4
Eberbach, Kloster Germany 76 C4
Eberswalde-Finow Germany 74 I4
Ebey's Landing N His Res USA 91 A1
Eboli Italy 78 B4
Ecab Mexico 95 F2
Echternach Luxembourg 65 B20
Ecija Spain 80 D2
Eckernförde Germany 74 E2
Ecouen France 72 H1
Ecrins Reg France 72 G4
Ecuador 54 A3
Edam Netherlands 65 B7
Ede Netherlands 74 A4
Edelsteinmine Germany 76 C3
Eden Riv UK 66 C2
Eden Germany 75 D5
Edgar Allen Poe N His USA 93 A4
Edinburgh Apt UK 66 B4
Edinburgh UK 66 B4
Edinburgh Castle His Sc UK 67 F2
Edirne Turkey 83 F2
Edison N His USA 93 A4
Edmonton Apt Canada 94 C2
Edmonton Canada 94 C2
Edremit Turkey 83 J5
Edson Canada 94 C2
Edzna Mexico 95 F1
Eelde Apt Netherlands 65 B4
Eemshaven Netherlands 65 B4
Eemshaven Netherlands 65 B8
Eferding Austria 75 I8
Effigy Mounds N Mon USA 93 A3
Efteling, Sprookjespark De Netherlands 65 B11
Egadi, Isole Sicily 78 E1
Eger Riv Germany 75 H6
Eggenfelden Germany 75 H8
Egglestone Abbey EH UK 67 F3
Egina I Greece 83 J7
Egmont UK 66 C1
Egypt 89 F4
Ehingen Germany 75 E8
Ehrwald Austria 77 F2
Eichstätt Germany 75 G8
Eider Riv Germany 74 E2
Eidfjord Cru Norway 59 A4
Eifel Reg Germany 76 C1
Eiger Mtn Switzerland 77 E2
Eigg Ferry UK 69 B1
Einbeck Germany 74 E5
Eindhoven Apt Netherlands 65 B11
Eindhoven Netherlands 65 B11
Einsiedeln Switzerland 77 E3
Eisenach Germany 75 F6
Eisenhower N His USA 93 A4
Eisenhüttenstadt Germany 74 J4
Eisenstadt Austria 77 D4
Eisleben Germany 74 G5
Eivissa Apt Ibiza 81 F3
Eivissa Cru Ibiza 59 C6
Eivissa I Balearic Is .....81 F
Eivissa Ibiza 81 F2
Ek Balam Mexico 95 F2
El Abrigo Canary Is. 80 B1
El Alamein Egypt 89 F1
El Altet, Elx Bch Spain 84 A9
El Ancón, Carboneras Bch Spain 84 A8
El Arenal, Jávea Bch Spain 84 A9
El Arish Egypt 89 F2
El Ashmûnein Egypt 89 F3
El Baúl Guatemala 95 F5
El Cabo de Gata Spain 80 D8
El Cargador, Alcalá de Chivert Bch Spain 84 A2
El Cayo Mexico 95 F3
El Cura, Torrevieja Bch Spain 84 A9
El Dosser, Cullera Bch Spain 84 A9
El Ejido Spain 80 D4
El Escorial UN C Spain 64 A9
El Espejo, Los Alcázares Bch Spain 84 A8
El Faiyûm Egypt 89 F1
El Faro, Cullera Bch Spain 84 A9
El Haouaria Tunisia 89 D2
El Jadida Morocco 89 E1
El Jem UN C Tunisia 64 A10
El Jem Tunisia 89 D4
El Khârga Apt Egypt 89 F3
El Khârga Egypt 89 F3
El Malhalla el Kubrâ Egypt 89 F1
El Malpais N Mon USA 92 A6
El Mansûra Egypt 89 F2
El Meco Mexico 95 F2
El Medano Canary Is. 80 B1
El Minya Egypt 89 F3
El Mirador Guatemala 95 F4
El Moharraq Egypt 89 F6
El Molinar Mallorca 81 G1
El Moro, Alcalá de Chivert Bch Spain 84 A2
El Morro N Mon USA 92 A6
El Nouzha Apt Egypt 89 F1
El Palo Spain 80 D7
El Palo-Dedo, Málaga Bch Spain 84 A8
El Paso USA 90 A6
El Peñón, Salobreña Bch Spain 84 A8
El Pilar Formentera 81 F4
El Pital Mexico 95 E2
El Portiguet, Alicante Bch Spain 84 A9
El Pozito Belize 95 F4
El Puerto de Sta Maria Spain 80 D5
El Qasr Egypt 89 F1
El Recati, Valencia Bch Spain 84 A9
El Rey Mexico 95 F2
El Rompido Spain 80 D1
El Salvador 58 B9
El Sebuca Egypt 89 F6
El Tajin Mexico 95 E2
El Tûr Egypt 89 F4
El Torro Mtn Menorca 81 H2
El Vendrell Spain 80 C3
El Zagázig Egypt 89 F2
Elba, Isola d' Italy 79 F10
Elbe Riv Germany 74 F3
Elberry Cove, Torbay Bch UK 68 A6
Elche Spain 81 E1
Elda Spain 81 E1

Elde Riv Germany 74 G3
Eldoret Kenya 89 G1
Eleanor Roosevelt N His USA 93 A4
Elephant Village Thailand 96 D4
Elephanta Caves UN C India 63 C2
Elephantine I. Egypt 89 F6
Eleuthera I Bahamas 58 B3
Elgin Cathedral His Sc UK 67 F1
Elgon, Mt N Pk Kenya 89 G1
Elgon, Mt Kenya 89 G1
Elia Crete 85 A13
Elia, Mikonos-Ano Meria Bch Greece 85 A13
Elia, Nikitas Bch Greece 85 A13
Elie Bch UK 68 A2
Elk I. N Pk Canada 94 C2
Elko USA 91 E2
Ellesmere I. Canada 54 A2
Ellmau Austria 77 F3
Ellora Caves UN C India 63 C2
Ellwangen Germany 75 F8
Elmdon Apt UK 66 D2
Elmshorn Germany 74 E3
Eloúnda Crete 83 J11
Eloúnda Bch Crete 85 A13
Elsass Reg France 75 C8
Elsehul Cru S Georgia 59 A10
Elsterwerda Germany 74 I5
Eltville Germany 76 C4
Eltz, Burg Germany 76 C3
Elvas Portugal 82 A2
Elx Spain 81 E1
Emden Germany 74 C3
Emilia-Romagna Adm Italy 79 F7
Emlichheim Germany 74 B4
Emmeloord Netherlands 65 B7
Emmen Netherlands 65 B8
Emmendingen Germany 75 C8
Emporda Reg Spain 80 C2
Empúries Spain 80 C2
Ems Riv Germany 74 C4
Emsland Reg Germany 74 C4
En Colom, Illa d' I Menorca 81 H1
En Vau, Marseille Bch France 84 A3
Engelberg Switzerland 77 E2
England UK 66 A2
English Channel .....69 D
Enkhuizen Netherlands 65 B7
Enkirch Germany 76 C3
Enna Sicily 78 E4
Ennerdale Water Lake UK 66 C1
Enns Riv Austria 77 F4
Enschede Apt Netherlands 65 B8
Enschede Netherlands 65 B8
Ensenada Apt Mexico 58 A4
Ensenada Mexico 91 E6
Entebbe Apt Tanzania 55 A5
Entenbühl Mtn Czech Rep./Germany 75 H7
Enz Riv Germany 75 D8
Epanomi Greece 85 A12
Epanomi Bch Greece 85 A12
Ephesus UN C Greece 64 A11
Epidaurus UN C Greece 83 J7
Épinal France 75 B8
Epirus Reg Greece 83 F1
Epping UK 66 E1
Equatorial Guinea 88 A3
Er Rachidia Morocco 89 E2
Eraclea Minoa Sicily 78 E3
Erbeskopf Mtn Germany 75 C7
Erculano Italy 78 B3
Erddig House NT UK 67 F4
Erdek Turkey 83 J3
Erding Germany 75 G8
Eressós Greece 83 J5
Erétria Greece 85 A13
Erétria Bch Greece 85 A13
Erfoud Morocco 89 E2
Erftstadt Germany 76 C2
Erfurt Germany 75 G6
Erice Sicily 78 E1
Ericeira Portugal 82 D1
Erie Canal N His USA 94 B10
Erie, Lake Canada/USA 90 A4
Eritrea 88 A2
Erl Austria 77 F3
Erlangen Germany 75 G7
Ermelo South Africa 88 B1
Ermióni Greece 85 A13
Ermónes Greece 83 G1
Ermónes, Gianades Bch Greece 85 A12
Erpeler Ley Hill Germany 76 C1
Erquy France 72 B2
Erstein France 75 C8
Erzgebirge Reg Germany 76 A2
Es Canutells Menorca 81 H4
Es Canyar Ibiza 81 F1
Es Delfins Menorca 81 H1
Es Grau Menorca 81 H4
Es Grau, Maó Bch Menorca 84 A9
Es Mercadal Menorca 81 H1
Es Migjorn Redones Gran St Cristóbal Menorca 81 H3
Es Pla Reg Mallorca 81 G2
Es Pujols Formentera 81 F4
Es Ribell, Son Servera Bch Mallorca 84 A9
Es Savina Formentera 81 F4
Es Tudóns, Naveta d' Menorca 81 H1
Esbjerg Ferry Denmark 69 C4
Esbjerg Denmark 74 H1
Escala, l' Spain 80 C2
Escambia Riv USA 91 D1
Escaut Riv France 65 B14
Esch-sur-Alzette Luxembourg 65 B20
Esch-sur-Sûre Luxembourg 65 B20
Eschwege Germany 75 F5
Eschweiler Germany 75 B6
Escondido USA 91 E6
Esfahan UN C Iran 63 A7
Esfahan Iran 87 D4
Esk Riv UK 66 C3
Eskisehir Turkey 83 F3
Esmeraldas Cru Ecuador 58 A3
Espalmador, Illa I Formentera 81 F4
Espardell, Illa I Formentera 81 F4
Espichel, Cabo Cape Portugal 82 D1
Espinhaço de Cão, Serra de Reg Portugal 82 E1
Espinho Portugal 82 A1
Essaouira Morocco 89 E1
Essen Germany 74 C5
Essex Adm UK 66 E2
Esslingen Germany 76 B6
Essonne Adm France 72 H3
Est, Bonassola Bch Italy 84 A3
Estany d'En Mas, Manacor Bch Mallorca 84 A9
Estartit, l' Spain 80 C2
Estellencs Mallorca 81 G1
Estepa Spain 80 D2
Estepona Spain 80 D4
Estérel, l' Reg France 72 F4
Estói Portugal 82 E7
Estonia 86 A1
Estoril Portugal 82 D1
Estrela, Serra da Reg Portugal 82 A2
Estuario do Tejo Ntr Res Portugal 82 D2

Etables France 72 B2
Étampes France 72 H3
Étang de Mateille, Gruissan Bch France 84 A2
Étang des Ayguades, Gruissan Bch France 84 A2
Ethiopia 88 A2
Ethiopian Highlands Mtns Ethiopia 88 A2
Etna, Monte Mtn Sicily 78 E2
Eton UK 66 E1
Euboea I Greece 83 J4
Eugene USA 90 A1
Eugene O'Neill N His USA 92 A1
Eupen Belgium 75 B6
Euphrates Riv Iraq/Syria/Turkey 87 D4
Eure Adm France 72 H1
Eure Riv France 72 H1
Eure-et-Loir Adm France 72 H3
Eure-et-Loire Adm France 72 C2
Eureka USA 91 E1
Europa, Punta de Cape Gibraltar 80 D6
Europe, Central 86
Europoort Netherlands 65 B10
Euskirchen Germany 76 C1
Eutin Germany 74 F2
Everglades N Pk, UN N USA 91 D8
Everglades Reg USA 91 D7
Evesham UK 66 D4
Evesham, Vale of UK 66 D4
Evia I Greece 83 J4
Evian-les-Bains France 72 G3
Evora UN C Portugal 64 A9
Evora Portugal 82 A3
Evreiaki, Paleókipos Bch Greece 85 A13
Evros Riv Greece/Turkey 83 J2
Evry France 72 H4
Ewa Beach Hawaiian Is. 91 C5
Ewaso Nyiro Riv Kenya 89 G2
Excelsior, Trieste Bch Italy 85 A4
Exeter Apt UK 70 A6
Exeter UK 70 A6
Exmoor N Pk UK 67 F6
Extremadura Adm Spain 80 A2

Fåborg Denmark 74 H1
Faenza Italy 79 F7
Faial I Azores 82 B1
Faial Apt Azores 82 B1
Faial Madeira 82 C2
Fair Isle I UK 70 A7
Fairmount Hot Springs Canada 94 C4
Fakse Bugt Bay Denmark 74 H1
Falcade Italy 79 F3
Falcone, Capo del Sardinia 78 D1
Faliráki Greece 83 J9
Faliráki *1* – *4*, Koskinoú Bch Greece 85 A13
Faliráki *5*, Koskinoú/Kalithiés Bch Greece 85 A13
Faliráki *A*-Kalithion, Kalithiés Bch Greece 85 A13
Faliráki *B*-Kalithion, Kalithiés Bch Greece 85 A13
Faliráki-Kastraki, Koskinoú Bch Greece 85 A13
Falkensee Germany 74 I4
Falkirk UK 66 B3
Falkland Is. 54 A3
False Bay South Africa 88 C5
Falster I Denmark 74 H2
Fanári Greece 83 J2
Fanári Bch Greece 85 A6
Fano Italy 79 F12
Fano I Denmark 74 H1
Fantasylandia Ibiza 81 F2
Far East Cruise Area 59 A8
Farafra Oasis Egypt 89 F3
Fareham UK 68 A6
Farewell, Cape Greenland 58 A4
Fargo USA 90 A3
Fargo USA 90 A3
Farinette, Vias Bch France 84 A2
Farnham Castle Keep EH UK 67 F6
Faro Apt Portugal 82 E7
Faro Adm Portugal 82 E7
Faro Portugal 82 E7
Faroe Is. 56 A1
Fasil Ghebbi UN C Ethiopia 63 A5
Fatehpur Sikri UN C India 63 C1
Father Marquette N Mem USA 93 A4
Fátima Portugal 82 A2
Faucigny Reg France 72 G2
Favàritx, Cap de Menorca 81 H2
Favignana, Isola Sicily 78 E1
Faye, Pas de la France 72 F2
Federal Hall N Mem USA 93 A4
Fegina, Monterosso Bch Italy 84 A3
Fehmarn I Germany 74 G2
Fehmarnbelt Str Germany 74 G2
Felanitx Mallorca 81 G4
Feldberg Mtn Germany 76 B6
Feldkirch Austria 77 F5
Felixstowe UK 66 E2
Felixstowe Ferry UK 69 C5
Fell Foot Park NT UK 66 C4
Feltre Italy 79 F3
Femer Bælt Str Germany 74 G2
Fenals, Lloret de Mar Bch Spain 84 A2
Fenouillèdes Reg France 72 E2
Fens Reg UK 66 D2
Fergana Basin Uzbekistan 86 A3
Fermanagh Adm UK 68 A3
Fernandina Beach USA 91 D3
Ferragudo Portugal 82 E6
Ferrara Italy 79 F7
Ferrara, Torrox Bch Spain 84 A8
Ferraria, Ponta da Cape Azores 82 B1
Ferreiras Portugal 82 E6
Ferreries Menorca 81 H1
Ferru, Monte Mtn Sardinia 78 D1
Ferté-Bernard, la France 72 C2
Fès Apt Morocco 89 E2
Fès UN C Morocco 64 A9
Fès Morocco 89 E2
Festung Germany 76 C2
Fetihye Turkey 83 J9
Feuchtwangen Germany 75 F7
Fichtelgebirge Reg Germany 75 H6
Fidenza Italy 79 F6
Fieberbrunn Austria 77 F3
Fiesch Switzerland 77 E6
Fiésole Italy 79 F11
Fife UK 66 B2
Figueira da Foz Portugal 82 A2
Figueres Spain 80 C2
Figuerolles, La Ciotat Bch France 84 A3
Figuig Morocco 89 E2
Fiji 55 A9
Filey Bch UK 68 A4
Filfla I Malta 79 G4
Filicudi, Isola Sicily 78 E2
Filzmoos Austria 77 F4
Finale Ligure Italy 84 A3
Findel Apt Luxembourg 65 B20
Finestrat Spain 81 E2
Finger Lakes Reg USA 94 B10
Finhaut Switzerland 77 E5
Finistère Adm France 72 B3
Finkenberg Austria 77 F7
Finland 56 A2
Finland, Gulf of 56 A3

Finsteraarhorn Mtn Switzerland 77 E6
Finsterwalde Germany 74 I5
Fire I. N Sea USA 93 A4
Firenze UN C Italy 64 A6
Firenze Italy 79 F11
Fishbourne Ferry UK 69 D8
Fisherman's Walk, Bournemouth Bch UK 68 A6
Fishguard UK 68 A5
Fishguard Ferry UK 69 B7
Fishnish Ferry UK 69 B2
Fiskárdo Greece 83 H2
Fiumarella, Isola di Capráia Bch Italy 84 A3
Fiume Liscia, Sta Teresa Gallura Bch Sardinia 84 A3
Fiume Piave Nord, Jésolo Bch Italy 85 A4
Fiume Piave, Jésolo Bch Italy 85 A4
Fiume Sile, Jésolo Bch Italy 85 A4
Fiumicino Cru Italy 59 C2
Fiumicino Italy 78 C3
Fiumicino (Leonardo da Vinci) Apt Italy 78 C3
Fjordland N Pk, UN N New Zealand 61 A9
Flachau Austria 77 F4
Flagstaff Lake USA 90 B2
Flaine France 72 G2
Flåm Cru Norway 59 A4
Flamborough UK 68 A4
Flamenca, Orihuela Bch Spain 84 A9
Flanders Reg Belgium/France 65 B13
Fleche, la France 72 C1
Fleece Inn NT UK 67 F5
Fleetwood Ferry UK 69 B5
Flensburg Germany 74 E2
Fleury-d'Aude France 84 A2
Flevoland Reg Netherlands 65 B7
Flevoland Adm Netherlands 65 B7
Flims Switzerland 77 E3
Floating market, Thon Buri Thailand 96 D1
Florence UN C Italy 64 A6
Florence Italy 79 F11
Florenville Belgium 65 B19
Flores I Indonesia 59 A8
Flores I Azores 82 B1
Flores Apt Azores 82 B1
Flores Guatemala 95 F4
Floriana Malta 79 G4
Florida Adm USA ....91 D
Florida Caverns S Pk USA 91 D2
Florida Citrus Tower USA 91 D5
Florida City USA 91 D7
Florida Keys USA 91 D7
Florida, Nice Bch France 84 A3
Florida, Straits of 58 B2
Florissant Fossil Beds N Mon USA 92 A6
Flumendosa Riv Sardinia 78 D4
Flumsberge Switzerland 77 E3
Flushing Netherlands 65 B10
Foce Agri, Scanzano Iónico Bch Italy 85 A11
Foce Cavone, Scanzano Iónico Bch Italy 85 A11
Foce Steria, Cervo Bch Italy 84 A3
Fóggia Italy 79 A2
Föhr I Germany 74 D2
Fóia Mtn Portugal 82 E2
Foix Reg France 72 E1
Foix France 72 E1
Folégandros I Greece 83 J7
Folgoët, le France 72 B1
Folkestone UK 66 E4
Folkestone Ferry UK 69 D4
Follónica Italy 79 F11
Fondi Italy 78 C4
Font Switzerland 77 E1
Font de sa Cala, Capdepera Bch Mallorca 84 A9
Font-Romeu France 72 E2
Fontainebleau UN C France 64 A6
Fontainebleau France 72 H4
Fontainebleau, Forêt de France 72 H4
Fontana Rossa Apt Sicily 78 E4
Fontanelle, Ostuni Bch Italy 85 A12
Fontenay UN C France 64 A6
Fontenay-le-Comte France 72 C3
Fontevraud France 72 C3
Fontonne Est, Antibes Bch France 84 A3
Fontonne Ouest, Antibes Bch France 84 A3
Fóppolo Italy 79 F2
Fora, Ilhéu de I Madeira 82 C2
Forbach France 75 B7
Ford's Theatre N His USA 93 A4
Forfar UK 66 B2
Forio Italy 78 B3
Forli Italy 79 F7
Formentera I Balearic Is 81 F4
Formentor Mallorca 81 G2
Formentor, Cap de Mallorca 81 G2
Former Soviet Union 86-87
Formia Italy 78 C4
Fornells Menorca 81 H2
Forst Germany 74 J5
Fort Beaufort South Africa 88 C4
Fort Bowie N His USA 92 A6
Fort Bragg USA 91 E1
Fort Caroline N Mem USA 93 D3
Fort Carré, Antibes Bch France 84 A3
Fort Clatsop N Mem USA 91 A1
Fort Davis N His USA 92 A6
Fort Donelson N Bat USA 93 A7
Fort Erie Canada 94 B9
Fort Frederica N Mon USA 93 A8
Fort Gadsden S His USA 91 D2
Fort George His UK 67 F1
Fort George Canada 94 A7
Fort Jefferson N Mon USA 91 D7
Fort Kent USA 90 B2
Fort Laramie N His USA 92 A2
Fort Larned N His USA 92 A6
Fort Lauderdale Cru USA 58 B2
Fort Lauderdale USA 91 D7
Fort Macleod Canada 94 C4
Fort Matanzas N Mon USA 91 D4
Fort McHenry N Mon USA 93 A4
Fort Myers USA 91 D5
Fort Myers Apt USA 91 D5
Fort Necessity N Bat USA 93 A4
Fort Nelson Canada 94 A5
Fort Pierce USA 91 D6
Fort Point N His USA 92 A1
Fort Pulaski N Mon USA 93 A8
Fort Raleigh N His USA 93 A8
Fort Ross S His USA 91 E3
Fort Scott N His USA 93 A7
Fort Smith N His USA 93 A7
Fort St John Canada 94 C1
Fort Stanwix N Mon USA 93 A4
Fort Steele Canada 94 C4
Fort Sumter N Mon USA 93 A8
Fort Union N Mon USA 92 A6
Fort Union Trading Post N His USA 92 A2
Fort Vancouver N His USA 91 A1
Fort Walton Beach USA 91 D2
Fort Washington Park USA 93 A4
Fort William UK 70 A2
Fort Worth USA 90 A6
Fort-de-France Cru Martinique 58 B11
Fortaleza Cru Brazil 58 A3
Forte dei Marmi Italy 79 F10
Forth Riv UK 66 B3
Forth, Firth of Est UK 66 B4

Forum, Nice Bch France 84 A3
Fos-sur-Mer France 84 A3
Fossanova, Abbazia di Italy 78 C4
Fossil Butte N Mon USA 92 A2
Fossil mammal sites UN N Australia 61 A9
Foula I UK 70 A7
Foulness I. UK 66 E2
Fountains Abbey UN C UK 64 A5
Foúrka Greece 85 A12
Foúrka Bch Greece 85 A12
Foúrnoi I Greece 83 J8
Frabosa Italy 79 F5
Framlingham Castle EH UK 67 F5
Framura Italy 84 A3
Francás, El Vendrell Bch Spain 84 A2
France 72-73
Franche-Comté Adm France 73 A1
Franconia USA 90 B3
Franeker Netherlands 74 A3
Frankenberg Germany 75 D5
Frankenstein, Burg Germany 76 C4
Frankenwald Reg Germany 75 G6
Frankfort USA 90 A7
Frankfurt am Main Apt Germany 76 C4
Frankfurt am Main Germany 76 C4
Frankfurt an der Oder Germany 74 J4
Fränkisch Alb Reg Germany 75 G7
Fränkische Saale Riv Germany 75 E6
Franklin Delano Roosevelt, Home of N His USA 93 A4
Franz Josef Land Is Russian Fed. 86 A2
Frasassi, Grotta di Italy 79 F12
Frascati Italy 78 C3
Fraser Riv Canada 94 C3
Fraser's Hill Malaysia 96 A2
Fraserburgh Bch UK 68 A1
Fraserburgh UK 70 A1
Fraserburgh South Africa 88 C2
Frauenfeld Switzerland 75 D9
Frederick Douglass Memorial Home USA 93 A4
Frederick Law Olmsted N His USA 93 A4
Fredericksburg & Spotsylvania Co Bat Mem USA 93 A4
Fredericton Canada 94 A8
Frederiksted Cru US Virgin Is. 58 B7
Freeport Cru Bahamas 58 B3
Freetown Apt Sierra Leone 55 A5
Freetown Cru Sierra Leone 59 A5
Fréhel, Cap France 72 B2
Freiberg Germany 75 I6
Freiberger Mulde Riv Germany 75 I6
Freiburg im Breisgau Germany 76 B8
Freidberg Germany 75 D5
Freilassing Germany 75 H9
Freising Germany 75 G8
Freital Germany 75 I6
Fréjus France 72 F4
Fréjus France 72 G4
Fréjus, Tunnel du France/Italy 72 G4
Fremont USA 91 E3
French Alps Mtns France ....73 G
French Guiana 54 A3
French Polynesia Is. 54 A1
Freshwater East Bch UK 68 A5
Fresno USA 91 E3
Freudenstadt Germany 76 B6
Friars Cliff, Christchurch Bch UK 68 A6
Fribourg Switzerland 77 E2
Friedrichshafen Germany 75 E9
Friendship Hill N His USA 93 A4
Friesland Adm Netherlands 65 B3
Friesoythe Germany 74 C3
Frisian Is., East Netherlands 74 A3
Frisian Is., West Netherlands 74 A3
Fritzlar Germany 75 E5
Friuli-Venezia Giulia Adm Italy 79 F4
Frobisher Bay Canada 94 A3
Frontenac P Pk Canada 94 B4
Frosinone Italy 78 C4
Fucino, Piana del Reg Italy 78 C2
Fuengirola Spain 80 D6
Fuerteventura I Canary Is. 80 B5
Fügen Austria 77 F3
Fukuoka Apt Japan 55 A4
Fulda Riv Germany 75 E5
Fulda Germany 75 E6
Fulpmes Austria 77 F6
Funchal Apt Madeira 82 C2
Funchal Cru Madeira 59 A4
Funchal Madeira 82 C2
Fungus Rock Malta 79 G1
Furnas Azores 82 B1
Furness Abbey EH UK 66 C3
Furness Fells UK 66 C4
Fürstenfeldbruck Germany 75 G8
Fürstenwalde Germany 74 J4
Furth Germany 75 H7
Fürth Germany 75 G7
Furtwangen Germany 76 B8
Füssen Germany 75 F9
Fyn I Denmark 74 F1

Gabbiano Azzurro, Roseto Capo Spúlico Bch Italy 85 A11
Gabbice Mare Italy 79 F12
Gabès Tunisia 89 D4
Gabès, Golfe de Tunisia 89 D4
Gabice Italy 79 F12
Gabon 88 A3
Gaborone Apt Botswana 55 A5
Gaeta Italy 78 C4
Gaeta, Golfo di Italy 78 C4
Gafsa Tunisia 89 D3
Gainesville USA 91 D3
Galapagos Is. 54 A3
Galapagos Is. Cru 58 A3
Galapagos Is. N Pk, UN N Ecuador 60 A3
Galati Romania 86 C2
Galicia Adm Spain 80 A1
Galileo Galilei Apt Italy 79 F11
Galle UN C Sri Lanka 63 C2
Gallion, Nice Bch France 84 A3
Gallipoli Turkey 83 J2
Gallipoli Peninsula Turkey 83 J2
Galtür Austria 77 F5
Galveston Cru USA 58 B1
Galveston USA 90 A7
Gamasa Egypt 89 F2
Gambia, The 88 A2
Gammarth Tunisia 89 D2
Gand Belgium 65 B14
Gander Apt Canada 54 A2
Gander Canada 94 A8
Gandía Spain 84 A9
Gandria Switzerland 77 E7
Ganges Riv India 87 D5
Gansbaai South Africa 88 C5
Ganzano di Roma Italy 78 C3
Gap France 72 G3
Garachico Canary Is. 80 B1
Garajonay N Pk, UN N Canary Is. 61 A4
Garamba N Pk, UN N Zaïre 61 A5
Garbi, Île Tunisia 89 D4
Garda, Lago di Italy 79 F7
Gardelegen Germany 74 G4
Garden Route Reg South Africa 88 C5
Gardiki Greece 83 G1
Gardone Riviera Italy 79 F7

Gargellen Austria 77 F5
Garibaldi P Pk Canada 94 C3
Garigliano Riv Italy 78 C4
Garissa Kenya 89 G4
Garmisch-Partenkirchen Germany 75 G9
Garonne Riv France 72 D1
Garonnette Val d'Esquières, Ste-Max'e Bch France 84 A3
Garsa, Chott el Reg Tunisia 89 D3
Garsdale Apt UK 66 B3
Gascony Reg France 72 A2
Gascoigne Canada 94 A8
Gaspé Peninsula Canada 94 A8
Gastoúri Greece 83 G1
Gata, Cabo de Cape Spain 80 D8
Gates of the Arctic N Pk, N Pres USA 92 A9
Gateway N Rec USA 93 A4
Gatineau Riv Canada 94 B2
Gatineau Park Canada 94 B2
Gatorland Zoo USA 91 D6
Gatwick Apt UK 66 E3
Gauley River N Rec USA 93 A8
Gavarnie France 72 D2
Gávdos I Greece 83 J10
Gaviotas-Boliches, Fuengirola Bch Spain 84 A8
Gávrio Greece 83 J7
Gaza Egypt 89 F2
Gaziantep Turkey 83 F3
Gazi Crete 85 A13
Gdansk Poland 86 B1
Gdynia Cru Poland 59 A4
Gdynia Poland 86 B1
Geddington: Eleanor Cross EH UK 67 F5
Gedi N Pk Kenya 89 G4
Gediz Riv Turkey 83 J6
Gedser Denmark 74 F2
Geelen Netherlands 65 B16
Geesthacht Germany 74 F3
Geiranger Cru Norway 59 A5
Geishügelhof Germany 76 C1
Geislingen Germany 75 E8
Gela Sicily 78 E4
Gela, Golfo di Sicily 78 E4
Gelderland Adm Netherlands 65 B7
Geldern Germany 74 B5
Gelibolu Turkey 83 J2
Gelibolu Yarimadasi Pen Turkey 83 J2
Gonâve, Île de la Haiti 58 B5
Gelnhausen Germany 76 B2
Gelnhausen Germany 75 E6
Gelsenkirchen Germany 74 C5
Gelugor Malaysia 96 B4
Gen Apt Switzerland/France 77 E6
Genádio Greece 83 J12
General Grant N Mem USA 93 A4
General Juan N. Alvarez Apt Mexico 95 E4
Geneva Apt Switzerland 77 E6
Geneva Switzerland 77 E5
Geneva, Lake Switzerland/France 77 E5
Genève Apt Switzerland 77 E5
Genève Switzerland 77 E5
Gengenbach Germany 76 B6
Gorizia Italy 79 F4
Genk Belgium 65 B15
Genoa UN C Italy 64 A6
Genoa Cru Italy 59 C2
Genoa Italy 79 F6
Genoa Apt Italy 79 F6
Genoa Cru Italy 59 C2
Génova Italy 79 F6
Gent Belgium 65 B14
Gent naar Oostende, Kanaal van Belgium 65 C2
Genting Highlands Malaysia 96 A2
George Apt Switzerland 77 E6
George South Africa 88 C7
George Land I Russian Fed. 86 A2
George Rogers Clark N His USA 93 A7
George Town Cru Cayman Is. 58 B5
George Washington Birthplace N Mon USA 93 A8
George Washington Carver N Mon USA 93 A7
George Washington Memorial Parkway USA 93 A4
George, Fort Canada 94 B9
Georgetown Apt Guyana 54 A3
Georgetown Malaysia 96 B2
Georgia 86 A2
Georgia Adm USA 90 A8
Georgian Bay Canada 94 B5
Georgian Bay Is. N Pk Canada 94 B5
Georgsmarienhütte Germany 74 D4
Gera Riv Germany 75 G5
Gera Germany 75 H6
Geraki Greece 83 J1
Gerakini, Poligíros Bch Greece 85 A13
Gérardmer France 75 B8
Gerlos Austria 77 F7
Gernsheim Germany 76 C4
Gerolstein Germany 76 C1
Gers Adm France 72 D2
Gersau Switzerland 77 E3
Gertak Sanggul Malaysia 96 B3
Gets, les France 72 G2
Gettysburg N Mil USA 93 A4
Ggantija UN C Malta 64 A10
Ggantija Malta 79 G1
Ghadames UN C Libya 64 A10
Ghajn Tuffieha Bay Malta 79 G3
Ghana 88 A2
Ghar Dalam Malta 79 G4
Gharb Malta 79 G1
Ghent Belgium 65 B14
Ghoumrassen Tunisia 89 D6
Giali I Greece 83 J8
Gianades Greece 85 A12
Giant's Causeway UN N UK 64 A4
Giardini-Naxos Sicily 78 E2
Giáros I Greece 83 J7
Gibidibar UN C Gibraltar 56 A13
Gibraltar Apt Gibraltar 56 A13
Gibraltar, Strait of 59 C5
Gibraltar 80 D6
Gibside Chapel and grounds NT UK 67 F3
Giens France 72 F3
Gießen Germany 76 B2
Giethoorn Netherlands 65 B8
Gifhorn Germany 74 F4
Gigaro, La Croix-Valmer Bch France 84 A3
Gigha Ferry UK 69 B2
Gijón Spain 80 A1
Gila Cliff Dwellings N Mon USA 92 A6
Gilfach yr Halen Bch UK 68 A5
Gioúra I Greece 83 J4
Girão, Cabo Cape Madeira 82 C1
Girolata Gulf UN N France 61 A4
Girona Spain 80 C2
Gisors France 72 H1
Gistel Belgium 65 C12
Githio Greece 85 A12
Githio Bch Greece 85 A12
Giulianova Italy 79 F12
Giurgiu Romania 86 C2
Giza UN C Egypt 64 A12
Giza Pyramids Egypt 89 F1
Gjirokastër Albania 86 D3
Glacier N Pk USA 92 A1

Glacier N Pk Canada 94 C4
Glacier N Pk USA 94 C4
Glacier Bay 58 A2
Glacier Bay N Pk, N Pres USA 92 A9
Glamis Castle UK 66 B2
Glan Riv Germany 75 C7
Glärner Alpen Mtns Switzerland 77 E3
Glasgow Apt UK 66 B3
Glasgow UK 66 B3
Glashütte Germany 75 I6
Glen 90 B3
Glen Canyon N Rec USA 92 A5
Glen Shee Reg UK 66 B2
Gleneagles Gf UK 66 B2
Glenridding UK 66 C2
Glenrothes UK 66 B2
Glens Falls USA 90 B3
Gletsch Switzerland 77 E3
Glifáda Greece 83 J7
Glifáda, Pélekas Bch Greece 85 A12
Glistra, Lárdos Bch Greece 85 A13
Glorenza Italy 79 F3
Gloria Dei (Old Swedes') Church N His USA 93 A4
Gloucester UK 66 D3
Gloucester Apt UK 66 D4
Gloucestershire Adm UK 66 D4
Glückstadt Germany 74 E3
Glyfos Melísinou, Asini Bch Greece 85 A12
Gmünd Austria 77 D3
Gmünd Austria 77 F4
Gmunden Austria 77 F4
Goa Cru India 59 A8
Goa UN C India 63 C2
Gobi Reg China/Mongolia 87 D3
Goch Germany 74 B5
Goderich Canada 94 B9
Godinne Belgium 65 B15
Goeree I Netherlands 65 B10
Gökçeada I Turkey 83 J2
Gold Coast Reg 59 A5
Golden Bay Malta 79 G3
Golden Gate N Rec USA 92 A1
Golden Ring Reg Russian Fed. 86 A2
Golden Sands Bulgaria 86 B2
Golden Spike N Mon USA 92 A1
Golden Valley UK 66 D3
Golfe-Juan France 72 F4
Golfo Aranci Sardinia 78 D2
Gomera I Canary Is. 80 B4
Gomera UN C India 63 C2
Gonàve, Île de la Haiti 58 B5
Gondar UN C Ethiopia 63 A5
Goodrich UK 66 D3
Goodrington's Sands, Torbay Bch UK 68 A6
Goodwood House UK 66 E3
Goose Bay Canada 94 A8
Göppingen Germany 75 E8
Gorda, Punta Cape USA 91 E1
Górdis Greece 83 G1
Gorée I. UN C Sénégal 63 A5
Göreme N Pk, UN C N Turkey 64 A12
Gorgona, Ísola di Italy 79 F10
Gorham USA 90 B3
Gorinchem Netherlands 65 B11
Gorizia Italy 79 F4
Gorky Reservoir Russian Fed. 86 C1
Görlitz Germany 75 J5
Gosau Austria 77 F4
Goslar Germany 74 F5
Gossilies Apt Belgium 65 B14
Göteborg Apt Sweden 56 A6
Göteborg Sweden 69 C4
Göteborg Cru Sweden 59 C2
Göteborg Ferry Sweden 69 F6
Gothenburg Apt Sweden 56 A6
Gothenburg Ferry Sweden 69 C4
Gotland I Sweden 56 A7
Göttingen Germany 74 E5
Gouda Netherlands 65 B11
Gough I. 55 A5
Goulimine Morocco 89 E3
Gouritsmond South Africa 88 C6
Gourock Ferry UK 69 B3
Gouves Bch Crete 85 A13
Gouves Crete 85 A13
Gouviá Greece 83 G1
Gouvia, Kérkira Bch Greece 85 A12
Goynük, Kemer Bch Turkey 85 A14
Gozo I Malta 79 G1
Graaff-Reinet South Africa 88 C4
Grächen Switzerland 77 E6
Graciosa I Canary Is. 80 B3
Graciosa I Azores 82 B2
Grado Italy 79 F8
Graham Bell I. Russian Fed. 86 A2
Grahamstown South Africa 88 C8
Grain Coast Reg 59 A5
Grampian Adm UK 68 A1
Grampians UK 66 A1
Grampians 66
Gran Cairo Mexico 95 F2
Gran Canaria I Canary Is. 80 B2
Gran Paradiso Mtn Italy 79 F5
Gran Sasso d'Italia Mtns Italy 78 C2
Gran Tarajal Canary Is. 80 B5
Granada UN C Spain 64 A9
Granada Spain 80 D3
Granby Canada 94 B8
Grand Bahama I. Bahamas 58 B3
Grand Batton Mtn France 75 C9
Grand Brière Reg France 72 B4
Grand Canyon N Pk, UN N USA 92 A5
Grand Erg Oriental Reg Tunisia 89 D5
Grand Falls 90 B2
Grand Harbour Malta 90 B3
Grand Isle UK 90 B3
Grand Lake Canada/USA 90 B2
Grand Portage N Mon USA 93 A3
Grand Roucas, Marseille Bch France 84 A3
Grand St-Bernard, Col du Pass Italy/Switzerland 77 E6
Grand Teton N Pk USA 92 A2
Grand Vallat, Martigues Bch France 84 A3
Grand-Morin, Vallée du Reg France 72 H4
Grand-Pressigny, le Ch France 72 C4
Grande Plage, Fos-sur-Mer Bch France 84 A3
Grande Prairie Canada 94 C2
Grange-over-Sands UK 66 C2
Grangemouth UK 66 B4
Granollers Spain 80 C2
Granville France 72 B2
Grasmere UK 66 C2
Grasmoor Mtn UK 66 C2
Grass Valley USA 91 E3
Grasse France 72 F4
Grave Bat Netherlands 65 B11
Grave, la France 72 G4
Gravenhurst Canada 94 B5
Gravesend UK 66 E4
Graz Austria 77 D4
Grazel, Gruissan Bch France 84 A2
Great Abaco I Bahamas 58 B3
Great America, Santa Clara USA 92 A1
Great Barrier Reef 59 A9
Great Barrier Reef UN N Australia 61 A9
Great Basin N Pk USA 92 A5
Great Bear Lake Canada 94 A2
Great Coxwell Barn NT UK 67 F5
Great Exuma I Bahamas 58 B3

Great Falls USA ....90 A
Great Fish Riv South Africa ....88 C
Great Gable Mtn UK ....66 C
Great Gorge Resort Action Park USA ....93 A
Great Inagua I Bahamas ....58 B
Gydan Reg South Africa ....88 A
Great Lakes Reg Canada/USA ....90 A
Great Malvern UK ....66 D
Great Oasis, The Egypt ....89 F
Great Plains USA ....90 A
Great Sand Dunes N Mon USA ....92 A
Great Slave Lake Canada ....94 A
Great Smoky Mountains N Pk, UN N USA ....93 A
Great Wall UN C China ....63 A
Great White Heron N W R USA ....91 D
Great Yarmouth: 4 South Quay NT UK ....67 F
Greater Antilles Is ....58 B
Greater London Adm UK ....66 E
Greater Manchester Adm UK ....68 A
Greece 83
Green Mountains USA ....90 B
Green Springs USA ....93 A
Greenbelt Park USA ....93 A
Greenland ....54 A
Greenland Sea ....59 A
Greenock UK ....66 B
Greifswald Germany 74
Greiz Germany ....75 H
Grenada Apt ....54 A
Grenada ....95 C
Grenadines, The Is ....58 B
Grenoble France ....72 C
Gréolières-les-Neiges France ....72 F
Gressoney Italy ....79 F
Greven Germany ....74 C
Grevenbroich Germany ....75 C
Grevesmühlen Germany 74
Griefswalder Bodden Bay Germany 74
Grifeu, Llançà Bch Spain ....84 A
Grignano, Trieste Bch Italy ....85 A
Grimaud France ....84 A
Grimaud Nord Bch France ....84 A
Grimentz Switzerland ....77 E
Grimmen Germany 74
Grimsby UK ....70 A
Grimselpass Switzerland 77
Grindelwald Switzerland ....77 E
Griz-Nez, Cap France ....66 E
Grizedale Forest UK ....66 C
Groix, Île de France ....72 B
Gronau Germany ....74 C
Groningen Apt Netherlands ....65 B
Groningen Adm Netherlands ....65 B
Groningen Netherlands ....65 B
Groot Riv South Africa ....88 C
Gros Morne N Pk, UN N Canada ....60 A
Gross-Gerau Germany ....76 C
Großer Arber Mtn Germany 75
Großer Inselsberg Mtn Germany 75
Grosseto Italy ....79 F
Großglockner Mtn Austria 77
Großrotte Italy ....79 F
Grotta Azzurra, Anacapri Bch Italy ....85 A
Grotta Romanelli, Castro Marina Bch Italy ....85 A
Grotta Zinzulusa, Castro Marina Bch Italy ....85 A
Gruissan France ....84 A
Grundy Lake P Pk Canada ....94 B
Grüsch Switzerland 77
Gruyères Switzerland ....77 E
Gryon Switzerland ....77 E
Grytviken Cru S Georgia ....59 A
Gstaad Switzerland ....77 E
Guadalajara Apt Mexico ....94 E
Guadalajara Mexico ....81 A
Guadaleste Spain ....81 E
Guadalmina-San Pedro, Marbella Bch Spain ....84 A
Guadalquivir Riv Spain ....80 D
Guadalupe Mountains N Pk USA ....92 A
Guadeloupe I ....95 C
Guadiana Riv Portugal/Spain ....82 E
Guadix Spain ....80 D
Guam I ....55 A
Guam Apt ....55 A
Guanajuato UN C Mexico ....62 E
Guanajuato Mexico ....95 E
Guangzhou Apt China ....55 A
Guangzhou Cru China ....59 A
Guantanamo Bay ....58 B
Guarani Jesuit missions UN C Argentina ....62 A
Guarda Portugal ....82 A
Guardamar del Segura Spain ....81 E
Guárdia Sanframondi Italy ....78 C
Guatemala ....95 A
Guatemala City Apt Guatemala ....54 A
Guatemala City Guatemala ....95 A
Guayaquil Apt Ecuador ....54 A
Guayaquil Cru Ecuador ....58 A
Gúbbio Italy ....79 F
Guben Germany ....74 J
Gubin Poland ....74 J
Gudvangen Cru Norway ....59 A
Guebwiller France ....75 C
Guebwiller France ....75 C
Guellala Tunisia ....89 D
Guelph Canada ....94 B
Guernsey I Channel Is. ....69 B
Guilford Courthouse N Mil USA ....93 A
Güímar Canary Is. ....80 B
Guincho Portugal ....82 D
Guinea ....88 A
Guinea, Gulf of ....59 A
Guinea-Bissau ....88 A
Guingamp France ....72 B
Guisborough Priory EH UK ....67 F
Gulf Islands N Rec USA ....91 D
Gulf of Mexico ....58 B
Gulf, The ....59 A
Gulfstream Park USA ....91 D
Gullane Bents Bch UK ....68 A
Güllük Turkey ....83 J
Gummersbach Germany ....75 C
Gümüslük, Bodrum Bch Turkey ....85 A
Günz Riv Germany ....75 F
Günzburg Germany ....75 F
Gunzenhausen Germany ....75 F
Gurnard UK ....68 A
Güstrow Germany ....74 H
Gütach Germany ....76 B
Gütach Germany ....76 B
Gütersloh Germany ....74 D
Guttenberg, Burg Germany ....76 C
Guyana ....54 A
Gwent Reg UK ....66 D
Gwent Adm UK ....66 D
Gwynedd castles and town walls UN C UK ....64 A
Gwydan Peninsula Russian Fed. ....86 A

Ha Long Bay UN N Vietnam ....61 A
Ha-ad Chao Samran Thailand ....96 D
Haardt Reg Germany 75

Hadamar Germany 76 C2
Haddington UK 66 B4
Haderslev Denmark 74 E1
Hadleigh Castle EH UK 67 F5
Hadrian's Wall UN C UK 64 A1
Hadrian's Wall, Museum and Fort NT UK 67 F3
Hadrian, Villa Italy 78 C1
Hagen Germany 74 C5
Hagenow Germany 74 G3
Hagerman Fossil Beds N Mon USA 92 A1
Hague, The UK 65 B6
Haguenau France 76 B6
Haifa Cru Israel 59 C8
Hailes Abbey NT UK 67 F5
Hainan I. 55 A8
Hainaut Adm Belgium 65 B14
Haines Cru USA 58 A2
Hainichen Germany 75 I6
Haiphong Cru Vietnam 59 A8
Haiti 95 D2
Hakodate Cru Japan 59 A8
Hal Saflieni Hypogeum UN C Malta 64 A10
Hal Saflieni Hypogeum Malta 79 G4
Halab Apt Syria 56 A16
Halab UN C Syria 64 A12
Halberstadt Germany 74 G5
Haldensleben Germany 74 G4
Haleakala N Pk Hawaiian Is. 91 C3
Haleakala Crater Mtn Hawaiian Is. 91 C3
Haleiwa Hawaiian Is. 91 C3
Half Moon I. Cru Antarctica 59 A10
Haliburton Highlands Reg Canada 94 B6
Halifax Apt Canada 54 A2
Halifax Cru Canada 58 A2
Halifax Canada 94 A8
Hálki I Greece 83 J12
Halkida Greece 83 J4
Halkida Bch Greece 85 A13
Halkidiki Reg Greece 83 J1
Hall in Tirol Austria 77 F2
Halle Germany 74 G5
Hallein Austria 77 F4
Halligyee Fogou tunnel EH UK 67 F6
Halstatt Austria 77 F4
Hamadan Iran 87 D4
Hamber P Pk Canada 94 C2
Hamburg Apt Germany 54 A2
Hamburg Cru Germany 59 A4
Hamburg Ferry Germany 69 C6
Hamburg Adm Germany 74 F3
Hamburg, Aue Germany 76 A1
Hameau Foce, St-Florent Bch Corsica 84 A3
Hameln Germany 74 E4
Hami China 87 D3
Hamilton Apt Canada 94 B9
Hamilton Cru Bermuda 58 A2
Hamilton UK 70 A3
Hamilton Canada 94 B9
Hamilton Grange N Mem USA 93 A4
Hamm Germany 74 C5
Hammam Lif Tunisia 89 D2
Hammamet Tunisia 89 D2
Hammamet, Golfe de Tunisia 89 D2
Hammelburg Germany 75 E6
Hammerfest Cru Norway 59 A4
Hammerfest Norway 59 A4
Hampi UN C India 63 C2
Hampshire Adm UK 68 A6
Hampstead UK 66 E1
Hampton N His USA 93 A4
Hampton Court UK 66 E1
Han-sur-Lesse Belgium 65 B19
Hana Hawaiian Is. 91 C4
Hanau Germany 76 B4
Haneda Apt Japan 55 A8
Hangklip, Cape South Africa 88 C5
Hanía Apt Greece 83 J10
Hanía Crete 83 J10
Hanía EOT Chrysi Akti Bch Crete 85 A13
Haniótis Greece 83 J1
Haniótis Bch Greece 85 A13
Hankey South Africa 88 C8
Hannover Apt Germany 54 A2
Hannover Germany 74 E4
Hannover Germany 74 E4
Hanoi Apt Vietnam 55 A8
Hanoi Vietnam 59 A4
Hanover USA 90 B3
Harare Apt Zimbabwe 55 A5
Hardangerfjord Cru Norway 59 A4
Harderwijk Netherlands 65 B7
Hardknott Pass UK 66 C3
Harlingen Netherlands 65 B3
Harlow UK 66 E1
Harlyn Bay, St Merryn Bch UK 68 A6
Harney Basin USA 91 E2
Harpers Ferry N His USA 93 A4
Harris I UK 70 A1
Harrisburg USA 90 A4
Harrogate UK 70 A4
Harry S. Truman N His USA 93 A7
Hartford Apt USA 54 B2
Hartford USA 90 A4
Hartlepool UK 70 A3
Harwich UK 66 E2
Harwich Ferry UK 69 C5
Harz Reg Germany 76 A1
Hase Riv Germany 74 C4
Hasselt Belgium 65 B15
Hastings UK 66 E4
Hat Yai Thailand 96 A2
Hatay Reg Turkey 83 F3
Hatfield UK 66 E1
Hatra UN C Jordan 64 A12
Hattusha UN C Turkey 64 A12
Haugesund Ferry Norway 69 C2
Haut Atlas Mtns Morocco 89 E2
Haute-Garonne Adm France 72 D2
Haute-Normandie Adm France 72 A1
Haute-Savoie Adm France 72 G2
Haute-Vienne Adm France 72 C4
Hautes-Alpes Adm France 72 G4
Hautes-Pyrénées Adm France 72 D2
Hauula Hawaiian Is. 91 C1
Havana Apt Cuba 54 A3
Havana UN C Cuba 62 A3
Havel Riv Germany 74 I3
Havel Riv Germany 74 H4
Havelland Reg Germany 76 A1
Havelte Netherlands 65 B8
Haverfordwest UK 68 A5
Haverthwaite UK 66 C4
Haw Par Dragon World Singapore 96 C3
Hawaii Adm USA 91 C
Hawaii I Hawaiian Is. 91 C8
Hawaii Volcanoes N Pk, UN N Hawaiian Is. 91 C8
Hawaiian Islands Cruise Area 58 A1
Haweswater Reservoir UK 66 C2
Hawford Dovecote NT UK 67 F5
Hawi Hawaiian Is. 91 C8
Hawkshead UK 66 C4
Hawkshead Courthouse NT UK 67 F3
Hay River Canada 94 A2
Hay-on-Wye UK 66 D3
Hayling Island West Bch UK 68 A6
Haywards Heath UK 66 E3
Head-Smashed-In Buffalo Jump UN C Canada 62 A2

Healdsburg USA 91 E3
Heard I. 55 A5
Hearst San Simeon S His Mon USA 91 E3
Heart of England UK 66 D
Heathrow Apt UK 66 E1
Hechingen Germany 75 D8
Heerenlogement Cave South Africa 88 C1
Heerenveen Netherlands 65 B3
Heerlen Netherlands 65 B16
Heide Germany 74 E2
Heidelberg Germany 76 B4
Heidenheim Germany 75 F8
Heilbronn Germany 76 B6
Heiligenberg, Schloss Germany 76 C4
Heiligenblut Austria 77 F8
Heiligenhafen Germany 74 G2
Heiligenstadt Germany 75 F5
Helena USA 90 A2
Helensburgh UK 66 B3
Helgoland I Germany 74 C2
Helgoländer Bucht Bay Germany 74 D2
Heliopolis Egypt 89 F2
Hellinikon Apt Greece 83 J4
Hells Gate N Pk Kenya 89 G3
Helme Riv Germany 74 G5
Helmond Netherlands 65 B11
Helmstedt Germany 74 G4
Helsinki Apt Finland 56 A3
Helsinki Cru Finland 59 A4
Helsinki UN C France 64 A3
Helvellyn Mtn UK 66 C2
Helwan Egypt 89 F2
Hendaye France 72 D1
Henderson Island UN N 60 A1
Hengelo Netherlands 65 B8
Hennebont France 72 B4
Henningsdorf Germany 74 I4
Herford Germany 77 E3
Hergiswil Switzerland 77 E3
Hergla Tunisia 89 D2
Herisau Switzerland 75 E9
Heritage Quay Cru Antigua 58 B7
Hermanus South Africa 88 C5
Hermiguero Mexico 95 F4
Herne Germany 74 C5
Herne Bay UK 66 E2
Herolds Bay South Africa 88 C7
Herrnsheim Germany 76 C4
Hertford UK 66 E1
Hertfordshire Adm UK 68 A5
Herzberg Germany 74 F5
Hesse Adm Germany 76 A2
Hessen Adm Germany 76 A2
Hesuncook Lake USA 90 B2
Hettstedt Germany 74 G5
Hever Castle UK 66 E3
Hexi Corridor China 87 D3
Hexrivierberge Reg South Africa 88 C6
Heysham Ferry UK 69 B5
Hialeah USA 91 D7
Hidcote Manor Garden NT UK 66 D4
Hiddensee I Germany 74 I2
Hierakonopolis Egypt 89 F6
Hierapolis Turkey 83 J6
Hierapolis-Pamukkale UN CN Turkey 64 A11
Hierro I Canary Is. 80 B4
High Street Mtn UK 66 C2
Highcliffe Castle, Christchurch Bch UK 68 A6
Highland Adm UK 68 A5
Highlands F Res Malaysia 96 B1
Highlands Hammock S Rec USA 91 D5
Hiiumaa I Estonia 86 A1
Hildburghausen Germany 75 F6
Hildesheim Germany 74 E4
Hildesheim UN C Germany 64 A6
Hilkarnassos Turkey 83 J9
Hill Head Bch UK 68 A6
Hilo Cru Hawaiian Is. 58 A1
Hilo Hawaiian Is. 91 C8
Hilvarenbeek Netherlands 65 B11
Hilversum Netherlands 65 B7
Himalaya Mtns China/Nepal 87 D5
Hinterglemm Austria 77 F3
Hintertux Austria 77 F7
Hios UN C Greece 64 A11
Hios I Greece 83 J5
Hios Greece 83 J5
Hios Apt Greece 83 J5
Hirschegg Austria 77 F1
Hirson France 65 B18
Hispaniola I. 58 B6
HLM, St-Florent Bch Corsica 84 A3
Ho Chi Minh City Apt Vietnam 55 A8
Ho Chi Minh City Cru Vietnam 59 A8
Hobart Apt Australia 55 A9
Hobart Cru Australia 59 A9
Hochbrig Switzerland 77 E3
Hochgolling Mtn Austria 75 H9
Hochgurgl Austria 77 F6
Hochob Mexico 95 F2
Hochsölden Austria 77 F6
Höchstdat Germany 75 F7
Hoek van Holland Netherlands 65 B10
Hoek van Holland Ferry Netherlands 69 C6
Hoekse Waard I Netherlands 65 B10
Hof Germany 75 G6
Hofgeismar Germany 74 E5
Hoge Veluwe N Pk Netherlands 65 B7
Hogger Reg Algeria 88 A1
Hohe Acht Mtn Germany 76 C1
Hohe Tauern Reg Austria 77 F7
Hohneck, Burg Germany 76 C4
Hohokam Pima N Mon USA 92 A5
Hokkaido I. 55 A8
Holliday, Vieste Bch Italy 85 A4
Hollókö UN C Hungary 64 A7
Hollywood, California USA 91 E6
Hollywood, Florida USA 91 D7
Holyhead UK 69 B5
Holyhead UK 70 A4
Holzgau Austria 77 F2
Holzminden Germany 74 E5
Homa Bay Kenya 89 G3
Homburg Germany 75 C7
Homestead USA 91 D7
Homestead N Mon USA 93 A3
Homosassa Springs S W Pk USA 91 D5
Honduras 58 B9
Honduras, Golfo de 58 B5
Hong Kong 55 A8
Hong Kong Apt. 55 A8
Hong Kong Cru 59 A8
Honiara Apt Solomon Is. 55 A9
Honiara Cru Solomon Is. 59 A9
Honister Pass UK 66 C1
Honningsvag Cru Norway 59 A4

Honolulu Apt Hawaiian Is. 91 C5
Honolulu Cru Hawaiian Is. 58 A1
Honolulu Hawaiian Is. 91 C6
Honshu I. 55 A8
Hoogeveen Netherlands 65 B8
Hoogezand Netherlands 65 B4
Hook of Holland Netherlands 65 B10
Hook of Holland Ferry Netherlands 69 C6
Hoorn Netherlands 65 B7
Hoover Dam USA 91 E4
Hope Canada 94 C3
Hope Bay Cru Antarctica 59 A10
Hope Cove, Inner Hope Bch UK 68 A6
Hopewell Culture N His USA 93 A4
Hopewell Furnace N His USA 93 A4
Horb Germany 75 D8
Horefto Greece 83 J4
Hormuz Iran 90 A2
Hormuz, Strait of 59 A7
Horn of Africa Reg Somalia 88 A2
Horn, Cape Chile 58 A3
Hornberg, Burg Germany 76 B4
Hornisgrinde Mtn Germany 76 B6
Horovice Czech Rep. 75 H7
Horseshoe Bend N Mil USA 93 A8
Horsey Windpump NT UK 67 F5
Horsham UK 66 E3
Horta Azores 82 B1
Horta Greece 83 J4
Hortas do Tabual Portugal 82 E5
Horton Court NT UK 67 F5
Hot Springs N Pk USA 93 A7
Hotan China 87 D3
Hôtel Belles Rives, Antibes Bch France 84 A3
Hotel Gergano, Vieste Bch Italy 85 A4
Hotel Jasmine, Diano Marina Bch Italy 84 A3
Hotel Madison, Ospedaletti Bch Italy 84 A3
Hotel Majestic, Diano Marina Bch Italy 84 A3
Hotel Majestic, Gabicce Mare Bch Italy 84 A3
Hotel Majola, San Bartolomeo al Mare Bch Italy 84 A3
Hotel Merinum, Vieste Bch Italy 85 A4
Hotel Tirreno, Érice Bch Sicily 85 A11
Hotel Venus, Gabicce Mare Bch Italy 84 A3
Hottentots Holland Ntr Res South Africa 88 C5
Hotton Belgium 65 B15
Houdan France 72 H3
Houlton USA 90 B2
Houmt-Souk Tunisia 89 D4
Houston Apt USA 54 B1
Houston USA 90 A1
Houston Canada 94 C1
Hovenweep N Mon USA 92 A6
Höxter Germany 74 E5
Hoy I UK 70 A7
Hoyerswerda Germany 74 J5
Hristani I Greece 83 J11
Hua Hin Thailand 96 D3
Huajuápan de León Mexico 95 E4
Huang He Riv China 87 D3
Huangshan N Pk China 61 A8
Huangshan UN C China 63 A8
Huascarán N Pk, UN N Peru 60 A3
Hubbell Trading Post N His USA 92 A6
Hudson Riv USA 90 B3
Huelgoat France 72 B1
Huelva Spain 80 D1
Huércal-Overa Spain 80 D4
Huéscar Spain 80 D4
Huexotla Mexico 95 E2
Hughenden Manor NT UK 67 F5
Hull Canada 94 B7
Hull Ferry UK 69 C5
Hull UK 70 A4
Humberside Adm UK 68 A4
Humboldt USA 70 A4
Hümmling, Der Hill Germany 74 C4
Hünfeld Germany 75 E6
Hungarian Plain Hungary 86 B2
Hungary 86 B2
Hunsrück Reg Germany 76 C3
Hunstanton UK 68 A4
Hunte Riv Germany 74 D4
Huntingtower Castle His Sc UK 67 F2
Huntly Castle His Sc UK 67 F1
Huntsville Canada 94 B5
Hurghada Egypt 89 F4
Hurghada Apt Egypt 89 F4
Huron, Lake Canada/USA 90 A4
Husum Germany 74 E2
Hutchinson South Africa 88 C3
Huy Belgium 65 B15
Hydra I Greece 83 J7
Hyères France 72 F3
Hyères, Îles d' France 72 F3
Hyères-Plage France 72 F3
Hylton Castle EH UK 67 F3
Hythe UK 66 E4

Ialisos Greece 83 J9
Ibbenbüren Germany 74 C4
Ibiza Apt Ibiza 81 F3
Ibiza Cru Ibiza 59 C6
Ibiza I Balearic Is. 81 F
Ibiza Ibiza 81 F2
Ice Age Scientific Reserve USA 93 A3
Iceland 55 A4
Ichkeul N Pk, UN N Tunisia 89 D1
Ichkeul N Pk Tunisia 89 D2
Ichpaatun Mexico 95 F4
Idaho Adm USA 90 A1
Idar-Oberstein Germany 76 C3
Idfu Egypt 89 F6
Idra I Greece 83 J7
Idroscalo, Marsala Bch Sicily 85 A11
Idstein Germany 75 D6
Ieper Belgium 65 B13
Ierápetra Crete 85 A13
Ierápetra Bch Crete 85 A13
Ifach, Peñon de Cape Spain 81 F
Ightham Mote NT UK 67 F6
Iglesias Sardinia 78 D3
Igls Austria 77 F6
Igoumenitsa Greece 85 A12
Iguaçu N Pk, UN N Brazil 60 A3
Iguala Mexico 95 E4
Igualada Spain 80 C3
Iguazu N Pk, UN N Argentina 60 A3
IJmuiden Netherlands 65 B6
IJssel Riv Netherlands 74 B4
IJsselmeer Lake Netherlands 65 B7
IJzendijke Netherlands 65 B10
Ikaria I Greece 83 J8
Ikil Mexico 95 F2
Il Porto, Ìsola di Capráia Bch Italy 84 A3
Île de Bandor Plage, Bandol Bch France 84 A3
Île de Bandor Soukana, Bandol Bch France 84 A3
Île de Porquerolles Bch France 84 A3
Île de Port-Cros, Hyères Bch France 84 A3
Île-de-France Adm France 72 A1
Ili Riv Kazakhstan 87 D2
Ille-et-Vilaine Adm France 72 B2
Iller Riv Germany 75 F9
Illetes Mallorca 81 G3
Illetes Bch Formentera 84 A9
Illinois Adm USA 90 A4
Illinois and Michigan Canal N Her Cor USA 93 A3
Ilm Riv Germany 75 G6

Ilmenau Germany 75 F6
Ilmenau Germany 75 H6
Imeros Greece 85 A6
Imeros Bch Greece 85 A6
Immenstadt Germany 75 F9
Imola Italy 79 F7
Imperatorskaya Gavan Russian Fed. 87 A6
Imperia Italy 79 F9
Imperial Palace, Beijing UN C China 63 A8
Imperial Palace, Peking UN C China 63 A8
Imst Austria 77 F6
Inca Mallorca 81 G1
Inchon Cru Korea, Rep. 59 A8
Independence N His USA 93 A4
Independence Hall, Philadelphia UN C USA 62 A2
India 55 A8
Indian Ocean 59
Indiana Adm USA 90 A3
Indiana Dunes N Lake USA 93 A3
Indianapolis Apt USA 54 B1
Indianapolis USA 90 A4
Indre Adm France 72 C4
Indre Riv France 72 C4
Indre-et-Loire Adm France 72 C2
Indus Riv Pakistan/China 87 D5
Inezgane Apt Morocco 89 E3
Infanta, Cape South Africa 88 C6
Infantado Portugal 82 D2
Ingenio Canary Is. 80 B2
Ingolstadt Germany 75 G8
Inland Sea Malta 79 G1
Inn Riv Germany 77 F3
Inner Hebrides Reg UK 66 A1
Inner Hope UK 68 A6
Innsbruck Apt Austria 77 F2
Innsbruck Austria 77 F6
Inousses I Greece 83 J5
Interlaken Switzerland 77 E3
International Peace Garden USA 92 A2
Inukjuak Canada 94 A7
Inuvik Canada 94 A1
Inverboyndie Bch UK 68 A1
Inverness UK 70 A1
Ioanina Apt Greece 56 A15
Ioanina Greece 83 G1
Ioánnina Greece 69 B2
Iona Ferry UK 69 B2
Ionian Is. Greece 83 G-H
Ionian Sea 59 C7
Ios Greece 83 J8
Ios I Greece 83 J8
Iowa Adm USA 90 A3
Ipiros Reg Greece 83 F1
Ipoh Malaysia 96 A2
Ipsos Greece 83 G1
Ipsos, Káto Korakiana Bch Greece 85 A12
Ipswich UK 70 A5
Iqaluit Canada 94 A3
Iráklia I Greece 83 J8
Iráklio Apt Greece 83 J11
Iráklio Crete 83 J11
Iran 87 D4
Irapuato Mexico 95 E1
Iraq 55 A7
Ireland 55 A4
Irian Jaya Reg 55 A9
Irish Sea UK 69 B
Irkutsk Apt Russian Fed. 55 A8
Irkutsk Russian Fed. 87 A5
Iroise Bay France 72 B1
Iron Gate Romania/Yugo, FR 86 C2
Ironbridge UK 66 D1
Ironbridge Gorge UN C UK 64 A5
Irrsdorf Austria 77 F4
Isar Riv Germany 75 H8
Isarco Riv Italy 79 F3
Ischgl Austria 77 F6
Ischia Italy 78 B3
Ischia, Ísola d' Italy 78 B3
Iseo, Lago d' Italy 79 F2
Isère Adm France 72 G3
Isère Riv France 72 G3
Iserlohn Germany 74 C5
Isfahan UN C Iran 63 A7
Isfahan Iran 87 D4
Isiolo Kenya 89 G2
Iskenderun Turkey 83 F3
Isla Cristina Spain 80 D1
Islamabad Apt Pakistan 55 A8
Islamorada USA 91 D7
Islay I UK 70 A2
Isle of Man 66 A1
Isle of Wight Adm UK 68 A6
Isle of Wight UK 70 A6
Isle Royale N Pk USA 93 A3
Isleham Priory Church EH UK 67 F5
Isles of Scilly Adm UK 68 A6
Islote de Hilario Canary Is. 80 B3
Ismâ'iliya Egypt 89 F2
Isna Egypt 89 F4
Isny Germany 75 F9
Iso Valley S Mon Hawaiian Is. 91 C3
Isola 2000 France 72 F2
Isola di Chianco, Vieste Bch Italy 85 A4
Isonzo Riv Italy 79 F4
Ispica, Cava d' Sicily 78 E4
Israel 55 A16
Istanbul Apt Turkey 83 J3
Istanbul Cru Turkey 59 C3
Istanbul UN C Turkey 64 A11
Istanbul Turkey 83 J3
Istria Reg Croatia 86 B2
Italian Lake District Reg Italy 78 A1
Italy 78-79
Itchan Kala UN C Uzbekistan 63 A6
Itéa Greece 85 A12
Ithaca I Greece 83 H2
Ithaki I Greece 83 H2
Itháki Greece 83 H2
Itter Austria 77 F3
Itzehoe Germany 74 E3
Ivanovo UN C Bulgaria 86 C1
Ivory Coast Reg 59 A5
Ivrea Italy 79 F5
Ixia Greece 83 J9
Ixiá, Ialisos Bch Greece 85 A13
Iximché Guatemala 95 F5
Ixkun Guatemala 95 F5
Ixtapa-Zihuatanejo Cru Mexico 58 B4
Ixtapa-Zihuatanejo Mexico 95 E3
Ixtapan del Oro Mexico 95 E3
Izamal Mexico 95 F2
Izapa Mexico 95 F5
Izmail Ukraine 86 C2
Izmir Apt Turkey 83 J5
Izmir Turkey 83 J5
Iznik Turkey 83 J3
Izníkgölü Lake Turkey 83 J3
Izúcar de Matamoros Mexico 95 E4

J.N. 'Ding' Darling N W R USA 91 D5
Jackson USA 90 A7
Jacksonville Apt USA 91 D3
Jacksonville USA 91 D3
Jade Gates Pass China 87 D3
Jaen Spain 80 D3

Jäffar, Cirque de Morocco 89 E2
Jagst Riv Germany 75 E7
Jakarta Apt Indonesia 55 A8
Jakarta Cru Indonesia 59 A8
Jalapa Mexico 95 E2
Jamaica 95 D1
James A. Garfield N His USA 93 A4
Jamestown N His USA 93 A8
Jan Mayen I. 55 A4
Jandia Playa Canary Is. 80 B5
Japan 55 A8
Japan, Sea of 59 A8
Jasper N Pk Canada 94 C2
Jasper Canada 94 C2
Java I. 55 A8
Java Sea 59 A8
Jávea Spain 81 E2
Jávia Spain 81 F2
Jawi Riv Malaysia 96 A6
Jaxartes Riv Turkmenistan/Uzbekistan 87 D2
Jean Blanc, Le Lavandou Bch France 84 A3
Jean Lafitte N His USA 93 A7
Jedburgh Abbey His Sc UK 67 F3
Jeddah Apt Saudi Arabia 55 A7
Jefferson USA 90 B3
Jefferson City USA 90 A7
Jefferson Nat. Expansion Mem. N Mem USA 93 A7
Jeffrey's Bay South Africa 88 C8
Jelling UN C Denmark 64 A2
Jelutong Malaysia 96 B2
Jena Germany 75 G6
Jerada Morocco 89 E2
Jerba Apt Tunisia 89 D4
Jerba, Île de Tunisia 89 D6
Jerejak, Pulau I Malaysia 96 B4
Jerez de la Frontera Spain 80 D5
Jerid, Chott el Reg Tunisia 89 D5
Jersey I Channel Is. 89 B6
Jerusalem UN C Jordan 64 A12
Jerusalem Israel/Jordan 89 F2
Jesuit mission ruins UN C Brazil 62 A3
Jesuítas-Cala, Pilar de la Horadada Bch Spain 84 A8
Jever Germany 74 C3
Jewel Cave N Mon USA 92 A2
Jiayuguan China 87 D3
Jimmy Carter N His USA 93 A8
Jinja Uganda 89 G1
Johannesburg Apt South Africa 55 A5
Johannesburg South Africa 88 B1
John D. Rockefeller Jr. Memorial Parkway USA 92 A2
John Day Fossil N Mon USA 91 A1
John F Kennedy Apt USA 54 B2
John F. Kennedy N His USA 93 A4
John F. Kennedy Center N Mem USA 93 A4
John F. Kennedy Space Center USA 91 D6
John Muir N His USA 92 A1
John Peel's Grave UK 66 C2
John Pennekamp Coral Reef S Pk USA 91 D7
Johnstown Flood N Mem USA 93 A4
Johor Baharu Malaysia 96 C1
Johor Strait Malaysia/Singapore 96 C2
Joliette Canada 94 B3
Jomo Kenyatta Apt Kenya 89 G3
Jönköping Apt Sweden 56 A6
Jonquera, la Spain 80 C2
Jordan 56 A16
Joshua Tree N Mon USA 91 E6
Josselin France 72 B4
Joubertina South Africa 88 C7
Joumâa Tunisia 89 D6
Juan de Fuca Strait Canada/USA 94 C3
Juan Fernandez, Islas 54 A3
Juan-les-Pins France 72 F4
Juan-les-Pins Arc-en-Ciel Bch France 84 A3
Juan-les-Pins Armorial Bch France 84 A3
Juan-les-Pins Le Bretagne Bch France 84 A3
Juan-les-Pins Le Provence Bch France 84 A3
Juist I Germany 74 B3
Julian Alps Mtns Slovenia 86 B2
Jülich Germany 75 B6
Jumilla Spain 81 E1
Juneau Cru USA 58 A2
Juneau USA 90 A10
Jungfrau Mtn Switzerland 77 E3
Jura I UK 70 A2
Jura Reg France 73 A1
Jura Adm France 72 G1
Jurong Bird Park Singapore 96 C1
Jurong New Town Singapore 96 C1
Juru Riv Malaysia 96 B4
Jüterbog Germany 74 I5
Juventud, Isla de la Cuba 95 D1
Jylland, Sønder Reg Denmark 74 E1

K. Gerakari Greece 85 A12
Kaala Mtn Hawaiian Is. 91 C5
Kaatsheuvel Netherlands 65 B11
Kabáh Mexico 95 F2
Kabin Buri Thailand 96 D2
Kabul Apt Afghanistan 55 A8
Kadan Czech Rep. 75 H6
Kaena Point Cape Hawaiian Is. 91 C5
Kahalui Hawaiian Is. 91 C5
Kahana Valley S Pk Hawaiian Is. 91 C5
Kahla Germany 75 G6
Kahler Asten Mtn Germany 75 D5
Kahoolawe I Hawaiian Is. 91 C7
Kahuku Point Cape Hawaiian Is. 91 C1
Kahului Cru Hawaiian Is. 58 A1
Kahului Hawaiian Is. 91 C3
Kahuzi-Biega N Pk, UN N Zaïre 61 A5
Kailua Hawaiian Is. 91 C6
Kailua Kona Cru Hawaiian Is. 58 A1
Kailua Kona Hawaiian Is. 91 C8
Kairouan UN C Tunisia 64 A10
Kairouan Tunisia 89 D4
Kaisersláutern Germany 76 C3
Kaiserstuhl Reg Germany 76 B7
Kaiwi Channel Hawaiian Is. 91 C3
Kakadu N Pk, UN CN Australia 63 A9
Kakamega Kenya 89 G1
Kalá Nerá Greece 85 A12
Kalá Nerá Greece 85 A12
Kalaá Kasbah Tunisia 89 D3
Kaladar Canada 94 B6
Kalafati, Ano Meriá Bch Greece 85 A13
Kalahari Desert Botswana/Namibia/S. Africa 88 A4
Kalalau Lookout Hawaiian Is. 91 C2
Kalamáki Greece 83 H3
Kalamáki Bch Greece 85 A13
Kalamaki, N. Kidonia Bch Crete 85 A13
Kalamáta Greece 83 F1
Kalamitsa, Kavála Bch Greece 85 A6
Kalamitsi, Síkia Bch Greece 85 A13
Kálamos I Greece 83 H1
Kalándra Greece 83 J1
Kalapana Hawaiian Is. 91 C8
Kálimnos I Greece 83 J8
Kaliningrad Russian Fed. 86 A1
Kalithées Greece 83 J9
Kalives Crete 85 A13
Kalives Bch Crete 85 A13
Kalkan Turkey 83 J6
Kalloni Greece 83 J4
Kaló Horió Crete 85 A13
Kaló Horió Bch Crete 85 A13

Index

Kalógria, Araxos Bch Greece 85 A12
Kaloko-Honokohau N His Hawaiian Is. 91 C8
Kamáres Greece 83 J7
Kamchatka Peninsula Russian Fed. 87 B7
Kaména Voúrla Greece 83 J4
Kaména Voúrla Bch Greece 85 A12
Kamenz Germany 75 J5
Kaminaljuyu Guatemala 95 F5
Kaminia, Skála Greece 85 A12
Kamiros Greece 83 J9
Kamloops Canada 94 C3
Kamnarok G Res Kenya 89 G1
Kampen Netherlands 65 B7
Kampoudi Bch Greece 85 A13
Kamuela Hawaiian Is. 91 C8
Kamyshin Russian Fed. 86 C1
Kanáli Greece 85 A12
Kanáli Greece 83 G1
Kanapitsa, Skiathos Bch Greece 85 A13
Kanchanaburi Thailand 96 D1
Kandel Mtn Germany 76 B8
Kandersteg Switzerland 77 E6
Kandy UN C Sri Lanka 63 C2
Kaneohe Hawaiian Is. 91 C6
Kaneohe Bay Hawaiian Is. 91 C6
Kang Kra Chan N Pk Thailand 96 D3
Kanoni Thermis, Pirgi Thermis Bch Greece 85 A13
Kanoni, Kérkira Bch Greece 85 A12
Kansai Apt Japan 55 A8
Kansas Adm USA 90 A6
Kansas City Apt USA 54 B1
Kansas City USA 90 A7
Kaohsiung Apt Taiwan 55 A8
Kapaa Hawaiian Is. 91 C2
Kapenguria Kenya 89 G1
Kappeln Germany 74 F2
Kaprun Austria 77 F4
Kara Sea 59 A6
Karachi Apt Pakistan 55 A8
Karadeniz Bogazi Str Turkey 83 J3
Karaganda Kazakhstan 86 A3
Karakoram Mongolia 87 D3
Karakoram Mongolia 87 D3
Karathonas, Nafplio Bch Greece 85 A12
Karavómilos Greece 85 A12
Karavómilos Bch Greece 85 A12
Karawanken Reg Austria 77 D3
Kardámena Greece 83 J8
Kardámila Greece 85 A13
Kareedouw South Africa 88 C7
Karelia Reg Russian Fed. 86 A1
Karfas, Thimiana Bch Greece 85 A13
Kariani Greece 85 A6
Kariani Bch Greece 85 A6
Karianous N Pk Kenya 89 G3
Kariega Riv South Africa 88 C3
Karimskoye Russian Fed. 87 A5
Káristos Greece 83 J4
Kárlovássi Greece 83 J8
Karlovy Vary Czech Rep. 86 B1
Karlsbad Czech Rep. 75 H6
Karlsruhe Germany 76 B6
Kärnten Adm Austria 77 D3
Karoo N Pk South Africa 88 C3
Karoo, Great Reg South Africa 88 C3
Karoo, Little Reg South Africa 88 C6
Kárpathos I Greece 83 J11
Kárpathos Greece 83 J11
Kárpathos Apt Greece 83 J11
Kars Turkey 83 F3
Karwandelgebirge Reg Austria 75 G9
Kas Turkey 83 F2
Kashgar China 87 D2
Kashi China 87 D2
Kassándra Pen Greece 83 J1
Kassándra, Kriopigi Bch Greece 85 A13
Kassel Germany 75 E5
Kasserine Tunisia 89 D3
Kassiópi Greece 83 G1
Kássos I Greece 83 J11
Kastós I Greece 83 H1
Kastraki, Asini Bch Greece 85 A12
Kástro Greece 83 J4
Kástro Greece 85 A12
Kástro Greece 85 A12
Kastrosykia, Kanáli Bch Greece 85 A12
Katakolon Cru Greece 59 C7
Katápola Greece 83 J8
Katavia Greece 83 J12
Katerinoskala, Peristasi Bch Greece 85 A13
Kathara Falirákiou, Kalithés Bch Greece 85 A13
Kathmandu Apt Nepal 55 A8
Kathmandu Valley UN C Nepal 63 C1
Katholiki, Afántou Bch Greece 85 A13
Katmai N Pk N Am USA 92 A9
Káto Korakiana Greece 85 A12
Kato Stavrós Greece 85 A13
Katong Singapore 96 C2
Katrine, Loch UK 66 B1
Kattegat Str 56 A6
Katwijk aan Zee Netherlands 65 B6
Katz, Burg Germany 76 C2
Kauai I Hawaiian Is. 91 C2
Kauai Channel Hawaiian Is. 91 C2
Kaub Germany 76 C4
Kaufbeuren Germany 75 F9
Kaula I. Hawaiian Is. 91 C1
Kaunakakai Hawaiian Is. 91 C3
Kavála Apt Greece 83 J1
Kavála Greece 83 J1
Kávos Greece 83 G1
Kávos, Lefkimi Bch Greece 85 A12
Kavourakia, Koskinoú Bch Greece 85 A13
Kavoúri Greece 83 J7
Kawaikini Mtn Hawaiian Is. 91 C2
Kaxil Uinic Belize 95 F4
Kayseri Turkey 83 F3
Kazakhstan 86 A3
Kazan Apt Russian Fed. 55 A6
Kazan Russian Fed. 86 A2
Kazanlâk UN C Bulgaria 64 A7
Kaziranga N Pk, UN N India 61 A8
Kéa I Greece 83 J7
Kebili Tunisia 89 D5
Keekorok Lodge Kenya 89 G3
Keene USA 90 B3
Kefaloniá I Greece 83 H2
Kefaloniá Apt Greece 83 H2
Keflavik Apt Iceland 55 A4
Kehl Germany 75 C8
Kehlheim Germany 75 G8
Kek Lok Si Temple Malaysia 96 B1
Kekaha Hawaiian Is. 91 C2
Keld Chapel NT UK 66 C2
Kelibia Tunisia 89 D5
Kelowna Canada 94 C4
Kemaman Malaysia 96 A2
Kemer Turkey 83 F2
Kemer Bch Turkey 85 A14
Kempley: St Mary's Church EH UK 67 F5
Kempten Germany 75 F9
Kenai Fjords N Pk USA 92 A9
Kendal UK 66 C4
Kenilworth Castle EH UK 67 F5

Kenitra Morocco 89 E2
Kennacraig Ferry UK 69 B2
Kennebec Riv USA 90 B2
Kenneburkport USA 90 B3
Kennesaw Mountain N Bat USA 93 A8
Kensington UK 66 E1
Kent Adm UK 66 E4
Kentucky Adm USA 90 A7
Kenwood: The Iveagh Bequest EH UK 67 F5
Kenya .....89 G
Kenya, Mt N Pk Kenya 89 G3
Kenya, Mt Kenya 89 G3
Keoladeo N Pk, UN N India 61 A8
Kerámi Greece 85 A13
Kerén Greece 83 H3
Kerio Valley G Res Kenya 89 G1
Kerkeneh, Iles Tunisia 89 D4
Kérkira Apt Greece 83 G1
Kérkira Cru Greece 59 C3
Kérkira I Greece 83 G1
Kérkira I Greece 83 G1
Kerkouane Tunisia 89 D2
Kerkuane UN C Tunisia 64 A10
Kermadec Is. 55 A9
Kéros Greece 83 J8
Kerpen Germany 75 B6
Kessingland Bch UK 68 A5
Keswick UK 66 C2
Ketchikan Cru USA 58 A2
Ketrzyn Poland 86 B1
Keukenhof Netherlands 65 B6
Keweenaw N His USA 93 A3
Key Biscayne USA 91 D7
Key Deer N W R USA 91 D8
Key Largo USA 91 D7
Key West Cru USA 58 B2
Key West USA 91 D7
Key West Apt USA 91 D7
Khabarovsk Apt Russian Fed 55 A6
Khabarovsk Russian Fed. 87 A6
Khajuraho UN C India 63 C1
Khami Ruins N Mon, UN C Zimbabwe 63 C1
Khao Chamao N Pk Thailand 96 D4
Khao Kheaw N Pk Thailand 96 D4
Khao Kheaw Zoo Thailand 96 D4
Khao Laem Mtn Thailand 96 D1
Khao Yai Nat Pk Thailand 96 D2
Khartoum Apt Sudan 55 A5
Khenifra Morocco 89 E2
Khiva Uzbekistan 86 A3
Khizi Pogost UN C Russian Fed. 64 A1
Khizi Pogost Russian Fed. 86 A2
Khwae Noi Riv Thailand 96 D1
Kicking Horse Pass Canada 94 C4
Kidderminster UK 66 D1
Kiedrich Germany 76 C4
Kiel Germany 74 F2
Kieler Bucht Bay Germany 74 F2
Kiev Apt Ukraine 56 A8
Kiev UN C Ukraine 64 A8
Kiev Ukraine 86 A1
Kigali Apt Rwanda 55 A5
Kihei Hawaiian Is. 91 C3
Kilauea Crater Mtn Hawaiian Is. 91 C8
Kilchoan Ferry UK 69 B2
Kilcreggan Ferry UK 69 B2
Kilimanjaro Apt Tanzania 55 A5
Kilimanjaro N Pk, UN N Tanzania 61 A5
Kilimanjaro, Mt Tanzania 89 G3
Killerton house and garden NT UK 67 F6
Killiecrankie, Pass of UK 66 B1
Killington USA 90 B3
Kilwa Kisiwani UN C Tanzania 63 C5
Kilyos Turkey 83 J3
Kimberley South Africa 88 B2
Kimi Greece 83 J4
Kimolos I Greece 83 J7
Kinal Guatemala 95 F4
Kinaros I Greece 83 J8
Kinbasket Lake Canada 94 C4
Kincardine UK 66 B4
Kinderdijk Netherlands 65 B10
Kineshma Russian Fed. 86 C1
King George I. Cru Antarctica 59 A10
King John's Hunting Lodge NT UK 67 F6
King William I. Canada 94 A2
King William's Town South Africa 88 B2
King's Lynn: St George's Guildhall NT UK 67 F5
Kings Canyon N Pk USA 91 E4
Kings Mountain N Mil USA 93 A8
Kings, Valley of the Egypt 89 F4
Kingsbarns UK 68 A2
Kingston Apt Jamaica 54 A3
Kingston Canada 94 B6
Kingston upon Hull UK 70 A4
Kingston-upon-Thames UK 66 E1
Kingstown Cru St Vincent 58 B11
Kini, Ano Siros Bch Greece 85 A13
Kinross UK 66 B2
Kinshasa Apt Zaïre 55 A5
Kinwarton Dovecote NT UK 67 F5
Kinzig Riv Germany 75 D8
Kióni Greece 83 H2
Kionia, Tinos Bch Greece 85 A13
Kiparissia Greece 85 A12
Kirby Muxloe Castle EH UK 67 F5
Kirchdorf Austria 77 F3
Kircheim Germany 75 E8
Kirchheim-Bolanden Germany 76 C4
Kiribati 54 A1
Kirkcaldy UK 66 B3
Kirkintilloch UK 66 B3
Kirkstone Pass UK 66 C2
Kirkwall UK 70 A7
Kirkwood South Africa 88 C8
Kirriemuir UK 66 B2
Kisii Kenya 89 G3
Kisite/Mpungu Marine N Pk Kenya 89 G4
Kismaros Crete 83 J10
Kissimmee USA 91 D6
Kisumu Apt Kenya 89 G3
Kisumu Kenya 89 G3
Kitale Kenya 89 G1
Kitchener-Waterloo Canada 94 B9
Kitinagen Germany 75 F7
Kiunga Marine G Res Kenya 89 G4
Kithira I Greece 83 J10
Kithira I Greece 83 J10
Kithira Apt Greece 83 J10
Kithnos I Greece 83 J7
Kitui Kenya 89 G4
Kitui, South G Res Kenya 89 G4
Kitzbühel Austria 77 F3
Kitzbüheler Alpen Mtns Austria 77 F3
Kitzingen Germany 75 F7
Kiungu Marine G Res Kenya 89 G4
Kivéri Greece 85 A12
Kivéri Bch Greece 85 A12
Kizil Adalar Is Turkey 83 J3
Kladno Czech Rep. 75 J6
Klaeng Thailand 96 D4
Klagenfurt Apt Austria 56 A10
Klagenfurt Austria 77 D3

Klamath Riv USA 91 E1
Klamath Falls USA 91 E1
Klamath Lake, Upper USA 91 E1
Klamath Mountains USA 91 E1
Klatovy Czech Rep. 75 I7
Klawer South Africa 88 C5
Kleinburg Canada 94 B9
Kleve Germany 74 B5
Klinovec Mtn Czech Rep. 75 I6
Klondike Gold Rush N His USA 92 A9
Klosters Switzerland 77 E4
Kluane N Pk, UN N Canada 60 A2
Knebworth House UK 66 E1
Knife River Indian Villages N His USA 92 A2
Knock Apt Ireland 56 A5
Knokke-Heist Belgium 65 C2
Knossos Crete 83 J11
Knott's Berry Farm USA 92 A5
Knowlton Church and Earthworks EH UK 67 F6
Knysna South Africa 88 C7
Knysna National Lake Area South Africa 88 C7
Ko Chang I Thailand 96 A1
Ko Khram I Thailand 96 A1
Ko Kut I Thailand 96 A1
Ko Lan I Thailand 96 A2
Ko Lanta I Thailand 96 A2
Ko Phangan I Thailand 96 A2
Ko Phoi I Thailand 96 D4
Ko Phuket I Thailand 96 A2
Ko Samae San I Thailand 96 D4
Ko Samet I Thailand 96 D4
Ko Samui I Thailand 96 A2
Ko Sichang I Thailand 96 D4
Ko Terutao I Thailand 96 A2
Ko Yao Yai I Thailand 96 A2
Kobe Cru Japan 59 A8
Kobenhavn Apt Denmark 56 A6
Kobern-Gondorf Germany 76 C1
Koblenz Germany 76 C2
Kobuk Valley N Pk USA 92 A9
Kochi Cru Germany 75 E7
Kodiak I. USA 92 A10
Kohunlich Mexico 95 F4
Koko Head Natural Park Hawaiian Is. 91 C6
Kokoni Greece 85 A12
Kokoni Bch Greece 85 A12
Koksijde-Bad Belgium 65 C1
Kola Peninsula Russian Fed. 86 A1
Kolding Denmark 74 E1
Kolguyev I. Russian Fed. 86 A1
Kolimbia, Afántou Bch Greece 85 A13
Kolimvári Crete 83 J10
Kolimvári Bch Crete 85 A13
Köln Germany 76 B1
Köln/Bonn Apt Germany 76 B1
Kolyma Riv Russian Fed. 87 B7
Kom Ombo Egypt 89 F6
Komi Reg Russian Fed. 86 A4
Kommeno, Kérkira Bch Greece 85 A12
Komodo N Pk, UN N Indonesia 61 A8
Komotini Greece 83 J2
Komsomol'sk-na-Amure Russian Fed. 87 A6
Komsomolets I. Russian Fed. 86 A4
Konarak UN C India 63 C2
Königs-Wusterhausen Germany 74 I4
Königswinter Germany 76 C1
Konstanz Germany 76 B8
Kontogialos, Pélekas Bch Greece 85 A12
Kontokali, Kérkira Bch Greece 85 A12
Konya Turkey 83 F3
Koolau Range Reg Hawaiian Is. 91 C5
Kootenay Riv Canada/USA 94 C4
Kootenay N Pk Canada 94 C4
Kora G Res Kenya 89 G4
Korat Plateau Reg Thailand 96 A1
Korbach Germany 75 D5
Korbous Tunisia 89 D2
Korea, DPR 55 A8
Korea, Rep. 55 A8
Korinós Greece 85 A12
Korinós Bch Greece 85 A12
Kórinthos Greece 83 J4
Korla China 87 D2
Korla China 87 D2
Kornelimünster Germany 76 B1
Korsør Denmark 74 G1
Kortrijk Belgium 65 B13
Kós Apt Greece 83 J8
Kós I Greece 83 J8
Kos I Greece 83 J8
Kosice Slovak Rep. 86 B1
Koskinoú Greece 85 A13
Kósta, Portohéli Bch Greece 85 A13
Kostroma Russian Fed. 86 A2
Kostrzyn Poland 74 J4
Kota Baharu Malaysia 96 A2
Kota Kinabalu Apt Malaysia 55 A8
Kota Kinabalu Malaysia 55 A8
Kotel'ny I. Russian Fed. 87 A6
Köthen Germany 74 G5
Kotlas Russian Fed. 86 A2
Kotlin I. Russian Fed. 86 A1
Kotor UN CN Yugo, FY 64 A7
Kotor Cru Italy 85 A9
Kotor Yugo, FR 86 B2
Kougaberge Reg South Africa 88 C7
Koukounariés, Skiathos Bch Greece 85 A13
Kouremenos, Palékastro Bch Crete 85 A13
Kourouta, Amaliáda Bch Greece 85 A12
Koutsounari, Agios Ioánnis Bch Greece 85 A13
Kouverta, Ermióni Bch Greece 85 A13
Kra, Isthmus of Reg Thailand 96 A2
Kraaifontein South Africa 88 C5
Krakatau G Res Indonesia 61 A8
Krakatau Ntr Res, UN N Indonesia 61 A8
Kraków Apt Poland 56 A7
Kraków Poland 86 B1
Kraków UN C Poland 64 A7
Kramsach Austria 77 F3
Kranebitten Apt Austria 77 F3
Krasnoyarsk Apt Russian Fed. 55 A6
Krasnoyarsk Russian Fed. 86 A4
Krefeld Germany 74 B5
Kremasti Greece 83 J9
Krems Austria 77 D4
Kreuzlingen Switzerland 75 E9
Kreuztal Germany 75 D6
Kriopigi Greece 85 A13
Kriopigi Bch Greece 85 A13
Kriti Greece 83 J10
Kritika, Kós Bch Greece 85 A13
Kritsa Crete 85 A13
Kronach Germany 75 G6
Kroonstad South Africa 88 B1
Kruger Reg South Africa 88 B1
Kruger N Pk South Africa 88 B1
Krumbach Germany 75 F8
Krusne Hory Czech Rep. 75 H6
Krym Reg 56 A12
Krym Reg 56 A12
Ksar Hadada Tunisia 89 D6
Ksar Hellal Tunisia 89 D4

Ksar Ouled Soltane Tunisia 89 D6
Kuala Lumpur Apt Malaysia 55 A8
Kuala Lumpur Malaysia 96 A2
Kuala Terengganu Malaysia 96 A2
Kuantan Cru Malaysia 59 A8
Kuantan Malaysia 96 A2
Kuching Apt Malaysia 55 A8
Kuching Cru Malaysia 59 A8
Kufstein Austria 77 F3
Kulmbach Germany 75 G6
Kumasi Ghana 89 E4
Kumamoto Apt Japan 55 A8
Kumamoto Japan 55 A8
Kumkapu Cru Turkey 59 C7
Kummbach Germany 75 G6
Kumasi Ghana 89 E4
Kumasi Ghana 89 E4
Kuujjuaq Apt Canada 54 A2
Kuwait 55 A7
Kuwait Apt 55 A7
Kuybyshev Reservoir Russian Fed. 86 C1
KwaZulu Natal Adm South Africa 88 B2
Kyani Akti, Préveza Bch Greece 85 A12
Kyle of Lochalsh Ferry UK 69 B1
Kyleakin Ferry UK 69 B1
Kyles Scalpay Ferry UK 69 B1
Kyll Riv Germany 76 C1
Kyoto UN C Japan 63 C2
Kyrgyzstan 86 A3
Kyushu I Japan 55 A8
Kyzl-Orda Kazakhstan 86 A3

l'Almadrava, Roses Bch Spain 84 A1
L'Almadrava, Vandellós i l'Hospitalet Bch Spain 84 A2
L'Almanarre Centre, Hyères Bch France 84 A3
L'Almanarre Nord, Hyères Bch France 84 A3
L'Ametlla de Mar Spain 84 A2
L'Ancresse UN Channel Is. 68 A3
L'Anglaise, Bandol Bch France 84 A3
L'Anse aux Meadows His Pk, UN C Canada 60 A2
L'Aquila Italy 78 C2
L'Aquila Italy 78 C2
L'Arenal, Vandellós i l'Hospitalet Bch Spain 84 A2
L'Argentière, La Londe-les-Maures Bch France 84 A3
L'Arrabassada, Tarragona Bch Spain 84 A2
L'Ayguade, La Londe-les-Maures Bch France 84 A3
L'Éléphant, Ste-Maxime Bch France 84 A3
L'Escalet, Ramatuelle Bch France 84 A3
L'Estany Gelat, Mont Roig del Camp Bch Spain 84 A2
L'Illa, Cullera Bch Spain 84 A9
L'Hyppodrome, Hyères Bch France 84 A3
L'vov Ukraine 86 A1
La Amistad Int Pk, UN N Costa Rica/Panama 60 A3
La Antilla Spain 80 D1
La Barra-Riera Chica, Sitges Bch Spain 84 A2
La Baule France 72 B4
La Botte, Andrano Bch Italy 85 A12
La Cala, Finestrat Bch Spain 84 A9
La Caleta, Vilaijoyosa Bch Spain 84 A9
La Canal Ibiza 81 F3
La Capte, Hyères Bch France 84 A3
La Chaux-de-Fonds Switzerland 77 E1
La Ciotat France 73 F2
La Conxa, Oropesa Bch Spain 84 A2
La Corniche-Lazaret, Sète Bch France 84 A2
La Coruña Apt Spain 59 C1
La Coruña Spain 80 A1
La Croix-Valmer France 84 A3
La Devesa, Valencia Bch Spain 84 A9
La Douane, La Croix-Valmer Bch France 84 A3
La Fortaleza UN C Puerto Rico 62 A3
La Fossa, Calpe Bch Spain 84 A9
La Fossette, Le Lavandou Bch France 84 A3
La Fougasse, Fréjus Bch France 84 A3
La Galite, Île de Tunisia 89 D1
La Garonne, Le Pradet Bch France 84 A3
La Garoupe, Antibes Bch France 84 A3
La Godille, Antibes Bch France 84 A3
La Gorguette, Sanary-sur-Mer Bch France 84 A3
La Goulette Tunisia 89 D2
La Granadella, Jávea Bch Spain 84 A9
La Grande Cosse, Vias Bch France 84 A2
La Grande-Motte France 84 A2
La Gravette, Antibes Bch France 84 A3
La Grilla, Roseto Capo Spúlico Bch Italy 85 A14
La Guaira Cru Venezuela 58 B7
La Guardia Apt USA 54 B2
La Herradura, Almuñécar Bch Spain 84 A1
La Isleta I Canary Is. 80 B3
La Jonica, Roseto Capo Spúlico Bch Italy 85 A11
La Laguna Canary Is. 80 B1
La Lave, Marseille Bch France 84 A2
La Linea Spain 80 D1
La Llana, San Pedro del Pinatar Bch Spain 84 A8
La Londe-les-Maures France 84 A3
La Madrague de St-Cyr-sur-Mer Bch France 84 A3
La Madrague, Hyères Bch France 84 A3
La Manga del Mar Menor Spain 81 G3
La Mans France 72 C2
La Mar Mexico 95 F3
La Marsa Tunisia 89 D2
La Mora, Tarragona Bch Spain 84 A2
La Nartelle, Ste-Maxime Bch France 84 A3
La Nave, Vernazza Bch Italy 84 A1
La Neuveville Switzerland 77 E2
La Orotava Canary Is. 80 B1
La Paille, Nice Bch France 84 A4
La Palma I Canary Is. 80 B4
La Paz Apt Bolivia 54 A3
La Paz Apt Mexico 54 A3
La Paz Cru Mexico 58 A3
La Playa de Mogan Canary Is. 80 B2
La Purisma Mission S His USA 91 E5
La Rada, Estepona Bch Spain 84 A8
La Rapita Mallorca 81 G4
La Redoute-Le Blockaus, Portiragnes Bch France 84 A2
La Redoute-Le Bosquet, Portiragnes Bch France 84 A2
La Ribera, Sitges Bch Spain 84 A2
La Rioja Adm Spain 81 A1
La Roche-en-Ardenne Belgium 65 B19
La Rochelle France 72 C3
La Roda, Altea Bch Spain 84 A9
La Romana, Alcalá de Chivert Bch Spain 84 A2
La Ronge Canada 94 A6
La Roqueta, Guardamar del Segura Bch Spain 84 A9
La Salis, Antibes Bch France 84 A3
La Savinosa, Tarragona Bch Spain 84 A2
La Secca, Monéglia Bch Italy 84 A1
La Seu d'Urgell Spain 80 C1
La Sorgente, Castro Marina Bch Italy 85 A11
La Spézia Italy 79 F10
La Tamarissière, Agde Bch France 84 A2
La Tortuga, Isla Venezuela 95 D7
La Tortuga, Isla Venezuela 95 D7
La Union Spain 81 G3
La Vega Canary Is. 80 B3
La Verna, Abbazia di Italy 79 F11
La Vieille, Le Lavandou Bch France 84 A3
La Zenia, Orihuela Bch Spain 84 A9
Laa an der Thaya Austria 77 E3
Laax Switzerland 77 E3
Labe Riv Czech Rep. 75 J6
Labe Czech Rep. 75 J6
Labná Mexico 95 F2

Labrador Reg Canada 94 A4
Labrador Sea 58 A2
Lac Mégantic Canada 94 B4
Laccadive Is. India 63 C2
Lachute Canada 94 B3
Lacock Abbey and Fox Talbot Museum NT UK 67 F6
Ladbury UK 66 D3
Ladispoli Italy 78 C1
Ladoga, Lake Russian Fed. 86 A1
Laganás Greece 83 H2
Lagartero Mexico 95 F5
Lago de Moreno Mexico 95 E1
Lagoa Portugal 82 E6
Lagoa Greece 83 J7
Lagonisi Greece 83 J7
Lagos Apt Nigeria 55 A5
Lagos Portugal 82 E6
Lagos Greece 85 A12
Lagos, Baia de Bay Portugal 82 E6
Lahaina Hawaiian Is. 91 C3
Lahn Riv Germany 76 B2
Lahnstein Germany 76 C2
Lahore Apt Pakistan 55 A8
Lahore UN C Pakistan 63 C1
Lahr Germany 76 B6
Laie Hawaiian Is. 91 C1
Laiguéglia Italy 84 A1
Laingsburg South Africa 88 C6
Lajes do Pico Azores 82 B1
Lake Chelan N Rec USA 91 A1
Lake City USA 91 D3
Lake Clark N Pk, N Pres USA 92 A10
Lake District UK .....66 C
Lake Louise Canada 94 C4
Lake Lucerne Switzerland 77 E3
Lake Malawi N Pk, UN N Malawi 61 A5
Lake Mead N Rec USA 92 A5
Lake Meredith N Rec USA 92 A6
Lake Nakuru N Pk Kenya 89 G3
Lake of the Woods Canada 94 A6
Lake Wales USA 91 D5
Lakeland USA 91 D5
Lakópetra Bch Greece 85 A12
Lakópetra Bch Greece 85 A12
Laksamana F Res Malaysia 96 B1
Lakshadweep Is India 63 C2
Lalibela UN C Ethiopia 63 A5
Lamaforca, Ostuni Bch Italy 85 A12
Lamanai Belize 95 F4
Lambert's Bay South Africa 88 C1
Lammermuir Hills UK 66 B4
Lampertheim Germany 75 D7
Lamu Kenya 89 G4
Lamu Kenya 89 G4
Lamu I. Kenya 89 G4
Lanai I Hawaiian Is. 91 C3
Lanai Apt Hawaiian Is. 91 C3
Lanai City Hawaiian Is. 91 C3
Lancashire Adm UK 66 A4
Lancaster UK 70 A4
Land of the Dogon UN N Mali 61 A3
Land of the Midnight Sun Cruise Area 59 A4
Landau Germany 75 D8
Landau in der Pfalz Germany 76 B6
Landeck Austria 77 F3
Landsberg Germany 75 F8
Landshut Germany 75 F8
Lanerbach Austria 77 F7
Langada Greece 83 J5
Langdale Fell UK 66 C2
Langeais Ch France 72 C2
Langeberg South Africa 88 C6
Langeland I Denmark 74 F2
Langenhagen Germany 74 E4
Langkawi I Malaysia 96 A2
Langnau Switzerland 77 E2
Languedoc-Roussillon Adm France 72 A2
Lanhydrock House and garden NT UK 72 C2
Lannemezan France 72 A3
Lansing USA 90 A3
Lante, Villa Italy 78 C1
Lanzarote I Canary Is. 80 B3
Lanzhou China 87 D3
Laon France 65 B18
Laos 96 A1
Laptev Sea 59 A6
Lara Turkey 85 A14
Lara plaji Bch Turkey 85 A14
Larantuka Cru Indonesia 59 A8
Lárdos Greece 85 A13
Largs UK 66 B3
Largs Ferry UK 69 B3
Larnaca Apt Cyprus 56 A10
Larne Ferry UK 69 B2
Larochette Luxembourg 65 B20
Larrau France 72 D1
Las Aves, Islas Venezuela 95 C6
Las Conchas-San Miguel, Almería Bch Spain 84 A1
Las Delicias, Águilas Bch Spain 84 A8
Las Galletas Canary Is. 80 B1
Las Marécottes Switzerland 77 E5
Las Marinas, Denia Bch Spain 84 A9
Las Marismas Reg Spain 80 D1
Las Palmas de Gran Canaria Apt Canary Is. 54 A4
Las Palmas de Gran Canaria Cru Canary Is. 59 A4
Las Palmas de Gran Canaria Canary Is. 80 B2
Las Rutas, Denia Bch Spain 84 A9
Las Vegas Apt USA 54 A1
Las Vegas USA 91 E4
Las Villas, Pilar de la Horadada Bch Spain 84 A8
Lassen Volcanic N Pk USA 91 E3
Lassithi Reg Crete 83 J11
Latina Italy 78 C4
Lattari, Monti Reg Italy 78 B3
Latvia 86 A1
Lauchammer Germany 74 I5
Lauf Germany 75 G7
Laurentians Reg Canada 94 B3
Lausanne Switzerland 77 E5
Lauter Riv Switzerland 75 C7
Lauterbach Germany 75 E6
Lauterbrunnen Switzerland 77 E5
Lava Beds N Mon USA 91 E1
Lavagna Italy 79 F6
Laval France 72 C3
Lavandou, le France 72 B3
Lavenham Guildhall NT UK 67 F5
Lávrio Greece 83 J7
Lázaro Cárdenas Mexico 95 E3
Lazio Adm Italy 78 C1
Le Barcarès France 84 A2
Le Bourget Apt France 72 H2
Le Brassus Switzerland 77 E1
Le Couchant, La Grande-Motte Bch France 84 A2
Le Croisic, Isola di Cápráia Bch Italy 84 A3
Le Havre Ferry UK 69 C2
Le Havre France 72 A1
Le Kef Tunisia 89 D1
Le Lavandou France 84 A3
Le Lido, Sete Bch France 84 A2
Le Locle Switzerland 77 E1
Le Mole, Agde Bch France 84 A2
Le Pradet France 84 A3
Le Roeulx Belgium 65 B14
Le Thillot France 75 B9

ebanon 56 A16
ebanon USA 90 B3
ecce Italy 79 A2
ach Riv Germany 75 F8
ch Austria 77 F5
echtaler Alpen Mtns Austria 77 F2
eeds UK 70 A4
eeds Castle UK 66 E4
eer Germany 74 C3
eeuwarden Netherlands 65 B3
efkáda I Greece 83 H1
efkáda Greece 83 H1
efkimi Greece 83 G1
eghorn Italy 79 F11
ehrte Germany 74 E4
eicester UK 66 D2
eicester: Jewry Hall EH UK 67 F5
eicestershire Adm UK 68 A5
eiden Netherlands 65 B6
eigh Bell Wharf, Southend-on-Sea UK 68 A5
eine Riv Germany 74 E4
eipzig Germany 75 H5
eipzig/Halle Apt Germany 74 H5
eiston Abbey EH UK 67 F5
eith UK 66 B4
enzerheide Switzerland 77 E4
eominster UK 66 D1
eominster USA 90 B3
eon Spain 80 A1
eon Mexico 95 E1
eonardo da Vinci (Fiumicino) Apt Italy 78 C3
eonberg Germany 75 E8
epitsa, Kiláda Bch Greece 85 A13
eonberg Germany 85 A12
eptokariá Greece 85 A12
eptokariá Bch Greece 85 A12
érici Italy 79 F10
érins, Îles de France 72 F4
ermoos Austria 77 F2
éros I Greece 83 J8
erwick Ferry UK 69 C1
erwick UK 70 A7
es Ayguades, Gruissan Bch France 84 A2
es Bioux Switzerland 77 E1
es Bormettes, La Londe-les-Maures Bch France ..84 A2
es Cabanes-de-Fleur, Fleury-d'Aude Bch France ..84 A2
es Cases, Alcanar Bch Spain 84 A2
es Chalets, Gruissan Bch France 84 A2
es Cigales, Grimaud Bch France 84 A3
es Deveses, Denia Bch Spain 84 A9
es Diablerets Switzerland 77 E6
es Laurons, Martigues Bch France 84 A3
es Lecques Ouest, St-Cyr-sur-Mer Bch France ..84 A3
es Lecques St-Come, St-Cyr-sur-Mer Bch France ..84 A3
es Mosses Switzerland 77 E6
es Playetes, Teulada Bch Spain 84 A9
es Quilles, Sète Bch France 84 A2
es Rives de Beauvaillon, Grimaud Bch France ..84 A3
esbos I Greece 83 J5
esbos Apt Greece 83 J5
esotho 88 A4
esser Antilles Is 58 B11
ester B. Pearson Apt Canada 94 B9
ésvos I Greece 83 J5
ésvos Apt Greece 83 J5
etocetum baths and museum NT UK 83 J9
etoon Turkey 83 J9
eucate, Étang de Lag France 72 E2
euk Switzerland 77 E6
euckerbad Switzerland 77 E6
euna Germany 75 H5
eutkirch Germany 75 F9
euven Belgium 65 B15
evant Reg 59 C8
evant, Île du France 72 F3
evante, Benidorm Bch Spain 84 A9
évanto Italy 79 F6
évanzo, Ísola de Sicily 78 E1
even, Loch UK 66 B2
evens Hall UK 66 C4
everkusen Germany 75 C5
évis Canada 94 B4
evitha I Greece 83 J8
evkás I Greece 83 H1
evkas I Greece 83 H1
evkosia Apt Cyprus 59 C8
ewes UK 66 E3
ewis I UK 70 A1
eysin Switzerland 77 E5
hasa Apt China 86 A3
hasa UN C China 63 C1
iani Ammos, Halkida Bch Greece 85 A13
iberia 88 A2
ibreville Apt Gabon 55 A5
ibya 88 A1
ibyan Desert Libya 88 A1
ichfield UK 66 D2
ichtenfels Germany 75 G6
iechtenstein 77 F5
iège Apt Belgium 65 B15
iège Belgium 65 B15
iège Adm Belgium 65 B16
ienz Austria 77 F8
ier Germany 65 B11
ignano Italy 79 F8
iguria Italy 79 F6
igurian Sea 59 C2
ihue Cru Hawaiian Is. 58 A1
ihue Hawaiian Is. 58 A1
ikoni Kenya 89 G4
ille Apt France 65 B13
ille France 65 B13
ille Belt Str Denmark 74 E1
illeshall Abbey EH UK 67 F5
illooet Canada 94 B3
ilongwe Apt Malawi 55 A5
ima Apt Peru 54 A3
ima UN C Peru 62 A3

Limassol Cru Cyprus 59 C8
Limburg Adm Netherlands 65 B12
Limburg Adm Belgium 65 B15
Limburg Germany 76 C2
Limité Commune, Antibes Bch France 84 A3
Limité de Commune, Antibes Bch France ..84 A3
Limni Greece 83 J4
Limnonari, Skópelos Bch Greece 85 A13
Limnos I Greece 83 J2
Limnos Apt Greece 83 J2
Limoges France 72 A2
Limone-Piemonte Italy 79 F5
Limousin Adm France 72 A2
Linares Spain 81 A2
Linariá Greece 83 J4
Linaro, Capo Italy 79 F11
Linate Apt Italy 79 F6
Lincoln UK 70 A4
Lincoln Boyhood Nat. Memorial N Mem USA ..93 A7
Lincoln Memorial N Mem USA 93 A4
Lincoln, Maine USA 90 B2
Lincoln, Nebraska USA 90 A3
Lincoln: Bishop's Palace EH UK 67 F4
Lincolnshire Adm UK 68 A4
Lindau Germany 77 F1
Lindbergh Field Apt USA 91 E6
Lindenfels Germany 76 B4
Lindisfarne Castle NT UK 67 F3
Lindos Greece 83 J12
Lindsay Canada 94 B5
Lingen Germany 74 C4
Linlithgow Palace His Sc UK 67 F2
Linoperámata, Rodiá Bch Crete 85 A13
Linz Apt Austria 75 A10
Linz Germany 76 C1
Linz Austria 77 D3
Lion, Golfe du 59 C2
Liouquet, La Ciotat Bch France 84 A3
Lipari, Ísola Sicily 78 E2
Lipari, Ísole Sicily 78 E2
Lipenska prehradní nadrz Lake Czech Rep. ..75 K8
Lippe Riv Germany 74 D5
Lippstadt Germany 74 D5
Lipsi I Greece 83 J8
Lisboa Apt Portugal 82 D2
Lisboa Cru Portugal 59 C5
Lisboa UN C Portugal 64 A9
Lisboa Adm Portugal 82 D1
Lisboa Portugal 82 D2
Lisboa e Vale do Tejo Adm Portugal 82 A2
Lisbon Apt Portugal 82 D2
Lisbon Cru Portugal 59 C5
Lisbon UN C Portugal 64 A9
Lisbon Portugal 82 D2
Lismore Ferry UK 69 B2
Lisse Netherlands 65 B6
Liternum Italy 78 B1
Lithuania 86 A1
Litohórou Greece 85 A12
Litohórou Bch Greece 85 A12
Litomerice Czech Rep. 75 J6
Little BAM Rail Russian Fed. 87 A6
Little Bighorn Battlefield N Mon USA 92 A2
Little Karoo Reg South Africa 88 C6
Little River Canyon N Pres USA 93 A2
Little Rock USA 90 A7
Littlehampton Bch UK 68 A6
Litvínov Czech Rep. 75 J6
Liverpool Ferry UK 69 B5
Liverpool Apt UK 70 A4
Liverpool UK 70 A4
Livigno Italy 79 F2
Livingston UK 66 B4
Livingstone Zambia 79 F11
Lixoúri Greece 83 H2
Ljubljana Apt Slovenia 56 A10
Ljubljana Slovenia 86 B2
Llafranc, Palafrugell Bch Spain 84 A2
Llancà Spain 80 C2
Llandanwg Bch UK 68 A5
Llanddona Bch UK 68 A4
Llanddwyn Bch UK 68 A4
Llangrannog Bch UK 68 A5
Llano Estacado USA 90 A6
Llevant Bch Formentera 84 A9
Llevant, Santa Pola Bch Spain 84 A9
Llevant, Serra de Reg Mallorca 81 G4
Llívia Spain 80 C1
Llobregat Riv Spain 80 C4
Lloret de Mar Spain 80 C4
Lloret, Lloret de Mar Bch France 84 A2
Lluc, Monestir de Mallorca 81 G1
Llucmajor Mallorca 81 G3
Lo Scoglio, Monterosso Bch Italy 84 A3
Löbau Germany 75 J5
Locarno Switzerland 77 E7
Lochaline Ferry UK 69 B2
Lochboisdale Ferry UK 69 A4
Loches Ch France 72 C4
Lochranza Ferry UK 69 B2
Locmariaquer France 72 B3
Locronan France 72 B3
Lodi Italy 79 F6
Lodore Falls UK 66 C2
Lodwar Kenya 89 G1
Lodz Poland 86 B1
Loerie South Africa 88 C8
Logan Apt USA 90 B3
Logroño Spain 81 A1
Lohmar Germany 76 B1
Löhne Germany 74 D4
Lohr Germany 76 B3
Loir Riv France 72 C2
Loir-et-Cher Adm France 72 C2
Loire Reg France 65 B19
Loire Riv France 72 C1
Loire Adm France 72 G1
Loire-Atlantique Adm France 72 C1
Loiret Adm France 72 C2
Loja Spain 80 D3
Lokwe Kangole Kenya 89 G1
Lolland Denmark 74 G2
Lom Bulgaria 86 C2
Lombardia Adm Italy 79 F6
Lombardsijde-Bad Belgium 65 C1
Lombardy Adm Italy 78 A1
Lomé Apt Togo 55 A5
Lomond, Loch UK 66 B3
London Reg UK 68 A5
London UK 70 A5
London Canada 94 A7
London: Biggin Hill Apt UK 70 A6
London: City Apt UK 66 E1
London: Gatwick Apt UK 66 E1
London: Heathrow Apt UK 66 E1
London: Luton Apt UK 66 E1
London: Stansted Apt UK 66 E1
London: Tower of London UN C UK 64 A5
London: Westminster UN C UK 64 A5
Londonderry Adm UK 68 A3
Londonderry UK 70 A3
Long Beach USA 91 E6
Long Crendon Courthouse NT UK 67 F5

Long I. Bahamas 58 B6
Long I. USA 90 A4
Long Kloof Reg South Africa 88 C7
Long Mynd, The Reg UK 66 D1
Long Point Cape Canada 94 B9
Longboat Key I USA 91 D5
Longfellow N His USA 93 A4
Longonot N Pk Kenya 89 G3
Longsands South, Tynemouth Bch UK 68 A3
Longtown Castle EH UK 67 F5
Longuyon France 65 B19
Longwy France 75 A7
Longyearbyen Cru Svalbard 59 A4
Löningen Germany 74 C4
Looe Key N Mar USA 91 D7
Lop Buri Thailand 96 A1
Loppem Belgium 65 C2
Lorch Germany 76 C4
Lord Howe I. 55 A9
Lord Howe Island group UN N Australia ..61 A9
Loreley Hill Germany 76 C4
Loreto Italy 79 F12
Lorient France 72 B3
Lörrach Germany 76 B7
Lorraine Adm France 73 A1
Lorsch UN C Germany 64 A6
Los Alcázares Spain 81 E3
Los Angeles Apt USA 91 E6
Los Angeles Cru USA 58 A2
Los Angeles USA 91 E6
Los Arenales del Sol Spain 81 E1
Los Cristianos Canary Is. 80 B1
Los Gigantes Canary Is. 80 B1
Los Glaciares N Pk, UN N Argentina 60 A3
Los Katíos N Pk, UN N Colombia 60 A3
Los Moros Mexico 95 E3
Los Narejos, Los Alcázares Bch Spain ...84 A8
Los Pocillos Canary Is. 80 B3
Los Rodeos Apt Canary Is. 80 B1
Los Roques, Islas Venezuela 95 D7
Losai G Res Kenya 89 G2
Lot Reg France 72 A2
Lothian Adm UK 66 B4
Lothiarika, Lárdos Bch Greece 85 A13
Lothringen Reg France 75 B8
Lotkipi Plain Kenya 89 G1
Loudéac France 72 B2
Loudun France 72 C3
Loughborough UK 66 D2
Loughwood Meeting House NT UK 67 F6
Louisiana Adm USA 90 A7
Louisville USA 90 A7
Loulan China 87 D3
Loulé Portugal 82 E7
Louny Czech Rep. 75 I6
Loup Riv France 72 F2
Loup, Gorges du France 72 F2
Lourdes Apt France 72 D2
Lourdes France 72 D2
Loutrá Greece 83 J7
Loutrá Edipsoú Greece 83 J4
Loutráki Greece 85 A12
Loutráki Bch Greece 85 A12
Lovosice Czech Rep. 75 J6
Low Newton Bch UK 68 A3
Lowell USA 90 B3
Lowell N His USA 93 A4
Lower Austria Adm Austria 77 D4
Lower Egypt Reg Egypt 89 F1
Lower Saxony Adm Germany 76 B1
Lowestoft South Bch UK 68 A5
Loweswater Lake UK 66 C1
Loxton South Africa 88 C3
Luanda Apt Angola 55 A5
Luang Po Ban Laem Thailand 96 C4
Lubaantun Belize 95 F4
Lübbecke Germany 74 D4
Lübben Germany 74 I5
Lübbenau Germany 74 I5
Lübeck USA 90 A6
Lübeck UN C Germany 64 A2
Lübeck Germany 74 F3
Lübeck-Travemünde Germany 74 F3
Lübecker Bucht Bay Germany 74 G2
Lubenec Czech Rep. 75 I6
Lubsko Poland 74 J5
Luc France 72 G3
Luc, le France 72 F3
Lucaya Cru Bahamas 58 A3
Lucca Italy 79 F11
Lucerne Switzerland 77 E6
Luchon-Superbagnères France 72 D2
Luckau Germany 74 I5
Luckenwalde Germany 74 I4
Luçon France 72 C3
Lude, le France 72 C1
Lüdenscheid Germany 75 C5
Ludlow UK 66 D1
Ludwigsburg Germany 76 B6
Ludwigshafen Germany 76 B4
Ludwigslust Germany 74 G3
Lugano Switzerland 77 E7
Lugano, Lago di Lake Italy/Switzerland ...77 E7
Lugo Orense Spain 80 A1
Lüneburg Germany 74 F3
Lüneburger Heide Reg Germany 76 A1
Lunéville France 75 B8
Luoyang China 87 D3
Luqa Apt Malta 79 G4
Lure France 75 B9
Lusaka Apt Zambia 55 A5
Lussac-les-Châteaux France 72 C4
Luton Apt UK 66 E1
Lütjensee Germany 75 H3
Luxembourg Apt Luxembourg 65 B20
Luxembourg 65
Luxembourg Belgium 65 B19
Luxembourg-Ville UN C Luxembourg 64 A6
Luxembourg-Ville Luxembourg 65 B20
Luxeuil-les-Bains France 75 B9
Luxor Apt Egypt 89 F4
Luxor Egypt 89 F4
Luz France 72 D2
Luzern Switzerland 77 E6
Lyakhov I. Russian Fed. 87 A6
Lydd Apt UK 66 E4
Lyddington Bede House EH UK 67 F5
Lydstep Bay Bch UK 68 A5
Lymington Ferry UK 69 D8
Lyndon B. Johnson N His USA 92 A6
Lyndon B. Johnson Mem. Grove N Mem USA ..93 A4
Lyon Apt France 73 G1
Lyon France 72 G1
Lyon-Satolas Apt France 77 F5
Lyveden New Bield NT UK

Macedonia, Former Yugoslav Republic of ..86 B2
Machakos Kenya 89 A3
Machaquilá Guatemala 95 F4
Machico Madeira ....82 C
Machico Madeira 82 A7
Mackenzie Delta Reg Canada 94 A1
Mackenzie Mountains Canada 94 A1
Mackerricher S Pk USA 91 E1
Macomer Sardinia 78 D1
Mâcon France 72 G1
Macquarie I. 55 A9
Macquarie I. Cru 59 A9
Madagascar 88 A4
Madara Rider UN C Bulgaria 64 A7
Maddalena, Ísola la Sardinia 78 D2
Madeira Apt Madeira ....82 C
Madésimo Italy 79 F2
Madison USA 90 A3
Madon Riv France 75 B8
Madone d'Utelle France 72 F2
Madonie Reg Sicily 78 E2
Madonna di Campiglio Italy 79 F3
Madras Apt India 55 A8
Madras Cru India 59 A8
Madrid Apt Spain 56 A9
Madrid Spain 81 A1
Madrid, Comunidad de Adm Spain 81 A1
Madurodam Netherlands 65 B6
Maes Howe tomb His Sc UK 67 F7
Mafra Portugal 82 D1
Magadan Russian Fed. 87 B7
Magadi Kenya 89 G3
Magadine Switzerland 77 E7
Magaliesburg Switzerland 81 G3
Magaliuf, Calvià Bch Mallorca 84 A9
Magdalen Is. Canada 94 A8
Magdeburg Germany 74 G4
Magellan, Strait of Chile 58 A3
Maggie L. Walker N His USA 93 A8
Maggiore, Lago Italy 79 F2
Maghágha Egypt 89 F3
Magny-en-Vexin France 72 H1
Magoules Greece 85 A12
Magritsa Greece 85 A12
Magrigialos Greece 85 A12
Maguelonne, Villeneuve-les-Mag'e Bch France ..84 A3
Mahabalipuram UN C India 63 C2
Mahdia Tunisia 89 D4
Mahé Apt Seychelles 55 A5
Mahé I Seychelles 59 A5
Mahón Apt Menorca 81 H4
Mahón Cru Menorca 59 C2
Mahón Menorca 81 H4
Mahrès Tunisia 89 D4
Maiami, Itéa Bch Greece 85 A12
Maidencombe, Torbay Bch UK 68 A6
Maidstone UK 66 E4
Main Riv Germany 76 B2
Main Beach, Teignmouth Bch UK 68 A6
Main-Donau-Kanal Germany 75 G7
Mainau Germany 75 E9
Mainburg Germany 75 G8
Maine Reg France 72 A1
Maine Adm USA 90 B2
Maine-et-Loire Adm France 72 C1
Mainland, Orkney I UK 70 A7
Mainland, Shetland I UK 70 A7
Maintenon France 72 H3
Mainz Germany 76 C4
Maister House NT UK 67 F4
Major, Puig Mtn Mallorca 81 G1
Majorca I Balearic Is. ....81 G
Makaha Hawaiian Is. 91 C5
Makakilo City Hawaiian Is. 91 C5
Makarska Croatia 86 B2
Makedonia Greece 83 F1
Makrigialos, Péfki Bch Crete 85 A13
Makryammos, Thássos Bch Greece 85 A13
Makrygiali, Igoumenítsa Bch Greece 85 A12
Makrys Gialos, Argostóli Bch Greece 85 A12
Makthar Tunisia 89 D1
Mal Pas, Benidorm Bch Spain 84 A9
Mala, Cap-d'Ail Bch France 84 A3
Malabo Apt Equatorial Guinea 55 A5
Malacca, Strait of 59 A8
Málaga Apt Spain 80 D7
Málaga Spain 80 D7
Malagueta Paseo Marítimo, Málaga Bch Spain ..84 A8
Malakonta, Erétria Bch Greece 85 A13
Malapesquera, Benalmádena Bch Spain ..84 A8
Malatya Turkey 83 F3
Malawi 88 A3
Malayan Highlands Reg Malaysia 96 C4
Malaysia 55 A8
Malbun Liechtenstein 77 F5
Malcésine Italy 79 F3
Malchin Germany 75 H3
Maldives 55 A8
Malé Apt Maldives 55 A8
Malé Cru Maldives 59 A8
Maléas, Akr. Capr Greece 83 J7
Máleme Crete 83 J10
Máleme Bch Crete 85 A13
Malgrat de Mar Spain 80 C4
Mali 88 A2
Mália Crete 83 J11
Malibu USA 91 E6
Malindi Kenya 89 G4
Malindi Apt Kenya 89 G4
Malindi Kenya 89 G4
Malindi Marine N Pk Kenya 89 G4
Malindi/Waitumu Marine G Res Kenya 89 G4
Mallaig Ferry UK 69 B1
Mallaig UK 70 A2
Mallorca I Balearic Is. ....81 G
Mallorca, Platjes de Bch Mallorca 81 G3
Malmédy Belgium 75 B6
Malmesbury South Africa 88 C5
Malmö Apt Sweden 56 A9
Malmö Cru Sweden 59 A4
Malmö Sweden 86 A3
Malpensa Apt Italy 79 F6
Malta ....79 G
Malta I Malta 79 G4
Malvern Hills UK 66 D3
Mamaia Romania 86 B2
Mambrui Kenya 89 G4
Mammoth Cave N Pk, UN N USA 93 A7
Mammoth Lakes USA 91 E4
Man, Isle of 66 C1
Mana Pools N Pk, UN N Zimbabwe 61 A5
Manacor Mallorca 81 G3
Managua Apt Nicaragua 54 A3
Manama Apt Bahrain 55 A8
Manassas N Bat USA 93 A4
Manaus Apt Brazil 54 A3
Manaus Cru Brazil 58 A3
Manaus Brazil 58 A3
Manchester Apt UK 70 A4
Manchester UK 70 A4
Manda I. Kenya 89 G4
Mandera Reg Kenya 89 G1
Mandera Kenya 89 G1

Manderscheid Germany 76 C3
Mándra Greece 85 A6
Mangana Greece 85 A6
Mángana Bch Greece 85 A6
Manila Apt Philippines 55 A8
Manila Cru Philippines 59 A8
Manila Philippines 94 A6
Manitoba Canada 94 B2
Manitoba, Lake Canada 94 A6
Maniwaki Canada 94 B2
Mannheim Germany 76 B4
Manorbier Bch UK 68 A5
Manosque France 72 F1
Manovo-Gounda St Floris N Pk, UN N C.A.R. ..61 A5
Manresa Spain 80 C3
Mansel I. Canada 94 A3
Mantes-la-Jolie France 72 H1
Mantova Italy 79 F7
Mantua Italy 79 F7
Manu UN N Peru 60 A3
Manzanar N His USA 92 A5
Manzanares, Los Alcázares Bch Spain ...84 A8
Manzanillo Cru Mexico 58 A3
Manzanillo Mexico 95 E3
Manzini Apt Swaziland 55 A5
Maó Apt Menorca 81 H4
Maó Cru Menorca 59 C2
Maó Menorca 81 H4
Maputo Apt Mozambique 55 A5
Mar de Cristal, Cartagena Bch Spain 84 A8
Maracaibo, Lago de Gulf Venezuela 58 B10
Maralal G Res Kenya 89 G1
Maranza Italy 79 F3
Marateca Riv Portugal 82 D2
Marathiá, Akr. Cape Greece 83 H3
Marathon USA 80 D6
Marathon USA 80 D6
Marbella Spain 80 D6
Marburg Germany 76 C4
Marcello Caetano, Barragem de Lake Portugal ..82 E2
Marche Adm Italy 79 F12
Marche-en-Famenne Belgium 65 B19
Marches, The Reg UK 78 B1
Marcianise Italy 78 B1
Marco I. USA 91 D7
Marco Polo Apt Italy 79 F8
Mardin Turkey 83 F3
Maremma Reg Italy 79 F11
Mareny de Vílxes, Sueca Bch Spain 84 A9
Mareth France 89 D6
Maréttimo, Ísola Sicily 78 E1
Marfa Point Malta 79 G1
Margarita, Isla Venezuela 95 D7
Margate UK 66 E2
Margate Bch UK 68 A5
Maria Laach Germany 76 C1
Mariana USA 91 D2
Mariánské Lázne Czech Rep. 86 B1
Maribo Denmark 74 G2
Marie Byrd Land Reg Antarctica 59 A10
Marignane Apt France 72 F3
Marilleva Italy 79 F3
Marina Bay Singapore 96 C4
Marina del Rey USA 91 E6
Marina di Massa Italy 79 F10
Marina di Pietrasanta Italy 79 F10
Marina Piccola Nord, Vieste Bch Italy 85 A4
Marina Piccola Sud, Vieste Bch Italy 85 A4
Marineland of Florida USA 91 D4
Marinella, Golfo di Sardinia 78 D2
Marineta Cassiana, Denia Bch Spain 84 A9
Mariposa USA 91 E3
Marismas, Las Reg Spain 80 D1
Maritime Museum Singapore 96 C4
Maritsa Riv Greece/Turkey 83 J2
Markerwaard Lake Netherlands 65 B7
Marktoberdorf Germany 75 F9
Marktredwitz Germany 75 H6
Marlboro USA 90 B2
Marloes, Milford Haven Bch UK 68 A5
Marlow UK 66 E1
Marmalete Portugal 82 E1
Marmara I Turkey 83 J3
Marmara, Sea of Turkey 83 J3
Marmarás, Néos Marmarás Bch Greece ..85 A13
Marmári Greece 83 J4
Marmaris Turkey 83 J5
Mármaro Greece 83 J5
Marmolada Mtn Italy 79 F3
Marne Riv France 72 H2
Marne au Rhin, Canal de la France 75 B8
Marónia Greece 83 J2
Marquet, Cap-d'Ail Bch France 84 A3
Marrakech Apt Morocco 89 E1
Marrakech UN C Morocco 64 A9
Marrakech Morocco 89 E1
Marroqui o de Tarifa, Punta Cape Spain ..80 D6
Marsabit G Res Kenya 89 G2
Marsabit Kenya 89 G2
Marsala Sicily 78 E1
Marsalforn Malta 79 G1
Marsalforn Bay Malta 79 G1
Máleme Crete 83 J10
Máleme Bch Crete 85 A13
Marsaskala Malta 79 G4
Marsaxlokk Malta 79 G4
Marsaxlokk Bay Malta 79 G4
Marseille Apt France 73 F3
Marseille France 72 F3
Marseille Cru France 72 F3
Marseille-Marignane Apt France 72 F3
Marshall Is. 55 A9
Marssum Netherlands 65 B3
Martha's Vineyard Cru USA 58 A2
Martigny-Ville Switzerland 77 E6
Martigues France 84 A3
Martin Apt France 82 E1
Martin Luther King Jr. N His USA 93 A8
Martin Van Buren N His USA 93 A4
Martinique 95 D7
Martorell Spain 80 C4
Mary Turkmenistan 86 A3
Mary McLeod Bethune Council House N His USA ..93 A4
Maryland Adm USA 90 A4
Maryport UK 66 C1
Masai Malaysia 96 C2
Masai Mara G Res Kenya 89 G3
Maseru Apt Lesotho 55 A5
Maseru Lesotho 88 B2
Maspalomas Canary Is. 80 B2
Massa Lubrense Italy 78 B1
Massa Marittima Italy 79 F11
Massachusetts Adm USA 90 A4
Massif Central Reg France 73 A2
Mastigouche P Res Canada 94 B3
Mataró Spain 80 C4
Matehuala Mexico 95 E1
Matese, Monti del Reg Italy 78 B1
Mateur Tunisia 89 D6
Matmata Tunisia 89 D6
Matrah Apt Egypt 89 F1
Matruh Egypt 89 F1
Mattawa Canada 94 B3
Matterdale Common UK 66 C1
Matterhorn Mtn Italy/Switzerland 77 E6

Mattersey Priory EH UK ... 67 F4
Maubeuge France ... 65 B18
Mauguio-Carnon France ... 84 A2
Maui I Hawaiian Is. ... 91 C3
Maui Apt Hawaiian Is. ... 91 C3
Mauléon France ... 72 D1
Mauna Kea Mtn Hawaiian Is. ... 91 C8
Mauna Loa Mtn Hawaiian Is. ... 91 C6
Maures, Massif des Reg France ... 72 F3
Mauricie N Pk Canada ... 94 B4
Maurienne Reg France ... 72 G4
Mauritania ... 88 A2
Mauritius Apt. ... 55 A5
Mauritius ... 88 A4
Maus, Burg Germany ... 76 C2
Mäuseturm Germany ... 76 C4
Maxglan Apt Austria ... 77 F4
Mayaguana Bahamas ... 58 B6
Mayapán Mexico ... 95 F2
Mayen Germany ... 76 C1
Mayenne Adm France ... 72 C1
Mayenne Riv France ... 72 C1
Mayenne France ... 72 C1
Mayotte I. ... 88 A3
Maythès Tunisia ... 89 D3
Mayrhofen Austria ... 77 F7
Mayshoß Germany ... 76 C1
Mazagón Spain ... 80 D1
Mazarrón Spain ... 81 E3
Mazatlán Cru Mexico ... 58 A3
Mazuria Reg Poland ... 86 B1
Mbale Uganda ... 89 G1
McCarron Apt USA ... 91 E4
McKinley Sea ... 58 A4
McLoughlin House N His USA ... 91 A1
McMurdo Station Cru Antarctica ... 59 A10
Mdina Malta ... 79 G4
Mdiq Morocco ... 89 E2
Mead, Lake USA ... 91 E4
Meadfoot, Torbay Bch UK ... 68 A6
Meaux France ... 72 H2
Mecca Saudi Arabia ... 88 D4
Mechelen Belgium ... 65 B14
Mecklenburg-Vorpommern Adm Germany ... 76 A1
Mecklenburg-Western Pomerania Adm Germany ... 74 H3
Mecklenburger Bucht Bay Germany ... 74 G2
Mecklenburgische Seenplatte Reg Germany ... 74 H3
Medenine Tunisia ... 89 D6
Medford USA ... 91 E1
Medina Saudi Arabia ... 87 D4
Mediterranean Cruise Area ... 59 C
Mediterranean Sea ... 59 C7
Medjez el Bab Tunisia ... 89 D2
Meerane Germany ... 75 H6
Meersburg Germany ... 76 B8
Megali Ammos, Skiathos Bch Greece ... 85 A13
Meganissi I Greece ... 83 H1
Megas Limnionas, Thimiana Bch Greece ... 85 A13
Megève France ... 72 G2
Megisti I Greece ... 83 J12
Meiningen Germany ... 75 F6
Meiringen Switzerland ... 77 E3
Meiringspoort Pass South Africa ... 88 C7
Meisenheim Germany ... 76 C4
Meißen Germany ... 75 I5
Meknassy Tunisia ... 89 D3
Meknès Morocco ... 89 E2
Mekong Riv China ... 87 D6
Melaka Cru Malaysia ... 59 A8
Melaka Malaysia ... 96 A2
Melanesia Is ... 59 A9
Melbourne Apt Australia ... 55 A9
Melbourne Cru Australia ... 59 A9
Melbourne USA ... 91 D6
Melchsee-Frutt Switzerland ... 77 E3
Meldorf Germany ... 74 E2
Melilla ... 88 A2
Melissáni Greece ... 83 H2
Melita Apt Tunisia ... 89 D4
Melívia Greece ... 83 J1
Mellègue Riv Tunisia ... 89 D1
Mellieha Malta ... 79 G1
Mellieha Bay Malta ... 79 G1
Melrose Abbey His Sc UK ... 67 F3
Melsungen Germany ... 75 E5
Melun France ... 72 H4
Melville Peninsula Canada ... 94 A3
Memmert I Germany ... 74 B3
Memmingen Germany ... 75 F9
Memphis Apt USA ... 54 B1
Memphis UN C Egypt ... 64 A12
Memphis USA ... 90 A7
Memphis Egypt ... 89 F1
Menaggio Italy ... 79 F2
Menara Apt Morocco ... 89 E1
Menden Germany ... 74 C5
Mendocino USA ... 91 E3
Menor, Mar Lake Spain ... 81 E3
Menorca I Balearic Is. ... 81 H
Menton France ... 72 F4
Menuires, les France ... 72 G4
Meppel Netherlands ... 65 B8
Meppen Germany ... 74 C3
Merano Italy ... 79 F3
Mercato Italy ... 78 B4
Mercier Dam Canada ... 94 B2
Méribel France ... 72 G4
Mérida Mexico ... 95 F7
Merlette France ... 72 G4
Merlimau, Pulau I Singapore ... 96 C3
Merritt I. N W R USA ... 91 D6
Mersch Luxembourg ... 65 B20
Mersea I. UK ... 66 E2
Merseburg Germany ... 75 H5
Merseyside Adm UK ... 68 A4
Mersin Turkey ... 83 F3
Meru N Pk Kenya ... 89 G2
Meru Kenya ... 89 G2
Merv Turkmenistan ... 87 D2
Meryemana Turkey ... 83 J9
Merzig Germany ... 75 B7
Mesa Verde N Pk, UN C USA ... 62 A2
Meski Morocco ... 89 E2
Méssi Greece ... 85 A6
Messina Sicily ... 78 E2
Messina, Stretto di Str Italy ... 78 E2
Messótopos Greece ... 85 A13
Mestá Greece ... 83 J5
Meta Italy ... 78 B3
Metamórfossi Greece ... 85 A13
Metamórfossi *1* Bch Greece ... 85 A13
Metamórfossi *2*, Ágios Nikólaos Bch Greece ... 85 A13
Metéora UN CN Greece ... 64 A11
Méthana I Greece ... 83 J7
Methil UK ... 66 B2
Methóni Greece ... 85 A12
Methóni Bch Greece ... 85 A12
Metóhi Greece ... 85 A12
Mettlach Germany ... 76 B3
Metz France ... 73 A1
Meuse Riv Belgium ... 65 B15
Meuse N France ... 75 A8
Meuse Valley Belgium ... 65 B15
Mexicali Mexico ... 91 E6
Mexican Riviera Cruise Area ... 58 A3

Mexico ... 54 A3
Mexico City Apt Mexico ... 94 E4
Mexico City UN C Mexico ... 62 B1
Mexico City Mexico ... 95 E2
Mfanganu I. Uganda ... 89 G3
Mgarr Malta ... 79 G1
Mhamid Morocco ... 89 E4
Miami Apt USA ... 91 D8
Miami Cru USA ... 58 B2
Miami USA ... 91 D7
Miami Beach USA ... 91 D7
Miami, Nice Bch France ... 84 A3
Michelstadt Germany ... 75 E7
Michigan Adm USA ... 90 A3
Michigan, Lake USA ... 90 A3
Micra Apt Greece ... 83 J1
Micronesia Is ... 59 A9
Micronesia, Fed States of ... 55 A9
Mid Atlantic, The Reg USA ... 90 A4
Mid Glamorgan UK ... 68 A4
Middelburg Netherlands ... 65 B10
Middelkirke-Bad Belgium ... 65 C1
Middlesbrough UK ... 70 A3
Midès Tunisia ... 89 D3
Midi-Pyrénées Adm France ... 72 A2
Midland Canada ... 94 B5
Midwest, The Reg USA ... 90 A3
Migjorn, Platja de Formentera ... 81 F4
Miguel Hidalgo Apt Mexico ... 95 E1
Mijas Costa Spain ... 80 D6
Mikonos Apt Greece ... 83 J8
Mikonos I Greece ... 83 J8
Mikra Mandínia Greece ... 85 A12
Mikra Mandínia Bch Greece ... 85 A12
Milan Apt Italy ... 79 F6
Milan UN C Italy ... 64 A6
Milan Italy ... 79 F6
Milano Apt Italy ... 79 F6
Milano UN C Italy ... 64 A6
Milano Italy ... 79 F6
Milano Maríttima Italy ... 79 F8
Milas Turkey ... 83 J9
Milazzo Sicily ... 78 E2
Mileai Greece ... 85 A12
Miletus Turkey ... 83 J8
Milford Haven UK ... 70 A5
Milford Sound Cru New Zealand ... 59 A9
Milia, Skópelos Bch Greece ... 85 A13
Militaire, Nice Bch France ... 84 A3
Millinocket USA ... 90 B2
Millom UK ... 66 C3
Milnthorpe UK ... 66 C4
Milos I Greece ... 83 J7
Milstatt Austria ... 77 F8
Miltenberg Germany ... 76 B4
Milton UK ... 91 D1
Milton Keynes UK ... 70 A5
Milwaukee Apt USA ... 54 B1
Milwaukee USA ... 90 A3
Mincio Riv Italy ... 79 F7
Mindel Riv Germany ... 75 F8
Mindelheim Germany ... 75 F8
Minden Germany ... 74 D4
Ming Village Singapore ... 96 C3
Mini Tunnel Magnan, Nice Bch France ... 84 A3
Minneapolis USA ... 90 A3
Minneapolis-St Paul Apt USA ... 54 B1
Minnesota Adm USA ... 90 A3
Minnis Bay, Birchington Bch UK ... 68 A6
Minorca I Balearic Is. ... 81 H
Minsk Apt Belarus ... 56 A7
Minsk Belarus ... 86 A1
Minster Leas, Sheerness Bch UK ... 68 A5
Minute Man N His USA ... 93 A4
Mira Riv Portugal ... 82 E2
Mirabel Apt Canada ... 94 B3
Miramare, Cervo Bch Italy ... 84 A3
Mirándola Italy ... 79 F7
Mirapolis France ... 72 H1
Mírina Greece ... 83 J2
Mirodato Italy ... 85 A6
Mirodato Bch Greece ... 85 A6
Mírtoan Sea Greece ... 83 J4
Mirtos Crete ... 85 A13
Mirtos Bch Crete ... 85 A13
Miseno, Capo Italy ... 78 B3
Miskito, Cayos Is Nicaragua ... 95 D5
Miskolc Hungary ... 86 B2
Mississauga Canada ... 94 B9
Mississippi Adm USA ... 90 A7
Mississippi Delta USA ... 90 A7
Mississippi Nord, Gabicce Mare Bch Italy ... 85 A4
Mississippi Sud, Gabicce Mare Bch Italy ... 85 A4
Missouri Adm USA ... 90 A7
Mistras UN C Greece ... 64 A11
Misty Fjords Reg ... 58 A2
Míthimna Greece ... 83 J5
Mítikas Greece ... 83 H1
Mítikas Greece ... 83 H1
Mitilíni Greece ... 83 J5
Mítla Mexico ... 95 E4
Mittelfranken Reg Germany ... 76 A2
Mittelland Reg Switzerland ... 77 E2
Mittellandkanal Germany ... 74 D4
Mittweida Germany ... 75 I5
Mixco Viejo Guatemala ... 95 F5
Mmabatho South Africa ... 88 A5
Mnajdra Malta ... 79 G4
Mobile USA ... 91 D1
Mobile Bay USA ... 91 D1
Modane France ... 72 G4
Modave Belgium ... 65 B16
Modena Italy ... 79 F7
Moder Riv France ... 75 C8
Moena Italy ... 79 F3
Moers Germany ... 65 B22
Mogadishu Apt Somalia ... 55 A5
Mogao Caves UN C China ... 63 A8
Moháčs Hungary ... 86 C2
Mohammed V Apt Morocco ... 89 E1
Mohammedia Morocco ... 89 E1
Mohendojaro UN C Pakistan ... 63 C1
Möhne Riv Germany ... 74 D5
Moi Apt Kenya ... 89 G4
Mojácar Spain ... 80 D4
Mojave Desert USA ... 91 E6
Mokapu Peninsula Hawaiian Is. ... 91 C6
Moknine Tunisia ... 89 D4
Mokuleia Baech Hawaiian Is. ... 91 C1
Molara, Isola Sardinia ... 78 D2
Moldavia Reg Moldova/Romania ... 86 B2
Molde Cru Norway ... 59 A4
Moldova ... 86 A1
Molise Adm Italy ... 79 A2
Moll Grec, L'Escala Bch Spain ... 84 A2
Molo Bernero, Monéglia Bch Italy ... 84 A3
Molo Centrale, Cervo Bch Italy ... 84 A3
Molo Sant'António, Spotorno Bch Italy ... 84 A3
Molo Sirio, Spotorno Bch Italy ... 84 A3
Molokai I Hawaiian Is. ... 91 C3
Molokai Apt Hawaiian Is. ... 91 C3
Mombasa Apt Kenya ... 89 G4
Mombasa Cru Kenya ... 89 A5
Mombasa Kenya ... 89 G4

Møn I Denmark ... 74 H1
Monaco ... 72 F2
Monaco, Le Pradet Bch France ... 84 A3
Monadnock Reg USA ... 90 B3
Monastir Apt Tunisia ... 89 D4
Monastir Tunisia ... 89 D4
Monção Portugal ... 82 A1
Moncarapacho Portugal ... 82 E8
Monchengladbach Germany ... 75 B5
Monchique Portugal ... 82 A2
Monchique, Serra de Reg Portugal ... 82 E2
Moncófar Spain ... 84 A9
Moncófar Bch Spain ... 84 A9
Mondello Sicily ... 78 E1
Mondorf-les-Bains Luxembourg ... 65 B20
Mondovì Italy ... 79 F5
Mondragone Italy ... 78 B1
Mondsee Lake Austria ... 77 F4
Mondsee Austria ... 77 F4
Monéglia Italy ... 79 F6
Monemvassia Greece ... 83 J7
Mongie, la France ... 72 D2
Mongolia ... 55 A8
Monmouth UK ... 66 D3
Mono Lake USA ... 91 E4
Monocacy N Bat USA ... 93 A4
Monolithi, Mitikas Bch Greece ... 85 A12
Monreale Sicily ... 78 E1
Monrovia Apt Liberia ... 55 A5
Monrovia Cru Liberia ... 59 A5
Mons Belgium ... 65 B14
Møns Klint Cape Denmark ... 74 H2
Monschau Germany ... 76 B1
Monsheim Germany ... 76 C4
Monster Netherlands ... 65 B6
Mont Blanc Mtn France/Italy ... 72 G2
Mont Blanc, Tunnel du France/Italy ... 72 G2
Mont Cenis, Col du Pass France ... 72 G4
Mont Roig del Camp Spain ... 84 A9
Mont Tremblant P Pk Canada ... 94 B4
Mont-Laurier Canada ... 94 B4
Mont-Mégantic P Pk Canada ... 94 B8
Mont-Orford P Pk Canada ... 94 B8
Mont-St-Bruno P Pk Canada ... 94 B8
Mont-St-Michel, le UN CN France ... 64 A5
Mont-St-Michel, le France ... 72 D2
Montabaur Germany ... 76 C2
Montacute House NT UK ... 67 F6
Montagnana Italy ... 79 F7
Montagu South Africa ... 88 C6
Montana Adm USA ... 90 A2
Montaña Blanca Canary Is. ... 80 B3
Montaña Clara I. Canary Is. ... 80 B3
Montanhãs Reg Portugal ... 82 A1
Montbéliard France ... 75 B9
Montblanc Spain ... 80 C3
Montchavin France ... 72 G2
Monte Albán UN C Mexico ... 62 B1
Monte Albán Mexico ... 95 E4
Monte Carlo France ... 72 F2
Monte Fogo, Serra de Reg Portugal ... 82 E7
Monte Gordo Portugal ... 82 E8
Monte Oliveto Maggiore, Abbazia di Italy ... 79 F11
Monte Rosa Mtn Italy/Switzerland ... 77 E6
Montecassino, Abbazia di Italy ... 78 C4
Montecatini Italy ... 79 F11
Montecorvino Italy ... 78 B4
Montefalco Italy ... 79 F12
Montego Bay Cru Jamaica ... 58 B9
Montegrotto Italy ... 79 F7
Montélimar France ... 72 G3
Montella Italy ... 78 B2
Montepulciano Italy ... 79 F11
Monterosso Italy ... 84 A3
Monterrey Apt Mexico ... 54 A2
Monteriggioni Italy ... 79 F11
Monterey USA ... 91 E3
Monterey Bay USA ... 91 E3
Montesárchio Italy ... 78 B2
Montevideo Apt Uruguay ... 54 A3
Montevideo Cru Uruguay ... 58 A3
Montezuma Castle N Mon USA ... 92 A5
Montgenèvre France ... 72 G4
Montgeoffroy Ch France ... 72 C1
Montgomery USA ... 90 A7
Monthey Switzerland ... 77 E5
Monticelli, Ostuni Bch Italy ... 85 A6
Montignies-Metz France ... 75 B7
Montijo Portugal ... 82 D2
Montilla Spain ... 80 D2
Montmélian France ... 72 G1
Montmagny Canada ... 90 B1
Montmélian France ... 72 G1
Montpelier USA ... 90 B3
Montpellier USA ... 90 B3
Montpellier France ... 73 A2
Montpoupon Ch France ... 72 C2
Montréal Cru Canada ... 58 A2
Montréal Canada ... 94 B7
Montréal: Dorval Apt Canada ... 94 B7
Montréal: Mirabel Apt Canada ... 94 B3
Montreux Switzerland ... 77 E5
Montrose UK ... 70 A2
Montserrat I ... 95 D3
Montserrat, Monestir de Spain ... 80 C3
Monza Italy ... 79 F6
Moorea Cru French Polynesia ... 58 A1
Moores Creek N Bat USA ... 93 A8
Moorfoot Hills UK ... 66 B4
Moosburg Germany ... 75 G8
Moosehead Lake USA ... 90 B2
Mooseonee Canada ... 94 A7
Moraira Spain ... 81 E2
Moraítika Greece ... 83 G1
Moravia Reg Czech Rep. ... 86 B1
Morbihan Adm France ... 72 B4
Morbihan, Golfe du Reg France ... 72 B4
Morcote Switzerland ... 77 E7
Moreton-in-Marsh UK ... 66 D4
Morelia UN C Mexico ... 62 B1
Morelia Mexico ... 95 E1
Morges Switzerland ... 77 E5
Morgins Switzerland ... 77 E5
Morgiou, Marseille Bch France ... 84 A3
Morhange France ... 75 B8
Morlaix France ... 72 B3
Morocco ... 89 E
Morristown N His USA ... 93 A4
Morro Bay S Pk USA ... 91 E5
Mortagne Riv France ... 75 B8
Mortole, Diano Marina Bch Italy ... 84 A3
Morzine France ... 72 G2
Mosbach Germany ... 76 B4
Moscow UN C Russian Fed. ... 64 A4
Moscow Apt Russian Fed. ... 56 A8
Moscow Russian Fed. ... 86 A2
Moscow-Volga Canal Russian Fed. ... 86 C1
Mosel Riv Germany ... 76 C3
Mosel Valley Germany ... 76 C3
Moselle Riv France ... 73 A1
Moshi Tanzania ... 89 G3
Mosi-oa-Tunya UN N Zambia/Zimbabwe ... 61 A5
Mosquitos, Costa de Reg Nicaragua ... 58 A9
Mossel Bay South Africa ... 88 C7
Most Czech Rep. ... 75 I6
Mosta Malta ... 79 G4

Motherwell UK ... 66 B3
Motril Spain ... 80 D7
Motul de San José Guatemala ... 95 F4
Moúdros Greece ... 83 J2
Moulin Ch France ... 72 C2
Moulouya Riv Morocco ... 89 E2
Moulton Packhorse Bridge EH UK ... 67 F5
Moúnda, Akr. Cape Greece ... 83 H2
Mount Nimba Ntr Res, UN N Guinea/Côte d'Ivoire ... 61 A5
Mount Ranier N Pk USA ... 91 A1
Mount Rushmore N Mem USA ... 92 A2
Mountain States, The Reg USA ... 90 A2
Mountain Zebra N Pk South Africa ... 88 C4
Moura Portugal ... 82 A3
Mourésí Greece ... 85 A12
Mouthwell, Outer Hope Bch UK ... 68 A6
Moutiers France ... 72 G2
Moyale Kenya ... 89 G2
Moyen Atlas Mtns Morocco ... 89 E2
Mozambique ... 88 A4
Mozambique Channel ... 59 A5
Mozambique Island UN N Mozambique ... 61 A5
Mpampati, Spartilas Bch Greece ... 85 A12
Mpoufou, Vrahási Bch Crete ... 85 A13
Mpouka, Lefkimi Bch Greece ... 85 A12
Mt Cook N Pk, UN N New Zealand ... 61 A9
Mt Desert I. USA ... 90 B4
Mt Nimba Ntr Res, UN N Guinea/Côte d'Ivoire 61 A5
Mt Ranier N Pk USA ... 91 A1
Mt Rushmore N Mem USA ... 92 A2
Mt Desert I. USA ... 90 B4
Muar Malaysia ... 96 A2
Muchavista, Campello Bch Spain ... 84 A9
Muck Ferry UK ... 69 A5
Mudanya Turkey ... 83 J3
Mugel, La Ciotat Bch France ... 84 A3
Mugla Turkey ... 83 J9
Muhammad, Râs Cape Egypt ... 89 F4
Mühlacker Germany ... 75 D8
Mühldorf Germany ... 75 H8
Mühlhausen Germany ... 75 F5
Muiden Netherlands ... 65 B7
Muir Woods N Mon USA ... 92 A1
Muirfield Gf UK ... 66 B4
Muizenberg South Africa ... 88 C5
Mujeres, Isla Mexico ... 95 F2
Muka Head Cape Malaysia ... 96 B1
Mulde Riv Germany ... 74 H5
Mulhacén Mtn Spain ... 80 D3
Mülheim Germany ... 74 B5
Mulhouse France ... 73 A1
Mull I UK ... 70 A2
Müllheim Germany ... 76 A6
Mummelsee Lake Germany ... 76 B6
Mumbles, The UK ... 66 D3
München Apt Germany ... 75 G8
München Germany ... 75 G8
Münden Germany ... 74 E5
Mundesley Bch UK ... 68 A4
Munich Apt Germany ... 75 G8
Munich Germany ... 75 G8
Munster France ... 73 A1
Münster Germany ... 74 C5
Münster/Osnabrück Apt Germany ... 74 A1
Münsterland Reg Germany ... 76 A1
Münzenberg Germany ... 76 B2
Muranga Kenya ... 89 G3
Murcia Spain ... 81 E3
Murcia, Región de Adm Spain ... 81 A2
Murg Riv Germany ... 75 D8
Müritz Lake Germany ... 74 H3
Murmansk Apt Russian Fed. ... 56 A6
Murmansk Russian Fed. ... 86 A1
Murnau Germany ... 75 G9
Muro Mallorca ... 81 G2
Murraysburg South Africa ... 88 C3
Mürren Switzerland ... 77 E2
Murten Switzerland ... 77 E2
Murtensee Lake Switzerland ... 77 E2
Muscat Apt Oman ... 55 A7
Muscat Oman ... 55 A7
Musoma Tanzania ... 89 G3
Müstair UN C Switzerland ... 64 A6
Müstair Switzerland ... 77 E4
Mut Egypt ... 89 F3
Mutters Austria ... 77 F6
Muyil Mexico ... 95 F2
Mwea G Res Kenya ... 89 G3
Mwnt Bch UK ... 68 A5
Myakka River S Pk USA ... 91 D5
Myanmar ... 55 A8
Mze Riv Czech Rep. ... 75 I7

N. Kidonia Crete ... 85 A13
Na Pali Coast S Pk Hawaiian Is. ... 91 C1
Naab Riv Germany ... 75 H7
Naalehu Hawaiian Is. ... 91 C8
Naarden Netherlands ... 65 B7
Nabeul Tunisia ... 89 D4
Nadi Apt Fiji ... 55 A9
Nador Morocco ... 89 E2
Nadur Malta ... 79 G1
Næstved Denmark ... 74 G1
Nafplio Greece ... 85 A12
Naftikos Omilos, Árgos Bch Greece ... 85 A12
Nagasaki Cru Japan ... 59 A8
Nagold Riv Germany ... 75 D8
Nagold bei Coburg Germany ... 75 G6
Nagold Reg Germany ... 76 B6
Nagpur Apt Japan ... 55 A8
Nahanni N Pk, UN N Canada ... 60 A2
Nahe Riv Germany ... 76 C4
Nailsworth UK ... 66 D3
Nain Canada ... 94 A4
Nairn Central Bch UK ... 68 A1
Nairobi Apt Kenya ... 89 G3
Nairobi N Pk Kenya ... 89 G3
Nairobi Kenya ... 89 G3
Nakhodka Russian Fed. ... 87 A6
Nakhon Nayok Thailand ... 96 D2
Nakhon Pathom Thailand ... 96 A1
Nakhon Ratchasima Thailand ... 96 A1
Nakhon Sawan Thailand ... 96 A1
Nakhon Si Thammarat Thailand ... 96 A2
Nakskov Denmark ... 74 G2
Nakum Guatemala ... 95 F4
Nakuru Kenya ... 89 G3
Nakuru, Lake N Pk Kenya ... 89 G3
Namib Desert Namibia ... 88 A4
Namibia ... 88 A4
Namur Adm Belgium ... 65 B15
Namur Belgium ... 65 B15
Nanjing UN C China ... 63 A8
Nancy UN C France ... 64 A6
Nancy France ... 73 A1
Nancy Apt France ... 75 B8
Nangis France ... 72 H4
Nanjing China ... 59 A8
Nanterre France ... 72 H1
Nantes Apt France ... 72 C1
Nantes France ... 72 C1
Nantucket Ferry UK ... 69 C2
Nantucket Cru USA ... 58 A2
Nanyuki Kenya ... 89 G3
Não, Cabo de la Cape Spain ... 81 E2
Napa Valley USA ... 91 E3
Napier Cru New Zealand ... 59 A9
Naples Apt USA ... 91 D5
Naples Cru USA ... 59 C2
Naples Italy ... 78 B3

Naples USA ... 91 D
Napléon, Route France ... 72 F
Nápoli Apt Italy ... 78 B
Nápoli Cru Italy ... 59 C
Nápoli Italy ... 78 B
Nápoli, Golfo di Italy ... 78 B
Napoule-Plage, la France ... 72 F
Naranjo Guatemala ... 95 F
Narbonne France ... 84 A
Narita Apt Japan ... 55 A
Naro Sicily ... 78 E
Narsarsuaq Apt Greenland ... 58 A
Narvik Cru Norway ... 59 A
Nasalot G Res Kenya ... 89 G
Nashua USA ... 90 B
Nashville USA ... 90 A
Nassau Apt Bahamas ... 54 B
Nassau Cru Bahamas ... 58 B
Nasser, Lake Egypt ... 89 F
Natchez N His USA ... 93 A
Natchez Trace Parkway USA ... 93 A
National Agricultural Centre UK ... 66 D
National Capital Region UK ... 93 A
National Exhibition Centre UK ... 66 D
National Mall, Washington USA ... 93 A
National Park of American Samoa N Pk AmS ... 96 C
National Stadium Singapore ... 96 C
Natron, Lake Tanzania ... 89 G
Nattawasaga Bay Canada ... 94 B
Natural Bridges N Mon USA ... 92 A
Nature's Valley South Africa ... 88 C
Nauders Austria ... 77 F
Naumburg Germany ... 75 G
Nauru ... 55 A
Navajo N Mon USA ... 92 A
Navarra, Comunidad Foral de Adm Spain ... 81 A
Navigatori, Jésolo Bch Italy ... 85 A
Nawiliwili Cru Hawaiian Is. ... 58 A
Náxos Greece ... 83 J
Náxos I Greece ... 83 J
Nazaré Portugal ... 82 A
Nazca UN C Peru ... 62 A
Ndjamena Apt Chad ... 55 A
Néa Fókea Greece ... 85 A1
Néa Ionia Greece ... 83 J
Néa Kessáni Greece ... 85 A
Néa Moní Greece ... 83 J
Néa Stíra Greece ... 83 J
Neápoli Greece ... 85 A1
Neápoli Bch Greece ... 85 A1
Nebraska Adm USA ... 90 A
Nechako Riv Canada ... 94 C
Neckar Riv Germany ... 76 B
Neckarsulm Germany ... 75 E
Nefta Tunisia ... 89 D
Néi Epivates Greece ... 85 A1
Néi Epivates Bch Greece ... 85 A1
Neidpath Castle UK ... 66 B
Nekhen Egypt ... 89 F
Nelson South Africa ... 88 C
Nelsport South Africa ... 88 C
Nelspruit South Africa ... 88 B
Nemi, Lagi di Italy ... 78 C
Nemours France ... 72 H
Nemrut Dag UN C Turkey ... 64 C
Neohóri Greece ... 85 A1
Neohóri Greece ... 85 A1
Néos Marmarás Greece ... 83 J
Nepal ... 55 A
Neptun Romania ... 86 B
Neptune, Antibes Bch France ... 84 A
Neptune, Nice Bch France ... 84 A
Nera Riv Italy ... 78 C
Nérantza France ... 72 H
Nérantza Bch Greece ... 85 A1
Nerjá Spain ... 80 D
Neryungri Russian Fed. ... 87 A
Ness Cove, Shaldon Bch UK ... 68 A
Nessebar UN C Bulgaria ... 64 A
Netherlands ... 65
Netherlands Antilles Is ... 54 A
Netley Abbey EH UK ... 67 F
Nette Riv Germany ... 76 C
Nettuno Italy ... 78 C
Nettuno, Grotta di Sardinia ... 78 D
Neu-Ulm Germany ... 75 F
Neubrandenburg Germany ... 74 I
Neuburg Germany ... 75 G
Neuchâtel Switzerland ... 77 E
Neuchâtel, Lac de Switzerland ... 77 E
Neufchâteau Belgium ... 65 B19
Neufchâteau France ... 75 B8
Neuleiningen Germany ... 76 B4
Neumagen-Dhron Germany ... 75 G
Neumünster Germany ... 74 G
Neunkirchen Germany ... 76 B3
Neuruppin Germany ... 74 H4
Neusiedler See Lake Austria ... 77 F
Neustadt Germany ... 75 F
Neustadt am Rübenberge Germany ... 74 E
Neustadt bei Coburg Germany ... 75 G
Neustadt i.H. Germany ... 74 F
Neustift Austria ... 77 F
Neustrelitz Germany ... 74 I3
Neuwied Germany ... 76 C1
Nevada Adm USA ... 91 E
Nevada City USA ... 91 E
Nevada, Sierra Mtns Spain ... 80 D
New Abbey Corn Mill His Sc UK ... 67 F
New Brunswick Adm Canada ... 94 A
New Caledonia Is ...
New England Reg USA ... 90 A
New Hampshire Adm USA ... 90 B
New Hazleton Canada ... 94 C
New Jersey Adm USA ... 90 A
New Kalabsha Egypt ... 89 F
New Mexico Adm USA ... 90 A
New Orleans Apt USA ... 54 B
New Orleans Cru USA ... 58 B
New Orleans USA ... 90 A
New Providence I Bahamas ... 58 B
New Quay UK ... 68 A
New Siberian Is. Russian Fed. ... 87 A
New Valley, The Egypt ... 89 F
New York Cru USA ... 58 A
New York Adm USA ... 90 A
New York USA ... 90 A
New York: John F Kennedy Apt USA ... 54 B
New York: La Guardia Apt USA ... 54 B
New York: Newark Apt USA ... 55 A
New Zealand ... 55 A
Newark USA ... 90 A
Newbury UK ... 70 A
Newcastle Apt UK ... 70 A
Newcastle Ferry UK ... 69 C
Newcastle-upon-Tyne UK ... 70 A
Newfoundland Adm Canada ... 94 A
Newfoundland I. Canada ... 94 A
Newgale Bch UK ... 68 A
Newhaven UK ... 66 E
Newhaven Ferry UK ... 69 C
Newmarket Canada ... 94 B
Newnham UK ... 66 D
Newport Cru USA ... 66 D
Newport UK ... 66 D
Newport USA ... 90 B

Newport Beach USA...91 E6
Newquay UK...70 A6
Nez Perce N His USA...92 A1
Ngai-Ndethya G Res Kenya...89 G4
Ngorongoro Con Area, UN N Tanzania...61 A5
Ngorongoro Crater Mtn Tanzania...89 G3
Nha Trang Cru Vietnam...59 A8
Niagara Falls USA...94 B9
Niagara Falls Canada...94 B9
Niagara Falls Wfall Canada/USA...94 B9
Niamey Apt Niger...55 A5
Nias Cru Indonesia...59 A8
Nicaragua...59 B9
Nice Apt France...73 F2
Nice Cru France...59 C2
Nice France...72 F2
Nice-Côte d'Azur Apt France...72 F2
Nicobar Is....55 A8
Nidda Riv Germany...75 E6
Nideggen Germany...76 B1
Nidri Greece...83 H1
Niebüll Germany...74 D2
Niederau Austria...77 F3
Niederbayern Reg Germany...76 A2
Niedere Tauern Reg Austria...77 F8
Niederlausitz Reg Germany...76 A1
Niederösterreich Adm Austria...77 D4
Niedersachsen Adm Germany...76 A1
Nienburg Germany...74 E4
Nieuwpoort Belgium...65 C1
Nieuwpoort-aan-Zee Belgium...65 C1
Nieves, Pico de las Mtn Canary Is....80 E2
Niger...88 A2
Nigeria...88 A2
Niihau I Hawaiian Is....91 C2
Nijar Spain...80 D4
Nijmegen Netherlands...65 B11
Nikitas Greece...85 A13
Nikitas Bch Greece...85 A13
Nikolayevsk Russian Fed....86 C1
Nile Riv Egypt...89 F3
Nile Delta Egypt...89 F1
Nile Valley Egypt...89 F
Nilometer Egypt...89 F6
Nim li punit Belize...95 F4
Nîmes France...73 A2
Ninety Six N His USA...93 A8
Ningbo Cru China...59 A8
Niokolo-Koba N Pk, UN N Sénégal...61 A5
Niort France...72 C3
Nipigon, Lake Canada...94 A7
Nipissing, Lake Canada...94 B1
Nisi, Paleá Epidavros Bch Greece...85 A13
Nispero Honduras...95 F6
Nissáki Greece...83 G1
Nissiros I Greece...83 J8
Nitra Slovak Rep....86 B1
Nitray Ch France...72 C2
Niue I...54 A1
Nivelles Belgium...65 B14
Nizhny Novgorod Russian Fed....86 A2
Noatak N Pres USA...92 A9
Nogent-le-Rotrou France...72 C2
Nohcacab Mexico...95 F2
Nohmul Belize...95 F4
Nola Italy...78 B1
Noli Italy...79 F5
Nolton Haven Bch UK...68 A5
Nong Nooch Garden Thailand...96 D4
Nonthaburi Thailand...96 D1
Noord Beveland I Netherlands...65 B10
Noord Brabant Adm Netherlands...65 B11
Noord Holland Adm Netherlands...65 B7
Noordoostpolder Netherlands...65 B7
Noordwijk aan Zee Netherlands...65 B6
Noordzee Kanaal Netherlands...65 B7
Nora Sardinia...78 D4
Nord, Gandia Bch Spain...84 A9
Nord, Lido di Metaponto Bernalda Bch Italy...85 A11
Nord, Peñiscola Bch Spain...84 A2
Nord, Torreblanca Bch Spain...84 A2
Nord-Ostsee-Kanal Germany...74 E2
Nord-Pas-de-Calais Adm France...72 A1
Norddeich Germany...74 D3
Norden Germany...74 C3
Nordenham Germany...74 D3
Norderney I Germany...74 F3
Norderstadt Germany...74 F3
Nordeste Azores...82 B1
Nordfriesland Reg Germany...74 D2
Nordhausen Germany...74 F5
Nordhorn Germany...74 C4
Nördlingen Germany...75 F8
Nordrhein-Westfalen Adm Germany...76 A1
Nordstrand I Germany...74 D2
Norfolk Adm UK...68 A5
Norfolk I....90 A8
Norfolk I....59 A9
Noril'sk Russian Fed....86 A4
Norman Wells Canada...94 A1
Norte Adm Portugal...82 B1
North Bay Canada...94 B1
North Bay, Scarborough Bch UK...68 A4
North Berwick UK...66 B4
North Cape...59 A4
North Cape Cruise Area...59 A4
North Carolina Adm USA...90 A8
North Cascades N Pk USA...91 A1
North Conway USA...90 B3
North Dakota Adm USA...91 D6
North Downs Reg UK...66 E3
North I....55 A9
North Land I. Russian Fed....86 A4
North Rhine-Westphalia Adm Germany...76 A1
North Saskatchewan Riv Canada...94 C2
North Sea Ferry UK...69 C
North Siberian Plain Russian Fed....87 A5
North Uist I UK...70 A1
North West Reg UK...68 A4
North West Adm South Africa...88 B1
North York Moors N Pk UK...67 F3
North Yorkshire Adm UK...68 A4
North-East Aegean Is. Reg Greece...83 J5
Northampton UK...70 A5
Northamptonshire Adm UK...68 A5
Northeast Passage Cruise Area...58 A2
Northeast, The Reg USA...90 A4
Northeim Germany...74 F5
Northern Cape Adm South Africa...88 B2
Northern Capitals Cruise Area...59 A4
Northern Hills Reg Thailand...96 A1
Northern Ireland UK...66 A1
Northern Mariana Is....55 A9
Northern Transvaal Adm South Africa...88 B1
Northington: The Grange EH UK...67 F6
Northumberland N Pk UK...68 A3
Northumberland Adm UK...68 A3
Northumbria Reg UK...68 A3
Northwest Territories Adm Canada...94 A2
Norway...56 A2
Norwegian Fjords Cruise Area...59 A4
Norwegian Sea...56 A2
Norwich Apt UK...70 A5
Norwich UK...70 A5
Nostra Señora de Guadalupe Portugal...82 E5

Nostra Senyora de Cura, Santuari de Mallorca...81 G4
Nosy Bé Cru Madagascar...59 A5
Noto, Golfo di Sicily...78 E4
Nottingham UK...70 A4
Nottinghamshire Adm UK...68 A4
Nouadhibou Apt Mauritania...55 A5
Nouakchott Apt Mauritania...55 A5
Nouméa Apt New Caledonia...55 A9
Nouméa Cru New Caledonia...59 A9
Nova Levante Italy...79 F3
Nova Scotia Adm Canada...94 A8
Novara Italy...79 F6
Novaya Sibir I. Russian Fed....87 B7
Novaya Zemlya Is Russian Fed....86 A3
Novelda Spain...81 E1
Novgorod Russian Fed....86 A1
Novi Sad Yugo, FR....86 C2
Novosibirsk Russian Fed....86 A4
Noyon France...65 B17
Ntamouchari, Mourési Bch Greece...85 A12
Ntrasiza, Portohéli Bch Greece...85 A13
Nubian Desert Sudan...88 A1
Nueß Germany...75 B5
Nuku'alofa Cru Tonga...59 A9
Nukus Uzbekistan...86 A3
Nunavik Reg Canada...94 A7
Nuneaton UK...66 D2
Nuoro Sardinia...78 D2
Nürburg Germany...76 C1
Nürburgring Germany...76 C1
Nuremberg Apt Germany...75 G7
Nürnberg Apt Germany...75 G7
Nürnberg Germany...78 D1
Nurra, La Reg Sardinia...78 D1
Nuuk Apt Greenland...54 A4
Nuw-weldberge Reg South Africa...88 C2
Nyali Kenya...89 G4
Nyborg Denmark...74 F1
Nyeri Kenya...89 G3
Nyfida, Polihnitos Bch Greece...85 A13
Nykøbing Denmark...74 G2
Nymans Garden NT UK...67 F6
Nyon Switzerland...77 E5

Oahu I Hawaiian Is....91 C5
Oakland USA...91 E3
Oasis de Nazaret Canary Is....80 B3
Oaxaca UN C Mexico...62 B1
Oaxaca Mexico...95 E4
Ob Estuary Russian Fed....86 A3
Oban Ferry UK...69 B2
Oban UK...70 A2
Ober Engadin Reg Switzerland...77 E8
Oberau Austria...77 F3
Oberbayern Reg Germany...76 A2
Oberfranken Reg Germany...76 A2
Obergurgl Austria...77 F6
Oberhausen Germany...74 B5
Oberhof Germany...75 F6
Oberinntal Reg Austria...77 F6
Oberlausitz Reg Germany...76 A1
Oberndorf Austria...77 F4
Oberösterreich Adm Austria...77 D3
Oberpfalz Reg Germany...75 H7
Oberpfalzerwald Reg Germany...75 H7
Obersaxen Switzerland...77 E3
Oberstdorf Germany...75 F9
Oberstein Germany...77 H4
Obertauern Austria...77 F8
Obertraun Austria...77 F8
Obervellach Austria...77 F8
Oberwesel Germany...76 C4
Ocala USA...91 D3
Ocean World Water Park Thailand...96 D4
Ochil Hills UK...66 B2
Ocho Rios Cru Jamaica...58 B6
Ochsenfurt Germany...75 G7
Ocmulgee N Mon USA...93 A8
October Revolution I. Russian Fed....86 A4
Oddicombe, Torbay Bch UK...68 A6
Odeceixe Portugal...82 E1
Odelette Portugal...82 E4
Odelouca Riv Portugal...82 E2
Ödemis Turkey...83 J6
Odense Denmark...74 F1
Odenwald Reg Germany...76 B4
Oder Riv Germany...74 J4
Odessa Apt Ukraine...56 A12
Odessa Cru Ukraine...59 C4
Odessa Ukraine...86 A1
Odiáxere Portugal...82 E6
Odra Riv Poland...74 J3
Oelsnitz Germany...75 H6
Ofanto Riv Italy...78 B2
Offenbach Germany...75 D6
Offenburg Germany...76 B6
Ofidoússa I Greece...83 J8
Ogaden Reg Ethiopia...88 A2
Ogdensburg USA...94 B7
Oglio Riv Italy...77 E8
Oglio Riv Italy...79 F6
Ognon Riv France...75 B9
Ohio Adm USA...90 A4
Ohre Riv Czech Rep....75 I6
Ohrid Yugo, FR....86 B2
Ohrid, Lake UN CN Mac, FYR...64 A11
Öhringen Germany...75 E7
Oise Adm France...72 H2
Oise Riv France...72 H2
Okanagan Riv Canada/USA...94 C4
Okeechobee, Lake USA...91 D6
Okefenokee Swamp USA...91 D3
Okha Russian Fed....87 A6
Okhotsk Russian Fed....87 A6
Okhotsk, Sea of Russian Fed....59 A6
Oklahoma Adm USA...90 A4
Oklahoma City USA...90 A4
Ol-Doinyo Swamp N Pk Kenya...89 G3
Öland I Sweden...56 A7
Olbia Sardinia...78 D2
Olbia Apt Sardinia...78 D2
Old Faithful Geyser USA...91 E3
Old Man of Coniston Mtn UK...66 C4
Old Orchard Beach USA...90 B4
Old Oswestry Hill Fort EH UK...67 F5
Old Sarai Netherlands...87 D1
Old Soar Manor NT UK...67 F6
Oldenburg Germany...74 D3
Oldenburg i.H. Germany...74 F2
Oldenzaal Netherlands...74 B4
Olhão Portugal...82 E7
Olhos de Água Portugal...82 E7
Oliena Sardinia...78 D2
Olifants Riv South Africa...88 C1
Olifants Riv South Africa...88 C1
Olimbiáda Greece...85 A13
Olimbiáda Bch Greece...85 A13
Ólimbos Greece...83 J11
Ólimbos Greece...83 J8
Olinda UN C Brazil...62 A3
Oliva Spain...84 A9
Olkhon I. Russian Fed....87 A6
Oloron-Ste-Marie France...72 D1
Olot Spain...80 C2
Olpe Germany...75 C5
Olten Switzerland...77 E3
Ölü Deniz Turkey...83 J9

Olympia UN CN Greece...64 A11
Olympia Greece...83 F1
Olympia USA...90 A1
Olympic N Pk, UN N USA...90 A1
Omaha USA...90 A3
Oman...59 A7
Oman, Gulf of...59 A7
Omiroupoli Greece...85 A13
Ommen Netherlands...65 B8
Omo Lower Valley UN C Ethiopia...63 A5
Omsk Russian Fed....86 A3
Onega, Lake Russian Fed....86 A2
Oneida Lake USA...94 B10
Ontario Adm Canada...94 A7
Ontario, Lake Canada/USA...94 B10
Oost Vlaanderen Belgium...65 B14
Oostduinkerke-Bad Belgium...65 C1
Oostende Apt Belgium...65 C1
Oostende Belgium...65 C1
Oostende Ferry Belgium...69 D4
Oosterbeek Bat Netherlands...65 B7
Opera, Nice Bch France...84 A3
Oporto Apt Portugal...56 A9
Oporto Cru Portugal...59 C4
Oporto Portugal...82 A1
Oppenheim Germany...76 C4
Opryland USA USA...93 A8
Oran Apt Algeria...56 A13
Orange UN C France...64 A6
Orange Free State Adm South Africa...88 B2
Orangeville Canada...94 B5
Oranienburg Germany...74 I4
Oranjestad Cru Aruba...58 B10
Orbe Switzerland...77 E1
Orcival France...73 A1
Oregon Adm USA...90 A1
Oregon Caves N Mon USA...91 A1
Orenburg Russian Fed....86 A2
Organ Pipe Cactus N Mon USA...92 A5
Orient Mallorca...81 G1
Orient Express Rail...86
Orihuela Spain...81 E3
Orinoco Delta Reg Venezuela...58 B11
Oristano Sardinia...78 D3
Oristano, Golfo di Sardinia...78 D3
Orkney Adm UK...70 A7
Orkney Is. UK...70 A7
Orlando Apt USA...91 D6
Orlando USA...91 D6
Orléans France...72 C2
Orléans, Île d' Canada...94 B4
Orly Apt France...72 H3
Ormea Italy...79 F5
Ormília Greece...85 A13
Ormond Beach USA...91 D4
Ormos Lo, Omiroupoli Bch Greece...85 A13
Ormuz Iran...87 D4
Orne Italy...79 F2
Oropesa Spain...84 A2
Óros, Ídi Mtn Crete...83 J10
Orosei Sardinia...78 D2
Orosei, Golfo di Sardinia...78 D2
Orta Italy...79 F2
Ortakent, Bodrum Bch Turkey...85 A13
Orte Italy...78 C1
Orthez France...72 D1
Ortisei Italy...79 F3
Orval, Abbaye-d' Belgium...65 B19
Orvieto Italy...78 C1
Orzola Canary Is....80 B3
Osaka Apt Japan...55 A8
Osawa Canada...94 B9
Osborne House EH UK...67 F6
Oslo Apt Norway...56 A7
Oslo Cru Norway...59 A4
Osnabrück Germany...74 D4
Ospedaletti Italy...79 F9
Oste Riv Germany...74 E3
Ostend Apt Belgium...65 C1
Ostend Belgium...65 C1
Ostend Ferry Belgium...69 D4
Osterholz-Scharmbeck Germany...74 D3
Osterode Germany...74 F5
Ostfriesische Inseln Is Germany...74 C3
Ostfriesland Reg Germany...74 A1
Ostia Italy...78 C3
Ostrava Czech Rep....86 B1
Ostrov Czech Rep....75 H6
Ostuni Italy...85 A12
Oswego Riv USA...94 B10
Oswego USA...94 B10
Oswiecim Poland...86 B1
Otava Riv Czech Rep....75 I7
Ottaviano Italy...78 B3
Ottawa Apt Canada...94 B3
Ottawa Riv Canada...94 B7
Ottawa Canada...94 B7
Ötztal Reg Austria...77 F6
Ötztaler Alpen Mtns Austria/Italy...77 F6
Ötztaler Alpen Mtns Austria/Italy...77 F6
Ouagadougou Apt Burkina Faso...55 A5
Ouarzazate Morocco...89 E4
Oudenaarde Belgium...65 B14
Oudewater Netherlands...65 B7
Oudna Tunisia...89 D2
Oudref Tunisia...89 D4
Oudtshoorn South Africa...88 C7
Oued Zem Morocco...89 E2
Ouerrha Riv Morocco...89 E2
Ouessant, Île d' France...72 B1
Oujda Morocco...89 E2
Oukaïmeden Morocco...89 E3
Oulu Apt Finland...56 A7
Ouranópoli Greece...83 J1
Ouranópoli Bch Greece...85 A13
Ouro Preto UN C Brazil...62 A3
Oursinières, Le Pradet Bch France...84 A3
Ourthe Riv Belgium...65 B15
Outão Portugal...82 D7
Outeniqua Mountains South Africa...88 C7
Outeniqua Pass South Africa...88 C7
Outer Hebrides Reg UK...66 A1
Outer Mongolia...68 A6
Overbecks Museum and garden NT UK...67 F6
Overflakkee I Netherlands...65 B10
OverIJssel Adm Netherlands...65 B8
Overloon Netherlands...65 B11
Ovest, Bonassola Bch Italy...84 A3
Ovest, Déiva Marina Bch Italy...84 A3
Oviedo Spain...80 A1
Owasco Lake USA...94 B10
Oxburgh Hall NT UK...67 F5
Oxford UK...70 A5
Oxfordshire Adm UK...68 A5
Oxkintok Mexico...95 F2
Oxnard USA...91 E5
Oxus Riv Kazakhstan...87 D2
Oxwych Bay Bch UK...68 A5
Oyster Bay South Africa...88 C8
Ozark Plateau USA...90 A7

Paar Riv Germany...75 G8
Paarl South Africa...88 C5
Pacheia Ammos, Paleohóra Bch Crete...85 A13
Pachuca Mexico...95 E2
Pacific Ocean...58
Pacific Palisades Hawaiian Is....91 C5

Pacific Rim N Pk Canada...94 C3
Pacific States, The Reg USA...90 A1
Padang Cru Indonesia...59 A8
Paderborn Germany...74 D5
Paderne Portugal...82 E7
Padova Italy...79 F7
Padre I. N Sea USA...93 A7
Padua Italy...79 F7
Paestum Italy...78 B4
Pago Pago Cru American Samoa...58 A1
Pagoi Greece...85 A12
Paharpur UN C Bangladesh...63 C1
Paignton, Torbay Bch UK...68 A6
Paillon Epi, Nice Bch France...84 A3
Paimpol France...72 B2
Pais Vasco Adm Spain...81 A1
Paisley UK...66 B3
Pajón Mexico...95 F3
Pakistan...55 A8
Palafrugell Spain...80 C2
Palais de la Mer, Nice Bch France...84 A3
Palamós Spain...80 C2
Palatka USA...91 D3
Palau Sardinia...78 D2
Paleá Epidavros Greece...85 A13
Paleá Epidavros Bch Greece...85 A13
Palékastro Crete...83 J11
Palenque UN C Mexico...62 B1
Palenque N Pk, UN C Mexico...62 B1
Palenque Mexico...95 F3
Paleo Faliro Greece...83 J10
Paleohóra Crete...83 J10
Paleokastritsa Greece...83 G1
Paleókipos Greece...85 A13
Palermo Apt Italy...78 E1
Palermo Sicily...78 E1
Páleros Greece...83 H1
Palestrina Italy...78 C3
Palm Beach Cru USA...58 B2
Palm Beach USA...91 D6
Palm Springs USA...91 E6
Palma de Mallorca Apt Mallorca...81 G1
Palma de Mallorca Cru Mallorca...59 C2
Palma de Mallorca Mallorca...81 G1
Palma del Rio Spain...80 D2
Pálmas, Golfo di Sardinia...78 D3
Palmela Portugal...82 D7
Palmyra UN C Syria...64 A12
Palmyra Syria...87 D4
Palo Alto Battlefield N His USA...93 A7
Palopo Cru Indonesia...59 A8
Palos, Cabo de Cape Spain...81 E3
Palouki, Amaliáda Bch Greece...85 A12
Pamir Mtns Tajikistan...87 D2
Pampelonne Chavarel, Ramatuelle Bch France...84 A3
Pampelonne Grand Vallat, Ramatuelle Bch France...84 A3
Pampelonne Neptune, Ramatuelle Bch France...84 A3
Pamplona Spain...81 A1
Pamporovo Bulgaria...83 J6
Pamukkale Turkey...85 A13
Panagía Bch Greece...85 A13
Panagiá Bch Greece...85 A13
Panama...95 D5
Panama Canal Panama...58 B9
Panama City Apt Panama...54 A3
Panama City USA...91 D2
Panarea, Ísola Sicily...78 E2
Panaro Riv Italy...79 F7
Pandeleimónas Greece...85 A12
Pandeleimónas Bch Greece...85 A12
Pangkor I Malaysia...96 A2
Panormos, Skópelos Bch Greece...85 A13
Pantai Aceh F Res Malaysia...96 B1
Pantelleria, Ísola di Italy...78 A2
Papa Nero, Mourési Bch Greece...85 A12
Papeete Apt French Polynesia...54 A1
Papeete Cru French Polynesia...58 A1
Papenburg Germany...74 C3
Papendorp South Africa...88 C1
Paphos Apt Cyprus...56 A16
Paphos UN C Cyprus...64 A12
Papikinou, Adámanta Bch Greece...85 A13
Papineau-Labelle P Res Canada...94 B3
Papua New Guinea...55 A9
Paradise Bay Cru Antarctica...59 A10
Paradise Bay Malta...79 G1
Paradise Bay Malta...83 J9
Paradisi Apt Greece...83 J8
Paraguay...54 A3
Parais, Villajoyosa Bch Spain...84 A9
Paralia Greece...85 A12
Paralia Bch Greece...85 A12
Paralia Mándras, Mándra Bch Greece...85 A6
Paralía Nagou, Kardámila Bch Greece...85 A13
Paralío Astros Greece...85 A12
Paramaribo Apt Suriname...54 A3
Parc Astérix France...72 B1
N pk du Manovo-Gounda St Floris UN N C.A.R....61 A5
Parchim Germany...74 G3
Parepare Cru Indonesia...59 A8
Parga, Ponta do Cape Madeira...82 C1
Paris France...72 H3
Paris: Charles de Gaulle Apt France...73 H2
Paris: Le Bourget Apt France...72 H2
Paris: Orly Apt France...73 H3
Paris: Seine UN CN France...64 A6
Parish Closes Reg France...72 B1
Parma Italy...79 F7
Páros Apt Greece...83 J8
Páros Greece...83 J8
Páros I Greece...83 J8
Parry Is. Canada...54 A2
Parry Sound Canada...94 B5
Partenen Austria...77 F5
Parthenay France...72 C3
Pasadena USA...91 E6
Pascagoula USA...91 D1
Pasewalk Germany...74 I3
Pasir Panjang Bay Malaysia...96 B3
Pasir Ras New Town Singapore...96 C2
Passage to India Cruise Area...59 A5
Pássaro, Capo Sicily...78 I8
Passau Germany...75 I8
Passendale Bat Belgium...65 B13
Pate I. Kenya...89 G4
Paterson South Africa...88 C7
Pátmos I Greece...83 J8
Pátra Greece...83 G1
Patras Greece...83 G1
Pattadakal UN C India...63 C2
Pattaya Cru Thailand...59 A8
Pattaya Thailand...96 D4
Patterdale UK...66 C2
Pátzcuaro Mexico...95 E1
Pau Riv France...72 D1
Pau France...72 D2
Paul de Serra Reg Madeira...82 C1
Paul Bridge South Africa...88 C7
Paulet I. Cru Antarctica...59 A10
Pavia Italy...79 F6
Pavia, Certosa di Italy...79 F6
Pavlodar Kazakhstan...86 A3
Pawai, Pulau Singapore...96 C3

Payerne Switzerland...77 E1
Pays Basque Reg France...72 D1
Pays de la Loire Adm France...72 A1
Pea Ridge N Mil USA...93 A7
Peace Riv Canada...94 C2
Peace River Canada...94 C2
Peak District Reg UK...66 A2
Peak District N Pk UK...67 F4
Pearl City Hawaiian Is....91 C5
Pearl Harbor Hawaiian Is....91 C5
Pearston South Africa...88 C4
Pébrier, Apt Bch France...84 A3
Pecos N His USA...92 A6
Pécs Hungary...86 B2
Peebles UK...66 B4
Peene Germany...74 I3
Péfki Crete...85 A13
Pefkohóri Greece...85 A13
Pefkohóri Bch Greece...85 A13
Pegnitz Riv Germany...75 G7
Pegnitz Germany...75 G7
Peguera Mallorca...81 G3
Peguera Romana, Calvià Bch Mallorca...84 A9
Peguera Tora, Calvià Bch Mallorca...84 A9
Peillon France...72 F2
Peiting Germany...74 F4
Peking Apt China...55 A8
Peking: Imperial Palace UN C China...63 A8
Pélagos I Greece...83 J4
Pelileo Ecuador...83 G1
Pellworm I Germany...74 D2
Pelopónnisos Reg Greece...83 F1
Pembroke Bch Channel Is....68 A8
Pembroke Ferry UK...69 B7
Pembroke Canada...94 B2
Pembroke Coast Reg UK...66 A2
Pembrokeshire Coast N Pk UK...67 F5
Penang Apt Malaysia...96 B3
Penang I Malaysia...96 B
Penara Bukit F Res Malaysia...96 B3
Penbryn Bch UK...68 A5
Pendennis Castle EH UK...67 F6
Peneda, Serra de Reg Portugal...82 A1
Penetanguishene Canada...94 B5
Penfche Portugal...82 A2
Peninsula Apt USA...91 E3
Peñíscola Spain...84 A2
Penjat, Illa des I Ibiza...81 F4
Penmar'ch, Pointe de Cape France...72 B3
Pennines Reg UK...66 A1
Pennsylvania Adm USA...90 A4
Pennsylvania Avenue, Washington N His USA...93 A4
Peno, Carqueiranne Bch France...84 A3
Penobscot Riv USA...90 B2
Penobscot Bay USA...90 B4
Penrhyn Castle NT UK...67 F4
Penrith UK...66 C2
Pensacola USA...91 D1
Penshurst Place UK...66 E3
Penticton Canada...94 C4
Pentland Hills UK...66 B4
Penzance Ferry UK...69 D1
Penzance UK...70 A6
Perai Riv Malaysia...96 B2
Pérama Greece...83 G1
Pereiro Portugal...82 E4
Pergamon Turkey...83 J5
Peristási Greece...85 A12
Peristéra I Greece...83 J4
Perl Germany...76 B3
Perleberg, Brandenburg Germany...74 G3
Perleberg, Niedersachsen Germany...74 G4
Perm Russian Fed....86 A2
Peroulades Greece...85 A12
Perpignan France...72 E2
Perros-Guirec France...72 B1
Perry's Victory & Inter'l Peace Mem. N Mem USA...93 A4
Persepolis UN C Iran...63 A7
Persian Gulf...87 D4
Perth Apt Australia...55 A9
Perth Cru Australia...59 A9
Perth UK...66 B2
Perth Canada...94 B6
Pertuis France...72 F1
Peru...54 A3
Perúgia Italy...79 F12
Pésaro Italy...79 F12
Pescara Italy...78 A2
Pesek, Pulau I Singapore...96 C3
Peshawar Apt Pakistan...55 A8
Pessáda Greece...83 H2
Petäjävesi UN C Finland...64 A3
Petaluma USA...91 E3
Petchaburi Thailand...96 D3
Peterborough Canada...94 B5
Petersburg N Bat USA...93 A8
Petit Bouchorel, Fréjus Bch France...84 A3
Petit Roucas, Marseille Bch France...84 A3
Petit St-Bernard, Col du Pass France/Italy...72 G2
Petra UN C Jordan...64 A12
Petralona Greece...83 J1
Petre, Point Cape Canada...94 B10
Petrified Forest N Pk USA...92 A6
Petroglyph N Mon USA...92 A6
Petropavlovsk-Kamchatsky Russian Fed....87 B7
Petrozavodsk Russian Fed....86 A2
Petworth House NT UK...67 F6
Pevensey Bay Bch UK...68 A6
Pevensey Castle EH UK...67 F6
Peveril Castle EH UK...67 F4
Peyrefite, Cerbère Bch France...84 A2
Pfalz Germany...76 C4
Pfälzer Wald Reg Germany...76 B4
Pfarrkirchen Germany...75 H8
Pfeiffer Big Sur S Pk USA...91 E3
Pforzheim Germany...76 B6
Pfullendorf Germany...76 B8
Phaestos Crete...83 J10
Phanat Nikhom Thailand...96 D4
Phanom Rung Thailand...96 A1
Philadelphia Apt USA...54 B2
Philadelphia USA...90 A4
Philadelphia: Independence Hall UN C USA...62 A2
Philae Egypt...89 F6
Philippi Greece...83 J1
Philippines...55 A8
Philippine Sea...55 A8
Philipsburg Cru St Maarten...58 B7
Phimai Thailand...96 A1
Phitsanulok Thailand...96 A1
Phnom Penh Apt Cambodia...55 A8
Phoenix Apt USA...90 A5
Phoenix USA...90 A5
Phra Buddha Sothorp Thailand...96 D1
Phra Pathom Chedi Thailand...96 D1
Phra Phutthabat Thailand...96 D2
Phuket Apt Thailand...55 A8
Phuket Cru Thailand...59 A8
Phuket Thailand...96 A2
Piacenza Italy...79 F6
Piancavallo Italy...79 F4
Piave Riv Italy...79 F3
Piazza Armerina Sicily...78 E4
Piazza Milano, Jésolo Bch Italy...85 A11
Picardie Adm France...72 A1

Picentini, Monti Reg Italy 78 B4
Pickens, Fort USA 91 D1
Pico I Azores 82 B1
Pico Apt Azores 82 B1
Picton Cru New Zealand 59 A9
Picton Canada 94 B6
Pictured Rocks N Lake USA 93 A3
Piedade, Ponta da Cape Portugal 82 E6
Piedmont Adm Italy 78 A1
Piedmonte Matese Italy 78 B1
Piemonte Adm Italy 78 A1
Piedras Negras Guatemala 95 F3
Pierce Reservoirs Singapore 96 C1
Pierre USA 90 A2
Pierrefonds France 72 H2
Pietermaritzburg South Africa 88 B2
Pietersburg South Africa 88 B1
Pietra Ligure Italy 79 F9
Pigadakia Bch Greece 85 A13
Pigi Crete 85 A13
Pigianos Kampos, Pigi Bch Crete 85 A13
Piketberg South Africa 88 C1
Pilaz Italy 79 F1
Piles Spain 84 A9
Piles Bch Spain 84 A9
Pilio Pen Greece 83 J4
Pilsen Czech Rep. 75 I7
Pin de Galles, Le Pradet Bch France 84 A3
Pinang Apt Malaysia 96 B3
Pinang Cru Malaysia 59 A8
Pinang I Malaysia ....96 B
Pinang Bird Park Malaysia 96 B2
Pinang Botanic Gardens Malaysia 96 B1
Pinang Hill Malaysia 96 B1
Pinang Island Bridge Malaysia 96 B4
Pinar, Cap d'es Mallorca 81 G2
Pine I. USA 91 D5
Pine Keys Is USA 91 D7
Pineda, la Spain 80 C3
Pinelands N Res USA 93 A4
Pinerolo Italy 79 F5
Pinnacles N Mon USA 92 A5
Pinneberg Germany 74 E3
Piombino Italy 79 F11
Pioner I. Russian Fed. 86 A4
Pipe Spring N Mon USA 92 A5
Pipestone N Mon USA 93 A3
Piráeus Cru Greece 59 C7
Piráeus Greece 83 J4
Piran Slovenia 79 F8
Pirgadikia Greece 85 A13
Pirgadikia Bch Greece 85 A13
Pirgi Thermiss Greece 85 A13
Pirin N Pk, UN N Bulgaria 61 A4
Pirmasens Germany 76 B5
Pirna Germany 74 H5
Pisa Apt Italy 79 F11
Pisa UN C Italy 64 A6
Pisa Italy 79 F11
Piscataway Park USA 93 A4
Piscine Eau de Mer, Cerbère Bch France 84 A2
Pissarelles, Cap-d'Ail Bch France 84 A3
Pissevaches, Fleury-d'Aude Bch France 84 A2
Pistóia Italy 79 F11
Pitcairn Is. 54 A1
Pitlochry UK 66 B1
Pitstone Windmill NT UK 67 F5
Pittsburgh Apt USA 54 B2
Pittsburgh USA 90 A4
Pittsfield USA 90 B3
Plage au Sud Port, St-Cyprien Bch France 84 A2
Plage Centrale, Canet-en-Rou'n Bch France 84 A2
Plage Centrale, Ste-Marie-la-Mer Bch France 84 A2
Plage Centre, Toreilles Bch France 84 A2
Plage d'en Baux, Port-Vendres Bch France 84 A2
Plage de la Corniche Tunisia 89 D2
Plage de la Coudalère, Le Barcarès Bch France 84 A2
Plage de la Marenda, Canet-en-Rou'n Bch France 84 A2
Plage de la Sardane, Argelès-sur-Mer Bch France 84 A2
Plage des Elmes, Banyuls-sur-Mer Bch France 84 A2
Plage des Pêcheurs, Collioure Bch France 84 A2
Plage Dorée Centre, Sanary-sur-Mer Bch France 84 A3
Plage du 1er Epi, Ste-Marie-la-Mer Bch France 84 A2
Plage du 2ème Epi, Ste-Marie-la-Mer Bch France 84 A2
Plage du 3ème Epi, Ste-Marie-la-Mer Bch France 84 A2
Plage du 4ème Epi, Ste-Marie-la-Mer Bch France 84 A2
Plage du Cala à Gogo, St-Cyprien Bch France 84 A2
Plage du camping, Ste-Marie-la-Mer Bch France 84 A2
Plage du Faubourg, Collioure Bch France 84 A2
Plage du Jimmy's, St-Cyprien Bch France 84 A2
Plage du Lido, Canet-en-Roussillon Bch France 84 A2
Plage du Lydia, Le Barcarès Bch France 84 A2
Plage du Mar Estang, Canet-en-Rou'n Bch France 84 A2
Plage du Mas Larrieu, Argelès-sur-Mer Bch France 84 A2
Plage du Racou, Argelès-sur-Mer Bch France 84 A2
Plage du Roussillon, Canet-en-Rou'n Bch France 84 A2
Plage du Sardinal, Canet-en-Rou'n Bch France 84 A2
Plage du Village, Le Barcarès Bch France 84 A2
Plage face station Total, St-Cyprien Bch France 84 A2
Plage Naturiste, Agde Bch France 84 A2
Plage Nord, Port-la-Nouvelle Bch France 84 A2
Plage Nord, Toreilles Bch France 84 A2
Plage P. de Secours no. 3, St-Cyprien Bch France 84 A2
Plage St Vincent Nord, Collioure Bch France 84 A2
Plage St Vincent, Collioure Bch France 84 A2
Plage Sud, Port-la-Nouvelle Bch France 84 A2
Plage Sud, Toreilles Bch France 84 A2
Plagne, la France 72 G2
Plaka, Drépano Bch Greece 85 A12
Plakas Crete 85 A13
Planachaux Switzerland 77 E5
Planicies Reg Portugal 82 A3
Plános Greece 83 H3
Plas Newydd house NT UK 67 F4
Plas-yn-Rhiw house and garden NT UK 67 F5
PLasy Czech Rep. 75 I7
Plata, Rio de la Est. 58 A3
Platamónes Greece 85 A12
Platamónas Bch Greece 85 A12
Plati Rivi Sicily 78 D3
Plátanias Crete 83 J10
Plátanias Bch Crete 85 A13
Platanias-Agia Paraskevi, Skiathos Bch Greece 85 A13
Platanitis, Marónia Bch Greece 85 A6
Plati Gialo, Mikonos Bch Greece 85 A13
Platja d'Aro Spain 80 C2
Platja d'Aro, Castell-Platja d'Aro Bch Spain 84 A2
Platja d'En Bossa Ibiza 81 F3
Platja de Muro Mallorca 81 G2
Platja de Muro Bch Mallorca 81 G2
Platja de Palma, P. de Mallorca Bch Mallorca 84 A2
Platja de Tossa, Tossa de Mar Bch Spain 84 A2
Platja dels Dols Mallorca 81 G4
Platja Gran, Palamós Bch Spain 84 A2
Platja Residence, Ostuni Bch Italy 85 A12
Platja Ribes Roges, Vilanova i I Bch Spain 84 A2
Platja Talamanca Ibiza 81 F2
Plattsburgh USA 90 B3
Platys Gialos, Argostóli Bch Greece 85 A12
Plau Germany 74 H3
Plauen Germany 75 H6
Plauer See Lake Germany 74 H3
Playa Blanca Canary Is. 80 B3

Playa de Las Americas Canary Is. 80 B1
Playa del Carmen Cru Mexico 58 B5
Playa del Carmen Mexico 95 F2
Playa del Inglés Canary Is. 80 B2
Playa Paraíso Canary Is. 80 B1
Plaz Dimou, Alexandroúpoli Bch Greece 85 A6
Plechy Mtn Austria/Czech Rep. 75 I8
Plessis-Bourré, le Ch France 72 C1
Plettenberg Bay South Africa 88 C7
Plitvice Lakes N Pk, UN N Croatia 61 A4
Plitvice Lakes Reg Croatia 79 F8
Ploërmel France 72 B4
Plomári Greece 85 A13
Plön Germany 74 F2
Plöner See Lake Germany 74 F2
Plouha France 72 B2
Plovdiv Bulgaria 86 B2
Plsek Czech Rep. 75 J7
Plymouth Cru Montserrat 58 B7
Plymouth Ferry UK 69 D2
Plymouth Apt UK 70 A6
Plymouth UK 70 A6
Plzen Czech Rep. 86 B1
Po Riv Italy 79 F7
Po Basin Reg Italy 79 F7
Podgorica Yugo, FR 86 B2
Poel I Germany 74 G2
Poiana Brasov Romania 86 B2
Poincaré, Nice Bch France 84 A3
Point Reyes N Sea USA 92 A1
Pointe Seraphine Cru St Lucia 58 B11
Pointe-à-Pitre Cru Guadeloupe 58 B7
Pointe-Noire Rep Congo 55 A5
Poitou Reg France 72 C3
Poitou-Charentes Adm France 72 A1
Poland 86 B1
Police Poland 74 J3
Poliegos I Greece 83 J7
Poligiros Greece 85 A13
Poligiros Bch Greece 85 A13
Polihnitos Greece 85 A13
Polihrono Greece 85 A13
Polihrono Bch Greece 85 A13
Póllica Mallorca 81 G2
Póllica Italy 85 A11
Polonnaruwa UN C Sri Lanka 63 C2
Polotsk Belarus 86 A1
Polumanac'h France 72 B1
Polynesia Is. 54 A1
Polzeath UK 68 A6
Pomerania Reg Poland 86 B1
Pommersche Bucht Bay 74 J2
Pompano Beach USA 91 D7
Pomposa Abbazia Italy 78 B3
Poniente, Benidorm Bch Spain 84 A9
Poniente-Almerimar, El Ejido Bch Spain 84 A8
Poniente-Sirena Loca, Adra Bch Spain 84 A8
Pont du Gard UN C France 64 A2
Pont-Aven France 72 B3
Pont-l'Abbé Apt Azores 82 E5
Pontal Cape Portugal 82 E5
Pontarlier France 72 G2
Ponte di Legno Italy 79 F3
Pontecagnano Italy 78 B3
Pontivy France 72 B4
Pontresina Switzerland 77 E8
Poole UK 68 A6
Poole Ferry UK 69 D2
Poperinge Belgium 65 B13
Popeye Village Malta 79 G1
Popocatepetl UN C Mexico 62 B1
Popocatepetl Mtn Mexico 95 E4
Pópoli Italy 78 C2
Poppit, St Dogmaels Bch UK 68 A5
Pordenone Italy 79 F4
Pornichet France 72 B4
Póros Greece 83 H2
Póros I Greece 83 J7
Poros, Eloúnda Bch Crete 85 A13
Porquerolles, Île de France 72 F3
Port Alberni Canada 94 C3
Port Askaig Ferry UK 69 B2
Port Aventura Spain 80 C3
Port Beaufort South Africa 88 C6
Port Blair Cru India 59 A8
Port Canaveral Cru USA 58 B2
Port Canaveral USA 91 D6
Port Charlotte USA 91 D5
Port Chicago Naval Magazine N Mem USA 92 A1
Port d'Addaia Menorca 81 H2
Port d'Alon, St-Cyr-sur-Mer Bch France 84 A3
Port d'es Torrent Ibiza 81 F1
Port d'es Torrent Bch Ibiza 81 F1
Port de Alcúdia Mallorca 81 G2
Port de Andratx Mallorca 81 G3
Port de Pollença Mallorca 81 G2
Port de Sagunto Bch Spain 84 A9
Port de San Miquel, St Joan de Labritja Bch Ibiza 84 A9
Port de Sóller Mallorca 81 G1
Port de St Miquel Ibiza 81 F2
Port de St-Ayguif, Fréjus Bch France 84 A3
Port Elizabeth Apt South Africa 88 C8
Port Elizabeth South Africa 88 C8
Port Ellen Ferry UK 69 B2
Port Everglades Cru USA 58 B2
Port Gallice, Antibes Bch France 84 A3
Port Grimaud France 84 A3
Port Hope Canada 94 B5
Port Issol, Sanary-sur-Mer Bch France 84 A3
Port Kelang Cru Malaysia 59 A8
Port Lockroy Cru Antarctica 59 A10
Port Louis Cru Mauritius 59 A5
Port Moresby Apt Papua New Guinea 55 A9
Port Moresby Cru Papua New Guinea 59 A9
Port of Spain Apt Trinidad 54 A3
Port of Spain Cru Trinidad & Tobago 58 B11
Port Pin, Marseille Bch France 84 A3
Port Roig, Son Servera Bch Mallorca 84 A9
Port Said Cru Egypt 59 C8
Port Said Egypt 89 F2
Port Shepstone South Africa 88 B2
Port Soif Bch Channel Is. 68 A8
Port Stanley Cru Falkland Is. 59 A10
Port Talbot UK 70 A5
Port Vell, Son Servera Bch Mallorca 84 A9
Port Victoria Cru Seychelles 59 A5
Port Vila Cru Vanuatu 59 A9
Port-au-Prince Apt Haiti 54 A3
Port-au-Prince Cru Haiti 58 B6
Port-Barcarès France 72 E2
Port-Cros, Île de France 73 F3
Port-Grimaud France 84 A3
Port-la-Nouvelle France 84 A2
Port-Leucate France 84 A2
Port-Pothuau les Salins, Hyères Bch France 84 A3
Port-Royal-des-Champs, Abbaye de France 72 H3
Port-Vendres France 84 A2
Portage la Prairie Canada 94 A6
Portalagre Portugal 82 A2

Portals Nous Mallorca 81 G3
Portbou Spain 80 C2
Portbou Bch Spain 84 A2
Porté-Puymorens France 72 E1
Porteghetto, Cervo Bch Italy 84 A3
Portela Madeira 82 D2
Portela de Sacavém Apt Portugal 82 D2
Portes, Punta de ses Cape Ibiza 81 F3
Porthmeor Bch UK 68 A4
Porthos Italy 78 B3
Portici Italy 78 B3
Portimão Portugal 82 E6
Portimão Apt Portugal 82 E6
Portinho da Arrábida Portugal 82 D2
Portinax Ibiza 81 F2
Portiragnes France 84 A2
Portland Apt USA 54 A2
Portland USA 90 B4
Portland, Maine USA 90 B4
Portland, Oregon USA 90 A1
Porto Apt Portugal 56 A9
Porto Cru Portugal 59 C1
Porto Portugal 82 A1
Porto Azzurro Italy 79 F11
Porto Canale Nord, Cesenático Bch Italy 85 A4
Porto Canale Sud, Cesenático Bch Italy 85 A4
Pórto Carras, Néos Marmarás Bch Greece 85 A13
Porto Cervo Sardinia 78 D2
Porto Colom Mallorca 81 G4
Porto Cristo Mallorca 81 G2
Porto da Cruz Madeira 82 C2
Porto Garibaldi Italy 79 F8
Porto Gulf UN N France 61 A4
Porto Lágos, Néa Kessáni Bch Greece 85 A6
Porto Limón Cru Costa Rica 58 B9
Porto Madryn Cru Argentina 58 A3
Porto Mont Cru Chile 58 A3
Porto Plata Cru Dominican Rep. 58 B6
Porto Moniz Madeira 82 C1
Porto Petro Mallorca 81 G4
Porto Pidocchio, Framura Bch Italy 84 A3
Porto Potenza Picena Italy 79 F12
Porto Pozzo, Sta Teresa Gallura Bch Sardinia 84 A3
Porto Rafael Sardinia 78 D2
Pórto Rafti Greece 83 J7
Porto Recanati Italy 79 F12
Porto Rotondo Sardinia 78 D2
Pórto Tórres Sardinia 78 D1
Porto Santo Apt Madeira 82 C2
Portobelo and San Lorenzo UN C Panama 62 A3
Portoferráio Italy 79 F10
Portofino Italy 79 F6
Portohéli Italy 83 J7
Portohéli Bch Greece 85 A13
Portoroz Slovenia 86 B2
Portoscuso Sardinia 78 D3
Portovénere Italy 79 F10
Portrush UK 68 A3
Portsmouth Cru Dominica 58 B11
Portsmouth Ferry UK 69 D3
Portsmouth UK 70 A6
Portsmouth USA 90 A4
Portugal 82
Posada Sardinia 78 D2
Posato, Monéglia Bch Italy 84 A3
Poschiavo Switzerland 77 E8
Poseidi, Kalándra Bch Greece 85 A12
Poseidon, Temple of Greece 83 J7
Posíllipo Italy 78 B3
Positano Italy 78 B3
Posada USA 78 B3
Poste de secours central, Valras Bch France 84 A2
Poste de secours, Narbonne Bch France 84 A2
Potala Palace UN C China 63 A8
Potamos, Mália Bch Crete 85 A13
Potenza Italy 78 B3
Potosi UN C Bolivia 62 A3
Potsdam UN C Germany 64 A4
Potsdam Germany 74 I4
Poverty Point N Mon USA 93 A4
Póvoa de Varzim Portugal 82 A1
Povoaçao Azores 82 B1
Powis Castle NT UK 67 F5
Powys Adm UK 70 A5
Poza Rica Mexico 95 E2
Poznan Poland 86 B1
Pozza di Fassa Italy 79 F3
Pozzallo Sicily 78 D3
Pozzuoli Italy 78 B3
Pra-Loup France 72 F2
Prachin Buri Thailand 96 D2
Prades France 72 E2
Præstø Denmark 74 H1
Prague Apt Czech Rep. 56 A6
Prague Czech Rep. 86 B1
Prague UN C Czech Rep. 75 J6
Praha Cru Czech Rep. 75 J6
Praia da Luz Portugal 82 E5
Praia da Rocha Portugal 59 C5
Praia da Rocha Portugal 82 E6
Praia das Macas Portugal 82 D1
Praia de Balaia Portugal 82 E7
Praia de Galé Portugal 82 E6
Praia de Oura Portugal 82 E7
Praia de Vale do Lobo Portugal 82 E7
Praia Grande Portugal 82 D1
Praia Parede Portugal 82 D1
Praia Verde Portugal 82 E8
Prainha Madeira 82 C2
Prambanan UN C Indonesia 63 A10
Pramousquier, Le Lavandou Bch France 84 A3
Pramouton France 72 F2
Prat d'en Fores, Cambrils de Mar Bch Spain 84 A2
Prat Mataou France 72 E1
Prato Italy 79 F11
Prats-de-Mollo France 72 E2
Prazeres Madeira 82 C1
Preetz Germany 74 F2
Premnitz Germany 74 H4
Prenzlau Germany 74 I3
Presqu'ile de Crozon Reg France 72 B1
Prerow Germany 74 H2
Prešov Czech Rep. 75 J7
Prestige Czech Rep. 75 I7
Preston UK 70 A4
Prestwick Apt UK 70 A3
Pretoria and Witwatersrand Adm South Africa 88 B1
Préveza Greece 83 H1
Příbram Czech Rep. 75 J7
Priene Turkey 83 J9
Prignitz Reg Germany 74 H4
Prince Albert South Africa 88 C6
Prince Albert Road South Africa 88 C6
Prince Alfreds Pass South Africa 88 C7
Prince Charles I. Canada 94 A3
Prince Edward I. Adm Canada 94 A8
Prince Edward I. 55 A5
Prince George Canada 94 C1
Prince of Wales I. Canada 94 A5
Prince Rupert Apt Canada 54 A2
Prince Rupert Cru Canada 58 A1
Prince Rupert Bay Cru Dominica 58 B11
Prince William I Pk USA 92 A5
Princes Is. Turkey 83 J3
Prínos Greece 85 A13
Prínos Dasylio, Prínos Bch Greece 85 A13
Pristina Yugo, FR 86 B2
Pritzwalk Germany 74 H3
Priverno Italy 78 B3
Prócida, Isola di Italy 78 B3

Profondeville Belgium 65 B15
Progreso Mexico 95 F2
Prophete, Marseille Bch France 84 A3
Provence Reg France 72 F1
Provence-Alpes-Côte d'Azur Adm France 73 A2
Providence USA 90 A4
Providence Apt USA 90 A4
Providencia, Isla de 95 D5
Prüm Germany 76 B3
Prūm Riv Germany 76 B3
Psakoudia, Ormília Bch Greece 85 A13
Psará I Greece 83 J5
Psaropoula Kanari, Ródos Bch Greece 85 A13
Psérimos I Greece 83 J8
Pte Rouge, Marseille Bch France 84 A3
Pu'uhonua o Honaunau N His Hawaiian Is. 91 C8
Pubblico Macello, Ospedaletti Bch Italy 84 A3
Pudent, Estany Lag Formentera 81 F4
Puebla UN C Mexico 62 B1
Puebla Mexico 95 E4
Puerto Ángel Mexico 95 E4
Puerto Banús Spain 80 D6
Puerto Barrios Guatemala 95 F6
Puerto de la Cruz Canary Is. 80 B1
Puerto de Mazarrón Spain 81 E3
Puerto del Carmen Canary Is. 80 B3
Puerto del Rosario Canary Is. 80 B5
Puerto Escondido Mexico 95 E4
Puerto Limón Cru Costa Rica 58 B9
Puerto Madryn Cru Argentina 58 A3
Puerto Mont Cru Chile 58 A3
Puerto Plata Cru Dominican Rep. 58 B6
Puerto Rey-El Playazo, Vera Bch Spain 84 B2
Puerto Rico Canary Is. 80 B2
Puerto Rico I. 95 D3
Puerto Vallarta Cru Mexico 58 A3
Puerto Vallarta Mexico 95 E1
Puglia Adm Italy 79 A2
Pugnochiuso, Vieste Bch Italy 85 A4
Puigcerdà Spain 80 C1
Pula Croatia 79 F8
Pulau Panjang Cru Indonesia 59 A8
Pulau Tikus Malaysia 96 B2
Pulpi Spain 84 A8
Punta Arciera, Anacapri Bch Italy 85 A11
Punta Arenas Cru Chile 58 A3
Punta Caleo, Póllica Bch Italy 85 A11
Punta Campitiello, Anacapri Bch Italy 85 A11
Punta Cannone, Isola la Maddalena Bch Sardinia 84 A3
Punta Carena, Anacapri Bch Italy 85 A11
Punta di Barbacale, Grado Bch Italy 84 A4
Punta Prima Menorca 81 H4
Punta Raisi Apt Sicily 78 E1
Punta San Giorgio, Isola la Maddalena Bch Sardinia 84 A3
Punta Umbria Spain 80 D1
Puntanella, Isola la Maddalena Bch Sardinia 84 A3
Puntarenas Cru Costa Rica 58 B9
Punxsutawney USA 90 A4
Pusan Apt Korea, Rep. 55 A8
Pusan Cru Korea, Rep. 55 A8
Putten I Netherlands 65 B10
Puttgarden Germany 74 G2
Puukohola Heiau N His Hawaiian Is. 91 C8
Puuwai Hawaiian Is. 91 C2
Pwllgwaelod Bch UK 68 A5
PWV Adm South Africa 88 B1
Pyongyang Apt Korea, DPR 55 A8
Pyramid Lake USA 91 E11
Pyrenees Mtns France/Spain ....72 D/E
Pyrénées-Atlantiques Adm France 72 D1
Pyrénées-Occidentales Reg France 72 D1
Pyrénées-Occidentales N Pk France 72 D2
Pyrénées-Orientales France ....72 E
Pyrénées-Orientales Adm France 72 E2

Qal'at al Jundi Egypt 89 F2
Qala Malta 79 G1
Qasr Amra UN C Jordan 64 A12
Qasr Ibrim Egypt 89 F6
Qatar 55 A7
Qattāra Depression Egypt 89 F1
Qawra Malta 79 G2
Qena Egypt 89 F4
Qikitaluk I Canada 94 A3
Quakenbrück Germany 74 F4
Quarry Bank Mill and Styal Country Park NT UK 67 F4
Quarteira Portugal 82 E7
Québec Apt Canada 94 B4
Québec Cru Canada 58 A2
Québec UN C Canada 62 A2
Québec Adm Canada 94 A7
Québec Canada 94 B4
Quedlinburg UN C Germany 64 A6
Quedlinburg Germany 74 G5
Queen Charlotte Is. Canada 94 A5
Queensland wet tropics UN N Australia 61 A9
Queenstown New Town Singapore 96 C2
Quéluz Portugal 82 D1
Quercianella Italy 79 F11
Querétaro Mexico 95 E2
Quesnel Canada 94 C1
Queyras Reg France 72 G4
Quezaltenango Guatemala 95 F5
Qufu UN C China 63 A8
Quiberon France 72 B4
Quillan France 72 E2
Quimper France 72 B3
Quimper Apt France 72 B3
Quimperlé France 72 B3
Quincy USA 91 E1
Quinta do Palheiro Ferreiro Madeira 82 C2
Quiriguá UN C Guatemala 62 B1
Quiriguá Guatemala 95 F6
Quito Apt Ecuador 54 A3
Quito UN C Ecuador 62 A3
Quseir Egypt 89 F4

Raasay Ferry UK 69 B1
Rabat Apt Morocco 89 E2
Rabat Malta 79 G4
Rabat Morocco 89 E2
Rabaul Cru Papua New Guinea 59 A9
Racó de L'Albir, Alfaz del Pi Bch Spain 84 A9
Racó de la Mar, Canet d'En Berenguer Bch Spain 84 A9
Radbuza Riv Czech Rep. 75 H7
Radebeul Germany 75 I5
Radium Hot Springs Canada 94 C4
Radnor Forest UK 67 F5
Radolfzell Germany 75 E9
Raf-Raf Tunisia 89 D1
Raffles Lighthouse Singapore 96 C3
Rafina Greece 83 H3
Ragian Castle Cadw UK 66 D2
Ragley Hall UK 66 D2
Ragusa Sicily 78 D3
Rähes Greece 85 A12
Rähes Bch Greece 85 A12
Rietini, Monti Reg Italy 78 C2
Rieti Italy 78 C2
Rietvlei South Africa 88 B2
Rieux France 72 D2
Rievaulx Abbey EH UK 67 F4
Rievaulx Terrace and Temples NT UK 67 F4
Riezlern Austria 77 F1
Rif Reg Morocco 89 E2
Rift Valley Africa 88 A3
Rift Valley Kenya 89 G1
Riga Apt Latvia 56 A1
Riga Latvia 86 A1
Rijeka Croatia 86 B2

Ramiers His Pk, UN C Haiti 62 A3
Ramla Bay Malta 79 G1
Ramonal Mexico 95 F4
Ramsey Abbey Gatehouse NT UK 67 F5
Ramsgate UK 66 E2
Ramsgate Ferry UK 69 D4
Rance Riv France 72 B2
Rangoon Apt Myanmar 55 A8
Rannoch, Loch UK 66 B1
Rapid City USA 90 A2
Raposeira Portugal 82 E5
Rapperswil Switzerland 77 E3
Rarotonga Apt Cook Is. 54 A1
Râs el Bar Egypt 89 F2
Râs Ghârib Egypt 89 F5
Râs Ghârib Apt Egypt 89 F5
Raso, Cabo Cape Portugal 82 D1
Rastatt Germany 75 D8
Rat Chaburi Thailand 96 D1
Rathenow Germany 74 H4
Rattenberg Austria 77 F3
Ratzeburg Germany 74 F2
Rauma UN C Finland 64 A3
Ravascletto Italy 79 F4
Ravello Italy 66 C3
Ravenglass UK 66 C3
Ravenglass Estuary UK 66 C3
Ravenna Italy 79 F8
Ravensburg Germany 75 E9
Rayon, Antibes Bch France 84 A3
Rayong Thailand 96 D4
Rayy Iran 87 D4
Raz, Pointe de Cape France 72 B1
Ré, Île de France 72 C3
Reading UK 70 A5
Recife Apt Brazil 54 A3
Recife Brazil 58 A3
Recife, Cape South Africa 88 C8
Recklinghausen Germany 74 C5
Recknitz Riv Germany 74 H2
Red Deer Canada 94 C4
Red Hill Patrick Henry N Mem USA 93 A8
Red Sea 59 A7
Redding USA 91 E1
Redeyef Tunisia 89 D3
Redgate, Torbay Bch UK 68 A6
Redon France 72 B4
Redwood N Pk, UN N USA 91 E1
Regen Riv Germany 75 H7
Regen Germany 75 I8
Régence, Nice Bch France 84 A3
Regensburg Germany 75 H7
Réggio de Calabria Italy 78 C2
Réggio nell'Emilia Italy 79 F7
Regina Canada 94 A6
Regnitz Riv Germany 75 G7
Reichenbach Germany 75 H6
Reichenstein, Burg Germany 76 C4
Reichenau UN C Germany 66 C3
Reichshardstein Ch Belgium 65 B16
Reinhardstein Tunisia ....
Remada Tunisia ....
Remagen Germany 76 C1
Remich Luxembourg 65 B20
Remiremont France 75 B5
Remscheid Germany 75 C5
Rendsburg Germany 74 F2
Reni, Ródos Bch Greece 85 A13
Rennes France 72 B4
Rennes Apt France 72 B4
Reno USA 91 E1
Reno Riv Italy 91 E3
Renon Italy 79 F3
Retamar, Almeria Bch Spain 65 B16
Rethel France 65 B16
Réthimno Crete 83 J10
Réthimno Bch Crete 85 A13
Réunion Apt 55 A5
Réunion I. 88 A4
Reus Spain 80 C3
Reuss Riv Switzerland 77 E3
Reutlingen Germany 75 E9
Revelstoke Canada 94 C4
Revelstoke, Mt N Pk Canada 94 C4
Reyes, Point USA 91 E1
Rheda-Wiedenbrück Germany 74 D5
Rhein Riv Germany 76 B6
Rhein Riv Switzerland 77 F4
Rhein-Main Apt Germany 76 C4
Rheinbach Germany 76 C1
Rheine Germany 74 C4
Rheineck, Burg Germany 76 C1
Rheinfels, Burg Germany 76 C4
Rheinhessen Reg Germany 76 C4
Rheinsberg Germany 74 H3
Rhens Germany 76 C1
Rhin Riv France 75 C8
Rhine Riv Germany 76 B6
Rhine Gorge Germany 76 C4
Rhineland-Palatinate Adm Germany 76 A2
Rhir, Cap Morocco 89 E3
Rhode Island USA 90 A4
Rhodes Apt Greece 83 J9
Rhodes UN C Greece 64 A11
Rhodes I Greece 83 J12
Rhodope Bulgaria 86 B2
Rhön Reg Germany 75 F6
Rhône Adm France 72 G1
Rhône Riv France 72 G3
Rhône Riv Germany 77 E6
Rhône au Rhin, Canal du France 75 C8
Rhône-Alps Adm France 73 A2
Rhoscolyn UK 68 A4
Rhosneigr UK 68 A4
Rhubodach Ferry UK 69 B2
Ribatejo Reg Portugal 82 A2
Ribe Denmark 74 G1
Ribeira Grande Azores 82 B1
Ribeira Grande Azores 82 B1
Ribnitz-Damgarten Germany 74 H2
Riccione Italy 79 F12
Richborough Castle EH UK 66 E2
Richelieu France 72 C1
Richelieu, Agde Bch France 84 A2
Richmond South Africa 88 C3
Richmond UK 66 C3
Richmond N Nat USA 93 A8
Ried Austria 75 I8
Riederalp Switzerland 77 E6
Riesa Germany 75 H5

ìla UN C Bulgaria....................................64 A7
ìla Reg Bulgaria......................................86 B2
ìmau, Pulau I Malaysia...........................96 B3
ìmini Italy..79 F12
ìngsted Denmark....................................74 G1
ìnia I Greece..83 J4
ìnteln Germany......................................74 E4
ìio Abiseo N Pk, UN N Peru....................60 A3
ìio Azul Guatemala.................................95 F4
ìio Bec Mexico..95 F4
ìio Carrubo, Ospedaletti Bch Italy...........84 A3
ìio Crosio, Ospedaletti Bch Italy..............84 A3
ìio Crovetto, Spotorno Bch Italy...............84 A3
ìio de Janeiro Apt Brazil..........................54 A3
ìio de Janeiro Cru Brazil..........................58 A3
ìio Formosa Ntr Res Portugal...................82 E7
ìio Jesus Guatemala................................95 F5
ìio Pellotta, Ospedaletti Bch Italy.............84 A3
ìio Platano B Res, UN N Honduras............60 A3
ìio Porrine, Ospedaletti Bch Italy..............95 E2
ìio Verde Mexico.....................................72 G4
ìisoul France..75 E8
ìiR Riv Germany.....................................96 D1
ìiver Kwai Bridge Thailand......................96 D1
ìiversdale South Africa............................88 C6
ìiverside Apt UK.....................................66 B2
ìiverside USA...91 E6
ìiviera Reg France/Italy..........................79 F10
ìiviera di Levante Reg Italy......................79 F10
ìiviera di Ponente Reg Italy.....................79 F9
ìixensart Belgium.................................65 B14
ìiyadh Apt Saudi Arabia.........................55 A7
ìoad Bay Cru Anguilla.............................58 B7
ìob Roy's Grave UK................................66 B1
ìobben I. South Africa.............................88 C5
ìöbel Germany..74 H3
ìobert E. Lee Memorial N Mem.................93 A4
ìobertson South Africa............................88 C6
ìobin Hood's Bay Bch UK.........................68 A3
ìobson, Mt Canada.................................94 C2
ìobson, Mt P Pk Canada..........................94 C2
ìocca di Papa Italy.................................78 C3
ìocce Nere, Sirolo Bch Italy.....................85 A4
ìoche Notre-Dame, Agde Bch France........84 A2
ìoche-Guyon, la France...........................72 H1
ìoche-Racan Ch France...........................72 C2
ìoche-sur-Yon, la France.........................72 C3
ìochefort Belgium..................................65 B19
ìochehaut Belgium.................................65 B19
ìochester Apt UK....................................66 E2
ìochester, Minnesota USA.......................90 A3
ìochester, New Hampshire USA................90 B3
ìochester, New York USA.........................90 A4
ìochford Apt UK.....................................66 E2
ìock Creek Park USA...............................93 A4
ìockland USA...90 B4
ìocky Mountain N Pk USA.......................92 A2
ìocky Mountains USA..............................90 A2
ìocky Mountains Canada.........................94 A5
ìocroi France...65 B18
ìocycany Czech Rep...............................75 I7
ìod Hill, Fort Canada..............................94 C3
ìöda Denmark..83 G1
ìödby Denmark......................................74 G2
ìodeia Croatia..85 A13
ìódos Apt Greece....................................83 J9
ìódos UN C Greece................................64 A11
ìódos Greece...83 J9
ìódos Greece...83 J12
ìoermond Netherlands...........................65 B12
ìoger Williams N Mem USA.....................93 A4
ìolandsbogen Germany..........................76 C1
ìoma Apt Italy..78 C3
ìoma UN C Italy.....................................64 A6
ìoma Italy...78 C3
ìomainmôtier Switzerland.......................77 E1
ìomania..86 B2
ìomanshom Switzerland.........................77 F1
ìomantic Coast Reg South Africa.............88 B2
ìome Apt Italy..78 C3
ìome UN C Italy.....................................64 A6
ìome Italy...78 C3
ìome USA...94 B10
ìomney Sands Bch UK.............................66 D3
ìomø I Denmark.....................................74 D1
ìomoranin-Lanthenay France...................72 C2
ìoncesvalles France................................72 D1
ìonda Spain...80 D6
ìonda, Serrania de Reg Spain..................80 D6
ìonda, Serrania de Reg Spain..................74 J1
ìonne Ice Shelf Reg Antarctica................59 A10
ìoosendaal Netherlands.........................65 B10
ìoosevelt Campobello Int Pk Canada........90 B2
ìoosevelt Home N His USA......................93 A4
ìoquetas USA...94 A8
ìoquetas de Mar Spain............................80 D8
ìøros UN C Norway..................................84 A2
ìosa Marina, Ostuni Bch Italy.................85 A12
ìosa, Monte Mtn Italy/Switzerland............77 E6
ìoscoff Ferry France................................69 D6
ìoscoff France..72 B1
ìoseau Cru Dominica...............................58 B11
ìosenheim Germany................................75 H9
ìoses Apt Spain......................................80 C2
ìoses Bch Spain......................................84 A2
ìosetano, Roseto Capo Spúlico Bch Italy...85 A11
ìoseto Capo Spúlico Italy........................85 A11
ìosetta Egypt...89 F1
ìosetta Mouth Riv Egypt.........................89 F1
ìosière, la France...................................72 G4
ìoss Ice Shelf Reg Antarctica..................59 A10
ìoss Lake N Rec USA...............................91 A1
ìoss Sea Antarctica................................59 A10
ìoss-on-Wye UK......................................66 D3
ìosslare Ferry Ireland.............................69 B6
ìostock Germany....................................74 H2
ìostov Veliky Russian Fed.......................86 A2
ìostov-on-Don Russian Fed.....................86 A2
ìota Spain...80 D5
ìotenburg Germany................................74 E3
ìoth Germany..75 G7
ìothaargebirge Reg Germany...................75 D5
ìothenburg ob der Tauber Germany..........75 F7
ìothesay Ferry UK..................................69 B2
ìothesay Castle His Sc UK.......................67 F2
ìott Riv Germany....................................75 I8
ìotta Primero Camping Tenuta, Grado Bch Italy...85 A4
ìottenburg Germany...............................76 B6
ìotterdam Apt Netherlands.....................65 B10
ìotterdam Netherlands...........................65 B10
ìotterdam UN C Netherlands...................69 C6
ìottumerplaat I Netherlands...................74 A1
ìottweil Germany...................................76 C3
ìoubaix France.....................................65 B13
ìouen France...72 H1
ìouge-Matawin P Res Canada..................94 B3
ìougemont Switzerland...........................77 E6
ìoussillon Reg France.............................72 E2
ìoviès France...83 J4
ìowallane Garden NT UK.........................67 F3
ìoya Reg France.....................................72 F2
ìoya Est, St-Florent Bch Corsica...............84 A3

Roya Ouest, St-Florent Bch Corsica...........84 A3
Royal Dockyard Cru Bermuda...................58 A2
Royal Leamington Spa UK.......................66 D2
Royal St George's Gf UK..........................66 E4
Royal Tunbridge Wells UK.......................66 E3
Royaumont, Abbaye de France.................72 H1
Roye France...65 B17
Rüdersdorf Germany...............................74 I4
Rüdesheim Germany...............................76 C4
Rudkøbing Denmark...............................74 F2
Rudolstadt Germany...............................75 G6
Rueil Malmaison France..........................72 H3
Rufford Abbey EH UK..............................67 F4
Rugby UK..66 D2
Rügen I Germany....................................74 B5
Ruhr Reg Germany..................................74 C5
Ruhr Riv Germany...................................74 C5
Ruivo, Pico Mtn Madeira.........................82 C1
Rum Ferry UK..69 B1
Rum I UK..70 A2
Ruma N Pk Kenya...................................89 G3
Rumina, Mojácar Bch Spain.....................84 A3
Runkel Germany.....................................76 C2
Runnymede NT UK.................................66 E1
Runswick Bay Bch UK.............................68 A3
Rur Riv Germany....................................76 B1
Ruse Bulgaria..86 C2
Russell Cave N Mon USA.........................93 A4
Russian Black Sea Coast Reg Russian Fed...86 A2
Russian Federation...............................86-87
Rüsslesheim Germany.............................75 D6
Rutland UK..90 B3
Ruvu Riv Tanzania..................................89 G3
Ruwenzori Mountains N Pk, UN N Uganda...61 A5
Rwanda..88 A3
Rybinsk Russian Fed..............................86 C1
Rybinsk Reservoir Russian Fed................86 C1
Rydal Mount UK.....................................66 C2
Ryde Ferry UK..69 D8
Ryde East Bch UK...................................68 A6
Ryde West Bch UK..................................68 A6
Rye UK..66 E4
Ryukyu Is..55 A8

Which Saint?

Each abbreviation (S, Sa, St, St', St-, Sta, San, Santa, São etc) has its own classification – be sure to check all the possible options.

's-Gravenhage Netherlands......................65 B6
's-Hertogenbosch Netherlands...............65 B11
S Andria Priu, Necropoli di Sardinia.........78 D2
S'Albufeira Menorca...............................81 H2
S'Algar Menorca.....................................81 H4
S'Arenal Menorca...................................81 G3
S'Arenal Gros, St Joan de Labritja Bch Ibiza...84 A9
S'Argamassa Ibiza.................................81 F2
S'Illot Mallorca......................................81 G1
S'Illot, St Joan de Labritja Bch Ibiza.........84 A9
S'Illot-Cala Moreia, St Llorenç Bch Mallorca...84 A9
Sa Boadella, Lloret de Mar Bch Spain.......84 A2
Sa Calobra Mallorca...............................81 G1
Sa Coma Mallorca..................................81 G1
Sa Coma, St Llorenç des Cardassar Bch Mallorca...84 A9
Sa Conca, Castell-Platja d'Aro Bch Spain...84 A2
Sa Conillera I Ibiza.................................81 F1
Sa Keo Riv Thailand................................96 D2
Sa Roqueta Bch Formentera....................84 A9
Sa Talaiassa de St Josep Mtn Ibiza..........81 F1
Saalbach Austria....................................77 F3
Saale Riv Germany.................................74 G5
Saalfeld Germany...................................75 G6
Saalfelden Austria..................................77 F4
Saanen Switzerland................................77 E6
Saanenmöser Switzerland.......................77 E6
Saar Riv Germany...................................76 B3
Saarbrücken Apt Germany.......................76 B3
Saarbrücken Germany.............................76 B3
Saarburg Germany..................................76 B3
Saaremaa I Estonia................................86 A1
Saarland Adm Germany...........................76 B3
Saarlouis Germany.................................76 B3
Saas Fee Switzerland..............................77 E6
Saba I..95 D3
Sabadell Spain.......................................80 C3
Sabanell, Blanes Bch Spain.....................84 A2
Sabáudia Italy..78 C4
Sabáudia, golfo di Italy...........................78 C4
Sabina Reg Italy.....................................78 C1
Sable, Cape USA....................................91 D7
Sablé-sur-Sarthe France..........................72 C1
Sablettes, Antibes Bch France..................84 A3
Sabratha UN C Libya.............................64 A10
Saccione, Chieuti Bch Italy.....................85 A4
Saché France...72 C2
Sachsen Germany...................................76 A2
Sachsen-Anhalt Adm Germany.................76 A1
Sächsische Schweiz Reg Germany.............75 J5
Sacramento Apt USA...............................91 E1
Sacramento Riv USA...............................91 E1
Sacramento USA....................................91 E3
Sacred Falls S Pk Hawaiian Is..................91 C5
Saduak floating market Thailand.............96 D1
Safaga Cru Egypt...................................59 A5
Safi Morocco..89 F1
Safi safari area UN N Zimbabwe...............61 A5
Safranbolu UN C Turkey..........................64 A12
Sagamore Hill N His USA........................93 A4
Sagarmatha N Pk, UN N Nepal.................61 A8
Sagres Portugal.....................................82 E5
Sagres, Ponta de Cape Portugal...............82 E5
Saguaro N Mon USA...............................92 A2
Sagunto Spain.......................................84 A9
Sahara Desert Africa..............................88 A1
Sahel Reg Africa.....................................88 A2
Sahel Reg Tunisia...................................89 D4
Sahr-i-Bahlol UN C Pakistan....................63 C1
Sahuayo Mexico.....................................95 E1
Saint Paul's Church N His USA.................93 A4
St Alban's Roman Wall EH UK..................67 F5
St Albans UK..66 E1
St Albans USA..90 B1
St Andrews UK..66 B2
St Andrews Cathedral and Castle His Sc UK...67 F2
St Andrews West Bch UK.........................68 A3
St Angelo in Fórmis Italy.........................78 B1
St Anton Austria.....................................77 F6
St Antoni de Portmany Ibiza....................81 F1
St Antoni, Calonge Bch Spain..................84 A2
St Antoni, Cullera Bch Spain....................84 A9
St Augustine USA...................................91 D4
St Barthélemy I......................................95 D3
St Bee's Head Cape UK............................66 C1
St Blais, Cape South Africa......................88 C6
St Blasien Germany................................76 B8
St Carles de Peralta Ibiza........................81 F2
St Catharines Canada.............................94 B9
St Catherine, Monastery of Egypt.............89 F4
St Christoph Austria...............................77 F1
St Climent Menorca................................81 H4
St Croix Riv USA.....................................90 B2
St Croix I. Int His USA.............................90 B2
St David's UK...68 A5

St Dogmaels UK.....................................68 A5
St Eustatius I...95 D3
St Feliu de Guixols Spain.........................80 C2
St Feliu, St Feliu de Guixols Bch Spain......84 A2
St Francis Bay South Africa......................88 C8
St Francis, Cape South Africa...................88 C8
St Fransesc de Formentera Formentera......81 F4
St Gallen UN C Switzerland......................64 A6
St Gallen Switzerland.............................77 F1
St George I. USA.....................................91 D2
St George I. USA.....................................58 A2
St George's Cru Bermuda........................58 A2
St George's Cru Grenada.........................58 B11
St George's Channel UK...........................69 B6
St Gilgen Austria....................................77 F4
St Goar Germany....................................76 C2
St Helena I..55 A5
St Helena Bay South Africa......................88 C1
St Helens Duver Bch UK...........................68 A6
St Helier Ferry Channel Is........................69 D6
St Jaume Mediterrani Menorca................81 H4
St Jean...94 B8
St Joan de Labritja Ibiza.........................81 F2
St Johann im Pongau Austria...................77 F4
St Johann in Tirol Austria........................77 F4
St John Riv Canada/USA.........................58 A2
St John Canada.....................................94 A8
St John's Apt Canada..............................54 A2
St John's Cru Antigua.............................58 B7
St John's Riv USA...................................91 D3
St John's Canada...................................94 A8
St Johnsbury USA...................................90 B3
St Josep de sa Talaia Ibiza.......................81 F1
St Julian's Malta....................................79 G4
St Kilda UN N UK....................................61 A4
St Kitts Apt...54 A3
St Kitts-Nevis..95 D3
St Lawrence St Canada...........................94 A8
St Lawrence Riv Canada..........................94 B4
St Lawrence I. USA.................................90 A10
St Lawrence Is. N Pk Canada...................94 B6
St Lawrence, Gulf of Canada....................58 A2
St Llorenç des Cardassar Mallorca............81 H4
St Lluis Menorca....................................81 H4
St Louis Apt USA....................................90 A7
St Louis USA..54 A3
St Lucia Apt St Lucia...............................95 D7
St Lucia...95 D3
St Maarten I..95 D3
St Märgen Germany................................76 B8
St Martin I..95 D3
St Mary's Ferry UK.................................69 D1
St Merryn UK...68 A4
St Michael's Mount NT UK.......................67 F6
St Miquel de Balansat Ibiza.....................81 F2
St Moritz Switzerland.............................77 E8
St Paul USA...90 A3
St Paul's Bay Malta................................79 G2
St Paul's Is. Malta..................................79 G2
St Paul, Île..55 A5
St Paul, Monastery of Egypt.....................89 F4
St Pere de Rodes Spain............................80 C2
St Pere Pescador Spain............................80 C2
St Peter Germany...................................76 B8
St Peter Ording Germany.........................74 D2
St Peter Port Ferry Channel Is..................69 D6
St Petersburg Apt Russian Fed.................56 A4
St Petersburg Russian Fed.......................59 A6
St Petersburg UN C Russian Fed...............64 A4
St Petersburg Russian Fed.......................86 A1
St Petersburg USA..................................91 D5
St Pierre Gf UK......................................66 D3
St Pierre et Miquelon..............................94 A8
St Pierre-la-Mer, Fleury-d'Aude Bch France...84 A2
St Pol, St Feliu de Guixols Bch Spain.........84 A2
St Pölten Austria....................................77 D4
St Rafael Ibiza.......................................81 F1
St Salvador, El Vendrell Bch Spain............84 A2
St Salvador, Santuari de Mallorca.............81 G4
St Sebastià, Sitges Bch Spain..................84 A2
St Telm Mallorca....................................81 G1
St Telm, Andratx Bch Mallorca.................84 A9
St Thomas Bay Malta..............................79 G4
St Tomàs Menorca..................................81 H3
St Ulrich Italy..79 F3
St Vincent Apt.......................................54 A3
St Vincent...95 D7
St Vincent I. USA....................................91 D2
St Vincent, Agde Bch France....................84 A2
St Vith Belgium....................................65 B16
St Wendel Germany................................75 C7
St Wolfgang Austria................................77 F4
St'Angelo dei Lombardi Italy....................78 B2
St'Antioco Sardinia.................................78 D3
St'Antioco, Isola di Sardinia.....................78 D3
St-Avold France......................................75 B7
St-Blaise Switzerland..............................77 E1
St-Brieuc France.....................................72 B2
St-Calais France.....................................72 B2
St-Cast France..72 B2
St-Clair, Le Lavandou Bch France.............84 A3
St-Cyprien France...................................84 A2
St-Cyr-sur-Mer France............................73 F3
St-Denis France......................................72 H1
St-Dié France...75 B8
St-Estèphe, Marseille Bch France.............84 A3
St-Étienne France...................................73 A2
St-Florent Corsica...................................84 A3
St-Francois Riv Canada...........................94 B4
St-Gaudens France.................................72 D2
St-Gaudens N His USA............................90 B3
St-Germain, Forêt de France....................72 H1
St-Germain-en-Laye France.....................72 H1
St-Gervais-les-Bains France.....................72 E1
St-Girons France....................................72 D2
St-Hyacinthe Canada.............................94 B4
St-Idesbald Belgium..............................65 C1
St-Jacut France......................................72 B2
St-Jean, La Ciotat Bch France...................84 A3
St-Jean-de-Luz France.............................72 D2
St-Jean-de-Luz France.............................72 D1
St-Jean-Pied-de-Port France.....................72 D2
St-Lary Soulan France.............................72 D2
St-Lizier France......................................72 E1
St-Louis France......................................75 C9
St-Malo Ferry France...............................69 D6
St-Malo France.......................................72 B2
St-Malo, Golfe de France.........................72 B1
St-Mathieu, Point de Cape France............72 B1
St-Maurice P Res Canada........................94 B3
St-Maurice Riv Canada............................94 B4
St-Maximin la Ste-Baume France..............72 E1
St-Nazaire France...................................72 B4
St-Omer France......................................65 B13
St-Paul France..72 F2
St-Pierre, Lac Canada.............................94 B4
St-Pol-sur-Ternoise France.......................65 B13
St-Quay-Portrieux France........................72 B2
St-Quentin France..................................65 B17
St-Raphaël France..................................72 F4
St-Savin-sur-Gartempe UN C France.........64 A5
St-Thégonnec France..............................72 B1
St-Tropez France....................................72 F4
Sta Caterina di Pittinuri Sardinia..............78 D1
Sta Caterina Valfurva Italy.......................79 F3

Sta Clara-a-Velha Portugal......................82 E2
Sta Cristina Valgardena Italy....................79 F3
Sta Cristina, Lloret de Mar Bch Spain........84 A2
Sta Cruz Madeira....................................82 C2
Sta Cruz das Flores Azores.......................82 B1
Sta Cruz de Graciosa Azores....................82 B2
Sta Cruz de la Palma Canary Is.................80 B4
Sta Cruz de Tenerife Cru Canary Is............59 A4
Sta Cruz de Tenerife Canary Is..................80 B5
Sta Eufémia, Faro di Cape Italy................78 C4
Sta Eulária del Riu Ibiza..........................81 F2
Sta Eulària, St Eulària del Riu Bch Ibiza....84 A9
Sta Líbera, Ostuni Bch Italy....................85 A12
Sta Margalida Mallorca............................81 G2
Sta Margherita di Pula Sardinia................78 D4
Sta Margherita Ligure Italy......................79 F6
Sta Maria I Azores..................................82 B2
Sta Maria Cápua Vetere Italy...................78 B1
Sta Maria, Cabo de Cape Portugal............82 E7
Sta Marinella Italy..................................78 C1
Sta Maria Riv Mexico..............................95 E2
Sta Ponça Mallorca................................81 G3
Sta Ponça, Calvià Bch Mallorca...............84 A9
Sta Rita Belize..95 F4
Sta Teresa Gallura Sardinia.....................78 D2
Sais Apt Morocco....................................89 E2
Saiwa Swamp N Pk Kenya.......................89 G1
Sakha Russian Fed..................................87 A6
Sakhalin I Russian Fed............................87 A6
Sakhira Tunisia......................................89 D4
Sakjiang, Pulau I Singapore.....................96 C4
Sakra, Pulau Singapore...........................96 C3
Sakramarkt Russian Fed..........................87 A4
Sal Apt Cape Verde.................................54 A3
Sal Apt Morocco.....................................80 D6
Saladar, Alicante Bch Spain.....................84 A9
Salamanca Apt Spain.............................80 A1
Salamanca Spain....................................80 A1
Salamanca Mexico..................................95 E1
Salamina I Greece...................................83 J4
Saldanha South Africa.............................88 C1
Saldanha Bay South Africa.......................88 C1
Salé Morocco..89 E2
Salé Apt Morocco....................................89 E2
Salem USA...90 A1
Salem Maritime N His USA.......................93 A4
Salerno Portugal.....................................82 E5
Salerno Italy..78 B4
Salerno, Golfo di Italy..............................78 B4
Salina Bay Malta....................................79 G2
Salina Cruz Mexico.................................95 E4
Salina, Isola Sicily...................................78 E4
Salinas Pueblo Missions N Mon USA.........92 A6
Salines, St Josep de sa Talaia Bch Ibiza....84 A9
Salir Portugal...82 E5
Salisbury USA..90 A6
Salisbury: Mompesson House UN C UK......67 F5
Salitron Honduras...................................95 F6
Salley Abbey EH UK................................67 F4
Salmonsdam Ntr Res South Africa............88 C6
Salò Italy..79 F7
Salobreña Spain.....................................80 D7
Salonga N Pk, UN N Zaïre.......................61 A5
Salonika Apt Greece...............................64 A11
Salonika Greece.....................................83 J1
Salou Spain...80 C3
Salso Riv Sicily.......................................78 E4
Salsomaggiore Italy................................79 F6
Salt Lake City Apt USA............................54 A2
Salt Lake City USA..................................90 A1
Salt River Bay N His US Virgin Is..............93
Salween Riv China/Myanmar....................87 D6
Salzach Riv Austria.................................77 F4
Salzburg Apt Austria...............................77 F4
Salzburg Adm Austria.............................77 F4
Salzburg Austria.....................................77 F4
Salzgitter Germany.................................74 F4
Salzwedel Germany................................74 G4
Samae San Thailand...............................96 D4
Samara Russian Fed................................86 A2
Samariás, Farági Crete............................83 J10
Samarkand UN C Uzbekistan...................86 A3
Sambre Riv Belgium..............................65 B14
Samburu G Res Kenya............................89 G2
Samedan Switzerland..............................77 E4
Samena, Marseille Bch France..................84 A3
Sámi Greece..83 H2
Samnaun Switzerland.............................77 F6
Samoëns France.....................................72 G2
Samora Riv Portugal...............................82 E2
Sámos Apt Greece..................................83 J8
Sámos I Greece......................................83 J8
Sámos I Greece......................................83 J8
Samothrace I Greece..............................83 J2
Samothráki I Greece...............................83 J2
Samsun Turkey......................................83 F3
Samut Prakan Thailand...........................96 D2
Samut Sakhon Thailand..........................96 D1
Samut Songkhram Thailand.....................96 D2
San Agustin Canary Is.............................80 D5
San Antonio USA....................................90 A6
San Antonio Missions N His USA..............92 A1
San Bartolomeo al Mare Italy...................84 A3
San Benedetto del Tronto Italy..................79 F12
San Bernardino Switzerland.....................77 E7
San Bernardino USA...............................91 E6
San Bernardino, Passo del Switzerland......77 E7
San Blas Mexico.....................................95 E2
San Blas Bay Malta.................................79 G1
San Blas, Cape USA................................91 D2
San Cándido Italy...................................79 F3
San Clemente I USA................................91 E6
San Cristóbal de las Casas Mexico............95 F3
San Cristóbal, Almuñécar Bch Spain.........84 A8
San Diego Apt USA.................................91 E6
San Diego Cru USA.................................58 A3
San Diego USA.......................................91 E6
San Diego Guatemala.............................95 F4
San Felice Circéo Italy.............................78 C4
San Francisco Apt USA............................91 E1
San Francisco Cru USA............................58 A3
San Francisco USA..................................91 E3
San Francisco Maritime N His USA............92 A1
San Gervasio Mexico...............................95 F2
San Gimignano UN C Italy.......................64 A6
San Gimignano Italy...............................79 F11
San Gottardo, Passo del Switzerland.........77 E3
San Javier Spain.....................................81 E3
San Joaquín Riv USA...............................91 E3
San Jose USA...91 E3
San José Apt Costa Rica...........................54 A3
San José USA...80 D8
San José, Nijar Bch Spain........................84 A8
San Juan Apt Puerto Rico.........................54 A3
San Juan UN C Puerto Rico......................62 A3

San Juan N His Puerto Rico......................93
San Juan Bautista USA............................91 E3
San Juan I. N His USA.............................91 A1
San Juan, Alicante Bch Spain...................84 A9
San Leo Italy...79 F12
San Leonardo, Ostuni Bch Italy...............85 A12
San Lorenzo, Monéglia Bch Italy..............84 A3
San Lorenzo, Vieste Bch Italy..................85 A4
San Luis Capistrano, Mission USA............91 E6
San Luis Obispo USA..............................91 E5
San Luis Potosí Mexico............................95 E1
San Mamete Italy...................................79 F2
San Marino..79 F12
San Martino di Castrozza Italy..................79 F3
San Mateo USA......................................91 E3
San Máuro Pascoli Italy...........................85 A4
San Michele al Tagliamento Italy..............85 A4
San Michele, Grotta di Italy.....................78 B2
San Michele, Rapallo Bch Italy................84 A3
San Miguel USA......................................91 E3
San Miguel de Allende Mexico..................95 E1
San Miguel I. USA...................................91 E5
San Nicolás de Tolentino Canary Is...........80 B2
San Nicolas I. USA..................................91 E5
San Nicolo', Lavagna Bch Italy.................84 A3
San Pawl il-Bahar Malta..........................79 G2
San Pedro Alcántara Spain......................80 D6
San Pedro del Pinatar Spain.....................81 E3
San Pedro Sula Honduras........................95 F6
San Pietro, Diano Marina Bch Italy...........84 A3
San Pietro, Isola di Sardinia.....................78 D3
San Remo Italy.......................................79 F9
San Rocque Spain...................................91 E5
San Salvador Apt El Salvador...................54 A3
San Salvador I Bahamas..........................58 B3
San Salvador El Salvador.........................95 F6
San Sebastián Spain...............................81 A1
San Sebastián Canary Is..........................80 B4
San Sebastiano, Diano Marina Bch Italy....84 A3
San Teodoro, Marsala Bch Sicily..............85 A11
San Viglio de Marebbe Italy.....................79 F11
San Vincenzo Italy..................................78 C1
San Vito lo Capo Sicily............................78 E1
Sana'a Apt Yemen..................................55 A7
Sana'a UN C Yemen...............................63 C7
Sanary-sur-Mer France...........................73 F3
Sanchi UN C India..................................63 C1
Sand Key I USA......................................91 D5
Sandbanks, Poole Bch UK........................68 A6
Sandend Bch UK.....................................68 A1
Sandown Bch UK....................................68 A6
Sandsend Bch UK...................................68 A3
Sandy Neck, Bude Bch UK.......................68 A6
Sanford, Florida USA..............................91 D6
Sanford, Maine USA...............................90 B3
Sangatte Channel Tunnel Terminal France..69 D4
Sangay N Pk, UN N Ecuador....................60 A3
Sangerhausen Germany..........................74 G5
Sani Greece..83 J1
Sani, Kassándra Bch Greece...................85 A12
Sani, Néa Fókea Bch Greece...................85 A13
Sanli Urfa Turkey...................................83 F3
Sanlúcar de Barrameda Spain..................80 D5
Sans-Souci UN C Haiti.............................62 A3
Santa Barbara USA.................................91 E5
Santa Barbara I. USA..............................91 E5
Santa Catalina I. USA..............................91 E6
Santa Clara USA.....................................91 E3
Santa Croce Porto, Trieste Bch Italy..........85 A4
Santa Cruz Apt Bolivia............................54 A3
Santa Cruz USA......................................91 E3
Santa Cruz I. USA...................................91 E5
Santa Fe USA...90 A6
Santa Monica Mtns N Rec USA.................92 A5
Santa Rosa USA......................................91 E3
Santa Rosa I. USA..................................91 D1
Santa Rosa I. USA..................................91 E5
Santa Rosa Xtampak Mexico....................95 F2
Santana Madeira....................................82 C2
Santana de Barra Portugal......................82 E2
Santander Ferry Spain.............................69 D5
Santander Spain.....................................81 A1
Santanyi Mallorca..................................81 G4
Santarém Cru Brazil................................58 A3
Santarém Portugal..................................82 A2
Santarém Adm Portugal..........................82 D2
Santes Creus, Monestir de Spain..............80 C3
Santiago Apt Chile..................................54 A3
Santiago Riv Mexico...............................95 E1
Santiago de Compostela Apt Spain...........56 A9
Santiago de Compostela UN C Spain.........64 A5
Santiago de Compostela Spain.................80 A1
Santiago de la Ribera Spain.....................81 E3
Santíssima Trinità di Saccargia Sardinia....78 D1
Santo da Serra Madeira...........................82 C2
Santo Domingo Apt Dominican Rep...........54 A3
Santo Domingo Cru Dominican Rep...........58 B6
Santo Domingo UN C Dominican Rep.........62 A3
Santo Estevão Riv Portugal......................82 D2
Santorini I Greece...................................83 J8
Santos Cru Brazil....................................58 A3
São Bartolomeu de Messines Portugal.......82 E2
São Brás de Alportel Portugal...................82 E2
São Jorge I Azores..................................82 B2
São Jorge Madeira..................................82 C2
São Marcos da Serra Portugal..................82 E2
São Miguel I. Azores...............................82 B1
Sao Miguel das Missoes UN C Brazil.........62 A3
São Paulo Apt Brazil...............................54 A3
São Teotónio Portugal.............................82 E1
São Tomé and Principe............................88 A3
São Vicente Cru Cape Verde....................59 A5
São Vicente Madeira...............................82 C1
São Vicente, Cabo de Cape Portugal.........82 E5
Saône Riv France....................................72 G1
Saqqara Egypt.......................................89 F1
Sara Buri Thailand..................................96 D2
Saragossa Spain....................................81 A1
Sarai Russian Fed...................................87 D1
Sarajevo Apt Bosnia-Herz........................56 A11
Sarajevo Bosnia-Herz..............................86 B2
Sarandë Albania.....................................83 G1
Sarasota USA...91 D5
Saratoga N His USA................................93 A4
Saratov Russian Fed...............................86 A2
Saratov Reservoir Russian Fed.................86 C1
Sardegna..78 D
Sardindida Plain Kenya...........................89 G2
Sardinia..78 D
Sargasso Sea...83 J11
Sárgerese Turkey....................................69 B6
Sark I Channel I......................................72 B2
Sarn Switzerland....................................77 E3
Saronic Gulf (Saronikós Kólpos) Greece......83 J7
Saronikós Kólpos (Saronic Gulf) Greece.....83 J7
Sarralbe France......................................75 C7
Sarrebourg France..................................75 C8
Sarreguemines France.............................76 B5
Sartenèje Belize......................................95 F4
Sarthe Riv France...................................72 C1
Sarthe Adm France.................................72 C2

Index

Sárti Greece 83 J1
Sárti Greece 85 A13
Sárti Bch Greece 85 A13
Sarzana Italy 79 F10
Saskatchewan Adm Canada 94 A6
Saskatoon Apt Canada 54 A2
Saskatoon Canada 94 A6
Sassari Apt Sardinia 78 D1
Sassari Sardinia 78 D1
Saßnitz Germany 74 I2
Satolas Apt France 72 G1
Sattahip Thailand 96 D4
Saudi Arabia 55 A7
Sauer Riv Germany 76 C3
Sauerland Reg Germany 75 D5
Sauerland Reg Germany 76 A1
Saugus Iron Works N His USA 93 A14
Sault Ste Marie Canada 94 A7
Saumur France 72 C1
Saundersfoot UK 68 A5
Sausalito USA 91 E3
Sausset-les-Pins France 84 A3
Sauveterre France 72 D1
Sàuze d'Oulx Italy 79 F5
Savannah USA 90 A8
Saverne France 75 C8
Savognin Switzerland 77 E4
Savoie Reg Switzerland 73 A2
Savoie Adm France 72 G2
Savona Italy 79 F6
Saxony Apt Germany 76 A2
Saxony-Anhalt Adm Germany 74 G4
Sayil Mexico 95 F2
Sbeitla Tunisia 89 D3
Scafell Pike Mtn UK 66 C1
Scala Eresou, Eressós Bch Greece 85 A13
Scala Kallonis, Kerámi Bch Greece 85 A13
Scalo Corniglia, Vernazza Bch Italy 84 A3
Scalpay Ferry UK 69 B1
Scandola Reserve UN N FRance 61 A4
Scanzano Iónico Italy 85 A11
Scanzano Nord, Scanzano Iónico Bch Italy 85 A11
Scanzano Sud, Scanzano Iónico Bch Italy 85 A11
Scarborough UK 70 A4
Scaricatore, Cesenático Bch Italy 85 A4
Scarpanto I Greece 83 J11
Scarpanto Bch Greece 83 J11
Schaalsee Lake Germany 74 F3
Schaffhausen Switzerland 76 B8
Schärding Austria 75 I8
Scharhörn I Germany 74 D3
Scharmützelsee Lake Germany 74 A4
Schauinsland Mtn Germany 76 B8
Scheidagg Switzerland 77 E2
Schelde Riv Belgium 65 B14
Scheveningen Netherlands 65 B6
Schiedam Netherlands 65 B10
Schiermonnikoog I Netherlands 65 A8
Schiltach Germany 76 B8
Schiphol Apt Netherlands 65 B7
Schisma, Eloúnda Bch Crete 85 A13
Schladming Austria 77 F4
Schleiden Germany 75 B6
Schleswig Germany 74 E2
Schleswig-Holstein Adm Germany 76 A1
Schluchsee Germany 76 C3
Schlüctern Germany 75 E6
Schneeberg Germany 75 H6
Schönburg Germany 76 C4
Schönebeck Germany 74 G4
Schönfeld Apt Germany 74 I4
Schongau Germany 75 F9
Schöningen Germany 74 F4
Schopfheim Germany 76 B8
Schouwen I Netherlands 65 B10
Schramberg Germany 75 D8
Schröken Austria 77 F5
Schruns Austria 77 F5
Schwabach Germany 75 G7
Schwaben Germany 75 F8
Schwäben Reg Germany 76 A2
Schwäbisch Gmünd Germany 75 E8
Schwäbisch Hall Germany 75 E7
Schwäbisch-Bayerisches Alpen'd Reg Germany 75 F8
Schwäbische Alb Reg Germany 75 E8
Schwandorf Germany 75 H7
Schwarzach Riv Germany 75 H7
Schwarze Elster Riv Germany 74 H5
Schwarzenberg Austria 77 F1
Schwarzwald Reg Germany 76 B8
Schwarzwaldbahn Germany 76 B8
Schwaz Austria 75 G9
Schwedt an der Oder Germany 74 J3
Schweinfurt Germany 75 F6
Schwerin Germany 74 G3
Schweriner See Lake Germany 74 G3
Schwetzingen Germany 75 D7
Schwielochsee Lake Germany 74 J4
Schwyz Switzerland 77 E3
Scialmarino, Vieste Bch Italy 85 A4
Scoglio della Galera, Roseto Capo Spúlico Bch Italy 85 A11
Scone Palace UK 66 B2
Sconser Ferry UK 69 B1
Scotia Sea 58 A3
Scotland UK 66 A1
Scott Base Cru Antarctica 59 A10
Scottish Borders Adm UK 66 A1
Scottish Highlands Reg UK 66 A1
Scottish Lowlands UK .....66 B
Scotts Bluff N Mon USA 92 A2
Scrabster Ferry UK 69 C3
Scunthorpe UK 70 A4
Scuol Switzerland 77 E4
Scutari Turkey 83 J3
Se Mesquida de Baix Mallorca 81 G2
Sea Life Park Hawaiian Is. 91 C6
Sea World of Ohio USA 93 A14
Sea World of Texas USA 92 A6
Sea World, Orlando USA 93 A8
Sea World, San Diego USA 92 A5
Seaford UK 66 E3
Seal, Cape South Africa 88 C7
Seascale UK 66 C3
Seattle Apt USA 54 A2
Seattle Cru USA 58 A2
Seattle USA 90 A1
Sebarok, Pulau I Singapore 96 C3

Seixal Portugal 82 D2
Selatan, Selat Str Malaysia 96 B4
Sele Riv Italy 78 B4
Sele, Piana dei Reg Italy 78 B4
Selenter See Lake Germany 74 F2
Sélestat France 75 C8
Seletar Reservoir Singapore 96 C1
Selinute Italy 78 E1
Sélestat France 75 C8
Seleucia Iraq 87 D4
Selinítsa Bch Greece 85 A12
Selinunte Sicily 78 E1
Seneca Lake USA 94 B10
Sénégal 88 A2
Senftenberg Germany 74 J5
Senigállia Italy 79 F12
Senlis France 72 H2
Sennen Gorge UK 68 A6
Sensa, Pulau I Singapore 96 C4
Sentosa, Pulau I Singapore 96 C4
Seoul Apt Korea, Rep. 55 A8
Sequoia N Pk USA 91 E4
Seraing Belgium 75 A6
Serangoon New Town Singapore 96 C2
Seraya, Pulau I Singapore 96 C3
Serengeti N Pk, UN N Tanzania 61 A5
Serengeti Plain Tanzania 89 G3
Séres Greece 83 J1
Serfaus Austria 77 F6
Sergeyev Posad Russian Fed. 86 A2
Sérifos I Greece 83 J7
Sérignan France 84 A2
Sérignan Plage Bch France 84 A2
Sérignan Plage Nature Bch France 84 A2
Serra de Capivara N Pk, UN CN Brazil 62 A3
Serra Órrios, Villaggio nuragico di Sardinia 78 D2
Serrant Ch France 72 C1
Ses Animas, Mirador de Mallorca 81 G1
Ses Figueretes Ibiza 81 F2
Ses Salines Mallorca 84 A9
Sesimbra Portugal 82 D2
Sessa Aurunca Italy 78 B1
Sestri Italy 79 F6
Sestriere Italy 79 F5
Sète France 84 A2
Sete Cidades, Caldeiras das Mtn Azores 82 B1
Setúbal Adm Portugal 82 D2
Setúbal Portugal 82 D2
Sevastopol Ukraine 86 A1
Severn Riv UK 66 D3
Severn Gorge UK 66 D1
Severnaya Zemlya Is Russian Fed. 86 A4
Severobaikalsk Russian Fed. 87 A5
Sevilla Apt Spain 80 D2
Sevilla UN C Spain 64 A9
Sevilla Spain 80 D1
Seville Apt Spain 80 D2
Seville Spain 80 D1
Seville UN C Spain 64 A9
Seville Spain 80 D1
Sèvre Riv France 72 C3
Sewall-Belmont House N His USA 93 A14
Seward Cru USA 58 A2
Seychelles 88 A3
Sfax Apt Tunisia 89 D4
Sfax Tunisia 89 D4
Sfintu Gheorghe Riv Romania 86 C2
Shaba N Res Kenya 89 G2
Shache China 87 D2
Shaldon UK 68 A6
Shalimar Gardens UN C Pakistan 63 C1
Shanghai Apt China 55 A8
Shanghai Cru China 59 A8
Shangri-La Menorca 81 H4
Shanklin Bch UK 68 A6
Shap UK 66 C3
Shap Abbey EH UK 66 C2
Shap Fells UK 66 C2
Shark Bay UN N Australia 61 A9
Sharm el Sheikh Egypt 89 F4
Shasta, Mt USA 91 E1
Shawnigan Canada 94 B4
Sheerness UK 66 E2
Sheffield UK 70 A4
Shenandoah N Pk USA 93 A8
Sheppey, Isle of UK 66 E2
Sherbrooke Canada 94 B8
Shetland Adm UK 68 A7
Shetland Is. UK 68 A7
Shetland Is. UK 68 A7
Shibam UN Y Yemen 63 A7
Shikoku I Japan 55 A8
Shiloh N Mil USA 93 A7
Shimba Hills G Res Kenya 89 G4
Shimoni Kenya 89 G4
Shinoússa I Greece 83 J8
Shipstern Belize 95 F4
Shiraz Iran 87 D4
Shoeburyness East Bch UK 68 A5
Shoshone Mountains USA 91 E4
Shrewsbury UK 66 D1
Shropshire Adm UK 68 A5
Shropshire Hills UK 66 D1
Shugborough Estate NT UK 67 F5
Si Racha Thailand 96 D4
Sian Ka'an B Res, UN N Mexico 60 A3
Sibiloi N Pk Kenya 89 G1
Sibiu Romania 86 B2
Sicié, Cap France 72 F3
Sicília .....78 E
Sicily .....78 E
Sidari Greece 83 G1
Side Turkey 83 F2
Sideros, Akr. Cape Crete 83 J11
Sidi Bou Saïd Tunisia 89 D2
Sidi Daoud Tunisia 89 D2
Sidi Ifni Morocco 89 E3
Sidlaw Hills UK 66 B2
Siebengebirge Reg Germany 76 B1
Sieg Riv Germany 75 C6
Siegburg Germany 76 B1
Siegen Germany 76 B2
Siegerwald Reg Germany 75 F7
Siena Italy 79 F11
Sierra Leone 88 A2
Sierra Madre del Sur Mtns Mexico 95 E4
Sierra Madre Occidental Mtns Mexico 95 E1
Sierra Madre Oriental Mtns Mexico 95 E2
Sierra Nevada Mtns Spain 80 D3
Sierra Nevada Mtns USA 91 E4
Sierre Switzerland 77 E6
Siesta Key I USA 91 D5
Siesta, Antibes Bch France 84 A3
Sífnos I Greece 83 J7
Sigmaringen Germany 75 E8
Sigiriya UN C Sri Lanka 63 C2
Signy Cru S Orkney Is. 59 A10
Sigri Greece 83 J5
Síkinos I Greece 83 J8

Silesia Reg Poland 86 B1
Silifke Turkey 83 F3
Silistra Bulgaria 86 C2
Silk Road .....87 D
Sille-le-Guillaume Ch France 72 C1
Síloso, Fort Singapore 96 C3
Síls Switzerland 77 E8
Silvaplana Switzerland 77 E8
Silver Sands, Aberdour Bch UK 68 A2
Silver Springs USA 91 D3
Silves Portugal 82 E6
Simbirsk Russian Fed. 86 A2
Simbruini, Monti Reg Italy 78 C2
Simcoe, Lake Canada 94 B5
Simei New Town Singapore 96 C2
Simen N Pk, UN N Ethiopia 61 A5
Siméto Riv Sicily 78 E4
Simi I Greece 83 J9
Simmer Riv Germany 76 C3
Simmern Germany 76 C3
Simon's Town South Africa 88 C5
Simplonpass Switzerland 77 E6
Sinai Reg Egypt 89 F2
Sinai, Mt Egypt 89 F4
Sinaia Romania 86 B2
Sines Portugal 82 A3
Sinéu Mallorca 81 G2
Singapore Apt 96 C2
Singapore Cru 59 A8
Singapore .....96 C
Singapore City Singapore 96 C4
Singapore Crocadilarium Singapore 96 C4
Singapore Science Centre Singapore 96 C1
Singapore Zoological Gardens Singapore 96 C1
Singapore, Straits of 96 C4
Singen Germany 75 D9
Sinharaja I Res, UN N Sri Lanka 61 A8
Sinis Reg Sardinia 78 D2
Sinop Turkey 83 F3
Sinsheim Germany 75 D7
Sintra Portugal 82 D1
Sintra, Serra de Reg Portugal 82 D1
Sinzig Germany 76 C1
Sion Switzerland 77 E6
Sioux Falls USA 90 A3
Sioux Lookout Canada 94 A7
Siraf Iran 87 D4
Sirmione Italy 79 F7
Sírna I Greece 83 J8
Sirolo Italy 79 F12
Síros I Greece 83 J7
Sirte, Gulf of 59 C7
Sisteron France 72 F1
Sistiana Italy 79 F4
Sitges Spain 80 C3
Sithonia Pen Greece 83 J1
Sitía Crete 83 J11
Sitia Bch Crete 85 A13
Sitka Cru USA 58 A2
Sitka N His USA 92 A9
Sittard Netherlands 75 A5
Sittard Netherlands 75 A5
Sivas Turkey 83 F3
Six Flags Great Adventure USA 93 A4
Six Flags Great America USA 93 A3
Six Flags Magic Mountain USA 92 A5
Six Flags Over Georgia USA 93 A8
Six Flags Over Mid-America USA 93 A7
Six Flags Over Texas USA 93 A7
Sizergh Castle NT UK 66 C4
Sjælland I Denmark 74 G1
Skagerrak Str 56 A6
Skagway Cru USA 58 A2
Skála Greece 83 H2
Skála Bch Greece 85 A12
Skála, Atalánti Bch Greece 85 A12
Skándzoura I Greece 83 J4
Skaneateles Lake USA 94 B10
Skanes Apt Tunisia 89 D4
Skara Brae stone age house His Sc UK 67 F7
Skeena Riv Canada 94 C1
Skenfrith Castle NT UK 67 F5
Skiathos Apt Greece 83 J4
Skiathos I Greece 83 J4
Skiddaw Mtn UK 66 C2
Skiddaw Forest UK 66 C2
Skínari, Akr. Cape Greece 83 H3
Skipsea Castle EH UK 67 F4
Skíros I Greece 83 J4
Skíti I Greece 85 A12
Skíthri, Skiathos Bch Greece 85 A12
Skocjan Caves UN N Slovenia 61 A4
Skópelos I Greece 83 J4
Skopje Apt Mac, FYR. 56 A11
Skopje Mac, FYR. 86 B2
Skorba Malta 79 G3
Skotina Greece 85 A12
Skotína Bch Greece 85 A12
Skowhegan USA 90 A4
Skrinkle Bch UK 68 A5
Skye I UK 70 A1
Slagelse Denmark 74 G1
Slave Coast Reg 59 A5
Slave Lake Canada 94 C2
Slave Lake, Lesser Canada 94 C2
Sleeping Bear Dunes N Lake USA 93 A3
Sliema Malta 79 G4
Slovak Republic 86 B1
Slovenia 86 B2
Slovak Republic 86 B1
Slubice Poland 74 J4
Småland-Farvandet Bay Denmark 74 G1
Smallhythe Place NT UK 67 F6
Smallwood Reservoir Canada 94 B4
Smeraldo, Grotta di Italy 78 B4
Smir-Restinga Morocco 89 E4
Smolensk Russian Fed. 86 A1
Snake Riv USA 91 E2
Snake River Plain USA 91 E2
Snake Temple, Pinang Malaysia 96 B3
Sneek Netherlands 65 B3
Snettisham Bch UK 68 A5
Snowdonia Reg UK 66 A2
Snowdonia N Pk UK 67 F4
Snowshill Manor NT UK 66 D4
Soave Italy 79 F7
Sochi Russian Fed. 86 A2
Socotra I 55 A7
Soest Germany 74 D5
Soestdijk Netherlands 65 B7
Soeste Riv Germany 74 C4
Sofia Apt Bulgaria 56 A11
Sofia Bulgaria 86 B2
Sohåg Egypt 89 F4
Soissons France 72 H2
Söke Turkey 83 J9
Sokolov Czech Rep. 75 H6
Solda Italy 79 F3
Sölden Austria 77 F6
Solingen Germany 75 C5
Soll Austria 77 F3
Sóller Mallorca 81 G1
Solomon Is. 55 A9
Solothurn Switzerland 77 E2
Soltau Germany 74 E4

Solvang USA 91 E5
Stavanger Ferry Norway .....69 C
Solynieve Spain 80 D3
Somalia 88 A2
Somerset Adm UK 68 A6
Somerset East South Africa 88 C4
Somerset I. Canada 94 A2
Somerset West South Africa 88 C5
Sömmerda Germany 75 G5
Son Bou de Baix Menorca 81 H4
Son Bou, Platja de Bch Menorca 81 H3
Son Moll Mallorca 81 G2
Son Moll, Capdepera Bch Mallorca 84 A9
Son Parc Menorca 81 H2
Son Saura, Es Mercadal Bch Menorca 84 A9
Son St Joan Apt Mallorca 81 G1
Son Servera Mallorca 84 A9
Son Xoriguer, Ciutadella Bch Menorca 84 A9
Sønder Jylland Reg Denmark 74 E1
Sønderborg Denmark 74 E2
Sonderhausen Germany 75 F5
Søndre Strønfjord Apt Greenland 55 A8
Songkhla Thailand 96 A2
Songo Mnara UN C Tanzania 63 A5
Sonneberg Germany 75 G6
Sonoma USA 91 E3
Sonora USA 91 E3
Sonthofen Germany 75 F9
Sooneck, Burg Germany 76 C4
Soontornpoo Monument Thailand 96 D4
Sopocani UN C Yugo, FY 64 A7
Sora Italy 78 C4
Sörenberg Switzerland 77 E2
Sorraia Riv Portugal 82 D1
Sorrento Cru Italy 59 C2
Sorrento Italy 78 B3
Souda Algeria 89 D1
Souflí Greece 83 J2
Soúnio, Akr. Cape Greece 83 J7
Soûr UN C Lebanon 64 A12
Sousse UN C Tunisia 64 A10
Sousse Tunisia 89 D2
South Africa 88
South America Cruise Area 58 A3
South Andaman I India 59 A5
South Bay, Scarborough Bch UK 68 A4
South Carolina Adm USA 90 A8
South China Sea 59 A8
South Dakota Adm USA 90 A2
South Downs Reg UK 66 E3
South East Reg UK 68 A6
South Georgia I 54 A3
South Glamorgan Adm UK 68 A5
South I. 55 A9
South I. N Pk Kenya 89 G1
South Landing, Flamborough Bch UK 68 A4
South Milton Sands, Thurlestone Bch UK 68 A6
South Pacific Cruise Area 58 A1
South Pacific Cruise Area 58 A1
South Pole Antarctica 59 A10
South Sandwich Is. 54 A3
South Uist I UK 70 A1
South Yorkshire Adm UK 70 A4
South, The Reg USA 90 A7
South-East England UK .....66 E
Southampton Ferry UK 69 D3
Southampton I. Canada 94 A3
Southampton Apt UK 69 A6
Southampton UK 70 A6
Southend-on-Sea Apt UK 66 E2
Southend-on-Sea UK 66 E2
Southern England Reg UK 66 A2
Southern Ocean 55
Southerndown Bch UK 68 A5
Southwark: George Inn NT UK 67 F5
Southwest, The Reg USA 90 A6
Southwold UK 68 A5
Souvala, Halkida Bch Greece 85 A13
Spa Belgium 65 B16
Spain 80-81
Spalmatore, Ísola la Maddalena Bch Sardinia 84 A3
Spánda, Akr. Cape Crete 83 J10
Spartel, Cap Morocco 89 E4
Spartilas Greece 83 G1
Spartivento, Capo Sardinia 78 D4
Speikeroog I Germany 74 C3
Speke Hall NT UK 67 F4
Spello Italy 79 F12
Sperlonga Italy 78 C4
Spessart Reg Germany 76 B4
Spetsai I Greece 83 J7
Spétses I Greece 83 J7
Speye UN C Germany 64 A6
Speyer Germany 76 B4
Sphinx Egypt 89 F1
Spiaggia Accíaroli Est, Póllica Bch Italy 85 A11
Spiaggia Accíaroli Ovest, Póllica Bch Italy 85 A11
Spiaggia Confine, Framura Bch Italy 84 A3
Spiaggia Pioppi, Póllica Bch Italy 85 A11
Spiaggia Principale, Grado Bch Italy 85 A4
Spiaggia San Lorenzo, Vieste Bch Italy 85 A4
Spiaggia Spagnola, Marsala Bch Sicily 85 A11
Spiez Switzerland 77 E2
Spitsbergen Cru Svalbard 59 A4
Spittal an der Drau Austria 77 F8
Split UN C Croatia 64 A7
Split Croatia 86 B2
Splügen Switzerland 77 E3
Spokane Apt USA 54 A2
Spokane USA 90 A1
Spoleto Italy 78 C1
Spongeorama USA 91 D5
Spontin Belgium 65 B15
Sporades, N Reg Greece 83 J4
Sportgastein Austria 77 F8
Spotorno Italy 79 F6
Spree Riv Germany 74 J5
Spremberg Germany 74 J5
Spring Hill USA 91 D5
Springe Germany 74 E4
Springfield USA 90 A3
Springfield Armory N His USA 93 A14
Springvale Bch UK 68 A6
Srebarna Ntr Res, UN N Bulgaria 61 A4
Sri Lanka 55 A8
Srinagar India 87 D3
Stabilimento Bikini, Vico Equense Bch Italy 85 A11
Stade Germany 74 E3
Stadskanaal Netherlands 74 B3
Staffordshire Adm UK 66 D1
Stáfylos, Skópelos Bch Greece 85 A13
Stagnone, ísola della Sicily 78 E1
Stagshaw Garden NT UK 67 F3
Stalos, N. Kidonía Bch Crete 85 A13
Stampalia I Greece 83 J8
Standen House NT UK 67 F6
Stansted Apt UK 66 E1
Stari Ras UN C Yugo, FY 64 A7
Starkenburg Germany 76 C3
Starnberg Germany 75 G8
Starnberger See Lake Germany 75 G9
Statue of Liberty N Mon, UN C USA 62 A2
Stavanger Apt Norway 56 A6

Stavanger Cru Norway .....59 A
Stavanger Ferry Norway .....69 C
Staverton Apt UK .....66 E
Stavoren Netherlands .....65 B
Stavrós Greece .....83 J
Stavrós Platania, Kato Stavrós Bch Greece 85 A1
Stazione Corniglia, Vernazza Bch Italy .....84 A
Stazione, Lavagna Bch Italy .....84 A
Ste-Agathe-des-Monts Canada .....94 B
Ste-Croix Switzerland .....77 E
Ste-Croix, Martigues Bch France .....72 F
Ste-Enghce France .....72 G
Ste-Marie-la-Mer France .....84 A
Ste-Maxime France .....72 F
Ste-Maxime-Ville Bch France .....84 A
Steamtown N His USA .....93 A
Steiermark Adm Austria .....77 D
Steinach Austria .....74 C
Steinfurt Germany .....74 C
Steinsel Luxembourg 65 B20
Stellenbosch South Africa .....88 C
Stelvio Italy .....79 F
Stenay France 65 B1
Stendal Germany .....74 C
Sterrenberg, Burg Germany .....76 C
Stes-Maries-de-la-Mer France .....84 A
Stettin Poland 86
Stettiner Haff Bay Germany/Poland .....74 J
Steyr Riv Austria 75
Steytlerville South Africa .....88 C
Still Bay South Africa .....88 C
Stirling UK .....66 B
Stirling Castle His Sc UK .....67 F
Stockholm Apt Sweden .....56 A
Stockholm Cru Sweden .....59 A
Stockholm UN C Sweden .....64 A
Stockton USA .....91 E
Stoke-on-Trent UK .....70 A
Stoke-sub-Hamdon Priory NT UK .....67 F
Stolberg Germany .....75 B
Stolzenfels, Schloss Germany .....76 C
Stonehenge UN C UK .....64 A
Stones River N Bat USA .....93 A
Stonington I. Cru Antarctica 59 A1
Store Bælt Str Denmark .....74 G
Stornoway Ferry UK .....69 B
Stornoway UK .....70 A
Stourhead Garden NT UK .....67 F
Stourton UK .....66 D
Stow-on-the-Wold UK .....66 D
Stowe USA .....90 B
Stra Italy .....79 F
Strakonice Czech Rep. 75
Stralsund Germany 74
Stranraer UK .....70 A
Stranraer Ferry UK .....69 B
Strasbourg UN C France .....64 A
Strasbourg France .....73 A
Stratford-upon-Avon UK .....66 D
Strath Earn Reg UK .....66 B
Strathclyde Adm UK .....66 A
Strathcona P Pk Canada .....94 C
Strathmore UK .....66 B
Stratton Mountain USA .....90 B
Straubing Germany .....75 H
Strausberg Germany 74
Stresa Italy .....79 F
Strete Gate, Dartmouth Bch UK .....68 A
Strimón Riv Greece .....83 J
Strómboli, Ísola Sicily .....78 E
Stromness Ferry UK .....69 C
Stroud UK .....66 D
Struisbaai South Africa .....88 C
Stubbenkammer Cape Germany 74
Stuben Austria .....77 F
Studenica UN C Yugo, FY .....64 A
Studley Royal Park UN C UK .....64 A
Sturgeon Falls Canada .....94 B
Stuttgart Apt Germany .....76 B
Stuttgart Germany .....76 B
Styria Adm Austria .....77 D
Su Nuraxi Sardinia .....78 D
Sucre UN C Bolivia .....62 A
Sud, Lido di Metaponto Bernalda Bch Italy 85 A11
Sudan .....88 A
Sudbury Canada .....94 G
Sude Riv Germany .....74 G
Sudety Czech Rep./Poland. .....86 B
Sudong, Pulau I Singapore .....96 C
Sueca Spain .....80 C
Suez Cru Egypt .....59 A
Suez Egypt .....89 F
Suez Canal Egypt .....89 F
Suez, Gulf of Egypt .....89 F
Suffolk Adm UK .....68 A
Suhl Germany .....75 F
Sukhothai UN CN Thailand .....63 A
Sukhumi Georgia .....86 A
Sulawesi I .....55 A
Sulina Riv Romania .....86 C
Sulmona Italy .....78 C
Sulz Germany .....75 D
Sulzbach-Rosenberg Germany .....75 G
Sumatra I .....55 A
Sumava Reg Czech Rep. 75
Sunapee USA .....90 B
Sundarbans N Pk, UN N India .....61 A
Sunderland UK .....70 A
Sundsvall Apt Sweden .....56 A
Sunny Beach Bulgaria .....86 C
Sunset Beach Hawaiian Is. .....91 C
Sunset Crater N Mon USA .....92 A
Super St-Bernard Switzerland .....77 E
Super-Sauze France .....72 F
Superior, Lake Canada/USA. .....94 A
Suphan Buri Thailand .....96 D
Surabaya Cru Indonesia .....59 A
Sûre Riv Luxembourg 65 B20
Surgut Russian Fed. .....86 A
Suriname .....54 A
Surrey Adm UK .....66 E
Susanville USA .....91 E
Susice Czech Rep. 75
Sussex, East Adm UK .....66 E
Sussex, West Adm UK .....66 E
Sutherland South Africa .....88 C
Sutlej Riv Pakistan/India. .....87 D
Sutton Scarsdale Hall EH UK .....67 F
Suva Cru Fiji .....59 A
Suwannee Riv USA .....91 D
Suzdal Russian Fed. .....86 A
Svechtari UN C Bulgaria .....64 A
Svendborg Denmark 74
Swabia Reg Germany .....76 A
Swakopmund Namibia .....88 B
Swaledale South Africa .....88 C
Swan Is. Honduras .....95 F
Swanage UK .....66 D
Swansea Ferry UK .....69 B
Swansea UK .....70 A
Swartberg Pass South Africa .....88 C
Swaziland 88
Sweden .....56 A
Swellendam South Africa .....88 C
Swindon UK .....70 A
Swinoujscie Poland .....74 J
Swiss Alps Mtns Switzerland .....77 E

Switzerland 77
Sydney Apt Australia 55 A9
Sydney Cru Australia 59 A9
Sylt I Germany 74 D2
Symond's Yat UK 66 D3
Syr Darya Riv Kazakhstan 87 D2
Syracuse Apt USA 54 B2
Syracuse Sicily 78 E4
Syracuse USA 56 A16
Syria 94 B10
Syzran Russian Fed. 86 C1
Szczecin Poland 86 B1
Szeged Hungary 86 B2

Taba Egypt 89 F2
Tabarka Tunisia 89 D1
Tabarka Apt Tunisia 89 D1
Tabasqueño Mexico 95 F2
Tabelbala Algeria 89 E4
Tabernes de Valldigna Spain 84 A9
Tabernes, Tabernes de Valldigna Bch Spain 84 A9
Table Bay South Africa 88 C5
Table Mountain South Africa 88 C5
Tabriz Iran 87 D1
Tadmur UN C Syria 64 A12
Tadmur Syria 87 D4
Tadrart Acacus UN C Libya 63 A5
Tafers Switzerland 77 E2
Tafilalt Reg Morocco 89 E4
Tafraoute Morocco 89 E3
Taggia Italy 79 F9
Tagliacozzo Italy 78 C2
Tagomago, Illa de I Ibiza 81 F2
Tahcob Mexico 95 F2
Tahcok Mexico 95 F2
Tahiti I French Polynesia 58 A1
Tahoe, Lake USA 91 E3
Tai N Pk, UN N Côte d'Ivoire 61 A5
Taipei Apt Taiwan 55 A4
Taishan Apt China 61 A8
Taishan UN N China 63 A8
Taiwan 55 A8
Taj Mahal UN C India 86 C1
Tajikistan 86 A3
Takht-i-Bakhi UN C Pakistan 63 C1
Taklamakan Desert China 87 D2
Talamanca Range UN N Costa Rica/Panama 60 A3
Talcy Ch France 72 C2
Taldy-Kurgan Kazakhstan 86 A4
Tallahassee USA 91 D2
Tallahassee Apt USA 91 D2
Tallinn Apt Estonia 56 A3
Tallinn Cru Estonia 59 A6
Tallinn Estonia 86 A1
Tamarinda Menorca 81 H3
Tamarit, Tarragona Bch Spain 84 A2
Tamariu, Palafrugell Bch Spain 84 A2
Tamegroute Morocco 89 E4
Tamerza Tunisia 89 D3
Tamiahua, Laguna de Mexico 95 E2
Tampa USA 91 D5
Tampa Cru USA 59 D5
Tampa USA 91 D5
Tampere Apt Finland 56 A3
Tampico Cru Mexico 58 B4
Tampico Mexico 95 E2
Tampines Singapore 96 C2
Tamworth UK 66 D2
Tan-Tan Morocco 89 E2
Tana Riv Kenya 89 G4
Tana River Primate G Res Kenya 89 G4
Tánaro Riv Italy 79 F5
Tanganyika, Lake Tanzania/Zaïre 88 A3
Tanger Apt Morocco 89 E2
Tanger Cru Morocco 59 C5
Tanger Morocco 89 E2
Tangermünde Germany 74 G4
Tangiers Apt Morocco 89 E2
Tangiers Cru Morocco 59 C5
Tangiers Morocco 89 E2
Tanjong Gertak Sanggul Cape Malaysia 96 B3
Tanjung Bunga Malaysia 96 B2
Tanjung Tokong Malaysia 96 B2
Tankwa-Karoo N Pk South Africa 88 C2
Tantâ Egypt 89 F1
Tantallon Castle His Sc UK 66 B4
Tanum UN C Sweden 64 A2
Tanzania 88 A3
Taormina Sicily 78 E2
Tapachula Mexico 95 F5
Taranto Italy 79 A2
Tarascon-sur-Ariège France 72 E1
Tarasp-Vulpera Switzerland 77 E4
Tarbert Ferry UK 69 B1
Tarbes France 72 D2
Tardieu, Ste-Maxime Bch France 84 A3
Tarentais Reg France 72 G2
Tarfaya Morocco 89 E2
Tarifa Spain 80 D6
Tarim Riv China 87 D2
Tarn Hows NT UK 66 C4
Taroudannt Morocco 89 E3
Tarpon Springs USA 91 D5
Tarquinia Italy 78 C1
Tarragona Spain 80 C3
Tarxien Temples Malta 79 G4
Tashkent Apt Uzbekistan 55 A6
Tashkent Uzbekistan 86 A3
Täsinge I Denmark 74 F2
Tasman Sea 59 A9
Tasmania I 55 A9
Tasmanian wilderness UN CN Australia 63 A9
Tassili n'Ajjer UN N Algeria 61 A5
Tassili n'Ajjer UN C Algeria 63 A5
Tataouine Tunisia 89 D6
Tatry Mtns Poland/Slovak Rep. 86 B2
Tatshenshini-Alsek P Wd Pk, UN N Canada 60 A2
Tattershall Castle NT UK 67 F4
Tatton Park NT UK 67 F4
Tauberbischofsheim Germany 75 E7
Taufstein Mtn Germany 75 E6
Taunus Reg Germany 76 C2
Tauranga Cru New Zealand 59 A9
Tavari, Messótopos Bch Greece 85 A13
Tavira Portugal 82 E8
Tavira, Ilha de I Portugal 82 E8
Tavolara, Isola Sardinia 78 D2
Tavollo, Gabicce Mare Bch Italy 85 A4
Taxco Mexico 95 E4
Taxila UN C Pakistan 63 C1
Taxila Pakistan 87 D5
Taxkorgan China 87 D2
Tay Riv China 66 B1
Tay, Firth of Est UK 66 B1
Tay, Loch UK 66 B1
Tayinloan Ferry UK 69 B2
Taymyr Peninsula Russian Fed. 87 A5
Tayshet Russian Fed. 86 A4
Tayside Adm UK 68 A2
Taza Morocco 89 E3
Tazumal El Salvador 95 F6
Tbilisi Apt Georgia 55 A6
Tbilisi Georgia 86 A2

Tchogha Zambil UN C Iran 63 A7
Teano Italy 78 B1
Tebay UK 66 C4
Tébessa Algeria 89 D3
Teesside Apt UK 70 A3
Tegel Germany 74 I4
Tegernsee Germany 75 G9
Tegge, Isola la Maddalena Bch Sardinia 54 A3
Tegucigalpa Apt Honduras 95 F6
Tegucigalpa Honduras 95 F6
Teguise Canary Is. 80 B3
Tehran Apt Iran 55 A7
Tehran Iran 87 D4
Tehuantepec, Golfo de Mexico 58 B8
Teide, Pico de Mtn Canary Is. 80 B1
Teignmouth UK 68 A6
Teith Riv UK 66 B1
Tejeda Canary Is. 80 B2
Tejo Riv Portugal 82 D2
Tekirova, Kemer Bch Turkey 85 A14
Tel Aviv-Yafo Apt Israel 56 A16
Telde Canary Is. 80 B2
Telford UK 66 D1
Tell el Amarna Egypt 89 F3
Teltow Germany 74 I4
Teluk Bahang Malaysia 96 B1
Teluk Bahang F Res Malaysia 96 B1
Teluk Duyung Bay Malaysia 96 B1
Teluk Kumbar Malaysia 96 B3
Teme Valley UK 66 D1
Témiscaming Canada 94 B1
Tempelhof Apt Germany 74 I4
Templin Germany 74 I3
Ten Thousand Is. USA 91 D7
Tenby North Bch UK 68 A5
Tenby South Bch UK 68 A5
Tenerife I Canary Is. 80 B1
Tenerife: North Apt Canary Is. 80 B1
Tenerife: South Apt Canary Is. 80 B1
Tennessee Adm USA 90 B1
Tensift Riv Morocco 89 E1
Teos Turkey 83 J5
Teotihuacan UN C Mexico 95 E2
Teotihuacan Mexico 95 E2
Tepic Mexico 95 E1
Teplice Czech Rep. 75 I6
Teposcolula Mexico 95 E4
Ter Riv Spain 80 C2
Ter Heijde Netherlands 65 B6
Teramo Italy 78 C2
Terceira Apt Azores 82 B2
Terceira I Azores 82 B2
Términi Imerese, Golfo di Sicily 78 E1
Ternate Cru Indonesia 59 A8
Terneuzen Netherlands 65 B10
Terni Italy 78 C1
Terracina Italy 78 C4
Terranova, Oliva Bch Spain 84 A9
Terrassa Spain 80 C3
Terrazza Mare, Grado Bch Italy 85 A4
Terreiro da Luta Madeira 82 C2
Terreros, Pulpi Bch Spain 84 A8
Terschelling I Netherlands 65 B3
Teruel UN C Spain 64 A9
Terzo Cavone, Scanzano Iónico Bch Italy 85 A11
Teskraia Tunisia 89 D1
Testa, Capo Sardinia 78 D2
Têt Riv France 72 E2
Teterow Germany 74 H3
Tétouan Morocco 89 E2
Teulada Spain 81 E2
Teutoburger Wald Reg Germany 74 D5
Tévere Riv Italy 78 C1
Tewkesbury UK 66 D4
Texas Adm USA 90 A6
Texel I Netherlands 65 B3
Tha Chin Riv Thailand 96 D1
Thaddeus Kosciuszko N Mem USA 93 A4
Thailand 96 A2
Thailand, Peninsular Reg Thailand 96 A2
Thames Riv UK 66 E1
Thames and Chilterns Reg UK 66 E2
Thames Estuary UK 66 E2
Thanet, Isle of UK 66 E2
Thanjavur UN C India 63 C2
Thann France 75 C9
Tharros Sardinia 78 D3
Thássos I Greece 83 J1
Thássos Greece 83 J1
Thatta UN C Pakistan 63 C1
The Courts garden NT UK 67 F6
The Needles Old Battery NT UK 67 F6
The Vyne NT UK 67 F6
The Weald Reg UK 66 E2
Thebes UN C Egypt 89 F4
Thebes Egypt 89 F4
Theinfelden Germany 76 B8
Thelle Reg France 72 H1
Theodore Roosevelt N Pk USA 92 A2
Theodore Roosevelt N His USA 93 A4
Theodore Roosevelt Birthplace N His USA 93 A4
Theodore Roosevelt Island N Mem USA 93 A4
Thermi Greece 83 J5
Thermia I Greece 83 J7
Thermisia UN C Greece 85 A13
Thermisia Bch Greece 85 A13
Thessalía Reg Greece 83 F1
Thessaloníki Apt Greece 83 J1
Thessaloníki UN C Greece 64 A11
Thessaloníki Greece 83 J1
Thessaly Reg Greece 83 F1
Thika Kenya 89 G3
Thimiana Greece 85 A13
Thinalío Greece 85 A12
Thionville France 76 B3
Thira Apt Greece 83 J8
Thira Greece 83 J8
Thira I Greece 83 J8
Thirlmere Lake UK 66 C2
Tholen I Netherlands 65 B10
Tholos, Arhángelos Bch Greece 85 A13
Thomas Hardy's Cottage NT UK 67 F6
Thomas Jefferson Memorial N Mem USA 93 A4
Thomas Stone N His USA 93 A4
Thompson Riv Canada 94 C3
Thon Buri Thailand 96 D1
Thonon-les-Bains France 72 G2
Thornton Abbey EH UK 67 F4
Thoronet, Abbaye du France 72 F3
Thorshavn Ferry UK 69 C1
Thouars France 72 C3
Thrace Greece/Turkey 83 F2
Threave Garden and estate NT Sc UK 67 F3
Three Shells, Southend-on-Sea Bch UK 68 A5
Threlkeld UK 66 C2
Thuburbo Majus Tunisia 89 D2
Thuille, la Italy 79 F1
Thun Switzerland 77 E2
Thunder Bay Canada 94 A7
Thuner See Lake Switzerland 77 E2
Thung Yai–Huai Kha Khaeng W Sanc, UN N Thai. 61 A3
Thur Riv Switzerland 75 D9
Thüringen Adm Germany 76 A2
Thüringer Wald Reg Germany 76 A2
Thuringia Adm Germany 76 A2

Thurlestone UK 68 A6
Thurso UK 70 A1
Thyon 2000 Switzerland 77 E6
Tianjin Cru China 59 A8
Tias Canary Is. 80 B3
Tiberias, Villa di Italy 78 C4
Tibesti Reg Chad/Libya 88 A1
Tibetan Plateau China 87 D5
Ticino Reg Switzerland 77 E7
Ticino Riv Switzerland 77 E7
Ticino Riv Italy 79 F6
Ticul Mexico 95 F2
Tiefenbronn Germany 76 B6
Tielt Belgium 65 C2
Tien Shan Mtns China/Kyrgyzstan 87 D2
Tienen Belgium 65 B15
Tierra del Fuego I 54 A3
Tignes France 72 G2
Tigris Riv Iraq/Turkey 87 D4
Tijuana Mexico 91 E6
Tikal N Pk, UN N Guatemala 60 A3
Tikal Guatemala 95 F4
Tikus, Pulau I Malaysia 96 B2
Tilburg Netherlands 65 B11
Tilbury UK 66 E1
Tilos I Greece 83 J9
Timbuktu UN C Mali 63 A5
Timgad UN C Algeria 64 A10
Timpanogos Cave N Mon USA 92 A1
Timucuan N His USA 93 A8
Tindari Sicily 78 E2
Tindouf Algeria 89 E3
Tinerhir Morocco 89 E2
Tinglev Denmark 74 E2
Tinos UN C Greece 83 J8
Tinos I Greece 83 J8
Tintagel Old Post Office NT UK 67 F6
Tintern Abbey Cadw UK 66 A2
Tipasa UN C Algeria 64 A10
Tioman I Malaysia 56 A11
Tirana Apt Albania 86 B2
Tirana Albania 86 B2
Tirano Italy 79 F3
Tire Turkey 83 J6
Tiree Ferry UK 69 B2
Tiree I UK 70 A2
Tirol Adm Austria 77 F3
Tirrénia I 79 F11
Tirso Riv Sardinia 78 D2
Titchfield Abbey EH UK 67 F6
Titisee Germany 76 B8
Titreyen Gol, Manavgat Bch Turkey 85 A14
Titusville USA 91 D6
Tivoli Italy 78 C2
Tiwi Kenya 89 G4
Tiya UN C Ethiopia 63 A5
Tizimin Mexico 95 F2
Tiznit Morocco 89 E3
Tlaxco Mexico 95 E2
Tobago I Trinidad & Tobago 58 B11
Tobago UN C Cuba 62 A3
Tobermory Ferry UK 69 B2
Todi Italy 79 F12
Todra, Gorges du Morocco 89 E2
Todtnau Germany 76 B8
Toftlund Denmark 74 E1
Toggenburg Reg Switzerland 77 E3
Togo 88 A2
Tokaj Hungary 86 B2
Tokelau I 54 A1
Tokyo Cru Japan 59 A8
Tokyo: Haneda Apt Japan 55 A8
Tokyo: Narita Apt Japan 55 A8
Tol'yatti Russian Fed. 86 C1
Toleant Mexico 95 E2
Toledo UN C Spain 64 A10
Toledo Spain 81 A2
Toledo USA 90 A3
Tolentino Italy 79 F12
Tolfa Italy 78 C1
Toló Greece 85 A12
Toló Bch Greece 85 A12
Toluca Mexico 95 E4
Toluca, Nevado de Mtn Mexico 95 E4
Tomar UN C Portugal 64 A10
Tombland UK 79 F3
Tonbridge UK 66 E3
Tønder Denmark 74 D2
Tonga 55 A9
Tongariro N Pk, UN N New Zealand 61 A9
Tongatapu Apt Tonga 55 A9
Tongatapu I Tonga 59 A9
Toniná Mexico 95 F3
Tönning Germany 74 D2
Tonto N Mon USA 92 A5
Topeka USA 90 A7
Topoxte Guatemala 95 F4
Torbay UK 68 A6
Torcross Bch UK 68 A6
Toreilles France 84 A2
Torgau Germany 74 J3
Torgelow Germany 74 J3
Torhout Belgium 65 C2
Torino Apt Italy 79 F5
Torino Italy 79 F5
Toronto Apt Canada 94 B9
Toronto Canada 94 B9
Tororo Uganda 89 G1
Torquay UK 70 A6
Torralba Portugal 82 E6
Torre Annunziata Italy 78 B3
Torre de Areas Portugal 82 E8
Torre de la Higuera Spain 80 D1
Torre de San Vicente, Benicácim Bch Spain 84 A2
Torre del Greco Italy 78 B3
Torre del Mar Spain 80 D7
Torre la Punta, Póllica Bch Italy 85 A11
Torre Valentina, Calonge Bch Spain 84 A2
Torreblanca Spain 84 A2
Torre, Fuengirola Bch Spain 84 A8
Torredembarra Spain 80 C3
Torredembarra Bch Spain 84 A2
Torredonjimeno Spain 80 D3
Torremolinos Spain 80 D7
Torrenostra, Torreblanca Bch Spain 84 A2
Torres, Calonge/Palamós Bch Spain 84 A2
Torrevieja Spain 81 E3
Torrox Spain 80 D7
Torsei, Framura Bch Italy 84 A3
Tortola Cru Brit Virgin Is. 58 B7
Tortona Italy 79 F6
Tortosa Spain 81 A1
Tortuga Mexico 95 F4
Torver UK 66 C4
Tosca, Kavála Bch Greece 85 A6
Toscana Italy 79 F11
Toshka Depression Egypt 89 F6
Tossa de Mar Spain 80 C4
Tossa de Mar, Tossa de Mar Bch Spain 84 C3
Toubkal, Jebel Mtn Morocco 89 E3
Toul France 75 A8
Toulon Cru France 59 C2
Toulon France 72 F3
Toulouse Apt France 56 A3
Toulouse France 72 A2
Touraine Reg France 72 C2
Tourcoing France 65 B13
Tourmalet, Col du Pass France 72 D2

Tournai Belgium 65 B14
Touro Synagogue N His USA 93 A4
Toury France 72 G4
Toussuire, la France 72 G2
Touws Riv South Africa 88 C6
Touws River South Africa 88 C6
Townsville Apt Australia 55 A9
Townsville Cru Australia 59 A9
Tozeur Apt Tunisia 89 D3
Tozeur Tunisia 89 D3
Traben-Trarbach Germany 76 C3
Trabzon Turkey 83 F3
Traeth cei Bach, New Quay Bch UK 68 A5
Traeth Crigyll, Rhosneigr Bch UK 68 A4
Traeth Harbwr, New Quay Bch UK 68 A5
Traeth y Dyffryn, Aberporth Bch UK 68 A5
Traeth y Gogledd, Aberystwyth Bch UK 68 A5
Traethgwyn, New Quay Bch UK 68 A5
Trafalgar, Cabo de Cape Spain 80 D5
Tragaki Greece 85 A12
Trail Canada 94 C4
Tramuntana, Serra de Reg Mallorca 81 G1
Trans-Siberian Railway 87
Transylvanian Alps Reg Romania 86 B2
Trápani Apt Sicily 78 E1
Trápani Sicily 78 E1
Tras os Montes Reg Portugal 82 A1
Trasimeno, Lago Italy 79 F11
Traun Riv Austria 75 I8
Traunsee Lake Austria 77 F4
Traunstein Germany 75 H9
Travemünde Cru Germany 59 A4
Travemünde Germany 74 F3
Trearddur Bay Bch UK 68 A4
Trébeurden France 72 B1
Trebinje UN C Croatia 87 D1
Trebizond Turkey 72 B1
Trégastel France 72 B2
Tréguier France 76 C1
Treis-Karden Germany 74 I1
Trelleborg Sweden 74 F2
Tremezzo Italy 79 F2
Trentino-Alto Adige Adm Italy 79 F3
Trento N Pk Italy 79 F3
Trento Italy 79 F3
Trenton USA 90 A4
Trenton Canada 94 B6
Tres Zapotes Mexico 95 E3
Tresaith Bch UK 68 A5
Treuchtlingen Germany 75 F8
Treviso Italy 79 F8
Treyarnon, St Merryn Bch UK 68 A6
Triador, Vinarós Bch Spain 84 A2
Trián, Ialisos Bch Greece 85 A13
zTriberg Germany 76 B8
Trier UN C Germany 64 A6
Trier Germany 76 C3
Trieste Italy 79 F8
Trieste, Golfo di Italy/Slovenia 79 F8
Trinidad I Trinidad & Tobago 58 B11
Trinidad UN C Cuba 62 A3
Trinidad and Tobago 95 D7
Tripoli Apt Libya 56 A14
Tristan da Cunha I 55 A5
Troc Pinell, Banyuls-sur-Mer Bch France 84 A2
Tróia Portugal 82 D2
Trois Rivières Canada 94 B4
Trokantero, Itéa Bch Greece 85 A12
Tromsø Apt Norway 55 A4
Tromsø Cru Norway 59 A4
Trondheim Apt Norway 56 A2
Trondheim Cru Norway 59 A4
Tróodos UN C Cyprus 64 A12
Troon South Bch UK 68 A3
Trossachs, The Reg UK 66 B1
Trossay Ch France 72 C2
Trostberg Germany 75 H8
Troullos, Skiathos Bch Greece 85 A13
Troutbeck UK 66 C4
Troy Turkey 83 J2
Truro UK 70 A6
Tsabou, Vourliotes Bch Greece 85 A13
Tsamakia, Mitlíni Bch Greece 85 A13
Tsampika, Arhángelos Bch Greece 85 A13
Tsampou, Vourliotes Bch Greece 85 A13
Tsavo East N Pk Kenya 89 G4
Tsavo West N Pk Kenya 89 G4
Tsilivi, Plános Bch Greece 85 A12
Tsingy Bemaraha Ntr Res, UN N Madagascar 61 A5
Tsitsikamma N Pk South Africa 88 C7
Tsitsikamma Mountains South Africa 88 C7
Tuas Singapore 96 C1
Tübingen Germany 76 B6
Tucson USA 90 A5
Tuktoyaktuk Canada 94 A1
Tula Mexico 95 E2
Tulancingo Mexico 95 E2
Tulbagh South Africa 88 C5
Tulcea Romania 86 C2
Tulum Mexico 95 F2
Tumacacori N Mon USA 92 A5
Tumbu Kenya 89 G4
Tummel Riv UK 66 B1
Tunis Apt Tunisia 89 D2
Tunis Cru Tunisia 59 C6
Tunis UN C Tunisia 64 A10
Tunis Tunisia 89 D2
Tunis, Golfe de Tunisia 89 D2
Tunisia ....89 D
Tupelo N Bat USA 93 A7
Turgay Basin Kazakhstan 86 A3
Turin Apt Italy 79 F5
Turin Italy 79 F5
Turkana, Lake Kenya 89 G1
Turkana, South G Res Kenya 89 G1
Turkey 83
Turkmenbashi Turkmenistan 86 A2
Turkmenistan 86 A2
Turks and Caicos Is. 95 D2
Turku Apt Finland 56 A3
Turkwel Riv Kenya 89 G1
Turnhout Belgium 65 B11
Turnov Czech Rep. 87 D3
Turpan China 87 D3
Turquoise Coast Reg Turkey 83 F2
Tusan / Kustur, Kusadasi Bch Turkey 85 A13
Tuscánia Italy 78 C1
Tuscany Adm Italy 79 F11
Tuskegee Institute N His USA 93 A8
Tuttlingen Germany 76 B8
Tutuila I French Polynesia 58 A1
Tuva Reg Russian Fed. 87 A5
Tuvalu 55 A9
Tuxpan Mexico 95 E2
Tuzigoot N Mon USA 92 A5
Tver' Russian Fed. 86 A2
Tweedsmuir P Pk Canada 94 C1
Twente Apt Netherlands 65 B8
Twin Falls USA 91 E2
Twistringen Germany 74 D4
Ty Mawr Wybrnant NT UK 67 F4
Tyndrum UK 66 A1
Tyne and Wear Adm UK 68 A3
Tynemouth UK 68 A3
Tyre UN C Lebanon 64 A12
Tyrone Adm UK 68 A5

Tyrrhenian Sea 59 C2
Tyumen Reg Russian Fed. 86 A3

UAE 55 A7
Uaxactún Guatemala 95 F4
Überlingen Germany 75 E9
Ubin, Pulau I Singapore 96 C2
Uckermark Reg Germany 76 A1
Ückermünde Germany 74 J3
Udine Italy 79 F4
Udon Thani Thailand 96 A1
Uecker Riv Germany 74 J3
Uelzen Germany 74 F4
Ufa Russian Fed. 86 A2
Uffington Castle EH UK 67 F5
Uganda 88 A3
Ugine France 72 G2
Uhlava Riv Czech Rep. 75 I7
Uig Ferry UK 69 B1
Uitenhage South Africa 88 C8
Uithuizen Netherlands 65 B4
Ujung Kulon N Pk, UN N Indonesia 61 A8
Ujung Pandang Cru Indonesia 59 A8
Ukraine 86 A1
Ulan Bator Apt Mongolia 55 A8
Ulan Ude Russian Fed. 87 A5
Ular, Pulau I Singapore 96 C3
Ulássai Sardinia 78 D4
Ullapool UK 70 A1
Ullswater Lake UK 66 C2
Ulm Germany 75 E8
Ulmen Germany 76 C1
Ulster Reg 66 A1
Uludag Mtn Turkey 83 J3
Ulundi South Africa 88 B1
Uluru N Pk, UN CN Australia 63 A9
Ulverston UK 66 C4
Ulysses S. Grant N His USA 93 A7
Umbria Adm Italy 78 A2
Umes UN C Norway 64 A2
Umtata South Africa 88 B2
Ungava Peninsula Canada 94 A3
Ungwana Bay Kenya 89 G4
Uniondale South Africa 88 C6
United Arab Emirates 55 A7
United Kingdom 66
United States 90
Universal Studios, Hollywood USA 92 A5
Universal Studios, Orlando USA 93 A8
Unst UK 70 A7
Unstrut Riv Germany 75 F5
Unter Engadin Reg Switzerland 77 E4
Unterfranken Reg Germany 76 A2
Unterinntal Reg Austria 77 F3
Unterwasser Switzerland 77 E3
Upington South Africa 88 B1
Uplands Apt Canada 94 B7
Uppark NT UK 67 F6
Upper Austria Adm Austria 77 D3
Upper Canada Village Canada 94 B7
Upper Egypt Reg Egypt 89 F4
Ural Mountains Russian Fed. 86 A3
Uranium City Canada 94 A6
Urbino Italy 79 F12
Urquhart Castle His Sc UK 67 F1
Uruapan Mexico 95 F1
Uruguay 54 A3
Urzig Germany 79 C3
Ürzig Germany 58 A2
US East Coast Cruise Area 59 D3
US Virgin Is. 58 B7
Usak Turkey 83 J6
Usedom I Germany 74 J3
Ushkani Is. Russian Fed. 87 A5
Ushuaia Cru Argentina 58 A3
Uskemen Kazakhstan 86 A4
Üsküdar Turkey 83 J3
USS Arizona Memorial N Mem Hawaiian Is. 91 C5
Ussé Ch France 72 C2
Ústí nad Labem Czech Rep. 75 J6
Ústica, Ísola di Sicily 78 E1
Ustyurt Plateau Kazahstan/Uzbekistan 86 A2
Utah Adm USA 90 A1
Utara, Selat Str Malaysia 96 B2
Utatlán Guatemala 95 F5
Utelle, Madone d' France 72 F2
Utica USA 90 A4
Utrecht Netherlands 65 B7
Utrecht Adm Netherlands 65 B7
Uxmal Mexico 95 F2
Uzbekistan 86 A3
Uzum I Turkey 83 J5

Vaasa Apt Finland 56 A3
Vác Hungary 86 C2
Vadehavet Bay Denmark 74 D1
Vágar Apt Faroe Is. 56 A1
Vai, Palékastro Bch Crete 85 A13
Val André, le France 72 B2
Val Camónica UN C Italy 64 A6
Val Camónica Reg Italy 79 F3
Val d'Isere France 72 G2
Val d'Oise Adm France 72 H1
Val di Mazara Reg Sicily 78 E1
Val di Noto Reg Sicily 78 E4
Val-Thorens France 72 G4
Valaam I Russian Fed. 86 A1
Valais Reg Switzerland 77 E6
Valbella Switzerland 72 D2
Valcabrère France 72 D2
Valdai Hills Russian Fed. 86 C1
Valdez Cru USA 58 A2
Valdivia Chile 91 D3
Vale de Parra Portugal 82 E6
Vale of Trent Reg UK 66 D2
Valençay Ch France 72 G3
Valence France 72 G3
Valencia Apt Spain 56 A13
Valencia Spain 81 A2
Valenciana, Comunidad de Adm Spain 81 A2
Valenciennes France 65 B14
Valkenburg Netherlands 65 B16
Valladolid Spain 80 A1
Valldemossa Mallorca 81 G1
Valle d'Aosta Adm Italy 79 F1
Valle de Bravo Mexico 95 E4
Valley Forge N His USA 93 A4
Valle dell'Erica, Sta Teresa Gallura Bch Sardinia 84 A3
Valle, Monterosso Bch Italy 88 C3
Valley of Desolation Reg South Africa 88 C3
Valley of the Kings Egypt 89 F4
Valleyfields Canada 94 B7
Valloire France 72 G4
Vallorbe Switzerland 77 E1
Valls Spain 80 C3
Valmorel France 72 G2
Valois Reg France 72 H2

Index

Valparaíso Cru Chile 58 A3
Valras France 84 A2
Vals Switzerland 77 E3
Valtournenche Italy 79 F1
Valverde Canary Is. 80 B4
Valverde Nord, Cesenático Bch Italy 85 A4
Valverde Sud, Cesenático Bch Italy 85 A4
Van Turkey 83 F3
Van, Lake Turkey 83 F3
Vancouver Apt Canada 94 C3
Vancouver Cru Canada 58 A2
Vancouver Canada 94 C3
Vancouver I. Canada 94 C3
Vandellòs i l'Hospitalet de l'infant Spain 84 A2
Vanderbilt Mansion N His USA 93 A4
Vanderhoof Canada 94 C1
Vänern Lake Sweden 56 A2
Vannes France 72 B4
Vanoise Reg France 72 G2
Vanuatu 55 A9
Var Riv France 72 F2
Var Adm France 72 F3
Vara, Pico da Mtn Azores 82 B1
Varador, Santa Pola Bch Spain 84 A9
Varcavello, Diano Marina Bch Italy 84 A3
Varkiza Greece 83 J7
Varna Apt Bulgaria 56 A11
Varna Cru Bulgaria 59 C3
Vars France 72 G4
Vascao Riv Portugal 82 E4
Vassiliki Greece 83 H1
Vassilikós Greece 83 H3
Vatera, Vríssa Bch Greece 85 A13
Vathy Greece 83 H2
Vatican City UN C 64 A6
Vatican City 78 C1
Vättern Lake Sweden 56 A6
Vaucluse Adm France 72 F1
Vaygach I. Russian Fed. 86 A3
Vazon Bay, Cobo Bch Channel Is. 68 A8
Vechta Germany 74 D4
Vechte Riv Germany 74 C4
Vedra, Illa es I Ibiza 81 F3
Veendam Netherlands 74 B3
Veere Netherlands 65 B10
Velanio, Skópelos Bch Greece 85 A13
Veldrif South Africa 88 C1
Veldenz, Schloss Germany 76 C3
Veleta, Pico de Mtn Spain 80 D3
Vélez Rubio Spain 80 D4
Vélez-Málaga Spain 80 D7
Velika, Melivia Bch Greece 85 A12
Velino Riv Italy 78 C2
Velletri Italy 78 C1
Vena, San Mauro Pascoli Bch Italy 85 A4
Vence France 72 F2
Vendée Adm France 72 C3
Vendôme France 72 C2
Veneciola, San Javier Bch Spain 84 A8
Véneta, Laguna Lag Italy 79 F8
Veneto Adm Italy 79 F7
Venézia Apt Italy 79 F8
Venézia Cru Italy 59 C2
Venézia UN C Italy 64 A6
Venézia Italy 79 F8
Venézia, Golfo di Croatia/Italy 79 F8
Venezuela 54 A3
Venezuela, Golfo de Venezuela 58 B10
Venice Apt Italy 79 F8
Venice Cru Italy 59 C2
Venice UN C Italy 64 A6
Venice Italy 79 F8
Venlo Netherlands 65 B12
Venta del Bancal,Mojácar Bch Spain 84 A8
Ventimiglia Italy 79 F9
Ventura USA 91 E5
Venzone Italy 79 F4
Vera Spain 84 A4
Veracruz Mexico 95 E4
Verbania Italy 79 F2
Verbier Switzerland 77 E6
Vercelli Italy 79 F6
Vercors Reg France 72 G3
Verdala Palace Malta 79 G4
Verden Germany 74 E4
Verdon Riv France 72 F1
Verdon, Basses Gorges du France 72 F1
Verdon, Grand Canyon du France 72 F1
Verdon, Martigues Bch France 84 A3
Vérendrye, la P Pk Canada 94 B2
Verga Greece 85 A12
Vergeron, La Croix-Valmer Bch France 84 A3
Vermont USA 90 B3
Vernazza Italy 79 F7
Vernon France 72 H1
Verona Italy 79 F7
Versailles UN C France 64 A6
Versailles France 72 H3
Verviers Belgium 65 B16
Vervins France 65 B18
Vesubie Reg France 72 F2
Vesuvio Mtn Italy 78 B3
Vesuvius Mtn Italy 78 B3
Vetralla Italy 78 C1
Veurne Belgium 65 C1
Vevey Switzerland 77 E5
Vexin Reg France 72 H1
Vézelay UN C France 64 A6
Vézère Valley UN C France 64 A6
Via del Saggitario, San Michele al Tag'o Bch Italy 85 A4
Via Delfino, San Michele al Tag'o Bch Italy 85 A4
Via Palmaria, San Bartolomeo al Mare Bch Italy 84 A3
Via Veneto, San Michele al Tag'o Bch Italy 85 A4
Viale dei Lauri, San Michele al Tag'o Bch Italy 85 A4
Viana do Castelo Portugal 82 A1
Vianden Luxembourg 65 B20
Viaréggio Italy 79 F10
Vias France 84 A2
Vic Spain 80 C2
Vicdessos France 72 E1
Vicenza UN C Italy 64 A6
Vicenza Italy 79 F7
Vichy France 73 A2
Vicksburg N Mil USA 93 A7
Vico Equense Italy 78 B3
Vico, Lago di Italy 78 C1
Victoria Cru Canada 58 A2
Victoria Malta 79 G1
Victoria Canada 94 C3
Victoria Apt Canada 94 C3
Victoria Falls UN N Zambia/Zimbabwe 61 A5
Victoria Falls Zambia/Zimbabwe 88 A4
Victoria I. Canada 94 A2
Victoria Lines Reg Malta 79 G4
Victoria, Lake Kenya/Tanzania/Uganda 88 A3
Victoria West South Africa 88 C3
Vidin Bulgaria 86 C2
Viechtach Germany 75 H7
Vieille Chapelle, Marseille Bch France 84 A3
Viella, Túnel de Spain 72 E1
Vienna Apt Austria 56 A11
Vienna Austria 77 D4
Vienne Adm France 72 C4
Vienne Riv France 72 C4
Vienne France 72 G1

Vientiane Apt Laos 55 A8
Viersen Germany 75 B5
Vierwald Stätter See Lake Switzerland 77 E3
Vieste Italy 85 A4
Vietnam 55 A8
Vietnam Veterans Memorial N Mem USA 93 A4
Vigévano Italy 79 F6
Vigo Cru Spain 59 C1
Vigo Spain 80 A1
Viking Bay, Broadstairs Bch UK 68 A6
Vila do Bispo Portugal 82 E5
Vila do Porto Apt Azores 82 B2
Vila do Porto Azores 82 B2
Vila Franca de Xira Portugal 82 D2
Vila Franca do Campo Azores 82 B1
Vila Nogueira de Azeitão Portugal 82 D2
Vila Real de Santo António Portugal 82 E8
Vilafortuny-Esquirol, Cambrils de Mar Bch Spain 84 A2
Vilafranca del Penèdes Spain 80 C3
Vilaine Riv France 72 B4
Vilamoura Portugal 82 E7
Vilanova i la Geltrú Spain 80 C3
Villa Bianchelli, Sirolo Bch Italy 85 A4
Villa Carlos Menorca 81 H4
Villa Sada, Ospedaletti Bch Italy 84 A3
Villach Austria 77 F8
Villaggio Cóppola Italy 78 B1
Villaggio Marzotto, Jésolo Bch Italy 85 A4
Villaggio Valtur, Ostuni Bch Italy 85 A12
Villagio Gattarella, Vieste Bch Italy 85 A4
Villahermosa Mexico 95 F3
Villajoyosa Spain 81 E2
Villamarina, Cesenático Bch Italy 85 A4
Villandry Ch France 72 C2
Villard-de-Lans France 72 G3
Villars Switzerland 77 E6
Villasimius Sardinia 78 D4
Villefranche-sur-Mer France 72 F2
Villefranche-sur-Sáone France 72 G1
Villena Spain 81 E1
Villeneuve Switzerland 77 E5
Villeneuve-les-Maguelonne France 84 A2
Villesavin Ch France 72 C2
Villingen-Schwenningen Germany 75 D8
Vilm I Germany 74 I2
Vilnius Apt Lithuania 56 A7
Vilnius UN C Lithuania 64 A3
Vilnius Lithuania 86 A1
Vils Riv Germany 75 H8
Vilshofen Germany 75 I8
Vilvoorde Belgium 65 B10
Vimperk Czech Rep. 75 I7
Vinarós Spain 81 A1
Vinarós Bch Spain 84 A2
Vinaroz Spain 81 A1
Vinaroz Bch Spain 84 A2
Vintzi, Náxos Bch Greece 85 A13
Vipiteno Italy 79 F3
Virgin Gorda Cru Brit Virgin Is. 58 B7
Virgin Is., Brit. 95 D3
Virgin Is., US 95 D3
Virgin Islands UN S Pk US Virgin Is. 93
Virginia Adm USA 90 A8
Virton Belgium 65 B19
Virunga N Pk, UN N Zaïre 61 A5
Visby Cru Sweden 59 A4
Visegrád Hungary 86 C2
Viseu Portugal 82 A1
Viso, Monte Mtn Italy 79 F5
Viterbo Italy 78 C1
Viti Levu I Fiji 59 A9
Vitória Gastiez Spain 81 A1
Vitré France 72 C1
Vitznau Switzerland 77 E3
Vittoriosa Malta 79 G4
Vittorio Véneto Italy 79 F4
Vivari, Drépano Bch Greece 85 A12
Vladimir Russian Fed. 86 A2
Vladivostok Apt Russian Fed. 55 A6
Vladivostok Cru Russian Fed. 59 A6
Vladivostok Russian Fed. 86 A2
Vlicha, Líndos Bch Greece 85 A13
Vlieland I Netherlands 65 B3
Vlihó Greece 83 H1
Vlissingen Netherlands 65 B10
Vlorë Albania 86 B2
Vltava Riv Czech Rep. 75 J6
Vöcklabrück Austria 75 I8
Vogelsberg Reg Germany 76 B2
Vogtland Reg Germany 75 H6
Voi Kenya 89 G4
Voile Blanche, Antibes Bch France 84 A3
Voilier, Nice Bch France 84 A3
Voiron France 72 G3
Vol'sk Russian Fed. 86 C1
Volary Czech Rep. 75 I8
Volcano Hawaiian Is. 91 C8
Volendam Netherlands 65 B7
Volga Riv Russian Fed. 86 A2
Volga Delta Reg Russian Fed. 86 A2
Volga, Cities of the Reg Russian Fed. 86 A2
Volgograd Apt Russian Fed. 55 A6
Volgograd Russian Fed. 86 C1
Volgograd Reservoir Russian Fed. 86 C1
Völklingen UN C Germany 64 A6
Völklingen Germany 75 B7
Vólos Greece 83 J4
Vólos Apt Greece 83 J4
Vólos Cru Greece 85 A12
Volterra Italy 79 F11
Volturno Riv Italy 78 B1
Vónitsa Greece 83 H1
Voorne I Netherlands 65 B10
Voramar-Almadrava, Benicàsim Bch Spain 84 A2
Vorarlberg Adm Austria 77 F1
Vordingborg Denmark 74 G1
Vorkuta Russian Fed. 86 A3
Voronezh Russian Fed. 86 A2
Vosges Reg France 75 C8
Voúla Greece 83 J7
Vouliagméni Greece 83 J7
Vourliotes Greece 85 A13
Vouvray France 72 C2
Voyage to the Glaciers Cruise Area 58 A2
Voyageurs N Pk USA 93 A3
Vrahási Greece 85 A13
Vraháti Bch Greece 85 A12
Vrassná Greece 85 A13
Vrassná Bch Greece 85 A13
Vredenburg South Africa 88 C1
Vredendal South Africa 88 C1
Vrine Albania 83 G1
Vrissa Greece 85 A13
Vromolimnos, Skiathos Bch Greece 85 A13
Vryburg South Africa 88 C3
Vukovar Croatia 86 C2
Vulcano, Ísola Sicily 78 A4
Vulkaneifel Germany 76 C1

W.A.C. Bennett Dam Canada 94 C1
Waal Riv Netherlands 65 B11
Wachadma Plain Kenya 89 G2
Waddenèilanden I Netherlands 79 B3
Waddenzee Sea Netherlands 65 B3

Waddington, Mt Canada 94 C3
Wagrain Austria 77 F4
Wahiawa Hawaiian Is. 91 C5
Waialua Hawaiian Is. 91 C5
Waianae Range Reg Hawaiian Is. 91 C5
Waikiki Hawaiian Is. 91 C6
Wailua Falls Hawaiian Is. 91 C4
Wailuku Hawaiian Is. 91 C3
Wailuku River S Pk Hawaiian Is. 91 C8
Waimanalo Beach Hawaiian Is. 91 C6
Waimea Hawaiian Is. 58 A1
Waimea Hawaiian Is. 91 C8
Waimea Bay Hawaiian Is. 91 C1
Waimea Canyon S Pk Hawaiian Is. 91 C2
Wainiha Hawaiian Is. 91 C2
Waipahu Hawaiian Is. 91 C5
Waipio Valley Hawaiian Is. 91 C1
Wajir Kenya 89 G2
Wakehurst Palace Garden NT UK 67 F6
Walachia Romania 86 B2
Walchensee Lake Germany 75 G9
Waldkirch Germany 76 B8
Waldkraiburg Germany 75 H8
Waldshut Germany 76 B8
Walensee Lake Switzerland 77 E3
Wales UK 66 A2
Walker Lake USA 91 E4
Wallis and Futuna Is. 55 A9
Walmer Castle and Gardens EH UK 67 F6
Walnut Canyon N Mon USA 92 A5
Walsall UK 66 D2
Walsertal, Grosser Reg Austria 77 F5
Walsrode Germany 74 E4
Walt Disney World Resort Complex USA 91 D5
Waltham Abbey Gatehouse and Bridge EH UK 67 F5
Walton Heath Gf UK 66 E3
Wang Phetburi Mtn Thailand 96 B2
Wang Takhrai N Pk Thailand 96 D2
Wang Takhrai Gardens Thailand 96 D2
Wangen Germany 75 E9
Wangerooge I Germany 74 C3
Wanneperveen Netherlands 65 B8
War in the Pacific N His Northern Mariana Is. 93
Warburg Germany 74 E5
Wardija Point Malta 79 G1
Waren Germany 74 H3
Warkworth UK 66 A1
Warnemünde Germany 74 H2
Warnow Riv Germany 74 H3
Warsaw Apt Poland 56 A7
Warsaw UN C Poland 64 A7
Warsaw Poland 86 B1
Warth Austria 77 F5
Warton Old Rectory EH UK 67 F4
Warwick UK 66 D2
Warwickshire Adm UK 66 D2
Washago Canada 94 B5
Washington Apt USA 54 B2
Washington USA 90 A1
Washington Adm USA 90 A4
Washington UK 66 A1
Washington Monument N Mem USA 93 A4
Washington Old Hall NT UK 67 F3
Washington, Mt USA 90 B3
Wassenaar Netherlands 65 B6
Wasserburg Germany 75 H8
Wasserkuppe Mtn Germany 75 E6
Wast Water Lake UK 66 C3
Wat Chayamangkalaram Malaysia 96 B2
Wat Phai Rong Wua Thailand 96 D1
Wat Phra Sriratana Mahathat Thailand 96 D3
Watcombe, Torbay Bch UK 68 A4
Waterloo Bat Belgium 65 B14
Waterport USA 94 B9
Watersmeet House NT UK 67 F6
Waterton Lakes N Pk Canada 94 C4
Waterton-Glacier Int Pc Pk Canada/USA .....94 A
Watertown USA 94 B10
Waterville USA 90 B4
Watford UK 66 E1
Wattenmeer Bay Germany 74 C3
Watumu Marine N Pk Kenya 89 G4
Watzmann Mtn Germany 75 H9
Waverley Abbey EH UK 67 F6
Waycross USA 91 D3
Weddell Sea Antarctica 59 A10
Wedel Germany 74 E3
Weeki Wachee Spring USA 91 D5
Weener Germany 74 C3
Weggis Switzerland 77 E3
Weiden Germany 75 H7
Weilburg Germany 76 C2
Weilheim Germany 75 G9
Weimar Germany 75 G6
Weinheim Germany 75 D7
Weir Farm N His USA 93 A4
Weiße Elster Riv Germany 75 H5
Weissenburg France 76 B6
Weißenburg Germany 75 F7
Weißenfels Germany 75 G5
Weißwasser Germany 74 J5
Welkom South Africa 88 B1
Welland Canal Canada 94 B9
Wellington Apt New Zealand 55 A9
Wellington Cru New Zealand 59 A9
Wells Gray P Pk Canada 94 C4
Wells-next-the-Sea Bch UK 68 A4
Wels Austria 77 D3
Welschap Apt Netherlands 65 B11
Wembury: The Old Mill NT UK 67 F6
Wemyss Bay Ferry UK 69 B3
Wenduine Belgium 65 C2
Wengen Switzerland 77 E2
Wenlock Edge Reg UK 66 D1
Wentworth UK 66 A1
Wernigerode Germany 74 F5
Werra Riv Germany 75 E5
Wertheim Germany 75 E7
Wertlach Riv Germany 75 F8
Wesel Germany 74 B5
Weser Riv Germany 74 E4
West Africa Cruise Area 59 A5
West Angle Bay Bch UK 68 A5
West Bay Bch UK 68 A4
West Bay Strand, Portrush Bch UK 68 A3
West Bromwich UK 66 D2
West Cliff, Whitby Bch UK 68 A3
West Coast N Pk South Africa 88 C1
West Country UK 68 A6
West Frisian Is. Netherlands 74 A3
West Glamorgan Adm UK 68 A5
West Highland Line Rail UK 66 B1
West Midlands Adm UK 66 D2
West Palm Beach USA 91 D6
West Point Cru Falkland Is. 59 A10
West Siberian Plain Russian Fed. 86 A4
West Virginia Adm USA 90 A4
West Vlaanderen Adm Netherlands 65 B12
West Wittering Bch UK 68 A6
West Yorkshire Adm UK 66 A1
Westende-Bad Belgium 65 C1
Westendorf Austria 77 F3
Westerbergland Reg Germany 74 E5
Westerland Germany 74 D2
Western Cape Adm South Africa 88 C6
Western Isles Adm UK 68 A1
Western Sahara 88 A1

Western Samoa 54 A1
Westerstede Germany 74 C3
Westerwald Reg Germany 76 B2
Westland N Pk, UN N New Zealand 61 A9
Westminster UN C UK 64 A5
Westminster UK 66 E1
Westminster: Jewel Tower EH UK 67 F5
Wetzlar Germany 76 B2
Weymouth Ferry UK 69 D2
Weymouth UK 70 A6
Weymouth Central Bch UK 68 A6
Whalley Abbey Gatehouse EH UK 67 F4
Whipsnade Zoo UK 66 E1
Whiskeytown-Shasta-Trinity N Rec USA 92 A1
Whistler Canada 94 C3
Whitby UK 68 A3
Whitby Bch UK 68 A3
White House, The USA 93 A4
White Mountains USA 90 B3
White River Junction USA 90 B3
White Sands N Mon USA 92 A6
White Sea Russian Fed. 59 A6
White Sea Russian Fed. 86 A2
Whitehaven UK 66 C1
Whitehorse Canada 94 A1
Whitesands, St David's Bch UK 68 A5
Whitman Mission N His USA 91 A1
Whitmore Village Hawaiian Is. 91 C5
Whitney, Mt USA 91 E4
Whitsunday Is. Cru Australia 59 A9
Whittier Cru USA 58 A2
Wick UK 70 A1
Widemouth Sand, Bude Bch UK 68 A6
Wied Riv Germany 76 C2
Wieliczka UN C Poland 64 A7
Wien Apt Austria 56 A11
Wien Adm Austria 77 D4
Wien Austria 77 D4
Wieringermeer Reg Netherlands 65 B6
Wies UN C Germany 64 A6
Wiesbaden Germany 76 C4
Wight, Isle of UK 70 A6
Wil Switzerland 75 E9
Wilczek Land I Russian Fed. 86 A3
Wild Coast Reg South Africa 88 B2
Wildbad Germany 76 B6
Wilderness National Lake Area South Africa 88 C7
Wildeshausen Germany 74 C4
Wildhaus Switzerland 77 E3
Wilhelmshaven Germany 74 D3
Wilkes Land Reg Antarctica 59 A10
Willandra lakes region UN CN Australia 63 A9
Willemstad Cru Curaçao 58 B10
William Howard Taft N His USA 93 A4
Williams Lake Canada 94 C3
Williston South Africa 88 C2
Williston Lake Canada 94 C1
Willowmore South Africa 88 C2
Wilson's Creek N Bat USA 93 A7
Wiltshire Adm UK 68 A6
Wiltz Luxembourg 65 B20
Winchelsea Bch UK 68 A6
Winchester UK 70 A6
Winchester City Mill NT UK 67 F6
Wind Cave N Pk USA 92 A2
Windermere Lake UK 66 C3
Windermere UK 66 C4
Windhoek Apt Namibia 55 A5
Windsor UK 66 E1
Windsor Canada 76 C1
Winnipeg Apt Canada 54 A2
Winnipeg Canada 94 A6
Winnipeg, Lake Canada 94 A6
Winnipesaukee, Lake USA 90 B3
Winsen Germany 74 E3
Winster Market House NT UK 67 F4
Winter Haven USA 91 D5
Winter Park USA 91 D6
Winterberg Germany 75 D5
Winterberg Reg South Africa 88 C4
Winterswijk Netherlands 65 B8
Winterthur Switzerland 77 D2
Wiscasset USA 90 B4
Wisconsin Adm USA 90 A3
Wiseman's Bridge, Saundersfoot Bch UK 68 A5
Wismar Germany 74 G3
Wissembourg France 76 B6
Witten Germany 74 C5
Wittenberge Germany 74 G4
Wittlich Germany 76 C1
Wittmund Germany 74 C3
Wittstock Germany 74 H3
Woking UK 66 E3
Wolf Trap Farm Park USA 93 A4
Wolfen Germany 74 H5
Wolfenbüttel Germany 74 F4
Wolfratshausen Germany 75 G9
Wolfsburg Germany 74 F4
Wolgast Germany 74 I2
Wolin I Poland 74 J3
Wolverhampton UK 66 D2
Wolvesley: Old Bishop's Palace EH UK 67 F6
Women's Rights N His USA 93 A4
Wood Buffalo N Pk, N Canada 60 A2
Woodbridge Bay Cru Dominica 58 B11
Woodlands New Town Singapore 96 C1
Woolacombe UK 68 A6
Worcester UK 66 D1
Worcester South Africa 88 C5
Wordsworth House NT UK 67 F4
Workington UK 66 C1
Worms Germany 76 C4
Worthing UK 66 E3
Wörgl Austria 75 H9
Wrangel I Russian Fed. 55 A6
Wrangell-St Elias N Pk, N Pres, UN N USA 92 A9
Wrangell, The Reg USA 92 A9
Wright Brothers N Mem USA 93 A4
Wroclaw Poland 86 B1
Wudang Mountains UN C China 63 A9
Wuhan Cru China 59 A8
Wunstorf Germany 74 E4
Wupatki N Mon USA 92 A5
Wuppertal Germany 75 C5
Würzburg UN C Germany 64 A6
Würzburg Germany 75 E7
Wurzen Germany 74 H5
Wusong Cru China 59 A8
Wutach Germany 76 B8
Wye Riv UK 66 D1
Wye Valley UK 66 D1
Wyoming Adm USA 90 A2
Wyre Forest UK 66 D1

Xeraco Spain 84 A9
Xewkija Malta 79 G1
Xi'an area UN C China 63 A4
Xiamen Cru China 59 A8
Xian China 87 D6
Xichmook Mexico 95 F2
Xlacach Mexico 95 F2
Xlendi Malta 79 G1
Xlendi Bay Malta 79 G1
Xpuhil Mexico 95 F3
Xultún Guatemala 95 F3
Xunantunich Belize 95 F4

Yakutsk Russian Fed. 87 A6
Yalova Turkey 83 J3
Yalta Cru Ukraine 59 C4
Yalta Ukraine 86 C1
Yamal Peninsula Russian Fed. 86 A3
Yamaska P Pk Canada 94 B8
Yangon Apt Myanmar 55 A8
Yangon Cru Myanmar 59 A8
Yangtze Riv China 59 A8
Yankee Harbour Cru Antarctica 59 A10
Yantai Cru China 59 A8
Yarkant China 87 D2
Yarmouth Ferry UK 69 D8
Yarmouth Castle EH UK 67 F6
Yaroslavl' Russian Fed. 86 A2
Yasawa Cru Fiji 59 A9
Yatta Plateau Kenya 89 G4
Yaverland Bch UK 68 A6
Yaxchilán Mexico 95 F3
Yaxhá Guatemala 95 F4
Yecla Spain 81 E1
Yekaterinburg Apt Russian Fed. 56 A3
Yekaterinburg Russian Fed. 86 A3
Yelapa Mexico 95 E1
Yell I UK 70 A7
Yellow Riv China 87 A7
Yellowhead Pass Canada 94 C3
Yellowknife Apt Canada 54 A2
Yellowknife Canada 94 A2
Yellowstone N Pk, UN N USA 92 A7
Yemen 54 A7
Yerevan Apt Armenia 55 A6
Yerevan Armenia 86 A2
Yishun New Town Singapore 96 C1
Yithion Cru Greece 94 C4
Yoho N Pk Canada 94 C3
Yokohama Cru Japan 59 A6
Yonne Adm France 72 H4
Yonne Riv France 72 H4
York UK 70 A4
York: Treasurer's House NT UK 67 F4
Yorkshire Reg UK 66 A1
Yorkshire and Humberside Reg UK 66 A1
Yorkshire Dales P Pk UK 67 F4
Yosemite N Pk, UN N USA 91 E3
Ypres Belgium 65 B13
Yucatán Channel 58 B5
Yucatán Peninsula Mexico 95 F2
Yucca House N Mon USA 92 A6
Yugoslavia, Federal Republic of 86 A2
Yukon Territory Adm Canada 94 A1
Yukon-Charley Rivers N Pres USA 92 A9
Yuma USA 91 E6
Yvelines Adm France 72 H4
Yverdon-les-Bains Switzerland 77 E2
Yvoir Belgium 65 B15

Zaabrugge Belgium 65 C2
Zaandam Netherlands 65 B7
Zacatecas Mexico 95 E1
Zaculeu Guatemala 95 F5
Zadar Croatia 86 B2
Zaghouan Tunisia 89 D2
Zagora Morocco 89 E4
Zagreb Apt Croatia 56 A11
Zagreb Croatia 86 B2
Záharo Greece 85 A12
Záharo Bch Greece 85 A12
Zaïre 88 A3
Zákinthos Apt Greece 83 H3
Zákinthos Greece 83 H3
Zákinthos Cru Greece 85 A12
Zákinthos Bch Greece 85 A12
Zakopane Poland 86 B1
Zambia 88 A3
Zandvoort Netherlands 65 B7
Zante I Greece 83 H3
Zante Greece 83 H3
Zanzibar Cru Tanzania 59 A5
Zaragoza Spain 81 A1
Zary Poland 74 K5
Zarzis Tunisia 89 D6
Zatec Czech Rep. 75 I6
Zaventem Apt Belgium 65 B14
Zebbug Malta 79 G4
Zeebrugge Ferry Belgium 69 C5
Zeeland Adm Netherlands 65 B10
Zehdenick Germany 74 I3
Zeitz Germany 75 H5
Zelená Hora UN C Czech Rep. 64 A7
Zell am See Austria 77 F4
Zell am Ziller Austria 77 F7
Zell, Baden Württemberg Germany 76 B6
Zell, Rheinland Pfalz Germany 76 C3
Zembra, Île Tunisia 89 D2
Zembretta, Île Tunisia 89 D2
Zerbst Germany 74 H5
Zermatt Switzerland 77 E6
Zernez Switzerland 77 E4
Zestienhoven Apt Netherlands 65 B10
Zeven Germany 74 E3
Zhiguli Hills Russian Fed. 86 C1
Zhoukoudian UN C China 63 A5
Zillertal Reg Austria 77 F7
Zillertaler Alpen Mtns Austria/Italy 77 F7
Zimbabwe 88 A4
Zinal Switzerland 77 E6
Zion N Pk USA 92 A5
Zittau Germany 75 J6
Zonnebeke Bat Belgium 65 B13
Zug Switzerland 77 E3
Zuger See Lake Switzerland 77 E3
Zugspitze Mtn Austria/Germany 77 F2
Zuid Beveland I Netherlands 65 B10
Zuid Holland Adm Netherlands 65 B10
Zülpich Germany 76 B1
Zuni-Cibola N His USA 92 A6
Zuoz Switzerland 77 E4
Zürich Apt Switzerland 56 A11
Zürich Switzerland 77 D2
Zürich Canada 94 C2
Zürich, Canton Switzerland 77 D2
Zürichsee Lake Switzerland 79 D4
Zurrieq Malta 79 G4
Zutphen Netherlands 65 B8
Zuurberg N Pk South Africa 88 C4
Zweibrücken Germany 76 B3
Zweisimmen Switzerland 77 E2
Zwickau Germany 75 H6
Zwickauer Mulde Riv Germany 75 H6
Zwijndrecht Netherlands 65 B11
Zwolle Netherlands 65 B8

TEACHING MAP : World

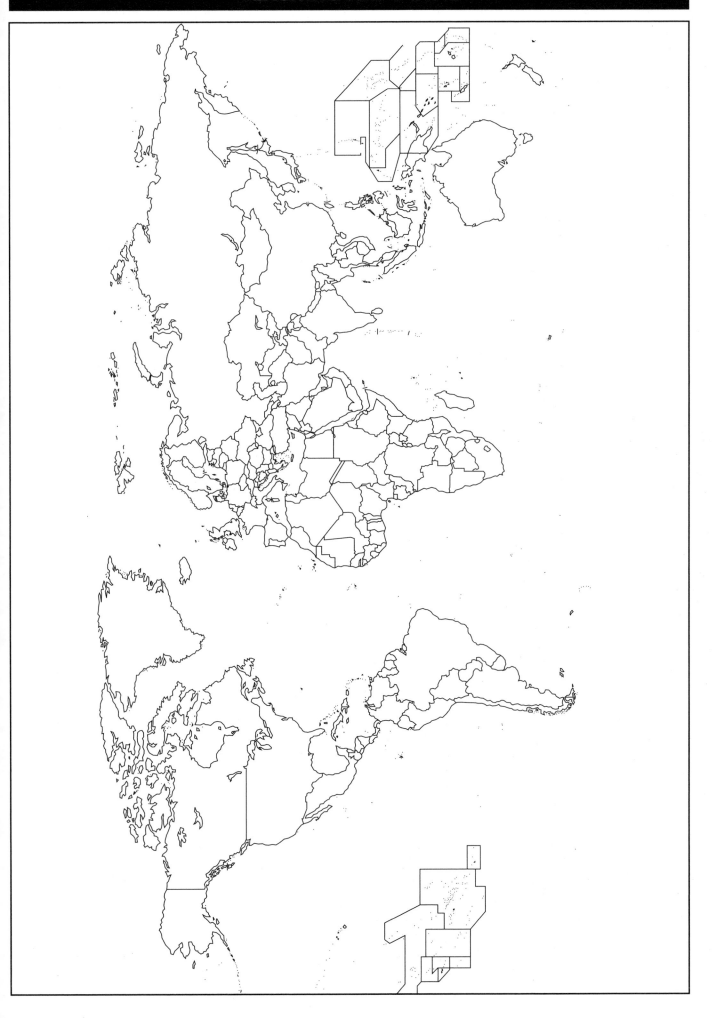

TEACHING MAP : Europe

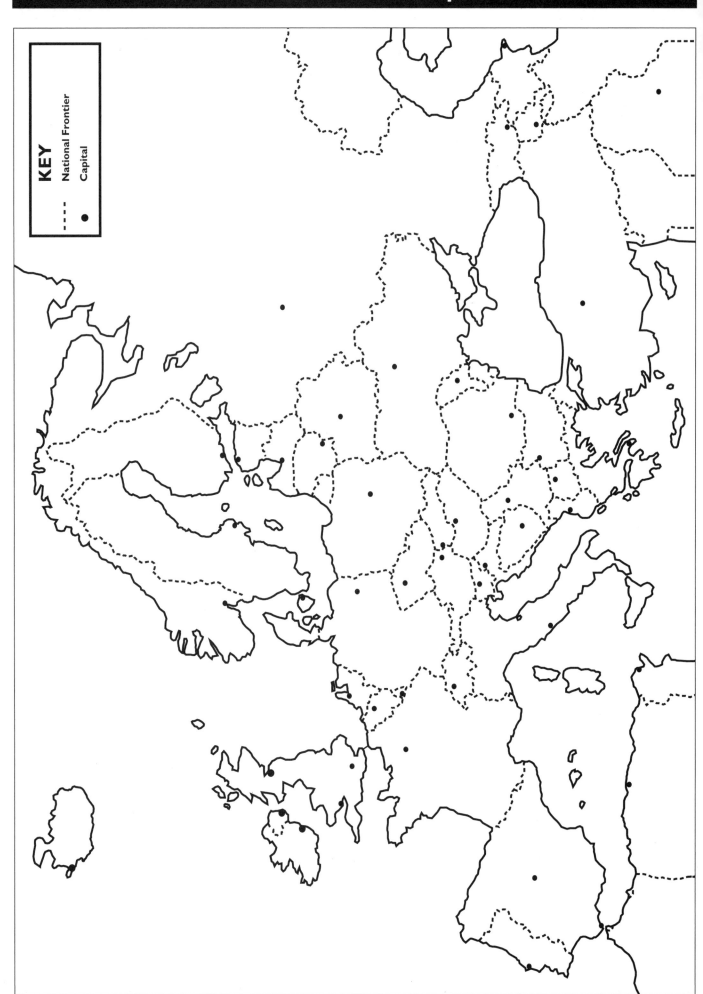

KEY

National Frontier

Capital

TEACHING MAP : UK

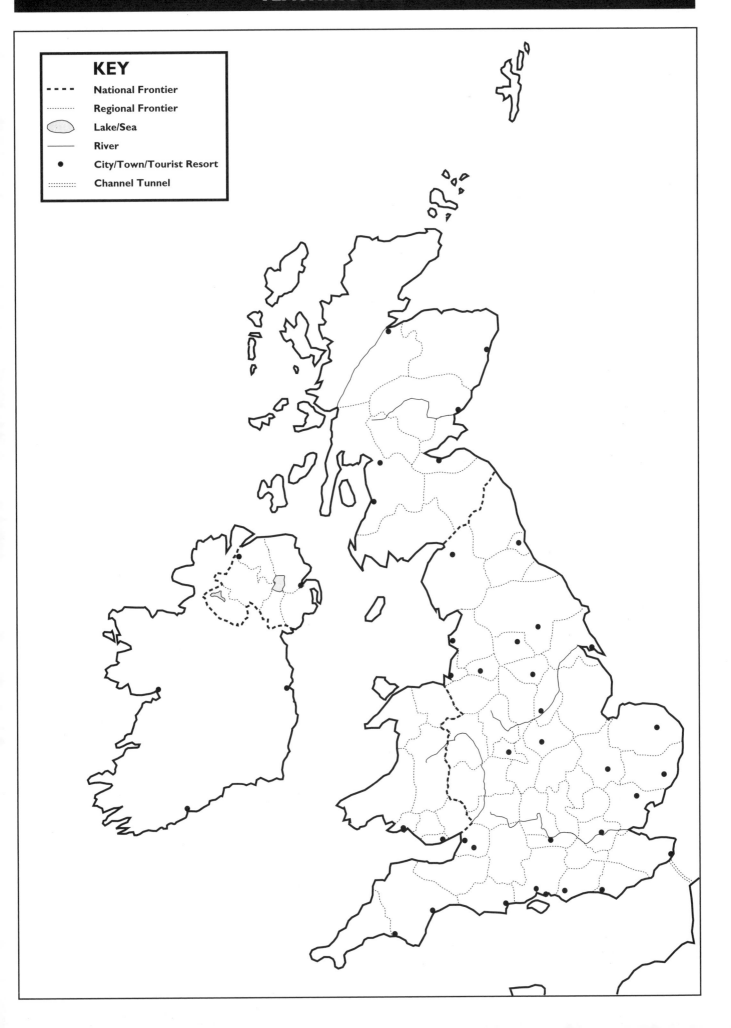

KEY

- - - - National Frontier
.... Regional Frontier
Lake/Sea
—— River
● City/Town/Tourist Resort
.... Channel Tunnel

TEACHING MAP : Germany

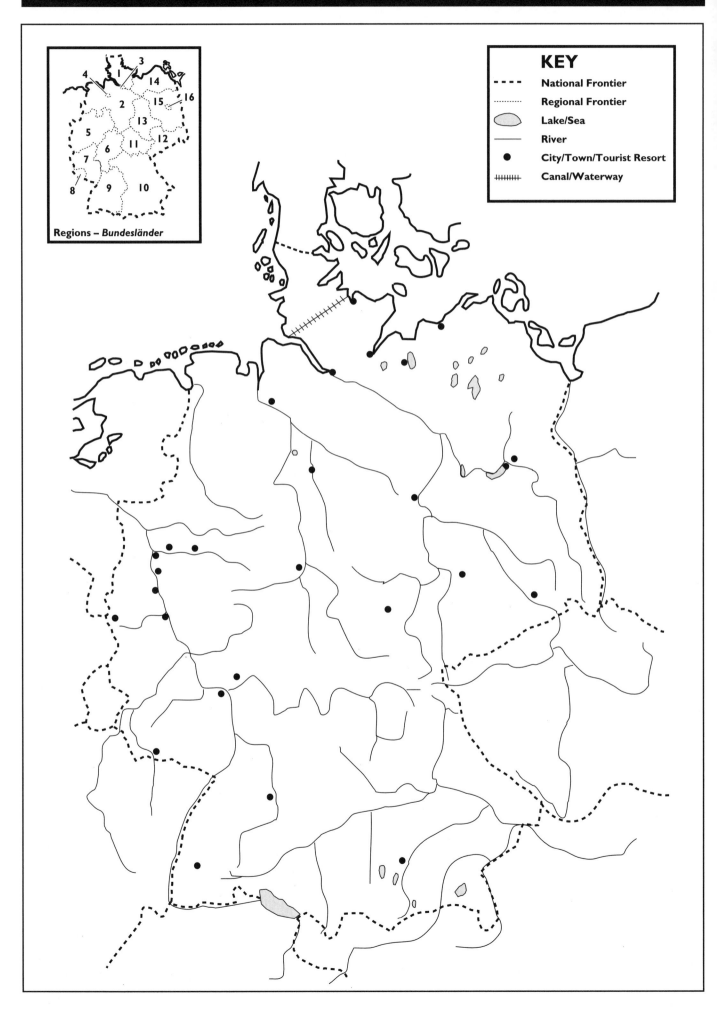

KEY

- - - - National Frontier
.... Regional Frontier
Lake/Sea
River
● City/Town/Tourist Resort
⊪⊪⊪⊪ Canal/Waterway

Regions – *Bundesländer*

TEACHING MAP : France

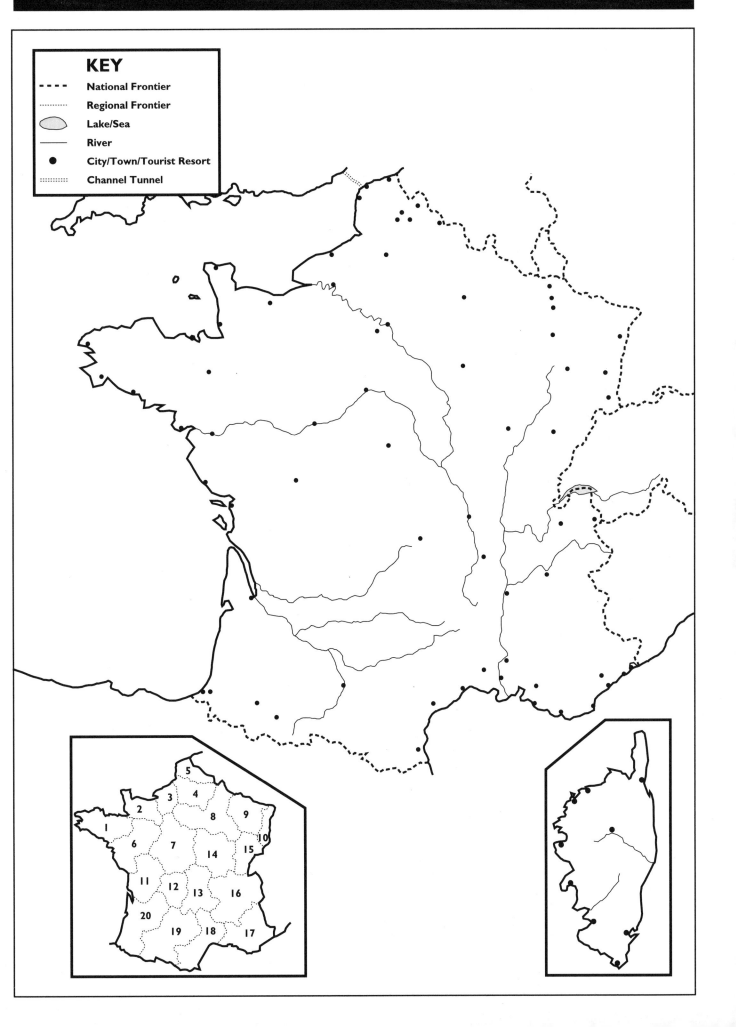

TEACHING MAP : France

KEY

- - - - National Frontier
.... Regional Frontier
Lake/Sea
River
● City/Town/Tourist Resort
:::::::: Channel Tunnel

TEACHING MAP : Iberia

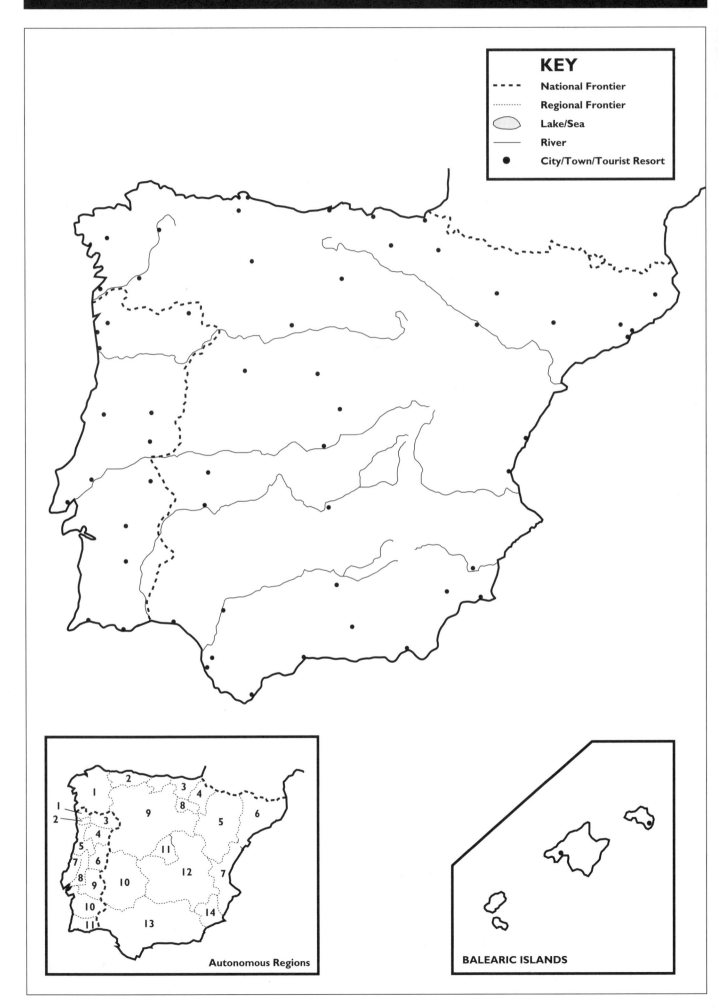

KEY

- - - - National Frontier
· · · · · · · Regional Frontier
Lake/Sea
——— River
● City/Town/Tourist Resort

Autonomous Regions

BALEARIC ISLANDS

TEACHING MAP : Iberian Islands

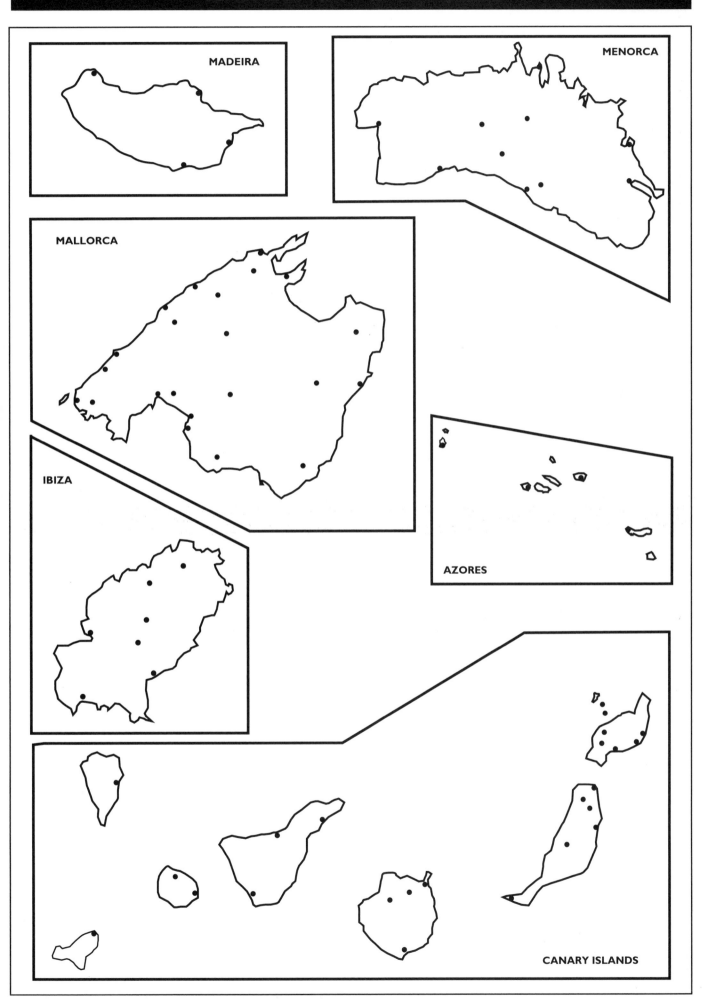

TEACHING MAP : Switzerland

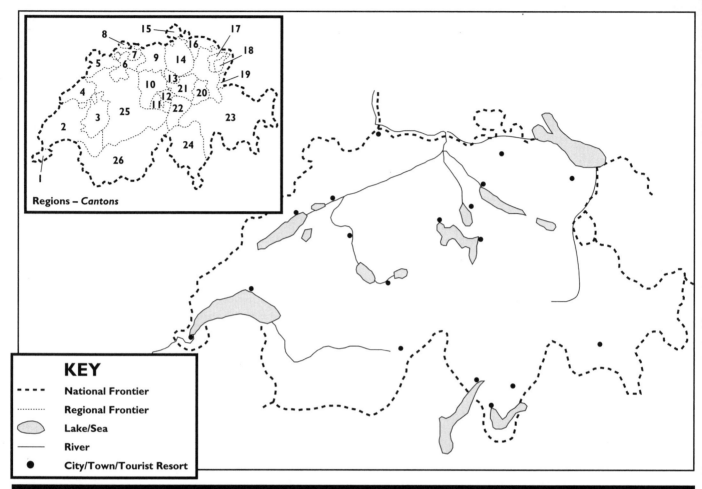

Regions – *Cantons*

KEY

- - - -	**National Frontier**
··········	**Regional Frontier**
⬭	**Lake/Sea**
——	**River**
●	**City/Town/Tourist Resort**

TEACHING MAP : Austria

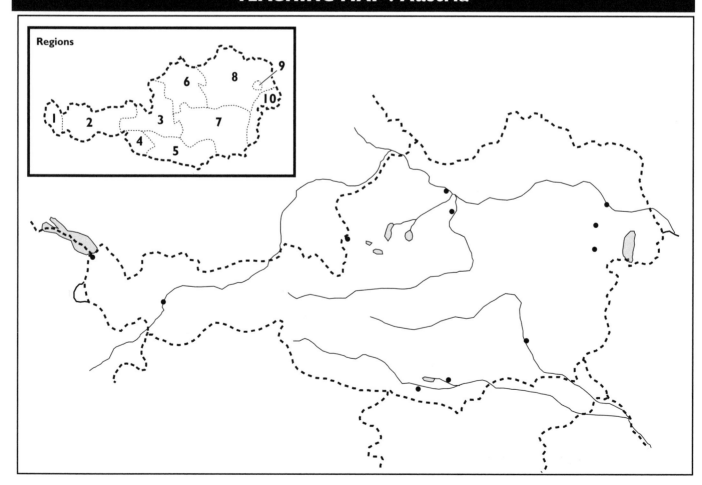

Regions

TEACHING MAP : Italy

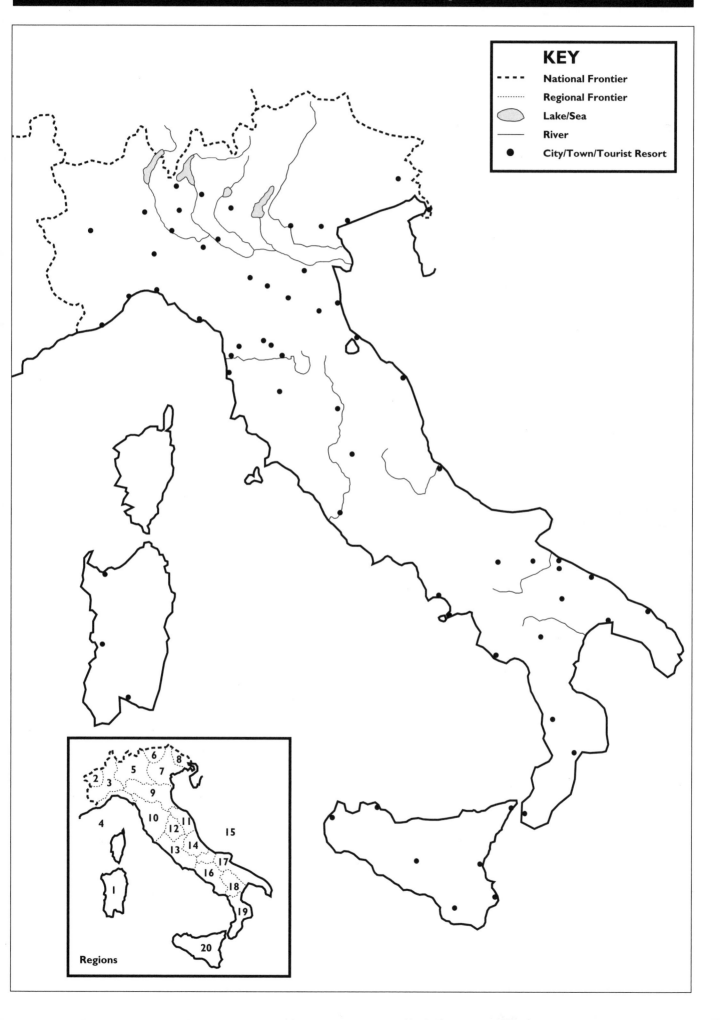

KEY

- – – – National Frontier
- ·········· Regional Frontier
- Lake/Sea
- ——— River
- ● City/Town/Tourist Resort

Regions

TEACHING MAP : Greece

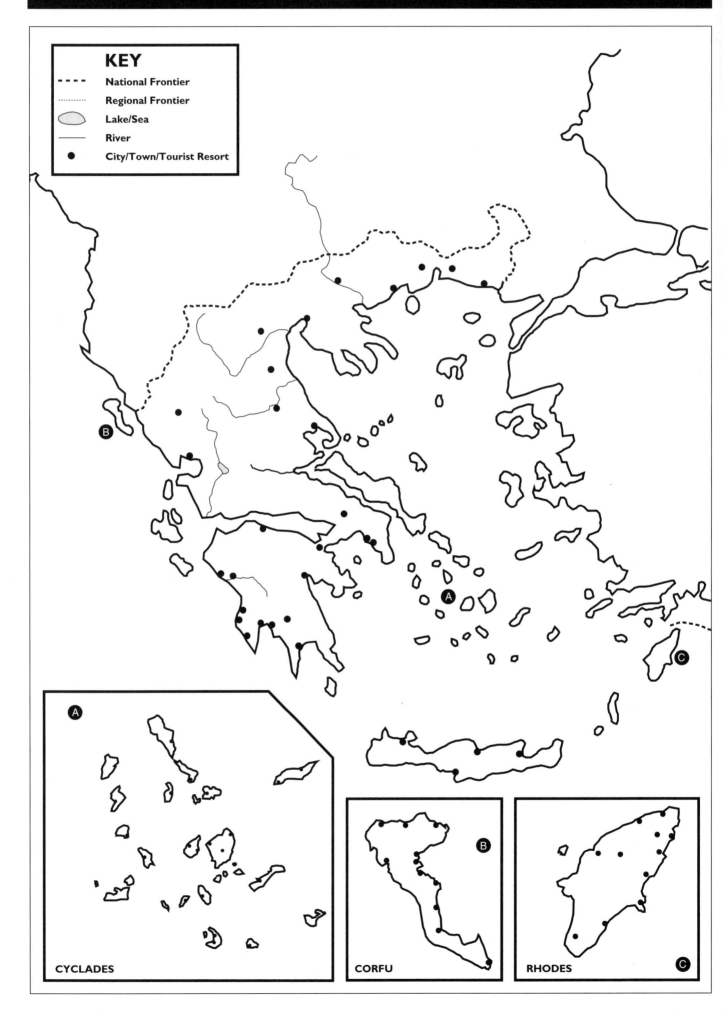

KEY

- - - - National Frontier
.... Regional Frontier
Lake/Sea
River
● City/Town/Tourist Resort

Ⓐ

Ⓑ

Ⓒ

Ⓐ

CYCLADES

CORFU Ⓑ

RHODES Ⓒ

TEACHING MAP : Central America & Caribbean

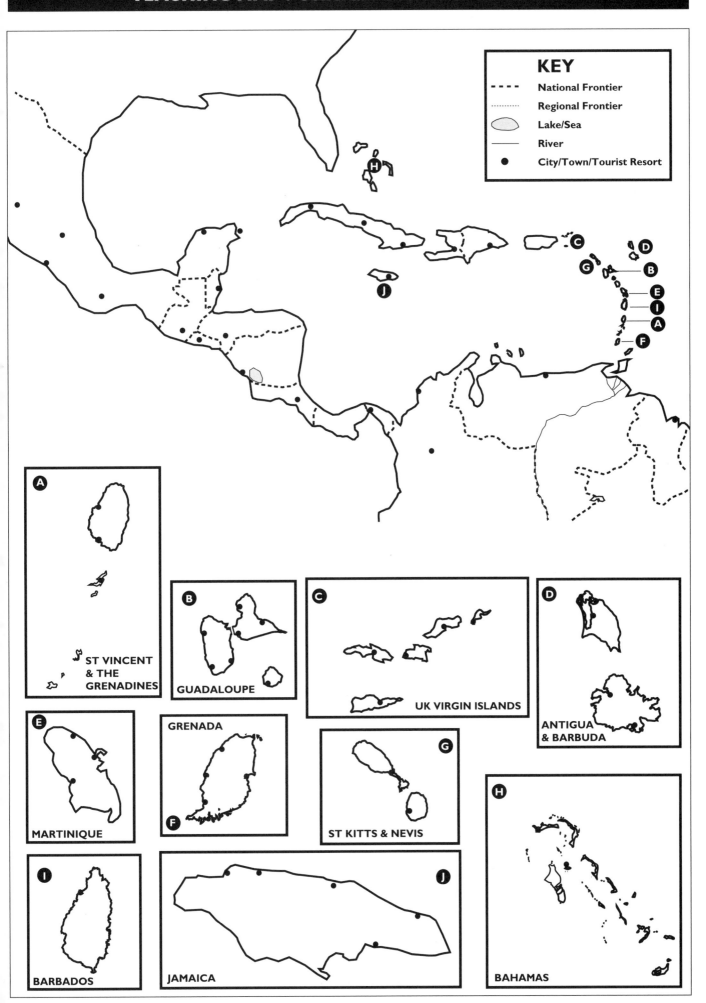

KEY

- – – – National Frontier
- .... Regional Frontier
- Lake/Sea
- —— River
- ● City/Town/Tourist Resort

A — ST VINCENT & THE GRENADINES

B — GUADALOUPE

C — UK VIRGIN ISLANDS

D — ANTIGUA & BARBUDA

E — MARTINIQUE

F — GRENADA

G — ST KITTS & NEVIS

H — BAHAMAS

I — BARBADOS

J — JAMAICA

TEACHING MAP : Canada

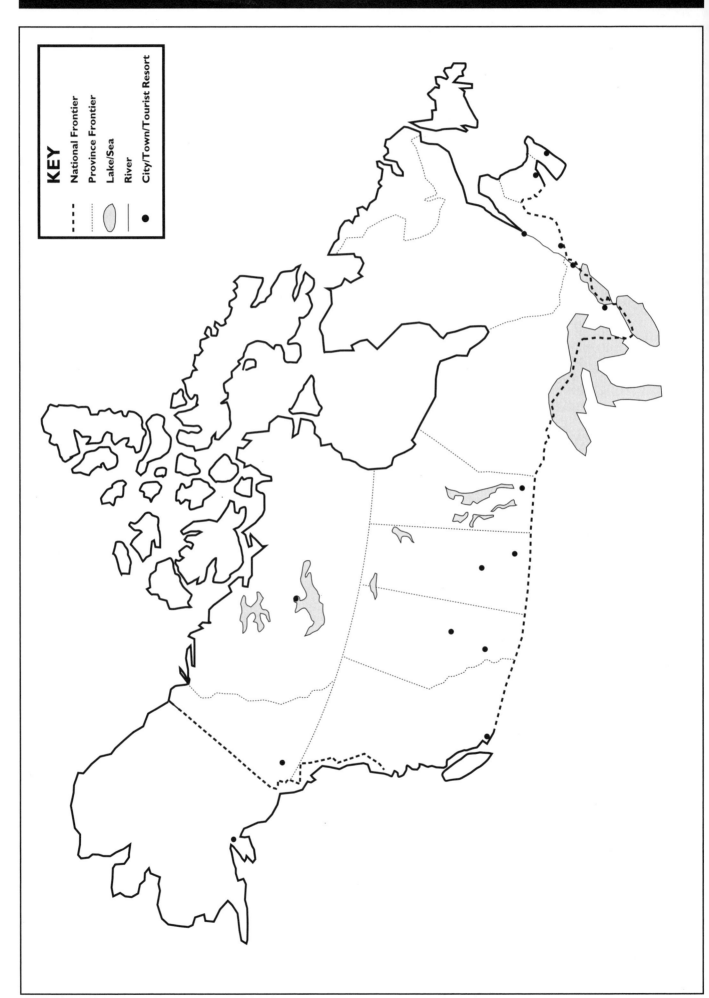

KEY

National Frontier
Province Frontier
Lake/Sea
River
● City/Town/Tourist Resort

TEACHING MAP : USA

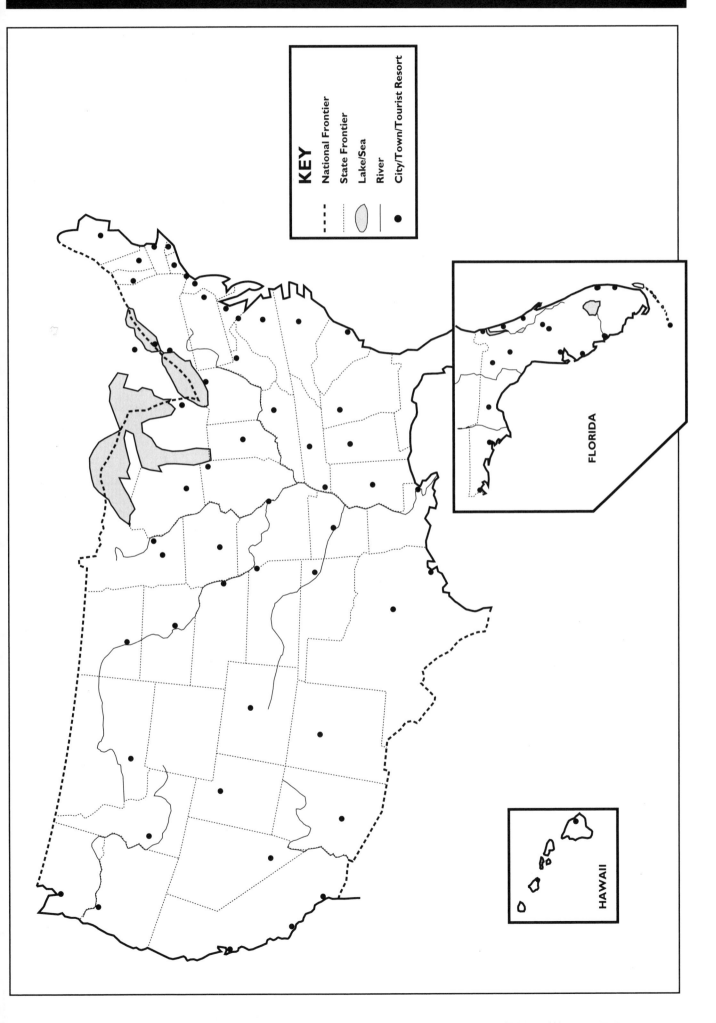

KEY

National Frontier
State Frontier
Lake/Sea
River
City/Town/Tourist Resort

FLORIDA

HAWAII

TEACHING MAP : North Africa & Israel

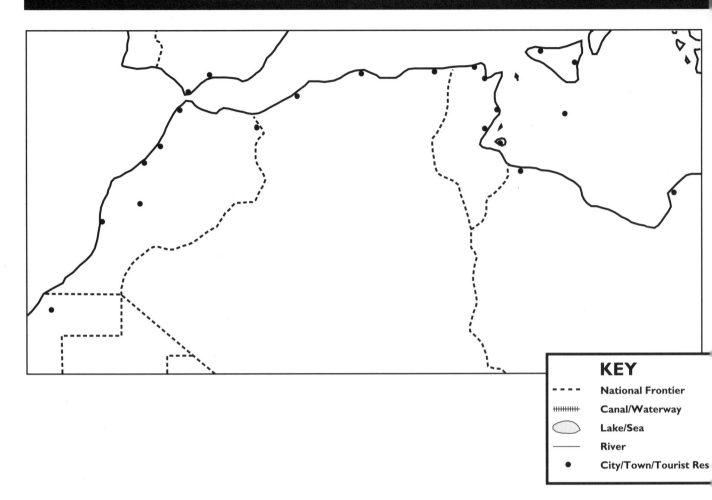

KEY

- - - - National Frontier
╫╫╫╫╫ Canal/Waterway
⬭ Lake/Sea
—— River
● City/Town/Tourist Res

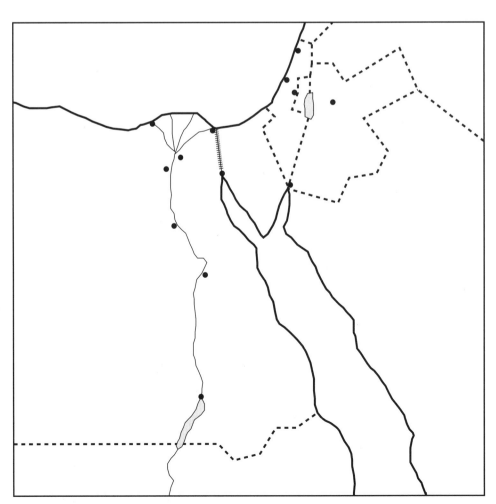

TEACHING MAP : Southern Africa

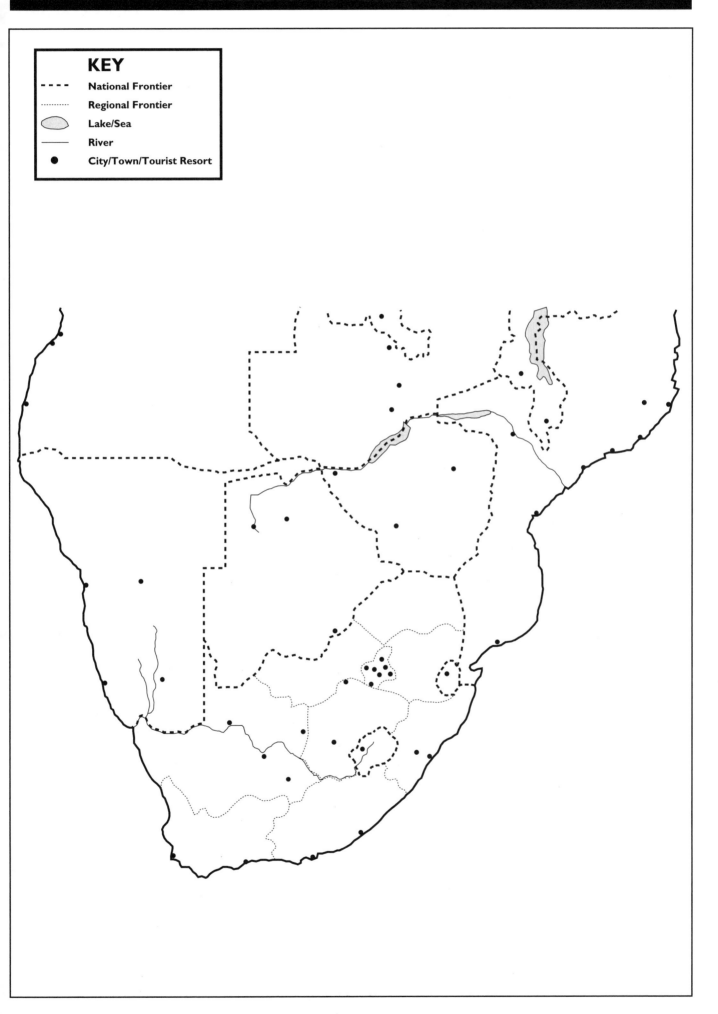

KEY

- - - - National Frontier
· · · · · · Regional Frontier
⬭ Lake/Sea
──── River
● City/Town/Tourist Resort

TEACHING MAP : Far East

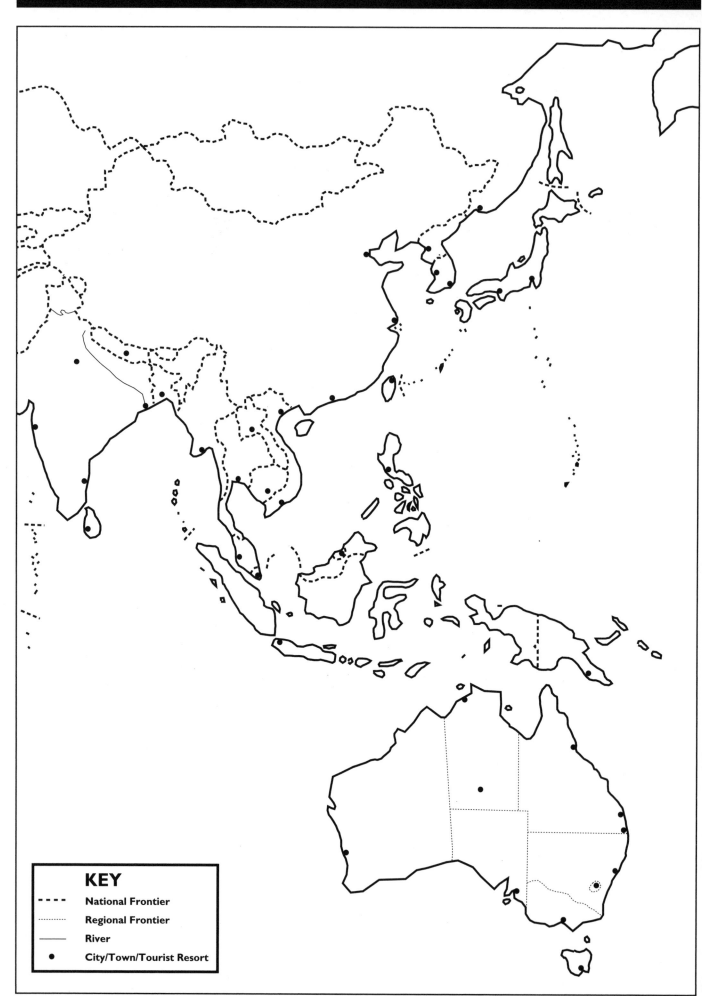

KEY

- - - - **National Frontier**
.... **Regional Frontier**
———— **River**
● **City/Town/Tourist Resort**